An Expanding World
Volume 22

Administrators of Empire

AN EXPANDING WORLD
The European Impact on World History, 1450–1800

General Editor: A.J.R. Russell-Wood

EXPANSION, INTERACTION, ENCOUNTERS
1 **The Global Opportunity** *Felipe Fernández-Armesto*
2 **The European Opportunity** *Felipe Fernández-Armesto*
3 **The Globe Encircled and the World Revealed** *Ursula Lamb*
4 **Historiography of Europeans in Africa and Asia** *Anthony Disney*
5 **Establishing Exceptionalism** *Amy Turner Bushnell*

TECHNOLOGY AND SCIENCE
6 **Scientific Aspects of European Expansion** *William Storey*
7 **Technology and European Overseas Enterprise** *Michael Adas*

TRADE AND COMMODITIES
8 **Merchant Networks in the Early Modern World** *Sanjay Subrahmanyam*
9 **The Atlantic Staple Trade** (Parts I & II) *Susan Socolow*
10 **European Commercial Expansion in Early Modern Asia** *Om Prakash*
11 **Spices in the Indian Ocean World** *M.N. Pearson*
12 **Textiles: Production, Trade and Demand** *Maureen Fennell Mazzaoui*
13 **Interoceanic Trade in European Expansion** *Pieter Emmer and Femme Gaastra*
14 **Metals and Monies in a Global Economy** *Dennis O. Flynn and Arturo Giráldez*
15 **Slave Trades** *Patrick Manning*

EXPLOITATION
16 **The Worlds of Unfree Labour** *Colin Palmer*
17 **Agriculture, Resource Exploitation, and Environmental Change** *Helen Wheatley*
18 **Plantation Societies in the Era of European Expansion** *Judy Bieber*
19 **Mines of Silver and Gold in the Americas** *Peter Bakewell*

GOVERNMENT AND EMPIRE
20 **Theories of Empire, 1450–1800** *David Armitage*
21 **Government and Governance of Empires** *A.J.R. Russell-Wood*
22 **Administrators of Empire** *Mark A. Burkholder*
23 **Local Government in European Empires** *A.J.R. Russell-Wood*
24 **Warfare and Empires** *Douglas M. Peers*

SOCIETY AND CULTURE
25 **Settlement Patterns in Early Modern Colonization** *Joyce Lorimer*
26 **Biological Consequences of the European Expansion** *Kenneth F. Kiple and Stephen V. Beck*
27 **European and Non-European Societies** (Parts I & II) *Robert Forster*
28 **Christianity and Missions** *J.S. Cummins*
29 **Families and the Expansion of Europe** *Maria Beatriz Nizza da Silva*
30 **European Intruders** *Murdo MacLeod and Evelyn Rawski*

THE WORLD AND EUROPE
31 **Facing Each Other** (Parts I & II) *Anthony Pagden*

Please note titles may change prior to publication

An Expanding World
The European Impact on World History 1450–1800

Volume 22

Administrators of Empire

edited by
Mark A. Burkholder

Routledge
Taylor & Francis Group
LONDON AND NEW YORK

First published 1998 in the Variorum Expanding World Series by Ashgate Publishing

Reissued 2018 by Routledge
2 Park Square, Milton Park, Abingdon, Oxon, OX14 4RN
711 Third Avenue, New York, NY 10017

Routledge is an imprint of the Taylor & Francis Group, an informa business

A Library of Congress record exists under LC control number: 98024125

ISBN 13: 978-1-138-31321-7 (hbk)
ISBN 13: 978-1-138-31323-1 (pbk)
ISBN 13: 978-0-429-45770-8 (ebk)

Contents

Acknowledgements

The chapters in this volume are taken from the sources listed below, for which the editor and publishers wish to thank their authors, original publishers or other copyright holders for permission to use their material as follows:

Chapter 1: John Leddy Phelan, 'Authority and Flexibility in the Spanish Imperial Bureaucracy', *Administrative Science Quarterly* V, no. 1 (Ithaca, NY, 1960), pp. 47–65. Copyright © 1960 by Administrative Science Quarterly. Reprinted by permission.

Chapter 2: Mark A. Burkholder, 'Bureaucrats', in ed. Louisa Schell Hoberman and Susan Migden Socolow, *Cities and Society in Colonial Latin America* (Albuquerque, 1986), pp. 77–103.

Chapter 3: Kenneth J. Andrien, 'The Sale of Fiscal Offices and the Decline of Royal Authority in the Viceroyalty of Peru, 1633–1700', *Hispanic American Historical Review* LXII, no. 1 (Durham, NC, 1982), pp. 49–71. Copyright © 1982 by Duke University Press. Reprinted with permission.

Chapter 4: M.A. Burkholder and D.S. Chandler, 'Creole Appointments and the Sale of Audiencia Positions in the Spanish Empire under the Early Bourbons, 1701–1750', *Journal of Latin American Studies* IV, no. 2 (Cambridge, 1972), pp. 187–206. Copyright © 1972 by Cambridge University Press.

Chapter 5: Jacques A. Barbier, 'Élites and Cadres in Bourbon Chile', *Hispanic American Historical Review* LII, no. 3 (Durham, NC, 1972), pp. 416–435. Copyright © 1972 by Duke University Press. Reprinted with permission.

Chapter 6: D.A. Brading, 'Government and Élite in Late Colonial Mexico', *Hispanic American Historical Review* LIII, no. 3 (Durham, NC, 1973), pp. 389–414. Copyright © 1973 by Duke University Press, Reprinted with permission.

Chapter 7: John Lynch, 'Intendants and Cabildos in the Viceroyalty of La Plata, 1782–1810', *Hispanic American Historical Review* XXXV, no. 3 (Durham, NC, 1955), pp. 337–362. Copyright © 1955 by Duke University Press. Reprinted with permission.

Chapter 8: Stuart B. Schwartz, 'Magistracy and Society in Colonial Brazil', *Hispanic American Historical Review*, L, no. 4 (Durham, NC, 1970), pp. 715–730. Copyright © 1970 by Duke University Press. Reprinted with permission.

Chapter 9: Stephen Saunders Webb, 'Army and Empire: English Garrison Government in Britain and America, 1569–1763', *William and Mary Quarterly* (3rd series) XXXIV, no. 1 (Williamsburg, VA, 1977), pp. 1–31. Copyright © 1977 by The Omohundro Institute of Early American History and Culture. Reprinted by permission of the author and The Omohundro Institute of Early American History and Culture.

Chapter 10: Ian Steele, 'Governors or Generals? A Note on Martial Law and the Revolution of 1689 in English America', *William and Mary Quarterly* (3rd series) XLVI, no. 2 (Williamsburg, VA, 1989), pp. 304–314. Copyright © 1989 by The Omohundro Institute of Early American History and Culture. Reprinted by permission of the author and The Omohundro Institute of Early American History and Culture.

Chapter 11: David W. Jordan, 'Sir Thomas Lawrence, Secretary of Maryland: A Royal Placeman's Fortunes in America', *Maryland Historical Magazine* LXXVI, no. 1 (Baltimore, MD, 1981), pp. 22–44. Copyright © 1981 by Maryland Historical Society.

Chapter 12: Jere R. Daniell, 'Politics in New Hampshire under Governor Benning Wentworth, 1741–1767', *William and Mary Quarterly* (3rd series), XXIII, no. 1 (Williamsburg, VA, 1966), pp. 76–105. Copyright © 1966 by The Omohundro Institute of Early American History and Culture. Reprinted by permission of the author and The Omohundro Institute of Early American History and Culture.

Chapter 13: Larry R. Gerlach, 'Customs and Contentions: John Hatton of Salem and Cohansey, 1764–1776', *New Jersey History* LXXXIX, no. 2 (Newark, NJ, 1971), pp. 69–72. Copyright © 1971 by the New Jersey Historical Society.

Chapter 14: John J. McCusker, 'Colonial Civil Servant and Counter-revolutionary: Thomas Irving (1738?–1800) in Boston, Charleston, and London', in John J. McCusker, *Essays in the Economic History of the Atlantic World* (London, 1997), pp. 190–221. Copyright © 1997 by John J. McCusker.

Chapter 15: Neil Rabitoy, 'Jonathan Duncan: A Lesson in Administrative Survival', *Asian Profile* VII, no. 5 (Hong Kong, 1979), pp. 443–449. Copyright © 1979 by the Asian Research Service.

Chapter 16: Dale S. Standen, 'Politics, Patronage, and the Imperial Interest: Charles de Beauharnais's Disputes with Gilles Hocquart', *The Canadian Historical Review* LX, no. 1 (North York, Ontario, 1979), pp. 19–40. Copyright © 1979 by the University of Toronto Press. Reprinted by permission of the University of Toronto Press Incorporated.

Every effort has been made to trace all the copyright holders, but if any have been inadvertently overlooked the publishers will be pleased to make the necessary arrangement at the first opportunity.

General Editor's Preface

A.J.R. Russell-Wood

An Expanding World: The European Impact on World History, 1450–1800 is designed to meet two objectives: first, each volume covers a specific aspect of the European initiative and reaction across time and space; second, the series represents a superb overview and compendium of knowledge and is an invaluable reference source on the European presence beyond Europe in the early modern period, interaction with non-Europeans, and experiences of peoples of other continents, religions, and races in relation to Europe and Europeans. The series reflects revisionist interpretations and new approaches to what has been called 'the expansion of Europe' and whose historiography traditionally bore the hallmarks of a narrowly Eurocentric perspective, focus on the achievements of individual nations, and characterization of the European presence as one of dominance, conquest, and control. Fragmentation characterized much of this literature: fragmentation by national groups, by geography, and by chronology.

The volumes of *An Expanding World* seek to transcend nationalist histories and to examine on the global stage rather than in discrete regions important selected facets of the European presence overseas. One result has been to bring to the fore the multicontinental, multi-oceanic and multinational dimension of the European activities. A further outcome is compensatory in the emphasis placed on the cross-cultural context of European activities and on how collaboration and cooperation between peoples transcended real or perceived boundaries of religion, nationality, race, and language and were no less important aspects of the European experience in Africa, Asia, the Americas, and Australia than the highly publicized confrontational, bellicose, and exploitative dimensions. Recent scholarship has not only led to greater understanding of peoples, cultures, and institutions of Africa, Asia, the Americas, and Australasia with whom Europeans interacted and the complexity of such interactions and transactions, but also of relations between Europeans of different nationalities and religious persuasions.

The initial five volumes reflect the changing historiography and set the stage for volumes encompassing the broad themes of technology and science, trade and commerce, exploitation as reflected in agriculture and the extractive industries and through systems of forced and coerced labour, government of empire, and society and culture in European colonies and settlements overseas. Final volumes examine the image of Europe and Europeans as 'the other' and the impact of the wider world on European *mentalités* and mores.

An international team of editors was selected to reflect a diversity of educational backgrounds, nationalities, and scholars at different stages of their professional careers. Few would claim to be 'world historians', but each is a recognized authority in his or her field and has the demonstrated capacity to ask the significant questions and provide a conceptual framework for the selection of articles which combine analysis with interpretation. Editors were exhorted to place their specific subjects within a global context and over the *longue durée*. I have been delighted by the enthusiasm with which they took up this intellectual challenge, their courage in venturing beyond their immediate research fields to look over the fences into the gardens of their academic neighbours, and the collegiality which has led to a generous informal exchange of information. Editors were posed the daunting task of surveying a rich historical literature and selecting those essays which they regarded as significant contributions to an understanding of the specific field or representative of the historiography. They were asked to give priority to articles in scholarly journals; essays from conference volumes and *Festschriften* were acceptable; excluded (with some few exceptions) were excerpts from recent monographs or paperback volumes. After much discussion and agonizing, the decision was taken to incorporate essays only in English, French, and Spanish. This has led to the exclusion of the extensive scholarly literature in Danish, Dutch, German and Portuguese. The ramifications of these decisions and how these have had an impact on the representative quality of selections of articles have varied, depending on the theme, and have been addressed by editors in their introductions.

The introduction to each volume enables readers to assess the importance of the topic *per se* and place this in the broader context of European activities overseas. It acquaints readers with broad trends in the historiography and alerts them to controversies and conflicting interpretations. Editors clarify the conceptual framework for each volume and explain the rationale for the selection of articles and how they relate to each other. Introductions permit volume editors to assess the impact on their treatments of discrete topics of constraints of language, format, and chronology, assess the completeness of the journal literature, and address *lacunae*. A further charge to editors was to describe and evaluate the importance of change over time, explain differences attributable to differing geographical, cultural, institutional, and economic circumstances and suggest the potential for cross-cultural, comparative, and interdisciplinary approaches. The addition of notes and bibliographies enhances the scholarly value of the introductions and suggests avenues for further enquiry.

I should like to express my thanks to the volume editors for their willing participation, enthusiasm, sage counsel, invaluable suggestions, and good judgment. Evidence of the timeliness and importance of the series was illustrated by the decision, based on extensive consultation with the scholarly community, to expand a series, which had originally been projected not to exceed eight volumes, to more than thirty volumes. It was John Smedley's initiative which gave rise to discussions as to the viability and need for such a series and he has overseen the publishing, publicity, and marketing of *An Expanding World*. As

General Editor, my task was greatly facilitated by the assistance of Dr Mark Steele who was initially responsible for the 'operations' component of the series as it got under way; latterly this assistance has been provided by staff at Variorum.

The Department of History,
The Johns Hopkins University

Introduction

Mark A. Burkholder[1]

The expansion of Europe overseas required the creation of institutions for governing the conquered peoples as well as the conquerors, their descendants, and later immigrants.[2] Portugal, Spain, England, and France faced this administrative challenge during the era of colonization. Though each crown responded differently, they all relied upon government officials to oversee royal interests in their colonies. This volume brings together a set of articles that illustrate the variety of imperial administrators, the ways in which they secured office, some of the pressures they experienced, and the opportunities they enjoyed as office-holders. The focus is almost exclusively on administrators in the New World both because all four countries had colonies there and because the periodical literature on the subject renders such an examination feasible although far from exhaustive. Despite a widely held belief that historians largely exhausted the subject of colonial administration long ago, in fact there has been relatively little written on the administrators themselves except for those of the highest rank and, aside from the Iberian colonies, almost no group biographies of bureaucrats have been written. The available historiography is skewed heavily toward the Americas in general and to Spanish and Anglo-America in particular. With the exception of Portuguese administration in Asia, moreover, European administration outside of the Americas was handled by companies rather than by royal bureaucracies. The materials gathered together in this volume thus reflect the existing historiography while exemplifying the nature of colonial rule wherever a European crown sent royal bureaucrats.

Portugal was the first European country to engage in sustained colonization, though its early African settlements were no more than fortified trading posts. However, Christopher Columbus's contract with the Crown of Castile to undertake his famous voyage to the west promised two administrative titles, those of viceroy and governor, along with administrative, taxation, and judicial responsibilities. When he proved a hopelessly inadequate administrator, the crown of Castile

---

[1] Mark A. Burkholder is Professor of History at the University of Missouri-St Louis. He thanks Theodore L. Listerman for his assistance in identifying the articles that follow and Suzanne Hiles Burkholder and Kristen M. Burkholder for their thoughtful and helpful comments on earlier drafts of the introduction. He also thanks the Department of History, the College of Arts and Sciences, the Center for International Studies, and the Graduate School at the University of Missouri-St Louis for their support.

[2] For a review of colonial administrative institutions, see the introduction by A. J. R. Russell-Wood in the companion volume on colonial administration.

curtailed many of his responsibilities and replaced him with a royal governor. Thus began European imperial administration in the New World.

Variations in the physical size and populations of the conquered and settled territories demanded significant differences in the complexity and extent of the colonial bureaucracies. Not surprisingly, however, all drew on institutions and personnel from the mother country and provided for executive, judicial, legislative, and taxation responsibilities. The earliest and largest bureaucracy was in Spanish America, geographically the most extensive and most populous region of European colonization in the New World. Royal administrators included viceroys, captains-general, and presidents, high court ministers, treasury officials, accountants, provincial administrators, customs officials, and local officials.

The bureaucracy in colonial Brazil was organized similarly, but developed more slowly and was far smaller in scale than that of Spanish America. The English and French colonies had even smaller and less sophisticated administrations. Each English colony had a governor, a provincial council, and customs officials and a few other royal appointees (in royal colonies), but only two, Sir Edmund Andros and Francis Nicholson, could be described as professional governors.[3] As a consequence of the modest population in the French colonies, there were few royal officials. After 1665 each French colony had a governor, an intendant, and a few minor bureaucrats. In 1763 the area known as New France had one governor-general, three provincial governors, an intendant, and some sub-delegates.[4]

What criteria and processes were involved in the selection of imperial administrators? Prior military service was important in the selection of the chief administrative official, and in the New World colonies nearly all chief executives, whatever their titles, were professional soldiers.[5] A law degree was indispensable for appointees to the regional high courts of Spanish America and Brazil and normally for intendants in the French colonies.[6] Magistrates named to the high court of Bahia usually had about fifteen years' experience as royal appointees in

---

[3] Andros was governor of New York, the Dominion of New England, Virginia, and acting governor of Maryland. Nicholson was governor of Maryland, Virginia, Nova Scotia, and South Carolina. Leonard Woods Labaree, *Royal Government in America: A Study of the British Colonial System before 1783* (New Haven, 1930; reprinted, Frederick Ungar Publishing Company, 1958), p. 41n.

[4] W. J. Eccles, *France in America* (New York, 1972), pp. 68–69.

[5] Ibid.; Stephen Saunders Webb, *The Governors-General: The English Army and the Definition of Empire, 1569–1681* (Chapel Hill, 1979); Bradley Benedict, 'El estado en México en la época de los Habsburgos', *Historia Mexicana*, XXIII, no. 4 (1974), 551–610.

[6] Mark A. Burkholder and D. S. Chandler, *From Impotence to Authority: The Spanish Crown and the American Audiencias, 1687–1808* (Columbia, Mo., 1977); Stuart B. Schwartz, *Sovereignty and Society in Colonial Brazil: The High Court of Bahia and its Judges, 1609–1751* (Berkeley and Los Angeles, 1981); W. J. Eccles, *The Government of New France* (Ottawa, 1971), p. 8.

municipal and provincial judgeships in Portugal.[7] There was no clear professional path for appointment to other positions and the one universal requirement was literacy. Once a person was named to a section of the Spanish imperial bureaucracy with multiple ranks such as the judiciary, promotion was typically based on seniority, although a record of particularly meritorious performance sometimes brought advancement.

Family status and connections at court were frequently more important than professional credentials in securing office but the most successful candidates often possessed all three. The long-serving governor-general of New France, Charles de Beauharnais, was the son of a naval officer and was related through blood and marriage to intendants in France. His cousin, the Count of Maurepas, was the Minister of Marine at the time of his appointment.[8] Placemen, men appointed because of their political connections, were common in the English colonies. Thomas Irving, for example, went to Boston in 1767 as Inspector-General of Imports and Exports and Register of Shipping of North America. Irving was from a noble landed family of Scotland and related to the third Duke of Queensberry, one of George III's favorites; according to McCusker, 'Ties of blood and kinship...greatly assisted his [Irving's] early career'.[9] One of the first creoles and the first native son named to an American audiencia, Alonso Bravo de Saravia, was the son of a civil judge of the Audiencia of Lima and received his education at Salamanca.[10] Ambrosia Cerdán y Pontero, named criminal crown attorney of the Audiencia of Chile in 1776, was the son of a minister of Spanish courts, grandson of a councilor of Castile, and nephew of a member of the Council of Orders.[11]

While family, court connections, and professional qualifications were important considerations for appointment, the ability to purchase an appointment or an office became, during certain periods of time, the primary qualification. This, not surprisingly, led to a relaxation of previous standards. For example, the sale of fiscal offices in Peru beginning in 1633 enabled younger, less experienced men to be named to positions in the Lima treasury office.[12] Seventeen year-old Juan Prospero de Solís Vango became a supernumerary judge of the Audiencia of Chile in 1707 when his father simultaneously bought an appointment as president of the Audiencia of Guadalajara.[13] This case underscores the extent to which the Spanish Crown sacrificed professional standards for financial assistance,

[7] Stuart B. Schwartz, see chapter 8 in this volume.

[8] S. Dale Standen, see chapter 16 in this volume.

[9] John J. McCusker, see chapter 14 in this volume.

[10] Mark A. Burkholder, see chapter 2 in this volume.

[11] Mark A. Burkholder, *Biographical Dictionary of Councilors of the Indies, 1717–1808* (Westport, Conn., 1986), pp. 28–29.

[12] Kenneth J. Andrien, see chapter 3 in this volume.

[13] Burkholder and Chandler, *From Impotence to Authority*, pp. 33n., 148n.

although Solís was explicitly prohibited from voting on the tribunal until he reached the age of majority (twenty-five years). The sale of appointments and offices ultimately affected a broad range of bureaucratic positions in the Spanish colonies until the practice ended in the middle of the eighteenth century.[14] The sale of office was also widespread in Brazil and bureaucrats such as Thomas Irving purchased posts in the English colonies as well.[15] Given the long-established venality of office holders in France, it is surprising that the French Crown sold no administrative or judicial positions in New France.[16]

While the first administrators were men born in Europe, the maturation of both the colonies and the descendants of the first settlers raised the issue of the colonists' participation in administration. The European governments considered men born and reared in the mother country more prone than those born in the colonies to support and enforce legislation beneficial to their interests and favoured them for high office in general and for the highest executive positions in particular. With few exceptions in Spain's empire, the highest ranking colonial officials, the viceroys of New Spain (Mexico), Peru, New Granada, and the Río de la Plata, were men born in Spain. Many had prior military experience. All claimed noble birth and most held or subsequently obtained titles of nobility.[17] In Brazil most governors-general were professional soldiers from the high nobility of Portugal. Nearly all governors were Portuguese as well and almost none of the few Brazilians named served in his home province.[18] More than eighty-five percent of the governors-general in the English colonies had prior experience as officers in the English army.[19] In the French colonies, the governors-general were professional soldiers and members of the nobility of the sword while the intendants were lawyers and from the nobility of the robe.[20] The chief executives, in sum, were almost always men with previous administrative experience who had been born in the mother countries.

Colonists, of course, sought administrative positions from the time the first generation of American-born males came of age. Their preferred course was to serve in the province or colony of their birth; there, as native sons, they would have long-established family and economic connections. If named to another colony, they would be considered outsiders much like appointees from Europe. While virtually excluded from the top executive positions, Americans were more

---

[14] Burkholder, see chapter 2 in this volume.

[15] Schwartz, see chapter 8 in this volume; McCusker, chapter 14 in this volume.

[16] Eccles, *France in America*, p. 75.

[17] Burkholder, see chapter 2 in this volume.

[18] Dauril Alden, *Royal Government in Colonial Brazil With Special Reference to the Administration of the Marquis of Lavradio, Viceroy, 1769–1779* (Berkeley and Los Angeles, 1968), p. 34.

[19] Stephen Saunders Webb, see chapter 9 in this volume.

[20] Eccles, *Government of New France*, p. 7.

successful in securing positions below the highest rank. The most successful even managed to obtain appointments in their home districts.

In Brazil and colonial Spanish America, the *relações* and *audiencias*, high courts of appeals and advisory bodies to the chief executives of their jurisdiction, had a number of American-born ministers. The high court of Bahia in Brazil had ten native sons who served between 1609 and 1759.[21] The first American-born Spaniard or creole to obtain an *audiencia* appointment did so in 1585, and after 1607 one or more creoles secured such an appointment in almost every calendar year.[22] Creoles in general and native sons in particular were notably successful when the Spanish Crown sold appointments to the courts. Increased reluctance to name creoles and especially native sons after 1750, however, reduced the number of creole appointees and produced intensified creole complaints about discrimination in appointments.[23]

Since the ministers on the high courts in Brazil and Spanish America served for life or the pleasure of the monarch, many remained at their posts for protracted periods of time. This long tenure in office gave the ministers extensive knowledge of local problems and, almost invariably, familial, kinship, and/or economic ties with members of the local elite in their districts.[24] A significant consequence was that as a group the members of the high courts were often more important than viceroys or other regional chief executives and only a foolish executive ignored their advice.

In contrast to Brazil and Spanish America, where high court judges were university-trained lawyers, New France depended for judicial rulings upon an intendant who was a lawyer.[25] In the English colonies, colonial governors and their provincial councils served as courts of appeal. The members of these councils were usually colonists, but formal legal training was not a requirement for appointment.[26]

The colonists' desire to serve in administrative positions frequently led to antagonism with outsiders, especially the European-born, who were named to office. While part of this was little more than resentment at being passed over for an appointment, native sons often considered European appointees to be far more interested in lining their pockets than providing effective administration. Studies of the placeman Sir Thomas Lawrence and customs official John Hatton illustrate the avaricious nature of many English officeholders in the colonies, and the consequent local opposition.[27]

---

[21] Schwartz, see chapter 8 in this volume, p. 729.

[22] Burkholder, see chapter 2 in this volume.

[23] Burkholder and Chandler, *From Impotence to Authority*.

[24] Ibid.; Schwartz, see chapter 8 in this volume.

[25] Eccles, *Government of New France*, p. 8.

[26] See Labaree, *Royal Government in America*, Chapter IX.

[27] David W. Jordan, see chapter 11 in this volume; Larry R. Gerlach, see chapter 13 in this volume.

The victims of greedy officeholders in Spanish America and Brazil were often the respective crowns and the native population. The corruption of officeholders in the Iberian colonies was almost legendary but, unlike British officials such as Thomas Irving, who anticipated advancing his career in England through service in the colonies, relatively few Iberian officeholders returned to the peninsula to occupy posts there. Fewer than one in seven judges on the high court in Bahia returned to serve on a council in Lisbon.[28] Prior to 1700 only eight ministers on the Spanish-American *audiencias* advanced directly to the Council of the Indies in Madrid, and only four others reached the Council after service on a Spanish court. Although advancement of ministers from the colonial courts to the Council increased after 1700, such promotion did not become routine until the 1770s.[29]

Because the opportunity to move from colonial to Spanish administration was very limited, numerous Spanish-born officials in the New World married into creole families. Thus Spaniards' colonial marital alliances enabled the locally born élite to share the benefits of ministers' greed. In contrast, some English officials treated the local population as a source of revenue to be milked until they could return to England.[30]

Imperial administrators' exploitation of, or integration into the local population was related to the length of their service. The most rapacious officials in colonial Spanish America were the notorious provincial administrators known variously as *corregidores, alcaldes mayores*, and *gobernadores*. Limited to three- to five-year terms, these officials used their positions to enrich themselves by serving as conduits for merchant houses in Mexico City and Lima. Through the power of their office they forced the natives of their district to purchase merchandise or, in some regions, mules; in other cases they coerced the natives into producing specific goods that they then purchased at below market prices. It appears that most of these officials served only one term. With only three to five years to get rich, they exploited the native population mercilessly. When the Spanish Crown began selling appointments of provincial administrator in 1677, the buyers had the additional pressure of recouping their purchase price as well as making a profit.[31]

In contrast to provincial officials, and executives of the larger jurisdictions who also received term appointments, members of the high courts, the treasury offices, and the accounting offices served for life unless they retired or were removed from office. Anticipating a lengthy term of office, they settled into the urban centre where they served and became, in most cases, permanent members

[28] Schwartz, see chapter 8 in this volume.

[29] Burkholder, *Biographical Dictionary of Councilors of the Indies.*

[30] Jordan, see chapter 11 in this volume.

[31] Burkholder, see chapter 2 in this volume.

of the community. The sale of fiscal offices begun in 1633 brought younger men into the system and reduced movement within it.[32]

Men sought imperial offices because government employment offered income, financial opportunities, and, at the higher levels, prestige. The case of Jonathan Duncan reveals the importance of continued employment to a colonial governor who had twice lost his fortune.[33] Many potential sources of income existed for imperial administrators. Legal income included salary and fees and varied substantially. However, lucrative illicit income was commonplace. In Spanish-America numerous high court magistrates were accused of the outright sale of judicial decisions.[34] Corruption in the treasury offices also appears to have been routine. Whether through active investment in contraband trade or the receipt of bribes to overlook it, officials throughout the Americas reaped the benefits of corruption. Customs officials such as John Hatton in the English colonies were notoriously corrupt.[35] At a higher level, Governor Benning Wentworth of New Hampshire made the transition from bankruptcy to substantial wealth by obtaining a portion of the illegal mast trade as well as his salary and fees.[36]

Receiving an appointment and actually serving were two different things and the use of lieutenants was a common practice in the English colonies. When the man named also had a post in England, he almost invariably employed a lieutenant in the colonies.[37] While provincial officials in the Spanish colonies sometimes used lieutenants, higher ranking officials filled their posts personally. They were, moreover, under strict injunction to assume their positions as soon as possible. The Crown ordered *audiencia* ministers named while in Spain to be prepared to embark for America within sixty days of obtaining their title of appointment.[38] Moreover, the Spanish Crown expected officials in the colonies to remain at their posts until they were replaced. To journey to Spain for whatever reason required a license which normally specified the period of time allowed. The English crown also granted its officials leave of absence and Thomas Irving obtained a six-month leave with pay in 1772 that was subsequently extended for an additional eighteen months.[39] On several occasions, Sir Thomas Lawrence was able to return to England from Maryland.[40]

---

[32] Andrien, see chapter 3 in this volume.

[33] Rabitoy, see chapter 15 in this volume.

[34] See Mark A. Burkholder, 'Honest Judges Leave Destitute Heirs: The Price of Integrity in Eighteenth-Century Spain' in Richard K. Matthews ed., *Virtue, Corruption, and Self-Interest: Political Values in the Eighteenth Century* (Lehigh, PA, 1994), pp. 247–269.

[35] Gerlach, see chapter 13 in this volume.

[36] Daniell, see chapter 12 in this volume.

[37] Labaree, *Royal Government in America*, p. 104.

[38] Mark A. Burkholder, *Politics of a Colonial Career: José Baquíjano and the Audiencia of Lima* (Albuquerque, 1980), p. 118.

[39] McCusker, see chapter 14 in this volume.

[40] Jordan, see chapter 11 in this volume.

Once in their positions, officials found themselves working under a variety of pressures.[41] Colonial chief executives arrived with instructions from their respective crowns. Frequently they found themselves in conflict with other officials.[42] Pressure from local families and economic interests were also important and a governor who supported local interests, such as the long-serving Governor Benning Wentworth of New Hampshire, could enjoy popularity while profiting personally.[43] The tension between serving royal interests while looking out for personal, family, and friends' interests was very real. Despite a variety of sanctions aimed at keeping officials in line, royal interests frequently suffered when bureaucrats participated in commerce and the local economy and married local women. In the Spanish and Portuguese empires, becoming a godparent to American-born children further extended bureaucrats' integration into local society.[44]

Bureaucrats in each empire sought to benefit their families, an objective that often included securing employment for their sons. New Hampshire governor John Wentworth, for example, represented the third generation of his family to hold the post.[45] Both Thomas Irving and his son William served as Inspector-General at different times.[46] Thomas Lawrence, the secretary of Maryland, later secured the same post for his son.[47] Numerous magistrates of the court of Bahia were sons of bureaucrats. Although more multi-generational high ranking bureaucratic families were present in Spain than in the Spanish colonies, overseas dynasties existed as well. Three generations of the Santiago Concha family served as ministers on Spanish American *audiencias*. Numerous examples also exist of bureaucrats marrying into other bureaucratic families.[48]

A description of the offices and responsibilities of imperial administrators based upon official job descriptions provides an impression of royal administrators belied by an examination of the officials themselves. Most imperial administrators with lifetime appointments were men who, with the exception of English placemen intent on enriching themselves and returning to England, eagerly entered the societies where they lived and worked. The higher their rank, the closer they were to the apex of those societies. An important consequence of the

---

[41] Phelan, see chapter 1 in this volume; see also John Leddy Phelan, *The Kingdom of Quito in the Seventeenth Century: Bureaucratic Politics in the Spanish Empire* (Madison, 1967).

[42] Standen, see chapter 16 in this volume, Jordan, see chapter 11 in this volume.

[43] Daniell, see chapter 12 in this volume.

[44] Schwartz, see chapter 8 in this volume.

[45] Daniell, see chapter 12 in this volume.

[46] McCusker, see chapter 14 in this volume.

[47] Jordan, see chapter 11 in this volume.

[48] Mark A. Burkholder and D. S. Chandler, *Biographical Dictionary of Audiencia Ministers in the Americas, 1687–1821* (Westport, Conn., 1982), pp. 317–319; Andrien, see chapter 3 in this volume.

administrators' integration into local societies was that they then served more as mediators between their crowns and the local populaces then overseers of royal legislation. Beset by conflicting pressures from other officials and institutions, most administrators served themselves, their families, and their friends more effectively than their royal employer.

Although historians have examined colonial administration for many years and published numerous fine institutional studies, they have paid significantly less attention to the bureaucrats themselves with the important exception of those who were chief executives. The selections in this volume emphasize the imperial administrators and their working environments rather than colonial administration in general. The Spanish Empire is particularly well-represented for it had the largest number of imperial administrators and its colonial bureaucracy was the first to develop fully.

John Leddy Phelan's 'Authority and Flexibility in the Spanish Imperial Bureaucracy' (chapter 1) provides a broad overview of the pressures on administrators within the colonial context. Although focused on colonial Spanish America, the article contains numerous insights which help in understanding the behaviour of administrators in other colonies as well. 'Bureaucrats' by Mark A. Burkholder (chapter 2) provides an overview of the types of officials present in the Spanish Empire. Kenneth J. Andrien's 'The Sale of Fiscal Offices and the Decline of Royal Authority in the Viceroyalty of Peru, 1633–1700' (chapter 3) and M. A. Burkholder and D. A. Chandler's 'Creole Appointments and the Sale of Audiencia Positions in the Spanish Empire under the Early Bourbons, 1701–1750' (chapter 4) document the sale of appointments for two important administrative institutions and indicate the implications of such sales. Jacques A. Barbier's 'Élite and Cadres in Bourbon Chile' (chapter 5) and D. A. Brading's 'Government and Élite in Late Colonial Mexico' (chapter 6) investigate the ties between the high level bureaucrats and local élites in two administrative centers. John Lynch's 'Intendants and Cabildos in the Viceroyalty of La Plata', 1782–1810 (chapter 7) discusses the impact of a new group of administrators, the intendants, on local government toward the close of the colonial era. Stuart B. Schwartz, 'Magistracy and Society in Colonial Brazil' (chapter 8) provides a prosopographical analysis of the members of the High Court of Bahia that documents their ties to the local elite.

Stephen Saunders Webb, 'Army and Empire: English Garrison Government in Britain and America, 1569–1763,' (chapter 9) supplies prosopographical information on the governors-general within a broader argument concerning the nature of colonial administration. Ian Steele, 'Governors or Generals? A Note on Martial Law and the Revolution of 1689 in English America' (chapter 10) raises some questions about Webb's argument. The remaining selections on English America illustrate common characteristics of English colonial administration through the lives and careers of individuals. These articles include: David W.

Jordan, 'Sir Thomas Lawrence, Secretary of Maryland: A Royal Placeman's Fortunes in America' (chapter 11); Jere R. Daniell, 'Politics in New Hampshire under Governor Benning Wentworth, 1741–1767' (chapter 12); Larry R. Gerlach, 'Customs and Contentions: John Hatton of Salem and Cohansey, 1764–1767' (chapter 13); and John J. McCusker, 'Colonial Civil Servant and Counter-revolutionary: Thomas Irving (1738?–1800) in Boston, Charleston, and London' (chapter 14). 'Jonathan Duncan: A Lesson in Administrative Survival' by Neil Rabitoy (chapter 15) outlines the conservative actions and attitudes of a governor of British Bombay. S. Dale Standen, in 'Politics, Patronage, and the Imperial Interest: Charles de Beauharnais's Disputes with Gilles Hocquart' (chapter 16), documents characteristics of bureaucratic behavior in New France.

Taken together, the selections in this volume illuminate both similarities and differences among the bureaucrats in the New World empires. With only rare exceptions they were born either in Europe or were descended from Europeans. Almost invariably, Spain, Portugal, England, and France relied upon men from the home country to serve as colonial chief executives. As a rule these executives were nobles and professional soldiers who had previously served their monarchs elsewhere. While numerous other high-ranking officials were also of European birth, men of European descent born in the colonies began to secure government positions and in some cases rose to offices just below the chief executive within decades after colonization began. Unless they served in the highest ranks of the administrative structure, colonial officials lacked formal prerequisites for appointment beyond literacy. An informal advantage, however, was the influence of prominent families and ties at court. Finally, there is little doubt that bureaucrats in all of the colonies, in turn, used their positions for personal gain. Aside from these generalizations, however, the differences among the bureaucrats are far more striking than the similarities.

The large population and geographic area of the Spanish colonies coupled with their comparatively early settlement by Europeans resulted in a larger and more fully developed administrative apparatus than in the English, French, or Portuguese colonies. The Spanish colonies were also more likely to have professional administrators who served in more than one colonial city or town. The ministers who served on the regional high courts and advisory bodies of Spanish and Portuguese America were uniformly men with university training in law. In New France intendants whose responsibility included the administration of justice normally had legal training. In the English colonies, however, legal training was not a prerequisite for judicial service.

Service in colonial office could result in advancement to a post in the mother country, but such an opportunity was greater for British officials and high-ranking Portuguese officials than for Spanish officials. Few Spanish colonial bureaucrats born in Spain succeeded in returning there until the late eighteenth century. Naturally bureaucrats born in the New World, and especially in colonial capitals, wanted to serve as native sons in their home districts and virtually none had a desire to serve in Spain itself.

A bureaucrat's interest in obtaining a post in the mother country and his perception of that possibility clearly affected the attitude he took in fulfilling his responsibilities. The phenomenon of the placeman anxious to enrich himself and return to a post in England had no counterpart in the Iberian colonies. In Spanish America an official sent from Europe was much more prone to marry a local woman and to sink social and economic roots into the district where he served. The consequence was a network of interest groups that bound bureaucrats, wholesale merchants, large landowners, and other members of the elite into mutually beneficial relationships that did little or nothing to advance royal interests.

With the exception of New France, which was lost to Britain as a result of the French and Indian War, one can argue that the looseness of royal control in the European colonies in the Americas facilitated the retention of empire. As long as the weight of colonial rule rested lightly on the local elites, loyalty to the metropolis was easily maintained. Thus while marriages between bureaucrats and local women often worked against short-term royal interests, these and other social and economic ties between officials and persons in the district of their employment encouraged bureaucrats to mitigate potentially negative consequences of royal dictates. Strict enforcement of unpopular legislation, on the other hand, could spell disaster for the metropolis, as England discovered when she faced the American Revolution.

From the appointment of Columbus as viceroy and governor in 1492 until the colonies became independent, colonial administrators were a characteristic feature of royal colonies in the New World. Some were efficient, effective, and honest; others were lazy, corrupt, and sought only personal gain. Some served but a brief term in office; others held royal appointments for life and at times served many decades. As a group, however, bureaucrats were essential for the preservation of extensive and long lasting European colonies in the New World.

Select Additional Bibliography

The selections in this volume will introduce the reader to colonial administrators, but numerous other works provide additional information and broader coverage. The starting place for identifying further material is *The American Historical Association's Guide to Historical Literature*, 2 vols., 3rd edition (New York, 1995). David P. Henige, *Colonial Governors from the Fifteenth Century to the Present: A Comprehensive List* (Madison, 1970) is valuable both for its list of governors and its bibliography.

For the Spanish Empire, Bradley Benedict's 'El estado en México en la época de los Habsburgos', *Historia Mexicana* XXIII, no. 4 (1974), pp. 551–610 illuminates the backgrounds and career characteristics of the viceroys of Habsburg Mexico. Two of the few biographies of viceroys in English focus on the sixteenth century: Arthur Scott Aiton, *Antonio de Mendoza, First Viceroy of New Spain* (Durham, N.C., 1927) and Arthur Franklin Zimmerman, *Francisco de Toledo, Fifth Viceroy of Peru, 1569–1581* (Caldwell, Idaho, 1938). J.I. Israel's *Race, Class and Politics in Colonial Mexico 1610–1670* (New York, 1975) highlights conflict at the viceregal level. Linda Arnold's *Bureaucracy and Bureaucrats in Mexico City, 1742–1835* (Tucson, 1988) is a comprehensive group portrait. Bernard E. Bobb's *The Viceregency of Antonio María Bucareli in New Spain, 1771–1779* (Austin, 1962) details the activities and policies of a late eighteenth-century viceroy. José María Restrepo Sáenz's *Biografías de los mandatarios y ministros de la real audiencia, 1671–1819* (Bogotá, 1952) provides biographical sketches of the chief executives and audiencia ministers of New Granada. Ministers of the Audiencia of Caracas are examined by Alí Enrique López Bohórquez in *Los ministros de la audiencia de Caracas, 1786–1810* (Caracas, 1984). Guillermo Lohmann Villena's group biography, *Los ministros de la audiencia de Lima en el reinado de los Borbones, 1700–1821* (Sevilla, 1974), is an extremely informative study of Peruvian ministers. John Jay TePaske, *The Governorship of Spanish Florida, 1700–1763* (Durham, N.C., 1964) provides a valuable examination of a key position. Kenneth J. Andrien breaks new ground on the appointment and careers of fiscal officials in *Crisis and Decline: The Viceroyalty of Peru in the Seventeenth Century* (Albuquerque, 1985). Mark A. Burkholder's *Politics of a Colonial Career: José Baquíjano and the Audiencia of Lima* (Albuquerque, 1980) follows the career of a minister near the close of the colonial era.

Jacques A. Barbier's *Reform and Politics in Bourbon Chile, 1755–1796* (Ottawa, 1980) highlights infighting among colonial administrators and city officials in Santiago, Chile, as well as illuminating the bureaucrats' social and economic ties there. Susan Migden Socolow has written a full account of the expanded bureaucracy of the Río de la Plata in *The Bureaucrats of Buenos Aires, 1769–1810: Amor al Real Servicio* (Durham, 1988).

The only empire-wide examination of a single group of bureaucrats in Spanish America is by Mark A. Burkholder and D.S. Chandler in *From Impotence to Authority: The Spanish Crown and the American Audiencias, 1687–1808* (Columbia, Mo., 1977). Their *Biographical Dictionary of Audiencia Ministers, 1687–1821* (Westport, Conn., 1982) provides corresponding biographical sketches of the ministers. Members of the Council of the Indies in the eighteenth century receive similar treatment in Burkholder's *Biographical Dictionary of Councilors of the Indies, 1717–1808* (Westport, Conn., 1986).

Two works are indispensable on colonial bureaucrats in Brazil: Stuart B. Schwartz's *Sovereignty and Society in Colonial Brazil: The High Court of Bahia and its Judges, 1609–1751* (Berkeley and Los Angeles, 1981) and Dauril Alden's

Royal Government in Colonial Brazil with Special Reference to the Administration of the Marquis of Lavradio, Viceroy, 1769–1779 (Berkeley and Los Angeles, 1968).

For the English colonies, Stephen Saunders Webb studies the governors-general at length in *The Governors-General: The English Army and the Definition of Empire, 1569–1681* (Chapel Hill, 1979). Stanley Nider Katz's *Newcastle's New York: Anglo-American Politics, 1732–1753* (Cambridge, Mass., 1968) examines a group of royal governors and their political environment. A sampling of the extensive number of biographies of individual governors and other officials includes: Mary Lou Lustig's *Robert Hunter, 1666–1734: New York's Augustan Statesman* (Syracuse, 1983); John A. Schutz's *William Shirley: King's Governor of Massachusetts* (Chapel Hill, 1961); Demond Clarke's *Arthur Dobbs Esquire, 1689–1765: Surveyor-General of Ireland Prospector, and Governor of North Carolina* (Chapel Hill, 1958); and Michael Garibaldi Hall's *Edward Randolph and the American Colonies, 1676–1703* (Chapel Hill, 1960).

For New France, W. J. Eccles has examined in detail the career of one governor in *Frontenac: The Courtier Governor* (Toronto, 1965). Louis Joseph Lemieux's *The Governors-General of Canada, 1608–1931* (London, 1931) provides brief sketches of the administrations of eighteen Governors-General of French Canada but little about the men themselves either before or after their appointments.

As the references above indicate, substantial scholarship is available on colonial administrators. Much of it, however, focuses on individuals, especially high-ranking officials placed in a political setting. This is especially true of the literature on governors in the English colonies. In contrast to the numerous individual studies, relatively few group biographies exist for specific categories of colonial bureaucrats. Those that do exist, moreover, are almost exclusively about high-ranking officials in the Iberian colonies. Opportunities abound, in short, for additional research on colonial administrators. By illuminating the lives and careers of the men responsible for administering Europe's first colonial empires, such research will enrich historians' appreciation of the nature of imperial administration and reveal in greater detail common and unique characteristics of the officials.

For Theodore L. Listerman
With Appreciation

1
Authority and Flexibility in the Spanish Imperial Bureaucracy

John Leddy Phelan

The approach to the Spanish colonial bureaucracy is that of the "conflicting standards analysis," first suggested by Andrew Gunder Frank. Given the ambiguity of goals and the frequent conflict among the standards, all the laws could not be enforced simultaneously. The prevalence of mutually conflicting standards, which prevented a subordinate from meeting all the standards at once, gave subordinates a voice in decision making without jeopardizing the centralized control of their superiors. Historians have traditionally assumed that the Spanish administration had a nonambiguous set of goals and that standards of conduct for its administrative agents were not mutually conflicting. The conflicting-standards hypothesis, however, provides a more satisfactory explanation of the wide gap between the law and its observance in the Spanish empire. Particular emphasis is given to an analysis of elements of centralization (the residencia *and the* visita*) and those of decentralization ("I obey but do not execute" formula). This approach not only applies to the Spanish-American administration; it may also throw some light on the structure and nature of several kinds of bureaucratic organizations.*

The author is associate professor in the Department of History at the University of Wisconsin-Milwaukee.

SOCIETAL and political stability was a predominant feature of Spain's vast overseas empire. In an age of slow communications Spain was able to preserve her widely scattered colonial dominions in both America and Asia against frequent foreign threats and occasional internal revolts without heavy reliance on military coercion.[1]

Two institutions were primarily responsible for the maintenance of a social status quo that endured for three centuries. They were the Spanish Catholic Church—and it was more Spanish than Roman—and the imperial bureaucracy. The effectiveness of these two institutions became apparent in the period following the wars of independence. Political emancipation swept away the imperial bureaucracy, and the Church emerged from the struggle with its traditional sources of power considerably undermined. Political instability resulted. The new republican ideology inspired by the American and the French revolutions did not fill the vacuum created by the abolition of the colonial bureaucracy and the weakening of the Church. Actually the military organization seized control after independence, and the various ideologies were scarcely more than a façade for masking this control.

In view of the predominate role of the colonial bureaucracy in creating conditions of durable social stability, the dynamics of this system merit some scrutiny. The aim of this essay is to examine the Spanish bureaucracy in terms of a thought-provoking hypothesis recently advanced by Andrew Gunder Frank. Although Frank's hypothesis was inspired by his study of the operation of the industrial system in the Soviet Union, his model illuminates the functioning of other bureaucratic systems as well.

THE HYPOTHESIS

Mr. Frank outlined his model as follows:

More than one hierarchal channel of communication is maintained. Multiple and, at least, in part conflicting standards are set by superiors for subordinates. Conflict may arise among standards set within each hierarchy as well as among those set by different hierarchies. Subordinates are free to decide which of the conflicting standards to meet, if any. However, subordinates are responsible to superiors for their performance with respect to all standards; and subordinates may be

[1]We would like to take this opportunity to express our appreciation to James D. Thompson, director of the Administrative Science Center at the University of Pittsburgh. This paper was discussed at a meeting of the Center May, 1959.

held responsible for failure to meet any standard. The relative importance of standards is neither well, nor completely defined, nor is it entirely undefined. The priority among standards is ambiguous. Subordinates make their assessment of priority to guide their decision making and task performance. Each subordinate appeals to those standards which are most in accord with his incentives and the circumstances of the moment and to those which are most likely to be invoked by superiors in evaluating his performance. Superiors in turn make their assessment of priority to guide their necessarily selective evaluation of subordinates' performance and enforcement of standards. The entire process is continuous: superiors modify the set of standards to comply with their changing objectives; subordinates adapt their decisions to changing standards and to changing circumstances; superiors enforce standards in accordance with the changing priority.[2]

In this model two outstanding features are flexibility and authority. Flexibility encompasses (1) the response of subordinates to changing objectives of their superiors, (2) the adaptability of subordinates to adjust to changing circumstances, and (3) the initiative of subordinates in sponsoring innovations. In this context of the term, authority means sensitivity of subordinates to their superiors' objectives rather than mere adherence to their rules. The Weberian distinction between formal rationality and substantive rationality is pertinent. Formal rationality refers to rational calculation and predictability based on adherence to specified procedures, which result in task performance; substantive rationality refers to the achievement of task performance itself regardless of the means employed. The bureaucratic systems under discussion exhibit substantive rather than formal rationality.

The multiplicity of standards permit superiors to make their ever-changing wishes felt by adding new standards or shifting the emphasis among existing ones. By their very incompatibility, multiple standards allow a wide latitude of discretion to subordinates, resulting in the decentralizing of decision making. Selective evaluation of performance and selective enforcement of standards makes the incompatibility among the standards operationally feasible.

[2]Andrew Gunder Frank, Goal Ambiguity and Conflicting Standards: An Approach to the Study of Organization, *Human Organization,* published by the Society for Applied Anthropology, 17 (1958–1959), 11.

This system also generates authority. Superiors can invoke, if they wish, one of the many standards that has not been met. Selective enforcement permits superiors to convert potential authority into real authority at any given time. Hence subordinates remain sensitive to the wishes, both formal and "real" of their superiors. The existence of multiple hierarchies and alternative channels of communications prevent subordinates from obstructing the upward movement of information about their own malperformance. By providing superiors with a wide fund of knowledge about conditions below, subordinates are made more responsible to their superiors.

In applying this hypothesis to the Spanish imperial bureaucracy, the structural features of the colonial administration must first be outlined. Then the kinds of standards imposed on the colonial magistrates by their superiors in Spain must be classified before the nature of the magistrates' response to the superiors can be assessed. Finally superiors' evaluation and enforcement of their subordinates' conduct in the colonies will be considered.

The illustrative data will be chosen from events connected with the Indian policy of the Crown during those decades spanning the end of the sixteenth and the beginning of the seventeenth century. The illustrative material could equally well have been selected from the eighteenth century. The essential organizational features of the bureaucratic system created by the Habsburg monarchs were not appreciably altered after the advent of the Bourbon dynasty in 1700. In the eighteenth century, however, the change of emphasis was the effort to make the system more efficient to increase the Crown's revenues. This study offers few new data. Its primary purpose is to outline a working hypothesis which may provide a new conceptual framework for fresh research.

THE STRUCTURE OF THE COLONIAL ADMINISTRATION

At the summit of the Spanish colonial bureaucracy was the king. Directly under the monarch was the Council of the Indies, exercising by royal delegation supreme jurisdiction over all phases of the colonial administration: legislative, financial, judicial, military, ecclesiastical, and commercial. Only at the top was the imperial bureaucracy highly centralized in the persons of the king and his Council. The Crown's agents in America and in the Philippines were the viceroys, the governors, and the Audiencia. The viceroys and the governors ostensibly held supreme sway in both civil and military matters;[3] in their territories they were the immediate representatives of the king. Command of the military establishment and the secular aspects of church government were under their jurisdiction. They nominated most of the lesser colonial officials subject to the eventual confirmation of the Council in Spain.

The centralization of authority in the viceroys and the governors was, however, more apparent than real. In various spheres the jurisdiction of those magistrates was rigidly limited. Many of the viceroy's subordinates as well as the judges of the Audiencia and the exchequer officials, who were his quasi peers, were appointees of the Crown. They corresponded directly with the Council. Under these circumstances the control of the viceroy over some of his subordinates and his quasi peers was frequently nominal. Although the viceroys had virtually unchallenged freedom in matters of routine administration, even in this their powers were limited; for every aspect of colonial life down to the most minute and insignificant details was regulated by a voluminous body of paternalistically inspired legislation issued by the Council. Viceroys and governors were under standing orders to enforce these mandates. These regulations were codified by 1681 in the celebrated *Recopilación de leyes de las reynos de los Indias*. In matters of policy the viceroys were supposed to refer all decisions to Spain.

The viceroy shared many of his powers with the Audiencia, the second hierarchy in the system. Those bodies were the highest court of appeal in their respective districts. The Audiencia also

[3]Before the eighteenth century there were two viceroyalties in the New World. That of New Spain embraced all of Spanish North America, and that of Peru included all Spanish South America. The viceroyalties were divided into Audiencia districts headed by a governor, a captain general, or a president. In the viceroyalty of New Spain there were Audiencia districts for Mexico City, Guadalajara, the Antilles, Central America, and the Philippines. Although the viceroy enjoyed greater social prestige than the chief magistrates of the Audiencia districts, the latter in their districts exercised substantially the same powers as the former did in theirs. For purposes of discussion the viceroys and the governors may therefore be included in the same classification.

served as an advisory council to the viceroy or governor and exercised certain legislative functions. In any clash between the two, ultimate authority usually rested with the viceroy. Yet a vacillating presiding officer or a refractory Audiencia could easily upset this rather delicate balance of jurisdictions.

In addition to the viceroys and the Audiencia the two other administrative hierarchies were the ecclesiastical and fiscal. Under the system of the *real patronato de las Indias* the king, as patron of the Church of the Indies, acted as the Pope's vicar in ecclesiastical administration. Royal agents administered ecclesiastical taxation, and they nominated all church dignitaries from archbishop to parish priest. Discipline and doctrinal matters were the only significant spheres beyond the immediate control of the Crown. Although the viceroy acted as vice-patron of the Church in his district, the ecclesiastical hierarchy enjoyed a wide degree of quasi-independent action. The prelates could appeal directly to the Council in Spain. They often played the viceroy off against the Council and vice versa.

In ecclesiastical administration the bishops were responsible to the king as patron of the Church of the Indies. In matters of faith, morals, and sacerdotal discipline, however, the episcopacy was accountable to the Pope, and under him the sacred congregations in Rome. There were no substantive conflicts between the Spanish Crown and the Holy See in the area of dogma and doctrine. Jurisdictional clashes, on the other hand, were endless and violent.

Nor was the authority of the bishops over all the priesthood unchallenged. The regular clergy, who initially bore most of the responsibility for converting the Indians, exercised powers often at variance with episcopal prerogatives.[4] This brief survey is meant only to suggest that the government of the Church in the Indies was of such a character as to constitute a partly independent and a partly interdependent hierarchy.

[4]For a survey of the *Patronato* see Clarence Haring, *The Spanish Empire in America* (New York: Oxford University Press, 1947), ch. x. For a discussion of the jurisdictional conflict between the episcopacy and the regular clergy in the Philippines see the author's book, *The Hispanization of the Philippines, Spanish Aims and Filipino Responses, 1565–1700* (Madison, Wis., 1959), pp. 32–35. The Inquisition, which did not have jurisdiction over the Indians, formed another semiautonomous administrative hierarchy inside the Church.

The officers of the royal exchequer, while of lower rank than the viceroys and the governors, were of co-ordinate authority in their sphere of administering royal revenue.

The viceroy, in reality, was the co-ordinator of the various administrative hierarchies. He served as the presiding officer of the Audiencia in its role as a Council of State, as vice-patron of the Church, and as president of the *junta superior de la real hacienda* (the exchequer office). Furthermore, the functions of each hierarchy were sometimes exercised by members of another. In the event of the sudden death of the viceroy, the Audiencia assumed supreme command of the government until a successor arrived from Spain. Archbishops sometimes served as viceroys. In spite of these occasional mergers of offices and the nominal centralization of power in the viceroy, the three other hierarchies retained a substantial amount of autonomous power, and each one was responsible directly to the Council of the Indies in Spain.

The Crown deliberately maintained several channels of communication with its colonial agents. The purpose was to ensure that superiors in Spain would have multiple sources of information as to actual conditions. As Clarence Haring has put it:

> The only real centralization was in the king and his Council in Spain. Spanish imperial government was one of checks and balances; not secured as in many constitutional states by a division of powers, legislative, judicial, executive, but by a division of authority among different individuals or tribunals exercising the same powers. There never was a clear-cut line of demarcation between the functions of various governmental agencies dealing with colonial problems. On the contrary, a great deal of overlapping was deliberately fostered to prevent officials from unduly building up personal prestige or engaging in corrupt or fraudulent practices.[5]

Motivated by an abiding distrust of its agents overseas, the Crown gradually fashioned during the course of the sixteenth century a complex bureaucratic pyramid with multiple, partly independent and partly interdependent hierarchies. Under this system the con-

[5]Haring, *op. cit.,* p. 122. This study is an authoritative account of the structural features of the colonial bureaucracy. See especially chs. vi, vii. Also, see Enríque Ruíz Guiñazú, *La magistratura indiana* (Buenos Aires, 1916); José María Ots Capdequí, *El estado español en las Indias* (Mexico, 1941); Ernesto Schäfer, *El consejo real y supremo de las Indias* (2 vols.; Seville, 1935).

flicts between the various bureaucracies were continuous and acrimonious, since their jurisdictions often overlapped. Internal conflicts within the bureaucracies themselves were perhaps somewhat less frequent, but did occur. In the ecclesiastical bureaucracy the tensions were particularly severe. The bishops and the secular clergy were pitted against the regular clergy, and conflict between the various orders of the regular clergy was not uncommon. The bishops and the Crown often clashed over jurisdictions.

THE NATURE OF THE STANDARDS IN THE SPANISH ADMINISTRATION

Standards refer to that multiplicity of pressures to which all colonial administrators had to adjust in order to survive in office. The most apparent standards were those interminable directives issued by the Council of the Indies. These mandates were often mutually contradictory. The incompatibility of the Council's directives in regard to the Indians stemmed in part from the Crown's desire to reconcile the needs of the natives and those of the colonists. The Spanish monarchs partially justified their sovereignty over the Indies from the missionary obligation to convert the Indians to Christianity. Both as infidels and even more so as "new Christians," their property rights and personal liberty merited some protection.[6] Furthermore the Church threw its considerable weight toward the protection of native rights. The spirit and intent of the Indian legislation of the Crown reflected the conviction that the Indians constituted an inferior group in society whose rights and obligations, however, deserved paternalistic protection. The conditions under which the Indians might render labor services to the colonists were minutely regulated in a voluminous body of legislation eventually codified in the *Recopilación,* but these edicts were more frequently honored in their breach than in their observance.

This wide gap between the law and its enforcement resulted

[6]For a discussion of the missionary justification of Spanish sovereignty in the Indies see the author's *The Millennial Kingdom of the Franciscans in the New World: A Study of the Writings of Gerónimo de Mendieta, 1525–1604* (University of California Publications in History, No. 52; Berkeley and Los Angeles, 1956), ch. i; also Some Ideological Aspects of the Spanish Conquest of the Philippines, *The Americas,* 13 (1957), 221–239.

partially from another source of pressure. Colonizing had to be made profitable for the Spanish colonists, and that meant some form of exploitation of native labor. The Crown usually sought to reconcile the welfare of the Indians and the general well-being of the colonial economy. Harmonized they sometimes were, but there were striking cases when the two objectives stood in naked conflict with each other. The economic crisis created by the diminution of the Indian population in Mexico after 1576 is one notable case in point; another one was the crisis in the Philippines (1609–1648) precipitated by the Hispano-Dutch war in the Orient.[7] There were also countless other cases in which magistrates in the Indies had to cope with mutually incompatible directives handed down by the Council in Spain.

The prevalence of mutually conflicting standards was further compounded by the ignorance of the central authorities as to actual conditions in the colonies. These local conditions could make the directives of the Council either impracticable or even impossible to enforce. In many cases the Council deliberately defied local conditions. The tendency of the central authorities was to eliminate regional differences, as the Council's aim was to standardize practices throughout the empire. Hence circular cedulas were often dispatched to all the Audiencias of the empire. Such a practice reflected the supreme indifference, if not the active hostility of the central authorities, to local conditions. The Philippines, for example, would be treated on occasion as if they were another Mexico.

In view of the Spanish procedure of assigning the same functions of government to different agencies, bureaucrats had to cultivate a sensitivity to the aims and the procedures of their peers in the other administrative hierarchies. In the sphere of Indian legislation, for example, the viceroys had to take into account the views of the clergy. The bishops in their ex officio role as protectors of the Indians could intervene in those cases where the economic demands of the state or the colonists encroached upon the religious welfare of the neophytes. Given their countless missions among the natives, the regular clergy also had a vested interest in all

[7]For the Philippine crisis see *Hispanization of the Philippines*, pp. 98–102.

matters pertaining to the welfare of the Indians. The officers of the exchequer were concerned with the fiscal aspects of Indian administration. A special responsibility of the Audiencia was the legal defense of the natives. In the administration of Indian affairs a viceroy or governor would be ill-advised not to take into account the viewpoints of his judicial, ecclesiastical, and fiscal peers. Decisions were often the result of tension and conflict, the consequence of the fact that the jurisdictions of these partly independent and partly interdependent hierarchies overlapped. Nor could the governors or viceroys ignore their subordinates. The middle-echelon officials, by virtue of their long tenures in office covering many administrations, were not without the means to influence the conduct of their superiors, the viceroys.

Although there was no organized and articulate press to serve as a vehicle of protest against bureaucratic incompetence, colonial subjects did not lack means for voicing their grievances. The wealthy and the educated often corresponded directly with the Council of the Indies. The Archivo General de Indias in Seville contains countless petitions and protests of corporate groups like town councils or class groups like encomenderos as well as memoranda from private citizens.

A system of incentives and penalties further encouraged colonial magistrates to adjust to the multiplicity of pressures. The offices in the colonial bureaucracy were in effect monopolized by peninsular Spaniards. They formed a class of career bureaucrats. They were likely to be sent to any region of the empire. Promotion and spoil were their incentives, as was assignment to a favored geographical location. Posts in an isolated and economically underdeveloped colony like the Philippines were considered far less desirable than stations in Mexico or in Peru, where a more agreeable climate and more lucrative emoluments of office attracted ambitious royal servants. Notwithstanding severe and widespread clashes of interests and values among the members of the system, colonial bureaucrats appeared to share an underlying esprit de corps that they belonged to a common body whose existence ought to be perpetuated. Most of the members seem to have been motivated to some significant degree by a feeling of personal involvement in the system's ultimate welfare. In addition to the incentives of advancement there was also a whole series of penalties. They ranged from reprimands, demotions, loss of office, fines, and criminal prosecution for those who miscalculated the pressures of a given situation.

All of these pressures—orders from Spain, local conditions, the peers and subordinates of bureaucrats, public opinion, incentives, and penalties—served to create a whole complex of standards, which guided and conditioned the conduct of colonial officialdom.

The very multiplicity and the often mutually contradictory character of the standards contributed both to maintaining authority and to providing flexibility. The issuing of new directives by superiors made those objectives known to their subordinates and hence contributed to the maintenance of authority, whose two components are knowledge by subordinates of the wishes of their superiors and compliance by subordinates. Multiplicity of standards also increased flexibility. Superiors had the opportunity to change directives and standards as the occasion demanded. In view of their contradictory nature, subordinates necessarily had a certain latitude in their choice of what standards to enforce.

FLEXIBILITY

There were a variety of ways in which colonial administrators responded to those manifold pressures created by mutually incompatible standards.

A well-documented example occurred in Mexico. New Spain's century of depression originated in the great epidemic of 1576–1579, in which the Indian population was massively diminished by the spread of contagious diseases against which they had no acquired immunity. The crisis was hastened by the accompanying rapid decline in available native labor, the increase of the non-Indian population (Spaniards and mestizos), and the extensive use of native labor by the regular and the secular clergy for their many architectural enterprises. Another factor complicating the plight of the Indians was a change in land use, in which a large portion of the land of central Mexico was removed from the production of maize and given over to the raising of livestock. The landscape of Mexico was radically altered by the advance of herds of cattle, sheep, and goats. The non-Indian population was determined to maintain its customary standard of living, with the result that the pressure on the rapidly diminishing Indians for increased grain production became almost intolerable. Stopgap measures such as the establishment of public granaries and a crude system of price fixing did not succeed in guaranteeing an adequate flow of foodstuffs to the cities.

The *repartimiento* (a system of compulsory draft labor) and the rise of a latifundia system based on Indian debt peonage by the middle of the seventeenth century arrested the contracting economy. Earlier, during the first administration of Velasco the Younger (1590–1595), the *repartimiento* was failing to draft enough labor from the steadily diminishing Indian population to meet even those demands which crown officials recognized as having a prior demand on what labor was available.

As the labor market was tightening, new orders arrived from Spain. The reform projects contained in the cedulas of November 24, 1601, and May 26, 1609, envisaged a drastic lightening of the labor burdens of the Indians. Motivating the crown's policy were a variety of considerations, ideological as well as humanitarian and economic. The Indians as recent converts to Christianity merited the Crown's special protection. Compassion for the plight of the Indians who were being decimated by famine, disease, and overwork was another factor. Thirdly, enlightened self-interest advocated measures of relief. The Indians must be preserved, for they were the colony's principal labor force. The viceroys, the Audiencia, and even the clergy did not discount the pertinence of these arguments. Yet the same officials realized that the implementation of the cedulas of 1601 and 1609 would only aggravate an already desperate crisis. Famine in the cities of New Spain instead of the threat of famine might ensue. In the face of conflicting standards, the responsible authorities in New Spain gave priority to the overall economic crisis rather than the specific plight of the Indians. Invoking a traditional formula of Spanish administrative procedure, the viceroys and the Audiencia obeyed but did not execute the orders of the Council.[8]

[8]For the demographic crisis see Lesley Byrd Simpson and Sherburne F. Cook, *The Population of Central Mexico in the Sixteenth Century (Ibero-Americana,* 31; Berkeley and Los Angeles, 1948); for the change in land use, Lesley B. Simpson, *The Exploitation of Land in Central Mexico in the Sixteenth Century (Ibero-*

The actual operation of this formula merits closer examination. Geographical isolation of the colonies, wide divergence in regional conditions, and only partial awareness of these conditions on the part of the central authorities made some such institutional device desirable. The formula's origins go back to the Roman law concept that the prince can will no injustice. The "I obey" clause signifies the recognition by subordinates of the legitimacy of the sovereign power who, if properly informed of all circumstances, would will no wrong. The "I do not execute" clause is the subordinate's assumption of the responsibility of postponing the execution of an order until the sovereign is informed of those conditions of which he may be ignorant and without a knowledge of which an injustice may be committed.

Presiding magistrates in the Indies were permitted by law to postpone the execution of royal orders whose implementation might create an injustice or undesirable social conflicts. Colonial administrators were required to justify immediately their conduct to the Council. The central authorities in return might reissue the orders in their original form, or they might modify them in accordance with the suggestions of the local authorities. The latter in turn might invoke the formula again in the hopes that by procrastination the unwanted proposals might be buried by bureaucratic inertia.[9]

Colonial administrators had to apply with discretion the "I obey but do not execute" formula. A reckless use of this power might arouse the ire of the Council. Offenders might incur any number of penalties, ranging from reprimands to demotions, to loss of office or imprisonment. The colonial bureaucrat constantly needed to strike a delicate balance between the orders of his superiors in Spain and the dictates of local pressures. Many a bureaucratic career ended in disgrace that could be traced back to a miscalculation of the relative importance of the pressures in a given situation. The Spanish colonial bureaucrat like his modern Russian counterpart had to orient himself to his superiors' "real" objectives, which were often not reflected in the actual instructions emanating from Spain.

Thus, the "I obey but do not execute" formula appears as an

Americana, 36; Berkeley and Los Angeles, 1952); for the economic crisis Woodrow Wilson Borah, *New Spain's Century of Depression (Ibero-Americana,* 35; Berkeley and Los Angeles, 1951).

[9]Haring, *op. cit.,* pp. 122–123.

institutional device for decentralizing decision making. Its frequent use enabled colonial officials to postpone indefinitely the execution of royal wishes. Furthermore, its operation reveals the more positive role of subordinates as policy makers. By postponing the execution of royal mandates and presenting fresh proposals, viceroys, Audiencia, and archbishops could influence the reformulation of their superiors' directives. New instructions from Spain often reflected to some extent, at least, the viewpoint of officials in the Indies.

The dialectic of the Spanish administrative system may be clarified by Hegelian formula. The thesis is the wishes of the Council embodied in its directives dispatched to the colonies. The antithesis is that complex of pressures or standards to which colonial administrators had to adapt, pressures often in conflict with the Council's instructions. The synthesis is what actually emerged. That was not only always a satisfactory but usually a workable compromise between what the central authorities intended and what local pressures would permit.[10]

The Spanish colonial administration was, in effect, a dynamic balance between the principles of authority and flexibility, in which the highly centralized decision making vested in the king and the Council was counterbalanced by some substantial measure of decentralized decision making exercised by bureaucratic subordinates in the colonies.

INSTRUMENTS OF CONTROL

If the "I obey but do not execute" formula gave colonial magistrates some measure of freedom in which to maneuver, other institutional devices made officers in the colonies sensitive to the wishes of their superiors in Spain. There were two institutional procedures by which superiors in Spain enforced standards and reviewed the performance of subordinates in the Indies. They were the *residencia* and the *visita.*

The *residencia* was a judicial review of the conduct of a magis-

[10]If local conditions gave officials in the Indies a comfortable freedom of action in enforcing mutually incompatible directives from Spain, these same conditions allowed the natives to be selective in their responses to the settled governmental policy of hispanizing indigenous culture. See *Hispanization of the Philippines,* pp. 153 ff.

trate at the end of his term of office. All appointees of the Crown with the notable exception of the clergy were required by law to submit to a *residencia* at the termination of their tenure. A specially designated *juez de residencia* conducted a public court of inquiry in which he heard all charges of malfeasance against the former incumbent. After receiving the latter's defense, the judge passed sentence and remitted his findings to the Council of the Indies for final review. Heavy fines, confiscation of property, imprisonment, or all three, were customary sentences in cases of grave misconduct in office. The fact that sentences in the Indies were often reversed or altered in Spain does suggest that decisions sometimes reflected the personal bias of the judges or that the official under investigation was able to bring to bear commanding influence at Court. Thus there was a Spanish counterpart to the Russian *blat*.[11]

The *visita* differed from the *residencia* in respect to procedure. Both devices, however, shared a common purpose, that is, to serve as agencies of royal control over subordinates in the colonies. The *residencia* was public and statutory. It took place at the end of a magistrate's term of office. The *visita,* on the other hand, was a secret inquiry which could be made at any time during a magistrate's incumbency. Generally applied as a crisis measure, it usually reflected the discontent of the central authorities with a specific situation in the colonies. The aim of the *visita* was to prod apathetic subordinates into taking more vigorous action, whereas the *residencia's* objective was to expose and to punish illegal practices. There were restricted *visitas* applying to a single official or to a single province, and there were general *visitas* in which an entire viceroyalty or an Audiencia district came under investigation. The visitor general could examine all aspects of administration. He might interrogate any magistrate from the viceroy or the archbishop downward. It is indeed a moot question as to whose authority was supreme during the term of the visitation—that of the viceroy or that of the visitor.[12]

[11]*Blat* in the Russian productive setup represents the element of personal influence which oils the wheels of the informal procurement system. See Frank, *op. cit.*, p. 9.

[12]Haring has an evaluation of both the *residencia* and the *visita, op. cit.*, pp. 148–157. Also see *Recopilación,* Bk. V, tit. xv (1681).

The opinion of the Marquis of Montesclaros, viceroy of Peru (1607–1615) has often been quoted. He likened the *residencia* and the *visita* to gusts of wind which one frequently encounters in the streets and in the public squares and which accomplish nothing but to raise the dust and refuse and cause everyone to cover his head. This bon mot may be an apt contemporary evaluation of the institution from the viewpoint of subordinates subject to investigation. Yet the perspective of the investigators, the Council of the Indies, was a different one. These twin procedures enabled superiors in Spain to enforce standards in the colonies and to review periodically the performance of subordinates. The *visita* functioned as a means of enforcing old standards, establishing new ones, or enunciating a new priority among existing standards. The *residencia* became an instrument for reviewing the past performance of subordinates. Both procedures were highly selective. Some standards were violated in order to enforce others, as the wide gap between the law and its observance in the colonies amply attests. Magistrates in the Indies, however, never for a moment forgot the existence of this highly institutionalized system of enforcement and review, however selective its application may have been in practice. Its operation certainly encouraged them to keep in harmony with their superiors' "real" wishes.

The key to this hypothesis about social organization lies in selective evaluation and selective enforcement. Selectivity makes a system with conflicts among the standards operationally feasible.

CONCLUSIONS

In summary, the operation of the Spanish colonial system apparently has some features common to the Soviet industrial system.

1. The members of both organizations were motivated to some significant degree by personal involvement in the system and its welfare.

2. Looking at the Spanish administration as a whole, one can see no single guiding goal or objective save that tendency common to all bureaucracies—the tendency toward self-perpetuation. Nor are there several goals commensurate with each other. Hence the goals are difficult to rank. The standards to which individual agents were subject often clashed with one other, and no clear-cut priority

among these standards was available for the agents. A notable exception to the over-all goal ambiguity of the Spanish system is the case of the Church. The spiritual welfare of the natives and the colonists was a clear-cut goal from which the Church could scarcely deviate, although various branches of the clergy clashed over the means of reaching that goal.

3. The Spanish system like the Russian was task-performance oriented.

4. Both systems are hierarchal and bureaucratic organizations.

5. In short, both administrations constitute multiple, partly interdependent and partly independent, hierarchies with mutually incompatible standards, selective enforcement of standards, and selective review of performance.

The fact that the Soviet productive system is undergoing intensive change while the Spanish administration was not does not seriously impair the over-all validity of the analogy between the two systems. The Spanish system was not static. Change there was, although it was slow in comparison to the quick tempo of change in the Russian industrial system. The Spanish administration possessed a feature lacking in the Soviet industrial organization, that of geographical distance. A one-to-two-year period ensued in the exchange of correspondence between the Council of the Indies and the colonial bureaucrats. This temporal hiatus contributed markedly to slowing down the pace of change in the colonies. As a consequence colonial magistrates had greater freedom in selecting their responses to orders from Spain than do officials in the Soviet productive system, dominated as it is by fast-moving change. More procrastination and a greater degree of venality probably prevailed in the Spanish system than in the Russian one, although unfamiliarity with the Russian sources makes it impossible to make a clear affirmation. A basic issue, which merits more attention, is how essential the element of change is to the hypothesis of conflicting standards and selective enforcement. The fact of geographical distance and its corollary of slow communications seems in the case of the Spanish colonial administration to replace rapid change as an assumption.

Historians have assumed that the Spanish bureaucracy like other bureaucratic organizations had only one goal or a set of commensurate goals and that standards of conduct for members were not mutually conflicting. If this assumption is cast aside in favor of goal ambiguity and conflicting standards, new light is thrown on the chasm between the law and its observance in the Spanish empire. The wide gap between the two was not a flaw, as has been traditionally assumed. On the contrary, the distance between observance and nonobservance was a necessary component of the system. Given the ambiguity of the goals and the conflict among the standards, all the laws could not be enforced simultaneously. The very conflict among the standards, which prevented a subordinate from meeting all the standards at once, gave subordinates a voice in decision making without jeopardizing the control of their superiors over the whole system.

This hypothesis, I suggest, can serve as a point of departure for monographic research that may provide us with a new and richer perspective on the working of the Spanish bureaucracy. Here only a few suggestions for future research will be outlined. In this essay the "downward" communication from superior to subordinate rather than the "upward" or "lateral" communication from subordinate to superior has been stressed. One aspect of this has already been touched upon. Subordinates did play a role in formulating the directives of their superiors through the advice and information they transmitted upward. It would be equally desirable to explore at greater depth the "horizontal" relations of the members of the various administrative hierarchies.

Since the standards set by the Council of the Indies were often mutually incompatible as well as in conflict with local conditions, the task of the historian is to evaluate the priority among those standards in any given situation. Which ones were enforced at the expense of others? In many cases a compromise emerged with token or partial enforcement of some standards. In this essay I have stressed some of the conflicts inherent in the Crown's Indian policy. Equally significant incompatibilities prevailed in other spheres of colonial administration.

In a sense this essay has been a "shakedown cruise." If this preliminary investigation proves anything at all, it justifies making further efforts. The various components of Frank's hypothesis now must be tested against a mass of documentary evidence in a concrete historical setting. The historian tries to preserve the flavor and uniqueness of individual human experience. My primary concern is not with bureaucracies as such, but with a particular bureaucracy during a specific time span. In a study of the dynamics of the Spanish imperial bureaucracy in which we are currently engaged, we have little doubt that Frank's hypothesis will provide a useful set of questions with which to interrogate the documents.[13] That the answers which will emerge from this interrogation may result in significant revisions of the original hypothesis is highly probable, but this net result ought not to obscure the creative role that such hypotheses play in stimulating fresh research.

[13]The specific topic of the book will be a study of the dynamics of the Spanish imperial bureaucracy as reflected in the career of a representative figure of that system. Antonio de Morga (1559–1636) was a vigorous, versatile, and articulate bureaucrat, who achieved distinction as a historian, a jurist, and a specialist in finance. The fact that he served in the Audiencias of Manila, Mexico, and Quito lends to this study something of an empire-wide dimension.

2
Bureaucrats
Mark A. Burkholder

Introduction

After a protracted series of attacks, each capable of causing death, Juan Dávalos y Toledo spoke briefly with the viceroy of Peru and his colleagues on Lima's *audiencia* (high court) on December 6, 1629. Two days later, at four o'clock in the morning, the *alcalde del crimen* (criminal judge of the audiencia) succumbed. His estate, seemingly little more than a few books, was so modest that in his last will and testament Dávalos had beseeched the Franciscans to bury him out of charity. Viceroy Conde de Chinchón was so moved by the judge's poverty that he personally provided 300 pesos to help with the funeral expenses. Following his example, the visitor general and the remaining audiencia ministers also contributed substantial sums. With similar generosity, the judge's creditors cancelled his debts. A Lima matron magnanimously offered the widow housing for her remaining years. On December 9, the viceroy, audiencia, tribunal of accounts, and other tribunals of Lima attended the funeral. After escorting the bereaved family home, the Conde de Chinchón drew from his pocket an appointment as *corregidor* (district governor) of Quispicanche for Pedro Dávalos y Toledo, the eldest son of the deceased, and informed Juan, a younger son, that an appointment as head of an infantry company in Callao soon would follow.

A continent away and a half-century later, cathedral bells clanged the alarm well before dawn on October 15, 1685. A warehouse on Calle Santo Domingo in Mexico City had burst into flames and firefighters were needed.

Stocked with sugar, olive oil, and cinnamon, the building burned for over two hours. The owner, Francisco de Rodezno, was a government auditor who had left the Old World for the New in 1677. Like many auditors in the late seventeenth century, Rodezno had purchased his appointment and subsequently devoted himself to wringing a profit from his investment. He married a woman from Puebla in the fall of 1680, and by the end of the decade had at least one son. Considered prosperous by 1689, Rodezno left a complex estate in Mexico City upon his death in the mid-1730s. By the time of his death, moreover, his American born and educated son José had been well-established for years. Undoubtedly aided by his father's cash, while still a minor José had purchased an appointment in 1710 as a supernumerary judge on the audiencia of Guatemala. Thus the immigrant auditor not only had prospered himself, but had placed his son in an even more prestigious position.

The length of Spanish rule in the Americas, the number of offices available, and the thousands of men who filled the posts make it possible to multiply such vignettes almost endlessly. Perhaps Andrés Pardo de Lago, a native of New Granada who served on the audiencias of Guadalajara and Mexico in the mid-seventeenth century, displayed even greater integrity than Dávalos. When laid to rest in his black robe of office and adorned with the distinctive hood and tassel of a doctor of civil law, Pardo was mourned by the archbishop, viceroy, audiencia, city council, tribunals, clerics, and "all the nobility of the realm" as a man renowned "for his great goodness and Christian proceeding."[1] Rodezno's use of office for personal benefit was probably modest compared to that of José Perfecto de Salas, who allegedly made over two million *pesos* during his long tenure as legal advisor to Viceroy Manuel de Amat in Peru in the late eighteenth century. Seen in broad perspective, however, the careers of Dávalos and Rodezno represent the ends of a continuum of attitude and action, stretching from those officials who perceived office as a public trust to those who viewed it as a source of private gain.

Both Dávalos and Rodezno displayed one characteristic common to officeholders in general and particularly obvious among those in high positions. For most of their adult lives, they had lived and worked, played and prayed, in cities. Officeholders' participation in urban social, economic, and political activities, as well as in administrative and judicial matters, placed them, as a group, in the mainstream of city life.

In Mexico City, Lima, Bogotá, Quito, and the other regional capitals of Spanish America, colonial bureaucracy reached full flower. Offices regularly outlasted the men who held them, and the number of posts increased over time. While family prominence might wax and wane, the recipients of the highest offices were, by virtue of their posts, members of the social and political elite of the capitals. Thus bureaucrats became an institutionalized part of the urban setting. Far more than the famous *conquistadores* (conquerors) the urban bureaucrats represented Spain's domination of the Indies; their presence was imprinted indelibly on the colonial landscape.

Founding an Imperial Bureaucracy

The discovery, exploration, and settlement of the New World presented the Spanish crown with traditional problems set in a new environment. Defense, the establishment and maintenance of royal authority, the extraction of revenue, and the provision of justice to a diverse population were just a few of the challenges that had appeared even before Christopher Columbus died. To meet them, the crown relied heavily upon bureaucrats scattered in the cities and towns that were founded in the wake of conquest. The immensity of the Indies made its division into more manageable units imperative. Within a few decades the crown had established an array of administrative entities of unequal size, shape, population, and importance.

The two major divisions from the sixteenth until well into the eighteenth century were the viceroyalties of New Spain and Peru. The northern viceroyalty encompassed land from the northern boundary of the province of Panama to what is presently the United States as well as to the Caribbean islands, and included part of the province of Venezuela. Even the Philippine islands fell under its jurisdiction. The viceroyalty of Peru included Panama and encompassed all Spanish possessions in South America, with the exception of a strip of Venezuela. When the crown created the viceroyalties of New Granada and the Río de la Plata in 1739 and 1776, respectively, it carved both from the viceroyalty of Peru.

The very size of the viceroyalties and the presence of rich mining regions in the heart of each has made them well known. However, the next largest territorial unit, the audiencia, was in many ways more important. Dating from 1511, with the establishment of a court and administrative body also called an audiencia in Santo Domingo, these territories increased in number as the empire expanded territorially, as well as in both white and *casta* (racially mixed) population. The last audiencia was created in 1787, when highland Peru became a separate administrative district with its capital in Cuzco. With this newest addition, the number of audiencias totaled thirteen. As the following list reveals, except for Cuzco and Guadalajara, each of the mainland audiencias became, with modest modifications, the geographic basis for an independent country in the nineteenth century, while its capital city became the national capital.

Audiencia District	Modern Counterpart
Mexico (and Guadalajara)	Mexico

Guatemala	Central America
Caracas	Venezuela
Bogotá	Columbia
Panama (until extinction in 1751)	Panama
Quito	Ecuador
Lima (and Cuzco)	Peru
Charcas (Chuquisaca)	Bolivia
Santiago	Chile
Buenos Aires	Argentina

The audiencias themselves were divided into smaller districts variously called *corregimientos, alcaldías mayores, gobernaciones,* and, in most of the Empire by 1790, *subdelegaciones*. Groups of the latter comprised intendencies which, from their creation in the late eighteenth century, formed intermediate-sized units within audiencias. The small districts were administered from capitals located in each. Disparate in size, population, and wealth, these provinces, especially the ones most distant from the audiencia capitals, were often subject to rapacious government by officials who were effectively beyond the reach of administrators residing in the audiencia capitals.

Cities, towns, and other municipalities of assorted names were the smallest and most numerous territorial units in the Empire. As did every other jurisdiction, these housed officials of varied titles and responsibilities. The number and importance of the officials, of course, were not the same in a viceregal capital as in a small provincial hamlet. While the latter might have only a handful of local posts, the number of royal offices alone reached over 400 in both Lima and Mexico City by the later eighteenth century.

Listing the territorial units from smaller to larger—municipalities, provinces, audiencias, viceroyalties, and Empire—suggests a pyramidal structure culminating in centralized authority in the hands of the monarch and his advisors in Spain. Reality belied this schema, however. A more accurate image is that of a group of wheels with their hubs in the audiencia capitals and their spokes extending outward to the provinces. The Spanish court, in turn, formed the hub of a wheel whose spokes were the audiencias. From this perspective, decentralization was pronounced in imperial administration.

An awareness of the principal administrative bodies in Spain is necessary in order to understand the imperial bureaucracy as a whole. The importance of the bureaucrats in the viceregal and audiencia capitals to the formulation, implementation, and modification of royal policy, however, makes it essential to focus more attention on the men who held office in the New World. What kinds of offices were there? What responsibilities did they entail? How did officials secure their appointments? Who were the officials, and from where did they come? What kinds of ties bound officials to each other and to the urban centers in which they served? These are some of the questions that will be discussed in the rest of this chapter.

Bureaucratic Organization

Viewed from a broad perspective, four major groups of officeholders provided administration and justice in the New World. Three of these four groups were resident in colonial cities. The highest ranking group was the central administration, based in the Council of the Indies and the House of Trade and located in Spain. In marked contrast to all other officials, few members of the central administration had ever been to the New World. Political administrators formed the second group. Viceroys, captains general, presidents, and provincial executives theoretically served term appointments that usually were less than six years in length. Professional bureaucrats formed the third, and in many ways the most powerful, group in the Indies. These judges, crown attorneys on audiencias, and ministers of the treasury (*caja real*) and accounting offices (*tribunales de cuentas*) held lifetime appointments, forfeited only for cause—such as a serious violation of professional ethics, flagrant abuse of office (usually for personal gain), or excessively scandalous behavior. Finally, there were numerous local and lesser royal offices ranging from chief constable to notary to inspector for weights and measures to city councilman. These were primarily fee-producing or largely honorific positions, and only a few carried even token salaries. Except for elected magistrates, or *alcaldes ordinarios,* incumbents in these posts normally held appointments for life, although many chose to leave office prior to their deaths.

Research on the men named to local and royal positions for the colonial period as a whole reveals that royal and private favors, inheritance, the crown's financial needs, and even "merit" were responsible for their appointments. The importance of each factor varied over time and depended on the office involved. In general, however, the crown's recurrent financial traumas had the greatest effect on appointments to these posts.

Maturation

The euphoria arising from conquest and treasure soon disappeared before the more mundane need to exploit the resources of the New World systematically. In the early decades of Spanish colonization, the crown normally created offices to meet specific needs. From its perspective, officials were necessary to oversee orderly expansion and settlement, provide general administration, mete out justice, collect and disburse taxes, perform ceremonial roles, and deal with local problems. As a general rule, the more responsible and central a post was to the exercise of royal authority, the more care the crown took in filling it; in other words, the crown displayed reluctance to relinquish control over a specific post in direct relation to that post's importance to administration, justice, the treasury, and defense. Financial distress, however, induced the crown to make exceptions to this general policy for immediate cash.

From the outset the crown used its undisputed power of patronage over the empire to pay for services with offices rather than money. As contemporaries expressed it, such a grant of office was a *merced,* a gift producing a source of income for its recipient that could be held until his death and, at times, passed on to his heirs. Thus, for example, Columbus, Pizarro, and Ponce de León received, among other benefits, offices as rewards for exploration, conquest, and settlement.

In Castile recipients of offices as mercedes could "renounce" them in favor of another person, an action that the crown routinely, although not necessarily, accepted and confirmed. With this precedent set, it was but a short step for persons favored with such posts in the Indies to realize immediate gain by privately selling and then publicly renouncing the office received.

Shortly after the conquest of New Spain, the crown took another step that it would repeat on countless subsequent occasions. In 1525, it gave Alonso Pérez de Valera the post of city councilman (*regidor*) for Mexico City in perpetuity. Other comparable appointments resulted both in an end to elected councilmen and, by 1529, in an excessive number of appointees. In short, even before the conquest of Peru was under way, individual purchase of office and inheritable posts existed in the New World.

The crown's view of offices for the Indies altered significantly in 1558. Again following the precedent set in Castile, it decided to sell offices for the Indies on its own account. While he continued to grant most posts as mercedes, Philip II, immediately following the crown's bankruptcy in 1557, introduced the concept of office as a *renta,* or source of income for the royal treasury. The first posts the crown sold were those of *escribano,* or notary, and *alférez,* or municipal standard bearer. The first position could be sold for life, the second in perpetuity if the price offered were sufficiently high.

The crown's alienation of offices expanded in 1581, when, in an effort to improve sales, Philip II agreed that all escribanos, both present and future, could renounce their posts once for a tax of one-third of the positions' value. Although he had sought earlier to open up more positions for sale, it was only after the defeat of the Armada in 1588 had exacerbated the crown's financial woes that, in 1591, the king approved the systematic sale of the post of regidor and related municipal positions for one lifetime.

A royal decree (*cédula*) issued in 1606 rounded out the sale of local offices, a process begun timidly in 1559. By 1606, the list of salable posts included the full range of fee-collecting, honorific, and municipal offices. The decree provided that present and future purchasers held the *oficios vendibles y renunciables,* as the group was known, in full propriety and enjoyed full rights of renunciation in perpetuity upon payment of appropriate taxes. Half of the value of a salable office was paid as a tax at the time of the first renunciation. Subsequently, the tax was one-third of the value of the post. While the decree alienated the positions from crown control, it instituted a steady source of revenue for the ever-depleted royal coffers. It also guaranteed, of course, that families could retain a given position for generation after generation. Entrenchment of local families in local office, in short, was blessed by law.

While peninsulars held the first positions of regidor and alcalde ordinario on the city councils of Mexico City and Lima, inheritance and sales soon brought a predominance of native sons. Men born in America, and probably almost exclusively in New Spain, comprised a majority of the aldermen in Mexico City from 1590 to 1699. Creole hegemony continued for the remainder of the colonial era. Indeed, faced with a virtual monopoly by native sons, in 1772, the crown created six elective positions of honorary alderman, three of which had to be filled by peninsulars. The result was that the city council elected three *radicados,* peninsulars entrenched in Mexico City society and more linked to local than to royal interests.

In Lima local families soon dominated the position of alderman for the same reasons as in Mexico City. A detailed examination of the men elected to the post of alcalde ordinario shows a shift from peninsular to native predominance as well. While only 13 of 70 alcaldes came from Peru in the years 1535 to 1599, the tables turned dramatically in the seventeenth century when peninsulars accounted for only 20 percent of the men elected and natives of Peru for 71 percent. Native son dominance continued to increase at the expense of peninsulars in the eighteenth and early nineteenth centuries, rising to 81 percent from 1700 to 1799 and to 88 percent from 1800 to 1821.

The local posts sold varied greatly in value, and thus in price. Alderman posts in Mexico City sold for amounts between 3,000 and 6,000 *pesos* in the late sixteenth century. With the provisions for inheritance set forth in 1606, however, the price quickly rose to 10,000 pesos. The value of office could decline over time as well. For example, a regimiento in Lima sold for 11,000 pesos in 1700, but only 6,000 pesos in 1760. The fee-earning capacity of some positions greatly enhanced their price. In 1737, for example, the post of chief notary (*escribano mayor*) of the Lima city council sold for 45,000 pesos. In contrast, the same post in Huancavelica in 1740 brought only 9,500 pesos. In Mexico City the post of chief constable (*alguacil mayor*) of the accounting tribunal in Mexico was highly prized. For 45,000 pesos paid in 1655, Pedro Mejía purchased the post, along with the rights to name a lieutenant to serve with him and to receive the salary of *contador mayor* (chief accountant of the tribunal of accounts). One of the highest prices paid in Lima for any position was 80,173 *pesos escudos* paid in 1702, by the Conde de San Juan de Lurigancho for the post of treasurer of the Lima mint. In 1629, a consortium of merchants had financed the purchase of the comparable post in Mexico City for 140,000 pesos.

From the year 1591, when oficios vendibles y renunciables began to appear as a separate item on the summary accounts for the central treasury in Mexico City, until 1808, the proceeds from the sales and taxes on these offices totaled over nine million pesos. While the average yearly income was some 42,000 pesos a year, the range varied from a high of 300,342 pesos in 1606–07 to a low of 826 pesos in 1614–15. As a greater proportion of income came to be generated not by the initial sale of office but by subsequent transfer, the income itself decreased. While annual revenue from the oficios vendibles y renunciables had exceeded 10,000 pesos nine times from 1591 to 1630, from 1631 to 1713 that sum was exceeded only four times, and subsequently never reached. After 1750, the mean annual yield for oficios vendibles in New Spain was under 24,000 pesos.

Excluded from the category of oficios vendibles y renunciables were precisely those positions that the crown rightly considered most central to its maintenance of authority, revenue, and security—those held by the political administrators and professional bureaucrats. Under unrelenting financial pressure, however, the crown gradually turned these offices too into a source of revenue, although it never alienated them in perpetuity.

As the Spanish crown's involvement in European wars repeatedly ravaged royal finances, the desire for offices and the crown's need for money came to coincide. Under continued financial pressure, the crown started selling appointments to treasury posts and the tribunals of accounts in 1633. Provincial administrative positions went on the block in 1677. A decade later, in late 1687, the systematic sale of audiencia appointments began. By 1700, the crown even had sold appointments for the office of viceroy.

The effect of the sale of offices and appointments on the composition of the bureaucracy and its activities cannot be overestimated. First, it determined who the bureaucrats would be. Service at home, if an appropriate position were available, was far more attractive both for peninsulars and for creoles than service in another district on either side of the Atlantic. Thus an immediate result of the sales was to increase the number of men who served in their home region (native sons) and other long-term residents in bureaucratic offices. The corollary to this was a diminution in the crown's ability to control the officeholders. In addition, the purchase of an office increased the pressure on the incumbent to emerge with not only a secure income, but a definite profit. Given the modest salaries associated with non-fee-earning positions, the temptation to resort to extralegal sources of income was irresistible for many bureaucrats. This, too, worked against the crown's interest.

Not far behind each conquistador in the New World was a royal official sent to secure and remit to Spain the crown's share of all treasure. While networks of provincial treasures were established for both New Spain and Peru, the central offices were located in Mexico City and Lima. By the seventeenth century the Lima treasury had three senior officials who collected taxes: a comptroller (*contador*) who oversaw collection and disbursement, a treasurer (*tesorero*) who actually handled the funds, and a business manager (*factor*) who was responsible for selling confiscated goods, collecting taxes paid in kind at public auction, stocking the armories in Lima and Callao, and handling any other commercial transactions associated with the treasury. Assisted by subordinates and often a supernumerary official awaiting a vacancy in a senior office, the *oficiales reales,* as the senior officials were known collectively, were responsible for the honest and efficient handling of the king's finances. In 1605, the crown ordered the establishment of tribunals of accounts in Lima, Mexico City, and Bogotá. Staffed by a small number of auditors, these tribunals were not only to serve as watchdogs for the treasury offices and accounts, but also to collect taxes in arrears from whatever source.

Treasury officials and auditors of the tribunals of accounts received lifetime appointments. While these officials almost always earned lower, and usually substantially lower, salaries than audiencia ministers, their compensation still was well above that earned by the average government employee. Because of the salary, the rank, the security, and, in some cases at least, the financial opportunities available for a person with access to government funds, there was considerable demand for appointments.

Prior to 1633, peninsulars secured far more appointments to the treasuries and tribunals of accounts than did creoles. If the case in Lima is representative, however, most of the peninsulars named were already resident in the Indies at the time of appointment. Viceregal recommendations were particularly important in the appointment of peninsulars as successive viceroys sought to secure posts for their friends and retainers. Only 2 creoles, both native sons, were among the 20 men who served on the tribunal of accounts in Lima from its opening in 1607 to 1633.

Before 1633, appointees were generally experienced public servants with prior service in local or provincial political offices, as functionaries in royal tribunals, or as treasury officers in regional sub-treasuries (*cajas*). In contrast to the background of audiencia ministers, an education at the university level was exceptional among these persons. It was experience that counted, and appointees to Lima often could boast many years of it, frequently outside the capital. For example, Bartolomé Astete de Ulloa left his native Spain for Peru at the age of twenty, arriving in 1598. Following military service and employment in minor posts, he became treasurer for the Potosí district. After working as factor and then, beginning in 1623, as *corregidor* (district governor) for Potosí, he became comptroller for the Lima treasury in 1628, a post he held until his death in 1662. Thus, three decades of service antedated his reaching the Lima treasury.

By 1633, in an effort to wring out still a few more pesos for the war-exhausted Spanish exchequer, the crown turned to the desperate expedient of systematically selling *hacienda* (royal treasury) posts, including those of treasurer and comptroller. Unlike the sale of oficios vendibles y renunciables, which was done in many cases at public auction, the sale of *hacienda* appointments was effected through private negotiation between the purchaser and the crown. The decision to sell the appointments resulted in an altered pool of candidates and a noticeable decline in the standards for appointees to the central treasury and tribunal of accounts in Lima. The Council of the Indies' fear that sales would result in the appointment of dishonest, incapable officeholders, with primary interests divorced from the crown's financial wellbeing, proved correct. The expansion of local ties that followed from sales weakened royal control of these important institutions and undermined efforts to implement increased taxation in the viceroyalty.

Appointees after 1633 were often younger and less experienced than their predecessors. This insured limited maturity and knowledge but, barring premature death, allowed for decades of service. In addition, as money replaced merit as the primary criterion for appointment, would-be purchasers sought the most coveted posts—those in Lima—with particular avidity. Native sons were especially anxious to secure the offices and, once in place, showed no desire to leave. As the previous promotion patterns fell into disuse, officials in regional subtreasuries remained in their backwaters and undoubtedly created or strengthened social, political, and economic ties to leading local families.

In the years from 1701 to 1744 alone, the crown sold at least 31 appointments of regent, auditor, and *oficial* (clerk) of the tribunal of accounts and central treasury in Mexico City. As elsewhere, native sons availed themselves of the crown's financial distress and paid cash for a lifetime post. In 1708, José Benito de Terreros Ochoa paid 5000 pesos escudos for a supernumerary position as auditor for the tribunal of accounts, with full salary and prequisites. Three years later his brother Antonio, already a *relator* (office of the court) for the audiencia of Mexico, secured an appointment as a supernumerary *oidor* (judge) on that tribunal, probably also for a cash payment. In 1740, Francisco Miguel de Berrio y Saldívar, another native son, purchased an appointment as auditor of the tribunal of accounts for 15,500 pesos fuertes.

The sales, of course, did give the crown immediate income. In the seventeenth century the price paid for appointments in the treasury office of Lima varied from 5,375 pesos to 18,750 pesos. Appointments in the tribunal of accounts cost from 2,500 to 20,000 pesos. The post of regent of the tribunal of accounts brought 26,000 pesos fuertes in 1733. Twelve years later Simón de Ontañón, Conde de las Lagunas, paid 31,200 pesos fuertes for a *futura,* or promise of succession, to the same position. The peak price for the office in Mexico City was paid in 1740, when Juan Chrisostomo de Barroeta gave 38,000 pesos fuertes for the appointment and the right to name a man to serve were he himself unable to do so.

The post of provincial administrator—variously called *alcalde mayor, corregidor,* and *gobernador*—was the next one sold. In the sixteenth century the crown had introduced provincial administrators who resided in the urban centers of the interior, both to provide sustenance for non-encomenderos and poor encomenderos (recipient of Indian labor and tribute) and to expand royal authority from the urban areas into the countryside and over the indigenous population. The posts were numerous—88 in Peru in 1633, and about 200 in New Spain. Although cases can be found of men serving or at least holding appointments as a provincial administrator in two or more locations, a single appointment and service of five years or less were more common. While the crown named lawyers to many corregimientos in Spain, in the New World it preferred men with military, or at least militia, backgrounds.

For about a century after the stabilization of these provincial positions in the years 1570 to 1580, most of the men named received their appointments from viceroys or other executives resident in the Indies. During the century dominated by viceregal rather than royal provision of the offices, the notorious system of *repartimiento de comercio* took root. Although located at varying distances from the viceregal capitals, provincial administrators were closely linked to them economically. Using goods advanced by merchants in Mexico City and Lima, the officials participated in the profitable repartimiento of merchandise by which Indians were forced to purchase mules, clothing, food, and other items, whether needed or not. In some regions at least, their production was subjected as well to monopolistic control by avaricious officials.

Some provincial administrators also were linked to viceregal capitals by reason of birth or residence there. In the seventeenth century, for example, some two dozen Lima-born alcaldes ordinarios of the capital served as corregidores during their careers. In New Spain and Peru, descendants of the conquistadores and early settlers were successful in gaining appointments as corregidor. The fact that viceroys enjoyed the right of patronage over the majority of the positions served to help them in their pursuit of appointment, despite the namings of viceregal retainers that occurred.

By 1677, an ever more financially desperate crown began to sell the appointments of corregidor and alcalde mayor. The result was that by 1700, nearly all of these positions had passed from viceregal to royal provision. As was the case with the treasury positions, the crown sold the appointments of corregidor and alcalde mayor on an individual basis, with the amount and terms of the agreement varying. In 1708, for example, Eugenio de Alvarado purchased an appointment to succeed Pedro de Alzamora as corregidor of the city of Trujillo in the viceroyalty of Peru for 6,000 pesos. For the price, Alvarado secured the right to name a lieutenant to serve for him and an assurance that the purchase was firm and that the crown would not renege by means of a subsequent reform. Nicolás Antonio Clerque, however, paid only 1,000 pesos for an appointment as corregidor of the Villa of Santa in Peru. The right to future possession of the much more desirable post of corregidor of Mexico City, and an accompanying rank of colonel, sold in 1731 for 16,000 pesos, while a 1735 appointment secured a futura as alcalde mayor of Tacuba for Mathías García de Gismeros for 1,000 pesos. García de Gismeros also obtained the right to name a lieutenant to serve in his place.

In contrast to the situation regarding local and treasury posts, creoles seem to have secured fewer, not more, provincial offices when the crown began to sell appointments in 1677. This may have been because wealthy and well-educated creoles, especially those who went to Spain, devoted their attention to securing either the more prestigious audiencia and treasury positions or hereditary offices. In addition, the close link between repartimiento of merchandise and provincial officials made it particularly advantageous for monopolistic merchants in Spain to loan purchase costs and travel expenses to men whom they knew personally and whom they could trust to distribute their goods—usually men born in Spain.

Term appointments meant that provincial officials rotated frequently. In contrast, audiencias displayed a notable continuity in personnel. The tribunals were the supreme courts of their districts and subject to appeal to the Council of the Indies only in cases involving major sums of money. Additionally, they had administrative and financial responsibilities. Arguably, the audiencias were the most important single civil institution in the colonies.

From the founding of the first audiencia in Santo Domingo in 1511 to 1808, just under 1,300 men were named to serve on the New World tribunals. Residing in capital cities that became the leading urban centers of the mainland American empire, these men comprised the most highly educated and professional branch of royal administration. Dressed in distinctive black robes, the ministers formed a prominent and highly visible part of urban life. In addition to performing judicial, legislative, and executive duties, they participated in parades, celebrations, funeral processions, baptisms, and other social activities. (See Figure 11.) Unlike the handful of American-born viceroys, none of whom served in the audiencia district of his birth, a number of these ministers secured audiencia appointments in their native districts.

Almost 75 years and just over 200 initial audiencia appointments had passed before the first creoles were named to New World tribunals. In 1585, Antonio Ribera Maldonado, a native of Mexico City, and Hernando de Saavedra Valderrama, a native of Lima, were selected for the courts in Manila and Mexico City, respectively. Given the still small number of creole men born prior to 1560, and thus having attained the minimum age of 25 years required for such a high appointment, these early selections demonstrated that place of birth would not prevent the American-born from receiving offices of high rank and responsibility. That Ribera and Saavedra were named to courts outside their home districts, on the other hand, accurately presaged that, regardless of general legislation calling for native-son appointments to office, the crown had little inclination to apply these requirements to the audiencias.

Only after naming two more creoles to tribunals outside their home districts did the crown appoint a native son. Alonso Bravo de Saravia secured an appointment to the audiencia of Lima, albeit to the junior position of alcalde del crimen in 1602. Alonso, the son of Melchor Bravo de Saravia, the eighth oidor or civil judge named to Lima, was born about 1570. As a boy he went to Spain with his parents, spending some years in the family home in Soria. Passing to the University of Salamanca, he secured the necessary formal education to qualify for an appointment. A Knight of Santiago since 1611, he was transferred from Lima to Mexico City in 1620 to serve as an oidor there.

Alonso Bravo's initial appointment as a native son was unique for 35 years. Indeed, prior to 1687, only six men began their audiencia careers in their home districts. Although very sparing with native son appointments, the crown nevertheless named Americans in every decade from the 1580s to the 1820s. After 1607, in fact, only twice prior to the conclusion of the War of the Spanish Succession in 1713, did more than two calendar years pass without at least one American appointment.

Table 4.1 shows three major periods of American appointments to the New World courts. Beginning with a cluster of American namings (four in 1610–11), the first period extends to the initiation of the systematic sale of audiencia appointments in late 1687. With creoles receiving nearly one of four initial appointments over most of the seventeenth century, a long and repeatedly reinforced record of American success had been established. During this period, Americans benefited from the availability of universities in the major cities of the New World, especially the University of San Marcos in Lima. Modeled on Spanish institutions, the leading universities of San Marcos and Mexico had offered the background in civil and canon law necessary for an audiencia position since the second half of the sixteenth century. As Table 4.2 indicates, South Americans in general and natives of Peru in particular dominated the ranks of American appointees during this period. The University of San Marcos provided the requisite credentials for most of these persons, as well as lobbying at court on behalf of its alumni. During this period, the practice of Americans traveling to Spain to advance their own cases was solidified. A protracted stay at court could yield valuable social, business, and even, for the American who married a peninsular woman, family ties. An audiencia appointment was an elusive goal, but the American who was well-connected at court and persistent in his efforts there had a much better chance of attaining it than did men who remained in the New World.

The appointment of *limeño* (Lima-born) Miguel Núñez de Sanabria as alcalde del crimen of the audiencia of Lima in November 1687, in return for 17,000 pesos initiated the second period, an Age of Impotence that lasted until 1750. For much of this period the crown was unable to staff the audiencias with the kind of appointees it preferred. Yielding to financial necessity, it followed a model already used for treasury posts and provincial administration positions and made individual arrangements with the purchasers. The price paid varied with the location of the office and the special conditions the buyer wanted. The highest price paid was paid by Domingo de Orrantia in 1749. Orrantia, a native of Lima, paid 47,500 pesos for an appointment as a supernumerary oidor and dispensations for being underage to serve the post, marry a native of the district, and hold property in the district. By contrast, in 1740, peninsular Juan José Martínez Patiño paid only 8,000 pesos for a supernumerary appointment as oidor for the audiencia of Guatemala.

The sales that began in 1687 enabled a record number of Americans, including unprecedented numbers of native sons, to reach New World courts.

Table 4.1 Origins of New Men Named to American Audiencias, 1610–1808

	1610–1687		1687–1750				1751–1808		Total	
			All Appointments		Initial Appointments*					
	No.	*(%)*	*No.*	*(%)*	*No.*	*(% of all Appointments)*	*No.*	*(%)*	*No.*	*(%)*
Peninsulars	108	(28.)	158	(50.5)	13	(8.2)	203	(76.)	469	(48.7)
Creoles	93	(24.2)	139	(44.4)	103	(74.1)	63	(24.)	295	(30.6)
Unknown**	184	(47.8)	16	(5.1)	5	(31.3)	—		200	(20.7)
Total	385	(100.0)	313	(100.0)	121	(38.7)	266	(100.0)	964	(100.0)

*Men who purchased their initial audiencia appointments and the percentage of purchasers. Another 12 men, all creoles, probably purchased their initial appointments.
**Nearly all ministers of unknown origin were undoubtedly peninsulars.

Table 4.2 District of Birth for Americans Named to American Audiencias, 1610–1808

	1610–1687		1687–1750			1751–1808		Total	
	No.	*N.S.**	*No.*	*N.S.**	**	*No.*	*N.S.*	*No.*	*N.S.*
Buenos Aires	—	—	—	—	—	3	—	3	—
Caracas	—	—	—	—	—	4	—	4	—
Chile	5	—	5	2	2	9	4	19	6
Charcas	7	1	6	2	—	3	—	16	3
Cuzco	—	—	—	—	—	1	—	1	—
Guadalajara	—	—	5	2	2	1	—	6	2
Guatemala	—	—	2	—	—	3	—	5	—
Lima	51	3	73	27	25	10	1	134	31
Manila	—	—	—	—	—	—	—	—	—
Mexico	6	—	26	11	8	5	—	37	11
Panama	7	—	6	4	2	—	—	13	4
Quito	3	—	3	3	3	1	—	7	3
Bogotá	7	1	4	1	1	11	3	22	5
Santo Domingo	4	—	8	1	—	10	1	22	2
Unknown	3	—	1	—	—	2	—	6	—
	93	5 (5%)	139	53 (38%)	43	63	9 (14%)	295	67 (23%)

*Native Sons. Named to home tribunal by *initial* appointment. Men who moved to their home tribunal with a second or subsequent appointment are *not* counted as native sons in this table.

**Native sons who purchased first audiencia appointment.

Table 4.1 highlights the greatly increased representation of Americans in general and the importance of sales in their appointments. Table 4.2 reveals both the continued preeminence of natives of Peru and the unprecedented number of appointments of native sons that resulted from sales. While sales did not account for all American entry to the courts, they were responsible for a substantial majority of the appointments of creoles named during the Age of Impotence.

The termination of sales at midcentury opened an Age of Authority that extended to 1808. During these years, marked by reforms in many areas, the crown pursued a steady and at times even dramatically enforced policy of increasing peninsular representation and reducing ties between ministers and the districts they served. Tables 4.1 and 4.2 reveal the impact of this policy and the resulting decline in creole appointments in general and native-son appointments in particular. Recognizing the impact of the policy which was followed after 1750, affected parties protested. Individuals who found their careers stymied objected, at times vociferously. Complaints and calls for change also came from city councils, as they perceived the loss of employment opportunities for local men and the reduction of local influence in administration.

By 1687, the sale of appointments for offices by contract with the crown had reached immense proportions. Seventy-five posts in the Viceroyalty of Peru were sold in that year. Although fewer sales occurred in the several years that followed, the total for 1688 to 1695 was over 230. As an appointment to the Council of the Indies already had been sold in 1675 for 50,000 *doblones* the only notable position that remained unsold was that of viceroy.

The office of viceroy held the greatest concentration of authority and responsibility in the New World. Established in New Spain in 1535, in a successful effort to curb the conquistadores and to establish royal authority, the office was extended to Peru in 1543. The crown created a third viceroyalty for New Granada in 1739, and a fourth for the Río de la Plata in 1776. As the pinnacle of authority within their respective domains, the viceroys bore the responsibility for financial, administrative, military, and judicial matters.

From 1535 to 1808, the crown gave regular appointments to only 92 men for the posts of viceroy for New Spain, Peru, New Granada, and the Río de la Plata. Especially in the beginning, it took special care to name men of impeccable social standing and demonstrated ability. Three of New Spain's first four viceroys, Antonio de Mendoza (1535–50), Luis de Velasco "The Elder" (1550–64), and Martín Enríquez de Almansa (1568–80), were strong and capable executives. Luis de Velasco "The Younger" (1590–95 and 1607–11) also earned high marks, but many of his successors were undistinguished. While these four men came from noble families, they were untitled. In contrast, an examination of their successors reveals that, except for one archbishop of Mexico, all prior to Baylio Fray María de Bucareli y Ursúa (1771–79) bore the titles of *conde* (count), *marqués* (marquis), or, in six cases, *duque* (duke). Many, moreover, belonged to a military order. Similar lustre accrued to viceroys in Peru, nine of whom, in fact, previously had served the office in New Spain.

From the sixteenth century on, many viceroys could claim military qualifications. The extension of European conflicts to the New World, in fact, led the crown to emphasize New World military experience in its appointments. One consequence of the crown's emphasis upon military ability and leadership demonstrated in the New World was a decline in the social background of the viceroys. New World service was rarely seen as desirable by the Europeans, and men without noble titles frequently held officerships. In general, the greater weight given to relevant ability over birth resulted in viceroys who, as a group, served their posts satisfactorily.

Although Mendoza, Velasco "The Elder," and Enríquez de Almansa served more than a decade each, the average tenure in office for seventeenth- and eighteenth-century viceroys in both New Spain and Peru was between six and seven years. In the new viceroyalties of New Granada and the Río de la Plata, the average tenure was comparable for the first but less than four years for the second. Extremes in length of service ran from the Conde de Superunda in Peru, who served just over 16 years in the office (1745–61), to the Duque de Veragua in New Spain (1673), who died within a month of reaching Vera Cruz. With only a few exceptions, viceroys were men born and reared in Spain.

Accorded lavish receptions upon arrival and housed in a palace on the central plaza, every viceroy by definition held the ranking social as well as political position in his capital city. Viceroys routinely traveled to their posts escorted by family, friends, and retainers. They expected and often sought to use their offices to benefit these persons, regardless of legislation to the contrary. The patronage they exercised, although reduced over time, offered opportunities to favor retainers as well as to gain substantial sums through the private sale of appointments and favors. Repeatedly, viceroys named retainers to lucrative commissions, appointed them to corregidor or other posts, and smiled beneficently when their minions married local encomenderas or their wives' ladies-in-waiting made favorable matches. By using their office in this manner, they set an example that other bureaucrats tried to emulate, to the best of their ability, for their own more limited staff and families.

Special emphasis must be placed on viceroys' limited tenure, for it contrasted with the lifetime appointments associated with most royal offices. While the king might transfer audiencia ministers and treasury officials at his pleasure, an appointment guaranteed them lifetime employment, barring dismissal for cause. In practice, audiencias, the central treasuries, and the tribunals of accounts regularly had ministers who had served longer in the regional capital than had the chief executive. Given the authority, prestige, and salary associated with their positions, in addition to the normal longer tenure, these ministers found themselves desirable marriage partners and in circumstances that enabled them to benefit financially from establishing local ties. Most who were not native sons—men born in the region in which they served—developed such ties and became *radicados,* and thus were more sympathetic to at least some local interests than they had been upon their arrival as outsiders.

In the last five years of the seventeenth century, the crown finally put its most important single administrative post on the block as well. With the sale of the appointment of Viceroy of Peru to the Conde de Cañete in the mid-1690s, the crown at last had traversed the full distance begun with the authorized sale of *escribanías* (notary public offices) in 1558. While no sale of an appointment of viceroy in the eighteenth century has been uncovered, the crown did sell appointments to the Council of the Indies during the War of the Spanish Succession and, on at least one occasion, again during the War of Jenkins' Ear.

By the middle of the eighteenth century the crown's improved finances enabled it to terminate the sale of audiencia appointments, governorships, corregimientos, alcaldías mayores, and treasury positions. The legacy of the earlier sales, however, would affect the composition of the bureaucracy until late in the century. Although within every decade the king had conferred some positions without monetary payment, it was precisely the widespread reliance upon sales as a fiscal device that brought the crown to the nadir of its control over the colonies. As a corollary, sales resulted in more access to power, both direct and indirect, for the local population in urban centers than had been the case since the crown first set about establishing a full-scale bureaucracy in the New World.

The Royal Bureaucrats

Bureaucrats and local officeholders were spread throughout the empire, with major concentrations of them present only in the audiencia and viceregal capitals. Lima and Mexico City, in particular, housed prominent bureaucracies whose presence was underscored frequently through the participation of the high-ranking bureaucrats in the innumerable processions that added color, excitement, and recreation to urban life. A religious celebration, the arrival or departure of a new viceroy or archbishop, a funeral, an *auto-da-fé* (public punishment of persons convicted by the Inquisition), and other occasions called for parades that brought people of all groups in society to participate or simply to gawk. (See Figure 12.) The public reception of a viceroy of Peru in 1674 was especially magnificent. Cavalry companies, representatives of the royal *colegios* (secondary schools) in Lima, of the University of San Marcos, and of the merchant guild, treasury officials, and audiencia ministers wearing their somber black robes of office passed before the viceroy, who was seated on a reviewing stand. When they had passed, the viceroy mounted a horse led by two city magistrates dressed in red velvet and joined the procession, riding near a large canopy held by the city aldermen. A company of lancers formed the rear guard. At different times aristocrats, members of the military orders, and brilliantly arrayed lackeys and pages were present. The formally attired royal and local officeholders located in the middle of the procession emphasized the symbolic as well as the tangible centrality of royal authority and bureaucrats in urban life.

The very location of principal offices on the central plazas underscored the importance of bureaucrats in colonial cities. Those officials who received direct appointments from the king to high-ranking and managerial positions formed the core of the bureaucracy: audiencia ministers, treasury officials, senior auditors, and, as they were created, the heads of separate major offices such as the tobacco monopoly. Below them were a host of support positions whose number increased slowly until the eighteenth century. Then, especially from around mid-century on, rapid expansion of the bureaucracy took place.

Despite the variety of responsibilities, salary, and perquisites they enjoyed, members of the royal bureaucracies in the capitals had several characteristics in common. That all bureaucrats were men was so obvious to contemporaries that it elicited no comment. Equally commonly assumed, but less rigorously enforced, was that bureaucrats would have acceptable social backgrounds. Legitimate birth and freedom from Moorish or Jewish blood were required, although occasionally celebrated bastards and men of less than pure Spanish descent did hold office.

The family backgrounds of government officials varied considerably within the peninsular and creole segments of society. Although no systematic examinations of the families of large groups of bureaucrats have been made, the variation present among fathers of audiencia ministers in Lima illustrates the range of backgrounds for those men who ascended to the peak of the bureaucracy. Army and militia officers, high-ranking bureaucrats, members of military orders, titled nobles, and merchants accounted for most of the identified fathers. The lowest position or status given was public escribano in Lima. One notable characteristic of native sons named to the audiencia of Lima from 1687 to 1750 was that nearly two-thirds of them were first-generation creoles on their paternal side. A "typical" native-son appointee to Lima during these years was the son of a peninsular father from the north of Spain and a mother from Lima. The father held a military commission or a post in local government. The family had sufficient resources to see the son through a legal education in Lima, and a trip to Spain, some time at court, and, probably, to provide at least a portion of the cost of an appointment.

Bureaucrats varied widely in age. Aside from audiencia ministers and officials who had started out as merchants, bureaucrats commonly began their careers in their teens or early twenties, at times working as *entretenidos* (apprentices) with little or no salary until death or promotion opened an entry position. Since the crown offered no retirement plan and normally considered retirement only for men who had become blind, deaf, or subject to debilitating illnesses, the bureaucracy always had a geriatric flavor.

The repeated entry of boys into the lower ranks of the bureaucracy is a reminder that educational qualifications ran the gamut from minimal literacy for positions in which reading and writing were necessary to university degrees through the doctorate held by some audiencia ministers. The academic prerequisite for matriculation in a university was proficiency in Latin, associated with completion of a course in rhetoric. Since memorization was a primary requirement for ultimately receiving a baccalaureate, boys of prodigious facility could graduate in their early teens. Small wonder that the careers of bureaucrats often began early.

The location of the most famous secondary schools in regional capitals meant that the students were drawn from less populated areas into the major urban centers. The famous Jesuit colegio of San Martín in Lima, for example, attracted students from nearly 20 separate places of birth in 1618. Among others, Chile, Panama, Chuquisaca, Quito, Paita, Saña, Arequipa, Cartagena, and several areas of Spain were represented, while a numerous contingent of students came from Lima itself. One implication of this was that students absorbed the attitudes and perspectives of the capital city well before they became bureaucrats. Most students undoubtedly emerged as confirmed urbanites, with interests and expectations based upon the pleasures and opportunities of the capital.

While some cities, most notably Buenos Aires, lacked universities, by the close of the colonial period 25 had been founded in America. Although a majority of these did not have all five of the major faculties (philosophy, theology, laws, canons, and medicine), as a group they provided thousands of young men with access to higher education, degrees, and the employment opportunities that followed. As many as 150,000 youths may have received degrees during the colonial period.

Bureaucratic positions provided an income, security, and, at least in the case of higher ones, prestige. The salaries paid varied greatly. Excluding those of the viceroys, who enjoyed princely sums that reached as high as 60,500 pesos, the range was still substantial. For most of the colonial period, audiencia ministers were the highest paid bureaucrats, with salaries that ultimately reached 5,000 pesos in Lima. Senior auditors on the tribunal of accounts in Lima received 3,645 pesos in 1774. Treasury officials earned slightly less with 3,240 pesos and several other auditors earned just over 2,000 pesos. The vast majority of employees, however, earned less than 1,000 pesos a year, a sum just slightly above the salary of a regular army captain.

The crown provided some variance in salaries, depending upon the location of the bureaucrat. According to the chief auditor for the Indies in 1772, Tomás Ortiz de Landazuri, Lima was the most desirable location for an audiencia minister. Not only was it the ranking tribunal in America, but the court enjoyed a generous salary, opportunities for extra compensation, a "pleasant climate," and a ready availability of consumer goods and foodstuffs. Mexico City, in contrast, had lower salaries, fewer commissions available, higher expenses, and a heavier workload.

The value of a salary (normally paid with some regularity) deserves emphasis. To produce the 5,000 peso salary received by audiencia ministers in Lima after the salary adjustment of 1776 would have required income-producing property worth as much as 100,000 pesos. Few persons commanded that much investment capital. And, aside from mortgages such as those issued by religious bodies, few investments would offer security comparable to the receipt of a government salary. Were salary the only attractive feature of the job, high officials undoubtedly still would have been viewed as attractive marital partners.

For low-ranking government employees, salaries were often modest at best. A single official who earned 500 pesos a year in Mexico City in the early nineteenth century was hard-pressed to make ends meet. Housing, meals and beverages, a servant (paid only five pesos a month), candles, boots and shoes, clothing, and the services of a barber consumed his salary. Given the additional expense that a family entailed, many bureaucrats never married.

There are no overall figures available on the percentage of bureaucrats who married. Most viceroys were married, although some were already widowers when they assumed office. Census data in the late colonial period for Mexico City reveal that approximately one-third of the bureaucrats remained single. It appears that marriage in the thirties or later was more common than early marriage among bureaucrats, a consequence of the modest salaries that most received.

Among the advantages of a high-ranking bureaucratic position for the single man was the possibility of marrying a wife who brought a rich dowry. When Mayor Bravo de Saravia married Juan Jiménez de Montalvo, an oidor of Lima, for example, she brought a dowry of 24,000 pesos. At about the same time, Agueda de los Rios i Lisperguer wed Blas de Torres Altamirano, bringing a dowry of 50,000 pesos. At least half of the audiencia ministers named from 1687 to 1808 were married, many to women born in the New World. The benefits that royal service could bring were related directly to one's rank in the bureaucratic hierarchy. Thus an audiencia minister was in a much better position to enrich himself than was a lesser official.

The range of salaries that government employees received meant that employees did not reside in one part of a capital alone. The pattern that existed was that of a fan, with the plaza mayor, or central square, providing the pivot. Fronting on the plaza in Mexico City, for example, were the cathedral and the viceregal palace. As in Lima, the viceroy living in the splendor of a rent-free palace provided the most conspicuous example of proximity to employment and centrality within the urban setting. A small number of other officials also resided in the buildings in which they worked, but they paid rent. The superintendent of the customs office in Mexico City, for example, paid 830 pesos annually for a small apartment in the customs building in the early nineteenth century.

A residence close to the center of a city was considered desirable, and higher ranking bureaucrats generally lived within easy walking distance of their offices. A few oidores in Lima lived as close as the adjacent block. Many lived within six blocks of the royal palace where they worked. In 1613, the postmaster general (*correo mayor*), several aldermen of the city council, and the administrator of the sales tax lived just two blocks away. Housing patterns in Mexico City, and probably elsewhere as well, provided well-integrated accommodations for a spectrum of social and economic groups. While the best paid officials might have private homes, most bureaucrats resided in apartment and tenement buildings spread throughout the city.

The salaries government employees received made them important purchasers of local services and of a wide range of consumer items. The more highly paid officials were expected to maintain a style of life appropriate to their positions. In consequence, they were among the urban buyers of slaves and imported luxury items as well as the employers of domestic labor.

Domestic slaves formed part of the household retinue for the wealthy and even for many persons of lesser means. From viceroy to clerks, many bureaucrats owned slaves. Those who went to Peru from Spain in the sixteenth century received a majority of the licenses granted to individuals to import slaves. The number of slaves that could be imported varied with the official's rank, with most being allowed two or three slaves. In addition, bureaucrats were free to purchase slaves in the New World. Slaves not only performed routine household duties, but also served for many years as armed escorts for high-ranking bureaucrats. Such public display both fed the officials' vanity and stimulated private citizens to emulate them. (See Figure 13.)

While most government salaries were modest, they offered at least minimal security for the employee. Coupled with a lifetime appointment, they made the bureaucrat in any post the envy of many contemporaries. For a position among those at the top of the bureaucracy, competition was extremely keen, and officeseekers (*pretendientes*) often went to great expense and devoted years of effort to secure the coveted office.

The viceroy of Peru's appointment of 52 corregidores from some 600 candidates in around 1670, confirms the existence of competition for office, especially office that offered possibilities of substantial gain within a brief period. Competition for high-ranking offices in the capital could be even stiffer. For posts that the crown filled directly, however, the locus of competition shifted from the regional capitals to the court itself.

Men from any region of the Empire were at a particular disadvantage in the pursuit of high-ranking positions. Characteristically, they most desired an appointment within their home district. They sought, in other words, to be native sons. Named to positions within another district, they normally would enter as outsiders, without social or economic ties to the region, in the same manner as would a peninsular. Even the largest bureaucracies in America, those in Mexico City and Lima, however, had few vacancies at the top.

In both the central treasury offices and audiencias, limited opportunity existed for appointment. From 1620 to 1700, only 20 treasury officials were named for the central treasury office in Lima. During the same year the King appointed 75 men for the 8 posts of oidor of the audiencia of Lima, and, coincidentally, an equal number of men as oidores of the audiencia of Mexico. Because some of the oidor appointments went to men already serving on these courts as alcaldes del crimen or *fiscales* (crown attorneys), the actual number of positions available on the tribunals was even smaller. Moreover, since death was the primary cause of vacancies, the vagaries of individuals' health resulted in periods of several years during which there were no openings.

In specific cases, and especially when it sold appointments, the crown would name supernumerary ministers or grant futuras, promises of a future regular appointment. This benefited the recipients, but ultimately resulted in even longer periods without appointments. From 1695 to 1699, for example, no new oidores were named for the audiencia of Lima. The practice, moreover, meant additional uncertainty for office seekers in general and a potentially greater burden for American applicants in particular.

Far more attention has been devoted to the movement of peninsulars to the New World than to that of creoles to Spain. For Americans who sought high office in the viceregal and audiencia capitals, however, a voyage to Spain and a sojourn at court, while not indispensable, could prove most helpful. The practice of traveling to Spain began early. While a few Americans matriculated at Salamanca or another Spanish university, many went principally to solicit office or other signs of royal largesse. What began as a trickle had turned into a steady stream by the seventeenth century.

High-ranking bureaucrats belonged by definition to the ruling elite of the capital cities in which they served. Their ability to pass on their status to their heirs, however, varied. The opportunities were probably greatest for those men who married following their appointment to office, and thus bestowed upon any children a life begun under the aura surrounding their employment. Ministers whose children were young at the time of their appointment could benefit almost as greatly. On the other hand, a minister who had been named late in life and whose children were already grown and employed at the time of his appointment was less able to help his heirs. Timing, in short, played a part in the transmission of elite status from bureaucrat to heirs.

Some bureaucrats were able not only to pass on high status but even to establish dynastic succession in the bureaucracy. Families such as that of limeño oidor Miguel Núñez de Sanabria, his son, oidor Gregorio Núñez de Rojas, and his grandson, oidor José Antonio Villalta y Núñez, served in the same branch of bureaucracy over generations.

Marriages could create webs of family ties within the bureaucracy that extended among several major regional capitals. The above-mentioned José Antonio Villalta y Núñez, oidor in Charcas, for example, married the daughter of Lima oidor José de Santiago Concha. The marriage gave him two brothers-in-law and a nephew were were audiencia ministers. Together the relatives served on the courts of Charcas, Chile, and Lima. Nephew José de Santiago Concha Jiménez Lobatón remained on Chile's tribunal until the Wars of Independence finally ousted him.

Family connections linked branches of the bureaucracy and bureaucrats, clerics, merchants, *hacendados* (large landowners), elected city officials, and other groups of society as well. Alcaldes of the Lima city council repeatedly were sons, grandsons, or sons-in-law of audiencia ministers. Often siblings achieved prominence in different branches of the local bureaucracy. Tomás de Querejazu y Mollinedo, brother of an oidor of Lima in the eighteeth century, belonged to the city's cathedral chapter. José Borda y Echevarría was the chief auditor of the tribunal of accounts and the brother of criminal judge Manuel Antonio de Borda. While not all audiencia ministers had ties to other officials, the familiar intermingling of royal and local office deserves emphasis as an arena for elite coalescence.

Prominent bureaucrats often were tied also through marriage and kinship to the most powerful financial interests of the colony in which they served. As an oidor of Mexico, Francisco Leandro de Viana married the daughter of a marqués and gained control over prosperous estates. José de Tagle, an oidor of Lima, was the son of one of the city's richest merchants, owned a major estate, rented out urban property, and was involved in commerce. His extended family and financial interests gave him links with nearly every major part of Lima society.

An important contemporary certification of family and personal lustre for much of the colonial era was membership in a military order—Santiago, Calatrava, or Alcántara. To enter an order, the candidate had to be granted membership by the king; be of legitimate birth and proven noble lineage, free from any trace of Jewish or Moorish blood, condemnation by the Inquisition, or employment in a base occupation; and possess sufficient economic resources to maintain the honor with dignity. Dispensation from meeting one of these personal prerequisites usually could be obtained for a price.

The number of members in the New World was never large, a fact that enhanced the attractiveness of entering an order. The viceregal capitals of Mexico City and Lima boasted the largest concentrations, but even in these cities the numbers were small. Mexico City had only 33 members in 1653; Lima had 40 in 1700. Both peninsulars and creoles entered the orders, but men of American birth counted for less than 5 percent (865 members) of the total. Men coveted membership in a military order, and many considered it an ample and adequate reward for protracted or unusual service to the crown.

High-ranking public officials, notably those on the audiencias, the treasuries, and the accounting tribunals, were conspicuous recipients of memberships in both the military orders and, later, the Order of Charles III. This civil order, established in 1771, with the specific purpose of recognizing meritorious civil servants, reduced the emphasis on noble ancestry; persons who could not have met a military order's genealogical tests were admitted on the basis of their bureaucratic service. As a result of its creation, few high-ranking bureaucrats entered military orders after mid-century, being admitted instead to the Order of Charles III.

Like those who held titles of nobility, bureaucrats who entered a military or civil order were unmistakably among the most prominent persons in urban centers, and formed part of the political and social elites of each regional capital. The marriages high bureaucrats and their children contracted, the property they owned, the income they enjoyed, the residences in which they lived, the carriages in which they rode, and their prominence in public parades and celebrations revealed their status. Some miners, merchants, and hacendados, especially in Mexico City in the late colonial period, were much wealthier, but high-ranking officials in every regional capital were powerful and visible representatives of royal authority. It took the Wars of Independence in the early nineteenth century to destroy the stability, flexibility, and general tranquillity that thousands of bureaucrats, both high and low, had labored to establish and then to preserve.

Notes

1. Gregorio M. de Guijo, *Diario, 1648–64*, 2 vols. (Mexico City: Editorial Porrua, 1952), 2: 15.

For Further Reading

Historians have paid more attention to governing and administrative institutions than to bureaucrats as individuals or a group. C. H. Haring, *The Spanish Empire in America* (New York: Oxford University Press, 1947), provides the classic discussion of government and administration at all levels. John Leddy Phelan, "Authority and Flexibility in the Spanish Imperial Bureaucracy," *Administrative Science Quarterly* 5:1 (June 1960): 47–65, explains in general terms how the system actually worked. Ernesto Schäfer, *El consejo real y supremo de las Indias*, 2 vols. (Seville: Escuela de Estudios Hispano-Americanos, 1935–47), provides a wealth of material, including lists of the councilors of the Indies, viceroys, captains-general, presidents, and audiencia ministers up to 1700. The influx of councilors with American experience is considered in Mark A. Burkholder, "The Council of the Indies in the Late Eighteenth Century: A New Perspective," *Hispanic American Historical Review* 56:3 (August 1976): 404–23.

J. H. Parry, *The Sale of Public Office in the Spanish Indies under the Hapsburgs* (Berkeley: University of California Press, 1953), is a useful brief discussion of the topic. His conclusions about the impact of sales on corruption have been challenged by John Leddy Phelan, *The Kingdom of Quito in the Seventeenth Century* (Madison, Wis.: University of Wisconsin Press, 1967). Francisco Tomás y Valiente, *La venta de oficios en Indias (1492–1606)* (Madrid: Instituto de Estudios Administrativos, 1972) is valuable for understanding the progression of sales from their Castilian precedents to 1606. Kenneth J. Andrien,

"The Sale of Fiscal Offices and the Decline of Royal Authority in the Viceroyalty of Peru, 1633–1700," *Hispanic American Historical Review* 62:1 (February 1982): 49–71, describes the adverse impact of the sales on royal authority in Peru. Although Saint Augustine was scarcely urban, Amy Bushnell, *The King's Coffers: Proprietors of the Spanish Florida Treasury, 1565–1702* (Gainesville, Fla.: University Presses of Florida, 1981) is the only full examination of any treasury in the Empire. Guillermo Lohmann Villena, *El corregidor de indios en el Perú bajo los Austrias* (Madrid: Ediciones Cultura Hispánica, 1957); Alfredo Moreno Cebrián, *El corregidor de indios y la economía peruana del siglo XVIII* (Madrid: Instituto Gonzalo Fernández de Oviedo, 1977); Alberto Yalí Román, "Sobre, alcaldías, mayores y corregimientos en Indias: Un ensayo de interpretación," *Jahrbuch für Geschichte von Staat, Wirtschaft, und Geselschaft Lateinamerikas* 9 (1972), 1–39; and Brian R. Hamnett, *Politics and Trade in Southern Mexico, 1750–1821* (Cambridge: At the University Press, 1971) are useful for studying provincial administration.

Few viceroys have received scholarly biographical treatment in English. However, Lewis Hanke, *Guía de las fuentes en el Archivo General de Indias para el estudio de la administración virreinal española en México y en el Perú, 1535–1700,* 3 vols. (Cologne: Böhlan Verlag, 1977), and *Los virreyes españoles en América durante el gobierno de la casa de Austria,* 12 vols. (Madrid: Biblioteca de Autores Españoles, 1976–80) presents relevant bibliography and invaluable documentation.

J. H. Parry, *The Audiencia of New Galicia in the Sixteenth Century* (Cambridge: At the University Press, 1948), Phelan, *The Kingdom of Quito;* and Constance Ann Crowder Carter, "Law and Society in Colonial Mexico: Audiencia Judges in Mexican Society from the Tello de Sandoval Visita General, 1543–1547" (Ph.D. diss., Columbia University, 1971); and, for Brazil, Stuart B. Schwartz, *Sovereignty and Society in Colonial Brazil: The High Court of Bahia and Its Judges, 1609–1751* (Berkeley: University of California Press, 1973) are modern treatments of audiencias. José María Restrepo Sáenz, *Biografías de los mandatarios y ministros de la real audiencia (1671–1819)* (Bogotá: Editorial Cromos, 1952); Abraham de Silva i Molina, *Oidores de la real audiencia de Santiago de Chile durante el siglo XVII* (Santiago de Chile: Imprenta Barcelona, 1903); and Guillermo Lohmann Villena, *Los ministros de la audiencia de Lima en el reinado de los Borbones (1700–1821)* (Seville: Escuela de Estudios Hispano-Americanos, 1974) present biographical information on ministers in three courts. Mark A. Burkholder and D. S. Chandler, *From Impotence to Authority: The Spanish Crown and the American Audiencias, 1687–1808* (Columbia, Mo.: University of Missouri Press, 1977) examine the nearly 700 ministers named to all New World tribunals as well as changes in appointees and appointment policy, and provide lists of appointees for 135 years. Biographical sketches of the individual ministers covered in *From Impotence to Authority* are in the same authors' *Biographical Dictionary of Audiencia Ministers in America, 1687–1821* (Westport, Conn.: Greenwood Press, 1982). The saga of a Peruvian's successful pursuit of an appointment to the Audiencia of Lima is told in Mark A. Burkholder, *Politics of a Colonial Career: José Baquijano and the Audiencia of Lima* (Albuquerque: University of New Mexico Press, 1980).

John Preston Moore, *The Cabildo in Peru under the Hapsburgs* (Durham, N.C.: Duke University Press, 1954) and *The Cabildo in Peru under the Bourbons* (Durham, N.C.: Duke University Press, 1966), and Dominic Azikiwe Nwasike, "Mexico City Town Government, 1590–1650: Study in Aldermanic Background and Performance" (Ph.D. diss., University of Wisconsin, 1972) consider local government in two centers of empire. Peter Marzahl, *Town in the Empire: Government, Politics, and Society in Seventeenth Century Popayan* (Austin, Tex.: University of Texas Press, 1978) examines a provincial town. For an analysis of the cabildo's response to urban crisis, see Louisa S. Hoberman, "Bureaucracy and Disaster: Mexico City and the Flood of 1629," *Journal of Latin American Studies* 6:2 (Fall 1974): 211–30.

A general treatment of the intendant system is Luis Navarro García, *Intendencias en Indias* (Seville: Escuela de Estudios Hispano-Americanos, 1959). Regional examinations include John Lynch, *Spanish Colonial Administration, 1782–1810: The Intendant System in the Viceroyalty of the Río de la Plata* (London: University of London Press, 1958); J. R. Fisher, *Government and Society in Colonial Peru: The Intendant System, 1784–1814* (London: The Athlone Press, 1970); D. A. Brading, *Miners and Merchants in Bourbon Mexico, 1763–1810* (Cambridge: At the University Press, 1971); and Hamnett, *Politics and Trade*. The only examination of a viceregal bureaucracy as a whole is Linda J. Arnold, "Bureaucracy and Bureaucrats in Mexico City, 1742–1835," (Ph.D. diss., The University of Texas, 1982).

Interrelationships among bureaucrats and local society can be discovered in Guillermo Lohmann Villena, *Los americanos en las órdenes nobiliarias (1529–1900),* 2 vols. (Madrid: Instituto Gonzalo Fernández Oviedo, 1947). The implications of such ties are developed in John Leddy Phelan, *The People and the King: The Comunero Revolution in Colombia, 1781* (Madison, Wis.: University of Wisconsin Press, 1978), and, as the best example of an integrated political history, Jacques A. Barbier, *Reform and Politics in Bourbon Chile, 1755–1796* (Ottawa: University of Ottawa Press, 1980).

3

The Sale of Fiscal Offices and the Decline of Royal Authority in the Viceroyalty of Peru, 1633–1700

Kenneth J. Andrien

The decision of the Spanish crown in 1633 to begin the systematic sale of high-ranking treasury appointments in the Indies had far-reaching consequences for the administration of royal finance in the Viceroyalty of Peru. The viceregal treasury, centered in Lima, exercised broad powers over financial matters in the realm; and the implementation of all crown revenue policies depended on the loyalty and efficiency of its officers. Throughout the seventeenth century, treasury officials (*Oficiales reales*) acted as political brokers: mediating between the financial demands of the crown and the frequent resistance of taxpayers in the viceroyalty to new government levies, and helping to maintain the political balance of power essential to the cohesion of the empire.[1] The sale of these important fiscal appointments after 1633 eventually tipped this balance pronouncedly in favor of local citizens as purchasers with strong local connections came to dominate the treasury.

The political changes brought about by the sales between 1633 and 1700 proved particularly damaging to royal authority in the Viceroyalty of Peru. The seventeenth century was a time of financial crisis for the Hapsburg monarchy, when officials in Madrid needed increased contributions from the viceregal treasury to help stem the economic and military decline of Spain in Europe.[2] Selling treasury offices yielded useful

1. John Leddy Phelan has argued forcefully that colonial audiencia officials played an important mediating role between the crown and its subjects in the Indies during the seventeenth century. Phelan's work does not focus on financial or economic matters, and, consequently, he does not discuss the role that treasury officials played in the political decision-making process in the Spanish empire. See John Leddy Phelan, *The Kingdom of Quito in the Seventeenth Century: Bureaucratic Politics in the Spanish Empire* (Madison, 1967), and "Authority and Flexibility in the Spanish Imperial Bureaucracy," *Administrative Sciences Quarterly* (Ithaca), 5 (June 1960), 47–65.

2. For an excellent summary of the crisis in Spain, see J. H. Elliott, *Imperial Spain, 1469–1716* (New York, 1963), pp. 317–381.

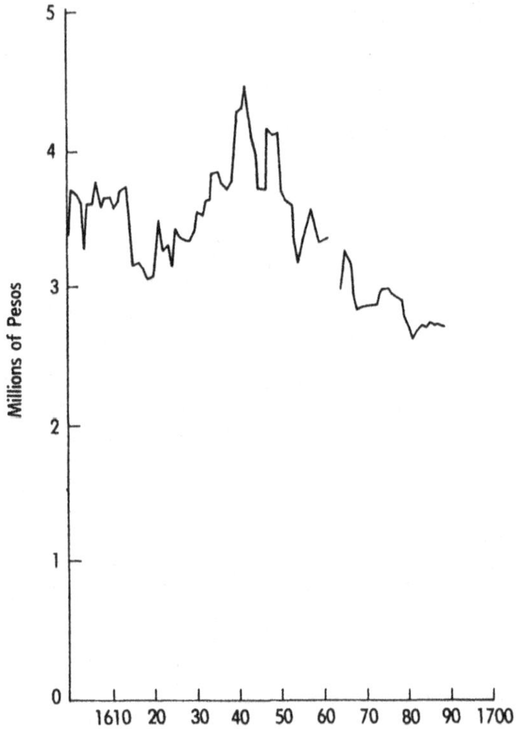

GRAPH I: Three-Year Moving Average of the Total Income Recorded in the Lima Treasury Office in Pesos de Ocho Reales. * Complete accounts for the years 1662–64 are missing from the AGI, Seville, and the AGN, Lima.

funds. At the same time, however, such sales allowed untrained, inefficient, and even dishonest officials to exercise power in this period of crisis. As a result, the sales begun in 1633 contributed to a steady decline in royal control over these officials, whose family, business, and political ties to magnates in the viceroyalty proved stronger than their allegiance to the king. In the end, the ministers of the Peruvian treasury failed to meet the pressing needs of the crown, and remissions of revenue to the metropolis steadily declined.

I.

Historians have long debated the consequences of selling bureaucratic offices in the Spanish Indies. J. H. Parry and Antonio Domínguez Ortiz content that the sale of public offices placed political power in the hands of inexperienced and incompetent men, who viewed their positions as

TABLE 1: Treasury Debts Accumulated by Royal Officials Serving in the *Caja* of Lima, 1620–79.

Treasury official	Years of service	Debts in pesos de ocho
Cristóbal de Ulloa	1620–25	750 pesos 6.5 reales
Juan López de Hernani	1620–26	1,120 pesos 7.5 reales
Leandro de Valencia	1613–26	470 pesos 1 real
Gerónimo Pamones	1625–28	370 pesos 1 real
Bartolomé de Osnayo	1628–31	1,309 pesos 3 reales
Sebastián Hurtado de Corcuera	1631–33	1,309 pesos 3 reales
Hernando Bravo de Lagunas	1633–38	1,095 pesos 4.5 reales
Pedro de Jaraba	1638–48	13,310 pesos 5 reales
Bartolomé Astete	1631–50, 1656–62	22,753 pesos 2.75 reales
Baltasar de Becerra*	1648–49	9,754 pesos 5 reales
Bartolomé Torres Cavallón*	1649–63	10,805 pesos 1.5 reales
Juan de Quesada*	1638–50, 1656–72	39,983 pesos 6.25 reales
Bartolomé de Solórzano**	1650–57	1,761 pesos 6.5 reales
Sebastián de Navarrete*	1651–56, 1663–82	27,516 pesos 6 reales
Francisco de Guerra*	1651–56, 1663–72	6,712 pesos 2 reales
Francisco de Colmenares	1659–1703	29,421 pesos 4 reales
Cristóbal de Llanos Jaraba*	1667–96	20,864 pesos 1.75 reales
Francisco Antonio de los Santos*	1679–1718	4,496 pesos 6.5 reales
		193,807 pesos 1.75 reales

* Men who purchased their appointments.

** Bartolomé de Solórzano served these seven years as supernumerary of the office. Before an opening developed for one of the senior positions, he was promoted to the tribunal of accounts.

sinecures rather than as public trusts.[3] For Parry and Domínguez, this process was one manifestation of the overall decline of the Spanish empire during the seventeenth century. Their conclusions have been modified significantly by Mark A. Burkholder and D. S. Chandler in their exhaustive prosopographical study of the colonial audiencias.[4] Burkholder and Chandler argue that creole appointments to the high courts increased

3. J. H. Parry, *The Sale of Public Office in the Spanish Indies under the Habsburgs* (Berkeley, 1953); and Antonio Domínguez Ortiz, "Un virreinato en venta," *Mercurio Peruano*, 49 (enero–febrero 1965), 46–51.

4. Mark A. Burkholder and D. S. Chandler, *From Impotence to Authority: The Spanish Crown and the American Audiencias, 1687–1808* (Columbia, 1977). See also Mark A. Burkholder and D. S. Chandler, "Creole Appointments and the Sale of Audiencia Positions in the Spanish Empire under the Early Bourbons, 1701–1750," *Journal of Latin American Studies*, 4 (Nov. 1972), 545–579. For an examination of creole influence in the late eighteenth century, see Mark A. Burkholder, "From Creole to Peninsular: The Transformation of the Audiencia of Lima," *HAHR*, 56 (Aug. 1976), 395–415; and Leon G. Campbell, "A Colonial Establishment: Creole Domination of the Audiencia of Lima During the Eighteenth Century," *HAHR*, 52 (Feb. 1972), 1–25. A recent study that examines the sale of corregimientos is Alberto Yalí Román, "Sobre alcaldías mayores y corregimientos en Indias," *Jahrbuch für Geschichte von Staat, Wirtschaft, und Gesellschaft Lateinamerikas*, 9 (1974), 1–39.

dramatically after the systematic sale of appointments in 1687. In addition, many peninsular Spaniards who purchased audiencia positions forged close alliances with citizens in their district and became *radicados en país*, or "firmly rooted in local society by social and economic ties."[5] Burkholder and Chandler's study clearly indicates that local influence in the audiencias did not necessarily signal the decline of the courts, but instead indicated a shift in the balance of power in the empire. The link that Burkholder and Chandler have established between the sale of audiencia positions and political change in the empire poses several important questions. For example, what was the impact of selling treasury appointments in the Indies after 1633? Was the rapid rise of local influence in the audiencias tied to the sale of offices begun in 1633? Did the consequences of selling bureaucratic offices vary in different areas of the empire? The aim of this study is to examine how such political changes in the two chief agencies of the royal treasury in the Viceroyalty of Peru, the tribunal of accounts and the central treasury office in Lima, led to a steady erosion of royal authority during the seventeenth-century imperial crisis.[6]

II.

The royal treasury played a crucial role in maintaining Spanish power and authority in the Viceroyalty of Peru. Throughout the seventeenth century, treasury officials collected the taxes that financed the empire and distributed this income according to the needs of the viceregal administration and the demands of the metropolitan government in Madrid. They also served as judicial officials and took part in the formulation and implementation of crown fiscal policies. Particularly during periods of financial distress within the empire, treasury officials were among the most powerful members of the viceregal government.

For Peru, the tribunal of accounts and the central treasury office in Lima formed the core of this fiscal bureaucracy. Along with the viceroy, who legally headed the treasury, these two agencies supervised or controlled most of the financial operations of the realm. In addition, the

5. Burkholder and Chandler, *From Impotence to Authority*, p. vii.

6. Information on the extent of local influence on treasury officials during the seventeenth century in New Spain may be found in Louisa S. Hoberman, "Merchants in Seventeenth-Century Mexico City: A Preliminary Portrait," *HAHR*, 57 (Aug. 1977), 482–486; Marta Espejo-Ponce Hunt, "The Processes of Development in the Yucatán, 1600–1700" in Ida Altman and James Lockhart, eds., *Provinces of Early Mexico: Variants of Spanish American Regional Evolution* (Los Angeles, 1976), pp. 46–47; and J. I. Israel, *Race, Class, and Politics in Colonial Mexico* (Oxford, 1975), and "Mexico and the General Crisis of the Seventeenth Century," *Past and Present*, 63 (May 1974), 33–57.

senior auditor of the tribunal and the officials from the central treasury office served with the viceroy and the senior oidor of the audiencia on the council of finance (*junta de hacienda*).[7] This council met every Thursday afternoon in Lima to set general policies and priorities for the various treasury offices (*cajas reales*) in Peru and Upper Peru. The *junta de hacienda* coordinated the operation of these widely scattered *cajas*, resolved problems of jurisdictional conflict, made decisions about debt collection, new tax levies, and government expenditures, and dispatched government visitas. The outcome of any financial reform measures designed to increase remissions of revenue to the hard-pressed Spanish crown in Europe ultimately depended on the successful completion of these duties.

Once the *junta de hacienda* established official policies for the viceregal treasury, the task of implementing these directives fell to the individual treasury offices. The crown established these in major mining, agricultural, commercial, military, and administrative centers of the realm; officials serving in them carried out the daily administrative chores of collecting taxes and paying government expenses in their districts. Each office was the center of an administrative orbit of considerable importance. Indeed, the operation of local government depended greatly on the honesty and efficiency of the officials attached to the royal treasury.

The most important treasury office in the Viceroyalty of Peru was that in Lima. Treasury officials in Lima not only collected taxes in their district and served on the important *junta de hacienda*, but also handled funds from other offices since the *caja* of Lima acted as a central clearinghouse for all *cajas subordinadas* in Peru and Upper Peru. At regular intervals the subordinate offices sent their fiscal accounts and surplus income to the central treasury (*caja principal* or *caja matriz*) in Lima.[8] The central office used these funds to pay the expenses of the viceregal administration and dispatched the rest to Spain.

Despite the considerable power of the treasury office in Lima, its administrative structure was quite simple during the seventeenth cen-

7. *Recopilación de leyes de los reynos de las Indias* (Hereinafter cited as *Recopilación*) (Madrid, 1681, repr. 1973), Libro VIII, tít. III, leyes 9,10,11,12,13; Libro II, tít. XVI, leyes 24, 159; Libro III, tít. III, ley 56; and Libro III, tít. XV, ley 52.

8. Surplus income refers to the income remaining after operating expenses for the *caja* had been deducted. The *cajas* of Potosí, Oruro, Otoca, La Paz, San Antonio de Esquilache (Chucuito), Charcas, and Carangas in Upper Peru, along with Huánuco, Pasco, Huamanga, Cuzco, Cailloma, New Potosí (Bombón), Trujillo, Cajamarca, Castrovirreyna, Arequipa, Arica, Piura y Paita, Chachapoyas, and Loja, sent their surplus income to Lima. The provinces of Tierrafirme, New Granada, Quito, Chile, and the Río de la Plata were separate political and bureaucratic units within the viceroyalty, and treasury offices in these regions never remitted surplus income to Lima.

tury. Three senior treasury officials collected the taxes: a comptroller (*contador*), a treasurer (*tesorero*), and a business manager (*factor*).[9] The comptroller supervised the income and expenditures of the *caja*, while the treasurer handled the actual receipt and payment of all authorized funds. The business manager sold all goods confiscated by the government and all taxes collected in kind at public auction, kept the armories in Lima and Callao stocked, and attended to any other commercial transactions involving royal money. One of these three senior officials also served, in rotation, at Callao to operate the customshouse and to oversee the military expenditures of the port. The treasury officer at Callao frequently received aid from a supernumerary (*supernumerario*) of the *caja*, who served as an adjutant at half-pay until one of the senior posts became vacant. In addition, each of the three senior officers had subordinates to assist him in his duties. The crown held the three senior officials collectively responsible for the administration of the treasury.[10]

Apart from administering the royal revenues, treasury officers possessed extensive judicial responsibilities as judges of the court of first instance in all fiscal suits. They commonly ruled on cases concerning taxes, debts, violations of fiscal legislation, corruption, and other fiscal matters. The three officers in Lima heard these cases as a group and had to render unanimous rulings. Even governors and corregidors had to yield to the treasury officers in fiscal cases.

After 1607 the task of supervising the financial dealings of all the treasury offices in the viceroyalty was entrusted to a special tribunal of accounts, located in the viceregal palace in Lima.[11] Each year all the treasury offices in the Audiencias of Lima, Quito, Charcas, Chile, and Panama sent copies of their accounts to the tribunal for audit. The tribunal also examined the accounts of the various individuals or agencies serving as tax farmers in the viceroyalty.[12] After completing these per-

9. Until 1620 the Lima office had a fourth senior position, an inspector (*veedor*). The *veedor* supervised the local mines and worked at the assay office. After 1620 the *veedor*'s duties were assumed by the other treasury officers. Juan de Peñalosa to King, Lima, 1683, Archivo General de Indias (hereinafter cited as AGI), Seville, Lima, leg. 290.

10. The crown held each treasury officer responsible for paying one-third of all fines charged against the office or any money missing from the strong box (*caja fuerte*). In certain extraordinary cases one official might be held culpable, but normally all three officers shared the guilt and the burden of repayment. Gaspar de Escalona Agüero, *Gazofilacio real del Perú*, Biblioteca Boliviana, tomo II, ser. I (1647; La Paz, repr. 1941), Libro I, parte II, cap. I, núms. 11, 12. (1647; La Paz, repr. 1941), Libro I, parte II, cap. I, núms. 11, 12.

11. Fray Buenaventura de Salinas y Córdoba, *Memorial de las historias del nuevo mundo, Pirú* (1639; Lima, repr. 1957), p. 152.

12. *Recopilación*, Libro VIII, tít. I, ley 5. The right to collect certain taxes was often farmed out to various individuals or groups for an established yearly fee or on a percentage basis. These tax-farming contracts (*asientos*) were granted for a limited period of time and were renewable. Such contracts were also common in Europe in the seventeenth century.

iodic audits, the tribunal sent a summary of its findings to the Council of the Indies, keeping copies for its own files in Lima. The tribunal of accounts also served as the final court of appeals in all cases relating to treasury activities in the realm.

Like the Lima treasury office, the tribunal of accounts had a small staff to fulfill its many responsibilities. Early in the seventeenth century only three senior auditors (*contadores mayores*), two lesser accountants (*contadores ordenadores*), and a few minor functionaries served in the tribunal in Lima.[13] By 1629 a backlog of unfinished accounts had accumulated, and the crown authorized the addition of two new accountants (*contadores de resultas*) in order to handle the back accounts and collect debts. Still, the workload of the agency proved beyond the capacity of its staff, and by 1651 the viceroy had added two more *contadores ordenadores* and also authorized the enlistment of several part-time accountants.[14]

To curb the considerable power of the treasury and tribunal officers, the crown imposed a host of laws regulating their behavior. Although many of the regulations were ignored during the seventeenth century, they served as a model of conduct for crown officials of the period. Fiscal officers could not, in law, hold another bureaucratic office, an encomienda grant, or serve in any public or private position that might hinder them from discharging their duties effectively.[15] Personal ties among members of the bureaucracy were forbidden, and intermarriage among the families of government officials was particularly discouraged.[16] Moreover, the law prohibited treasury officers from engaging in commercial ventures. They could not borrow money, or own mines, sugar mills, or land without the consent of their superiors.[17] Authorities in Madrid were adamant in forbidding fiscal officials to use their political position for personal gain or to turn royal funds to their own use.[18] Most of these

13. Tomás de Ballesteros, *Tomo primero de las ordenanzas del Perú* (Lima, 1685), Libro I, tít. XXVII, ordenanza 1.

14. On Sept. 9, 1651, the viceroy of Peru, the Conde de Salvatierra, provided the crown with the following list of the staff of the tribunal of accounts and their salaries: three *contadores mayores* and a supernumerary, each earning 2,250 pesos ensayados; two *contadores de resultas*, each earning 1,250 pesos ensayados; four *contadores ordenadores*, two named by the crown earning 1,000 pesos ensayados, and two viceregal appointees earning 500 pesos ensayados; one *contador* to work at the desk of the account books (*mesa de libros*), earning 400 pesos ensayados; and three *contadores entretenidos*, earning 300 pesos ensayados. Conde de Salvatierra to King, Lima, Sept. 9, 1651, AGI, Lima, leg. 55.

15. Ismael Sánchez Bella, *La organización financiera de las Indias: Siglo xvi* (Seville, 1968), pp. 145–148; and *Recopilación*, Libro VIII, tít. II, ley 13.

16. Sánchez Bella, *La organización financiera*, p. 147; and Escalona Agüero, *Gazofilacio real*, Libro I, parte II, cap. XVII, núm. 4; Libro II, parte II, cap. XVI, núms. 1–3.

17. Sánchez Bella, *La organización financiera*, p. 147.

18. Escalona Agüero, *Gazofilacio real*, Libro I, parte II, cap. XVII, núms. 1, 2; Libro II, parte I, cap. XVI, núm. 2.

prohibitions extended to the wives and sons of the bureaucrats. The *contadores* of the tribunal were also prohibited from meeting collectively outside the chambers of the viceregal palace.[19] Even a short trip beyond the confines of their district had to be approved by the viceroy or the president of the audiencia. When accused of breaking any of these laws, fiscal officials in Lima were suspended from office until the charges were resolved. If found guilty, an official might be obliged to forfeit his office, his personal property, or even his life.

It is not surprising that the crown sought to regulate closely the power of officials serving on the tribunal of accounts and in the treasury office in Lima. Any measure that undermined the power and loyalty of these two agencies could alter dramatically the political balance of power in the empire.

III.

Authorities in Madrid recognized many of the dangers of selling treasury appointments, and only reluctantly approved the policy in 1633.[20] The debate on the measure was most heated in the Council of the Indies. Members of the council warned the king that the sales might allow unqualified, incompetent, or corrupt men to gain these important offices. The councillors cautioned the king to weigh the "merits" of the purchasers against the "considerable amounts of money" offered to meet the "urgent needs" of the financially pressed royal treasury.[21] In addition, the council recognized that the policy was a sharp break with the past. The crown had openly sold some hereditary and transferable offices (*oficios vendibles y renunciables*) at public auction as early as 1559, but these sales involved only minor posts: those for scribes, notaries, and some municipal offices.[22] Treasury officers, however, had extensive financial and judicial powers and received high salaries.[23] Ultimately, only under pressure from Philip IV and his chief minister, Conde Duque de Olivares, did the councillors approve the sales. Faced with bankruptcy and military defeat, the Madrid government decided to sell treasury appointments, regardless of the consequences.[24]

19. Ibid., Libro II, parte I, cap. XVI, núm. 9.

20. Consulta, Madrid, Apr. 27, 1633, AGI, Indiferente general, leg. 757.

21. Ibid.

22. Parry, *Sale of Public Office*, pp. 1–5.

23. In addition, treasury offices could not be passed on to an heir or later sold by the original purchaser, unless these provisions were stated specifically in the official appointment title (*título*).

24. The list of saleable offices expanded to include corregimientos in 1678 and audiencia judgeships in 1687. By 1700, even the offices of viceroy of New Spain and Peru

The crown derived considerable income from the sales and continued them throughout the seventeenth century. It was able to command particularly high prices for seats on both the tribunal of accounts and the central treasury office in Lima. Sales of the offices were made through individual private transactions, rather than at auction, and the receipts went directly to the Spanish treasury.[25] There was no predetermined price list, however, and the amounts charged for each position varied considerably over the years.[26] The price of a post in the Lima treasury office fluctuated between 5,375 and 18,750 pesos.[27] In the tribunal of accounts, the office of *contador mayor* commanded the highest prices—from 9,000 to 20,000 pesos. The lesser positions of *contador de resultas* and *contador ordenador* cost between 2,500 and 8,750 pesos.[28] Since all senior offices in the Lima *caja* were legally equal, no such price differential obtained there. In fact, if no position in the office was vacant, the buyer could purchase a future (*futura*), which entitled him to assume the first available opening in the office, whether it was that of treasurer, comptroller, or factor. Purchasers in the tribunal, on the other hand, usually received a future for one of the three specific *contador* positions. In the *caja* other considerations, such as the immediate financial position of the crown, or the political influence of the purchaser, his past record, his qualifications, and his eagerness to buy an appointment, were the factors that influenced prices. A Spaniard, Dr. Bartolomé Torres Cavallón, purchased a future in Lima, for example, in 1646 for only 6,000 pesos, but he had an advanced academic degree and boasted a distinguished record of government service in Spain and the Indies.[29] On the other hand, a young native son of Lima, Francisco Antonio de los Santos,

---

were sold. Guillermo Lohmann Villena, *El corregidor de Indios en el Perú bajo los Austrias* (Madrid, 1957), p. 130; Burkholder and Chandler, *From Impotence to Authority*, p. 19; and Domínguez Ortiz, "Un virreinato en venta," 46–51.

25. Consulta, Madrid, Apr. 27, 1633, AGI, Indiferente general, leg. 757.

26. In 1692 the viceroy, the Conde de Monclova, provided the crown with a list of office prices to serve as a guide for selling appointments to the major treasury *cajas* in the viceroyalty. Conde de Monclova to King, Lima, Aug. 5, 1692, AGI, Lima, leg. 89. The list is also cited in Manuel Moreyra y Paz Soldán and Guillermo Céspedes del Castillo, *Virreinato peruano: Documentos para su historia. Colección de cartas de virreyes, Conde de Monclova*, 3 vols. (Lima, 1954–55), I, 221.

27. The prices for the treasury offices in the Viceroyalty of Peru may be found in the following locations: Títulos de oficiales reales, Madrid, AGI, Lima, leg. 1070; and Títulos de Indias, Madrid, Archivo General de Simancas, Simancas (hereinafter cited as AGS), Dirección general del tesoro, Inventarios 1, 2, 24.

28. The prices for posts on the tribunal of accounts in Lima may be found in the following locations: Títulos de contadores del tribunal de cuentas, AGI, Lima, leg. 1123; and Títulos de Indias, AGS, Dirección general del tesoro, Inventarios 1, 2, 24.

29. Consulta, Lima, Madrid, Apr. 13, 1646, AGI, Lima, leg. 7.

paid the sum of 14,400 pesos for his future in 1680.[30] This was consistent with the crown's policy of discouraging native sons from serving in the highest echelons of the colonial bureaucracy. In short, each transaction was negotiated separately and the receipts received by the crown varied with individual circumstances.

The prices charged by the crown for appointments to the subordinate treasury offices tended to be lower than those for a similar post in Lima. An appointment in the important mining center of Oruro cost between 8,000 and 10,000 pesos. By comparison, a similar post in a less productive mining area like Bombón varied in price from 2,000 to 5,600 pesos.[31] The average cost of an appointment in the Lima office, meanwhile, was approximately 10,000 pesos, while a post as *contador mayor* on the tribunal of accounts averaged nearly 12,000 pesos.

Despite the considerable income accruing to the crown from the sale of treasury offices in Peru, opposition to the practice continued in the Council of the Indies. Although the councillors recognized the king's legal right to sell public offices in any of his kingdoms, they continued to press for an end to the policy. They feared the sales would allow dishonest and inept men to gain high office during a particularly difficult period in Spain's fiscal affairs. This was bound to damage the efficiency and responsiveness of the viceregal treasury at a time when the crown desperately needed funds from the Indies. In 1667 the president of the council, the Conde de Peñaranda, seemed obsessed with the problem. In secret instructions to the viceroy-designate for Peru, the Conde de Lemos, Peñaranda warned him to beware of opponents on the tribunal of accounts because: "I know little of the subjects who are on it; the offices were bought, and thus the officials show no respect for you."[32] The situation, Peñaranda feared, could undermine the viceroy's position in Lima, hinder attempts to reform the treasury, and ultimately weaken the entire imperial system.

IV.

The Council of the Indies had good reason to fear the consequences of selling appointments to the tribunal of accounts and the treasury in

30. Título de Francisco Antonio de los Santos, Madrid, Dec. 4, 1680, AGI, Lima, leg. 1070.

31. Moreyra y Paz Soldán and Céspedes del Castillo, *Virreinato peruano*, I, 221; and Títulos de oficiales reales de Bombón, Madrid, AGI, Lima, leg. 1070.

32. Lewis Hanke and Celso Rodríguez, eds., *Los virreyes españoles en América durante el gobierno de la casa de Austria*, Biblioteca de Autores Españoles, 6 vols. (Madrid, 1979), IV, 243.

THE SALE OF FISCAL OFFICES 59

Peru. The deteriorating financial position of the crown, which led to the sales in 1633, eventually resulted in officials in Madrid reducing their vigilance in the recruitment and promotion of crown ministers. As a consequence, inexperienced men with strong local connections came to dominate these two agencies, and to prejudice their operation during the years when the Spanish crown most desperately needed greater contributions from the Indies to shore up the financial position of its treasury.

One unforeseen effect of the sales in Lima was to undermine the viceroy's power of patronage over the appointment of treasury officials. Although the king had the legal right to name officials to serve in the viceregal treasury, most of those who purchased offices were already resident in the Indies. In the case of these candidates, the crown had usually had to rely on the advice of the viceroy. Historically the law allowed the viceroy of Peru to make any necessary interim appointments to the treasury, and he frequently offered suggestions about permanent appointments to these important agencies. Naturally the viceroy used his influence in Madrid to ensure that his friends and retainers (*criados*) staffed these posts.[33] After the sales began, however, treasury appointments were negotiated through private transactions between the crown and the purchaser. In some cases the viceroy was not even consulted.

33. The careers of seventy-five members of the tribunal of accounts and the treasury office were examined for this study. This was the total number of *títulos* found in the AGI, AGS, and the Archivo General de la Nación, Lima (hereinafter cited as AGN). Since interim appointments and part-time officials usually did not receive a *título*, they were not included in the study. For the tribunal, the *títulos* were found from 1605, when the agency was founded, until the end of the century. For the *caja*, *títulos* were found only for the period from 1613 until the end of the seventeenth century. Of these seventy-five *títulos*, thirty-one were issued before 1633 and forty-four after that date. All but eight of the forty-four *títulos* granted after sales began were sold by the crown. Prosopographical information on these bureaucrats came from the following sources: Títulos de Indias, Madrid, AGI, Lima, legs. 1070, 1123; Consultas, Madrid, AGI, Lima, legs. 3–13; Cartas de los virreyes, Lima, AGI, Lima, legs. 33–91; Visitas, Lima, AGI, Lima, legs. 109, 115, 276, 280–290, 573, and Indiferente general, 595, 1692; Títulos de Indias, Madrid, AGS, Dirección general del tesoro, Inventarios 1, 2, 24; Manuscritos, Z-222, B-1107, Biblioteca Municipal de Lima (hereinafter cited as BM); Protocolo, ante Francisco Sánchez Becerra, AGN, leg. 1699, fol. 338; Testimonios, Lima, AGN, Superior gobierno, 4; and Testimonios, Lima, AGN, ex-Archivo Histórico del Ministerio de Hacienda y Comercio; Burkholder and Chandler, *From Impotence to Authority*; Hanke and Rodríguez, *Los virreyes*, I–VI; Guillermo Lohmann Villena, *Los americanos en las órdenes nobiliarias, 1529–1900*, 2 vols. (Madrid, 1947); Guillermo Lohmann Villena, *El Conde de Lemos, Virrey del Perú* (Madrid, 1946); Manuel de Mendiburu, *Diccionario histórico-biográfico del Perú*, 14 vols. (Lima, 1874); Joseph Mugaburu and Francisco Mugaburu, *Chronicle of Colonial Lima, 1640–1697*, trans. by Robert R. Miller (Norman, 1975); Pedro Rodríguez Crespo, "Sobre parentescos de los oidores con los grupos superiores de la sociedad limeña (a comienzos del siglo xvii)," *Mercurio Peruano* (julio–septiembre 1964); Juan Antonio Suardo, *Diario de Lima, 1629–1639*, 2 vols. (Lima, 1936); and Luis Varela y Orbegoso, *Apuntes para la historia de la sociedad colonial* (Lima, 1905).

For example, in 1634 a prominent Lima merchant, Juan de Quesada y Sotomayor, went to Spain on business and used the opportunity to negotiate the purchase of an appointment as treasurer in the Lima *caja*, without the prior knowledge of the viceroy, the Conde de Chinchón. When word of the appointment finally reached Lima in 1637, Chinchón wrote a stormy letter to Madrid denouncing Quesada. He objected to merchants' serving in the treasury, especially Quesada, who had many outstanding debts in the city and little training or talent for the job.[34] Quesada's generous offer of 18,750 pesos for the post impressed authorities in Madrid, and they overruled Chinchón's objections.[35] In other cases the crown clearly worked more closely with the viceroy in filling fiscal appointments, and a few viceregal *criados* still received the posts. José de Bernal, a secretary of the viceroy, the Duque de La Palata, received a position as *contador mayor* of the tribunal in 1697, but he was an exceptionally well-qualified man and was not obliged to pay for his appointment.[36] Too often viceregal *criados* like Bernal could not afford to outbid wealthy *radicados* for the powerful and prestigious posts. As the financial distress of the crown grew, authorities in Madrid were more likely to sell the offices for the highest possible price, regardless of the man's qualifications or the recommendations of the viceroy. As a consequence, local magnates in Lima stood a good chance of putting their own candidates in office, even without the support of the viceroy. In all likelihood, as these native sons and *radicados* became less dependent on the viceroy for their appointments, they also became less responsive to his will. This indirect curtailment of the viceroy's patronage power and influence probably hindered efforts to raise taxes in the viceroyalty.

The sale of appointments to the Lima treasury office led to a significant increase in the number of local personnel recruited to serve the crown. Before the sales, the crown favored Spanish-born candidates with few previous ties in the city. In the twenty-year period before 1633, the crown appointed only two creole ministers, Leandro de Valencia and Juan de Guzmán. Valencia came from a prominent conquistador family that had settled in Lima, while Guzmán was from a notable Huánuco family with a tradition of government service.[37] The remaining eight men who held office in the *caja* apparently came from Spain. When sales

34. Conde de Chinchón to King, Lima, May 17, 1637, AGI, Lima, leg. 48.

35. Quesada's offer was the highest price received by the crown for an appointment in the Lima *caja* during the seventeenth century.

36. Hanke and Rodríguez, *Los virreyes*, VII, 148; and Título de José de Bernal, Madrid, Sept. 9, 1697, AGI, Lima, leg. 1123.

37. Lohmann Villena, *Los americanos*, I, 120; and Consulta, Madrid, Jan. 16, 1613, AGI, Lima, leg. 3.

began, two *radicados*, Juan de Quesada y Sotomayor and Baltasar de Becerra, were among the first purchasers.[38] Both were wealthy merchants who had long lived in the city. By the end of the century, the crown routinely approved sales to native sons of Lima. In fact, the last three appointments to the treasury office during the century went to Limeños, Cristóbal de Llanos Jaraba, Francisco Antonio de los Santos, and Francisco de Arnao y Granados.[39] Apparently the financially destitute government of Charles II had little choice but to sell these offices to eager native sons, who were usually willing to pay high prices for the honor and prestige that went with their positions.

The sale of treasury appointments also had a direct impact on the staffing of the tribunal of accounts. The tribunal was considered a chamber (*sala*) of the Audiencia of Lima, the highest judicial authority in the realm, and the crown only reluctantly named native sons and *radicados* to that body. Between the establishment of the agency in 1607 and the inauguration of sales in 1663, authorities in Madrid named only two men identified as creoles, Hernando de Santa Cruz y Padilla and José de Jaraba y Arnedo, to the tribunal of accounts. Both were prominent native sons. Santa Cruz y Padilla was a successful and well-connected merchant, who helped found the consulado in 1613. Jaraba used the good name of his powerful father, Pedro de Jaraba y Vivar, a former treasury officer in Lima, to obtain his appointment.[40] Obviously the crown felt such prominent local figures would prove trustworthy. After 1633, however, the crown seems to have become less selective. Between 1633 and 1660 it sold so many *futuras* that as many as six or seven men held them and were waiting to take the first available opening as *contador mayor*.[41] Of the twelve men who bought futures on tribunal offices between 1633 and 1660, only two have been identified as peninsulars.[42] Like their col-

38. Título de Baltasar de Becerra, Madrid, Oct. 17, 1636, AGI, Lima, leg. 1070; Bartolomé Astete de Ulloa and Juan de Quesada y Sotomayor to King, Lima, Apr. 6, 1650, AGI, Lima, leg. 57; and Conde de Chinchón to King, Lima, May 17, 1637, AGI, Lima, leg. 48.

39. Título de Cristóbal de Llanos Jaraba, Madrid, Aug. 7, 1655, AGI, Lima, leg. 1070; Título de Francisco Antonio de los Santos, Madrid, Apr. 12, 1680, AGI, Lima, leg. 1070; and Título de Francisco de Arnao y Granados, Madrid, Dec. 20, 1680, AGI, Lima, leg. 1070.

40. Rodríguez Crespo, "Sobre parentescos," 52; and Lohmann Villena, *Los americanos*, II, 128.

41. Título de Alvaro de Alarcón, Madrid, Mar. 24, 1653, AGS, leg. 24–167–37. According to a cédula of May 17, 1678, the crown ordered the viceroy of Peru, the Conde de Castellar, to reduce the size of the tribunal by asking four auditors, Bartolomé de Solórzano, Juan de San Miguel y Solier, Alvaro de Alarcón, and Andrés de Mieses y Espinosa, to step down and accept corregimientos. Hanke and Rodríguez, *Los virreyes*, V, 212–213.

42. The origins of two other purchasers could not be determined.

leagues seeking a post in the treasury office, creoles and even native sons were apparently willing to outbid peninsular claimants for the posts. Apparently, the high prices they were willing to pay also led officials in Madrid to ignore any legal obstacles to their holding office. One Limeño, Alonso Bravo de la Maza, purchased an appointment in 1649, while holding an encomienda in the district, a clear violation of the law.[43] Another, Alvaro de Alarcón, received a dispensation from the crown to buy a position on the tribunal while his father, Sebastián de Alarcón, served as an oidor in the Audiencia of Lima.[44] By the second half of the century, when these purchasers gained numerical superiority in the tribunal of accounts, it had become a stronghold of local power and authority in Lima.

Most of the men who bought positions in the tribunal of accounts and the Lima treasury office were younger and claimed less experience than their predecessors. The majority of the twenty-two men who held positions in the tribunal before 1633 had had strong credentials.[45] It was not unusual for a man like Juan Bautista de Aramburu to serve for two decades as a functionary in the *contaduría mayor de hacienda* before taking a post in Lima.[46] Other members of the tribunal served for extended periods in the viceroyalty. Diego de Meneses and Hernando Bravo de Lagunas, for instance, served terms as treasury officers in the Lima *caja* before receiving a post as *contador mayor*. Likewise, the men serving in the Lima treasury office before the sales were usually competent bureaucrats, who had served in other key government positions in Spain and the Indies.[47] This changed in both agencies, however, after sales commenced. In the tribunal, the new appointees usually had little training in government accounting matters. Most had only limited experience as soldiers, aldermen, or, in a few cases, as corregidors and members of the consulado. It was not unusual that a young native son, Alonso Bravo de la Maza, should have used his family's considerable wealth and influence in Lima to secure an appointment as *contador mayor*, despite his lack of experience and training. The same problems appeared in the Lima treasury office. Of the nine men who bought appointments in Lima dur-

43. Mendiburu, *Diccionario*, III, 126.

44. Título de Alvaro de Alarcón, Madrid, Mar. 24, 1653, AGI, Lima, leg. 1123.

45. The backgrounds of seven men could not be determined. Data on the remaining officials who served during the period are sufficient to suggest that their credentials were strong.

46. Consulta, Madrid, Aug. 22, 1639, AGI, Lima, leg. 5.

47. In the period from 1613 to 1633, only one man, Juan López de Hernani, claimed any significant government experience in Spain before receiving an appointment in the Lima treasury office. The rest of the appointees had served in the Indies, usually outside Lima.

ing the century, only Bartolomé Torres Cavallón and Cristóbal de Llanos Jaraba had strong bureaucratic backgrounds.[48] The remainder had little experience before gaining an appointment. An unusual case occurred in 1641 when the father of Sebastián de Navarrete managed to purchase an appointment for his fifteen-year-old son, with the understanding that the boy would not begin serving until his twenty-fifth birthday.[49] Some of these inexperienced officials, such as Navarrete, had to serve apprenticeships as supernumeraries in the *caja*, but by the end of the century even this precaution was ignored. In short, the standards of the crown in filling treasury appointments declined markedly after 1633.

The entry of inexperienced men into the Lima treasury office clearly disrupted patterns of promotion in the agency. Before the sales began, treasury officers had usually served in a number of lesser positions outside of Lima before moving to the capital. The career of Bartolomé Astete de Ulloa was in many respects typical. Before coming to serve as comptroller of the Lima *caja* in 1631, Astete had worked in several government posts, including those of treasurer, factor, and corregidor of the rich mining district of Potosí.[50] In addition, especially competent members of the treasury office had had the opportunity to impress the viceroy and perhaps gain a lucrative promotion. Two treasury officers, Diego de Meneses and Hernando Bravo de Lagunas, were elevated to the tribunal of accounts, and treasurer Sebastián Hurtado de Corcuera managed to secure an appointment as president of the Audiencia of Panama.[51] After the sales began, however, these patterns of *ascenso* were altered. The sale of positions made it difficult to gain a promotion on merit alone. From 1633 to 1700, not a single member of the *caja* received a promotion from the office. The net result was that members of the treasury office usually received their jobs at a younger age and held them until retirement or death. Before the crown began selling these appointments officials had usually spent from three to ten years in office. After the sales commenced, the purchasers held office for twenty years or more. As a result, even well-trained peninsular officials, like Astete, could spend enough time in the city to become *radicados*. The only exception to this pattern

48. Consulta, Madrid, Apr. 13, 1648, AGI, Lima, leg. 7; and Título de Cristóbal de Llanos Jaraba, Madrid, Aug. 7, 1655, AGI, Lima, leg. 1070.

49. Título de Sebastían de Navarrete, Madrid, Mar. 24, 1641, AGS, leg. 1–15–30.

50. Título de Bartolomé Astete de Ulloa, Madrid, July 14, 1628, AGI, Lima, leg. 1070; Consulta, Madrid, Apr. 11, 1628, AGI, Lima, leg. 5; and Consulta, Madrid, July 7, 1650, AGI, Lima, leg. 7.

51. Relación de servicios de Fernando Bravo de Lagunas, Lima, May 30, 1637, AGI, Lima, leg. 109; Consulta, Madrid, Dec. 26, 1619, AGI, Lima, leg. 4; and Suardo, *Diario*, II, 84.

of long tenures in office was Baltasar de Becerra, who died less than a year after assuming his duties in Lima.[52] After assuming the post his father had bought him, Sebastián de Navarrete served nearly thirty years in Lima (but he died in disgrace after being exiled to Mexico for malfeasance in office).[53] Treasury officers served at the king's pleasure, and, after purchasing an office in Lima, most held the post for life. To gain a promotion, an official needed money and influence rather than a strong service record. Consequently, officers in the *caja* of Lima had little incentive to work honestly, efficiently, and loyally.

The crown did not have enough time between 1607 and 1633 to establish a clear-cut *ascenso* for the tribunal of accounts, but problems similar to those found in the treasury office emerged after sales began. Again, appointments generally went to younger men, who served long terms in office. In addition, only two men who began serving in the agency before 1633, Juan Bautista de Aramburu and Francisco Gómez Pradera, received promotions to the post of *contador mayor*, the pinnacle of the viceregal treasury hierarchy. All others who held that position had bought it. As in the treasury office, money and influence came to outweigh ability and experience in gaining a post.

Purchasers of offices used their long tenures in Lima to develop and sustain strong political, social, and economic ties in the city. In time, most of the bureaucrats probably had little desire for a promotion if it meant leaving behind these important connections in the capital. A senior treasury post in the tribunal or the *caja* provided a handsome salary, a high social position, and access to considerable political power. Local interest groups eagerly sought personal and professional alliances with these officials in order to gain influence over government policy. Treasury officials were also eager to augment their wealth and power by developing and consolidating ties with important local citizens. All this had existed before 1633, but the deteriorating financial position of the crown and the acquisition by ambitious young *radicados* and native sons of fiscal positions accelerated the processes and facilitated the integration of these officials into colonial society.

Some links between treasury officials and prominent citizens in Lima solidified even before the bureaucrats took office. Each employee in the Lima *caja*, for example, had to post a security bond (*fianza*) before assuming his duties.[54] Since the bond frequently was between 20,000 and

52. Bartolomé Astete de Ulloa and Juan de Quesada y Sotomayor to King, Lima, Apr. 6, 1650, AGI, Lima, leg. 57.

53. Mugaburu and Mugaburu, *Chronicle*, p. 273.

54. Members of the tribunal of accounts did not post a *fianza*.

45,000 pesos, the treasury officers commonly found it impossible to put up the entire amount themselves. Occasionally relatives or friends in Spain posted the bond, but more commonly local citizens performed the favor. Ten contributors met the bond of Cristóbal de Llanos Jaraba in 1665, including several merchants, family members, and two oidores of the audiencia, Juan de Retuerta and Martín de Zavala.[55] Of course, the payment of a *fianza* did not necessarily wed the royal official to the interests of his bondsmen (*fiadores*), but it did provide an obvious link between government officials and prominent local citizens. Young native sons like Llanos Jaraba already had such ties before they took office, but the *fianzas* reinforced them.

Family and marriage ties formed an even more important bond among treasury officials and local interest groups. Officials frequently had relatives among the most important families of Lima. Among those who were not native sons of the city, Juan de Quesada y Sotomayor had the strongest family connections in the capital. Members of his clan had preceded him to Peru after the conquest and, by the seventeenth century, several of them had accumulated fortunes of more than 250,000 pesos.[56] When fiscal officers lacked strong family ties or simply wished to extend them, they frequently searched for favorable marriages. The power and influence of the officials made them attractive matches for the daughters of the rich and powerful in Lima. Young Francisco de Colmenares, for example, married a rich widow, Silveria Hermosa de Chillón. The marriage was apparently arranged for political and economic reasons: gossips in Lima continually whispered of the couple's frequent quarrels and the beatings Colmenares meted out to his wife. Furthermore, the young official lived openly with his mistress.[57] Apart from marrying for money, officials also chose their mates in order to cement political alliances. Sebastián de Navarrete's wife was the granddaughter of Juan de Loayza Calderón, an oidor of the Lima audiencia; and Juan Fermín de Izu, a *contador mayor* in the tribunal, married Antonia de Ibarra, the daughter of Gregorio de Ibarra, a wealthy merchant and a member of the Lima Inquisition. Her brother, Alvaro de Ibarra, would later become an oidor of the Lima audiencia and serve as chief aide (*privado*) to Viceroy Conde de Lemos.[58] Family ties were also evident within the staff of the treasury itself. Cristóbal de Llanos Jaraba was factor of the Lima *caja* at the same time that his first cousin, José de Jaraba y Arnedo, served as *contador*

55. *Fianza* de Cristóbal de Llanos Jaraba, Lima, Sept. 22, 1683, AGI, Lima, leg. 290.
56. Varela y Orbegoso, *Apuntes*, p. 182.
57. Lohmann Villena, *Conde de Lemos*, pp. 385–386 n.24.
58. Suardo, *Diario*, I, 190; and Lohmann Villena, *Conde de Lemos*, p. 135 n.27.

mayor on the tribunal of accounts.[59] In short, treasury officials developed a network of interpersonal relationships that helped to bind them to other prominent politicians, merchants, miners, farmers, and clergymen.

Economic relationships further linked officials in the tribunal of accounts and the treasury office in Lima with local magnates. More than one-third of the taxes collected in the Lima office were administered by tax farmers. Private individuals, groups, or organizations usually collected these taxes for an established yearly fee or on a percentage basis. It was frequently a very profitable enterprise. Officials in the tribunal and the treasury office had considerable influence in awarding the contracts to tax farmers, checking their accounts, and negotiating contract renewals. The sale of these offices to men with strong local connections provided an opportunity to favor friends, relatives, and business associates. The possibilities for kickbacks, favors, and other forms of corruption were numerous.

There is also evidence that the native sons and *radicados* serving in the central treasury office and the tribunal of accounts participated directly in illegal economic ventures. Juan de Quesada y Sotomayor provides only the most obvious example of these activities. Before he assumed his duties as the treasurer of the Lima *caja* in 1637, Quesada was a notable merchant in the city. He lived in an ostentatious style, and when his daughter María married in 1636, he provided a dowry of 25,000 pesos.[60] This was an exorbitant sum for a man about to assume an office that paid only 2,500 pesos in annual salary. After holding office for only one year, however, Quesada used his influence to become an admiral of the Pacific armada, and in 1648 he even gained command of the treasury fleet to Panama.[61] These positions allowed an enterprising merchant like Quesada the opportunity to supplement his salary by consorting with contrabandists operating in the Pacific, smuggling unregistered silver from Callao, and extorting bribes from his fellow merchants trading in legal and contraband goods.

The sale of fiscal appointments in Lima gave local interest groups the opportunity to gain influence within the viceregal government. Partisan interests in Lima had always tried to coopt government officials and forge alliances to influence government policies. By the second half of the century, *radicados* and native sons had gained control over both the tribunal of accounts and the Lima *caja*. Such ministers were unlikely to support unpopular new tax levies initiated by the crown to aid the hard-

59. Lohmann Villena, *Los americanos*, I, 243.
60. Inquisition records, Seville, Apr. 13, 1636, BM, Manuscritos, Z-222.
61. Mugaburu and Mugaburu, *Chronicle*, p. 23.

pressed Madrid government. When the crown began the systematic sale of other bureaucratic appointments, such as corregimientos and audiencia judgeships, in the 1680s, the political power of local partisan groups in the viceroyalty was already well established.

V.

The sale of treasury appointments in 1633 set in motion a series of political changes that contributed to a steady erosion of royal authority in the Viceroyalty of Peru. During the first half of the seventeenth century, the declining position of the Hapsburg monarchy in Europe led officials in Madrid to frame a series of revenue measures for the Viceroyalty of Peru, including new tax levies, forced donations, loans, composition of land titles (*composiciones de tierras*), and the sale of annuities (*juros*) and public offices. In order to implement these measures, the crown needed loyal dedicated servants in the chief agencies of the fiscal bureaucracy, the tribunal of accounts and the treasury office in Lima. At this juncture, however, crucial financial decisions in Lima were entrusted to officials who often proved inefficient, corrupt, and strongly tied to local partisan interests hostile to heavy tax levies. As the metropolis declined, treasury officials drew closer to local magnates in order to maintain their own wealth and status. In the end royal authority over the viceregal treasury deteriorated, remissions of revenue to Spain declined, and the financial problems of the crown worsened.

A major administrative problem resulting from the sales of offices was a decline in efficiency, particularly in the tribunal of accounts. The tribunal had never proved as effective in supervising the royal treasury as officials in Madrid had hoped, but problems intensified after 1633. In 1664, royal inspectors reported that officials serving in the tribunal of accounts were not capable of performing their duties. The inspectors found Andrés de Mieses, a *contador mayor,* incompetent. Other members who had purchased their posts, such as Joseph de Bolívar, seldom came to work in the tribunal chambers.[62] The influx of less competent auditors and the tolerance of absentee officials made it impossible for the Madrid government to maintain adequate checks on the activities of the royal treasury during these vital years.

Similar problems plagued the treasury office in Lima. In 1659 royal inspectors found several officials incompetent. Bartolomé Astete de Ulloa

62. The inspectors also found that Juan Bautista de Aramburu was often absent working at his other job as a professor at the University of San Marcos, while Bartolomé de Solórzano was away serving as corregidor of Chilques y Masques. Neither had purchased his post. Francisco Antonio de Manzolo to King, Lima, 1664, AGI, Lima, leg. 280.

was knowledgeable, but at sixty-two he was too old and sickly to serve as comptroller without the aid of colleagues. The inspectors judged Bartolomé Torres Cavallón, Sebastián de Navarrete, and Francisco de Colmenares too stupid, inexperienced, or lazy to work effectively in the office.[63] All except Astete had purchased their appointments. Further proof of these problems came in 1696 when Visitor General Juan de Peñalosa reported that debts owed the Lima treasury had increased dramatically by 1650. As Table I indicates, those who purchased their appointments after 1633 allowed large debts to accumulate.[64] The declining standards of efficiency after the sales began exacted a considerable price in lost revenues; it was a price the crown could ill afford to pay.

The declining level of government efficiency after 1633 gave local treasury officials increased freedom in the administration of the royal revenues. This decline in royal authority in turn made possible greater political corruption. One of the outstanding cases of this corruption occurred in the central treasury office in Lima. For many years treasury officials in Lima had failed to collect all debts (*alcances*) owed the royal treasury, and these began to reach considerable sums during the second half of the century. Finally, in 1650, members of the perpetually backlogged tribunal of accounts began investigating the problem and uncovered a debt of 45,409 pesos on the Lima accounts for the year 1647 alone.[65] The shortage was too large to ignore, and a special investigation, headed by Pedro Vásquez de Velasco, a judge of the audiencia, was begun. The treasury officials held responsible for the debt, Bartolomé Astete de Ulloa and Juan de Quesada y Sotomayor, protested their innocence and blamed their deceased colleague, Baltasar de Becerra. The embarrassed officials reported that in recent years they had met the immediate expenses of the *caja* by borrowing from the personal savings of Becerra, a man of considerable wealth. When the yearly remissions of silver arrived from the subordinate offices, Becerra simply took crown revenues as repayment. They reasoned that in 1647, when Quesada was absent in Callao and the elderly Astete was ill, Becerra, who was serving as supernumerary of the office, must have taken funds in excess of the original loans.

Quesada and Astete blamed the entire incident on the crown's policy of selling future appointments to the *caja*. Becerra had been the first to purchase a future in 1636; by 1647 three other men were in line behind

63. Conde de Alba to King, Lima, Sept. 10, 1659, AGI, Lima, leg. 280.

64. Juan de Peñalosa to King, Lima, Sept. 15, 1696, AGI, Lima, leg. 288.

65. Tribunal of accounts to King, Lima, Apr. 15, 1651, AGI, Lima, leg. 57.

66. Bartolomé Astete de Ulloa and Juan de Quesada y Sotomayor to King, Lima, Apr. 6, 1651, AGI, Lima, leg. 57.

him waiting for a vacancy in the office.[67] Astete and Quesada alleged that these three men, Sebastián de Navarrete, Francisco de Guerra, and Bartolomé Torres Cavallón, had conspired with Becerra to create the scandal in 1647 in order to replace them. Furthermore, the two treasury officials charged that the royal investigator, Pedro Vásquez de Velasco, was in league with Navarrete, Guerra, and Torres Cavallón. According to Astete and Quesada, the investigator had obtained most of his incriminating evidence from the three future holders, while he was their guest in Callao.[68]

The case was a complicated and confusing one, but ultimately the Council of the Indies chose to punish Astete and Quesada. The law held all three treasury officials responsible for any uncollected debts. Their excuses, moreover, did not account for an additional sum of 58,361 pesos that the tribunal and the investigator had found missing for the period 1648–50. Becerra, who died early in 1649, could not be blamed for this shortage.[69] Nevertheless, in the end, the investigators in Lima collected 25,000 pesos from the estate of Baltasar de Becerra and found another 46,400 pesos in a chest carelessly pushed aside in a corner of the treasury office itself. The two treasury officers had no explanation for these hidden or mislaid funds, and continued to blame everything on Becerra. The final verdict held Quesada, Astete, and their *fiadores* responsible for all the additional missing funds. The two treasury officials were also fined 2,500 pesos each and suspended from office for four years.[70]

Officials in Madrid viewed the corruption and confusion in the Lima office with great alarm. In 1662, Philip IV and the Council of the Indies dispatched a visita general to the viceroyalty to reassert royal control over the colonial treasury. Authorities in Madrid gave Visitor General Juan de Cornejo broad powers to investigate the competence, performance, and loyalty of members of the audiencia, the tribunal of accounts, and the central treasury office. Cornejo was also instructed to examine the administration of the sale of indulgences (*cruzada*), the commercial taxes (*avería, alcabala,* and *almojarifazgo*), and the sale of public offices. Cornejo was also to account for increases in defense expenditures that the crown found worrying.

When Cornejo arrived in Lima on September 8, 1664, he received a cordial reception from the viceroy, the Conde de Santisteban.[71] Santisteban had been conducting his own study of the problems of the vice-

67. Ibid., Sept. 15, 1651, AGI, Lima, leg. 57.
68. Ibid.
69. Tribunal of accounts to King, Lima, Apr. 15, 1651, AGI, Lima, leg. 57.
70. Ibid.
71. Mugaburu and Mugaburu, *Chronicle*, p. 88.

regal treasury, and was appalled by the decline in tax revenues and the accumulation of uncollected debts. Accordingly, he was basically sympathetic to Cornejo's mission. Officials in the audiencia, the tribunal of accounts, and the treasury, however, resented any curtailment of their power and viewed the visitor general with suspicion and hostility. When Cornejo began investigating reports of abuse of power, corruption, and inefficiency, many of these high-ranking officials in Lima turned against him. The comptroller of the Lima *caja*, Francisco de Colmenares, openly referred to the visitor general as "Juan Cuernejo" and feuded bitterly with him in the audiencia chambers.[72] Hostility to the visita became intense after Santisteban's death in early 1666. Officials in Lima complained to Madrid about Cornejo's attempts to assume many of the prerogatives of the viceroy and accused him of high-handedness and lavish spending. The visitador's conflict with local officials finally contributed to his recall. He left the city on December 10, 1666, his mission an utter failure.[73] He had apparently been defeated by a combination of his own arrogance and the weakened position of the crown in the viceroyalty.

The final indication of the decline in royal authority in Peru was the drop in tax revenue flowing into the viceregal treasury. Royal revenues at the Lima *caja* declined steadily after 1664 (see Graph I).[74] The principal cause of this was the falling silver output of the mining provinces of highland Peru and Upper Peru, particularly Potosí. The efforts of financial reformers during the reign of Philip IV to levy new imposts to offset this decline and expand the tax base of the viceregal treasury had failed by 1664. New taxes on other productive sectors provoked strong opposition in Peru, and treasury officers relied instead on measures more acceptable to local taxpayers such as borrowing, withholding funds normally remitted to Spain, and selling land titles, *juros*, and offices. Although these expedients allowed treasury officers to meet their immediate expenses, they never provided a consistent or permanent source of funds to counterbalance the decline in mining taxes.[75] In addition, measures such as sales of *juros* and borrowing encumbered the treasury with debts and made fiscal solvency increasingly the product of the goodwill of local magnates. As, by the 1660s, even these sources of revenue became scarce, government income levels dropped and remissions of revenue to Spain fell even farther. The sale of treasury appointments was

72. Lohmann Villena, *Conde de Lemos*, p. 385 n.24.

73. Mugaburu and Mugaburu, *Chronicle*, p. 107.

74. For further details on the decline of royal revenues in the Viceroyalty of Peru, see Kenneth J. Andrien, "The Royal Treasury and Society in Seventeenth Century Lima" (Ph.D. Diss., Duke University, 1977), pp. 29–64.

75. Ibid., pp. 50–52.

not the sole cause of these financial problems, but it was a contributing factor. The native sons and *radicados* who gained control of the central treasury office and the tribunal of accounts made the policy decisions that doomed the reform program. As one historian has noted: "A weak government cannot adequately tax. Without taxes, political administration becomes even weaker."[76] Although the crown began selling fiscal appointments to gain revenue, the measure ultimately weakened the treasury in Peru and lessened the crown's power to draw revenue from the viceroyalty. The needs of the metropolis and the solvency of the viceregal government itself were sacrificed by the fiscal officials of the crown who came to power after 1633.

The administrative and financial problems related to the sale of treasury appointments continued into the next century. Between 1700 and 1745, for example, the crown managed to negotiate the sale of eighteen appointments to the tribunal of accounts and nine appointments to the central treasury office in Lima.[77] According to Jorge Juan and Antonio de Ulloa, writing in 1749, the ultimate effect of the sales of offices was to undermine royal authority in the viceroyalty. In fact, Juan and Ulloa stated that the viceregal government was so riddled with abuses that:

> Those governing Peru are presented with the pleasant prospect of absolute authority growing ever larger and more ostentatious, of precious metals to satisfy their lust and greed, and of people who ingratiate, enrich, and shower praise on the least deserving. These three factors are the poison which chokes and destroys good government in those kingdoms.[78]

When by 1750 Ferdinand VI finally ended the systematic sale of most high-ranking bureaucratic offices in Peru, he made a great contribution toward reversing the damage begun in 1633.

76. Miles Wortman, "Government Revenue and Economic Trends in Central America, 1787–1819," *HAHR*, 55 (May 1975), 277.

77. Relación de los empleos de justicia, políticos, y de real hacienda de los dominios de el Perú, que se han concedido por servicio pecuniario desde el año de 1700 al de 1746, Madrid, Mar. 31, 1746, AGI, Indiferente general, leg. 525. The author would like to thank Mark A. Burkholder and D. S. Chandler for making these data available to him.

78. Jorge Juan and Antonio de Ulloa, *Discourse and Political Reflections on the Kingdoms of Peru*, ed. and trans. by John J. TePaske and Besse A. Clement (Norman, 1978), p. 247.

4

Creole Appointments and the Sale of Audiencia Positions in the Spanish Empire under the Early Bourbons, 1701–1750

M.A. Burkholder and D.S. Chandler

Soon after Philip V assumed the Spanish throne in 1700, he began selling appointments of *oidor, alcalde del crimen*, and *fiscal* for the American audiencias.[1] By 1750 he and his successor Ferdinand VI had sold about one-fourth of all appointments; the Crown added over 1,000,000 pesos to the treasury by resorting to this expedient.[2] Primarily through purchasing judicial appointments, numerous creoles (Spaniards born in America) entered these prestigious tribunals. Although an occasional scholar has noted individual sales or creoles serving on an audiencia, historians have neither recognized the extent nor explored the implications of these occurrences.[3] Rather, they have stressed the exclusion of Americans from high office

* The authors wish to thank Duke University for the awards which made research for this article possible and also Professor John J. TePaske for his helpful comments on an earlier draft.

[1] An *audiencia* was an appellate court with administrative and advisory responsibilities. Its jurisdiction extended throughout a territorial unit also called an audiencia. *Oidores* were judges of the audiencias; they handled civil and criminal cases except in Lima and Mexico where they were civil magistrates alone, criminal cases being the responsibility of the *alcaldes del crimen* who were present only in these two courts. The *fiscal* was the crown attorney and carried the particular charge of defending royal interests in financial questions.

[2] The evidence for these sales comes from two principal sources. In 1746 the Marqués de la Ensenada ordered the Secretariats of New Spain and Peru to form registers of all salaried positions sold during the reign of Philip V. These registers are in the Archivo General de Indias (hereafter AGI), Sección V, Indiferente General (hereafter Indiferente), *legajos* 525, 526, and 1847. They contain the names, dates, prices, and conditions of the sales made for each audiencia. The titles (*títulos*) of office in the Archivo General de Simancas (hereafter AGS), Sección XXIII, Dirección General del Tesoro (hereafter XXIII), Inventario 2, legajos 1 through 14 and 16 through 38, and Inventario 24, legajos 173 through 182 corroborate the lists in nearly every case and contain additional information on sales and appointments. The data on sales and creole appointments in this article is based primarily on these sources.

[3] For examples of single sales, see Marcelin Defourneaux, *Pablo Olavide ou l'afrancesado (1725–1803)* (Paris, 1959), pp. 36–7, and G. Desdevizes du Dézert, *L'Espagne de l'ancien régime*, Vol. II, *Les institutions* (Paris, 1899), 149. J. M. Ots Capdequí recognized the sale of some oidorships in *El estado español en las Indias* (4th ed., Mexico, 1965), p. 48.

throughout the viceregal period and linked it to the coming of independence in the early nineteenth century. This article will point out the extent and conditions of the sales and creole appointments made between 1701 and 1750, the last year of recorded sales; it will also indicate how creoles suffered discrimination despite receiving 40 per cent of the audiencia appointments.

The sale of public office in the Spanish Empire falls into two broad divisions; hereditary and transferable offices sold through public auction (*oficios vendibles y renunciables*) and salaried offices that could not be bequeathed or transferred and were sold through private contract between the Crown and purchaser. In his important study *The Sale of Public Office in the Indies Under the Hapsburgs*, J. H. Parry devoted most of his attention to offices of the first group—notarial, ' miscellaneous fee-earning ', and municipal.[4] He did point out, however, the seventeenth-century growth of the sale of the salaried offices comprising the second group.

Although the Crown disliked and opposed selling salaried offices on principle, its penury encouraged using these financial, administrative, and judicial positions as a source of revenue. Overriding the opposition of the Council of the Indies, the King commonly sold treasury positions by the mid-seventeenth century, although not at auction.[5] The sale of provincial governorships followed soon afterwards, also proceeding through private contract between purchaser and Crown.[6] Continuing fiscal need pressed the Crown into further expanding the offices available for purchase, and by the end of the seventeenth century it had sold not only positions on the audiencias but even the exalted office of viceroy for both Peru and New Spain.[7]

Sales of the highest positions on the audiencias—those of *oidor*, *alcalde del crimen*, and *fiscal*—did not fall under the classification of *oficios vendibles y renunciables*. Rather, they were individual transactions made with-

4 *Ibero-Americana*, no. 37 (Berkeley, 1953), pp. 6–47.

5 The Council of the Indies was the supreme court for the Crown's possessions in America (or " the Indies " as the Spaniards called it) and the Philippines. It also had administrative and advisory responsibilities.

6 Parry, *Sale of Public Office*, pp. 51–5.

7 For examples of the sale of positions on the American audiencias under the Habsburgs, see Jorge Tovar Velarde, ' La Audiencia de Lima 1705–1707. Dos años de Gobierno criollo en el Perú ', *Revista histórica* (Lima), tomo XXIII (1957–8), 355, 361, 369; Antonio Domínguez Ortiz, ' Un virreinato en venta ', *Mercurio peruano* (Lima), año XXXIX, vol. XLIX, núm. 453 (enero-febrero de 1965), 46; Richard Konetzke, *Colección de Documentos para la Historia de la Formación Social de Hispanoamérica 1493–1810*, 3 vols. (Madrid, 1953–62), III, tomo I, 34–9, 49–50; Ernesto Schäfer, *El Consejo real y supremo de las Indias*, 2 vols. (Sevilla, 1935–47), II, 191. Antonio Domínguez Ortiz revealed the sale of the office of viceroy of New Spain and Peru in the 1690s in ' Un virreinato en venta ', pp. 46–51.

out provision for inheritance or resale of the office.[8] Unlike members of the sovereign courts in France during the Old Regime, purchasers of audiencia positions did not enjoy any special proprietary right to their seats; once members of the magistracy, they were treated the same as those appointed on merit.[9] With normal honorable service, a purchaser could expect the same promotions to higher tribunals as his fellows.

The sale of appointments to American audiencias did not go unchallenged. The Council of the Indies protested against attempts to debase the professional bench by sale or by granting judicial positions as dowries for hapless noblewomen.[10] By the end of the seventeenth century, however, it had become clear that financial exigency surpassed any objections the Council could voice. Although Charles II had ordered in 1689 that no office related to justice or the royal exchequer was to be sold, three years later he authorized continuing the sale of all offices in the Indies.[11] Deploring this practice, the Council marshalled its arguments in a brief (*consulta*) of 9 November 1693 pointing out that justice was a spiritual matter and could not be sold and that the Indies were in 'absolute ruin' as a consequence of these sales. Since the buyers of high offices sought only to make a profit, abuses arose uncurbed by the Crown owing to the infrequent fleets and great distance separating the court from the Indies. Furthermore, this practice meant ignoring colonists who could legitimately expect to hold office. In addition, the Council observed that the quantity of sales, including second and third *futuras*, meant that the prices had dropped to the point that the sales no longer provided a good source of revenue.[12] These arguments, and the Council's plea that if the King must sell offices he should at least withhold those of justice and military government, failed to have any effect. The Crown declared that despite its recognition of the dangers involved and the desire to end this means of obtaining revenue, the perilous circumstances

[8] The term 'servicio' described the cash payment. Although this term has far broader implications, in this instance it meant simply the monetary 'service' rendered to the Crown in a time of financial distress.

[9] Franklin L. Ford, *Robe and Sword: The Regrouping of the French Aristocracy after Louis XIV* (New York, Harper & Row, 1965), pp. 105–15.

[10] Konetzke, *Colección de Documentos*, II, tomo I, 359–61, 402–4, 418–19. Examples of men who received their appointments as part of their wives' dowries include Alonso de Zárate y Verdugo (*alcalde del crimen*, Audiencia of Lima, 1660) and José Tello de Meneses (supernumerary *oidor*, Audiencia of Guadalajara, 1664). Schäfer, *op. cit.*, I, 488, note 2 and 496 note 4.

[11] Cited in 'Consulta del consejo de las Indias sobre los inconvenientes que resultan en beneficiar los oficios en Indias, y especialmente los puestos de justicia y gobierno', Madrid, 9 November 1693. Published in Konetzke, *op. cit.*, III, tomo I, 34–9.

[12] A *futura* was the promise of appointment to a given office at a future date, usually after the death of the incumbent. The Crown made over 525 appointments from 1650 to 1700. Schäfer, *op. cit.*, II, Appendix II, 443–524.

of the realm made the sales necessary to avoid even worse consequences.[13] Thus, in the closing years of Habsburg rule, the Crown had accepted the sale of high judicial office as an unfortunate but unavoidable necessity. The coming of the Bourbons to Spain did not immediately change this policy. Despite a decree in 1701 cancelling the appointments of those persons who held *futuras* or were supernumerary appointees not actually serving, Philip V was soon selling positions in the audiencias.[14] The desire for instant cash overcame legal restraints and moral reservations.

The sale of appointments to the American audiencias in the eighteenth century brought many creoles into the tribunals. As modern historians have become increasingly aware, the great emphasis given to the events of the sixteenth century and to the closing decades of the vice-regal period in Spanish America has obscured many important developments in the seventeenth and early eighteenth centuries. In the question of royal judicial appointments, insufficient investigation of this middle period has forced scholars to generalize about appointments made throughout the entire colonial period on the basis of research limited to its beginning and end. The theme voiced in 1849 by the Mexican statesman and historian Lucas Alamán concerning creole exclusion from the most prestigious positions in America has been repeated for over a century with little critical examination of its application at particular times or in the different audiencias.[15]

Despite occasional indications of creoles holding numerous high positions, comments on colonial administration have generally echoed those of Alamán.[16] The dominant picture is that Spaniards consistently held a near monopoly of the most prestigious American offices. In concluding his study

13 Konetzke, *Colección de Documentos*, III, tomo I, 34–9.

14 For an example of the reform decree of 6 March 1701 at work, see AGS, XXIII, 24-173-48, Buen Retiro, 8 July 1703. A supernumerary was an extra minister above the number authorized by law. In most cases he moved into a regular (*de numero*) position upon the death of an incumbent.

15 Peninsular Spaniards, Alamán avowed, held 'almost all the high positions'. All but four of 170 viceroys and fourteen of 602 captains-general and presidents prior to 1813 had been born in Spain. Only 105 of 706 bishops had been Americans, and these had generally served dioceses of secondary importance. The number of Americans who had been *oidores* and canons did not alter the generalization. Lucas Alamán, *Historia de Méjico desde los primeros movimientos que prepararon su independencia en el año de 1808 hasta la época presente* (5 vols., Mexico, 1849–52), I, 12–14 and notes 6 and 7 on pp. 12–13. An important contemporary statement of creole exclusion from power was Simón Bolívar's famous 'Jamaica letter' of 1815.

16 The large number of creoles holding high office in Chile has been pointed out by Bailey W. Diffie, *Latin American Civilizations: Colonial Period* (New York, 1967), p. 489; and by Jaime Eyzaguirre, *Ideario y ruta de la emancipación chilena* (Santiago, 1957), pp. 55–6. John J. TePaske's work on Peru in the early eighteenth century has led him to deny the traditional view for Peru and to raise the question of its validity elsewhere.

The Audiencia of New Galicia in the Sixteenth Century, J. H. Parry generalized that '*oidores* were almost always born and always trained in Spain'.[17] John Lynch, examining colonial administration in its closing decades, noted that the new positions of intendant and subdelegate were 'legally reserved to peninsular-born Spaniards, who now, as always, monopolized the highest offices in Church and State'. This legal reservation was representative of the royal policy 'which consistently debarred creoles from political service'.[18] Although recognizing that a few creoles did become *oidores*, John Leddy Phelan extended his comments beyond the early seventeenth century in Quito and emphasized the '*de facto* exclusion of the creoles from the ranks of the professional magistracy' and 'the failure to grant any high offices to the creoles in the Indies'.[19] Scholars have only recently begun to question the hoary hypothesis of creole exclusion, principally focusing attention on individual audiencias.[20] This work, however, centers on the second half of the eighteenth century and leaves the initial decades of Bourbon rule largely unexplored.

The Crown appointed 108 creoles to 136 audiencia positions between 1701 and 1750, 40 per cent of the total.[21] These figures reveal far more creole appointments than scholars have traditionally imagined. The high

[17] (Cambridge University Press, 1948), p. 195.

[18] *Spanish Colonial Administration, 1782–1810: The Intendant System in the Viceroyalty of the Río de la Plata* (London, 1958), p. 77. As John R. Fisher notes, however, in his more recent study: 'The idea that creoles were excluded from government is a misleading oversimplification'. *Government and Society in Colonial Peru: The Intendant System 1784–1814* (London, 1970), p. 8.

[19] *The Kingdom of Quito in the Seventeenth Century: Bureaucratic Politics in the Spanish Empire* (Madison, 1967), p. 145.

[20] In his recent work *Miners and Merchants in Bourbon Mexico 1763–1810* (Cambridge University Press, 1971), David A. Brading recognized the importance of numerous creoles on the Audiencia of Mexico in mid-century. John L. Phelan noted creole dominance in the Audiencia of Santa Fé de Bogotá in his review of Germán Colmenares, *La Provincia de Tunja en el Nuevo Reino. Ensayo de Historia Social (1539–1800)*, *The Hispanic American Historical Review*, LI, no. 3 (Aug. 1971), 515. See also Mark A. Burkholder, 'José Baquíjano and the Audiencia of Lima' (unpublished Ph.D. dissertation, Duke University, 1970), pp. 62–9.

[21] This represents the minimum confirmed number of creoles. The authors believe that further research may push the figure even higher. The Crown did not usually refer to a nominee's place of birth unless there was some reason. For instance, in 1742 the King appointed Antonio de Villaurrutia y Salcedo as *oidor* in Santo Domingo. There is no mention of Villaurrutia's origin on the title of office, so he would normally appear as a peninsular in our statistics. He is recorded as a creole, however, because Rafael Matos Díaz, in 'Hombres de America, los Villaurrutia', *Anales de la Sociedad de Geografía e Historia de Guatemala*, XXXI (enero-diciembre, 1958), 167–73, identifies Villaurrutia as a creole, born and educated in New Spain. In addition to archival sources, Guillermo Lohmann Villena, *Los Americanos en las ordenes nobiliarias (1529–1900)*, 2 vols. (Madrid, 1947) was particularly valuable in identifying creoles.

percentage of Americans named, however, is misleading in its implication that discrimination against creoles was scarcely evident in audiencia appointments during the first fifty years of Bourbon rule. In fact nearly two-thirds of the creoles appointed had to purchase their appointments, these purchases forming a disproportionate share of 81 per cent of the sales made. Thus, while the Crown was willing to name Americans to the audiencias, it frequently demanded monetary payment for the appointment and for exemptions from laws restricting local social and economic connections which were more relevant to a creole named to his home province than to a *peninsular* (Spaniard from Spain). Indeed, during times of crisis under the early Bourbons, creole *letrados* (university trained lawyers) with wealth enough to pay for the privileges had perhaps as good a chance of gaining appointment to an American audiencia as did their peninsular counterparts. While it would be patently impossible to deny peninsular control of the audiencias in 1550 or 1800, scholars have erred in following The Liberator Simón Bolívar's lead and equating peninsular dominance with creole exclusion. It is one thing to recognize peninsular primacy during most periods and another to attribute to Spaniards effective monopolization of the American audiencias throughout the entire viceregal period. The first fifty years of Bourbon rule clearly show that, although they suffered discrimination, creoles were definitely not excluded from audiencia positions.

Philip V and Ferdinand VI sold at least 88 of 346 appointments made to the American audiencias from 1701 to 1750. Sales of these appointments did not proceed regularly throughout these years, but occurred in two definite periods of great strain on the royal treasury: 1706–11 and 1740–50. As Graph A reveals, Philip and Ferdinand made all but three of the sales in these seventeen years.[22]

Although the buyers paid varying amounts and received different privileges, their purchases fell into two major categories: regular (*de numero*) and supernumerary. The man who bought a regular position filled an existing vacancy. A supernumerary was an extra minister who, nevertheless, often served until a vacancy appeared in the limited number of regular places. Occasionally the Crown sold a *futura* to a position, but except in the case of fiscales, the *futurario* or holder of the *futura* seemed to enjoy the same general prerogatives as a supernumerary. To understand why pur-

[22] In 1704 Philip V sold a supernumerary oidorship in Lima to Juan de Peralta y Sanabria, but this isolated case preceded the commitment in 1706 to sell audiencia seats as a regular policy (AGI, Indiferente, legajo 525); the other two sales were to Manuel Antonio Borda y Echevarría (AGS, xxiii, 2-30-351, San Ildefonso, 11 July 1736) and to Pedro Bravo del Rivero in 1733 (AGI, Lima, legajo 1082); the two sales in the 1730s were made during the War of the Polish Succession; all three men were creoles.

chased appointments took different forms and why the number of sales was limited, one must appreciate the sizes of the audiencias. During the first half of the eighteenth century, the tribunals of Lima and Mexico were normally authorized to have 8 *oidores*, 4 *alcaldes del crimen*, and 2 *fiscales*, 1 each for criminal and civil cases.[23] In the other 9 audiencias, there were generally 4 or 5 *oidores* and 1 *fiscal*. Taking the 11 tribunals together, normally there were 76 positions of *oidor*, *alcalde del crimen*, and *fiscal*.[24]

Members of an audiencia served their posts at the pleasure of the King and could plan on spending the remainder of their careers in the high judiciary. The bureaucratic ideal of a promotion pattern, as stated in the *Laws of the Indies*, provided for elevating ministers from the minor audiencias to the viceregal tribunals of Lima and Mexico.[25] If this law were consistently followed, openings for new ministers would appear only in the minor audiencias. In fact, the Crown sometimes appointed an inexperienced lawyer to fill a vacancy in Lima or Mexico.[26] In either case, however, the number of vacancies available depended upon the mortality rate among the ministers more than anything else.

Frequently the Crown had a very limited number of positions to fill in a given year. Having made seven appointments in 1700, for example, the King appointed only one *oidor* in 1701 and three in 1702. After a flurry of appointments in 1710 and 1711, there were only three in 1713, and one each in 1714, 1715, and 1716. If only a few or perhaps no vacancies existed at the time that the Crown wished to raise revenue through the sale of audiencia positions, the government resorted to selling supernumerary appointments and the less frequent *futuras*.

Supernumerary appointees did not enjoy standard privileges or responsibilities. Three major matters appearing in every supernumerary's title of office, however, involved salary, the extent of actual service on the audiencia, and movement into a regular place. Provisions for salary varied from no compensation while the appointee was a supernumerary to the more fre-

[23] Because of the great pressure of business and the resultant long delays in hearing cases, in 1737 the Crown authorized a special one-time augmentation in the Audiencia of Mexico of four *oidores* and two *alcaldes del crimen*. This brought Mexico's total to twelve *oidores* and six *alcaldes del crimen* and allowed the operation of three separate chambers. The titles of office in the AGS reveal that these extra appointments were indeed made; the audiencia was allowed to return to its normal complement by attrition. Consulta of the Council of the Indies, February 2, 1737, AGI, Mexico, legajo 452.

[24] *Recopilación de leyes de los reinos de las Indias*, 3 vols. (Madrid, 1943), libro 2, título 15, leyes 2 through 12.

[25] *Ibid.*, libro 2, título 2, ley 34.

[26] For example, Juan de Echavarría Zuluaga as *oidor* in Lima (AGS, XXIII, 2-5-46, Buen Retiro, 3 July 1708); and Clemente del Campo y Zárate as *alcalde del crimen* in Mexico (AGS, XXIII, 2-26-108, Cazalla, 25 June 1730).

quent full payment beginning from the time he was sworn into office.[27] The Crown required most supernumeraries to begin service immediately. When a vacancy appeared in the ranks of the regular ministers, a supernumerary could advance to fill it, generally on the basis of his *antigüedad*, or seniority.

During the years from 1706 to 1711 and from 1740 to 1750, only a small number of regular positions on American audiencias became vacant at times when the Crown desperately needed money. Consequently, in the first great period of sales, the Crown appointed 48 supernumeraries, 5 *futuras*, and only 14 regular ministers. Of the 67 total appointments, it sold 39 supernumerary, 3 *futura*, and 7 regular for sums totaling over 350,000 pesos. Of these 49 positions sold, creoles purchased at least 37. 86 per cent of the creoles gaining audiencia positions during these years purchased them. After 1711 the sale of audiencia positions abruptly ceased for over twenty years. The superabundance of ministers in the Indies was reflected in the temporary drop in the number of appointments; in the six years from 1712 to 1717, only ten were made. In the succeeding years through to 1739, the Crown made 153 appointments, selling but two for a total of 49,000 pesos. A renewal of sales began, however, in the following year. From 1740 to 1750 the Crown appointed 40 supernumeraries, 3 *futuras*, and 34 regular ministers. Of these 77 total appointments, the King sold nearly half: 31 supernumerary, 2 *futura*, and 4 regular for a yield of over 700,000 pesos. Of the 37 positions sold, creoles purchased at least 32. Of the 42 creoles gaining positions in this period, 76 per cent purchased them; in contrast, only 15 per cent of the 33 peninsulares had to pay for their appointments. Driven by the financial burdens of war, the Bourbons yielded to selling audiencia positions and to appointing numerous creoles desirous and capable of buying them. (See Graphs A and B.)

As the Crown had indicated in the 1690s, it was reluctant to sell judicial positions, and only severe economic strain could provoke such a distasteful action. Philip V's view corresponded to the Habsburg position, and the Council of the Indies during his reign gave evidence again of its concern with maintaining the professional quality of the American judiciary. As soon as the War of the Spanish Succession had ended, Philip made good Charles II's promise to stop selling audiencia positions. With few lapses, the

[27] For example, Francisco de Casa Alvarado was to receive full salary as a supernumerary *alcalde del crimen* in Mexico (AGI, Indiferente, legajo 1847); Juan José Martínez Patiño was to receive half salary as a supernumerary *oidor* in Guatemala (AGS, XXIII, 2-32-273. San Ildefonso, 28 July 1740); Martín de Recávarren, appointed a supernumerary *oidor* in Panama, was to receive no salary until he held a regular position (AGS, XXIII, 2-3-67, 23 May 1707).

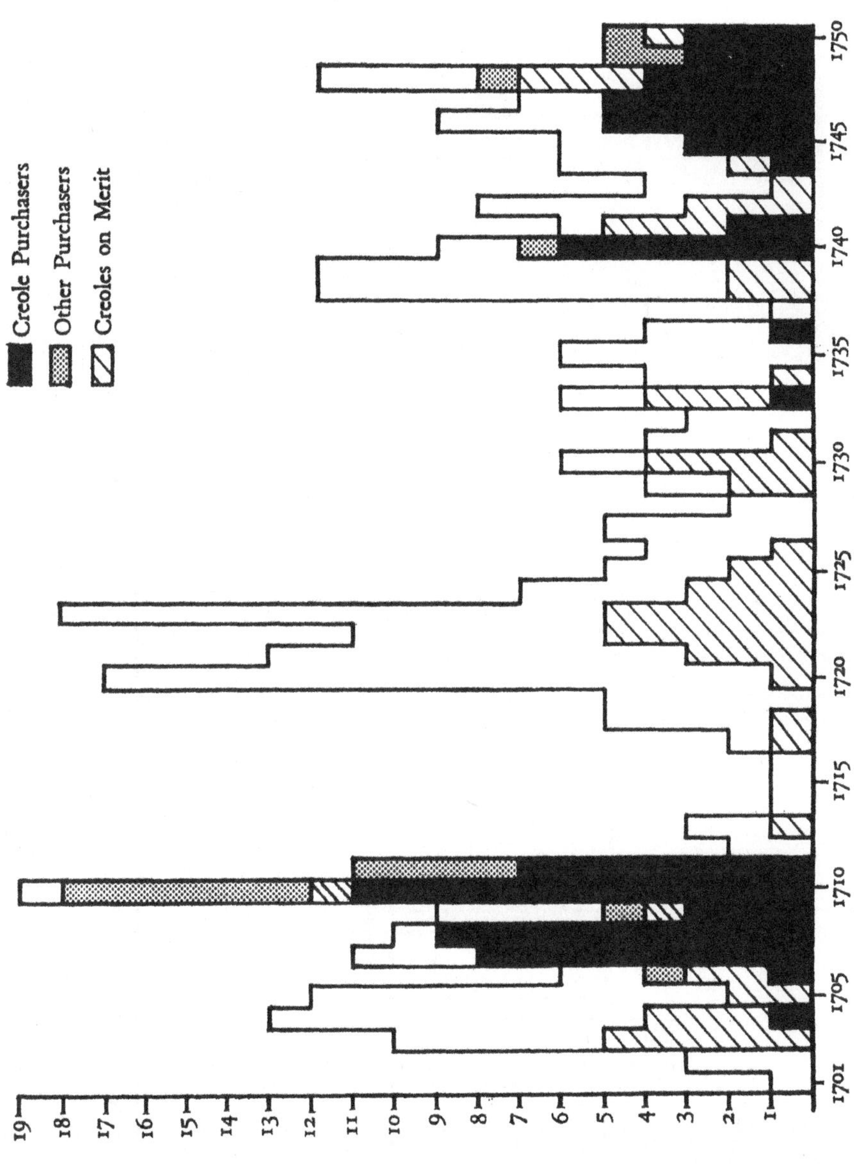

GRAPH A

Number of appointments

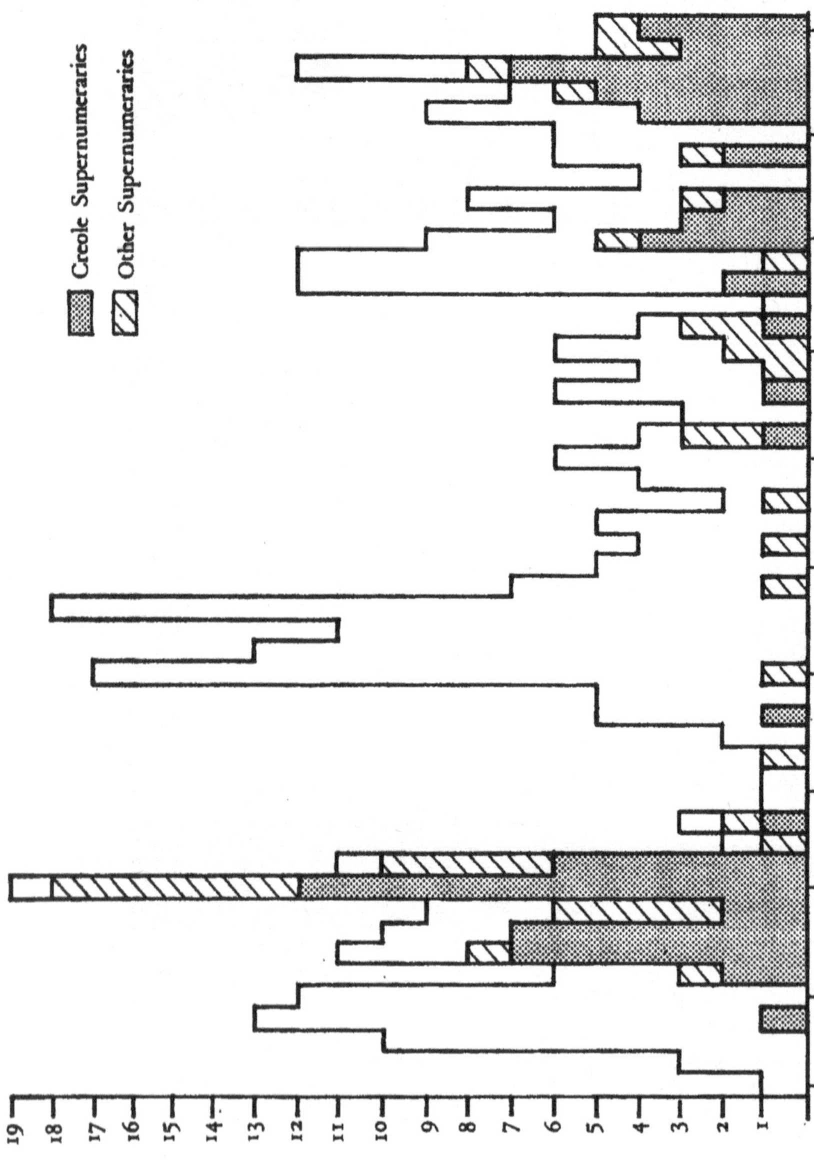

GRAPH B

Number of appointments

Bourbon maintained his aversion to selling these offices until the general European wars, beginning in 1739 with the War of Jenkins' Ear, again created great financial strain.

The decision to resume the sale of audiencia positions in the 1740s came only after considerable soul-searching and debate. A strong faction within the royal government, composed mainly of high judicial bureaucrats of the various councils, remained unalterably opposed to the sale of judicial and treasury appointments in America.[28] Their arguments continued unchanged from the seventeenth century and were based on a semi-religious concept of justice. The Council of the Indies stated this position most clearly in an opinion written for the King in 1737, a time of lingering financial difficulty for the Crown due to the recently ended War of the Polish Succession.[29]

The Council declared that not only audiencia posts but all offices involving the administration of justice and treasury affairs should be awarded solely on the basis of individual merit. This sweeping statement touched all governorships, treasury offices, and district administrators—in short, the Council would return to Philip II's position that only fee-producing and non-salaried offices not involving judicial authority or the royal fisc could be sold. The arguments in defense of this position ring with theological concepts that sound sophistical to a modern ear. The Council related the story of an interview between St Thomas Aquinas and the Duchess of Brabant during which the lady asked the learned doctor if she could legally and morally sell the offices of justice within her realm. The Saint replied that, strictly speaking, such sales were legal as she was the temporal lord, but only when sold at moderate prices and to subjects qualified for the posts. He reasoned that the most worthy servants often were found among the poor, and that prices should be kept within their means. The royal councillors of Philip V then proceeded to marshal the legal persuasions of 'Theodosius, Justinian, Severus, Trajan, and others'. Justice, being a divine attribute of sovereignty, was not a saleable commodity; the King's most sacred obligation was to render it to his subjects. The sale of such positions would result in the prostitution of justice as the purchaser recouped his investment from the King's flock.

The Council of the Indies, therefore, opposed the sale of judicial office but stipulated that it might be considered legal if certain conditions were fulfilled: the purchaser must meet the normal requirements for appointment to such a post (for audiencia positions this meant being a *letrado*); the

[28] Phelan noted this 'professional *esprit de corps*' in the Council of the Indies in the 1640s. *Kingdom of Quito*, pp. 129–31.

[29] Consulta of the Council of the Indies, 21 Aug. 1737, AGI, Mexico, legajo 1970. The next three paragraphs are based on this document.

price must be moderate; and the financial need of the government truly great. The Council then proceeded, however, to suggest that these provisions were unrealistic. It pointed out that in the past (*en lo antiguo*) the amounts paid for such positions had more than doubled, violating the requirement for moderate prices. Furthermore, in practice such sales were self-defeating; if, by some miracle, the admonition to sell at moderate prices could be observed, no real financial benefit would accrue to the treasury. Therefore, the Council recommended that the government stop selling judicial and treasury posts; improved administration of justice and more honest tax collection would more than compensate for the loss of income. The councillors could not resist a jibe at what they regarded as the notorious office-selling practices of the French, and congratulated themselves that such was not the case in Spain.

The royal response to this recommendation echoed that of Charles II forty-five years earlier; the Crown frankly admitted the validity of the Council's argument but stressed the grave financial difficulties of the state.[30] The King had no choice but to continue the sale of most salaried positions in America. In line with previous declarations, he promised the early cessation of the practice when the crisis eased, and pledged a continuation for the time being of the ban on the sale of audiencia positions.

The outbreak of the War of Jenkins' Ear, however, forced a re-evaluation of the sale of judicial offices in America. A note of December 1739 suggested the resumption of the sale of audiencia positions, subject always to the requirement that only those fully qualified for the posts be allowed to purchase them.[31] Although the documentation is incomplete, there is enough evidence to indicate that the years 1740 and 1741 saw a clash of priorities within the government over the sale of these posts.[32] Letters between members of the Council of the Indies in April and May of 1740 record the King's recent decision to resume the sale of audiencia posts in America.[33] In July of that year the Council appealed to the King to postpone selling judgeships and military governorships, and in 1741 the King informed the tribunal that he had changed his mind and would not sell audiencia positions.[34]

A few years later, however, Philip again reversed his decision. The record

[30] An unsigned note in *ibid.* expresses the royal decision.

[31] Unsigned memorandum to the Marqués de Villarias, Buen Retiro, December 1739, AGI, Mexico, legajo 1970.

[32] Marqués de Villarias to José de la Quintana, El Pardo, 25 Feb. 1741, in *ibid.*, mentions the loss of pertinent papers in a recent fire at San Ildefonso.

[33] Fernando Verdes Montenegro to José de la Quintana, Buen Retiro, 13 May 1740, in *ibid.*

[34] Consulta of the Council of the Indies, 18 July 1740, with an addendum dated 28 March 1741 expressing the royal will, in *ibid.*

of sales bears out this change of policy: the Crown sold seven of nine audiencia appointments in 1740 and two of six in 1741. A gap of several years followed for which there is no record of such transactions. As financial difficulties increased, however, the royal scruples must have yielded, for the King countenanced the sale of one of six positions in 1744 and resumed selling offices in earnest the following year. In the six-year period from 1745 to 1750, the hard-pressed monarchy realized over 500,000 pesos by selling 27 of 44 audiencia appointments for America. As in the period from 1706 to 1711, the sales in the 1740s displayed the individual nature of each transaction.

When the Crown sold high judicial positions, it frequently granted not only the office, but also dispensations from various laws that might inconvenience the purchaser. These dispensations included permission to marry a native of the audiencia district or to own property there. If the purchaser were himself a native of the district, he received an exemption from this disability.[35] Occasionally the Crown even overlooked the youthfulness of an appointee and allowed minors to receive office. Several examples will illustrate the variety of the appointment terms and the different dispensations provided.

On 21 May 1707 the King named Juan Francisco de la Peña y Flores to be an *alcalde del crimen* in the Audiencia of Mexico. Peña paid 3,000 *doblones* for this honor and the accompanying provisions. The decree entitled him to serve, whether or not a vacancy existed when he arrived in New Spain. If there were no vacancy, he was, nevertheless, to receive full salary while serving as a supernumerary *alcalde del crimen* until a regular position became available. Furthermore, if he should not take office, he or his heirs would receive a refund of the 2,000 *doblones* 'down payment' he had made in Spain. Following his payment of the final 1,000 *doblones* in Mexico, Peña could marry a native of the district. Finally, as the result of an additional 800 pesos *escudos*, he obtained a decree in October 1707, removing the impediment of serving in the audiencia district in which he had been born.[36]

Three years later, Nicolás Chirino Vandeval also obtained appointment as a supernumerary *alcalde del crimen* in Mexico for a *servicio* of 7,000 pesos. Along with the position, Chirino obtained dispensations, for both he and his wife were natives of New Spain. The decree stated that he could

[35] Although the Crown both granted freely and sold natives dispensations in order to serve on the audiencias of their births, there was no law in the *Recopilación* explicitly denying natives the right to serve at home. AGI, Audiencia of Lima, legajo 620, Comment of the *mesa* to 19 Feb. 1794.

[36] AGI, Indiferente, legajo 1847.

take office immediately and receive full salary. Finally, the King declared the position and dispensations safe from any future reform decree (such as those of 1691 and 1701 which cancelled supernumerary appointments). If the creole did not take possession of his place, the Crown promised to refund the amount he had paid.[37]

The lengths to which the Crown would go for revenue is illustrated by the simultaneous appointment of father and son to positions in America. For their payment of 38,000 pesos in 1709, Philip V named Juan Prospero de Solís Vango *oidor* of the Audiencia of Chile and his father, Toribio Rodríguez de Solís, president of the Audiencia of Guadalajara. Since the *oidor* was of minor age, he was prohibited from voting in matters of justice until he had reached twenty-five years. Regardless of this limitation on his service, however, the youth was to receive full salary and begin his seniority from the date he took the oath of office in Santiago.[38]

An even more striking family relationship appeared in the Audiencia of Mexico in 1741. American-born Ambrosio Eugenio Santaella y Melgarejo paid 17,500 pesos for the post of *alcalde del crimen supernumerario*. One of the dispensations he received covered the fact that his father was already serving as *oidor* on the same tribunal. The only limitation mentioned in the son's title of office denied him promotion to the civil chamber of the body as long as his father was still a member.[39]

Other equally complex appointments appeared between 1740 and 1750. José de Tagle y Bracho, for example, paid 16,000 pesos to the Crown in 1740 for an appointment as *oidor* of the Audiencia of Charcas. He was to serve in the audiencia as a supernumerary if no vacancy existed in the regular positions and was to draw full salary.[40] A title issued in the following July modified Tagle's first appointment. In consideration of an additional 8,000 pesos delivered 'for the urgencies of the war', Philip appointed Tagle as a supernumerary *oidor* in the Audiencia of Lima. In addition to the position, Tagle received dispensations for being under age and a native of Lima. He was also granted the right to hold property and marry within the district. Finally, the young creole was to receive half-salary until he moved into the first vacant position.[41]

A similar case occurred several years later. On 8 July 1745 the title of office appeared naming the *limeño* Manuel de Zurbarán y Allende *oidor* in the Audiencia of Charcas. For this position and accompanying dispensa-

[37] *Ibid.*

[38] AGI, Indiferente, legajo 526.

[39] AGS, XXIII, 2-33-6, El Pardo, 12 Feb. 1741.

[40] AGS, XXIII, 2-32-277, San Ildefonso, Aug. 1740.

[41] AGS, XXIII, 2-33-114, Buen Retiro, 18 July 1741.

tions, Zurbarán paid the treasury 21,000 pesos. In addition to the office, he received permission to marry a native of the audiencia district, to own real estate there, and to remain in Lima for two months to settle urgent family affairs before proceeding to his post.[42] Later that year, another title appeared, changing the appointment to supernumerary *oidor* of Lima with the right to claim the first vacant regular position. Health considerations and, undoubtedly of far greater significance, an additional 12,000 pesos paid to the treasury provided the stimuli behind this alteration. As an additional dispensation, Zurbarán was now allowed to serve in Lima, despite having been born and raised there. His salary, however, would begin only when he actually moved into one of the regular positions.[43]

One of the most unusual dispensations granted struck at the foundation of the entire professional judiciary—the requirement that magistrates be *letrados*. In 1711, Juan Bautista Sánchez de Orellana, a native of Quito, purchased an appointment as supernumerary *oidor* in that audiencia for 1,500 *doblones*. There were inadequacies in his legal education, however, that invalidated his claim to be a school-trained lawyer, perhaps the most basic prerequisite for audiencia positions.[44] The Crown allowed Sánchez to take his seat on the body but denied him a vote and gave him a period of one year in which to remedy the defect in his education. Sánchez, however, drew full salary and enjoyed seniority from the date of his occupancy.[45]

The close relationship between Spanish involvement in expensive wars and the sale of audiencia posts in the first half of the eighteenth century has already been noted. The geographical distribution of the sales was also related to the international situation. During the two periods of audiencia sales, English sea power was the primary threat to Spanish possessions in America. Accordingly, the highest percentage of appointments sold occurred in the less threatened inland or Pacific coast audiencias of Lima, Quito, Chile, Charcas, and Guadalajara; the lowest percentages can be found in those of Manila, Mexico, Santa Fé de Bogotá and Santo Domingo, areas more likely to be attacked.[46] In highly exposed Santo Domingo, the King did not sell a single audiencia post in the eighteenth century. The decision

[42] AGS, XXIII, 2-35-95, Buen Retiro, 8 July 1745.

[43] AGS, XXIII, 2-35-104, San Lorenzo, 29 Oct. 1745.

[44] AGS, XXIII, 2-12-29, Zaragoza, 13 April 1711.

[45] Six years later the Crown issued an order removing the creole from his post because he had failed to complete his legal education. The King returned the purchase price. AGS, XXIII, 2-20-62, Aranjuez, 18 May 1722.

[46] The percentage of appointments sold for each audiencia (rounded to the nearest whole number) are: Santo Domingo, 0%; Santa Fé, 7%; Manila, 11%; Mexico, 19%; Guatemala, 24%; Panama, 28%; Lima, 34%; Charcas, 40%; Quito, 40%; Guadalajara, 41%; and Chile, 42%.

in 1742 to replace several elderly members of that audiencia with younger and more able men clearly reflected the royal concern with the quality of administration at Santo Domingo in a time of foreign threats.[47] In the midst of its financial difficulties, the Spanish government voluntarily committed itself to the expense of retirement pensions so that the tribunal would be better prepared to meet crises.

Geographical imbalance was even more obvious in the audiencia sales from 1740 to 1750 than it had been in the earlier period. The King made one sale in Guatemala in 1740, one in Mexico in 1741, and another in Santa Fé de Bogotá in 1748; there were none in Manila during this period and, of course, none in Santo Domingo. By contrast, the same period saw five sales each in Quito and Guadalajara, seven in Charcas, and nine in Lima.[48]

Information revealing the percentage of creoles on the various audiencias is less complete than that concerning sales, but it is possible to arrive at general figures indicating regional variations.[49] The audiencias lowest in the percentage of sales for the entire period, those of Santo Domingo, Santa Fé, Mexico, and Manila, show creole appointments of between 11 and 35 per cent of their totals and averaging about 18 per cent. For the period from 1740 to 1750, creoles accounted for between 14 and 50 per cent of the appointments to these tribunals, or an average of about 30 per cent. On the other hand, the five audiencias highest in sales for the half-century show that from 32 to 68 per cent of the appointments went to creoles, averaging about 56 per cent. During the 1740s, these same five courts received creoles in proportions of from 57 to 100 per cent for an average of about 77 per cent. Not surprisingly, the density of creole appointments corresponds roughly to the density of sales.

The attitude of the Council of the Indies in 1740 reveals the significance of this geographical distribution of sales and creoles. Military considerations were clearly present when the Council linked audiencia posts with certain governorships in its attempts to dissuade the King from selling important

[47] AGS, XXIII, 2-34-40, Aranjuez, 31 May 1743; 24-181-21, San Ildefonso, 18 Sept. 1742; and 2-33-370, San Ildefonso, 26 Sept. 1742.

[48] The percentages of sales for the eleven-year period 1740-50 are: Santo Domingo, 0%; Manila, 0%; Mexico, 12%; Guatemala, 12%; Santa Fé, 25%; Panama, 50%; Chile, 67%; Lima, 69%; Guadalajara, 71%; Charcas, 78%; and Quito, 83%. The percentage for Santa Fé is unnaturally high because there were only four appointments there during the decade, one of which was sold.

[49] The percentages of creoles during the entire period are as follows: Santo Domingo, 11%; Santa Fé, 17%; Manila, 11%; Mexico, 35%; Guatemala, 9%; Panama, 55%; Lima, 55%; Charcas, 68%; Quito, 56%; Guadalajara, 32%; and Chile, 68%. The figures for the period 1740-50 are: Santo Domingo, 14%; Manila, 33%; Mexico, 50%; Guatemala, 0%; Santa Fé, 25%; Panama, 50%; Chile, 83%; Lima, 100%; Guadalajara, 57%; Charcas, 78%; and Quito, 67%.

positions in America. The councillors prepared a list of governorships and presidencies that had been excluded from sale since 1717 for reasons of security.[50] Almost all of these posts were on the islands of the Caribbean and Gulf of Mexico or on the mainland areas bordering those seas, the areas of maximum military threat and the lowest rates of sales of audiencia positions and creole appointments. In the correspondence between the Council and the Crown in 1740, references to the military risks of sales of important posts were almost as significant as legal and theoretical arguments.[51]

Other reasons may have influenced the distribution of creole appointments and audiencia sales. The presence in Lima, for example, of more wealthy young men with the ambition for the honors of office than could be found in Santo Domingo may have played a part; also the possibility exists of different approaches in the Council's administrative branches for New Spain and Peru to the sales issue and the question of creoles in high office in America. There is little doubt, however, that military security was one important consideration in the distribution of these sales and creole nominations.

The amount paid for an audiencia position in the eighteenth century underwent a steady increase, bearing out one of the arguments the Council of the Indies had used against the sales in 1737. Anyone who has worked with the flexible monetary values of the colonial period in Spanish America will realize that the comparisons drawn and the averages calculated here are no more than approximations; the extent of the increase in real terms cannot be established without an exhaustive study of cost-of-living indices in the various parts of Spanish America, a project beyond the scope of this article. The salaries received by audiencia judges, however, provide a useful standard of comparison.[52]

There was no scale or 'price list' established for the various audiencias. The highest prices in both periods of sales can be found in Lima, but the varying amounts paid for appointments to that viceregal capital and between Lima and other tribunals reveal that each sale was very much an individual case, a fact illustrated by the examples presented earlier. Among other things, the price depended on the Crown's financial difficulties at the time, the different dispensations requested, the buyer's qualifications, and his ability and eagerness to purchase. Because of the individual circumstances

[50] Nota de los empleos . . . que desde el año de 1717 se han excluydo del beneficio por las razones que militan por ello, Buen Retiro, 1 June 1740, AGI, Mexico, legajo 1970.

[51] José de la Quintana to the Marqués de Villarias, Buen Retiro, 28 Aug. 1740; also, consulta of the Council of the Indies, 18 July 1740, in *ibid.*

[52] Information on the salaries paid the judges comes from their titles of office in AGS, XXIII.

governing each sale, one can only generalize about the movement of prices. A few cases of high prices might represent the purchaser's willingness to aid his sovereign as much as his desire for position; a financial 'service' to the Crown in a time of crisis was something to be proud of, and the fact of purchase was not usually hidden.

In the period of the War of the Spanish Succession, prices ranged between 4,000 and 20,000 pesos in America and from 2,000 to 3,000 in Manila, a less desirable location. In Lima, the area of highest sale prices, the average was about 12,000 pesos.[53] Annual salaries on the Audiencia of Lima at this time were almost 5,000 pesos (1,350,000 *maravedís*), so purchasers paid the equivalent of about one to four years' salary for their positions, exclusive of the tax of the *media anata* or of the *anata entera* required of some during the war years.[54] Prices in Mexico show a lower range. There the rate varied from 4,000 to 14,000 pesos, the average being about 8,000, while salaries were about 3,000 pesos annually (800,000 *maravedís*).[55] As in Lima the sale price was roughly equivalent to from one to four years' salary. In the nine lesser audiencias, Charcas and Chile show the second highest sale prices between 1706 and 1711, with a range of 7,000 to 16,000 pesos. These were areas of high living costs and the salaries of the judges were approximately 5,000 pesos in each case. Positions in these two provinces were also valuable as the most likely areas from which promotions to Lima originated. Sales for other minor audiencias showed decidedly lower prices, none being over 8,000 pesos. In these tribunals, the salaries ranged from 2,000 to about 3,300 pesos yearly, which meant that the prices of seats in these bodies also did not vary considerably from the ratio of one to four years' salary.

[53] For instance, Juan Antonio de Mena Caballero purchased a position as *alcalde del crimen* in Lima for four thousand doblones (AGS, XXIII, 24-174-301, July 1708); Alvaro Cavero Medina as *oidor supernumerario* for sixteen thousand pesos (AGS, XXIII, 2-9-17, Corella, 2 July 1711); Bartolomé de Munarriz as *alcalde del crimen* for five thousand doblones (AGS, XXIII, 2-4-31, Buen Retiro, 20 July 1708); and Francisco de los Santos as a supernumerary *alcalde del crimen* in 1707 for four thousand pesos (AGI, Indiferente, legajo 525). A peso was equal to eight reales or 272 maravedís while a doblón equalled four pesos.

[54] The *media anata* was a tax of one half of the first year's salary while the *anata entera* was a tax of the first full year's pay. Requiring either tax, of course, added to the amount the Crown was able to realize immediately from its sale of positions. For a summary of the *anata entera* decree of 4 Oct. 1704, see the title of office of Pedro Antonio Echaves y Rojas as *fiscal futurario* in Lima (AGS, XXIII, 2-8-134, Madrid, 11 Jan. 1710).

[55] For representative Mexican appointments, see the titles of Diego Francisco de Castañeda as *alcalde del crimen supernumerario* for five thousand pesos (AGS, XXIII, 2-9-34, Zaragoza, 21 March 1711); Tristán Manuel de Rivadeneyra as supernumerary *oidor* for fourteen thousand pesos (AGS, XXIII, 2-5-147, Buen Retiro, 30 Sept. 1708); Agustín Franco de Toledo as supernumerary *oidor* for eight thousand pesos (AGS, XXIII, 2-8-4, Madrid, 18 July 1710); and Francisco de Oyanguren as *fiscal futurario* for two thousand *doblones* (AGS, XXIII, 2-8-39, Madrid, 22 April 1710).

By contrast, the prices of the 1740s showed a considerable increase although salaries rose only in Mexico (to 4,000 pesos). As a general rule, the 1740 prices began at or slightly above the maximum rates for the earlier period. Thus, the price that year in Lima was 21,000 pesos, while the judge's robe sold for 16,000 pesos in Charcas, 8,000 pesos in Guatemala and Guadalajara, and 7,000 pesos in Quito. The resumption of heavy sales in the second half of the decade saw prices rise to a maximum of 47,500 pesos in Lima, 40,000 in Charcas, and over 20,000 in Quito, Chile, and Santa Fé. The top price in Guadalajara rose from 8,000 to 14,000 pesos in the same period. By 1750, then, purchasers everywhere were paying the equivalent of from four to nine years' salary, a sizable increase over 1740 and the earlier period. The royal need for cash and the thirst for honors and position among *letrados* in Spain and America combined to push prices steadily upward.

Traditionally most scholars have maintained that the Spanish Crown did not sell high judicial offices and almost completely excluded creoles from audiencia positions. During the reigns of the first two Bourbons, however, the Crown did sell appointments and did name many creoles to serve in the Indies. Just as the Habsburgs, the Bourbons were reluctant to sell judicial offices but would do so when facing severe financial crisis. From 1701 to 1750 Philip V and Ferdinand VI sold nearly a quarter of the appointments to American tribunals and named creoles to fill roughly two-fifths of all audiencia posts.

The creoles had greater impact on the high courts in America than numbers alone would suggest. Had American appointments been spread evenly over time and region, peninsular Spaniards would probably have retained their dominance at all times. In fact, the Crown largely limited creole admissions to the two periods of sales; nearly two-thirds of the creole appointments occurred during these seventeen years. This concentration enabled Americans to dominate several audiencias for a number of years after 1750.[56] Although creoles obtained an important minority of these ministerial appointments between 1701 and 1750, they nevertheless continued to suffer from discrimination. The number of creole sales provides clear evidence of this discrimination; over 60 per cent of the American appointees had to purchase their positions in contrast to only 11 per cent of

[56] José de Gálvez commented on the creole majority in Mexico during his *visita*. See his Informe, que el Sor Visitador ha dado a S.E. con fecha de 31 de Diz.e de 1711 (a copy of Gálvez' inspection report to Viceroy Bucareli), AGI, Mexico, legajo 1509. See also Brading, *Miners and Merchants*, part I. For Lima see M. A. Burkholder, 'From Creole to Peninsular: The Transformation of the Audiencia of Lima', *The Hispanic American Historical Review*, Vol. LII, no. 3 (August, 1972).

the peninsulars. The Bourbons again followed Habsburg precedent in favoring peninsular *letrados*.

The creole appointments and the sale of high judicial offices raise questions that only detailed examination of each American audiencia will resolve. Since purchasers of positions naturally desired to regain their often heavy payments and most creoles appointed to serve in their home districts enjoyed ties with the local aristocracy, the question of impartial justice arises immediately. A second question concerns the implications of accustoming creoles to the exercise of authority. *Limeños* protested repeatedly when after 1776 the Crown began to regain control over the Audiencia of Lima, control virtually abdicated through previous sales and creole appointments.[57] The audiencia appointments made in the first half of the eighteenth century raise two final questions: how widespread was the practice of selling appointments to high salaried offices throughout the colonial period; and what percentage of these administrative positions did creoles hold? Only investigation of appointments throughout the entire bureaucracy will provide answers to these questions and shed new light on the place of creoles in viceregal society and its relationship to the origins of the Wars of Independence.

[57] *Ibid*

5

Élite and Cadres in Bourbon Chile

Jacques A. Barbier

IN RECENT YEARS historians have begun to question the traditional belief that colonial Latin American government was autocratic and centralized. In the process of this reevaluation features such as corruption, which had previously been treated as weaknesses of the political system, have come to be regarded as hidden strengths. Today theoretical articles emphasize that the "corruption" of the administration provided the local population with an opportunity for political influence. Colonial officials are presented, therefore, as having been responsive to local pressures, and having enjoyed considerable autonomy from central authorities.[1] Such arguments conclude that corruption was a safety valve for the empires. The creole who surreptitiously wielded influence, it is argued, was not likely to demand formal control of the government.

These theoretical discussions have been confirmed by regional studies. The predominant tendency has been to argue that the roots of corruption were to be found in an informal structure of primary interpersonal relations established between members of the elite and royal officials. While the formal structure of government placed the Indies in a classic colonial position by forcing administrators to be loyal to outside authorities, "the informal structure allowed colonial interest groups to treat magistrates as simply another source of power subject to alliance and cooptation."[2]

1. For examples of this type of work see John L. Phelan, "Authority and Flexibility in the Spanish Imperial Bureaucracy" *Administrative Sciences Quarterly*, 5 (June 1960), 47-65; Frank Jay Moreno, "The Spanish Colonial System: a Functional Approach," *Western Political Quarterly*, 20 (June 1967), 308-320; Magali Sarfatti, *Spanish Bureaucratic-Patrimonialism in America* (Berkeley, 1966); S. N. Eisenstadt, *The Political Systems of Empire* (New York, 1963), pp. 222-272. Phelan has produced a significant modification of this last theoretical work in his book *The Kingdom of Quito in the Seventeenth Century* (Madison, 1967), pp. 320-337.

2. Stuart B. Schwartz, "Magistracy and Society in Colonial Brazil," *HAHR*, 50:4 (November 1970), 729-730. For other works demonstrating the existence of these colonial establishments see Phelan's *Kingdom of Quito*; Leon G. Campbell, "A Colonial Establishment: Creole Domination of the Audiencia of Lima in

This situation, in which the administrative cadres were related in so many ways to the local elite that they could not provide impartial administration, is presumed by many authorities to have come to an end because of the reforms of Charles III and Pombal. One recent writer on the period, for example, describes the Bourbon dynasty as carrying out a revolution in government that destroyed "that small colonial establishment which had hitherto governed . . ."[3]

We cannot know if such a result was characteristic. With few exceptions political histories do not exist for the colonial period. We know a great deal about laws and institutions but next to nothing of the petty, often sordid, intergroup struggles that determined who was truly in command in each of the colonies. Lacking such basic work regional differences in political patterns cannot be known. Yet it is precisely such knowledge which is needed to evaluate the impact of the Bourbon reforms. An examination of their impact on elite influence in various areas is particularly vital because of the recent tendency to see such influence as the preserver of the empire.

There is reason to believe that the results of such an examination would vary from one region of the Indies to another.[4] Indeed, if the general effect of the Bourbon reforms was to force the creole elite permanently out of positions of political power, if they prevented it from creating primary interpersonal relations between itself and the administrative cadres, then the Chilean case was aberrant in the extreme. An examination of marital patterns demonstrates that in Chile the period of Bourbon reforms was characterized by an increasingly high degree of interrelation between the elite and the administrative

the Late Eighteenth Century," *HAHR*, 52:1 (February 1972) 1-25; and D. A. Brading, *Miners and Merchants in Bourbon Mexico* (New York, 1971).

3. Brading, *Miners and Merchants*, pp. 34-35.

4. The evidence on this matter is somewhat contradictory. Brading argues for a destruction of the colonial establishment in Mexico. J. R. Fisher in *Government and Society in Colonial Peru: the Intendant System, 1784-1814* (London, 1970) and "The Intendant System and the Cabildos of Peru, 1784-1810," *HAHR*, 49:3 (August 1969), 430-453, finds the creoles took advantage of the increased power of the cabildos. Ralph Lee Woodward Jr. in his article "Economic and Social Origins of the Guatemalan Political Parties," *HAHR*, 45:3 (August 1965), 544-566, sees struggle for power between creole groups continuing within the context of the new institutions. In Guatemala reform may have only provided the local elite with new political vehicles. Mark A. Burkholder in an article on Peru "From Creole to Peninsular: the Transformation of the Audiencia of Lima," in this issue of *HAHR*, concludes that the creoles lost one of their chief bastions of power due to the reforms. The present article is drawn from a larger work, made possible by a grant from the Doherty Fellowship Committee, which concludes that the reforms created new modes of political expression without significantly curbing creole influence in Chile.

cadres. At the same time, far from being forced out of office-holding, the elite benefited from the opportunities created by the phenomenal extension of the bureaucracy during this period, and came to value government posts and relations with officials more than ever before.[5]

No evaluation of the elite's ties or influence can be attempted without a clear idea of who belonged to it. For colonial Chile this is difficult to determine because a scholarly social history of the group remains to be written.[6] Although it would be difficult to make up a complete list of all elite families, there are a few who have long been recognized as belonging to the group. These are families whose heads held a title of nobility (*título de Castilla*) or an entailed estate (*mayorazgo*).[7] The purchase of a title of nobility by the head of a family, or the establishment of an entail, is strong evidence of a lineage's high social status. A title was a particularly heavy expense, one that could not be borne save by the very rich. For a man who did not have impeccable credentials the price rose steeply, so that only the very wealthy, very noble, or very well connected could aspire to purchase one. An entail, on the other hand, was designed to safeguard for the head of a family the property on which ultimately the status of the lineage depended. Often established in prejudice of the material interests of most of the children of the founder, an entail can be taken as a demonstration that the status of the family was sufficiently high to warrant the sacrifice.[8] In short, an individual responsible for securing a

5. For the increase in the Chilean bureaucracy during the reform period see Fernando Silva Vargas, "La visita de Areche en Chile y la subdelegación del regente Álvarez de Acevedo," *Historia* (Santiago), 6 (1967), 153-191.

6. The most famous work on the Chilean elite is that of Alberto Edwards, *La fronda aristocrática* (Santiago, 1928), which is more journalistic than historical. It speaks of the eighteenth century as a period during which the old families of *conquistadores* and *encomenderos* were replaced and absorbed by new families of merchants and entrepreneurs. Unfortunately, insightful as it is, the work of Edwards does not provide a formula by which one can decide who belonged to this bourgeois aristocracy.

7. The importance of titles and entails to the elite of Santiago was pointed out by Domingo Amunátegui Solar in his work *La sociedad chilena del siglo xviii: mayorazgos i títulos de Castilla* (3 vols.; Santiago, 1901-1904), I, xii-xxi. In other areas of the Indies different criteria of elite membership might have to be adopted.

8. Entails were founded by giving in usufruct to one heir property representing the *tercio* and *quinto* of the estates of the founders. The individual enjoying this special status was normally the first-born son. While such a division of property could result even without the creation of an entail if one of the heirs were given a *mejora* of the above portions, the injustice of the division of property was often accentuated if an entail was formed. Often the founder forced other children into entering regular orders and renouncing their portion so that the entail might be larger. The effects were particularly baneful for the grandchildren of the founder.

TABLE I. CHRONOLOGICAL LIST OF TITLES, ENTAILS, AND MAJOR VÍNCULOS IN SANTIAGO SOCIETY WITH FAMILY NAMES OF HOLDERS

Date	Creation	Family
1684	M. de la Pica	Irarrázaval
1685	C. de Sierra Bella	Mesía
1693	Torres entail	Mesía
1702	M. de la Cañada Hermosa	Marín de Poveda, Ruiz de Azúa
1703	Cerda entail	Cerda
1728	Irarrázaval entail	Irarrázaval
1728	M. de Villapalma	Calvo de Encalada
1736	Larraín entail	Larraín
1744	Aguirre entail	Aguirre
1748	Azúa entail	Ruiz de Azúa
1752	Toro Mazote entail	Caldera
1755	M. de Montepío	Aguirre
1755	M. de Casa Real	García Huidobro
1756	García Huidobro entail	García Huidobro
1763	C. de Quinta Alegre	Alcalde
1763	Valdés entail	Valdés
1768	Lecaros entail	Lecaros, Larraín
1770	C. de la Conquista	Toro Zambrano
1778	Balmaceda entail	Fernández de Balmaceda
1779	Rojas entail	Rojas
1780	Larraín y Rojas entail	Rojas de Larraín, Larraín
1783	Ruiz Tagle entail	Ruiz Tagle
1785	Prado entail	Prado
1887	M. de Larraín	Larraín
1789	Toro Zambrano entail	Toro Zambrano
1789	Aguila y Rojas entail	Herrera
1791	Alcalde *vínculo*	Alcalde

title or entail for his family was classifying it as belonging in the highest social stratum.

This study is restricted to the central administration of Chile, therefore this discussion limits itself to considering those titles and entails which were created or secured by individuals who had a close connection to the city of Santiago, and who founded families which became established there. In all there were 27 creations, making up 18 distinct combinations.[9]

These titles and entails came into existence between 1684 and 1791. However, they were not evenly distributed over the entire period. Around 1755 there is a definite increase in the tempo of creations. In

9. The information in Table I is from Amunátegui Solar, *La sociedad chilena.* Following the practice of that author I treat the Alcalde *vínculo* as a *mayorazgo* because of its large size and disregard others of that class on the grounds that they were neither entails in law nor large enough to have the same social result as an entail. Titles which did not become established in the Santiago area are not included in this treatment nor are titles and entails that were established after 1796. Family names given in Table I are only for the holders in the period between 1755 and 1796.

fact the frequency of foundations after 1755 is twice that of the period preceding that date. The year 1755 is important in the social history of Chile because it marks the start of a period of inflation of honors. For titles this is quite clear. They cluster in the period after that date because it was only after 1755 that the crown allowed Chileans to buy them on advantageous terms.[10] For entails the phenomenon is not so clear. There are two separate clusters of entail foundations, one of four in the period between 1744 and 1756, and another of eight between 1778 and 1791. The other six creations were widely scattered. Although entails seem to become more frequent after 1744, an examination of the matter in detail reveals the primacy of the date 1755.

The Aguirre entail, founded in 1744, came eight years after the foundation of the Larraín entail in 1736, and that in turn came eight years after the foundation of the Irarrázaval entail in 1728. The speed-up in foundations after 1744 is an illusion. The Toro Mazote entail, created in 1752, came only as a belated enforcement of the will of Andrés de Toro Mazote y Cifuentes, who died in 1706.[11] The creation of the Azúa entail again is not really new, since it was meant to benefit the future heirs of the Marquesado de la Cañada Hermosa. These were clearly already members of the elite. Lastly, the 1756 creation of the García Huidobro entail resulted from the acquisition of the title of Marqués de Casa Real by the head of that family in 1755. It was meant only to enable future heirs of the title to maintain themselves in dignity, and thus did not involve the entry of a new family into the elite. If only truly new creations ordered during this period are considered, there is a gap of eleven years between the distinctions secured by the Aguirre and García Huidobro families.

If we consider the creations between 1755 and 1770, on the other hand, we see a clear pattern of new families reaching distinction. Of the seven titles and entails created in this period, only one was a mere addition to the distinctions held by a family that already belonged to the elite. Considering the period between 1778 and 1791, out of nine creations only one, a title, was secured to distinguish further a family whose entail predated 1755. Another two entails were created to bolster the status of families acquiring titles in the 1755 to 1770 period. The remaining six were genuinely new.

10. As a financial expedient to aid in the creation of new towns, crown officials sent a set of blank *títulos de Castilla* to the presidency of Chile. Although some had been dispatched to Chile previously, it was only in 1755 that some of these were sold in the country itself. See Diego Barros Arana, *Historia jeneral de Chile* (16 vols.; Santiago, 1884-1902), VI, 198-199.

11. Amunátegui Solar, *La sociedad chilena*, I, 183-217.

In short, titles and entails became more frequent after 1755. The families belonging to the Chilean elite can therefore be divided into two groups: the old elite, which achieved these distinctions before a trend to secure them set in, and the new elite, which did so afterwards.

Looking at the men who were responsible for securing these distinctions for their families, it is clear that the two groups had different origins. The first title created for a resident of Chile, that of Marqués de la Pica, was given to a direct descendant of a President of the Audiencia of Chile, Melchor Bravo de Saravia. The first Marqués de la Pica had succeeded to family entails and *señoríos* in Spain, and held an encomienda and vast estates in Chile. He served for several years in military posts (rising to *sargento mayor general* and *maestre de campo general*), and married one of his daughters to a Chilean President, Francisco de Meneses. These official connections recur in many other of the first group of creations. The Irarrázaval entail was founded by the head of a family whose senior branch in Spain had risen to the grandeeship through military service. Founded by a companion of Ercilla, this was one of the more distinguished families in the country. More directly connected with royal service were the titles of Conde de Sierra Bella, granted to a President of Charcas, Marqués de la Cañada Hermosa, granted to a President of Chile, and the entail of Azúa, founded by an Archbishop of Bogotá to benefit his brother, a member of the Audiencia of Chile.[12]

Other founders of old elite lineages, while they engaged in trade, enjoyed official connections like those mentioned above. The entail tied to the title of Sierra Bella, for instance, was founded by a merchant who held the post of treasurer of the *Santa Cruzada*. His political influence served to increase and preserve his wealth. The same proved true in the case of Diego de Encalada y Orozco, first Marqués de Villapalma, who although he engaged in trade also secured two Peruvian *corregimientos* and the command of the Chilean cavalry. The cases of the entails founded for the Larraín and Aguirre families show similar characteristics. That of Larraín was founded by a Spanish merchant who bought the post of President of Quito, while the Aguirre entail was the creation of a merchant who was the administrator of the Chilean tobacco monopoly.[13]

It is striking that out of the creations and foundations made before

12. *Ibid.*, I, 18-34, 130-155, 183-217, 231-329, 343-360; III, 153-180. The Cerda entail was founded by a lawyer who did not hold a permanent post in the administration. He was active in politics, however. The Toro Mazote entail was founded by a member of a family of first settlers.

13. *Ibid.*, I, 1-58, 289-433; II, 1-22; III, 343-378.

1755, three were by presidents of audiencias and four by other high officials. A total of nine out of eleven had administrative antecedents. Of the eleven, at least five engaged in commerce, including two of the presidents of audiencias, and only three could trace their ancestry in Chile back to the sixteenth century. In short, they were relatively new men, connected to official circles, and often characterized by an interest in trade. This surely indicates that the process of replenishment of the Chilean elite was a long established one.

Looking at the creations and foundations made after 1755 (and ignoring those that served only to adorn already existing ones), one finds a different situation. Of the eleven individuals responsible for them, seven were merchants, one was a priest, another the daughter of a merchant, yet another a landowner belonging to a family long established in Chile, and the last a Spanish-born *oidor*. Except for the *oidor*, the only one of these subjects who held royal office was Francisco García Huidobro, first Marqués de Casa Real, who was allowed to establish the royal mint of Santiago as a private speculation and consequently held the title of Treasurer of the establishment.[14] Of the ten families involved, five were recently arrived from Spain, two recently arrived from Peru, two descended from obscure soldiers who reached Chile around 1600, and one descended from a treasury official who arrived at about the same time.[15]

There is a definite tendency for this later group to come from more obscure stock and to engage in trade in a more prominent way. More to the point, however, the founders of these titles and entails lacked the high level of political involvement of the earlier group. The founders of titles and entails before 1755 were either administrators who became local notables, or merchants who became administrators and then local notables in turn. Only two out of eleven are exceptions to this pattern. In the foundations and creations made after 1755, only two out of eleven follow the same route. It might seem therefore that this method of rising into high colonial society lost importance during the course of the eighteenth century. Since the entry of administrators into the elite is part of a pattern of interdependence which made crown officials sensitive to colonial desires, it might appear that at least this part of the structure of informal control broke down during the period.

An analysis of the marital patterns of both old and new aristocrats puts this development in proper relief. In this analysis, the only individuals considered are those who received titles or founded entails, their

14. *Ibid.*, II, 72-116.

15. *Ibid.*, I, 379-401, 432-437; II, 72-129, 187-210, 243-259, 279-296, 309-344, 373-389, 405-414; III, 7-49, 273-285.

brothers and sisters, their heirs and heirs apparent, and the brothers and sisters of these successors. All collateral branches have been disregarded on the grounds that they may have suffered an erosion of status because of their genealogical distance from the head of the family. In all, there were 182 people falling within these categories and known to have married before 1808. They entered into a total of 201 marriages which (excluding duplications due to in-group marriages) involved a total of 347 separate individuals.[16]

These 347 people are not a sample. They are the total number of those appearing in genealogies who meet the qualifications set. As such, they constitute a population and therefore can be treated statistically, although our interest, of course, is less with quantitative than with qualitative factors. Of particular interest are the types of marriages the members of the group entered into. The overall pattern of marriages is in keeping with the background of the old elite. Out of 201 marriages, 22% took place within the elite, 8% with members of families whose titled head lived outside of Chile, and 27% with royal officials and their relatives. A clear majority of the marriages, 115 out of 201, were either within the status group or into official circles.[17]

Breaking down the figures further, there seems to have been a growing cohesion over the years between the older and newer group of aristocrats. Thus, while before 1755 the old elite chose mates from the new elite only 3% of the time, after 1755 they did so 12% of the time.

A more serious indication of this change is the growing similarity between the marital patterns. Before 1755 18% of the marriages of the

16. The data on which all of the following statistical work is based is taken from genealogies. The work of Amunátegui Solar was taken as the base for determining entail founders, holders, and their relations in the first degree. Modifications and additions to the resulting list have been made from the truly superior genealogy of Juan Luis Espejo, *Nobiliario de la antigua capitanía general de Chile* (Santiago, 1967). The work was first published in two volumes in 1917 and was based in part on private collections which are no longer in existence. Chile is endowed with a rich genealogical literature, one far too voluminous to cite extensively. When other sources were lacking I consulted the not always reliable works of Enrique Torres Saldamando, *Los títulos de Castilla en las familias de Chile* (Santiago, 1894), and Luis de Roa y Urzúa, *El reyno de Chile* (Valladolid, 1945), as well as the masterful one of Guillermo Lohmann Villena, *Los americanos en las órdenes nobiliarias* (Madrid, 1947). I also looked at family histories to confirm the information found in these works of collective genealogy. While other Chilean collective genealogies were consulted they did not prove useful either because of notorious weaknesses, because the information in them was not in my time period, or simply because they were redundant.

17. Appendix I. Included in all the computations for the tables and appendices were the marriages of the founders and holders of entails and titles and their relatives within the first degree.

TABLE II. MARITAL PATTERNS OF THE CHILEAN ELITE BEFORE 1808[a]

Period	To Old Elite	To New Elite	To Officials	To "First Family"	To Other Titled	To Others
Before 1755	13.5%	10.4%	14.5%	20.8%	9.4%	31.5%
After 1755	5.7%	15.2%	38.2%	4.8%	6.7%	29.5%
Both Periods	9.5%	12.9%	26.9%	12.2%	8.0%	30.3%

[a]Because the figures are averaged to the nearest tenth of one percent in this and succeeding tables their sum is not always 100%.

TABLE III. MARITAL PATTERNS OF THE CHILEAN ELITE BEFORE 1755

Group	To Old Elite	To New Elite	To Officials	To "First Family"	To Other Titled	To Others
Old Elite	17.9%	3.0%	19.4%	20.9%	13.5%	25.4%
New Elite	3.4%	27.6%	3.4%	20.7%	0.0%	44.8%

old elite took place within the group, 14% with families whose titled heads resided outside of Chile, 21% into families of Chilean conquistadores and first settlers (here termed "first families"), and 19% with families of officials. They married with the new elite only 3% of the time and with others 25% of the time. Of the new elite marriages during the same period, 28% took place within the group, 3% with officials and relatives of officials, 21% within "first families," only 3% to old elite families, and 45% with others. Whereas the older group tended to secure government officials and their relatives as marital partners before 1755, the newer group did not. The newer group chose partners with no inheritable status 45% of the time, as opposed to only 25% in the older group. Further, the two groups did not tend to marry into each other. Clearly they were separate social groups before this date.

After 1755 these differences tended to disappear. While from that date the old elite no longer chose mates from within itself, 12% came from the newer group, 5% from families whose titled head resided outside of Chile, 5% from "first families," no less than 49% from officials and their relatives, and 29% from other families. After 1755 the new elite married 9% of the time with the older group, 17% with itself, 8% into families whose titled head resided abroad, 5% with members of "first families," 31% with officials and their relatives, and 30% with others.[18]

18. Appendix II.

TABLE IV. MARITAL PATTERNS OF THE CHILEAN ELITE AFTER 1755

Group	To Old Elite	To New Elite	To Officials	To "First Family"	To Other Titled	To Others
Old Elite	0.0%	12.2%	48.8%	4.9%	4.8%	29.3%
New Elite	9.4%	17.2%	31.3%	4.7%	7.9%	29.7%

Before 1755 the two groups of aristocrats had different marital patterns. This ceased to be the case thereafter. Indeed, during the last part of the eighteenth century they shared a common pattern characterized by clannishness and a high rate of intermarriage with the families of members of the bureaucracy. This development signals the entry of the new group into the true elite of the province. It married into the old line families and adopted their criteria as to what were desirable marriages, even as previously it had imitated old elite behavior by buying land, founding entails, and seeking titles. Significantly, as it rose the new elite began to seek marital relations with administrative personnel, and neglected marital opportunities with wealthy, newly established merchants.[19] So pronounced was the tendency to restrict marriages to the few families in the elite and those of equivalent status, or to officials and their relatives, that in the post-1755 period such marriages accounted for 66% of all those entered into by the group. Officials and their relatives by themselves were chosen 38% of the time.[20] Before 1755 officials and relatives had made up only 19% of the marital partners of the old elite and less than 15% of the mates of both groups.[21]

In short, far from decreasing, marital ties between the elite and officials increased during the years of the Bourbon reforms. With this increase there was a concomitant rise in the opportunities for an official to be swayed in his actions by the interests of his relations. The ironic aspect of the situation is that it came about in large part because of the reform effort itself. Many new posts were created in Chile during the late eighteenth century, and a goodly number of the new officials married locally. Such families as Cerda, Azúa, and Toro married their daughters to men holding posts which would not have existed but for the administrative reforms.[22]

19. Juan Ricardo Couyomdjian, "Los magnatos chilenos del siglo xviii," *Revista Chilena de Historia y Geografía*, no. 136 (1968), 315-322.

20. Appendix I.

21. Appendix II.

22. A daughter of the *mayorazgo* Cerda married Ramón del Pedregal, who was *administrador general* of the Santiago customs house. Rita Azúa profited directly

Even the enforcement by José de Gálvez of the regulation prohibiting *oidores* to marry within the area of their jurisdiction served to create opportunities for the elite. The Marqués de Villapalma by himself married no less than four of his daughters to members of the Audiencia of Chile. This could only take place because of the policy of transferring such men after their marriage, for otherwise so many men would not have held office in Santiago. Of course an anticipated marriage could have as much influence on a *fiscal* or *oidor* as a consummated one, and in view of the large dowries involved (which did not change hands until after the marriage), perhaps more. The vendetta of two of the future sons-in-law of the Marqués with the corregidor Zañartu of Santiago, a man despised by the creoles, is very suggestive.[23] The policy of transfer was implemented for Chile only during the *visitas* of Areche and Escobedo. By 1787 *oidor* Urriola was arranging to marry a niece of the Marquesa de Montepío, and Urriola was not transferred.[24] It is doubtful that implementation of the old prohibition or its abandonment changed very much.

Clearly ties with the administration remained much desired by the elite of Chile during the late eighteenth century. The reforms did not effectively prevent marital ties from being consummated. Another example of the aristocracy's covetousness of official connections comes with the incidences of outright entry of members of the elite into royal service. Although kept very busy by his business interests, the Conde de la Conquista held for a time the post of Superintendent of the Santiago mint. Others who entered the administration were the third Conde de Quinta Alegre, who made a career in the same bureau; the Marqués de Montepío, who ran the tobacco monopoly; the Conde de Sierra Bella, who became an *oidor* of Lima; and the Marqués de Casa

from the *visita* by marrying its *contador* in Chile, Pedro Dionisio Gálvez. This individual later rose to the post of *contador decano* of the *Tribunal Mayor de Cuentas* of Peru (see Amunátegui Solar, *La sociedad chilena*, III, 188). The Conde de la Conquista married all of his daughters to royal servants. Mariana de Toro married first José Antonio de Armaza, inspector in the customs house of Santiago, and second Marcos Alonso de Gamero, director of the tobacco monopoly; María Inés married a line military officer as did her sister María Josefa; and María Mercedes married the superintendent of the Santiago mint, Carlos Vigil de Miranda (see *ibid.*, III, 43-49).

23. *Fiscal* of the Council of the Indies, May, 1778, Santiago de Chile, Manuscritos y Copias de D. José Toribio Medina, vol. 196, pp. 217-262; and *fiscales* of Chile to José de Gálvez, November 18, 1777, vol. 196, pp. 352-354 (henceforth cited as SM). Some of these judges were moved to the Audiencia of Lima where they came into contact with their Peruvian relatives and business partners or those of their fathers-in-law. This merely changed the locus of the problem without altering its substance.

24. Anonymous letter, December 7, 1793, SM, vol. 211, pp. 307-320.

Real, who gave up ownership of the Santiago mint in return for hereditary possession of the post of *alguacil mayor* and chancellor of the Audiencia.[25] Besides such civil posts, almost all members of the aristocracy who were not clerics entered into the militia forces once these were given a regular organization.

The most important result of the reforms, insofar as their effect on the attitudes of the elite is concerned, may indeed have been to change subtly its feelings about royal service. Before the changes instituted during the terms of Julián de Arriaga and José de Gálvez as Minister of the Indies, high ranking positions available to residents of Chile were restricted to a few financial and judicial posts. Other high ranking offices would have required a social status, intimacy with court life, and broad administrative experience which could not have been achieved in remote Chile. Even in the case of judicial positions, which some members of the elite did secure, it was at a disadvantage. Having a secure social and economic position, few of its members saw any advantage in following the career of a *letrado,* particularly since before the creation of the University of San Felipe it required years of study in Lima, and in most cases a subsequent trip to the Peninsula to secure a post. The administrative positions open to Chileans were by and large not lucrative, and those that were valuable required an absence from Santiago for the term of office. Many were unwilling to leave their affairs in the hands of agents for very long. Thus the Conde de la Conquista refused the governments of both La Serena and Chiloé because his business kept him at home, and repeatedly during the eighteenth century Chileans refused offers of Peruvian *corregimientos.*[26]

Although it is clear that members of Chilean elite sought government posts, it is equally evident that they did not covet all posts. Indeed, before the reforms honorifics were more prized. Thus hereditary

25. *Título* of Superintendent of the mint to the Conde de la Conquista, Chile, Archivo Nacional, Archivo de la Real Audiencia, vol. 2139, piece 11 (henceforth cited as RA). Letter of Ambrosio O'Higgins to the Ministry of Finance and Commerce of August 16, 1794, Chile, Archivo Nacional, Archivo de la Capitanía General, vol. 786, letter 243 (henceforth cited as CG). The name of the Marqués de Montepío occurs repeatedly as administrator of the *estanco*. See *fianzas* of September 9, 1760 and June 19, 1764 in Chile, Archivo Nacional, Archivo de los Escribanos de Santiago, vol. 574, pp. 88 v.-89 and 145 v-146. (henceforth cited as ES). The previous administrator, José Ignacio Herquiñigo, had been the husband of Rosa de Aguirre of the Marqués' family. See document dated July 3, 1764 in ES, vol. 576, pp. 42-44. See also Amunátegui Solar, *La sociedad chilena,* III, 285-300. For the García Huidobro family see final act of foundation of their entail, September 20, 1782 in ES, vol. 847, pp. 265 v.-266.

26. Royal Order of August 4, 1780, SM, vol. 293, no. 8901. For a biographical sketch of the career of the Conde de la Conquista see Jaime Eyzaguirre, *El conde de la Conquista* (Santiago, 1951).

or renunciable offices with little practical power or emoluments had been avidly sought, along with encomiendas, titles of nobility, and knighthoods in the military orders. The only notable exceptions were cabildo posts, which left one open to disagreeable experiences. The creation of new posts of general political and fiscal administration in Santiago, however, meant that there were high posts available in the city which did not require legal training or relegating the interests of one's family to others. These were immediately sought by the local aristocracy. The creole Manuel de Salas, writing to his friend José Antonio de Rojas in Madrid to secure a title of nobility, gave him this advice:

> Your father has done me the favor of showing me your letters and told me something of your personal aspirations. Because I have the advantage of seeing things from closer up, today I will take the liberty of warning you (and your father says the same) that a title is not the object you should seek . . . but rather one of the honorific and lifetime employments to which one who is not conversant with the law can aspire, as for instance the *Contaduría Mayor*, the Superintendency of the mint, or the Direction of the tobacco monopoly, or another of the subordinate offices. . .[27]

Indeed, this attitude seems to have been widespread. The head of the senior branch of the house of Larraín requested an office of importance in Santiago as a reward for his services and those of his ancestors, and only failing this was he willing to accept a title. It is a fact that after the sale of the last of the four titles sent to the President of Chile in 1755 (all of which were sold at very reasonable terms), there was little demand for any more.[28]

The high valuation which came to be placed on government posts during the late eighteenth century indicates that securing such an office may have been as sure a way for a Chilean to enter the elite as buying a *título de Castilla.* This in turn helps to explain why administrators did not tend to secure titles after 1755. By virtue of their offices alone they belonged to the elite. Although a couple of them did hold *títulos*

27. Letter of Manuel de Salas to José Antonio de Rojas, October 4, 1774, in Chile, Archivo Nacional, Fondo Varios, vol. 118, pp. 60-61 (henceforth cited as FV).

28. Three letters from President Benavides to Agustín de Larraín dated December 18, 1781, November 6, 1782, and May 21, 1784, are most revealing on the kind of hard bargain the creoles wished to drive with the crown for a title of nobility. See CG, vol. 774, letters 99 and 157, and vol. 775, letter 157. The title of Marqués de Larraín was the last one sold in Chile.

de Castilla, such families as Rozas, Salas, Guzmán, Recabarren, Aldunate, and Santiago Concha did not need to crown their posts with a title. The acceptance as sons-in-law by titled and entail-holding Chileans clearly demonstrated their high status.

After the reforms, as before, administrators could establish families that entered the elite. As never before, members of the elite sought administrative positions, and more than before, the two groups intermarried. It would seem, under the circumstances, that informal relations between the two groups should have continued to provide opportunities for the elite to influence the administration.

Client-patron relationship and other patterns characteristic of relations between the two groups persisted through the reign of Charles III. Thus one finds José Antonio de Rojas, bitter as he was against the Spanish administration, paying court to Regent Álvarez de Acevedo, and becoming more bitter in the process. *Oidores* clearly continued to accept favors from residents of Chile. Before the reign of Charles III, *oidor* Juan Verdugo had used an intermediary in buying property, a custom developed to a fine art by *fiscal* José Perfecto de Salas in the early years of the reign. Shortly after the death of the King, Regent Moreno was furnishing his home with "borrowed" pieces from the brother-in-law of the *mayorazgo* Cerda, Ramón del Pedregal.[29]

Such favors clearly opened the way for some special pleading. Thus when Francisco Borja de Araoz found himself in a conflict with President Benavides which was to come before the Audiencia, he asked his brother-in-law, Ignacio de la Carrera, to use his good offices. Carrera sent his sister Damiana to visit all the *oidores*, had the dossier in the case (illicitly) shown him by the *relator*, whom he held in his power, and used the information thus acquired to forearm his protector, Regent Álvarez de Acevedo. Such cases were quite common.[30]

Despite the administrative reforms of the Bourbon period, the complaints against the close relations of Audiencia members with local kin groups did not cease. Thus the *contador mayor* of Chile, Silvestre García, in 1774 called attention to the many ties of *oidores* with the local power structure.

29. Letter of José Antonio de Rojas (fragment, n.d.) in FV, vol. 157, pp. 194-197 v. Contracted sale of a *chacra* by Juan Verdugo, February 6, 1755 in ES, vol. 669, p. 100 v.-103. Wife of Pedregal vs. estate of Regent Moreno, March 10, 1792 in RA, vol. 2430, pieces 11 and 13. For the long and corrupt career of *fiscal* José Perfecto de Salas see Ricardo Donoso, *Un letrado del siglo xviii: D. José Perfecto de Salas* (2 vols.; Buenos Aires, 1967).

30. Letter of Ignacio de la Carrera to Francisco de Borja de Araoz, March 2, 1781, in FV, vol. 237, no. 4571.

> By their marriages here, infinite [numbers] of relatives, the connections and haciendas that they have, and by their maximum opposition to that which is . . . advantageous to royal finances, all is reduced to becoming a [victim] of their passion . . .[31]

This particular Audiencia was purged in its entirety in 1776; nevertheless, the above accusation was repeated twenty years later after the completion of the reforms of José de Gálvez. Despite the changes in personnel and organization, the *oidores* were still accused of protecting their relatives. Among those enjoying this favor were members of eleven related clans, including the dowager Marquesa de Montepío and the entail-holding Caldera family.[32] There is ample reason to doubt that the changes made resulted in an increased independence of *oidores* from local ties.

Indeed, one need do no more than look at the Audiencia's personnel. On the accession of Charles III to the throne of Spain, in addition to its normal membership the Audiencia of Chile included three *oidores supernumerarios*. Because of this overstaffing, no new appointments to the Santiago bench were made for nearly twenty years. During this period, the Audiencia's membership was reduced through death and retirement, but the lack of new blood nevertheless created a high degree of continuity which made the *oidores* all the more formidable. This Audiencia establishment reached a peak of influence in the 1760s. Those who sat on the Santiago bench in this period had strong Chilean ties.

The *oidor decano* was Martín de Recabarren, a native of Cuba. He arrived in Chile in 1716 as *oidor interino*. Recabarren was married to the Peruvian-born Isabel Pardo de Figueroa, niece of the Marqués de Casafuerte, Viceroy of Mexico. His eldest son, José, became the fifth Conde de Villaseñor by inheritance through his mother. Among his daughters, Margarita married the Marqués de Villapalma, and Juana became wife of the son and heir of the Marqués de la Cañada Hermosa.[33]

Juan de Balmaceda was a childless peninsular-born *oidor*. Like bishops, however such men were wont to have nephews, and Balmaceda had two. The first, Pedro Fernández Balmaceda, was a wealthy mer-

31. Secret letter of Silvestre García to Minister of the Indies Julián de Arriaga, January 31, 1774, in SM, vol. 195, pp. 312-313.

32. Anonymous letter of denunciation, December 7, 1793, in SM, vol. 211, pp. 317-320; anonymous letter of denunciation sent to Godoy, January 8, 1794, in SM, vol. 213, pp. 1-3.

33. Espejo, *Nobiliario*, pp. 635 and 683-684.

chant and estate owner who held an entail founded by his uncle. He also founded one of his own. The other, Juan Francisco Ruiz Clavijo de Balmaceda, was safely esconced by his uncle in the administration of the tobacco monopoly. While not tied to native families, Balmaceda, through the entail he founded and the nephews he established in Chile, clearly had many material interests in common with them.[34]

Oidor Gregorio Blanco de Laisequilla was in a similar situation. A *peninsular*, Blanco made up for his lack of children by having a prominent nephew, Joaquín de la Plaza. De la Plaza was a wealthy merchant and married a daughter of the Marqués de Casa Real.[35]

The last *oidor de número*, José Clemente de Traslaviña, was a native of Peru. Unlike the others he seems to have had no son, nephew, or wife who tied him to the ruling elite. He was, however, distantly related to his colleague Melchor de Santiago Concha, and chose to live out his years in Chile after retiring.[36]

Of the *oidores supernumerarios*, Juan Verdugo was a native of Chile. Verdugo married into the Valdivieso family, which settled in Chile from the Río de la Plata during mid-century. His daughter and sole heiress, Francisca de Paula, married the Chilean Ignacio de la Carrera and was the mother of the redoubtable Carrera brothers of the War of Independence.[37]

Domingo Martínez de Aldunate was born in Santiago and had numerous brothers and sisters domiciled there, one of whom was dean of the cathedral chapter. Through his nephews and children, Aldunate was particularly well connected in Chilean society. His nephew, José Antonio Martínez de Aldunate y Garcé, was vicar general of the diocese of Santiago in the lifetime of his uncle, and rose to be Bishop of Huamanga and later of Santiago. Juan Miguel Martínez de Aldunate y Garcé (brother of the above) married an aunt of the Marqués de Larraín. Of his nieces one married a Marqués de Montepío, another the brother of the Conde de la Conquista, and a third the *regidor* Santa Cruz y Silva of the cabildo of Santiago. Of his own children, Josefa married the rich peninsular-born merchant Pedro Fernández Palazuelos, Manuel and Francisco married into the family of the Marqués de la Pica, Isabel into that of the Marqués de la Cañada Hermosa, and Rosa into the mercantile Errázuriz family. Another son,

34. *Ibid.*, pp. 142 and 144-146.
35. *Ibid.*, pp. 171 and 652-653.
36. Roa y Urzúa, *Reyno de Chile*, p. 882. See also Espejo, *Nobiliario*, p. 736.
37. Espejo, *Nobiliario*, pp. 216 and 834. See also Chile Archivo Nacional, Archivo de D. Benjamín Vicuña Mackenna, vol. 3, piece 2.

José Santiago, was to follow his father to a judgeship on the Audiencia of Santiago in 1796.[38]

The last of the *oidores* was Melchor de Santiago Concha, a *limeño* born into a distinguished family of judges. His father, half-brother, and two brothers-in-law all served in the Audiencia of Lima. While an *oidor* in Charcas, Santiago Concha married a daughter of the Marqués de Rocafuerte, president of that audiencia. In 1775 he married his daughter Nicolasa to Nicolás de la Cerda, holder of the Cerda *mayorazgo*. His eldest son, José Maria (a native of Santiago), was to marry one of the children of this union, and became *oidor* of Chile in 1794.[39]

The *fiscal* of Chile during this period was José Perfecto de Salas, a native of Buenos Aires. He had married María Josefa Corbalán, a member of one of the three dominant families of the province of Cuyo (at that time still subject to Chile). He protected and eventually married one daughter to the first holder of the Rojas *mayorazgo*. Through a series of client-patron relationships Salas became a dominant political figure in Santiago.[40]

Of eight members of this Santiago Audiencia of 1759, only two were Spaniards. With the death of Recabarren and Blanco Laisequilla and the retirement of Balmaceda, the balance was further shifted to the benefit of creoles. At the time of the near rising against the tax reforms introduced by the interim *contador mayor* Gregorio González Blanco in 1776, the Audiencia was 100% creole. Every one of the five men had bought his post.[41]

Soon after the nomination of José de Gálvez as Minister of the Indies, this creole-run Audiencia was purged. In part this was the result of the conviction of the *Contaduría General de Indias* that the tribunal was the chief stumbling block to fiscal reform in Chile. In greater part the policy resulted from the negative personal experience of Gálvez with the audiencias of New Spain, and as such was only a small part of the general reform that he envisaged.[42] During the

38. Arturo Fontecilla Larraín, "Los Aldunate de Chile," *Boletín de la Academia Chilena de la Historia*, no. 6 (1935), 303-317.

39. Espejo, *Nobiliario*, pp. 736-738. Santiago Concha was transferred to Chile. In Santiago, after a series of disputes as to his status, it was decided that he would serve as the most junior of the *oidores supernumerarios* although at full pay. See Royal Cédula of June 25, 1768, in CG, vol. 724 IV, pp. 76-76 v.

40. On the career and family of Salas see Donoso, *Un letrado del siglo xviii*. See also Jorge Comandran Ruiz, "Las tres casas reinantes de Cuyo," *Revista Chilena de Historia y Geografía*, no. 126 (1958), 77-127.

41. Silvestre García to Julián de Arriaga, January 31, 1774, in SM, vol. 195, p. 312. See also Donoso, *Un letrado*, I, 46-47.

42. Nestor Meza Villalobos, *La conciencia política chilena durante la monarquía*

month of July 1776, *fiscal* José Perfecto de Salas was notified of his transfer as *oidor* to the *Audiencia de Contratación* in Cádiz, and the *oidores* Traslaviña, Verdugo, and Aldunate were transferred to Lima, the first as *oidor* and the other two as *alcaldes de crimen.* Combined with the later transfer of *oidor* Santiago Concha and the previous retirement of *oidor decano* Balmaceda, these changes removed the entire previous membership of the Santiago Audiencia.[43]

The men who replaced these creole *oidores* were not tainted with local ties, and thus the purge temporarily achieved its ends. Soon these new appointees were transferred, however, and individuals with creole connections began to sit once more on the Santiago bench. As was already seen, there were four separate attempts by the Marqués de Villapalma to infiltrate the Santiago bench through his daughters' marriages. The dowager Marquesa de Montepío had more luck when she married a niece to *oidor* Luis de Urriola.

During the tenure of Gálvez himself, a number of creoles were named to the Audiencia. Urriola was Panamanian, *oidor* Tadeo Diez de Medina was a *charqueño*, as was *fiscal* Joaquín Pérez de Uriondo. By 1788, three out of six appointees were creoles. This creole representation was further strengthened by the nomination of a New Grenadine regent (Moreno y Escandón) to replace the Spanish-born Álvarez de Acevedo. Of course these creoles were all foreign to Chile. By 1794-1796 Chileans were again being appointed to the Santiago bench. Significantly, they came from the Aldunate and Santiago Concha families which had been purged in 1776. Because there was a tendency to promote *peninsulares* out of Chile and leave creoles in place, these soon gained great influence by reason of seniority. The system of promotions itself eventually brought one of the sons-in-law of

(Santiago, 1958), pp. 188-189; Barros Arana, *Historia jeneral*, VI, 377-378, note 37; Donoso, *Un letrado*, I, 424-435.

43. Royal Orders of February 2, 1776, in CG, vol. 727, p. 74; and of March 22, 1776, in CG, vol. 722, pp. 90-91; Donoso, *Un letrado*, I, 435-439; see also instructions of Jáuregui in Royal Order of August 4, 1776 and *Reales Despachos* of Traslaviña, Verdugo, and Aldunate, all dated July 27, 1776, as in CG, vol. 727, p. 150; see also letter of Jáuregui to Gálvez of September 5, 1777 in DG, vol. 779, p. 82. The situation which was being remedied was to a degree accidental. Because of the financial problems of the crown during the reign of Ferdinand VI, a number of creoles were able to buy positions on the Audiencia. The overstaffing which resulted perpetuated the consequences of this momentary situation into 1776. After becoming aware of the deleterious effects of the policy, the crown endeavored to limit the local ties of the *oidores* and the number of native judges. To achieve these ends without blatant discrimination it adopted three separate policies: 1) the transfer of judges who married locally; 2) the regular promotion of judges by the *ascenso* system; 3) the appointment of a number of creoles to courts in Spain. These measures failed to produce the expected results.

the Marqués de Villapalma back to Chile as regent of the Audiencia.

The crown tried to limit the number of native judges in Chile by offering petitioners posts in Spain itself. Thus José Ignacio de Guzmán, whose father had rejected a post on the Audiencia of Santa Fé, had to accept one in the Chancellery of Granada.[44] Nonetheless, the crown allowed some Chileans to serve as judges in their native lands. Between 1796 and 1810 there were always at least two Chilean *oidores* on the court. This does not mean that the frequent appointment of Spaniards to the Audiencia was popular with native Chileans. On the contrary, aristocrats trained to value official connections to bolster their status must have been frustrated at being unable to monopolize offices and office-holders. However, their frustration says more about their aspirations then about their real power.

Indeed, it is important to distinguish between offices and influence. The inability to monopolize offices may have been an important factor in bringing about independence. Influence, however, was based on cooptation of the cadres rather than their displacement. There is no evidence that this process of cooptation was stymied by the Bourbon reforms. Although the degree of control of, if not participation in, the Audiencia decreased after 1776, and the tribunal itself lost power, the elite found ample consolation in penetrating the bureaucracy created by the *visitas.*

In Chile the elite married into families of officials and enticed the latter to reciprocate throughout the Bourbon period. Indeed, the increased size of the bureaucracy allowed elite families to increase their rate of marriage with the administrative cadres. The aristocrats of Santiago continued to enter the royal administration up to the time of independence. In 1810 Chileans serving in top positions in the city included the *oidores* José Santiago Martínez de Aldunate and José de Santiago Concha; the Superintendent of the mint, José Santiago Portales; the Administrator General of the customs house, Manuel Manso; and the Bishop, José Antonio Martínez de Aldunate.[45] This does not mean that a few creoles were not dissatisfied with their personal lack of success. Such men as Manuel de Salas and José Antonio de Rojas, who were to be important in the movement for independence, clearly were. It does mean that we must not overestimate the results of the reform movement. The practices which enabled the elite to coopt the cadres continued. Consequently, special influence by creoles on the administration remained an outstanding feature of political life.

44. Jaime Eyzaguirre, *Ideario y ruta de la emancipación chilena* (Santiago, 1969), p. 56, note 47.

45. *Ibid.*, p. 57.

The elite of Santiago became even more closely knit during the Bourbon period; it demonstrated a high degree of willingness to enter into marriage alliances with outsiders who had achieved high positions; and it expected to wield influence through informal means. Far from being a time of new politics, therefore, the late eighteenth century may well have been a golden age for the practice of the old.

At the same time it is clear that there are close analogies between the political behavior of this colonial elite and that of the group which governed the country in the national period. In their clannishness, in their willingness to absorb the powerful of whatever origins, in their greater regard for position than for wealth, in their search for office and relations with officials, the colonial elite set the style for independent Chile.

APPENDIX 1. MARITAL PATTERNS OF TITLED AND ENTAIL-HOLDING FAMILIES DIVIDED BY PERIODS[a]

	Before 1755	After 1755	Both Periods
To Old Elite	13.5%	5.7%	9.5%
To New Elite	10.4%	15.2%	12.9%
To Other Titled (Chilean Branches)	4.2%	4.8%	4.5%
To Other Titled (Non-Chileans)	5.2%	1.9%	3.5%
To Resident Oidorial Families	1.0%	14.3%	8.0%
To Non-resident Oidorial Families	4.2%	4.8%	4.5%
To Other Officials	9.3%	19.2%	14.4%
To "First Family"	20.8%	4.8%	12.4%
To Others	31.3%	29.5%	30.3%

[a]Because the figures in these appendices are averaged to the nearest tenth of one percent, their sum is not always 100%.

APPENDIX 2. MARITAL PATTERNS OF TITLED AND ENTAIL-HOLDING FAMILIES DIVIDED BY GROUPS AND PERIODS

	Before 1755		After 1755	
	Old Elite	New Elite	Old Elite	New Elite
To Old Elite	17.9%	3.4%	0.0%	9.4%
To New Elite	3.0%	27.6%	12.2%	17.2%
To Other Titled (Chilean Branches)	6.0%	0.0%	2.4%	6.3%
To Other Titled (Non-Chileans)	7.5%	0.0%	2.4%	1.6%
To Resident Oidorial Families	1.5%	0.0%	24.4%	7.8%
To Non-resident Oidorial Families	6.0%	0.0%	9.8%	1.6%
To Other Officials	11.9%	3.4%	14.6%	21.9%
To "First Family"	20.9%	20.7%	4.9%	4.7%
To Others	25.4%	44.8%	29.3%	29.7%

6
Government and Élite in Late Colonial Mexico

D.A. Brading

COLONIAL MEXICO WAS A SOCIETY of Orders or Estates. According to Roland Mousnier, stratification and status in such a society are determined by the privileges, functions and comparative esteem of the various estates rather than by the hierarchy of economic class or relation to the marketplace.[1] New Spain presents a complicated variant of this type of society in that the functional distinctions of Europe were replaced by an ethnic stratification based upon the five Estates of Spaniards, mestizos, mulattoes, Indians and blacks. These categories indicated only the approximate genetic character of an individual and are best regarded as definitions of civic and fiscal status.[2] As descendants of the conquering nation, Spaniards constituted the noble estate within this colonial scale, exercising a virtual monopoly of all appointments in Church and State. By the close of the eighteenth century, however, through natural increase, intermarriage and the silent intrusion of mestizos and mulattoes, this stratum had come to comprise about 18 percent of the Mexican population.[3] Defined by occupation, at least three-quarters

Editor's note: This essay is a revised version of a paper presented by Professor Brading at the December 1972 meetings of the American Historical Association. Some of the themes which it explores are already familiar to readers of his *Miners and Merchants in Bourbon Mexico, 1763-1810.* The editors are pleased to publish the present essay as, like the companion piece by John N. Kennedy, it adds new material to and represents a further step toward a new synthesis of the recent work of various scholars on late colonial elites.

1. See Roland Mousnier, *Les hiérarchies sociales de 1450 a nos jours* (Paris, 1969). Sections of his discussion are reproduced in Mousnier, *Peasant Uprisings in Seventeenth Century France, Russia and China* (New York, 1970), pp. 3-31, 153-178, 233-272.

2. See also Lyle N. McAlister, "Social Structure and Social Change in New Spain," *HAHR*, 53:3 (August 1963), 349-370; Woodrow Borah, "Race and Class in Mexico," *The Pacific Historical Review*, 22 (1954), 331-342; Richard M. Morse, "The Heritage of Latin America," in Louis Hartz, *The Founding of New Societies* (New York, 1964), pp. 135-146.

3. D. A. Brading, *Miners and Merchants in Bourbon Mexico, 1763-1810* (Cambridge, Eng., 1971), pp. 14, 19-24.

of all American-born Spaniards belonged to the upper ranks of the populace rather than to any elite. One consequence of the expansion, not to say dilution of the Spanish group, was that only the *peninsulares,* immigrants from the metropolis, and a reduced number of Creole families possessed the quintessential nobility of their estate.

At the forefront of the Spanish estate stood the *gente decente,* the respectable, the quality. No single criterion such as ownership of land or common legal privilege governed entrance into this heterogeneous colonial elite, which numbered less than 5 percent of the Mexican population. Instead, it comprised most European Spaniards, all clergymen, qualified doctors, lawyers and notaries, the royal bureaucracy, merchants, hacendados and successful silver miners. As such, its membership derived from the operation of the three distinct principles of ethnic nobility, legal privilege and wealth. The metropolitan origin of the *peninsulares,* be they officials or merchants, conferred an assured elite status which led them to dismiss any creole claims to superiority. Then again, the clergy, by reason of the *fuero* which exempted them from all civil jurisdiction, and their education, possessed a social position second to none. Similarly the merchants, organized into a guild with its court and *fuero,* enjoyed an acceptance more reminiscent of Boston than of Madrid. By contrast, the place of the landowners within the elite was ambiguous and difficult to define. Ownership of a great estate brought more prestige than legal status. In general, the Mexican hacendado lacked the privileges, the fiscal exemptions and the command of political office that was associated with gentry status in Europe. There was no *fuero,* no specific quality or title of nobility that went with ownership of an hacienda. In effect, New Spain was dominated by the network of towns rather than by an aristocracy of the countryside, and town councils, the chief institution of local society, were rarely headed by landowners. As far as can be ascertained, hacendados consorted on relatively equal terms with the local clergy, royal officials and prosperous merchants.[4] All such calculations of rank, however, are in part vitiated by the absence in New Spain of that elaborate round of public functions, balls, receptions and hunts which in Europe at this period constituted Society and which served as an open forum wherein individual and family status could be appraised and compared.[5]

4. For a vigorous statement of this position, see Frank Safford, "Social Aspects of Politics in Nineteenth-Century Spanish America: New Granada, 1825-1850," *Journal of Social History,* 5:3 (Spring, 1972), 344-370.

5. H. G. Ward, *Mexico in 1827* (2 vols., London, 1828), II, 715. "I have said nothing about the organization of society in Mexico, because, in fact, there is none."

In this essay, I propose (1) to analyze the composition of the Mexican elite during the eighteenth century and to trace the different patterns of social mobility exhibited by its creole and *peninsular* members; (2) to examine creole participation in the bureaucracy; (3) to discuss the allocation of political benefits to the different sections of the Mexican elite; and (4) to scan the changes wrought by the attainment of independence. A major theme throughout is the economic and political debility of the Mexican hacendado. To illumine the drift of the argument, I find it instructive to begin with an English comparison.

II

Some years ago Lawrence Stone presented a brilliant visual image of Tudor England.[6] He compared English society of the 1540s to the United Nations Building at New York. The overwhelming majority of the population—up to 95 percent—inhabited the podium. Its great lateral extension, with many corridors and several floors, offered a considerable range of horizontal movement, between both districts and occupations, and included a limited chance of upward social ascent. Towering above the masses were several status groups which occupied the skyscraper, defined for the most part by the amount of land they owned. Inside the tower an infrequent elevator connected the levels, carrying, however, more passengers on the downward journey than in the reverse direction. Outside the skyscraper, exposed to the winds, ran four ramps, labelled Law, Office, Church, and Commerce, up which individuals climbed to the height permitted by their talents and fortune, whereupon they entered the skyscraper through the purchase of land. Professor Stone concluded with a contrast to the England of 1700, which he claimed could be best illustrated by San Gimignano, a town standing on a hill with a series of vertical towers rising above the cluster of houses beneath. By then, each economic and status group had its own elevator and hierarchy, running independently of the central tower of landownership.

Bourbon Mexico more closely resembled Tudor than Hanoverian England. At least 95 percent of its population lived at the base of the social scale, denied much opportunity of upward social mobility beyond the prescribed limits open to *la plebe*. Within this range, however, there existed distinct economic strata. A silver miner earning 350 pesos a year or a *ranchero* with land and livestock worth 500 pesos

6. Lawrence Stone, "Social Mobility in England, 1500-1700: Conference Paper," *Past and Present*, 33 (1966), 16-50.

differed markedly from an hacienda peon paid a maize ration and an annual wage of 48 pesos, and still more from a vagrant hired hand gaining 2 reales a day where and when employment could be found. These variations at times bisected the hierarchy of ethnic estates; but they form a subject in themselves and here is not the occasion to explore them.[7]

Lifting our view to the inhabitants of the social skyscraper, we find that in Mexico as in Tudor England fortunes created in commerce, mining and public office were generally invested in the purchase of landed estates. Unfortunately as yet we lack an adequate characterization of the Mexican hacendado of the eighteenth century. By 1810, with 4,945 listed haciendas and estancias, there were probably little more than 4,000 families who belonged to the landlord class. Within this limited number we must distinguish a mere hacendado, holding a single estate worth about 20-50,000 pesos, from a great magnate, owner of a chain of haciendas collectively valued at anywhere between 300,000 and a million pesos. At both levels this class experienced financial difficulties of such proportions as to constitute a downwardly mobile sector in society. The Marquises of San Miguel de Aguayo, with entails covering half of Coahuila, barely supported their inherited debts of nearly half a million pesos. Smaller fry were soon sold up. In his study of the Valley of Oaxaca, William Taylor has found that those haciendas for which he possessed complete records, on average changed hands five times during the eighteenth century. In León my own research yields a somewhat lower value; there, a sample of 25 haciendas averaged four sales over the period 1700-1860. The causes of this turnover in ownership, precipitous by European standards, have yet to be fully defined; tentatively, we may advance three factors: (1) The testamentary system. Entails were uncommon and primogeniture forbidden by law. Since the physical partition of haciendas was normally impractical or forbidden by mortgage contracts, the equal division of a fortune among all heirs frequently required the sale of an estate. (2) Ecclesiastical mortgages and annuities. Over the years many haciendas had been so burdened that all their income went for the payment of interest. In a sample of 27 haciendas, Taylor calculated the sum of clerical charges at 67 percent of their total capital value.[8] (3) The relatively low and uncertain rate of agricultural profit.

7. Manuel Abad y Queipo, "Escritos," José María Luis Mora, *Obras sueltas* (México, 1963), pp. 208-209.

8. For list of haciendas see Fernando Navarro y Noriega, *Memoria sobre la población del reino de Nueva España* (Míxico, 1943), foldpaper. For the Marquisate of San Miguel, Vito Alessio Robles, *Coahuila y Texas en la época colonial* (Míxico, 1938), pp. 503-508. For Oaxaca, William B. Taylor, *Landlord and Peasant in Colonial Oaxaca* (Stanford, 1972), pp. 141-142, 251.

With exports denied by reason of transport costs, the great estates derived their income from sales to the fairly limited urban markets. Enrique Florescano has argued that competition from small producers —*rancheros* and Indian villages—forced the haciendas to rely for profit upon the intermittent years of scarce harvests when they could release their stored grain at high prices.[9] Whatever the cause, and no doubt each region followed a different pattern, the colonial hacienda did not constitute a firm foundation for the establishment of a stable American nobility or gentry.

The chief vehicles of upward economic mobility were commerce and mining. Apart from the windfall of marriage to an heiress, the commonest way of making a fortune was to open a shop. Reliable figures as to the number of merchants, as distinct from mere dealers, cannot be readily obtained. In 1791 the census listed 1,384 *comerciantes* in Mexico City, a term which probably included the *cajeros* or apprentices; only 85 men, however, chose to vote in the *Consulado* elections of 1787. In much the same year, Guanajuato, the leading silver-mining town, housed no more than 162 merchants and 149 *cajeros,* while the entire intendancy supported about a thousand persons described as *comerciantes.*[10] In all, I should be surprised if over 10,000 merchants and *cajeros* were to be found in New Spain at this time. Needless to say, great differences existed in the scale of enterprise. Many traders finished an arduous life worth only a few hundred pesos; the most successful usually built upon family relations and business connections which provided early access to credit and capital. With few exceptions, once accumulated, mercantile capital was invested in the purchase of landed estates.

One remarkable feature of colonial commerce requires emphasis. All available evidence suggests that the wealthiest merchants in both the capital and the chief provincial towns were immigrants from the Peninsula. An inspection of the 1791-92 census shows that in the Bajío about half of all *comerciantes* and *cajeros* were European Spaniards. In all, the immigrant community of these years, excluding members of the religious orders, did not number more than 9,250 persons, of whom a mere 400 were women. About a quarter of this number (and over half the females) resided in Mexico City. The remainder clustered in the major urban centers—314 persons in Guanajuato, 249 in Oaxaca, 190 in Querétaro, 113 in Orizaba, 93 in Jalapa, 51 in Toluca, 40 in

9. Enrique Florescano, *Estructuras y problemas agrarios de México* (1500-1821 (México, 1971), pp. 125-128.

10. For Mexico City, see Alexander von Humboldt, *Ensayo político sobre el reino de la Nueva España* (México, 1966), pp. 579. For *Consulado* elections and Guanajuato, see Brading, *Miners and Merchants,* pp. 117, 254. Also, Archivo General de la Nación (hereafter cited as AGN), Historia 523, ff. 76, 90.

San Miguel el Grande, and 19 in San Juan del Río. A scattered sample of jurisdictions, mainly located in the Bajío but including Toluca, Orizaba and Jalapa, reveals that under a fifth of these men lived in the countryside. At least 55 percent of all immigrants and probably more, entered trade.[11] (See Table I). European settlement in New Spain thus could be graphically represented as a network of urban knots connected by the fine lines of commercial credit and family relation. In the last resort, it was probably more in his person than by reason of his occupation that the gachupín merchant enjoyed social acceptance.

Silver-mining can be compared to a primitive open hoist moving at dizzying speed, onto which men jumped at their peril. Most novices crashed to their ruin; the few survivors, however, often rose to the highest levels of colonial society. The extreme volatility of this profession prevents any easy calculation of number, all the more since the 1792-93 census does not distinguish between the great mine-owners and mere technicians or prospectors. Wages at all levels were high, with skilled pick and blast men forming a labor aristocracy. In all, I doubt whether the industry, in both its refining and mining sectors, employed more than a thousand persons with the pretension or possibility of elite status.

Viewed as an economic system our model offers few surprises. The significance of the export sector lay in its profitability, rather than in the total value of its product. Only through mining and the importation of luxury goods (all European cloth can be reckoned a luxury) could great fortunes be readily assembled.[12] But mining was a peculiarly speculative business and trade a decidedly tedious one, and in each occupation success depended upon personal flair not easily transmitted to children who were educated to consider themselves gentlemen. In the absence of banks, joint stock companies and national debt bonds, the only sure investments were in land, urban property and the Church. In general, therefore, a continuous process was in motion whereby surplus capital accumulated in the export sector was sunk in the purchase of landed estates, there to be slowly dissipated through conspicuous consumption, testamentary partition, clerical bequests and seasonal losses.

Regarded as a social system, the model contains some unusual features. In Western Europe also wealthy urban merchants, them-

11. These are my calculations based upon an examination of AGN, Padrones, vols. 5, 19-24, 26, 30-31, 34-37, 39, 41-42; see also Navarro y Noriega, *Memoria*, p. 64-65.

12. See Jonathan V. Levin, *The Export Economies* (Cambridge, Mass., 1960), pp. 7-12.

TABLE I. Occupations of Peninsular Spaniards in Selected Areas of Mexico 1791-92.

	Merchants	Cajeros	Dealers	Miners	Hacendados	Managers, Farmers	Royal Officials	Military	Artisans	Professions	Unknown & Misc.	Totals	Source: AGN, Padrones, vol. no.
Guanajuato	77	72	22	90	—	3	28	2	8	4	8	314	30–31
Querétaro	61	45	5	—	21	10	12	15	13	8	12	203	39
Oaxaca	103	60	6	2	7	4	28	5	4	9	21	249	13
Orizaba	16	7	29	—	3	18	31	5	7	4	9	128	20
Jalapa	27	17	22	—	2	8	9	2	5	3	16	111	19
Celaya	22	10	1	—	10	5	10	7	1	3	—	69	26
San Miguel	13	17	—	—	3	—	7	—	—	—	—	40	36
San Felipe	4	2	3	—	5	4	—	—	—	—	—	18	34
Dolores	2	4	—	—	—	5	2	—	—	—	—	13	24
Silao	11	4	1	1	1	—	3	—	—	2	—	23	42
Irapuato	5	3	—	1	3	4	5	—	—	—	3	24	37
Pénjamo	5	3	—	—	—	14	4	—	—	—	—	26	41
Acámbaro	10	2	—	—	2	—	2	—	—	—	—	16	23
Toluca	8	12	—	—	8	1	7	15	—	1	5	57	21
San Juan del Río	10	4	—	1	—	8	5	2	1	—	—	31	35
Totals	374	262	89	95	65	84	153	53	39	34	74	1322	

The term "merchant" translates *comerciante*. With *cajeros* are grouped *dependientes*. "Dealer" translates *tratante*; in this group are included *tenderos* and *vinateros*. Miners include refiners. The military mainly consisted of veteran soldiers assigned to train the militia; unfortunately it includes some militia officers without other stated occupation. Under the term artisan are grouped 11 *obrajeros* of Querétaro, presumably men of some wealth. With the professions—doctors, lawyers, notaries etc.—are listed 10 secular priests; members of the religious orders were not included in the census. The large number of Crown employees is accounted for by Guanajuato and Oaxaca being intendancy capitals and Orizaba a center of the tobacco monopoly.

Source: AGN, Ramo de Padrones. All entries include the *partido* or district subordinate to the respective towns, with the one exception of Oaxaca, where the census stopped at the city limits.

selves often the sons of impecunious gentry or prosperous peasants, frequently bought the estates of impoverished noblemen. The rise and fall of such families was a commonplace in the literature of this period.[13] In New Spain, however, this circular movement, so often a journey spread over three generations from the countryside to the town and back again, was interrupted. The *peninsular* immigrants who dominated commerce ascended the social scale, the creole landowners descended it. Silver mining attracted both groups and injected a feverish quality into the scene, with a few miners, creoles among them, becoming millionaires and the majority ending their days without reward. Needless to say, the downward progress of the creole upper class often stretched across more than the proverbial three generations, and no doubt in some cases skilful management averted total ruin. The general trend, however, remains unmistakable.

Equally startling to a European observer is the rapidity with which families moved up and down the social scale. To take the aristocracy as a yardstick, we find that of the 49 new titles of nobility granted in Mexico over the years 1700-1810 no less than 26 went to miners and merchants and 21 to immigrants, excluding officials from the latter calculation. Yet despite initial fortunes often worth over half a million pesos, several newly ennobled families did not weather the passage of time. In 1775 an official inquiry into the tax debts of the aristocracy found that some titles had been renounced because the current descendants were poverty-stricken.[14] The Marquis of San Clemente, a leading miner of Guanajuato, died virtually bankrupt, and his grandson, who wished to marry a maid-servant, relinquished all claim to the title. It is significant that when the Counts of Pérez Gálvez and Casa Rul, two Malagueño immigrants enriched by marriages to mining heiresses, sought to create landed patrimonies, they bought entire chains of haciendas from the descendants of the Marquis of Altamira and from the second Count of Regla, titles respectively conferred in 1704 and 1768.[15]

The downward social mobility of so many elite families obviously exacerbated the tension which characterized the relations of the *peninsulares* and the creoles. By the close of the seventeenth century

13. See Pierre Goubert, *Beauvais et le Beauvaisis de 1600 a 1730* (2 vols., Paris, 1960), I, 206-222, 334-348. A concise contemporary analysis was made by John Millar, *The Origin of the Distinctions of Ranks* (Edinburgh, 1779), reprinted in William C. Lehmann, *John Millar of Glasgow, 1735-1801* (Cambridge, Eng., 1960), pp. 290-291. See also Brading, *Miners and Merchants*, pp. 208-214.

14. "La nobleza colonial en la segunda parte del siglo XVIII," in Archivo General de la Nación, *Boletín*, 13 (1942), 541-590.

15. Brading, *Miners and Merchants*, pp. 105, 120, 208, 264-265, 297-298.

both travellers and viceroys commented upon their mutual antipathy.[16] Apparently the two branches of the Spanish nation resident in Mexico had developed distinct social identities. The stereotypes of their respective characters bear a remarkable similarity to the social psychology of colonial Europeans defined by O. Mannoni in his classic study of twentieth-century Madagascar.[17] The European Spaniard had to prove his elite status by achievement; his arrogance sprang from the conviction of his superiority to the colored masses about him, an attitude which was confirmed by his command of the chief avenues leading to financial success. By contrast, the upper-class American Spaniard was born a gentleman and demonstrated his superior status by conspicuous consumption. The peculiar bitterness of the situation came from the creole knowing that he was trapped on a downwardly moving economic escalator, his descendants doomed to lose their rank in society.

An acute sense of displacement, or best to say, disinheritance, lay deep within the Mexican mind, with its collective roots reaching back to the late sixteenth century when encomendero families found their social position challenged and in many cases overshadowed by new waves of immigrants enriched through mining, trade or public office. As early as 1599, Gonzalo Gómez de Cervantes exclaimed: "those who but yesterday served in shops, taverns and other low jobs now today possess the best and most honorable positions in the country, whereas gentlemen and descendants of the men who conquered and settled it are poor, humiliated, disfavored and cast down."[18] The most poignant of these laments came from Baltasar Dorantes de Carranza: "Oh Indias! Madre de extraños, abrigo de forajidos y delincuentes, patria común a los innaturales, dulce beso a los recién venidos . . . Madrasta de vuestros hijos y destierro de vuestros naturales, azote de los propios . . ."[19] A generation later, the Peruvian chronicler, Antonio de la Calancha, expressed the same sentiment in an equally untranslatable formula: "los nacidos en ella (Peru) son peregrinos en su

16. G. F. Gemelli Carreri, *Viaje a la Nueva España* (2 vols., México, 1955), I, 45; *Instrucciones que los virreyes de Nueva España dejaron a sus sucesores* (2 vols., México, 1873), I, 101-103.

17. O. Mannoni, *Prospero and Caliban. The Psychology of Colonization* (2nd edition, New York, 1964), pp. 97-109, 125-28.

18. Gonzalo Gómez de Cervantes, *La vida económica y social de Nueva España al finalizar el siglo XVI* (México, 1944), p. 94.

19. Baltasar Dorantes de Carranza, *Sumaria relación de la cosas de la Nueva España* (México, 1902), pp. 113-114; see also Jorge Alberto Manrique, "La época crítica de la Nueva España a través de sus historiadores," in *Investigaciones contemporáneas sobre historia de México* (México and Austin, Texas, 1971), pp. 101-124.

patria; los advenedizos son los herederos de sus honras."[20] How often, even until the Revolution of our century, was the Mexican intellectual to echo these declarations! Over the years the initial hostility towards newcomers was to deepen into set patterns of prejudice invoked even by the children of later settlers against all immigrants to New Spain. It is noticeable that the chief exponents of creole patriotism—Calancha, Eguiara y Eguren, Clavijero and Bustamante—were all sons of *peninsulares.*

If creole resentment rarely exploded into overt political action, it was presumably because in each generation the most gifted Mexicans of the upper classes entered the priesthood, and there, in the multiple functions of the ministry, in preaching, lecturing and writing, in the administration of the sacraments and the direction of conscience, and in the management of the financial resources of the Church, found an ample field for the exercise of their talents. In effect, the American clergy acted as the moral and intellectual leaders of colonial society. The *gachupín* merchant, disdainful of creole business ability, accepted their spiritual guidance with the greatest complacency and encouraged his children to enter the Church. By 1810 the clergy comprised 4,229 secular priests and 3,112 friars. Actual parish benefices numbered 1,073 besides another 107 cathedral prebendaries.[21] Viewed as a source of employment, the Church overshadowed all other professions. In 1804 the Audiencia counted a mere 386 registered lawyers in Mexico, of whom only 210 were in practice. Similarly notaries and qualified physicians (as distinct from *escribientes* and *cirujanos*) each numbered about 150 persons for the entire country.[22]

Judged in secular light as a career or livelihood, the Church served as a haven for the impecunious creole without the financial means to support his social pretensions; and for the most talented it offered a path of promotion. Income derived from the ecclesiastical tithe, from parish fees and from the five percent interest paid on the multitude of *capellanías* and other endowments charged on haciendas and urban

20. Antonio de la Calancha, *Corónica moralizada del orden de San Augustín en el Perú* (Barcelona, 1639), p. 72.

21. Fernando Navarro y Noriega, *Memoria sobre la población,* foldpaper; see also his *Catálogo de los curatos y misiones de la Nueva España* (México, 1943), pp. 44, 50; Mariano Torrente, *Historia de la revolución hispano-americana* (3 vols., Madrid, 1829), I, 46-48.

22. For number of lawyers see Archivo General de Indias (hereafter cited as AGI), México 1811, Audiencia to Council of Indies, October 21, 1806. The intendency of Guanajuato, with about a tenth of the Mexican population, had 9 physicians and 11 notaries; in addition there were 51 doctors and 63 notaries in Mexico City. See Humboldt, *Ensayo político,* p. 579, and AGN, Historia, v. 523, ff. 76, 90.

property. A considerable part of Church capital came from landowners and merchants who established *capellanías* as perpetual annuities for those of their descendants who entered the priesthood.[23] In this fashion, many an hacienda yielded an income to families who years before had relinquished formal ownership of the estate. At one level a major cause of the economic debility of the landowning class, at another level the Church employed much of its income to support the children of the same class who chose to become priests or nuns. Full comprehension of this intimate symbiosis, as much as the effect of clerical celibacy upon the composition of the colonial elite, awaits further research. An instructive exercise would be to calculate how much accumulated capital went into the construction of the churches, convents and altars which are still the architectural glory of Mexico.

III

As yet our description lacks a political dimension. What were the relations of the royal bureaucracy and the colonial elite? First let us clarify our terms. S. N. Eisenstadt has defined the polity of the Spanish Empire as a historical bureaucracy, a system of government associated in continental Europe with dynastic absolutism and which succeeded the patrimonial and feudal regimes of the Middle Ages. In his study of the Audiencia of Quito, John L. Phelan has demonstrated the utility of this Weberian category.[24] No longer mere household servants of the Crown, the bureaucracy acted as a semi-autonomous body jealous of its professional prerogatives, and as such can be viewed as an interest group comparable to the territorial aristocracy, the Church or the urban elites. Within most polities of this type Crown officials had the tendency to assimilate to the condition of the aristocracy.

Here we must guard against the habit of applying grand abstractions to small groups of people. Until the Bourbon reforms of the late eighteenth century the Spanish Crown depended upon a mere handful of officials to govern its American empire. In New Spain the entire judicial bureaucracy, *i.e.*, the salaried members of the audiencias of Mexico and Guadalajara, numbered about 20 persons. The fiscal bureaucracy was equally exiguous. The court of audit and the treasuries

23. François Chevalier, *La formación de los grandes latifundios en México* (México, 1956), pp. 204-208.

24. I here follow John Leddy Phelan, *The Kingdom of Quito in the Seventeenth Century* (Madison, 1967), pp. 320-327. See S. N. Eisenstadt, *The Political Systems of Empires* (New York, 1963). For a brilliant analysis of dynastic absolutism see Hans Rosenberg, *Bureaucracy, Aristocracy and Autocracy. The Prussian Experience 1660-1815* (2nd edition, Boston, 1966).

did not employ more that 60 men above the level of mere clerks.[25] Save for the frontier patrols and the port guards, there were no armed forces worthy of mention. The district magistrates, the *alcaldes mayores* and corregidores, did not fulfill any known criterion of bureaucracy. With the accession of the Bourbon dynasty all pretense at paying what was already deemed a derisory salary was abandoned, so that these magistrates, 150 in number, had to subsist upon the meager fruits of justice or else engage in illegal trade.[26] Appointed for periods of three to five years, without professional qualification or tradition, these officials viewed their positions as mere prebends, as an opportunity for personal enrichment.

Interest in colonial government has largely centered about the question of creole exclusion from public office. The traditional notion, still enshrined in most textbooks, stemmed from the debates at the Cortes of Cádiz in 1811 when the American deputies compiled lists to demonstrate the derisory number of native-born viceroys and archbishops. Although even then their evidence was challenged by Juan López de Cancelada, their contentions were eagerly embraced by propagandists for independence. Later publication of colonial documents confirmed the current orthodoxy.[27] As early as 1604 a Mexican viceroy commented: "It is common opinion that of necessity only descendants of the Conquerors should serve as corregidores. . ."[28] At the start of the eighteenth century, Dr. Juan Antonio de Ahumada addressed an outspoken memorial to Philip V, demanding that all Crown appointments in America should be reserved for the natives of that hemisphere, to the heirs, so he argued, of the men who had conquered it. Without the hope of public office, young creoles lacked incentive to study and sank back into idleness and vice, becoming mere "pilgrims in their homeland."[29] In 1771 the ayuntamiento of Mexico City reiterated his arguments with equal vehemence. They frankly dismissed European Spaniards as foreigners in Mexico, and hence sought a creole monopoly in the royal bureaucracy.[30]

25. The court of audit then employed 14 permanent accountants and a varying number of supernumeraries. There were still only 10 treasuries. Brading, *Miners and Merchants*, p. 55; Joaquín Maniau Torquemada, *Compendio de la historia de la real hacienda de Nueva España* (México, 1914), pp. 6-8.

26. Brading, *Miners and Merchants*, p. 48.

27. Juan López de Cancelada, *El Telégrafo Americano* (Cádiz, 1812), pp. 133-142; José Miguel Guridi Alcocer, *El Censor Extraordinario* (Cádiz, 1812), pp. 1-26.

28. *Instrucciones que los virreyes de Nueva España dejaron a sus sucesores*, (México, 1867), pp. 249, 255.

29. Juan Antonio Ahumada, *Representación política-legal a la Magestad del Sr. D. Felipe V en favor de los españoles americanos . . .* (Madrid, 1725).

30. The 1771 memorial is printed in Juan E. Hernández y Dávalos, *Colección de documentos para la historia de la guerra de independencia de México de 1808 a 1821* (6 vols., México, 1877-82), I, 427-455.

Recently, however, the traditional view has been challenged and in part refuted. In a series of four articles, all published in 1972, Leon Campbell, Mark Burkholder, Jacques Barbier, and D. S. Chandler demonstrated that during the eighteenth century, creole membership in the American audiencias was common and at times predominant. My own inspection of the Mexican court pointed in the same direction.[31] It has been conclusively proved that during the 1760s the majority of *oidores* in the audiencias of Lima, Santiago de Chile and Mexico were creoles. This preponderance was of relatively recent origin. It derived from the extraordinary decision of the first Bourbons to sell audiencia judgeships to qualified bidders. Between 1701-50 a quarter of all new appointments were sold, with a heavy concentration of such transactions occurring in the 1740s. During this period Americans received two-fifths of all places, the majority—less than two-thirds—obtaining their office through purchase. In Lima and Santiago de Chile, most creole *oidores* were intimately linked by descent, marriage or financial interest to the landowning elite of these capitals. Here, as with cabildo membership, sale of office ironically opened the way to a form of representative government. By 1770 most American audiencias represented the rich and powerful families of their respective provinces.

The Audiencia of Mexico displayed the same characteristics as its counterparts in Lima and Chile. In 1767, of the eleven men with ascertained backgrounds (there were twelve places) eight were creoles and three *peninsulares,* although at least three of these creoles had European fathers, with the parent of another coming from the Canary Islands. Although only half of the American *oidores* were born in the provinces subject to the Mexican court, another two came from Jalisco, and a third, a native of Guatemala, was educated in Mexico City. No less than five *oidores,* including two *peninsulares,* were directly connected through marriage or by descent to the titled nobility. Equally important, at least five judges were the children of government officials, two being the sons of *oidores.* Evidence as to their individual wealth is not available; education and talent, however, constituted an important role in their advancement. At least four were educated at the famous Jesuit College of San Ildefonso in Mexico City.[32] Two creoles,

31. Leon G. Campbell, "A Colonial Establishment: Creole Domination of the Audiencia of Lima during the Late Eighteenth Century," *HAHR,* 52:1 (February 1972), 1-25; Mark A. Burkholder, "From Creole to *Peninsular*: The Transformation of the Audiencia of Lima," and Jacques A. Barbier, "Elites and Cadres in Bourbon Chile," both in *HAHR,* 52:3 (August 1972), 395-415, 416-435; M. A. Burkholder and D. S. Chandler, "Creole Appointments and the Sale of Audiencia Positions in the Spanish Empire under the Early Bourbons 1701-1750," *Journal of Latin American Studies,* 4 (1972), 187-206.

32. Brading, *Miners and Merchants,* pp. 40-44.

Francisco Javier de Gamboa and Joaquín de Rivadeneyra had spent considerable time in Spain, where both made their reputation upon the publication of substantial books. The Mexican *oidores* thus formed a tightly knit elite group, with similar social backgrounds and education; one or two were distantly related by marriage.

With the paucity of prosopographical studies, it is still premature to generalize from the one instance of the audiencias. The success of American Spaniards in buying their way onto the bench implies a lack of competition from wealthy lawyers in Madrid. By contrast, the high profits expected from the *alcaldías mayores,* in particular those which produced cochineal, probably awakened *peninsular* avarice. In this case, sale of office may well have worked against creole participation. In point of fact, we know remarkably little about the social background of these magistrates. Similarly, the sources of recruitment into the fiscal bureaucracy are equally obscure. Only future research will settle such questions.

No discussion of colonial government can afford to ignore the role of the Church. Dependent upon the Crown for beneficed appointment and promotion, the clergy formed a parallel administrative bureaucracy which, judged as a system of social control, operated far more effectively than the secular magistracy. The Church dominated the intellectual and spiritual life of the country and in addition provided that range of welfare services—schools, colleges, hospitals, asylums and orphanages—which is now supported by the State. It collected its own tax—the tithe—and ran its own courts. Ecclesiastical judges did not confine their attention to cases of clerical discipline or spiritual transgression; in instances of default in payment of either tithes or interest upon Church mortgages they could also order the embargo and auction of private property.[33] More generally, it was to the 1,073 parish priests rather than to the 150 *alcaldes mayores* that the populace looked for guidance and leadership. In the same fashion, it was to the clergy that both Crown and the upper classes appealed when the masses went out on riot.[34] The mission role of the Jesuits and Franciscans in frontier pacification requires no comment. Despite their importance, we know virtually nothing about the social composition of the Mexican clergy save that at some ill-defined moment in the seventeenth century secular benefices below the rank of bishop became a creole monopoly. For what it is worth, we may note that during the

33. N. M. Farriss, *Crown and Clergy in Colonial Mexico 1759-1821* (London, 1968), pp. 94-96, 152-154, 165-168.

34. In Tehuantepec the mere appearance of the Bishop of Oaxaca in episcopal attire apparently quieted an Indian rebellion. See Brian R. Hamnett, *Politics and Trade in Southern Mexico 1750-1821* (Cambridge, Eng., 1971), p. 13.

1790s at least four sons of audiencia judges were members of the cathedral chapter of Mexico.[35]

To convert the American Empire into a more profitable possession, Charles III and his ministers relied upon the classic instruments of absolutist monarchy: the soldier and the tax collector. A small regular army of about 10,000 men was organized for permanent duty in New Spain, the rank and file mainly recruited from the districts in which they were stationed. The fiscal bureaucracy experienced an unprecedented expansion with the augmentation of old institutions such as the treasuries and the court of audit, and the creation of new departments such as the tobacco monopoly, the excise service and the intendancies. The 1791-92 census listed 311 persons in Mexico City as *empleados de real hacienda* and another 105 in the Guanajuato intendancy, figures superior to the combined total of lawyers, physicians and notaries in each district.[36] I estimate that as a consequence of the Bourbon reforms the number of well-paid permanent places in the colonial bureaucracy quadrupled. The emphasis remained upon revenue collection. Apart from the installation of 12 intendants as provincial governors, local government was neglected, being farmed out to subdelegates, the new version of the *alcaldes mayores,* who were expected to subsist upon a five percent commission of tribute collected from their Indian and mulatto subjects.

The recent research mentioned above has confirmed that Charles III and José de Gálvez as Minister of the Indies actively sought to reduce creole participation in both Church and State. High officials in the tobacco monopoly and the excise service were brought directly from the Peninsula. Through a variety of devices the creole share of audiencia places was cut to about a third or quarter of the total membership. Similarly, about a third of the prebendaries of the archiepiscopal chapter were eventually occupied by Europeans.[37] Once again, caution is advisable when interpreting incomplete evidence. The increase in government activity undoubtedly gave employment to many creoles who at an earlier period would have petitioned in vain for some kind of office. Then again, creole exclusion mainly operated at the highest level. Nearly all the parochial clergy continued to be locally

35. These were Andrés Luis Fernández de Madrid, Juan José Gamboa y Urrutia, Ciro Ponciano Villaurrutia, and Joaquín José Ladrón de Guevara; in addition José Cayetano Foncerrada was brother to an *oidor* appointed a little later. *Títulos de Indias. Catálogo XX del Archivo General de Simancas* (Valladolid, 1954), pp. 168-176.

36. Humboldt, *Ensayo político,* p. 579; AGN, Historia 523, ff. 76, 90.

37. See note 31; also Juan López de Cancelada, *El Telégrafo Americano,* pp. 139-141.

recruited. A case in point was the colonial army. An inspection of the officer record sheets for 1798-1800 reveals that the six regiments and one battalion of the central force (we exclude from our calculations the scattered companies of the north) were led by 268 officers with ranks of ensign to captain. Of these men 112 were peninsulares, 28 Americans from other colonies, and the remaining 128 natives of Mexico. As might be expected, however, all save one of the colonels were Europeans.[38] (See Table II.) It was against this discrimination that the Mexico City Ayuntamiento complained in 1771, and again in 1776. In effect, when the American deputies at the Cortes of Cádiz protested against creole exclusion from public office, they denounced the policy of the past generation rather than the practice of the entire colonial period.

TABLE II. Creole and Peninsular Officers in New Spain's Army 1798-1800.

	Regular Regiments				Militia Regiments		
Rank	Peninsular	Mexican Creole	Creoles from Other Colonies	Totals	Peninsular	Mexican Creole	Totals
Colonel	4	—	—	4	6	9	15
Lt. Colonel	8	1	—	9	13	5	18
Captain	40	31	3	74	76	78	154
Lieutenant	28	55	4	87	76	90	166
Sub-Lieut. & Ensign	44	42	21	107	57	119	176
Cadet	9	39	29	77	6	16	22
Reg. Adjutant	1	2	—	3	26	7	33
Reg. Lieut.	—	—	—	—	27	13	40
Totals	134	170	57	361	287	338	624

The regular force comprises: four infantry regiments, Corona, Nueva España, México and Puebla; the infantry battalion of Veracruz; and two dragoon regiments of Puebla and México. The militia force comprises: seven infantry regiments of México, Puebla, Tlaxcala, Tres Villas (Córdoba, Orizaba and Jalapa), Toluca, Valladolid, and Celaya; three infantry battalions of Oaxaca, Guanajuato and Guadalajara; eight dragoon regiments of Querétaro, Príncipe, Pátzcuaro, Puebla, Nueva Galicia, Reina, San Carlos and San Luis; and the lancer squadrons of Veracruz. For rank and file enlistment see Humboldt, *Ensayo político*, pp. 554-57.

Source: Hojas de servicio in Archivo General de Simancas, Guerra moderna, legajos 7274-77.

In the case of the upper bureaucracy, tantalizing hints of a more subtle kind of change can be found. Many of the chief ministers of

38. My own calculations based on the *hojas de servicio* found in Archivo General de Simancas, Guerra moderna, legajos 7274-77.

Charles III–Campomanes, Floridablanca, Roda and Gálvez–were *manteistas*; that is to say, at university by reason of their inferior social rank they were denied entrance into the prestigious *colegios mayores* administered by the Jesuits, whose pupils traditionally secured the lion's share of government appointments.[39] Now for seventeenth-century Spain, Richard Kagan has demonstrated the existence of a *letrado* nobility, a hereditary bureaucratic elite, recruited from families of noble status, which despite possession of landed entails, drew their chief sustenance, generation by generation, from their virtual monopoly of high public office.[40] Were the senior officials in New Spain recruited from a colonial extension of this *noblesse de robe?* Here it is relevant to recall that no less than five of the Mexican *oidores* in 1767 were sons of royal officials. The current dean of the audiencia, Domingo, Valcárcel, a peninsular who served in New Spain from 1721 until his death in 1783, clearly sprang from this class. His brother, his father and both his grandfathers were members of the Council of Castile.[41] Then again, the fact that most colonial judges and leading churchmen had been trained by the Jesuits no doubt increased their dislike of the new regime. These class antagonisms and family connections often stretched across the Atlantic into the ministries at Madrid and bisected the usual distinctions of creole and peninsular.

Equally important, Charles III and his ministers relied upon a different kind of trained intelligence to administer the projected expansion in government activity. The Hapsburgs had recruited the bureaucracy from the law faculties of the leading universities. In important matters of state they took counsel with theologians and used the arguments of scholastic philosophers. In the first decades of the eighteenth century the Mexican audiencia still formed the only pool of reliable public servants available to administer the complex operations of the mint and the mercury monopoly. But after the Gálvez visitation, a new breed of official appeared on the scene, by origin army officers and accountants, men without a university or legal education, yet with a formation and discipline more than adequate for the efficient conduct of state business.[42] The key institution here is presumably the army and the training received by its officers. The military background of the last viceroys and most intendants demonstrates the sig-

39. Richard Herr, *The Eighteenth Century Revolution in Spain* (Princeton, 1958), pp. 25-26; Jean Sarraílh, *La España ilustrada* (México, 1957), pp. 209-211.

40. Richard L. Kagan, "Universities in Castile 1500-1700," *Past and Present*, 49 (1970), 44-71.

41. For Valcárcel, see AGI, Mexico 1371, Bucareli to Arriaga, November 26, 1773.

42. Brading, *Miners and Merchants*, p. 44

nificance of this transition. Needless to say, since Gálvez doubted creole capacity as much as he suspected their loyalty, he recruited the majority of this new type of bureaucrat, especially the revenue officials, from the Peninsula.

IV

In addition to decisions about the occupancy of public office, a political system also deals with the allocation of scarce economic resources. The historical bureaucratic polities all had to come to terms with the powerful vested interests of the traditional elite groups. In Eastern Europe, for example, the absolute monarchies of this period based their new-found authority upon a close alliance with the territorial aristocracy and gentry. Landowners enrolled in the army and the civil service and in many instances acted as provincial governors. In exchange for their support, the monarchy confirmed and extended their feudal jurisdiction over the peasantry.[43] So too, Lawrence Stone has emphasized how many noble families in England owed their rise in fortune to attendance at the Tudor and Stuart court which served as a veritable fount of favor, privilege and office.[44] Given the lavish expenditure expected from the aristocracy, it can be argued that in pre-modern economies the maintenance of great landed fortunes required the exercise of political power or material assistance from the State.

In sixteenth-century Mexico the Spanish grandees who became viceroys maintained an open court and acted as the leaders of encomendero society. Within their hand lay the reversion of vacant encomiendas, the right to grant title for vast tracts of land, and the duty of appointing most *alcaldes mayores*. It is noticeable that at this time many royal officials became wealthy men. In the last resort, however, the viceregal court was but a pale simulacrum of its Madrid original. Once the period of initial settlement was past, it no longer acted as a dynamic center of autonomous political action. Save at its periphery the empire faced remarkably few external or internal challenges; piracy never threatened mainland possession. In consequence the Crown relied upon the audiencias and the Church to maintain law and order; there was no attempt to mobilize the landowning class for military or administrative service; the function of the colonies within the

43. Rosenberg, *Bureaucracy, Aristocracy and Autocracy*, pp. 29-45. Henry Kamen, *The Iron Century. Social Change in Europe 1550-1660* (London, 1971), pp. 178-180, 214-228, 430-433.

44. Lawrence Stone, *The Crisis of the Aristocracy, 1558-1641* (Oxford, 1965), pp. 398-445.

imperial system was to provide revenue and to serve as a market for Spanish goods.

The predicament of the creole elite now becomes apparent. The persistent clamor for public office—expressed with an emotional intensity quite at variance with the limited range of places available—sprang not so much from a craving for bureaucratic employment as from a desire for political power and its perquisites. The creole sense of grievance stemmed from the historic failure of the first conquerors and encomenderos to establish a seigneurial society in New Spain. The Spanish Crown's refusal to grant perpetual encomiendas and its insistence upon cash remuneration for repartimiento workers denied the Mexican landowner a supply of free or even cheap labor. The precipitous fall in silver production in the years after 1630, when coupled with the long demographic decline of the central region, produced a widespread economic crisis, which far from creating a feudal society simply bankrupted many landowners, forcing them either to abandon or to sell their estates.[45] The comparison with Russia is instructive. There too the nobility and gentry faced financial ruin at the beginning of the seventeenth century. But the Tsars intervened to rescue them by reducing the peasantry to the condition of serfs with the obligation to work for their masters without recompense. In later years it established a state bank to grant loans to the nobility at low rates of interest.[46] For similar assistance the creole landowner pined in vain.

But what of debt peonage, that much advertised Mexican equivalent of serfdom? For the hacendado in need of cheap labor it was a remarkably poor substitute. More of an inducement than a bond, it required the outlay of a considerable sum in cash or in goods to a group of laborers who might well abscond without repayment of the loan. In any case, these peons still had to be fed a weekly maize ration and to be paid a monthly wage at the going rate.[47] It was for this reason that many landlords preferred to rent much of their land and to hire workers at harvest time upon a daily basis. Apart from the frontier exigencies of the far north, Mexican landowners rarely exercised political or judicial authority over their workers. Most Indians, for example, continued to reside in villages governed by their own elected

45. For a possibly contrary view, see François Chevalier, *La formación de los grandes latifundios en México*, pp. 226-233; but see also P. J. Bakewell, *Silver Mining and Society in Colonial Mexico* 1: *Zacatecas, 1546-1700* (Cambridge, Eng., 1971), pp. 115-121.

46. Jerome Blum, *Lord and Peasant in Russia from the Ninth to the Nineteenth Century* (Princeton, 1961), pp. 259-276, 376-385.

47. Charles Gibson, *The Aztecs under Spanish Rule* (Stanford, 1964), pp. 233-236, 249-256.

leaders and magistrates. In consequence, unlike the feudal manor or the serf-estate of Eastern Europe, the Mexican hacienda had to survive upon its economic merits as a unit of production, unassisted either by seigneurial rights or the free labor of resident serfs. By 1700 it was not uncommon to find landlords in debt to their workers.[48] Small wonder that the turnover in ownership was so rapid; it was the price paid for political impotence.

The class which benefited most from the policies of the Spanish monarchy was the colonial merchants. Already by the 1670s their advance in social prestige was the subject of viceregal comment. The ensuing century (until 1778) formed their heyday. The *consulado,* the merchant guild, now farmed the collection of the *alcabalas* for a contracted sum. At much the same time the great silver merchants took over the management of the mint, and from this vantage point dominated the credit structure of the silver-mining industry.[49] Then again, in 1678, the power to appoint *alcaldes mayores* was taken from the viceroy so that these offices could be auctioned to the highest bidder in Madrid. As late as 1754 the Cádiz firm of Pardo and Freire bought the rights to no less than three magistracies: Querétaro, Guanajuato and Tehuacán.[50] With the Bourbon refusal to pay salaries to *alcaldes mayores,* these officials were driven to become traders, issuing goods and cash on credit to their unfortunate subjects, who stood menaced with imprisonment and flogging for any failure to meet their obligations. To finance these *repartimientos de comercio,* most magistrates relied upon merchant backers, resident in Mexico or the provincial towns. It was in this enforced distribution of merchandise rather than in debt peonage that the political authority of the Crown was most obviously utilized, not to say prostituted, for the financial profit of a particular economic class. It was precisely the same practice which most provoked popular unrest, leading in some cases to open rebellion.[51] Thus the immigrant *almaceneros,* the very embodiment of commercial capitalism, emerged as the dominant figures within the colonial

48. D. A. Brading, "The Structure of Agricultural Production in the Mexican Bajío during the Eighteenth Century," paper presented at the International Congress of Americanists (Rome, 1972).

49. Robert Smith, "Sales Taxes in New Spain, 1575-1770," *HAHR,* 28:1 (February 1948), 2-37; Brading, *Miners and Merchants,* pp. 170-172; P. J. Bakewell, *Zacatecas,* pp. 212-215.

50. *Handbook of Middle American Indians. Volume 12, Guide to Ethnohistorical Sources: Part One,* ed. by Howard Cline (Austin, 1972), p. 78; Guillermo Lohmann Villena, *El corregidor de indios en el Perú bajo los Austrias* (Madrid, 1957), pp. 126-131; AGI, Mexico, 689, March 30, 1754.

51. Hamnett, *Politics and Trade in Southern Mexico, 1750-1821,* pp. 11-23.

economy, enjoying a social status equal to that of the upper bureaucracy and the territorial magnates.

An essential part of the Bourbon revolution in government launched under Charles III was the destruction of the commercial monopoly exercised by great import houses of the capital. The promulgation of *comercio libre* in 1778 opened the way for a free flow of trade between the chief ports of the Peninsula and the American possessions. In Mexico new *consulados* were set up in Guadalajara and Veracruz. At the same time the regime attempted to free the productive sectors from the former reliance upon merchant credit. *Repartimientos de comercio* were prohibited and a finance bank was established to aid the mining industry. In all this, there was little to assist the landowning class. Instead, the favored child of the government was the silver miner, whose endeavors were now encouraged by a positive battery of inducements, both financial and institutional. A private jurisdiction, a central court, a technical college, a new code of law, numerous individual tax rebates, titles of nobility—all this fell into the lap of the fortunate miner. By contrast, apart from the removal of a few export duties, nothing was directly undertaken to assist agriculture or the landowning class. Indeed the inflexible enforcement of ecclesiastical amortization after 1804 led to the embargo and auction of many haciendas. The later Bourbons strove to release the productive capacity of the colony from the restrictions imposed during the Hapsburg era. But it was still the export sector, silver mining and not agriculture, which benefited the most from the new order.

One great exception can be advanced to this proposition. Through the recruitment of militia forces the Crown sought to mobilize the political loyalty of the wealthy classes. A commission in the militia conferred an extensive *fuero*; it brought both social distinction and some quasi-political influence. A full colonelcy—which could be purchased for about 40,000 pesos together with an unspecified gratuity for the Viceroy—carried the address of *vuestra señoría*, the same as that enjoyed by an *oidor*.[52] In return, some great landowners, especially in the North, obtained command and military jurisdiction over a force often in part recruited from their own estates. Here as elsewhere sale of office opened the door to extensive creole promotion. The sixteen regiments and three battalions of the militia were led by 496 officers

52. For the colonial army see María del Carmen Velázquez, *El estado de guerra en Nueva España, 1760-1800* (México, 1958); Lyle N. McAlister, *The "Fuero Militar" in New Spain, 1764-1800* (Gainesville, Fla., 1957); Brading, *Miners and Merchants*, pp. 324-327.

TABLE III. Colonels and Lieutenant-Colonels in New Spain's Militia 1798-1800.

Regiments	Colonels	Lieutenant-Colonels
Cavalry		
Querétaro	Pedro Ruiz Dávalos (Brigadier)[a]	— —
Príncipe	Count of Pérez Gálvez	Francisco de Septién y Arce
Puebla	Marquis of Moncada	*Ignacio Maneiro*[a]
Reina	*Narciso de la Canal*	*Juan de Lanzagorta*
Pátzcuaro	*Francisco Menocal*	*José Bernardo Foncerrada*
San Luis	*Count of Peñasco*	Ángel Prieto de la Maza
San Carlos	*Manuel Rincón Gallardo*	Francisco Miguel de Aguirre
Nueva Galicia	*Ignacio Obregón*	Juan Francisco Calera
Infantry		
México	*Joaquín Benito de Medina*	*Miguel de Otero*
Puebla	Joaquín Gutiérrez de los Ríos (?)	*Mariano Diez de Bonilla*
Valladolid	Diego Rul	Juan José Martínez de Lejarza
Tres Villas	*José Manuel de Zeballos*	Marcos González Joaquín de Castillo y Bustamante
Tlaxcala	Lorenzo Angulo Guardamino	— —
Toluca	*Marquis of Rivascacho*	Manuel García Alonso
Celaya	Juan Fernández Munilla	Manuel Fernández Solano
Battalions		
Guanajuato	— —	Manuel García de Quintana
Oaxaca	— —	Juan Francisco Echarri
Guadalajara	— —	Francisco de Escobedo y Devía
Veracruz	— —	Manuel Rengel

[a] Names in italics are creoles, the remainder are *peninsulares*.

The Marquis of Moncada was a Sicilian; Francisco Menocal a native of Havana; Diego Rul and Manuel Rincón Gallardo later became the Count of Casa Rul and the Marquis of Guadalupe. Joaquín Gutiérrez de los Ríos is described as a native of Córdoba; probably he came from the Spanish city rather than from the Mexican town of that name, as the surname "Gutiérrez de los Ríos" had been associated with Spanish Córdoba for centuries.

Source: Hojas de servicio in Archivo General de Simancas, Guerra moderna, legajos 7274-76.

of the ranks ensign to captain, of whom 209 were *peninsulares* and 287 creoles, a ratio of about forty to sixty. (See Table II.) More important, no less than 13 creoles (compared to 20 *peninsulares*) held the rank of colonel or lieutenant colonel.[53] (See Table III.) As yet we lack material for any analysis of the social background of these officers. Among the 15 full colonels were four noblemen and another two who later received titles. Two men had made their fortunes in trade, and another three were mining millionaires. Both colonels of the San Luis Potosí

53. My own calculations based upon the record sheets for 1798-1800 found in Archivo General de Simancas, Guerra moderna, leg. 7274-77.

brigade, the Count of Peñasco and Manuel Rincón Gallardo (later Marquis of Guadalupe) were creole landowners with vast estates in that zone. At the same time, the great number of *peninsulares* at all levels of the militia reinforces our notion of their standing in colonial society.

V

The manner in which each country in Spanish America attained independence affected its history for a generation to come. In South America patriot armies disbanded after defeating the royalist forces in open battle, and their place was taken by district militia subject to local landowners. Officers who chose a professional military career rarely gained access to high public office. Instead, both Argentina and Venezuela were governed by caudillos, the political agents of the landowning class. The gaucho regiments that swept Rosas to power in Buenos Aires were recruited from the workers resident on his family estates.[54]

In Mexico the lower clergy called out the masses behind the banner of Our Lady of Guadalupe in a movement which at times resembled a peasant jacquerie. But it was the *peninsulares*, the ethnic nobility within New Spain's spectrum of Estates, and not the rich who were the chief target of popular hatred. Nevertheless, their material interests threatened, the great hacendados rallied to the Crown to suppress this priest-led rebellion. In the absence of European troops (the first expeditionary forces arrived in 1812) the viceroy had to depend upon young upper-class creoles to officer the rapidly expanded colonial army, men who over the years came to adopt the ethos and career of the professional soldier. It was these royalist officers who first supported Iturbide's declaration of independence, and then, with the tumultuous decade of the 1820s once past, effectively ruled Mexico until the Reform. Presidents Bustamante, Barragán, Herrera, Paredes, and López de Santa Anna all passed their early manhood in combat against the insurgency. Their equivalents in South America were not caudillos like Rosas or Páez, but rather the military presidents of Peru and Bolivia—Gamarra, Santa Cruz, Ballivián, and Castilla—all one-time officers in the royalist forces of Goyeneche.[55] After independence, with expendi-

54. Horacio C.E. Giberti, *Historia económica de la ganadería argentina* (Buenos Aires, 1954), pp. 118-127; Jorge M. Mayer, *Alberdi y su tiempo* (Buenos Aires, 1963), pp. 71-76; Robert L. Gilmore, *Caudillism and Militarism in Venezuela, 1810-1910* (Athens, Ohio, 1964), pp. 122-146.

55. Alberto María Carreño, *Jefes del ejército mexicano en 1847* (México, 1914); Thomas Ewing Cotner, *The Military and Political Career of José Joaquín de Herrera, 1792-1854* (Austin, 1949). For Peru see Manuel de Mendiburu, *Biografías de generales republicanos*, ed. by Félix Denegri Luna (Lima, 1963).

tures which frequently absorbed up to four-fifths of the national budget, the Mexican army constituted a virtually autonomous power structure, unrepresentative of any one economic class, which not merely paralleled but in many instances dominated the civil authority of the state.

Military predominance only partially accounts for the evident debility of the political system. As much as Argentina, Mexico experienced the struggle between the towns and the wilderness so eloquently described by Sarmiento. Old insurgents like Juan Álvarez in Guerrero still haunted the back-country and the mountainous periphery. At the same time, however, the network of provincial capitals housed ambitious politicians, backed by considerable state revenue and urban militia, anxious to preserve their local autonomy. Neither group of leaders possessed the resources or power to break the hegemony of the regular army. Then again, the Church, with prestige undermined by its activity during the civil wars, asserted its independence from the State despite the constitutional endorsement of Catholicism as the established religion. In effect, the Bourbon Republic or Regency, as some choose to name this period, lacked that intangible but quite necessary quality of legitimacy.[56] The old habits of civil obedience and social deference had been lost; new bonds of loyalty and interest were slow to emerge. The result was bitter stasis, a political system of institutionalized disorder with an empty throne at its center. The monarchy had been destroyed but the republic had yet to find its soul, or best to say, its constitutive principle.

With political malaise went chronic economic depression and social dissolution. The old stratification according to ethnic Estates was slowly transformed into a hierarchy of economic class. At the level of the elite, however, Mexico remained a society of Orders. The clergy and the army preserved their *fueros*, their exemption from the common jurisdiction of the Republic. When Dr. Mora interpreted the course of politics as a conflict of the Church and army against the States, he wished to emphasize the persistence of the ancien régime.[57] At the same time, the influence of the productive classes, of landowners, miners, merchants and industrialists, was counterbalanced by the rise of lawyers and intellectuals, scions of the professional class, who sought political office both to advance their principles and to assure them-

56. The best political analysis of this period is still Francisco Bulnes, *Juárez y las revoluciones de Ayutla y de Reforma* (2nd edition, México, 1967). The term Bourbon Republic I take from John Womack, "Mexican Political Historiography 1959-1969" in *Investigaciones contemporáneas sobre historia de México*, pp. 484-485.

57. José María Luis Mora, *Obras sueltas*, pp. 55-82.

selves a livelihood, if not a fortune. Save perhaps during the last decades of the *Porfiriato,* Mexico was never to be governed by the simple alliance of the economic classes. Upon the urban intellectual proletariat—to use a favorite term of Francisco Bulnes—fell the mantle of the historical bureaucracy; whether they ever cared to convert it into a cover for what Max Weber called legal domination is a matter for debate.[58]

The disruptive effect of the economic depression cannot be overestimated; it brought widespread unemployment for the masses and thrust many of the upper class into debt. Agriculture emerged from the insurgency with many of the great estates in ruin, their livestock slaughtered and their barns and dams destroyed. Land values, already depressed by the amortization decree of 1804, declined still further, with the consequence that the burden of ecclesiastical mortgages relative to capital assessment became all the more oppressive. In the Bajío and adjacent areas a perceptible trend towards the subdivision of haciendas has been noted.[59] Given their bankrupt condition, it can come as no surprise to learn that as a class landowners exercised relatively little political influence. A sympathetic commentator, Carlos María de Bustamante, lamented their absence from Congress and deplored their public incapacity.[60] The great conservative of the epoch, Lucas Alamán, sought in vain their effective, united support. Instead his reactionary coalition was built upon an alliance of the Church, the army and the industrial interest.[61]

The traditional vehicles of social advancement—silver-mining and commerce—also experienced a profound change. Many of the great enterprises which had dominated the mining industry were wrecked by the insurgency. Gross national production fell to less than half the 1805 peak, a level not to be permanently surpassed until the 1870s. Extensive investment of British capital restored many mines to working order, although a substantial recovery in output did not begin

58. Bulnes described the political problem of post-independence Mexico as: "Clase propietaria hipotecada, Iglesia rica, Estado pobre. Abundantes clases medias, profesionales, famélicas, ecclesiásticas y militares." Francisco Bulnes, *El porvenir de las naciones hispano-americanas* (México, 1899), p. 253.

59. José María de Jáuregui, *Discurso en que se manifiesta que deben bajarse los réditos a proporción del quebranto que hayan sufrido en la insurrección los bienes y giros de los deudores* (México, 1820); Jan Bazant, *Los bienes de la iglesia en México, 1856-1875* (México, 1971), pp. 340-348; Luis González, *Pueblo en vilo* (México, 1968), pp. 85-86, 94-97; D. A. Brading, "The Structure of Agricultural Production in the Mexican Bajío" (see note 48).

60. Carlos María de Bustamante, *Continuación del cuadro histórico de la revolución mexicana* (4 vols., México, 1953-63), II, 160-162; Mariano Otero, *Obras* (2 vols., México, 1967), I, 28-32, 40-41.

61. Lucas Alamán, *Documentos diversos* (5 vols., México, 1947), III, 264-265.

before the late 1840s. It seems safe to assume that few Mexican fortunes were created in silver-mining before that decade.[62] At the same time the expulsion of the last remaining Spanish merchants in 1827 and 1829 permitted a fresh wave of immigrants to seize control of the import trade. But these British, French and German merchants differed from their gachupín predecessors in that they rarely established families which entered the social elite of Mexico.[63] The French came closest to this pattern, but even during their Porfirian heyday they never rivalled the previous *peninsular* command of the main avenues of upward social mobility.

All available evidence thus suggests that the process of elite recruitment and social change which we deem characteristic of New Spain cannot be readily applied to the Mexico of Santa Anna. True, the great estate continued to absorb as much credit as it could obtain. The difference lay in the debility of the export sector and the intrusion of foreign investment. Capital accumulated in mining and trade no longer flowed so abundantly into domestic agriculture. The chief contrast, however, centered upon the more active role of the State. Monies which previously would have been shipped abroad to finance the military ventures of the Spanish monarchy now stayed at home to fructify in native pockets. Whether mere occupancy of public office enriched many politicians is doubtful. On the other hand, speculation in national debt operations brought great wealth to an entire group of merchant–financiers, the infamous *agiotistas*. Then again, the men who established the new mechanized textile industry depended upon government credit and tariff protection to assure the success of their venture.[64] At last, therefore, political power was deployed to advance the economic interests of at least one section of the Mexican elite.

62. M. P. Laur, "De la métallurgie de l'argent au Mexique," *Annales des Mines*, 6th series, 20 (1871), 38-317; Robert W. Randall, *Real del Monte. A British Mining Venture in Mexico* (Austin, 1972), pp. 73-85, 201-219.

63. Lucas Alamán, *Historia de Méjico* (5 vols., México, 1969), V, 552-554.

64. Robert A. Potash, *El banco de Avío de México* (México, 1959).

7

Intendants and Cabildos in the Viceroyalty of La Plata, 1782–1810

John Lynch

IN DECEMBER, 1807, the cabildo of Buenos Aires, conscious of the prestige it had earned in the recent defence of the region against the British expeditions which had invaded the Río de La Plata, petitioned the crown to grant it the title of "Defender of South America and Protector of the Cabildos of the Viceroyalty of La Plata." The petition was written by its legal adviser, Mariano Moreno, and the eloquent document which he submitted to Madrid contained a remarkable request by the cabildo to act as the recognized leader and mouthpiece of the other cabildos of the viceroyalty, the channel through which they could direct their complaints to higher authorities.

> "We learn by bitter experience in these dominions the constant practice followed by governors in general of humbling and depreciating the cabildos. Ignorant of their noble origin . . . they openly boast of vilifying them, and there is hardly a governor or subdelegate who does not consider it a supreme demonstration of his authority to scorn and despise the cabildos."[1]

An earlier criticism of the treatment accorded to the cabildos in the era of the intendants had been made by Viceroy Croix of Peru in 1789 when he argued that the intendants had completely alienated the municipalities by an intolerant intrusion into their affairs.[2] These assertions were echoed by later writers, and historians have generally agreed that the centralization of authority imposed by the Ordinance of Intendants, whatever its results at the level of efficiency, was a retrogressive move from the point of view of municipal self-government. The administration of public works and even of justice, it

Research in Spanish archives was carried out with the help of the George Scott Scholarship awarded by the University of Edinburgh.—Ed.

[1] M. Moreno, *Escritos* (ed. R. Levene, 2 vols., Buenos Aires, 1943), I, 162-163.

[2] Croix to Valdes, May 16, 1789, Archivo General de Indias, Sevilla (cited hereinafter as AGI), Indiferente General, leg. 1714. See L. E. Fisher, *The Intendant System in Spanish America* (Berkeley, Calif., 1929), pp. 87-88.

is argued, was almost completely assumed by the intendants,[3] while the financial autonomy previously enjoyed by the cabildos was radically diminished by the complex exchequer system which was now established.[4]

But even if it is granted that the great reforms of Charles III gave the intendant the initiative in town government, it does not follow that he took this initiative from the cabildos, for he could not take what they did not have. By the beginning of the eighteenth century the heroic age of the cabildos was a thing of distant memory in all parts of the Spanish empire, and not least in its southernmost provinces. The days when the cabildo of Buenos Aires could offer vigorous and successful opposition to its governors were over.[5] Theoretically the legal position of the cabildos was well defined. The city appointed its judges, administered its property and exercised its moderate local functions. But in practice the legal theory was infringed by the very authority which was supposed to maintain it. By law the election of *alcaldes ordinarios* had to be submitted to the confirmation of viceroys, presidents, governors, or *corregidores,* who were ordered not to hinder the free election of any cabildo members either by interference or by influence.[6] Governors, however, abused this right of confirming elections by using it as opportunity to revise or annul them, and they even adopted the habit of filling vacancies directly by their own appointments. In 1706 the cabildo of Buenos Aires complained to the king that Governor Maldonado had filled six vacancies in this way. Another governor, Valdés Inclán, dissatisfied with the legal municipal elections, appointed his own *regidores* without even consulting the cabildo, and in spite of a royal resolution sustaining the rights of the cabildo he threatened to fine those councillors who resisted him.[7] The practice of sale of office completed the ruin of the municipal system and, in the words of a modern historian, "undoubtedly contributed to the apathy and incompetence of municipal government in many of the towns of the Indies."[8] In Buenos Aires the proprietary councillors formed the

[3] W. W. Pierson, "Some reflections on the cabildo as an institution," *HAHR,* V (1922), p. 595; see also C. H. Haring, *The Spanish Empire in America* (New York, 1947), p. 177.

[4] Emilio Ravignani, *Historia constitucional de la república argentina* (2nd ed., 3 vols., Buenos Aires, 1930), I, 75-77.

[5] For examples of earlier municipal vigor and independence see A. Garreton, *La municipalidad colonial* (Buenos Aires, 1933), pp. 345-388.

[6] *Recopilación de leyes de las Indias* (Madrid, 1791), V. iii. 10. and IV. ix. 7.

[7] J. A. García, *La ciudad indiana* (Buenos Aires, 1900), pp. 164-165.

[8] J. H. Parry, *The Sale of Public Office in the Spanish Indies Under the Hapsburgs* (Berkeley and Los Angeles, 1953), p. 70.

majority of the cabildo and this was precisely the faction which allied itself to the governors.[9] At the same time exchequer officials, in direct defiance of all the laws, frequently got themselves or their friends elected to cabildo offices. The abuses became so extreme that the governor of Buenos Aires in 1739 requested the king to abolish altogether the elections of alcaldes in Santa Fe, Corrientes, and Montevideo, for the meager functions they performed did not justify the electoral disputes which they caused.[10]

A vigorous policy could not be expected from such bodies. Even in their modest local functions—the administration of their funds, public works, price regulations, inspection of prisons—their authority was subordinate to that of the governor. It was no part of the policy of an absolute monarchy to nurture vigorous municipalities, and neither in fact nor in theory was independence countenanced. The legal role of the cabildo was that of a counsellor:

> "It is only to give its advice to those who have the supreme authority, and it has neither power nor competence to order or determine or put into execution its opinion or deliberations, but has to refer all these to the corregidor . . ."[11]

This dependence on higher authorities induced a subservience and inertia that can be read in every line of the minutes of the cabildos. The cabildo of Santiago del Estero frequently received messages from the governor of Tucumán ordering a certain line of action, and invariably these directives were received with submission. Its *actas capitulares*, barbarously written, are full of the most humdrum routine such as prison inspection and licence granting, and are often brought to a fruitless close with the monotonous formula "and there being no business to attend to . . ." Any fundamental work, such as the reconstruction of the town reservoir, would take years to accomplish, and Santiago suffered from periodic shortages of water between 1748 and 1778 precisely because problems of this magnitude were so dilatorily tackled.[12] In Buenos Aires, it is true, the cabildo showed a spasmodic energy in looking after the interests of its citizens. It often bestirred itself over food supplies, but it was powerless to regulate them on its own and needed to seek the co-operation

[9] García, *La ciudad indiana*, pp. 168-169.

[10] Ricardo Levene, *Los orígenes de la democracia argentina* (Buenos Aires, 1911), pp. 124-125.

[11] G. Castillo de Bobadilla, *Política para corregidores* (Madrid, 1775) II, 172.

[12] *Actas capitulares de Santiago del Estero* (cited hereinafter as *ACSE*) (4 vols., Buenos Aires, 1942-46), II, 41-434; III, 197.

of the governor to enforce decisions.[13] Even in Buenos Aires, however, initiative was the exception, passivity the norm.

The fatal condition of the cabildos can be traced to two basic causes: they lacked any firm basis of popular representation, and they lacked adequate financial resources. The direct intrusion of governors in municipal elections has already been noticed. This burden was, if anything, increasing on the eve of the intendant system.[14] Moreover, the viceroy was reaffirming in unambiguous terms his right of confirming elections, and assuring similar rights to his subordinate governors.[15] But the oligarchic composition of the cabildos themselves was an even greater drag on municipal development. There were not infrequent complaints that the councillor class was itself "fixing" elections. Any ideas the cabildos had of changing the electoral system were liable to be retrogressive. The cabildo of Buenos Aires, for example, would have liked more than the three proprietary regidores which it already had. But there was no incentive for citizens to buy the office, for in return for sacrifice in time and money there was no prospect of their lining their own pockets from the empty municipal coffers. It was suggested, therefore, that those regidores who were elected should be elected for a term of six years, and that the alcaldes should be allowed re-election before their first term of office had been judged in residencia.[16] The idea was submitted to the governor, and there it died a natural death, but the incident shows that, far from desiring a greater representative character, the cabildos of this period were actually inclined to make themselves a closer oligarchy than they already were.

They were also losing what little control they had over their own membership. A governor could in theory and often did in practice suspend a councillor whom he considered guilty of a civil misdemeanor. This was unquestioned. But the cabildo had long enjoyed the right of granting its members licenses of leave of absence of up to one year or even longer with the approbation of the governor. This right was used without challenge throughout the first half of the eighteenth century, but it was summarily rejected by a *real provisión* issued by the Audiencia of Charcas in 1774, which prohibited any cabildo member from taking leave of absence without the express license of the governor or of the audiencia.[17]

[13] *Acuerdos del extinguido cabildo de Buenos Aires* (cited hereinafter as *ACBA*) (47 vols., Buenos Aires, 1907-34), serie III, vol. i, pp. 405-407, Acuerdo del 22 de Abril 1754.

[14] *ACSE,* IV, 60-63, 152, 155, for examples in Santiago in 1779-81.

[15] *ACBA,* III. v. 617-631; *ACSE,* IV, 225-227.

[16] *ACBA,* III. iv. 244, Feb. 25, 1771; III. iv. 247, Feb. 28, 1771.

[17] *Ibid.,* III. v. 148, Oct. 5, 1774; III. v. 327-332.

The cabildos might have been able to withstand this increasing pressure on their position had they enjoyed a strong economic foundation, but lack of any financial influence was itself probably the most fundamental cause of their sterility in this period. The poverty of the cabildos was endemic. What income they had was limited to the *propios,* or rents from municipal land and property, and a few local taxes derived from the granting of licences of various kinds. Direct taxation could only be imposed for some specific public object, and was limited to 55 pesos except by consent of the audiencia, which could raise it to 200 pesos; otherwise the approval of the crown was required.[18] In 1708 the revenue from the municipal propios of Buenos Aires amounted to no more than 320 pesos a year. By 1751 this had increased to 844 pesos, but as the procurator pointed out, this was still an inadequate fund for local government, and in February of that year the cabildo requested the Council of the Indies for permission to extend rentable land. By a royal cédula of 1760 authority was given to charge five pesos on all built-up sites on the common ground in the city. But to go ahead and collect it was another matter. The cabildo had to make repeated requests to the governor to issue the necessary order to implement the cédula, but such was his unconcern that it was 1766 before the first rents were collected, and for many years their collection was surrounded with difficulties and hindrances.[19] Further propositions were made by the cabildo to increase its propios, but royal permission was difficult to obtain. Meanwhile municipal activity was brought to an almost complete standstill. In February 1768 the cabildo was still lamenting its notorious lack of funds, "since with the *arbitrios* which it now has it can hardly cover the bare and essential yearly expenses." Eventually it was reduced to asking for voluntary contributions from citizens. The response was not very promising, and in December 1777 it asked the viceroy for a loan of 8000 pesos to cover various expenses, but met with a refusal.[20] A similar tale of poverty emerges from the pages of the council meetings of the cabildo of Santiago del Estero, and the story can be implemented from the records of other provincial cabildos. In the province of Tucumán the *sisa* tax was never fully paid before 1783.[21] The yearly income of Mendoza from propios in the third quarter of the eighteenth century was only

[18] *Recopilación,* IV. vii. 7, 14; IV. xv. 3.

[19] *ACBA,* III. i. 28, Feb. 15, 1751; III. ii. 652; III. iv. 25, 27, 32.

[20] *Ibid.,* III. ii. 179, 284; III. iii. 528, 549-553, 587-588; III. vi. 155-156, 160, Dec. 15, 1777.

[21] Superintendant Fernández to José de Gálvez, Minister of the Indies, May 15, 1783, Carta 714, AGI, Aud. de Buenos Aires, leg. 356.

400 pesos, that of San Juan 200, while San Luis had none at all.[22] In the province of Cochabamba in Upper Peru only the cabildos of Cochabamba and Mizque possessed propios and arbitrios; other towns were completely devoid of this income.[23]

Financial control means little when there are scanty finances to control. But not only was municipal revenue meager, its appropriation was for the most part prescribed. The very management of their own funds was so hedged around with restrictions that it is impossible to speak of the "financial autonomy" of the cabildos in the period before the intendants.[24] Without previous consent of the audiencia or of the provincial governor, extraordinary appropriations or assignments of wages from revenue were limited to the minute figure of 3000 maravedis.[25] Governors were quick to pounce upon any deviations from this law. When the cabildo of Buenos Aires appointed a paid archivist in April 1772, assigning him 200 pesos a year, the governor decreed that it was legally incapable of disposing of its own funds in this way, and the cabildo had no alternative but to submit to the law.[26]

The picture presented by the cabildos in the third quarter of the eighteenth century was not, then, an impressive one. An occasional cry of protest indicated that a flame of independence still flickered, but it was a cry of despair and signified impotence. It can be read in the words of the cabildo of Santiago del Estero:

> "We debated the best way to seek a remedy against the despotisms of the chiefs of this province and their absolute government, the outrages they inflict on officials and other subjects . . . their complete immunity from punishment . . . "[27]

They decided to complain to the king through their attorney in Madrid, and no more is heard of the matter. Three years later, in 1776, the cabildo of Asunción del Paraguay submitted a long list of complaints against Augustín Fernando Pinedo, governor of Paraguay, accusing him of oppression, nepotism, maladministration of

[22] José Torre Revello, *El marqués de Sobre Monte, gobernador-intendente de Córdoba y virrey del Río de la Plata* (Buenos Aires, 1946), Apendice III, pp. xci, xciii, xcv.

[23] Intendant Viedma to Marqués de Bajamar, May 18, 1792, AGI, Aud. de Buenos Aires, leg. 140.

[24] Both Levene and Ravignani use this expression. See Levene, *La revolución de mayo y Mariano Moreno* (2 vols., Buenos Aires, 1946), I, 131-132; and Ravignani in introduction to *Actas capitulares de Concepción del Río Cuarto* (Buenos Aires, 1943), p. 9. This work is cited hereafter as *ACCRC*.

[25] *Recopilación*, IV. xiii. 2.

[26] *ACBA*, III. iv. 285-286, 422, 459-460.

[27] *ACSE*, III, 365-366, Nov. 29, 1773.

royal revenues, private commercial activities and many other crimes. But Gálvez, the Minister of the Indies, did not offer an opinion, and it was not until 1785, that is precisely in the period of the intendancies, that the complaints against Pinedo were really entertained.[28] While Santiago and Asunción were complaining of despotism, from Upper Peru came a faint plea for more government. In 1781 the cabildo of La Plata petitioned the Crown to move the seat of the viceroyalty there because of the lack of government in the province and its propensity to disorder, so great was its distance from Buenos Aires. Not surprisingly, the request was coldly received in Madrid where it was pointed out that the president of the audiencia had adequate authority for dealing with the problems of Upper Peru.[29]

Any evidence of strength or independence on the part of the cabildos was abnormal and ephemeral. Yet twenty years later, between approximately 1800 and 1810, in almost all the main cities of the viceroyalty of La Plata vigorous cabildos were in conflict with the local political authorities and challenging them on many issues. Sometime between the 1770's and the end of the century the cabildos found a new lease of life. This coincided precisely with the period of the intendancies.

It is true that the centralizing policy pursued by Charles III and his ministers did not augur well for the cabildos. The municipality of Buenos Aires showed an evident desire to share in the increase of political powers assigned to the area with the creation of the new viceroyalty in 1776, a desire which was encouraged by Cevallos, the first viceroy, who relied on the support of the cabildo for initiating his new policy, and who responded completely to its demands for freer commerce.[30] But five years' experience under Superintendant Fernández, before the Ordinance of 1782 inaugurated the full intendant system, dashed any hopes the cabildo may have had of the arrival of a new period in municipal government. Fernández kept cabildo activity carefully confined, as one example will show. There was in Buenos Aires a war fund amounting to more than 25,000 pesos and used for maintaining three militia battalions in the province. This fund was administered by the exchequer, but it had originally been collected and managed by the cabildo of Buenos Aires. When Fernández heard that the cabildo was pressing the viceroy to return the fund to its jurisdiction, he immediately sought con-

[28] Cabildo of Asunción del Paraguay to Gálvez, July 29, 1776, AGI, Aud. de Buenos Aires, leg. 48; Royal Order Nov. 24, 1785, *loc. cit.*

[29] Cabildo of La Plata, Feb. 15, 1781, AGI, Aud. de Buenos Aires, leg. 151.

[30] Cabildo of Buenos Aires to Cevallos, July 22, 1777, AGI, Aud. de Buenos Aires, leg. 157.

firmation from Madrid of his own exclusive control of this revenue as head of the exchequer in the viceroyalty. This was assured him by royal order of March 9, 1779.[31]

The cabildo of Buenos Aires had political as well as financial pretensions. In April 1778, claiming to speak on behalf of all interests and classes in the city, it uttered a genuine cry of distress at the impending departure of Viceroy Cevallos to whom it attributed all the recent progress made in the affairs of the province, and implored him to remain in office while an extension of his appointment was sought from the crown.[32] This representation was made after the publication of the appointment of Viceroy Vertiz and was therefore interpreted in Madrid as an affront to the prestige and reputation of the new viceroy and as setting an extremely dangerous precedent. Superintendant Fernández was instructed to examine the minutes of the cabildo and take note of all the events of the incident and the names of the members who were its promoters. As a result of Fernández's enquiry and advice two councillors, Judas Josef de Salas and Bernardo Sancho de Larrea, were banished to the Falkland Islands for a year after which they were to reside in Mendoza, while the other nine cabildo members who had signed the representation were prohibited from exercising office for seven years.[33]

The cabildos, therefore, had no reason to welcome any extension, still less formalization, of the intendant system by the Ordinance of Intendants of 1782. Yet it was obvious that they themselves were incompetent to deal with the type of administration which local government was lacking and which the new system was meant to supply. The colonial municipal oligarchy treated and resolved the affairs of the city according to the same criterion as they dealt with their own personal affairs. But with the extension of commerce and increase in population this simple domestic machinery was no longer adequate to cope with the new administrative problems which were arising, nor were merchant-councillors competent to resolve them. The time had passed when they could miss sessions because there was nothing to do. Building, public works, hygiene, finance and justice were all clamoring for prompt attention and needed a

[31] Fernández to Gálvez, Dec. 1, 1778, AGI, Aud. de Buenos Aires, leg. 473; R. O. Mar. 9, 1779, *loc. cit.*

[32] *ACBA*, III. vi. 204-205, April 9, 1778.

[33] Fernández to Gálvez, Feb. 5, 1779, and R. O. Reservada May 28, 1779, AGI, Aud. de Buenos Aires, leg. 308. See also *ACBA*, III. vi. 427-429, Sept. 10, 1779. Vertiz secured royal pardon for the offenders (R. O. Mar. 10, 1790), and the two exiles were brought back, *Ibid.*, III. vi. 572-574.

treatment for which the cabildos had no precedent and their members no skill.[34] This is the context in which the intendancy system must be judged. In view of the evidence showing the legal and practical weakness of the cabildos on the eve of the intendancy system, it is unreal to consider the problem in terms of local institutions being absorbed by centralizing officials. The criterion of any judgment on the cabildos in the new era will be whether the intendants made the cabildos more active and whether they allowed them to co-operate in the work they were doing.

It has been maintained that the cabildos lost part of their authority because the alcaldes and regidores appointed by them had to be confirmed in office by the intendant.[35] In fact there was no substantial change. By the Laws of the Indies the ultimate authority for confirmation of municipal elections was the viceroy.[36] This law was expressly annulled by the Ordinance of Intendants, and the power of confirmation was reserved exclusively to the intendants who were to ensure that "the said offices be assigned to individuals who are judged most suitable for the fair administration of justice and for the proper security of the revenues of my royal treasury . . ."[37] This system operated until 1787 when by royal cédula of November 29 it was annulled and the right of confirming the election of alcaldes ordinarios was restored to the viceroy. In cities where there were audiencias, and for fifteen leagues around them, the president of the audiencia was to confirm the alcaldes in office. In small towns viceroys could authorize intendants to do this with subsequent central confirmation.[38] But whatever changes were made the cabildos themselves neither lost anything nor gained anything from the point of view of legal rights.

In practice, however, there were far less abuses under the new régime. Between 1784 and 1789 the intendants of Salta regularly confirmed the elections in Santiago del Estero without any intrusion. In 1790 the intendant annulled the election of Juan José Iramaín as junior alcalde on the ground that he was already subdelegate of exchequer and as such was precluded from municipal office by the Ordinance of Intendants. He ordered the cabildo to make a new appointment, which was done without demur and this time ap-

[34] R. de Lafuente Machain, *Buenos Aires en el siglo XVIII* (Buenos Aires, 1946), pp. 10-11.

[35] Ravignani, *Historia constitucional,* I. 75.

[36] *Recopilación,* V. iii. 10.

[37] *Ordenanza de Intendentes de Buenos Aires,* 1782, art. 8.

[38] Viceroy Loreto to Porlier, Carta 41, May 1, 1788, AGI, Aud. de Buenos Aires, leg. 76. See Fisher, *Intendant System,* pp. 94, 107.

proved.[39] In the event of a disputed election the cabildo of Santiago would voluntarily offer the case for solution to the intendant.[40] In general the intendants only cancelled elections on strictly legal and not on political grounds. For example, Intendant Rodríguez of Córdoba approved the 1806 elections in Concepción except that of Josef Francisco Tisera as alcalde ordinario on account of the distance he resided from the city and of the fact that he had a tobacco *estanco* which would suffer from lack of attention—to the detriment of the royal revenue. The cabildo agreed without comment and proceeded to elect another alcalde whom the intendant confirmed in office.[41] In fact whenever royal authority was brought to bear on cabildos in these matters it was likely to be in the interests of purer elections; a residencia on councillors of Santiago who had served between 1778 and 1790 disclosed that some regidores were very susceptible to bribery and would sell their votes to aspirants to office. Punishments in these cases varied from deprivation of votes to monetary fines.[42]

In Santiago any diminution of the already weak representative basis of the cabildo came not as a result of pressure from the intendant but on the initiative of the cabildo itself. The traditional electoral procedure in Santiago was as follows: at the end of the year the cabildo met to choose six citizens "of education and intelligence" who were admitted to the council to assist in the election of the new cabildo. This system was followed until 1786 when, on the pretext of avoiding dissension which the admission of citizens was alleged to cause, the existing cabildo omitted this first stage and itself made the elections for the following year. This procedure was then approved by the intendant.[43] On the other hand, when in 1797 Intendant Sobremonte created the town of Concepción del Río Cuarto and endowed it with a cabildo he did this in a more democratic manner than earlier founders of towns had followed. Instead of founding the cabildo by direct appointment,[44] Sobremonte authorized the citizens themselves to make the first elections, and instructed his commissioners only to supervise. His two commissioners summoned the most suitable and substantial citizens on January 1, 1789; the latter elected the regidores who in turn chose the alcaldes.[45]

[39] *Ord. Ints.*, art. 73; *ACSE*, IV. 504-506, 511.

[40] *Ibid.*, IV. 423-425, Jan. 25, 1788.

[41] *ACCRC*, 230, 232.

[42] *ACSE*, IV, 557-568.

[43] *Ibid.*, IV, 53-55, 99, 349-350, 353.

[44] *Recopilación*, IV. iii. 10.

[45] A. C. Vitulo, "Fundación de la Villa de Río Cuarto," *Boletín del instituto de investigaciones históricas*, XVII (Buenos Aires, 1933-34), pp. 156-157; Vitulo, *ACCRC*, p. 37 note 2.

But it was the cabildo of Buenos Aires which maintained most vigilance over its own composition, and came to resent interference not only from the intendant but also from higher political authorities. In the elections of 1788 it elected Manuel Antonio Warnes as senior alcalde. Superintendant Sanz approved all the other appointments but annulled that of Warnes and ordered the cabildo to make another one. Sanz's real objection to Warnes was personal dislike combined with a political distrust of what he called his "*espíritu revoltoso.*"[46] The cabildo, however, would not retreat, and appealed to the audiencia which upheld its election and confirmed Warnes in office.[47] In the election of 1792 it was Viceroy Arredondo who forbade the election of Warnes, but this was on the legal grounds that there was a law suit against him, and although the cabildo protested vigorously it had to obey.[48] Nevertheless, it carried its protest to the Crown and received a royal cédula of December 24, 1795, disapproving of Arredondo's exclusion of Warnes from the elections as being against the spirit of the municipal ordinances of Buenos Aires.[49]

At the same time the cabildo was securing more control of its own members. A royal cédula of May 8, 1789, conceded to the cabildos the privilege of hearing renunciations of office. When, therefore, Martín Alzaga, procurator-elect for 1790, obtained exemption from office from the viceroy, the cabildo of Buenos Aires insisted on its rights and enforced his acceptance.[50] On August 21, 1794, Benito González de Rivadavia, regidor and *depositario general* of the cabildo of Buenos Aires, was exiled by the Audiencia of Buenos Aires to Córdoba. On the 22nd the cabildo protested that he had been banished on no more specific ground than that of public security, and, what was more significant, that no notice had been given to the cabildo on a matter affecting its own members: in particular it was complained that Rivadavia had been forced to leave without giving an account of the municipal deposits he held. These objections were made to the viceroy, who was supporting the action of the audiencia, and were continued unremittently—three representations were made between August 22 and September 3—until the viceroy issued an order on October 26 authorizing the return of Rivadavia so that he could give an account of his deposits to the cabildo.[51]

[46] Sanz to Porlier, Jan. 2, 1788, AGI, Aud. de Buenos Aires, leg. 364.

[47] Warnes to Porlier, reservada duplicado, Jan. 8, 1778, AGI, Aud. de Buenos Aires, leg. 445. See also *ACBA*, III. viii. 454-455.

[48] *ACBA*, III. x. 9-13.

[49] *Ibid.*, III. xi. 76-77.

[50] *Ibid.*, III. ix. 246, Jan. 26, 1790.

[51] *Ibid.*, III. x. 363, 424-425.

While the cabildo elections were subject to less intromission by higher authorities during the first stages of the intendant period, their financial basis was also becoming more secure. It is true that the Ordinance of Intendants circumscribed the already slender control they had over their own finances. These were now subject to inspection by the *Junta Superior de Hacienda* in Buenos Aires which could ask the intendants for information concerning municipal finance and communicate its measures to them through the account-general of municipal finance, who was also secretary of the junta. The intendants were instructed on taking office to ask each of the cities and towns within their jurisdiction for an exact account of their funds and of the municipal taxes. From this information the intendants were to draw up a provisional ordinance for municipal finance and submit it to the Junta Superior which in turn was to report it to the Crown. A municipal junta was to be established in each Spanish colonial city and town for the control of financial matters; this was composed of the senior alcalde ordinario, who was to preside over it, two regidores and the procurator-general, but it was supposed to be a distinct body from the cabildo which was forbidden to interfere with it in any way. The business of the junta was to conduct the sale of offices connected with municipal finance, and lease the town revenues to collectors. The intendants were to supervise the proceedings of the municipal juntas in order to prevent abuses, though if the juntas had any complaints against the intendants' measures they could appeal directly to the Junta Superior. In the smaller divisions of the provinces the subdelegate had much the same supervision over municipal finance as the intendants had in the provincial capital.[52]

The financial authority of the cabildos was circumscribed to this moderate degree not from any conscious anti-municipal policy, but simply in the interests of greater efficiency and by the creation of a more detailed administrative machine. They were not completely deprived of financial powers. The cabildos chose from among their own members the two regidores who were to serve on the municipal junta, and the alcaldes were already cabildo appointees.[53] The rule of submitting the accounts to the cabildo was adhered to.[54] In a small town like Santiago del Estero the two bodies were virtually identical and the cabildo simply turned itself into the finance committee for certain purposes:

"We the cabildo . . . having assembled as president and members of

[52] *Ord. Ints.*, arts. 23-44.

[53] *ACBA*, III. viii. 282.

[54] *Ibid.*, III. vii. 401-402.

the municipal junta of propios and arbitrios of this city to treat of matters pertaining to it, determined to consider the business of bringing the taxable wine-stores at the disposal of this city up to the number of eight . . ."[55]

It is clear in fact that the cabildo of Santiago considered its own interests and that of the junta identical, and, far from regarding it as a rival, it was as ready to defend it as it was to defend itself whenever there was unwarranted interference on the part of the subdelegate.[56]

By the new system the interests of efficiency were better served than they had previously been. At the same time the most important single fact in the life of the cabildos in this period was the increase in their funds. This can be ascribed in many cases precisely to the activity of the intendants. The quickest results were obtained in Córdoba and owed their existence to Intendant Sobremonte, who was able to report in November 1785:

> "The propios of this city have risen in the past year to 1040 pesos: the year previously they only amounted to 525 pesos. And according to what I have proposed to the Junta Superior for their increase, sufficient quantities can now be assigned to meet its needs, to complete the municipal buildings and other useful and decorative works."[57]

He also had proposals for increasing the propios of the other towns of his province. His methods did not involve any spectacular creation of new taxes but simply a more thorough collection of existing ones, a thing which the cabildo had never been able to accomplish on its own. By this method he was able to triple the propios of Córdoba in his first five years of office there.[58] The result in practical terms was seen in the new growth of public building in Córdoba.

Buenos Aires had completely outgrown its financial resources, and there the situation required not only a rigorous collection of existing taxes but also the creation of completely new ones. Superintendant Sanz spared no pains to increase municipal revenue. He kept the cabildo on its toes by periodically demanding a statement of revenue accounts.[59] And soon after he took office he requested a formal statement from the cabildo containing its precise requirements in matters of taxation. This was the opportunity the cabildo had been waiting for all during the century. In a long and far from clear report

[55] *ACSE*, IV, 340, Aug. 23, 1785.
[56] *Ibid.*, IV, 300-301, Aug. 4, 1784.
[57] Sobremonte to Loreto, Nov. 6, 1785, printed in Torre Revello, *Sobre Monte*, Apendice, p. xcix.
[58] Sobremonte to Sanz, April 5, 1786, AGI, Aud. de Buenos Aires, leg. 363; Revello, *op. cit.*, p. 33.
[59] *ACBA*, III. vii. 473, Jan. 22, 1785.

the cabildo outlined its needs: new taxes amounting to more than 11,000 pesos were proposed and a substantial increase in existing propios were suggested. The proposals were considered by the Junta Superior, presided over by the superintendent, and on February 29, 1788, it conceded new taxes on a scale which the cabildo had been demanding in vain for years. Authority was granted for taxes on hawkers' stalls, gaming saloons, weights and measures and at an increased rate on built-up areas on the common land. Twenty-two taxable wine stores were added to the eight which were already assigned to the cabildo, at the rate of 25 pesos each one.[60] Moreover, the Junta Superior tackled the chronic inability of the cabildo to collect its own taxes by prodding it to a stricter sense of duty in this respect. For instance, it demanded an explanation from the cabildo for its failure to collect the duty on the *Corredores de Lonja* (a sort of merchant exchange) to which it had been entitled ever since the foundation of the city.[61]

It was not a tale of unrelieved progress. In January 1792 at the instance of certain citizens the viceroy suspended the tax on occupiers of common-land, in spite of a strong protest from the cabildo.[62] On February 17, the cabildo was driven to ask the viceroy for a further increase of propios and arbitrios, but the financial support they had enjoyed under Superintendant Sanz was not so assured after the suppression of the independent superintendency in 1788.[63] Nevertheless, the increased taxative powers conceded by Sanz in the 1780's gradually began to bear fruit, and the funds in the municipal treasury steadily rose:[64]

Year	*Pesos*	*Reales*
1798	9668	3
1799	15298	4½
1800	10674	1¾
1802	15903	¼
1805	23431	1¾

But the new municipal prosperity was not shared by every town. The story of Santiago del Estero continued to be one of crippling poverty. When the cabildo was organizing road repairs and improving the town hall for the viceroy's visit of inspection in 1789, it had

[60] *Ibid.*, III. viii. 196-209, 363, 496-497.

[61] *Ibid.*, III. viii. 497

[62] *Ibid.*, III. x. 30. But by Sept. 25, 1792, this must have been restored, for the cabildo was requesting powers to increase it, *ibid.*, III. x. 129-133.

[63] *Ibid.*, III. x. 47.

[64] *Ibid.*, III. xi. 79, 497; IV. i. 41, 279; IV. ii. 685.

to report that there were no funds available for this work from the regular municipal revenue. Santiago still suffered from what the intendants in Buenos Aires and Córdoba were trying to reform—an inability to collect its own taxes and control its own collectors. The senior alcalde for 1788 did not collect the propios for that year, so that in 1789 the cabildo had to inform the intendant of Salta that it had nothing with which to defray the expenses of public administration ordered by him.[65] The inference to be drawn is that only the immediate presence of the intendant in his provincial capital was sufficient to stimulate the cabildos and that the others fared ill under the subdelegates.

Revenue in Potosí was in a much healthier state. In April 1787 the town propios had a fund of 7,960 pesos. In 1788 the annual revenue was 2,139 pesos from the sisa tax and 2,314 pesos 2½ reales from the propios. In all, therefore, the municipal treasury was in possession of 12,413 pesos 2½ reales.[66] To put this income to profitable use Intendant Pino Manrique, in consultation with the cabildo, proposed to the Junta Superior in Buenos Aires a scheme for investing it in a public store, which would relieve the town of the necessity of buying its most essential foodstuffs in so-called *canchas* at exorbitant prices. This sort of financial activity was authorized by the Ordinance of Intendants.[67] But in spite of the repeated applications of Intendant Pino Manrique, the Junta Superior took no resolution on the matter, and he was forced to report the situation to the home government.[68] The result of his complaint was a salutary devolution of power. By royal cédula of September 14, 1788, it was decided that in order to avoid such delays to useful projects the investment of municipal funds in all the colonies should in future be made on the proposal of the intendants of the cabildos, and with the approbation of the audiencia, to which, and not to the Juntas Superiores, the proposal should be submitted.[69]

With the validity of their elections more assured, and their finances clearly if fitfully improving, the cabildos entered upon a period of greater activity in public administration. The initiative

[65] *ACSE*, IV, 452-453, Jan. 7, 1789.

[66] Intendant Pino Manrique to Porlier, Mar. 16, 1788, AGI, Aud. de Charcas, leg. 439.

[67] *Ord. Ints.*, art. 41.

[68] Pino Manrique to Porlier, *loc. cit.*, AGI, Aud. de Charcas, leg. 439.

[69] Loreto to Porlier, Carta 85, Jan. 20, 1789, AGI, Aud. de Buenos Aires, leg. 77; *ACBA*, III. ix. 21; *ACSE*, IV, 471-472. But apparently this order was not efficiently enforced: see Mata Linares (Regente of the audiencia) to Porlier, May 21, 1791, and Aud. of Buenos Aires to Crown, June 15, 1803, AGI, Aud. de Buenos Aires, leg. 152.

generally came from the intendant, but this was not a question of removing the faculties of the cabildo; rather was it the necessity of making them do things which they should have done before but had neglected. In January 1779, for example, Superintendant Fernández made the cabildo of Buenos Aires undertake an inspection of weights and measures in the interests of the consumer. This task had of course always been open to the cabildo but only now was it undertaken.[70] Superintendant Sanz pushed the cabildo along even more vigorously, consulting it on various points of public interest, and inviting a profusion of reports on matters such as the regulation of supplies and prices, public works, taxes, rights of citizens, and economic affairs.[71] Meanwhile the cabildo pursued its own work of inspection in the service of the public, but there were many instances where by the nature of things it could not act alone but needed the assistance of higher political authorities. That assistance was generally forthcoming, and the vigilance of the cabildo would be implemented by a proclamation from the superintendant or the viceroy. In March 1791, for example, the cabildo of Buenos Aires informed the viceroy that many ranchers were slaughtering infected cattle for consumption and requested a prohibition of this activity. Arredondo issued a proclamation ordering the ranchers to take adequate precautions and detailing the *ministros de los corrales* to undertake inspections.[72]

But this mutual co-operation between cabildo and governor did not extend to every branch of municipal administration. It did not extend to town planning and public works. By an order issued in agreement with the viceroy on February 14, 1785, Superintendant Sanz removed all competence from the municipal officials in matters of street regulation and public building, and reserved all executive power in these affairs to himself and his officials.[73] His motives were greater efficiency and speed, and he specifically maintained the right of the cabildo to give advice and to put forward ideas. When the superintendancy was suppressed in 1788 the viceroy did not go back on this order, and he himself assumed the faculties of the superintendant. But the concentration of work was too much for him, and it was inevitable that the cabildo's own *diputado de policia* (gen-

[70] *ACBA*, III, vi, 491-492, Feb. 5, 1780; III, vi, 500-501, Mar. 3, 1780.

[71] *Ibid., passim.*

[72] *Documentos para la historia argentina*, Facultad de Filosofía y Letras, Universidad de Buenos Aires (Buenos Aires, 1913-), IV, 119, Mar. 31, 1791. Cited hereafter as *DHA*.

[73] *DHA*, IX, 181-182, Sanz to Cabildo, Feb. 14, 1785. This had already been the practice since the beginning of 1784.

erally the third regidor) should in practice assume more power in this field. But this could not make good the need for a full-time official in charge of public works. Consequently, on August 1, 1799, the viceroy appointed Martín Boneo *intendente de policía* in Buenos Aires, subject to the viceroy and charged with street registration, enumeration and censorship, duties which were later extended to more general public works.[74] He soon came into conflict with the cabildo when he requested that its mayordomo should be placed at his orders and disposal. The cabildo bluntly refused and carried its point. But its real objection was the very principle of the new establishment, and it was not slow to carry its protests to the viceroy. The viceroy supported the intendant and reported to the government that he was doing useful work. Meanwhile the cabildo obstructed Boneo's work and appealed to Madrid with such success that a royal cédula of January 16, 1804, ordered Boneo to resign his post and return to Spain, singular evidence that South American cabildos were not without influence in the metropolis.[75] The viceroy replaced him by Antonio de las Cagigas. The cabildo now implicitly recognized that a full-time official in charge of public works was essential, for it reported to the viceroy that it had no objection to this appointment, but insisted that the appointee "ought to proceed in his commission with the intervention and knowledge of this illustrious cabildo or of the *junta municipal* . . ."[76] Its persistence was rewarded, for it was now allowed to appoint two councillors to audit the income and expenditure of funds destined for public works, and Cagigas had to regulate his account with them.[77] Even in the sphere of public works, therefore, the cabildo was never completely excluded in this period. Furthermore, growth of business was shown by the fact that it had to decide in January 1790 to increase its meetings to two each week.[78]

The history of Córdoba under the rule of its first intendant, Sobremonte, reveals a similar tale of invigoration and mutual cooperation. Until the arrival of Sobremonte, the cabildo consisted of eight members. He enlarged it to twelve, and initiated a subscription among members, heading it himself, to pay for repairs to the town hall. Drawing on his experience as viceregal secretary under Vertiz in Buenos Aires, he instituted the system of *comisarios*

[74] *ACBA*, III. xi. 471-472; IV. i. 162.

[75] *Ibid.*, III. xi. 493-494; IV. i. 39-40, 46-47, 402-418. Cabildo to Crown, May 26, 1803, and R. C., Jan. 16, 1804, AGI, Aud. de Buenos Aires, leg. 14.

[76] *ACBA*, IV. i. 436, July 3, 1804.

[77] *Ibid.*, IV. i. 499-500, Oct. 11, 1804; IV. ii. 12, Jan. 7, 1805.

[78] *Ibid.*, III. ix. 259-260, Jan 29, 1790.

de barrios; six of these were appointed by the cabildo from among the citizens to see to the execution of orders for the improvement of the city, police and security, control of beggars, and traffic supervision. Already in 1786 the cabildo was remarking on the zeal of the new intendant. Sobremonte worked well with the municipality, which in turn gave support and co-operation. Through the initiative of Sobremonte, the cabildo contracted with the *hacendados* of the province to supply an adequate amount of meat every year at fair prices, free of alcabala and all other taxes.[79]

In the neighboring intendancy of Salta del Tucumán a similar effort on the part of the intendant to stimulate municipal activity can be discerned, though the plans were less well defined and the policy was less vigorous. In December 1785 the intendant requested from the cabildo of Santiago del Estero a report on its various activities. The cabildo was apparently becoming more conscious of social problems in the town, and was developing a scheme of poor relief, the details of which are not clear. Two years later the intendant requested the remittance within two months of statistics of the size of the town, its population and racial composition, its agricultural and mineral products. Without waste of time, the cabildo collected and forwarded the required information. Thus in their task of collecting data and information for submission to Spain, the intendants had to seek the collaboration of the cabildos. In turn, the intendants passed on general news and information to the cabildo, which was thus the means of distributing to the people constitutional and political news from Spain.[80] And for all the predominance of the intendant in the economic affairs of his province, the cabildo of Santiago could still look after its own economic interests: in January 1786 it forbade the export of grain from the district because of the bad harvest.[81]

The cabildos themselves were not slow to show their appreciation of the intendants, and during the first fifteen years of the regime there flowed from the municipalities an impressive stream of eulogies of their political superiors. The cabildo of Mendoza described Sobremonte as its "*nuevo fundador,*" and in August, 1788, sent a long and glowing account of his services, requesting from the Crown his retention in office, "because his extraordinary activity and tireless zeal combined with his integrity and enlightened political ideas have contributed advantageously to the general prosperity, progress

[79] I. Garzón, *Crónica de Córdoba* (Córdoba, 1898), pp. 14-15, 43, 341-345.
[80] *ACSE,* IV, 344, 405-406, 463.
[81] *Ibid.,* IV, 351-352.

and administration of these remote and loyal dominions.''[82] In 1790 the cabildo of Córdoba decided to send a testimonial of Sobremonte's merits and services to the king.[83] The good impression left by Sobremonte lasted long. When he was appointed temporary viceroy the cabildos of Córdoba, San Juan, Mendoza, and San Luis petitioned the Crown to confirm him permanently in office. And even after his conduct during the first British invasion of the Río de la Plata in 1806, when he not only failed to organize the defence of Buenos Aires but also deserted his capital, the cabildo of Córdoba defended him in a message to the king dated August 29, 1806.[84]

In 1789 the cabildo of Salta del Tucumán reported on the good services of Intendant Mestre in all branches of government, and asked the king to prolong his term of office. Particular praise was given to his completion of a ''magnificent town hall'' and its division into decent and comfortable offices where the alcaldes and other officials could work with proper formality.[85] The cabildo of Potosí reported on the new system of government in 1786, and, in terms disappointingly vague, declared that the intendancy system had had beneficial results in restoring public peace, stimulating industry, and formulating new municipal legislation. Special praise was given to Intendant Pino Manrique's administration in public works, commerce, mines, and exchequer. The cabildo was of the opinion that only the intendancy system had been able to provide a strong government in unruly Potosí.[86] In 1793 the cabildo of La Plata informed the Crown of the good services of President-Intendant Joaquín del Pino, his zeal in reorganizing the hospital and personally visiting the sick, his reform of prison conditions, his efforts to promote public works, and his success in increasing royal revenues.[87]

The cabildo of La Paz showed a particular readiness to support the intendancy system, and was in fact concerned that it was not operating to full advantage in this distant province. The cabildo was quite alive to the fact that what La Paz suffered from was a lack of permanency in its governors: there was a continual change

[82] Memorial del Cabildo de Mendoza, Aug. 26, 1788, AGI, Aud. de Buenos Aires, leg. 50. Part of this is printed in Revello, *Sobre Monte*, p. 35, where the dispatch is misdated.

[83] Garzón, *op. cit.*, p. 23.

[84] *Ibid.*, pp. 78, 90-94.

[85] Cabildo of Salta to Crown, July 29, 1789, AGI, Aud. de Buenos Aires, leg. 143.

[86] Cabildo of Potosí to Crown, Feb. 4, 1786, British Museum, London, Egerton MS 1813, fols. 76v-78. Cited hereafter as BM.

[87] Cabildo of La Plata to Crown, Jan. 28, 1793, AGI, Aud. de Buenos Aires, leg. 45.

of appointments, and no intendant completed a full term of office. In 1795 La Paz was enjoying the rule of a temporary intendant, Fernando Sota, a naval captain and a man whom the cabildo considered intelligent, experienced, and well versed in the affairs of the province and of the viceroyalty. So concerned was the cabildo to retain his services that it offered 25,000 pesos to the Spanish treasury for the war fund on condition that Soto's appointment be confirmed and prolonged.[88] In August of the following year the cabildo sent a further and more substantial account of Soto's administration and renewed its previous request and offer. It was supported by the Audiencia of Charcas, but it failed to move the home government. Nevertheless his successor, Intendant Burgunyo, also earned the support of the cabildo and its gratitude for an increase in municipal revenue.[89]

The cabildo of Asunción del Paraguay forwarded in 1798 a long report on the services of Intendant Rivera, whom it described as a "prudent and zealous governor," and supplied a detailed account of his administration and policy in military, frontier, Indian and financial affairs, concluding with an appreciation of his régime in no uncertain terms.[90]

This reaction of the cabildos of the viceroyalty of La Plata to the activity of the intendants could be supported by an even more striking body of evidence from the viceroyalty of Peru. In 1786, for example, the cabildo of Lima submitted a report on the work of the superintendent and on his treatment of the cabildo which is convincing both in its generalizations and its particulars and which augured extremely well for future co-operation between the two bodies. Grateful testimonials came also from the cabildos of Huancavelica and Arequipa.[91]

A cabildo which criticizes intendants is likely to be giving its real opinion when it praises them, and thus these testimonials are convincing precisely because they are not indiscriminate. The very cabildos which praise the intendants with whom they can work, do

[88] Cabildo of La Paz to Crown, Dec. 17, 1795, AGI, Aud. de Charcas, leg. 436.

[89] Cabildo of La Paz to Príncipe de la Paz (Godoy), Aug. 31, 1796, and Audiencia of Charcas to Crown, Dec. 25, 1795, AGI, Aud. de Charcas, leg. 436. Cabildo of La Paz to Crown, Dec. 11, 1798, AGI, Aud. de Buenos Aires, leg. 37.

[90] Cabildo of Asunción to Francisco de Saavedra, Nov. 19, 1798, AGI, Aud. de Buenos Aires, leg. 48.

[91] Cabildo of Lima, Mar. 31, 1786, Cabildo of Huancavelica, April 11, 1788, Cabildo of Arequipa, Dec. 30, 1788, AGI, Aud. de Lima, leg. 802. The remarks of the cabildo of Lima are the best commentary on the criticisms of Viceroy Croix mentioned above: "Desde qe. el Sor. Intendente se pósesionó del empleo empesó a dirigir oficios a este Illo. Ayuntamiento para que se meditase, y confiriese todo lo que exigia su atencion, y p̄rovidencias consultandolo inmediatamente para expedirlas con prontitud, y opŏrtunidad."

not hesitate to protest against those whom they oppose. In the 1780's and 1790's esteem and co-operation was the norm. But in the first decade of the 19th century in almost every part of the viceroyalty of La Plata the cabildos were at loggerheads with their intendants. The revival of political consciousness and public spirit which was evident in the municipalities in this era was then turned against the intendants who had helped to nurture it, or rather against their successors. This apprenticeship in opposition was in turn an invaluable preparation for the approaching revolution for independence. The change from collaboration to distrust was due to two causes. The quality of the intendants appointed to the colonies declined in proportion as the quality of patronage in Madrid declined: the difference between Sobremonte and González in Córdoba is the measure of the difference between the government of Charles III and Gálvez and that of Charles IV and Godoy. Moreover, encouraged by their association with the work of the intendants and by the respect with which the early intendants treated them, the cabildos became more sure of themselves and began to resent the tutelage of their superiors. Anxious to control the funds which the intendants had made possible and to direct the work which the intendants had initiated, they reacted against their masters and began to claim more share of local government.

Hostilities in Chuquisaca began as early as 1796. In November of that year the cabildo submitted to Madrid a lengthy complaint against what it described as the violation of its authority and ursurpation of its jurisdiction by President-Intendant Joaquín del Pino, whose conduct it had commended only three years previously. Pino was in fact a fair-minded administrator, and in this case the initiative came from the cabildo. It protested that its right of appointing the town doctor had been violated by the intendant, who, with the support of the fiscal of the Audiencia of Charcas, Victorián de Villava, had removed its nominee and appointed his own. In the sphere of public works the intendant had rejected a contract given by the cabildo to one of its regidores for the repair of a bridge at an estimate of 500 pesos, and commissioned a contractor of his own choice at 600 pesos, which the cabildo considered an exorbitant charge on the town funds. Generalizing from these and other particulars, the cabildo made an eloquent appeal for independence and municipal liberty, for freedom of votes and acceptancy of majority decisions, ending with the remark: "We now feel that the city is no longer represented in its cabildo but in the vote of the fiscal and the will of the president.''[92]

The cabildo asked the crown for a judgment, and a royal cédula of September 15, 1787, requested the Audiencia of Charcas to collect information and forward its opinion. The audiencia accepted the intendant's case that he had authority in matters of public welfare, and judged that the complaints of the cabildo were unjustified.[93] It would be a mistake to regard the attitude of the cabildo in this case as entirely progressive, or the result of the intendant's policy entirely oppressive. The cabildo regretfully reported that its authority and prestige had suffered so much from these rebuffs that the offices of regidores could no longer find purchasers and had consequently depreciated greatly in value. Thus there were no longer any proprietory councillors, and they all had to be elected annually.[94] The intendant had unwittingly liberalized the municipal régime but the cabildo of Chuquisaca was quite unconscious of the irony.

In Córdoba the happy period of co-operation between intendant and cabildo came to an end in 1798, when a series of electoral disputes between the cabildo and the temporary intendant initiated a period of administrative sterility.[95] The situation worsened with the arrival of the new intendant, José González, a man of choleric disposition and domineering temperament. He was sworn into office on December 4, 1803, and one of his first acts was to demand that all the records of the municipal archive should be copied so that he could be precisely informed about the privileges of the cabildo. The latter considered that its province was being invaded and yielded with such reluctance that the intendant dropped the matter. A few days later the cabildo took the initiative and demanded that the intendant pay the 10,000 pesos security to which he was bound by the title of his appointment. Gonzales retorted that ''it ought not to waste the precious time of its sessions in useless affairs.'' Nevertheless the cabildo stuck to the point and informed the viceroy repeatedly until by September 1805 the intendant had fulfilled his obligation.[96]

In a note of June 11, 1804, González informed the cabildo that it

[92] Cabildo of La Plata to Crown, Nov. 20, 1796, AGI, Aud. de Charcas, leg. 589.

[93] R. C. Sept. 15, 1797, and Informe de la Audiencia de Charcas, July 25, 1800, AGI, Aud. de Charcas, leg. 589.

[94] Cabildo of La Plata to Crown, Nov. 20, 1796, *Ibid.*

[95] Garzón, *op. cit.*, pp. 61-63, 391-406.

[96] *Ibid.*, pp. 75-80.

was "no more than a representative economic body, incapable of determining anything itself without the intervention of the governor."[97] The reply of the cabildo was to draw a comparison between the régime of Sobremonte and the present state of affairs. But there was no improvement under the next intendant, Gutiérrez de la Concha, who took office on December 28, 1807. An immediate election dispute ensured that for the whole of 1808 the cabildo was dominated by a party hostile to the intendant. This feud was nourished by an excessive legal formalism and petty disputes over public ceremonial and precedence which were a perennial breeding ground of bad feeling in Spanish colonial society, especially in the small isolated communities of the interior.[98] Then, in the elections of January 1809, the two cabildo nominees for senior alcalde and procurator were refused confirmation by the intendant who appointed others in their place. In the subsequent appeal the cabildo's case was defended by Mariano Moreno, then a lawyer in Buenos Aires and relator of the audiencia. He declined to labor the point that a majority vote decided municipal elections and that this obliged the superior authorities to confirm the choice of the cabildo unless there were legitimate legal objections, and went on to argue that "the most precious prerogative of the cabildos is the private right of electing the councillors who are to compose it," a privilege too important to remain exposed to capricious usurpation or to a "stroke of despotism."[99]

Comparable tension also existed in La Paz, where the genesis of the revolution of 1809 which deposed the intendant lay mostly in cabildo activity.[100] La Paz was in a state of unrest from 1805 onwards, and this became more acute in the early months of 1809 when news arrived of revolutionary developments in Buenos Aires. In March the intendant reported that the cabildo had been occupied in secret nocturnal sessions.[101] Simultaneously the Spanish authorities started squabbling among themselves. Dávila, the temporary intendant, accused the inspector of the exchequer in La Paz, González de Prada, of engaging in subversive activities and of planning, in conjunction with certain members of the cabildo, to remove Dávila from the intendancy and substitute himself.[102] These assertions need

[97] *Ibid.*, p. 80. [98] *Ibid.*, pp. 85-86, 103-104, for examples.

[99] Moreno, *Escritos*, I, 302, 311. In a similar case in Corrientes in January 1808 Moreno used like arguments on behalf of the cabildo, *Ibid.*, I, 171-180.

[100] M. M. Pinto, *La revolución de la intendencia de la Paz en el virreynato del Río de la Plata, con la ocurrencia de Chuquisaca* (Buenos Aires, 1909), p. 57.

[101] Intendant Dávila to Viceroy Liniers, Mar. 17, 1809, Biblioteca Nacional, Madrid, MS 13150, fol. 2v.

[102] Dávila to Liniers, Nov. 17, 1808, Bishop of La Paz to Liniers, Nov. 16, 1808, Bishop of La Paz to Dávila, Oct. 27, 1808, *Ibid.*, fols. 5-9.

not be taken at their face value: it was probable that Dávila was trying to hide financial mismanagement or even peculation, and resented the inspection of González; the latter denied the charges and claimed that they arose out of personal malice. But the latent hostility between intendant and cabildo is obvious, and the cabildo was able to take advantage of the evident disunity among the authorities. After the events of May 25 and 26 in Chuquisaca where the audiencia deposed the intendant, the conspirators came out into the open. Under the direction of a mestizo soldier, Pedro Domingo Murillo, the commandant of the fort, the revolutionaries deposed the intendant and the cabildo took charge of the government in La Paz. Later it constituted itself as a junta, under the presidency of Murillo. The insurgents tried to clothe the action of revolt in loyal terms. On September 16 the cabildo wrote to the viceroy affirming their loyalty to him and to Ferdinand VII, and assuring him of the continuation of municipal government.[103] Then, calling itself a representative junta, the cabildo initiated proceedings against Intendant Dávila before the audiencia of Charcas in order to clarify the events of the insurrection of July 16, and to affirm its loyalty. But this maneuver made little progress, nor did the representations deceive anyone in Buenos Aires.[104] The viceroy advised the cabildo of La Paz to maintain government until the arrival of a new intendant and meanwhile to restore the ministers whom they had deposed.[105] But this advice was simply a cloak for more violent action. The viceroy of Peru sent an army against the insurgents; by the end of October the junta was overthrown, and Murillo and his companions were put to death without mercy.

But the most vigorous defence of municipal liberty and opposition to arbitrary government came from the cabildo of Buenos Aires. Relations between the viceroy and cabildo deteriorated precisely under the régime of Sobremonte, whose character and behaviour underwent a strange metamorphosis after his appointment as viceroy in April, 1804. The part played by the cabildo in the critical events of the summer of 1806 when Buenos Aires was invaded by a British expedition, and its role in the reconquest, gave it a moral ascendancy over the viceroy which it was able to turn to good account. The viceroy refused to confirm the elections of 1807, arguing that in the critical circumstances of another imminent invasion experienced councillors should remain in office yet another year. The cabildo re-

[103] Cabildo of La Paz to Cisneros, Sept. 16, 1809, *Ibid.*, fols. 21-22.

[104] *Ibid.*, fols. 24-30.

[105] Cisneros to Cornel, Aug. 22, 1809, BM, Add. MS 32,609, fols. 157-160.

jected this argument and appealed to the audiencia; as Sobremonte was nowhere to be found at the time the audiencia confirmed the elections within two days, and the viceroy sent a lame approval later.[106] Sobremonte's answer to the British invasion of the Río de la Plata was to collect the treasury and make for Córdoba on the pretext of going to raise troops. In 1807 he was arrested by deputies of the cabildo of Buenos Aires near Montevideo and detained in a monastery in Buenos Aires. He was then deposed by the cabildo and the audiencia, and the latter was left temporarily as the depositary of royal authority.

Meanwhile the cabildo's denouncement of maladministration became more and more outspoken. Already on July 3, 1806, it had written to its attorney in Madrid reporting Sobremonte's conduct in the early period of the crisis. Then in secret dispatches to Madrid in May and July 1807 it instructed its attorney to impede the appointment of Santiago Liniers, the hero of the reconquest of Buenos Aires, as viceroy, for it considered him ill-suited for the command of the viceroyalty.[107] In a representation to the government dated September 13, 1808, it requested the appointment of a worthy viceroy, and stated its conviction that

> "Corruption in all departments of government has arrived at its extreme . . . Justice is administered without any subjection to the law; administration knows no rules; the exchequer is managed without economy and with criminal indolence; . . . for many years America has had to suffer corrupt and despotic leaders, ignorant and venal ministers, inefficient and cowardly soldiers."[108]

The vigorous example set by Buenos Aires in these years appealed to the other towns of the viceroyalty, and a growing consciousness of their rights and duties radiated to the other cabildos. Buenos Aires came to be regarded as a leader and protector in municipal politics. When the cabildo of Asunción del Paraguay planned to form a constitution for itself modelled on that of Buenos Aires, and submitted its scheme to the audiencia, the latter requested the cabildo of Buenos Aires to furnish a copy of its ordinances and constitutions for its information. In December, 1805, the audiencia ordered the

[106] *ACBA,* IV. ii. 389-421. See also J. M. Saenz Valiente, "Los alcaldes de Buenos Aires en 1806," *Boletín del instituto de investigaciones históricas,* XVII (1933-34), pp. 105-118. In the cabildo of 1806 Europeans formed the majority; only four were creoles, *Ibid.,* p. 101.

[107] *ACBA,* IV. ii. 533, 643.

[108] Cabildo of Buenos Aires, Sept. 13, 1808, AGI, Aud. de Buenos Aires. leg. 157.

cabildo to submit a similar record to the municipality of Córdoba.[109] In April 1807 the cabildo of Asunción was in conflict with the newly appointed temporary intendant of Paraguay, and naturally sought the patronage of the cabildo of Buenos Aires for its appeal before the audiencia.[110] For their part almost all the cabildos in the viceroyalty, and many beyond, rallied around Buenos Aires with generous gifts of money in 1807 for the repulse of the British invasions.[111] By now the metropolis was conscious of its ascendancy, and in December 1807, in requesting the title of "Defender of South America and Protector of the Cabildos of the Viceroyalty of La Plata," it posed as the leader of municipal life in the viceroyalty, the benefactor who could help its poor neighbours, "the organ whereby the complaints of the cabildos reach Your Majesty and through which they receive Your graces."[112] Buenos Aires was already prepared for its role in the revolution for independence.

[109] *ACBA*, IV. ii. 151, 192.
[110] *Ibid.*, IV. ii. 529.
[111] *Ibid.*, IV. ii. 490-650.
[112] Moreno, *Escritos*, I, 162-164, Dec. 30, 1807.

8

Magistracy and Society in Colonial Brazil

Stuart B. Schwartz

THE GOVERNMENT and society of the Portuguese empire formed two interlocking systems of organization. In one of them a metropolitan-directed administration, characterized by categorical and impersonal relations, joined the individual or corporation to the political institutions that constituted formal government. In the other system interpersonal primary relations were based on extended families and kinship groups (*parentelas*), shared corporate or social status and goals, and common economic interests. To understand properly the operation of government in colonial Brazil one must examine the interaction of these two systems and the relations of government employees with other socioeconomic groups. The following analysis will deal with the Portuguese professional bureaucrats, not only as performers of specific political functions but also as dynamic participants in the complex relations that made up Brazilian colonial society.

For historical and theoretical reasons magistrates formed the core of the Portuguese imperial bureaucracy. At the center of each town in the Portuguese empire stood the *pelourinho* (pillory), symbol of justice and royal authority. Its location at the core of the community bespoke the Portuguese medieval concept of kingship which stressed the role of the monarch as dispenser of justice and protector of the poor and weak.[1] This close identification of King and Justice led quite naturally to the embodiment of royal authority in the judicial-administrative officers of the realm. This group, the magisterial bureaucrats, rose to power with the dynastic revolution of 1383 that brought the House of Aviz to the Portuguese throne.[2] Thereafter, the demands of royal centralization and the development of a

[1] Martim de Albuquerque, *O poder político no renascimento português* (Lisbon, 1968), 146, 152.

[2] Henrique da Gama Barros, *História da administração pública em Portugal* (2nd ed., 11 vols., Lisbon, 1945-1954), III, 256-258; Marcello Caetano, "As Cortes de 1385," *Revista Portuguêsa de História*, V (1951), 5-86. See also António Borges Coelho, *A Revolução de 1383* (Lisbon, 1965).

councillor structure of government depended increasingly on the magisterial bureaucrats. What resulted was a kind of symbiotic relationship, since the importance of the magistrates as a class proceeded directly from royal authority, while the King relied on the performance and loyalty of the magistrates to achieve and maintain this authority.

The rise of the magisterial bureaucracy did not go unnoticed or unchallenged. Other groups in Portugal, the landed and military nobility and the metropolitan municipal councils, opposed the social ascendancy of the bureaucrats and the concomitant political dominance of the Crown. This opposition was often expressed as anti-legal sentiments, criticism of lawyers and scribes who seemed to inherit without effort the privileges of the nobility in Portugal and the conquests of the soldiers beyond the Algarve.[3] By the mid-seventeenth century the parties to the conflict were ardently debating the relative value of arms or letters to the empire. Magnates in Portugal, soldiers in India, and sugar planters in Brazil all complained against lawyers and the legal class.[4] Their protestations were in vain, for although the military nobility continued in high positions in colonies and councils, much of the business of empire and the structure of government had come irretrievably into the hands of the professional bureaucrats.[5]

[3] In defense of "Letters" see João Pedro Ribeiro, *Preferencia das letras ás armas* (Lisbon, 1645), and "Información en la causa de los estudios de Portugal" (Madrid, 1633), ms 4162 in the Biblioteca Nacional de Madrid (BNM). The best exposition of the contrary opinion is in Francisco Manuel de Mello, *Espanáforas de Várias História Portuguêsa* (Coimbra, 1931), 20-21. It is interesting to note that at the Cortes of Thomar (1581) one of the demands which the nobility made on Philip II of Spain was that nobles be employed in high colonial posts rather than lawyers, as had become the custom. The King's answer was evasive. See *Capítulos do Stado da Nobreza*, Archivo General de Simancas (AGS) Estado, Negociaciones de Portugal 427.

[4] The typical charges were that justice was expensive and slow and that magistrates engaged in a good deal of the seventeenth- and eighteenth-century equivalents of ambulance chasing. Such complaints often moved colonial councils in Portugal to consider placing a limitation on the number of magistrates and abolishing overseas tribunals. Suggestions to abolish the High Court of Goa were heard in 1688, and the Marquis of Pombal suspended that tribunal temporarily between 1750 and 1759. See Biblioteca Geral da Universidade de Coimbra (BGUC), Cod. 548 (Lisbon, June 10, 1688), f. 23 and Carlos Renato Gonçalves Pereira, *História da administração da justiça no Estado da Índia* (2 vols., Lisbon, 1965). For anti-legal sentiments in India see Diogo do Couto, *O soldado prático* (2nd ed., Lisbon, 1954), 30-32; for similar statements about metropolitan Portugal, Francisco Rodriguez de Silveira, *Memorials de um soldado da Índia (1585-1634)* (Lisbon, 1877), 191-193; and for Brazil, Engel Sluiter (ed.), "Report on the State of Brazil 1612," *HAHR*, XXIX (November 1949), 518-562.

[5] Paulo Merea, "Da minha gaveta: Os secretários do Estado do antigo

In theory, the Portuguese monarch made all political decisions. In practice, however, the complexities of government forced him to lean heavily on various administrative and advisory councils, especially for those matters requiring specific knowledge or technical competence. In the daily process of decision-making the King's signature often became a rubber stamp for conciliar suggestions. Two Secretaries of State at court acted as intermediaries between King and councils, but they did not assume any significance until the union of Spain and Portugal in 1580. Rarely did they influence policy, and in colonial affairs it was only after 1750 and the rise of the Marquis of Pombal that Colonial Secretaries replaced the Overseas Council as creators of policy.

Unlike the Spanish government, that of Portugal never fully divided its conciliar system by geographical areas or between metropolis and colonies. Thus, between 1550 and 1808 there were three specifically colonial councils: the Treasury Council (Conselho da Fazenda, 1594-1641), the India Council (Conselho da Índia, 1604-1614), and the Overseas Council (Conselho Ultramarino, 1642-1808). None of these ever controlled all aspects of Imperial government,[6] and other bodies continued to play a part in colonial affairs. The Board of Conscience (Mesa da Consciência e Ordens) resolved moral and theological problems in both metropolis and colonies, handling matters as diverse as student riots at Coimbra and ecclesiastical benefices in Brazil. More central to this study, a Board of Justice (Desembargo do Paço) exercised in its sphere appointive, regulatory, and policy formation functions throughout the empire.

Designed as the apex of the judicial system, the Board of Justice had responsibility for the recruitment, promotion, procedures, and standards of the magisterial bureaucrats. Despite considerable jurisdictional conflict with the specifically colonial councils, the Board of Justice never relinquished its control over the judicial-administrative aspects of government.[7] In effect, the goals and standards of the magisterial bureaucrats were established and maintained by professionals who had risen to the Board of Justice. As a result, the

regímen,'' *Boletim da Faculdade de Direito da Universidade de Coimbra*, XL (1964), 173-189. The post of colonial secretary was created in 1736.

[6] Curiously the Treasury Council and the Overseas Council have never received monographic treatment. On the India Council see Francisco Paulo Mendes da Luz, *O Conselho da Índia* (Lisbon, 1952).

[7] *Anais da Biblioteca Nacional de Rio de Janeiro* (*ABNR*), XXXIX, 94-95, is a consulta of the Conselho Ultramarino of 1661 noting conflicts with the Desembargo do Paço. Mendes da Luz, *O Conselho* deals with conflicts between that organ and the Desembargo do Paço.

bureaucracy enjoyed a degree of autonomy, professionalism, and relatively high standards.

In the New World, the magisterial bureaucrats shared authority with other branches of government in a complex arrangement of checks and balances. After 1621 Portuguese America was divided into two large administrative units, the States of Maranhão and Brazil.[8] Each was ruled by a governor-general and subdivided into a number of captaincies administered by governors who also bore the title of captain. These officers, usually military men of aristocratic background, formed an executive group as direct representatives of the Crown. Although the captaincies were theoretically centralized symmetrically under the governor-general, centralization and symmetry were never achieved. Governors-general in Bahia often found it impossible to control subordinate governors in Rio de Janeiro and Pernambuco.[9] Moreover, all officials and in fact "even the meanest vassal" were encouraged to communicate directly with the King thus providing him with multiple sources of information while allowing subordinate and coordinate officials a certain degree of autonomy.[10]

Within the formal table of organization the magistrates constituted a second level of administration, balancing the authority of the governors and checking the independence of the municipal councils (*câmaras*), which characteristically represented dominant local interest groups. The first royal magistrate (*ouvidor geral*) arrived in Brazil in 1549 to perform his traditional functions as judge and defender of royal prerogatives. Relatively inefficient successors followed, and not until 1609 was a larger group of magistrates sent to Brazil.[11] In that year, as the result of judicial reform instigated by Spain in Portugal, a high court or Relação staffed by ten magistrates (*desembargadores*) and a number of minor officials arrived in Brazil.

[8] The State of Maranhão remained a separate entity until 1774. Judicial-administrative matters were appealed from Maranhão to the metropolitan Casa da Suplecação rather than to the Relação of Bahia.

[9] Dauril Alden, *Royal Government in Colonial Brazil* (Berkeley, 1968), 30-44.

[10] The Overseas Council made a special point of encouraging such correspondence and it rigorously reprimanded any official who tried to limit it. See Arquivo Histórico Ultramarino (AHU), Bahia papeis auvlsos caixa 4, 1ª série não catalogoda (April 26, 1645). Powerful individuals in Brazil, however, occasionally bribed ship captains not to carry such reports to Portugal as the "Rezoes g. darão os moradores para não se extinguir a Relação" clearly states. See Biblioteca Nacional de Lisboa (BNL), Coleção Pombalina 647, ff. 69-72.

[11] Stuart B. Schwartz, "The High Court of Bahia: A Study in Hapsburg Brazil 1580-1630" (Ph.D. dissertation, Columbia University, 1968), especially chapter 1. The number was increased to twelve in 1658. See *Documentos Históricos da Biblioteca Nacional de Rio de Janeiro* (*DHBNR*), LXVI, 146.

The Relação became the core of the magisterial bureaucracy in Brazil. Eventually provincial magistrates (*ouvidores*) in the captaincies and after 1696 royal municipal magistrates (*juizes de fora*) also served, but they remained professionally and jurisdictionally below the high court.[12]

A myriad lesser officials at the captaincy and municipal levels characterized the lower echelons of government. As early as 1552, the perceptive Jesuit, Manuel da Nóbrega, pleaded for more colonists and fewer government employees who wanted "nothing more than to do their time and collect their pay . . ., and as this is their principal goal they do not love the land and all their affection is for Portugal."[13] By the seventeenth century Brazilians held many of these offices, but the effect of the change was not wholly invigorating. Colonials were anxious to become a "child of the paymaster" (*filho da folha*) and the tendency was for these offices to multiply without improving in performance.[14]

Offices in the lower echelons of government were often rife with venality and incompetence. These posts were traditionally granted as rewards or favors; the usual response of the Crown to a legitimate petition was to promise "some office of justice or the treasury." Under both the Hapsburgs and the Braganças there was considerable purchase of office, often with hereditary control.[15] Pluralism (holding more than one office) was condoned and the use of deputies (*serventia*) a common practice.[16] Instances of municipal councillors

[12] Sebastião da Rocha Pitta, *História da América portuguêsa* (Lisbon, 1880), 242-243. Juizes de fora should not be confused with the nonprofessional elected municipal judges, the *juizes ordinários*.

[13] Serafim Leite (ed.), *Cartas do Brasil e mais escritos do P. Manuel da Nóbrega (opera omnia)* (Coimbra, 1955), 114.

[14] Offices multiplied for various reasons. Governors and magistrates often tried to get their friends and relatives on the payroll. Moreover, the sale of offices became a source of revenue for the Crown. See for example *DHBNR*, XXXVIII. D. João de Castro to Ouvidor Christovão Soares Reimão. Unfortunately, there is no study on the sale of office in the Portuguese empire. For posts requiring technical competence (reading and writing) it was usually stipulated that the applicant be apt. In Brazil this was often impossible to enforce. Although an *alvará* of November 13, 1642 stated that only those people who could read and write could serve as judges, circumstances forced the Crown to abandon this position.

[15] For example, among the offices sold in Rio de Janeiro in 1664 were probate judge (juiz dos orfãos); court clerk (escrivão da correição); bailiff (meirinho da correição); and three notarial offices. *ABNR*, XXXIX, 104-105.

[16] Pluralism was not permitted among the magisterial bureaucrats although they sometimes inherited or purchased minor offices which they sold or rented. Desembargador João Elizeu de Sousa owned a treasury office in Cachoeira, Bahia.

and elected judges who were functional illiterates and of notaries who could scarcely sign their own name occurred from time to time.[17]

Such incompetence was unknown, however, within the ranks of magisterial bureaucrats, whose central role in the formal structure of government and royally sanctioned position as guardians of that structure rested on their competence and professionalization. A short discussion of the professional and private lives of these men, therefore, may illumine our analysis.[18]

The Board of Justice administered a personal and professional examination to all those seeking entry into the ranks of the royal bureaucracy. The applicant was expected to be a graduate in civil or canon law from the University of Coimbra with at least two years of practice as a lawyer.[19] Socially he was expected to be the legitimate son of honorable and orthodox parents. More precisely, anyone who had artisan or shopkeeper forebears or whose family was tainted with the blood of "New Christian, Moor, Mulatto, or other infected race" was theoretically prohibited from royal service.[20] The extent

---

Arquivo Nacional de Torre do Tombo (ANTT), Chancelaria de D. João V, Livro 78, f. 63v.

[17] Arquivo Público de Estado da Bahia (APEB), Ordens Régias Livro 5, No. 38. King to D. João de Lencastre, Governor of Brazil (Lisbon, February 15, 1698) noted that even though rural judges could not read or write, it did not matter as long as their clerks could do so.

[18] The following analysis is based on the collective biographies of the 167 magistrates (desembargadores) who served in the High Court (Relação) of Bahia from 1609 to 1759. See José António Caldas, *Notícia geral da toda esta capitania da Bahia desde o seu descombrimento até o presente ano de 1759* (Salvador, 1959). For biographical information the series Leitura dos Bachareis in the Arquivo Nacional de Torre do Tombo (ANTT) was most helpful and when deficient the records of matriculation (*verbetes*) in the Arquivo da Universidade de Coimbra filled many gaps. Professional careers were traced in the ANTT chancellery books of Felipe II, III, D. João IV, Afonso VI, Pedro II, João V, and José I. Also the Livro dos assentos dos bachareis do Desembargo do Paço, BGUC, Cod. 644 proved helpful. The following categories were used in tabulating this material: place and date of birth; father's occupation; university degree; date of entry into royal service; positions held before entering the Bahian tribunal; date of entry in the Relação; posterior service; special characteristics (e.g., membership in a military order, marriage in Brazil, etc.).

[19] José Justiano Andrade e Silva, *Collecção chronológica da legislação portugueza (1603-1700)* (10 vols., Lisbon, 1854-1859), IV (June 19, 1649).

[20] Sons of those artisan guild members who had been elected to the joint artisan assembly (Casa de vinte quatro) were eligible to serve in the royal bureaucracy. See Andrade e Silva, *Collecção*, IV (December 16, 1644), VI (May 26, 1663). Four desembargadores in Brazil were the sons of members of the Casa do vinte quatro. Five others were allowed into the service despite other "impediments." On the Casa do vinte quatro see Franz-Paul Langhans, *As Corporações dos Ofícios Mecânicos. Subsídios para a sua história* (2 vols., Lisbon, 1943).

to which a friend at court or family connections influenced career patterns is obscure, but it seems unlikely that positions of magisterial rank were bought outright. Some nepotism was institutionalized, since the sons of magistrates were given preferential treatment.[21] Clandestine purchase and nepotism, however, did not imply a complete breakdown of performance or standards, since the required competence examination by the Board of Justice insured at least minimal qualifications of all appointees. Still, personal influence vied with seniority as the principal requisite for promotion. Performance was evaluated by successful completion of the incumbency examination (*residência*), and thus a premium was placed on adherence to norms rather than on innovation or outstanding achievement.

The magistrates who served in Brazil between 1609 and 1759 came from social groups of middle rank. In a statistical sample of 100 high court magistrates, the sons of merchants, soldiers, and artisans were more numerous than those who claimed noble (*fidalgo*) origins. Far more significant, 13 percent were the sons of minor and municipal officials and 22 percent of university-trained lawyers and bureaucrats. In fact, a legist class is represented in these figures. Sons followed fathers into the university and then into royal service. These men often married the daughters of other bureaucrats so that endogamy and class perpetuation became identifiable characteristics of the group. *Filho da pez sabe nadar* (the fish's son knows how to swim), the Portuguese equivalent of "the apple doesn't fall far from the tree" was often true. A good illustration was António Rodrigues Banha, who entered the high court of Bahia in 1729 and whose father and maternal grandfather had both preceded him in that tribunal. Such a case was not uncommon in Portuguese bureaucracy.[22]

The typical high court magistrate in Brazil entered royal service at age 26. First he served a three-year term in Portugal as a royal municipal judge. Then he was moved to another town and reap-

[21] There are many examples of this. Pero Nogueira Coelho, magistrate in India, petitioned for a metropolitan post "as your Majesty usually gives . . . to people of quality and especially to sons of desembargadores." See BGUC, Cod. 460, *Consulta* of the Board of Justice (January 26, 1636), ff. 59-61. In Brazil, Cristovão Salema de Carvalho asked for a position and was granted it because his father was a desembargador. During the following century, Manuel da Costa Bonicho was made desembargador in Bahia because his father was a successful magistrate. Cf. *DHBNR*, LXVI, King to Count of Odemira (June 5, 1655), 88; BGUC, Cod. 709 (December 20, 1712), f.149.

[22] His father was Dionízio de Azevedo e Arevalos, who entered the High Court of Bahia in 1713. His maternal grandfather and namesake was António Rodrigues Banha, who had entered the tribunal in 1680 and who had married a Brazilian.

pointed at the same level or promoted as provincial magistrate (ouvidor) for a similar term. After about 15 years of service on the average, the magistrate expected promotion to a high court, and it was precisely at this juncture that, prior to 1680, most of the magistrates came to Brazil. Before that date many tried to avoid Brazilian service, but by the end of the century a post in the Bahian high court was ardently sought as an important step up the promotional ladder, and the excess of deserving magistrates forced the Crown to make supernumerary appointments.[23] After six to eight years of service in Brazil the bureaucrat could expect to return to a position in the Oporto Relação and the Supreme Court of Appeals (Casa da Suplicaçâo) in Lisbon.[24]

This career pattern meant that the age of the average high court magistrate on arrival in Brazil was 42 and that he had been seasoned by fifteen years of professional experience. These men, therefore, were senior magistrates of proven competence and loyalty. In the last years of the sixteenth century direct promotion from subordinate colonial positions to posts in the Relação became common. After 1682, 42 percent of those who served in the Bahian tribunal had previous colonial experience and 70 percent of these in Brazil. Thus only at the end of the century did a colonial sub-system begin to form, and even then prior or subsequent service in the metropolis was never excluded to colonial magistrates.[25]

Only in rare and exceptional cases did magistrates who had served earlier in Portuguese India discharge professional duties in Brazil.[26] However, those who served in the West African colonies—

[23] Of the first ten appointed in 1609 nine sought to be excused from what seemed to be occupational exile. By the end of the seventeenth century, however, the title of desembargador do Brasil was sought by and granted to overseas ouvidores. Supernumerary appointments were made as early as 1705, although they were not fully regularized until 1718. See Schwartz, "The High Court," chap. II; ANTT, Chancelaria D. Pedro II, Livro 23, f. 119; Livro 29, f. 236; BGUC, Cod. 709, f. 154.

[24] Out of the desembargadores who saw service in Portugal after returning from Brazil, 83 percent reached Oporto and 52 percent served in the Casa da Suplicação.

[25] After 1680 magistrates began to arrive in Brazil as ouvidores without previous metropolitan experience.

[26] The expeditions were Jorge Seco de Macedo, who was appointed chancellor of the Bahian tribunal in 1655 after service in India and in the Casa da Suplicação, and Ignácio Dias Madeira, sent from Goa to Brazil in 1736. See AHU, Bahia papeis auvlsos caixa 6, 1ª não catalogada (November 27, 1654); ANTT, Chancelaria D. João V, Livro 92, f. 312 (November 25, 1736). Joaquim Veríssimo Serrão (*Do Brasil filipino ao Brasil de 1640* [São Paulo, 1968]) claims that Antão de Mesquita also served in India but Veríssimo Serrão has confused him with another man of the same name.

Angola, Cabo Verde, São Tomé, and Guiné—were often promoted to the Bahian high court. There were, in effect, two colonial channels of promotion, which we can call the Indian Ocean and the Atlantic Ocean branches. Both were integrated into the metropolitan system, but they remained distinct from each other. Only 15 percent of the magistrates who saw service in Brazil rose to conciliar positions in Portugal. This fact indicates that the highest levels of government were filled by officials who had risen by direct metropolitan appointment or through the Indian Ocean branch. If the magistrates in Brazil perceived this inequality, they may have been more willing to exploit their immediate position for personal gain since adherence to bureaucratic norms did not insure the achievement of their highest professional aspirations.

Although the ecclesiastical bureaucracy lies beyond the scope of this discussion, the function of the Church as an administrative arm should at least be noted. The King exercised control of the Church in matters temporal, and churchmen, both regular and secular, performed tasks of direct benefit to royal government. The influence of the Church pervaded society, and for many Brazilians the parish stood as the most immediate and recognizable institution of organization. Moreover, despite much jurisdictional conflict between civil and ecclesiastical officials in the colony, Church doctrine generally supported the Crown and the dominant theory of government.

Control over the official hierarchy, over colonial officials and colonial affairs depended on regulation, jurisdictional overlap, multiple lines of communication, and shared, if not conflicting, powers. Blurred and disputed lines of authority meant constant reference to Portugal and arbitration by metropolitan councils. Statutes and royal commands combined with periodic and extraordinary investigations (*devassas*) to stop abuses, insure honesty, and assure compliance with expected behavior. Each official from viceroy to doorkeeper of the customshouse lived under the shadow of a terminal examination (*residência*) which would come at the end of his incumbency,[27] and this too was expected to check misbehavior in office.

In this system of countervailing powers and institutionalized mechanisms of metropolitan control, the Relação and the subordinate royal magistrates were the principal cogs. Considered by the Crown as the most loyal and efficient body of officials, they were charged

[27] A typical residência can be seen in the documents printed in *Livro primeiro do govêrno do Brasil 1607-1633* (Rio de Janeiro, 1958), 333-411.

with preventing the dominance of any political and economic force in the colony, while maintaining the prerogatives and standards of the Crown. It was the magisterial bureaucrats who conducted the various investigations and the judicial review and who staffed special advisory councils and administrative boards.[28] To control the magistrates, the Crown depended on certain regulatory powers of the governor-general within the system of checks and balances and on the multiple lines of communication. Probably to an even greater degree, the Crown looked on the professional standards and goals of the magistrates, on mechanisms such as rotation in office, and on their collective ties to royal power as means of keeping them subservient to royal desires.

These men of non-noble gentry and professional backgrounds hoped to find in the promotional channels of the bureaucracy a means for status gratification and social ascendancy. Upper magistrates considered themselves the social equals of the titled and landed nobility in Portugal. By the eighteenth century jurists argued that the study of law literally enobled an individual. Also by the accretion of rewards and titles the professional bureaucracy began to identify with the attitudes and aspirations of their former class and political rivals.[29] A certain amount of group consciousness, however, kept the magisterial bureaucrats from becoming simply integrated into the nobility. The means by which they sought to fulfill their particular status and financial desires within their professional position form the links between formal and informal government in Brazil.

The Crown was not unaware of these personal and class aspirations and realized that the role of the magistrates in the formal structure of government would be compromised by extra-professional contacts. Thus the Crown tried to isolate the bureaucrats from the pressures of individual, familial, or class interests. Statutes sought to separate the judges from Brazilian society by limiting their residence, social relations, dress, and habits. No magistrate, for example, was to marry in the area of his jurisdiction or to enter into

[28] The governor-general appointed desembargadores for special investigations and circuit tours of inspection. Magistrates were made members of bodies such as the Mint or, after 1759, the Boards of Inspection which regulated agricultural commerce. In the course of time magistrates acquired additional duties. By 1730 the position of Ouvidor carried with it the position of Provedor and Juiz dos órfãos.

[29] On these claims to nobility see Francisco de Almeida e Amaral Bottelho, *Discursos jurídicos em que se contém várias matérias úteis aos principantes com os assentos da Caza da Supplicação* (Lisbon, 1790), 97-111.

business there.[30] To lift the magistrates above society the Crown invested them with great authority, paid them substantial salaries, and granted them membership in the honorific military orders.[31]

These measures, designed to reinforce the authority and effectiveness of the magistrates in a society deeply respectful of ascriptive status, had two unforseen consequences. First, the bureaucrats, with their shared university background, esprit de corps, and group consciousness, could articulate policies or desires independent of the Crown's goals.[32] This, however, they rarely did. More commonly the magistrates used their authority and prestige for personal or familial aggrandizement. Though salaries were high, graft and malfeasance, for example, did not disappear. Instead the access to more capital increased the opportunities for magistrates to invest in prohibited business ventures. Seen from another angle, the dignity, authority, and wealth of the magistrates did not isolate them at all from an awed society. Quite to the contrary, their prestige made them seem more attractive allies to important socio-economic groups, especially the dominant planter oligarchy. The role—or more exactly roles—of the magistrates presented a paradox. On the one hand, disinterested magisterial bureaucrats formed the keystone of the formal governmental structure erected by the Crown. But on the other, they pursued individual and collective goals and entered into a variety of personal relations that openly conflicted with their expected professional behavior.

Brazil contained various means for creating an extensive "social genealogy"—the web of both kin and other primary relations.[33] Curiously, just as Church doctrine and officials had bolstered the formal political structure, so Church-sponsored marriage, godparent-

[30] Fernando Mendes de Almeida (ed.), *Ordenações filipinas (1603)* (3 vols., São Paulo, 1957), I, tit. xcv; Andrade e Silva, *Coll. chron.*, I, 113, 295. After 1615 all married magistrates sent to Brazil were expected to bring their wives. On the limitations of commerce see BGUC, Cod. 71, f. 134, Law of August 29, 1720.

[31] The chancellor's salary was second only to that of the governors-general. The desembargadores not only received respectable salaries, but were also given expense accounts while on circuit tours and life insurance provisions for their families. Appointment to the Court in Brazil often carried with it promise of a membership in one of the military orders and of a position in a superior tribunal in Portugal.

[32] S. N. Eisenstadt, "The Political Orientations of Bureaucracies in Centralized Empires," *Essays in Comparative Institutions of Social Change* (New York, 1965), 216-250.

[33] This term is used and explained in the excellent analysis by Anthony Leeds, "Brazilian Careers and Social Structure: An Evolutionary Model and a Case History," *American Anthropologist*, LXVI (December 1964), 1329.

age, and religious brotherhoods supplied vital integration to the informal structure. Although expressly forbidden by law, high court and lesser magisterial bureaucrats in Brazil did marry Brazilians.[34] Twenty-six magistrates of the Bahian High Court (15%) married in Brazil, and although the social origins of all the brides have not been ascertained, it is clear that many were daughters of the planter oligarchy or of other government officials.[35] A second institution for creating social linkage was that of ritual godparentage (*compadrio*) which created close ties and placed mutual obligations on all parties concerned. Magistrates, their retainers, relatives, and friends also entered into these ritual relationships, thereby extending their obligations and influence.[36] It should be made clear, however, that the nature of Brazilian society and the social aspirations of the magistrates limited most of these personal relations to the highest strata of colonial society. Chances are slim indeed that the marginal mulatto, the enslaved Negro, or even the Portuguese cobbler ever became the compadre or the brother-in-law of a magistrate.[37]

In their search for financial gain and status positions concomitant with their rank, the magisterial bureaucrats in Brazil also cre-

[34] The marriage of magistrates was prohibited by an *alvará* of November 22, 1610 which was reinforced by a law of March 24, 1734. Cf. Andrade e Silva, *Coll. chron.*, I, 295; BGUC, Cod. 711 (March 24, 1734). In order to marry within the area of his jurisdiction, a magistrate had to petition for special permission such as that granted to Manoel Pinto da Rocha in 1611. See ANTT, Chancelaria Filipe II, privilégios, Livro 2, f. 196v. Failure to obtain this permission could result in suspension and recall. See BGUC, Cod. 708 (November 27, 1728), f. 27.

[35] The majority of the brides were Bahians and Pernambucans. For example, Antão de Mesquita married the daughter of Paulo Bezzera, a Pernambucan sugar planter and member of the town council of Olinda. António José de Afonseca Lemos wed a Bahian lady whose father was a municipal councillor in Salvador. The Brazilian-born magistrate Simão Álvares da Penha married the sister of the renowned Jesuit Father António Vieira whose father was a senior clerk in the Relação of Bahia.

[36] I am sure that extensive research in the Arquivo de Cúria Metropolitana do Salvador would reveal many references to the participation of magistrates and other officials in ritual godparentage relationships. My brief probe in the summer of 1967 turned up the following item: Paróquia de Vitória, Livro dos bautizados (1630-1713) Desembargador Belchior Ramires de Carvalho served as godparent for Gonçalo, son of plantation owner, Antônio Gomes and his wife Ana Maria de Castelo Branco (December 4, 1694).

[37] Studies on the Brazilian family show clearly that lower income and status groups are less able to maintain extended family structures. Compliance with ideal patterns is therefore limited to upper class individuals and families. See Emílio Willems, "The Structure of the Brazilian Family," *Social Forces*, XXXI (1953), 346. Charles Wagley, summarizing a number of community studies, notes the same phenomenon in *The Latin American Tradition* (New York, 1968), chapter VI, "Kinship Patterns in Brazil."

ated a secondary layer of nonritualized relationships. High court magistrates often served on the board of directors in the honorific Holy Brotherhood of Mercy (Misericôrdia) and sometimes controlled its senior position of Provedor.[38] The Misericôrdia counted among its brothers the wealthiest and socially most prominent members of Bahian society, and thus the opportunity for friendship and personal interaction between the magistrates and certain groups was increased.[39] Moreover, ritualized and nonritualized primary relations tended to become concentrated in the same individuals and reinforce each other. Of the six magistrates who served as Provedor of the Misericôrdia of Salvador five were married to Brazilian women and the sixth was Brazilian-born. Either these men had used family connections to obtain the position, or their family connections made others in the society more ready to accept them.

Many magistrates also engaged in business activities—whale fishing, slave trading, commerce, and plantations—entering into contracts and partnerships. Some, like Pedro de Cascais and Caetano de Brito de Figuereido, went deeply into debt, while others, like the Bahian-born Cristóvão de Burgos, became fabulously wealthy.[40] In our discussion their success or failure is a secondary concern. What is important is the existence of these extraprofessional activities and the accompanying network of personal relations that they imply.

Blood and ritual ties, business enterprise, favoritism, and venality could all be viewed strictly as violations of expected behavior which hampered the normal operations of government. At the same time these mechanisms permitted primary relations to penetrate into a highly rationalized system of categorical and impersonal ones. Despite royal attempts to eliminate these "deviancies," these primary

[38] Magistrate Manoel Pinto da Rocha became Provedor of the Misericôrdia in 1621 or 1622. See Arquivo da Santa Casa da Misericôrdia da Bahia (ASCMB), Livro I do Tombo 40 (June 30, 1622), f. 25. In 1716 the Crown noted that for the previous five years the position of Provedor of the Misericôrdia had been held by magistrates who had spread about a good deal of money to insure their election. The Crown ordered that desembargadores could serve on the Board of the Misericôrdia but not as Provedor. AHU, Conselho Ultramarino, Cod. 247, King to the Viceroy of Brazil (September 26, 1716), ff. 68-69.

[39] A. J. R. Russell-Wood, *Fidalgos and Philanthropists* (Berkeley, 1968) is the basic study of the Misericôrdia of Salvador.

[40] Cascais owed 256,400 reis (almost a year's salary) to Pedro Viegas Giraldes. ASCMB, Livro do Tombo I, Testament of Pedro Viegas Giraldes (1637), ff. 125v.-126. APEB, Ordens Régias Livro 21, N. 24c indicates the large debts which chancellor Caetano de Brito de Figuereido contracted with a Bahian merchant and which he refused to pay for nine years. Cristóvão de Burgos was described in 1675 as "o mais afazendado na terra" in Arquivo da Câmara Municipal do Salvador, Livro 159, King to the Câmara (March 18, 1675).

relations which constituted and constitute so much of Portuguese and Brazilian life continued to prevail. Indeed, they gave an unintended flexibility to government and facilitated the resolution of problems on the local level when official channels were too slow or obstructed.

The colonial bureaucrats, seen from the standpoint of a virtuous governor, metropolitan councillors, or even those colonials who had no personal ties with them, often appeared to violate the required standards of their vocation. To be sure, they were never totally absorbed and always capable of pursuing independent or royal interests. Still, the dominant socio-economic groups in the colony never found the royal bureaucrats beyond the reach of colonial pressures or ignorant of colonial desires. Local interests could be expressed and implemented through the web of primary relations, so that policy-making was never simply a matter of royal fiat and bureaucratic compliance.

In effect, the existing social and political organization could accommodate modifications in the structure of colonial society such as the economic ascendency of an urban mercantile class after 1730. Through the formation of social alliances with the bureaucracy, groups and individuals could acquire social legitimacy and the security of powerful friends and relatives. Thus within the formal table of government—a static pattern of organization—new interests could be articulated by the creation of new groupings. These changing social patterns provided, therefore, a dynamic element in the relationship of society to bureaucracy.

This is not to ignore the difficulties created by individual and collective abuses. Tax evasion, graft, faulting on debt payments, and especially misuse of authority were charges often brought against magisterial bureaucrats in Brazil. Occasionally a magistrate could be fairly described as was one royal municipal judge in Pará—"the most evil and perverse man by nature, habit, and design that has until now been honored with the authority of an official." But generally the system of checks and balances kept magisterial activities within bounds, while their professional goals, their loyalty to the Crown, and their personal interests prevented them from becoming the tools of any one colonial group or faction.

Although statutes prohibited Brazilians from serving in the Bahian Relação or in subordinate royal positions in Brazil, the law was bent to meet colonial demands. Between 1653 and 1753 ten Brazilian-born magistrates served in the Relação and others held positions as provincial judges.[41] This practice did not stop even after an attempt in 1663 to eliminate such violations of the law.[42] In fact, when a second Relação was established at Rio de Janeiro in 1752, the man selected for its senior position (*chanceler*) was the Bahian, João Pacheco Pereira, former provincial magistrate of Ouro Preto.[43] Moreover, the Crown took special pains to inform Brazilians that they were not excluded from royal employ in other colonies or in the metropolis, a fact in which the colonials took considerable pride.[44]

Ten Brazilian-born magistrates in the High Court, twenty-six married to Brazilian women, thirty-five who had served previously in Brazil, others related to former governors of Minas Gerais and Pernambuco, and still others who had fathered illegitimate children in the colony—the network of these personal relations was wide indeed.[45] Offended parties in Brazil might censure individual magistrates, but the royal bureaucracy never seemed a distant and oppressive imperial tool to the Brazilian oligarchy. Instead, Brazilians themselves hoped to matriculate their sons in Coimbra and find a career for them in the bureaucracy. These opportunities may at times have been more apparent than real, but there seems little doubt that the theoretically open nature of the professional bureaucracy muted the distinctions between colonials and peninsulars. While the formal structure of administration placed Brazil in a

[41] Luiza da Fonseca, "Bachareis Brasileiros-Elementos biográficos (1635-1830)," *Anais. IV Congresso de História Nacional* (11 vols., Rio de Janeiro, 1951), XI, 113-405, makes extensive use of the Leitura dos Bachareis and lists hundreds of Brazilians with Portuguese law degrees.

[42] After the reestablishment of a Brazilian high court in 1652 a number of Brazilians filled magisterial posts. Because of the abuses caused by conflict of interests the Crown prohibited Brazilians from serving in that tribunal in 1667. Both the Câmara of Salvador and the Jesuits complained of this discrimination, and it is apparent that the Board of Justice did not continue it. The pertinent documents are published in Serafim Leite, *História de companhia de Jesus no Brasil* (10 vols., Lisbon, 1938-1950), VII, 195-199.

[43] The practice of appointing Brazilians in Rio was continued. See Mário de Sampaio Ribeiro, "O Rio de Janeiro em 1783 segundo o chanceler da sua Relação, Conselheiro José Luís França," *Anais da Academia Portuguêsa da História*, ii series, XV (1965), 29-87.

[44] Rocha Pitta, *História da América Portuguêsa*, "Pessoas naturaes do Brasil, que exerceram dignidades e governos ecclesiásticos e seculares na pátria e fóra d'ella," 334-336.

[45] Desembargador Belchior de Sousa Vilas Boas fathered an illegitimate child in Bahia. See ANTT, Chancelaria João V, Legitimações, 133 f. 30. Even today in Brazil individuals can often identify between 50 and 500 relatives in the *parentela* or extended family. Wagley, *Latin American Tradition*, 190. Colonial genealogies such as Pedro Taques de Almeida Paes Leme, *Nobilarchia Paulistiana*, were in a sense recognition of the importance of such personal relations.

classic colonial position, the informal structure allowed colonial interest groups to treat the magistrates as simply another source of power subject to alliance and cooptation.

After 1750 the administration under the Marquis of Pombal changed much of the formal governmental structure, and his policies resulted in the creation of new interest groups and the restructuring of old alliances. In essence, however, most of the informal structure remained unchanged. Royal government in colonial Brazil was never efficient but it never totally collapsed. Magisterial bureaucrats played the crucial though often unintended role of balancing colonial and metropolitan interests.

9

Army and Empire: English Garrison Government in Britain and America, 1569 to 1763

Stephen Saunders Webb

Since 1924 Charles M. Andrews's essay, "Conditions Leading to the Revolt of the Colonies," has exercised a controlling influence over historians' understanding of the origins of the American Revolution. In this essay Andrews declared:

> The year 1763 has always and rightly been considered a great turning point in the history of America's relations with the mother country. . . . [B]y her victory over France, Great Britain obtained peace and a securely established imperial status. . . . In the past men had spoken of "empire," meaning the self-sufficient empire of the mercantilists rather than a thing of territory, centralization, maintenance, and authority. After 1763, however, territorial empire came into real and visible existence, and writers, both British and colonial, became aware that "imperialism" meant something more than commerce and colonies and that the colonial problem, with which they were familiar only in its mercantile aspects, had taken on a distinctly territorial and political form.

Portions of this essay were presented at the seminar of the Charles Warren Center for Studies in American History, Harvard University, May 1975; the Taft Interdisciplinary Lectures in History and Political Science, University of Cincinnati, March 1976; and the annual meeting of the Organization of American Historians, St. Louis, April 1976. Mr. Webb wishes to express his appreciation to the audiences for their comments, and to acknowledge with thanks the arrangements by Donald Fleming, Henry D. Shapiro, Pauline Maier, and Alden T. Vaughan. He also wishes to note helpful criticisms by David Ammerman, Bernard Bailyn, Norman S. Fiering, Merrill Jensen, Alison Olson, I. K. Steele, and Linda M. Webb. The present essay is a precis and projection of portions of *The Governors-General: The English Army and the Definition of the Empire, 1569-1681,* to be published by the University of North Carolina Press for the Institute of Early American History and Culture.

Andrews pointed out that this "new and untried policy of imperialism" had "autocratic" and "paternal" elements. Its promoters "advocated the use of force or the employment of a policy of coercion." After 1763, therefore, "British statesmen affronted in one way or another the colonies in America, because they were thinking in terms, not of accepted mercantilism but in those of the new imperialism."[1]

Reinforcing the orthodoxy of his pioneering historical generation, Andrews persuaded virtually all subsequent historians of early America that "imperialism and not mercantilism was the first cause of the eventual rupture"; that imperialism was inaugurated after 1763; and that it was not in accord with "the principles or methods of the old British colonial policy." Indeed, in his final statement on the subject, published in 1938, Andrews asserted that, in the classic sense of rule and control by a state over dependencies, " 'imperial' and 'imperialism'. have no place in the vocabulary of our early history." Although historians have since challenged the significance of 1763 as a turning point in British policy toward America, and although they have debated the degree of change that occurred during and after "the great war for the empire," they have acquiesced nonetheless in the dictum that, before that war, England's had been a "commercial and colonial policy" which was altered to a military and metropolitan policy, with revolutionary results. Thus historians have gone on assessing the Anglo-American empire in a commercial framework, one laden with whig political assumptions and late nineteenth-century economic concepts. The result has been to obscure both the political and the economic realities of Anglo-American history, as well as to unduly restrict the study of the causes of the Revolution.[2]

From its beginning, English colonization was as much imperial as it was mercantile, and English colonial policy was as much military as it was commercial. Of course, English attitudes toward the colonists (and vice versa) were also shaped by the ties of family and place, by Christian and classical ideologies, and by the growth of the state. All of these influences,

[1] Charles M. Andrews, *The Colonial Background of the American Revolution*, rev. ed. (New Haven, Conn., 1931), 122, 123, 126-127, 128.

[2] *Ibid.*, 129; Charles M. Andrews, *The Colonial Period of American History* (New Haven, Conn., 1934-1938), IV: *England's Commercial and Colonial Policy*, 7, n. 1. Here (pp. 5, 7) we also find the decisive statements: "England's interest in these colonies was not political but commercial" and "colonies were not looked upon as the stuff out of which an empire was to be made, but rather as the source of raw materials. . . . No one at this time took any other view." The view which Andrews summarized was earlier expressed by George Louis Beer, *The Old Colonial System, 1660-1754*, Pt. I: *The Establishment of the System, 1660-1688* (New York, 1913), vii. Beer defined "colonial system" as "that complex system of regulations whose fundamental aim was to create a self-sufficient empire of mutually complementary

however, tended to promote Anglo-American empire at least as much as they enhanced transatlantic commerce. The forces fostering imperialism were most clearly summarized in the political role of the English army and in the administrative careers of its officers commanding colonies, the governors-general. Their imperial influence was coeval with colonization itself. The empire that they organized originated almost two centuries before the onset of the American Revolution in 1763. It achieved constitutional definition a century prior to its dissolution in 1783. In Anglo-America commercial considerations, while always present, were dominant only occasionally. More often the imperial ethos prevailed in English thinking about the provinces, and imperialism had economic as well as bureaucratic and military bases. The coexistence of these policy extremes, and their continual competition for political influence, provide the terms of analysis for Anglo-American relationships. It is time to end the "commercial and colonial" monopoly of interpretation. In reassessing Anglo-America, historians must recognize the fact of empire embodied in the governors-general and applied through garrison government.[3]

The present essay sets forth some themes of this reassessment. First, it reexamines the Tudor military foundations of English empire. The essential element in the definition of empire is the imposition of state control on dependent peoples by force. The instrument of that imposition is the army. There are no empires without armies. Second, this reinterpretation notes the development of "garrison government"—that is, militarized and centralized provincial administration—particularly during the English Civil Wars and the Interregnum. Third, the essay observes that throughout the Protectorate, and during most of the Restoration, paramilitary power relationships were

economic parts." For the continued dominance of the "commercial and colonial" interpretation of Anglo-American history see such recent and well-regarded studies as Michael Kammen, *Empire and Interest: The American Colonies and the Politics of Mercantilism* (Philadelphia, 1970), esp. chap. 1; Alison Gilbert Olson and Richard Maxwell Brown, eds., *Anglo-American Political Relations, 1675-1775* (New Brunswick, N.J., 1970), esp. fig. 2; and Thomas C. Barrow, *Trade and Empire: The British Customs Service in Colonial America, 1660-1775* (Cambridge, Mass., 1967), esp. 1-3. Andrews has not gone unchallenged, at least in private: "James Truslow Adams, in a long correspondence [1922], demonstrated that the word and the concept [of "empire"] had been extensively used prior to that year [1763], in contemporary literature, and that no latter-day misreading of England's colonial relations was being committed by speaking of 'empire' during that period." A. S. Eisenstadt, *Charles McLean Andrews: A Study in American Historical Writing* (New York, 1956), 127. As Andrews's subsequent publications and those of his students show, he was not convinced.

[3] Evidence for this reassessment appears at large in Stephen Saunders Webb, *The Governors-General: The English Army and the Definition of the Empire, 1569-1681* (Chapel Hill, N.C., forthcoming).

applied over ever-widening territorial areas, first in the British Isles and then in England's overseas provinces.

The Anglo-American empire thus created was formalized by 1681. At this early date, a century before the winning of independence by thirteen of the continental colonies, Anglo-American relations were already dominated by an imperial system whose principal agents were the governors-general—officers of the English army who constituted nine-tenths of the royal provincial governors during the adolescence of the "old Empire," 1660-1727. By 1727, however, the imperial militarization finally impressed upon England's colonies by Marlborough's subordinates was being overlaid, if not undone, by the commercial and colonial policies long advocated by "country" politicians and "city" merchants, and finally effected by the Walpole regime. The renewal of imperial war at the close of the era of "salutary neglect" opened the penultimate phase in the struggle of armed imperial authority with commercial motivation and colonial autonomy. "The great war for the empire" at last realized the imperial ambitions of two centuries, but at the price of provoking the resistance of the colonial elites and the revenge of imperial rivals which combined as the American Revolution.

The political and administrative usefulness of military men had been impressed on English sovereigns during their long obsession with the conquest of France. Continental experience had endowed the monarchy with an imperial title, an imperial ambition, and an imperial instrument. By the reign of Henry VIII, military governors, assisted by councils of military, fiscal, and secretarial officers, controlled the European possessions of "the imperial crown of England." "Governors"—the English title is of Tudor coinage—commanded garrisons in provincial capitals. Their troops marched out from urban citadels to enforce the orders the governor received from the crown and to collect the taxes he levied for the crown. English soldier-administrators used the forceful methods they had learned in France to subject England itself to royal authority. This process was concluded at Naworth in 1569, when the governor of the Berwick citadel and the soldiers of his garrison shot down the feudal followers of the northern earls. The crisis of the Elizabethan regime was thus decided in favor of royal, central government.[4]

[4] C. G. Cruickshank, *The English Occupation of Tournai, 1513-1519* (Oxford, 1971), esp. 33-66. I thank Wallace T. MacCaffrey for directing me to this source. See his comments in "Place and Patronage in Elizabethan Politics," in S. T. Bindoff *et al.*, eds., *Elizabethan Government and Society: Essays Presented to Sir John Neale* (London, 1961), 107, and in MacCaffrey, *The Shaping of the Elizabethan Regime* (Princeton, N.J., 1968), 343. See also R. R. Reid, "The Rebellion of the Earls, 1569," Royal Historical Society, *Transactions*, N.S., XX (1906), 175-176, 179, 180; Sir C[uthbert] Sharpe, ed., *Memorials of the Rebellion of 1569* (London, 1840), 17, 67, 74n, 76, 84, 92, 103, 117, 160-161n, 219-220, 313, 382, 413.

In 1585 Tudor governors and garrisons sailed overseas once more as Spain replaced France in English enmity. Holding fortified commercial towns in the formerly Spanish Netherlands, the English soldier-administrators discovered that wealth followed the flag—that Spain, and through her all of Europe, was enriched by the spoil of conquered kingdoms in America. English officers observed that imperial rivalry would make them the agents of an English authority extended over England's neighbors and overseas, as well as the instruments of crown control over England itself.[5]

To the army's domestic police function and its American ambition, the reconquest and colonization of Ireland between 1550 and 1622 added agrarian and societal duties. The Irish "first phases of modern English imperialism" led to the implementation of the classic colonial model: by 1609 "the custom of plantation in colonies, whereby the Roman plant was removed into the soil of other nations," was imposed in Munster and in Ulster as a central component of English imperialism. Plantation government was defined on the Roman model, modified by the European conciliar tradition: "For Government, let it be in the Hands of one, assisted with some Counsell: and let them have Commission, to exercise Martiall Lawes, with some limitation."[6] Governor, council, and martial law—such was the prescription for English empire in America in the coming century.

[5] See the letters in *Calendar of the Manuscripts of the Most Hon. The Marquis of Salisbury* .... (Historical Manuscripts Commission, *Ninth Report* [London, 1893-1970]), Pt. IV, 293, 503, 512, 581, Pt. V, 450, Pt. VI, 538-539, Pt. VII, 13, 57; Francis Bamford, ed. and trans., *A Royalists' Notebook* . . . (London, 1930); C. G. Cruickshank, *Elizabeth's Army,* 2d ed. (Oxford, 1966), esp. 14-44, 290-291; R. B. Wernham, "Elizabethan War Aims and Strategy," in Bindoff *et al.*, eds., *Elizabethan Government,* 348; J. E. Neale, "Elizabeth and the Netherlands, 1586-7," *Essays in Elizabethan History* (New York, 1958), 170-201; Richard Arthur Preston, *Gorges of Plymouth Fort, Governor of New England* . . . (Toronto, 1953); and Thomas Elyot, *The boke named the Governour* . . . (London, 1531).

[6] Francis Bacon brought the lessons of Irish plantation into the consciousness of the English establishment sixteen years after the events cited here, just as the crown was taking over Virginia government, when he amended his essay on the greatness of kingdoms and added one "Of Plantations," both quoted here from *The Essayes or Counsels, Civill and Morall, Of Francis Bacon Lo. Verulam, Viscount St. Alban* (London, 1625), 176, 202; English Books, 1475-1640 (microfilm, University of Michigan, Ann Arbor, Mich.); Howard Mumford Jones, "Origins of the Colonial Idea in England," American Philosophical Society, *Proceedings,* LXXXV (1942), 451-459; David Beers Quinn, "Sir Thomas Smith (1513-1577) and the Beginnings of English Colonial Theory," *ibid.*, LXXXIX (1945), 543-560; Quinn, "The Munster Plantation: Problems and Opportunities," Cork Historical and Archaeological Society, *Journal,* 2d Ser., LXXI (1966), 19-40, esp. 23, 32. I am indebted to Prof. William Smyth of St. Patrick's College, Maynooth, for a copy of the Munster item. See also Nicholas P. Canny, "The Ideology of English Colonization: From Ireland to America," *William and Mary Quarterly,* 3d Ser., XXX (1973), 575-598.

In their memories and in their orders, English army officers carried imperial ideas across the Atlantic. Trained in arms and administration in the cities and citadels of France and in the Netherlands, experienced in Irish conquest and plantation, these officers came to command the palisaded plantations of Jamestown and Henrico; St. Mary's, Sagadahoc, and Saybrook; Plymouth and Piscataqua; Charlestown and Cambridge—all in North America—and the even more embattled outposts in the West Indies: Providence, St. Kitts, and Barbados. As scattered settlements grew, touched, and required governmental organization, military units helped define political jurisdictions. In Virginia local squads gave way to plantation companies, and these were subsequently amalgamated into county commands. The association of township militia companies in regiments was fundamental to county definition in Massachusetts. And all around the Atlantic circuit of the English empire, town government reflected Netherlands garrison practices and obeyed the orders of Netherlands veterans.

The model was established not only at Jamestown, the capital of a dominion in the making, with its triple bastions and uniformed guards, but also at tiny Plymouth, ordered within its palisade, lying down the hill beneath its fort, with "pateroes" pointing from the guard post at the town intersection, its men organized by Captain Standish, mustering by squads for guard duty, fire fighting, and religious worship. This simple model was easily duplicated in Captain Graves's Charlestown, Captain Dudley's Cambridge, Captain Endecott's Salem, Captain Gardiner's Saybrook, Captain Mason's Hartford. Each of these towns was defined by "watch and ward." Each was a militarized node of English conquest and colonization in America. The governmental institutions of England's colonies, whether in Ireland, the West Indies, or North America, thus were shaped by military men, intent on establishing security and imposing social order within their jurisdictions, and determined to spread crusading Christianity and English authority over conquered territories and "native" peoples. Here were elements of empire.[7]

On the American continent, Virginia was from the first what it would

[7] Darrett B. Rutman, "A Militant New World, 1607-1640: America's First Generation, Its Martial Spirit, Its Tradition of Arms, Its Militia Organization, Its Wars" (Ph.D. diss., University of Virginia, 1959), is the fullest study of the military bases of the early English settlements on the continent. On the Irish connections and precedents see n. 6 above. On Dudley and Cambridge see William Andrew Polf, "Puritan Gentlemen: The Dudleys of Massachusetts, 1576-1686" (Ph.D. diss., Syracuse University, 1973), 6-7, 18, 30-33, 40, 42. Arthur Percival Newton, *The Colonising Activities of the English Puritans* (New Haven, Conn., 1914), discusses the Providence and Tortuga settlements. See also Newton's *The European Nations in the West Indies, 1493-1688* (London, 1933); Vincent T. Harlow, *A History of Barbados, 1625-1685* (Oxford, 1926); and Alan Burns, *History of the British West Indies*, 2d ed. rev. (London, 1965).

continue to be, the bellwether of English empire. It was the continental colony that contributed most to the development of an imperial constitution, and prior to the outbreak of the English Civil Wars it especially exemplified the effect, and the limits, of military ideas and institutions in the early English colonies. Virginia's beginnings suggest a general Anglo-American pattern. With a heroism reminiscent of archaic eras, Capt. John Smith, soldier, adventurer, imperialist, played out in Virginia a socially significant scene from the militant drama of his life. His ideas were institutionalized, and the colony's society stabilized, by a quartet of Netherlands veterans who subjected Virginia to the continent's first English and imperial code, the "Lawes Divine, Morall and Martiall." Subsequent testimony about Virginia by soldier-advisors and military officials illustrated the influence of army administrators over the "plantations," the "natives," and the "colonists" (all terms that these officers derived from Irish conquest and colonization, and applied to the definition of early American experience). The soldier-statesmen of Virginia also defined the fundamental and perennial divisions of English expansionist thought by strongly contrasting their imperial and authoritarian programs for Virginia with more legislative, legalistic, civilian, commercial, and oligarchical colonial concepts.

Captain Smith militarized Virginia government. Nothing else could be expected of a man whose experience had led him to equate social order with army discipline. In 1596, aged sixteen, Smith had run away from his merchant master and apprenticed himself to war. "When France and Netherlands had taught him to use his Armes," he came home to camp in the fields of his native Lincolnshire, run courses with his lance, and read Machiavelli and Marcus Aurelius on the interrelations of force, morality, and empire. The year 1601 found him fighting for the German empire against the Turkish empire, and for Christianity against Islam. In the siege, storm, and defense of central European citadels, and by cultivating their governors and serving in their garrisons, Smith—and many other English cavaliers—learned the socially stabilizing use of the garrisoned government center. Such a fortified central place, he observed, "could bee of no great strength, yet it keepes all them barbarous Countreyes about it in admiration and subjection."[8]

[8] Edward Arber and A. G. Bradley, eds., *Travels and Works of Captain John Smith: President of Virginia, and Admiral of New England, 1580-1631*, II (Edinburgh, 1910), 581, 816, 823, 828, 854-855. On the character of this work, and the forthcoming edition of Smith's writings by Philip L. Barbour, author of the standard biography, *The Three Worlds of Captain John Smith* (Boston, 1964), see Wesley Frank Craven, "A New Edition of the Works of Captain John Smith," *WMQ*, 3d Ser., XXIX (1972), 479-486. For full details on the colony see Craven, *The Southern Colonies in the Seventeenth Century, 1607-1689* (Baton Rouge, La., 1949), esp. 72-73 for Smith's role, and Richard L. Morton, *Colonial Virginia*, 2 vols. (Chapel Hill, N.C., 1960).

Eager to help found an English empire in which he might serve, and desiring a capital to command, Smith first visited Ireland and then, in December 1606, sailed for Virginia as a member of the first American colonial council. At Jamestown factionalism, starvation, and Indian war produced a reaction toward absolutism among the colonists, whom Smith addressed as "Fellow Soldiers." Taking command, the captain forced the adoption of the military plantation model of society which had been developed by the English conquerors of Ireland from their European garrison experience: "the Church was repaired; the Store-house recovered; buildings prepared for the Supplyes we expected; the Fort reduced to a five-square forme; the order of the watch renewed; the squadrons . . . trained; the whole Company every Saturday exercised," both to awe the natives and to discipline the English. So Smith pioneered in America the pattern of imperial settlement: "the effect of a Cittadell, or the true modell of a Plantation."[9]

The survival of citadels and plantations depended on the military ability of their commanders or "governors." "What is requisite to be in a Gouvernour of a plantation?" Smith was asked. Aggressiveness, he answered. In a world of warring empires, on American seas and Dutch battlefields, "many hundreds of brave English Souldiers, Captaines and Gentlemen" had found that "peace was onely but an empty name," and security was better won by war than purchased by tribute. Brains as well as bravery were essential in governors, Smith contended, for "there is no misery worse than [to] be conducted by a foole, or commanded by a coward." Leader and led were subordinate parts of an imperial whole, "obedient to government and their Soveraigne, as duty required." To promote the cause of disciplined national expansion, Smith concluded, England's military governors should emulate the Spanish conquistadors "that advanced themselves from poore Souldiers to great Captaines, their posterity to great Lords, and their King to be one of the greatest potentates on earth, and the fruits of their labours his greatest glory, power, and renowne."[10]

Before Captain Smith's imperial dream could be realized, much social building would be required of the English empire's "hammerors and rough masons . . . I mean our old soldiers trained up in the Netherlands." Smith's executive model was officially adopted for Virginia government in 1609, and he himself was succeeded by three Netherlands veterans, each of whom had been knighted in battle, had captained a garrisoned town, and had served in Ireland. These three—Virginia's "Lord Governour and Captaine General," Sir Thomas West (Lord de la Warr); the lieutenant general, Sir Thomas Gates; and the provost marshal and deputy governor, Sir Thomas Dale—

[9] Arber and Bradley, eds. *Travels and Works of Smith*, II, 387, 392, 433-434, 900.

[10] *Ibid.*, 964-965.

carried Virginia from Smith's garrisoned beginnings to plantation permanency. Their political principles and social definitions were expressed in the code "For The Colony In Virginea Brittannia Lawes Divine, Morall and Martiall, etc." This code the veterans compiled with the aid of another Netherlands officer, William Strachey, secretary of the colony, from the martial law of the English army in the Netherlands and from Sir Thomas Smythe's regulations for the Ulster military plantation.[11]

Determined to "proceede by martial lawe accordinge to your commission as of most despatch and terror and fittest for this governement," the military administrators of Virginia made themselves absolute by defining all adult males as soldiers. The soldier's oath bound each armed settler "to serve his Prince, and obey his officers: for the true order of warre is fitly resembled to true religion ordeined of God, which bindeth the souldier to observe justice, loyaltie, faith, constancie, patience, silence, and above all, obedience." As religion enforced every soldier's obedience to "his Colonel or Governor," so that commander (like his king) pictured himself as a Biblical patriarch. Responsible to God, "as knowing assuredly that all the crimes and trespasses of his people under him shall be exacted at his hands," the military governor enforced the "Lawes Divine, Morall and Martiall" that made it death to criticize his sacred person. His authority was restricted only by his own military oath—to "perform [in] all Integrity [and] uprightnesse, Justice and sincere administration of the discipline and Lawes in all causes and cases, for the good of the Colony or Colonies . . ."—and by the physical limits of his power. These two factors compelled every governor-general to rely primarily on his own example—"a lively pattern of industry, order and comliness"—to secure the public good, while reserving for emergencies "the power and Sword of Justice and authority."[12]

By 1618, after four years of local peace, amidst the first flush of tobacco prosperity and during control of the Virginia Company by partisans of parliamentary authority, the "Lawes Divine, Morall and Martiall" had been displaced. There ensued that degraded command, unregulated settlement, and concentration on individual economic aggrandizement at the cost of order, community, and security, that led to the massacre of 1622. "The cause of the massacre was the want of marshall discipline," John Smith told a

[11] *Dictionary of National Biography*, s.v. "Gates, Sir Thomas," and "West, Sir Thomas." On Sir Thomas Dale see Darrett B. Rutman, "The Historian and the Marshal," *Virginia Magazine of History and Biography*, LXVIII (1960), 284-294; Jones, "Origins of the Colonial Idea," Am. Phil. Soc., *Procs.*, LXXXV (1942), 453; Craven, *Southern Colonies*, 91-92, 98, 103, 105-107; David H. Flaherty, ed., *For the Colony in Virginea Brittania Lawes Divine, Morall and Martiall, etc.*, comp. William Strachey (Charlottesville, Va., 1969), 9.

[12] Flaherty, ed., *For the Colony in Virginea*, comp. Strachey, xii-xix, 13-14, 27, 42-46, 60-62, 85-86.

royal commission of enquiry. Deficiencies of "marshall discipline," the captain explained, included a variety of social and political elements: dispersed settlement compounded the shortage of soldiers, and there were too many councilors and counsels, both in England and Virginia. Their number exacerbated the destabilizing, discordant results of overfrequent changes of executive. Moreover, the councilors' disunity reemphasized the Virginia executive's lack of military authority.[13]

Even those English observers of Virginia's plight who did not share Smith's conviction that the crown should institute direct royal rule in Virginia and restore a military governor and government, backed by a regular garrison, nonetheless repeated the martial commonplaces of the age, which Smith from the first had applied to the colony. In a deathbed letter to his son—Sir Francis Wyatt, governor of Virginia—George Wyatt recalled that Virginia had begun as a combination of Roman "colony" and English "plantation." It was designed to force "Barbarians to Civilitie and Christianitie." A settlement among savages, Wyatt concluded, should have continued to concentrate on "Soldgership, afore better deservinge wel, now more to be respected[,] which neclected hathe cost you so deare."[14]

The elder Wyatt was a veteran of the contest with Spain in the Netherlands. To direct observation of the Spaniards' European military practice he added reading about their American colonial experience. Both supported his call for compact, socially gradated, militarily ordered, fortified settlements in Virginia. These were to be connected, protected, and dominated by three garrisoned cities. The whole colony should be ruled, Wyatt suggested, by a well-guarded, loyally counseled governor-general, commanding armed forces modeled on the Greek phalanx and the Roman legion. These formations, the old soldier observed, had "spreade their branches even over the world": they were the shade trees of empire. In advocating the "feedfight" and by applying Xenophon's hunting techniques to guerrilla war against the natives, as well as by recommending that firearms be substituted for polearms (most useful against cavalry which the natives did not have; unwieldy in the forests where they dwelt), Wyatt adapted classic tactics to Virginia. His prescriptions for well-garrisoned urban places, for legionary-type entrenchments, and for elaborate drill, however, all required far greater resources than those which his son commanded in the colony.[15]

[13] Arber and Bradley, eds., *Travels and Works of Smith,* II, 572-578, 591; Craven, *Southern Colonies,* 11-114, 123-127, 133-135.

[14] Arber and Bradley, eds., *Travels and Works of Smith,* II, 588-590; Craven, *Southern Colonies,* 145-147; J. Frederick Fausz and Jon Kukla, eds., " A Letter of Advice to the Governor of Virginia, 1624," *WMQ,* 3d Ser., XXXIV (1977), 112-116.

[15] Fausz and Kukla, eds., "Letter of Advice," *WMQ,* 3d Ser., XXXIV (1977), 118-122. On the Roman army's nightly entrenchments see Cornelius Tacitus, *The*

Francis Wyatt did revive military plantation practices after the massacre of 1622, but they continually conflicted with commercial and localist drives, as Capt. George Donne reported in 1638. Having fought for the Protestants in France and against the Spaniards in the West Indies, Donne was commissioned muster-master general and provost marshal of Virginia in 1637. In the following year he presented to Charles I "two Consideracions without which this sound limbe of your confirmed Empire cannott bee fast joynted to the full bodie." The first was a "Serious Strict observation" of those laws and rules especially suited to colonies. The second was "ready Instruction in the use of armes." Both should be required in a colonial constitution, "An Injunction by Authority imposed," to which colonial assent need not be secured by the crown. Armed authority would both enforce colonial order and accomplish the conquest of neighbors and natives, for domestic peace and foreign conquest had been "the chiefe Glorye and firmity of the Roman Empire."[16]

Military government, Donne asserted in terms that had become imperialist commonplaces, would check the "search for growing rich to soone" which was producing unsuitable political ambition in colonial and commercial elites, leading to contention with executive authority and "a Competition with a Governor for Superiority." Unwise dependence on "the Wills and counsailes of Men of Trade" had produced oligarchic license and conciliar pretensions. Monarchical and military political prescriptions of the sort the king wished to revive at home and overseas in the later 1630s, therefore, "disquieted the Composition of some Mynds in Virginia and of too many (as it appeares) in England." Anglo-American opposition to the executive had other springs also. The provost marshal told the king that, as in old England so in New England, religious dissent had induced political treason. Thus this imperial officer anticipated that social aspiration, political ambition, and religious enthusiasm would excite civil war.[17]

Within three years Donne's fears became fact: a civil war, inimical alike to monarchy, army, and empire, destroyed the authority of the English executive in America. By forcing the development of autonomous colonial elites and institutions, and by providing a republican ideology, the Civil Wars became the essential precondition of American independence. For example,

Histories, trans. Kenneth Wellesley (Baltimore, 1964), 108, n. 1. On the Virginia population at the date of Wyatt's letter see Irene W. D. Hecht, "The Virginia Muster of 1624/5 as a Source for Demographic History," *WMQ*, 3d Ser., XXX (1973), 65-92.

[16] T. H. Breen, ed., "George Donne's 'Virginia Reviewed': A 1638 Plan to Reform Colonial Society," *WMQ*, 3d Ser., XXX (1973), 449-466, esp. 449-450, 455, 456, 458. See also Craven, *Southern Colonies*, 148-419, 153-155.

[17] Breen, ed., "George Donne's 'Virginia Reviewed,'" *WMQ*, 3d Ser., XXX (1973), 459, 460, 463-464.

Sir William Berkeley was recommissioned governor of Virginia in 1641 by a monarch suffering from a reaction against his absolutism, and recommissioned by an exiled prince in 1650. He was stripped of the military authority possessed by his veteran predecessors. He was reduced to being merely first among equals in the colony's council. He lost the institutional model which a strong English executive provided the dependencies, and he was deprived as well of monarchical support for his provincial government. Concurrent with the abasement of executive authority throughout the empire by civil war, provincial autonomy was enhanced by the political aggression of acquisitive elites. They took control of the now-dominant local institutions of the provincial council and the county courts, and their outport commercial connections with England were as antimetropolitan as their politics. Anglo-American republicanism—oligarchic, localist, autarchic alike in religion and commerce—successfully challenged monarchical centralization of politics and imperial uniformity in church and commerce during the imperial civil wars of the 1640s and of the 1770s and 1780s.[18]

While executive authority shrank overseas, a centralizing reaction against the social disintegration and political factionalization of civil war strengthened the institutions of garrison government in England. There, during the 1640s, both royalist and parliamentary military governors sought to pacify their commands by establishing the authority of one or the other of the competing central governments. They thereby introduced a metropolitan focus into local politics. The governors made "court" and "country" partisanships the polarities of English provincial politics by forcing local leaders either to defend local autonomy or to support state sovereignty. Thus they forecast the shape of Anglo-American politics as well. In Nottingham from 1644 to 1646, as in Virginia from 1676 to 1681, local partisanships were sublimated in the struggle to determine the dimensions of metropolitan authority in provincial life. Established elites saw the continuation of their sway in the maintenance of local autonomy. Aspirant outgroups tied their

[18] Samuel R. Gardiner, *History of England from the Accession of James I to the Outbreak of the Civil War, 1603-1642*, rev. ed. (London, 1900); Newton, *Colonising Activities;* Caroline Robbins, *The Eighteenth-Century Commonwealthman: Studies in the Transmission, Development and Circumstances of English Liberal Thought . . .* (Cambridge, Mass., 1959); Perez Zagorin, *The Court and the Country: The Beginning of the English Revolution* (New York, 1970); L. H. Butterfield *et al.*, eds., *Diary and Autobiography of John Adams*, I (New York, 1964), 314-316; Stephen Saunders Webb's review of Zagorin, *The Court and the Country*, in *WMQ*, 3d Ser., XXVIII (1971), 129-133; "The king's instructions to Sir William Berkeley as the governor of Virginia," Aug. 9, 1641; commission of the king to Berkeley, June 3, 1650; king's instructions to Berkeley, Sept. 12, 1662, C. O. 5/1354, 224-241, 243-252, 270-280, Public Record Office.

ascent to an expansion of the central government's local role. Appeals to London to resolve the contest for local power produced gubernatorial commissions that divided authority between the executive and elements of the local elite organized as a council. In these commissions, consultative and judicial roles were always reserved to the councilors, but the preponderance of power was held by the governor in the form of extensive military authority.[19]

The governors used their military authority to patronize their supporters. They not only personified but also developed a professional administrative class—governmental "men of business"—and they helped to organize an alternative elite to the traditional governing class by paying particular attention to "the middling sort" of people. These were the heart of the governors' militias, the friends of public order. Their approval of executive authority contrasted with the arrogance and independence of the provincial elites and the anarchism of the poor. The governors' social rebalancing, political reorganization, and paramilitary administration were financed in part by local requisitions and taxes, collected by the governor for the state and spent by him for military purposes. Further support for prerogative politics came from central government grants to localities. These were disbursed by the governor largely to pay himself, his staff, his garrison, and their local suppliers. Increased governmental revenue and expenditure provided politically directed economic alternatives in agriculture, clothing, processing, shipping, and finance. These new economic opportunities tended to be monopolized by the growing official "interest" of officers, administrators, court-connected merchants, and farmer-suppliers. Garrison government, whether of nation, province, town, or colony, required the recruitment and organization of masses of men and money, supplies and food, that laid the economic basis of prerogative politics. Merchant-bankers, clothiers, manufacturers, recruiters, and farmers all stood to profit from garrison government.[20]

[19] On Nottingham see Lucy Hutchinson, *Memoirs of the Life of Colonel Hutchinson, governor of Nottingham* . . . , ed. Rev. Julius Hutchinson, rev. by C. H. Firth (London, 1906 [orig. publ. 1806]), 214-215, 220, 222, 427, hereafter cited as *Memoirs of Hutchinson.* The 1681 parallels in Virginia (and Jamaica) are recorded in "orders of the king-in-council, Jan. 16, 1681[/2], and other preliminaries to Lord Culpeper's instructions . . . , Jan. 27, 1681[/2]," C.O. 5/1356, 411, 39-60; W. Noel Sainsbury *et al.*, eds., *Calendar of State Papers, Colonial Series, America and the West Indies* (London, 1862-), *1681-1685*, 157-158, nos. 321, 322; 167-168, nos. 331, 332; hereafter cited as *Calendar of State Papers, Col. Ser.*; "Virginia in 1681-82," *VMHB*, XXVII (1919), 327-328, 330, 331, 332; *ibid.*, XXVIII (1920), 43, 46; "The king's commission and instructions to Sir Thomas Lynch as governor-general of Jamaica," Aug. 6, Sept. 8, 1681, C.O. 138/4, 1-15, 17-39, Public Record Office.

[20] Some representative sources are *Memoirs of Hutchinson;* Rev. John Webb. *Military Memoirs of Colonel Birch, Sometime Governor of Hereford* . . . , ed. Rev. T. W. Webb, Camden Society, N.S. VII (Westminster, 1873); Wallace T.

Twenty-six veterans carried the Civil War institutions of garrison government to ten different colonies, seven in America and in the West Indies, and one each in Europe, North Africa, and India. These officers had governed a dozen different English cities, towns, and citadels. They subsequently served thirty terms in governorships overseas. Among New World colonies, Jamaica, Barbados, New York, and Virginia were especially influenced by the administration of these civil warriors.[21]

In the British Isles, the Celtic kingdoms felt the rough hand of English paramilitary rulers after 1649, as Oliver Cromwell extended the principles and practices of garrison government from England to the conquest, pacification, and development of Ireland and Scotland. His officers then transferred experiences of military government, widened and intensified by Irish and Scottish application, to the overseas units of the empire. So the forceful local administrations of the English Civil Wars were transmuted into an Anglo-American imperial system by royalist and parliamentary officers alike, and by the military executives of the Commonwealth and of the Protectorate.

Basing empire in conquest, Cromwell's legions had massacred Irish urban garrisons and "pacified" the Irish countryside with fire and sword. More constructively, they renewed urban garrison government and agricultural military plantation. Together, these operations supported an army of

MacCaffrey, *Exeter, 1540-1640: The Growth of an English County Town* (Cambridge, Mass., 1958); Richard W. Cotton, *Barnstaple and the Northern Part of Devonshire during the Great Civil War, 1642-1646* (London, 1889); Edward, earl of Clarendon, *The History of the Rebellion and Civil Wars in England* (Oxford, 1819); John Corbet, *An Historical Relation of the Military Government of Gloucester* . . . (London, 1645); Andrew Marvell, "The First Anniversary of the Government under O. C.," lines 279-282.

[21] The colonies include Barbados, Bombay, Dunkirk, Tangier, Jamaica, the Leeward Islands, New York, New Jersey, Nova Scotia, and Virginia. Army officers of the Civil Wars and Interregnum who afterwards governed overseas provinces had commanded Gainsborough, Chester, Belvoir Castle, Monmouth, Cannon Frome, Worcester, Gloucester, Carlisle, Carmarthen Castle, York, Newark, and Hull, in addition to at least three English counties, Cumberland, Westmoreland, and Northumberland. Civil warriors commissioned by the crown to command colonies included Francis Lord Willoughby of Parham; Sir Richard Dutton; James Ley, earl of Marlborough; Sir Gervase Lucas; Sir Edmund Harley; Henry Norwood; Edward D'Oyley; Sir Charles Littleton; Sir Edward Massey; Sir Thomas Modyford; Edward Morgan; Sir Thomas Lynch; Charles Howard, earl of Carlisle, and his brother, Sir Philip Howard; Sir Charles Wheeler; Christopher Codrington, Sr.; Richard Nicolls; Francis Lovelace; Sir Thomas Temple; Henry Mordaunt, second earl of Peterborough; Sir Tobias Bridge; John Lord Belasyse; Sir Henry Chicheley; Herbert Jeffreys; John Fitzgerald; John Middleton, earl of Middleton; Sir Jonathan Atkins; Thomas Hickman, Lord Windsor; and Robert Walters. Massey, Philip Howard, and Walters either did not come out or did not serve, and are not tallied in the text above. Alison Gilbert Olson, *Anglo-American Politics, 1660-1775: The Relationship between Parties in England and Colonial America* (New York, 1973), 33, notes that John Leverett was a Cromwellian captain and governor of Nova Scotia.

occupation and administration. As frontier police, militia cadres, and seaport patrols, English soldiers redistributed land, regulated political activity, and collected customs. Officer-executives were regularly shifted from Irish posts to provincial service elsewhere in the British Isles and in Dunkirk, Tangier, Jamaica, Barbados, Massachusetts, New York, and Maryland as well. Repeated Irish revolts insured that Ireland continued to employ the English army's largest reserve as a garrison. So Ireland educated both governors-general and an increasing variety of other officer-administrators, down to the American Revolution. Five officers, who afterwards commanded Jamaica, New York, and Tangier, had served in Ireland before 1660. During the Restoration they were succeeded in Ireland by six officer-executives who later went out to govern New York, New England, and the Leeward Islands. Between 1689 and 1727 fifteen or more veterans of William III's Irish war also served as royal governors in Virginia, Gibraltar, Minorca, Jamaica, Barbados, the Leeward Islands, Nova Scotia and Newfoundland, and New York and Pennsylvania.[22]

The first of these classes of Irish military administrators, trained as much in social as in military discipline under Cromwell, Monck, and Jones, had gone on to complete their unification of the British Isles by the conquest of

[22] Major sources of information on Anglo-Irish administration in this period include *Calendar of the Manuscripts of the Marquess of Ormonde* (Hist. MSS Comm., *Fifteenth Report*, N.S. [London, 1902-1920]); Charles Firth and Godfrey Davies, *The Regimental History of Cromwell's Army* (Oxford, 1940); Thomas Carte, *An History of the Life of James Duke of Ormond . . . To which is added . . . a very valuable collection of letters . . .* (Oxford, 1851); and Richard Bagwell, *Ireland under the Stuarts and during the Interregnum* (London, 1916). Governors-general Edward D'Oyley, Thomas Dongan, William Brayne, Robert Venables, and John Fitzgerald served in Ireland before 1650. Restoration officer governors of American and West Indian colonies, who had held Irish posts, included Sir Edmund Andros, Sir Charles Wheeler, Sir William Stapleton, Benjamin Fletcher, Richard Ingoldsby, and Thomas Foulke. Fletcher and Ingoldsby also served in Ireland after 1688 and were joined there by such imperially important officers as Roger Elliot and Alexander Spotswood, the half-brother who served in Sir Beville Grenville's regiment; Richard Kane; William O'Brien, second earl of Inchiquin; James Kendall; Francis Russell; Thomas Caulfield; Richard Phillips; Richard Brewer; Thomas Handasyde; and Robert Hunter. Percy Kirke and George Hamilton, earl of Orkney, also received appointments. Although no English army commission appears for Richard Coote, earl of Bellomont, he governed Co. Lentrim for William III before commanding New York and Massachusetts under commissions signed by the lords justices (regents). Prof. Robert C. Ritchie informs me that Bellomont had commanded a company of English soldiers in the Netherlands for the prince of Orange (William III) in 1687. Additional MSS 41820, 273, British Library, formerly the British Museum. The continuing influence on American settlement, society, and politics of the army and the plantations in Ireland is shown in John Christopher Guzzardo, "Sir William Johnson's Official Family: Patron and Client in an Anglo-American Empire" (Ph.D. diss., Syracuse University, 1975), esp. chap. 2.

Scotland. They were suspicious of merchant motivations, and the public order they imposed on the Scots was biased in favor of yeomen and tradesmen. It was distinguished, even among garrison governments, by its high degree of centralization and militarization. In the period 1654-1658 officer-governors carried the paternalist, regulatory, and coercive tendencies, developed in Scotland, to Jamaica, where they survived to find expression in the imperial constitutional formulations of 1681. After 1688, Williamite repression in Scotland trained seven soldiers who subsequently ruled Virginia, New York, Barbados, and Jamaica. The Union of 1707 refreshed the flow of army administrators from Scotland to the American provinces (and vice versa). Therefore another half-dozen or more veterans of Scottish garrisons, several of whom were themselves Scots, were commissioned as governors-general in America before 1727. Whether in expanding the frontier westward, as did Col. Alexander Spotswood, or in interrelating provincial and metropolitan political groups, as the earl of Orkney did, Scots officers had an especially marked influence on Virginia in the early eighteenth century.[23]

While this routine transfer of officers from governments in the three British kingdoms to the empire's American provinces continued until the American Revolution, it had begun much earlier, with the Commonwealth's punitive expeditions to Barbados in 1651 and to Virginia in 1652. Next the Protectorate tried to unite the British Isles and every English colony into a

[23] C. H. Firth, ed., *Scotland the Commonwealth: Letters and Papers Relating to the Military Government of Scotland, from August 1651 to December 1653*, XVIII (Edinburgh, 1895); C. H. Firth, ed., *Scotland the Protectorate: Letters Relating to the Military Government of Scotland from January 1654 to June 1659*, XXXI (Edinburgh, 1899); Firth and Davies, *Regimental History;* T[homas] Birch, ed., *A Collection of the State Papers of John Thurloe, Esq. Secretary, to the Council of State and the two Protectors Oliver and Richard Cromwell . . .*, 7 vols. (London 1742); Osmund Airy, ed., *Gilbert Burnet's History of My Own Time . . .*, I (Oxford, 1897), xxxiv, 108-109, 186, 195; Robert Lemon *et al.*, eds., *Calendar of State Papers, Domestic Series . . .* (London, 1856–1872), *1654*, 211, hereafter cited as *Calendar of State Papers, Dom. Ser.* The garrison government of Scotland before 1660 produced five governors-general: William Brayne, Tobias Bridge, and the earls of Middleton, Rutherford, and Carlisle. The last of these, as governor-general of Jamaica, was a central figure in the 1681 settlement. When William III repeated Cromwell's subjugation of Ireland and Scotland, he gave experience in forceful government of the latter to subsequent governors-general of Virginia, Barbados, the Leeward Islands, Jamaica, and Gibraltar. These were the earl of Orkney (an absentee executive); William Forbes, master of Forbes; Henry Worsley; David Colyear, earl of Portmore; Richard Brewer; Thomas Handasyde; and John Johnson. After the Union, the staff for Scotland's military government included such sometime colonial governors-general as Charles DuBorgay; the earl of Orkney; Thomas Whetham; John Campbell, duke of Argyll; Sir William Gooch; Lord George Forbes; Charles Dilke; and, returning from Virginia, Alexander Spotswood.

single transatlantic state, directed by its military executive to the reduction of the Spanish empire. This "Western Design" was planned by a Barbadian, Thomas Modyford. It was directed by a commissioner from the New English Plymouth, Edward Winslow. Its settlers were recruited by a Massachusetts officer, Daniel Gookin. The governors of Irish plantations and Scottish citadels, Robert Venables and William Brayne, commanded expeditionary regiments drawn from London and the Leeward Islands. The widespread residences of its officers and men attest to the geographic scope of the Protector's imperial vision. It produced the massive expedition of 1654 that attacked Hispaniola, conquered Jamaica, and so revived and intensified military plantation and garrison government in America after the imperially decadent era of the early Stuarts and the disintegrative period of the Civil Wars. The imperialists of the Restoration would force a reluctant Charles II to recognize the political and administrative necessity of adopting the Cromwellian system of territorial control and political administration. Thus they would keep provincial government, in Britain and overseas, a military preserve.[24]

As this decision was especially apparent in colonial government, so it was an especially contentious issue in colonial policy. From the outset of English colonization, military-imperial and civilian-commercial elements had competed for domination of English expansion overseas; but never was that

[24] In addition to the sources for the Protectorate, Puritan colonization, and the West Indies, cited above, see C. H. Firth, ed., *The Narrative of General Venables . . .*, Camden Society, LX (London, 1900); Frank Cundall and Joseph L. Pietersz [eds.], *Jamaica under the Spaniards. Abstracted from the archives of Seville* (Kingston, Jam., 1919); "Papers Relative to the West Indies, 1654-1682," Add. MSS, 11410; "Papers Relative to English Colonies in America and the West Indies, 1627-1699," Egerton MS, 2395, Brit. Lib.; Arthur P. Watts, *Une Historie des Colonies anglaises aux Antilles, de 1649 à 1660* (Paris, 1924); C. H. Firth, ed., *The Clarke Papers. Selections from the Papers of William Clarke*, Camden Society, N.S. LXI, III (London, 1899), 205; *Calendar of State Papers, Col. Ser., 1574-1660*, 415 ff., nos. 229-232; Samuel Rawson Gardiner, *History of the Commonwealth and Protectorate, 1649-1656*, II (London, 1903); Granville Penn, *Memorials of the Professional Life and Times of Sir William Penn, Knt.*, II (London, 1833); Edward Long, *The History of Jamaica or General Survey of the Ancient and Modern State of that Island . . .*, I (London, 1774); S. A. G. Taylor, *The Western Design: An Account of Cromwell's Expedition to the Caribbean* (Kingston, Jam., 1965). On the re-adoption of the Cromwellian system see Allen B. Hinds, ed., *Calendar of State Papers and Manuscripts relating to English Affairs, existing in the archives and collections of Venice . . ., 1659-1661* (London, 1864); Wilbur C. Abbott, "English Conspiracy and Dissent, 1660-1674," *American Historical Review*, XVI (1909), 503-528, esp. 503; Airy, ed., *Burnet's History*, I, 276-277; K. H. D. Haley, *The First Earl of Shaftesbury* (Oxford, 1965), 155; and J. S. Clarke, ed., *The Life of James the Second, King of England, etc., Collected out of memoirs writ of his own hand . . .* (London, 1816).

struggle more severe than in the first fifteen years of the Restoration. Control of colonial policy, and of overseas investment and direction of money and men, fluctuated between the devotees of the Tudor-Cromwellian imperial tradition and those who sought to negate the militarist and statist outcome of the Interregnum and to reaffirm instead commercial freedom and local autonomy. From the eve of the Restoration, Anthony Ashley Cooper, afterwards earl of Shaftesbury, headed those who wished to ally particularist "country" politicians with the anti-governmentalists among the "city" merchants and with the clients of both groups among the colonial oligarchs. By 1674 Shaftesbury had defined the proto-whig commercial and colonial program, most notably restated twenty-five years later by his secretary, John Locke, and finally realized by the Walpoles after 1722.[25]

That whig and commercial dominance was so long delayed, however, only emphasizes the profundity of the monarchical and imperial triumph of 1675. The fall of Shaftesbury, and the dissolution of the council of foreign plantations of which he was president, opened imperial administration to the reformed, revitalized, and royalist committee of the Privy Council for the plantations (the so-called "Lords of Trade and Plantations"). This committee was chaired on occasion by the duke of York, afterwards James II, always the personification of unbending monarchy, militarism, and empire. It was influenced by the earl of Danby, who tied an administration aggressive overseas and absolutist at home to a vision of English national achievement. The Privy Council committee was informed, and so directed, by a secretariat first drawn from council, customs, treasury, and the army by Sir Robert Southwell and afterwards developed by William Blathwayt, the imperial fixer. The imperialists' achievement in the six years after 1675 was summarized by the constitution for the empire which they formalized in 1681.[26]

[25] Hale, *First Earl of Shaftesbury;* Clarke, ed., *Life of James the Second;* C. M. Andrews. *British Committees, Commissions, and Councils of Trade and Plantations, 1662-1675*, Johns Hopkins University Studies in Historical and Political Science, XXVI (Baltimore, 1908), 9-151; *Calendar of State Papers, Col. Ser., 1669-1674*, 541-542, nos. 1185, 1186; 545-546, no. 1197; 567-568, nos. 1251, 1252; 575, no. 1264; draft commissions and instructions to the earl of Carlisle as governor-general of Jamaica, Mar. 23, 1673/4, C.O. 138/1, 171-185; E. E. Rich, "The First Earl of Shaftesbury's Colonial Policy," Royal Hist. Soc., *Trans.*, 5th Ser., VII (1957), 47-70; Percy Lewis Kaye, *English Colonial Administration Under Lord Clarendon, 1660-1667*, Johns Hopkins Univ. Studies in Hist. and Pol. Sci., XXIII (Baltimore, 1905); Ralph Paul Bieber, "The British Plantation Councils of 1670-4," *English Historical Review*, XL (1925), 93-106; E. S. de Beer, ed., *The Diary of John Evelyn* (London, 1959); Andrew Browning, *Thomas Osborne Earl of Danby and Duke of Leeds, 1632-1712*, 3 vols. (Glasgow, 1951). Contrast Olson, *Anglo-American Politics*, 51: "Shaftesbury's main interest was not so much in colonial policy as in the procedures by which it was created."

[26] In addition to the sources cited in n. 25 above, see the reference of the draft of the Virginia charter from the Shaftesbury council to the Privy Council committee, Oct. 19, 1675, C.O. 5/1355, 33-42, and note its constitutional consequences.

That accomplishment primarily depended upon the work of three generations of governors-general in defining and establishing English military and imperial authority, both in the British Isles and overseas. Between the restoration of Charles II in 1660 and the death of George I in 1727, the crown commissioned 206 commanders-in-chief of royal provinces overseas. Almost nine in every ten (87.5 percent) of these appointees were English army officers prior to their promotion to the command of colonies. The commissions carried the rank of colonel in the royal army and local rank as general. The prior military service of the governors-general was not nominal, nor was it merely the attribute of social status. These officers had served an average of ten years as captains, or at higher rank, before being promoted to governorships. About 65 percent of the veterans who became governors-general had already had extensive garrison service in the British Isles, and often in England's possessions as well. In the royal garrisons they acquired the administrative skills, worked out the social policies, and practiced the paramilitary, prerogative politics that had helped stabilize England itself, the most turbulent society of seventeenth-century Europe, and that made these veterans of garrison government effective agents of imperialism.[27]

Through these officers the English executive shaped an empire between 1654 and 1681. Its principles were territorial conquest and plantation, political coercion and centralization. Ever-expanding territories were seized from imperial rivals or were reclaimed by the state either from private proprietors or from those local oligarchies that claimed royal sanction for their rule but refused to obey the crown's commands. The conquest of Jamaica in 1655 and of New York in 1664, the subsequent reversion of Barbados and the Leeward Islands from proprietary to royal rule, and the royalization of Virginia government are Restoration cases in point. With cumulative and lasting effect on provincial polities, both in the British Isles and in America and the

[27] Many of these officers' names appear in Charles M. Andrews, ed., "List of Commissions, Instructions, and Additional Instructions Issued to the Royal Governors and Others in America," American Historical Association, *Annual Report for the Year 1911*, I (Washington, D.C., 1913), 393-528. Additional names appear in David P. Henige, *Colonial Governors from the Fifteenth Century to the Present: A Comprehensive List* (Madison, Wis., 1970). More governors-general are named in the entry books of the secretaries of state and of the several colonies, especially S.P. 44, Public Record Office. In addition see Charles Dalton, ed., *English Army Lists and Commission Registers, 1661-1714*, I-II (London, 1892-1904), and Dalton, *George the First's Army, 1714-1727* (London, 1912); Arthur S. White, *A Bibliography of Regimental Histories of the British Army* (London, 1965); *Guide to the Reports of the Royal Commission on Historical Manuscripts, 1911-1957* (Hist. MSS Comm., 3 vols. [London, 1966], Pt. II); Anthony J. Gaber, "Check List of English Newspapers and Periodicals before 1801 in the Huntington Library," *Huntington Library Bulletin*, 2 (1931), 1-66; and Narcissus Luttrell, *A Brief Historical Relation of State Affairs . . .* (Oxford, 1857). Fuller details on 200 of the governors-general appear in an appendix to Webb, *Governors-General*.

West Indies, the English executive sought to impose a classic, avowedly Roman, imperial system on its dependencies.[28]

Proconsular government of provinces in the interest of the "imperial princes" of England played upon the regional, cultural, and familial ties between Englishmen at home and overseas; and the provincial executives also made political and social use of the mercantile acts designed to define the relationships between the merchants of the metropolis and their colonial correspondents. Thus the military cousinage of the Moncks and the Modyfords, and the government service connection of the Nicholas and D'Oyley families, were powerful in Jamaica. In Virginia the influence of the military, banking, and factoring house of Jeffreys had imperial political results equaled only by the Anglican Morrisons or the Gloucestershire Norwoods and Berkeleys.

The political interplay of family, fortune, and profession produced a transatlantic imperial interest, premised on the crown's ability to patronize, protect, and direct its provincial officers (most of whom were both military and economic leaders in their communities) and to require their obedience to royal orders. This primitive "military-industrial complex" meant that arms and munitions for provincial forts and militias were the most common subject of solicitation at court by colonial agents in the seventeenth century. The crown's provision of military supplies, together with the military salaries it paid the army officers commanding colonies, was the largest fiscal cost of empire. Royal commissions reiterated the military bias of empire by directing the governors-general to give the largest share of their attention to militia discipline, drill, and command. The social policy enjoined by these commissions opposed land engrossment and poll taxes. Instead, the governors-general were ordered to favor food crops and excise taxes. The dispersion of

[28] In addition to the Jamaica sources cited in n. 24 see Harlow, *History of Barbados;* A. P. Thornton, *West-Indian Policy under the Restoration* (Oxford, 1956); Frank Cundall, *The Governors of Jamaica in the Seventeenth Century* (London, 1936); C. S. S. Higham, *The Development of the Leeward Islands under the Restoration, 1660-1688* . . . (Cambridge, 1921); Andrews, *Colonial Period,* III: *The Settlements,* 1-138; Stephen Saunders Webb, "William Blathwayt, Imperial Fixer: From Popish Plot to Glorious Revolution," *WMQ,* 3d Ser., XXV (1968), 3-21; and Webb, "William Blathwayt, Imperial Fixer: Muddling Through to Empire, 1689-1717," *ibid.,* XXVI (1969), 373-415. On the Roman example see "Conditions by Sir Thomas Modyford for strengthening His Majesty's Interest in the West Indies" [1671], C.O. 138/1, 136; Robert Latham and William Matthews, eds., *The Diary of Samuel Pepys,* IV (Berkeley and Los Angeles, 1971), 217; Quinn, "Sir Thomas Smith," Am. Phil. Soc., *Procs.,* LXXXIX (1945), 545, 546-547; Quinn, "Muster Plantation," Cork Hist. and Archaeol. Soc., *Jour.,* 2d Ser., LXXI (1966), 22; and Caroline Robbins, "The 'Excellent Use' of Colonies. A Note on Walter Moyle's Justification of Roman Colonies, *ca.* 1699," *WMQ,* 3d Ser., XXIII (1966), 620-626.

population caused by unproductive, speculative landholding and by commercial agriculture, and the penalty placed on the poor and on families by poll taxes, were opposed by the governors-general in order to encourage farm families to settle closely in self-sustaining settlements. Such settlements could support a numerous militia, capable of self-defense and subject to garrison government discipline.[29]

Other military institutions than the provincial militias expressed the imperialists' agrarian, authoritarian, paramilitary social policy. The regimental plantations of Cromwellian soldiers defined the settlement patterns of Jamaica and so shaped the island's social structure. In Virginia a regiment of Charles II's Guards, elements of which stayed in the colony for seven years, helped a succession of governors-general displace Berkeleyan oligarchs and repress Baconian rebels, clearing a social middle ground for aspirant, but obedient, planter-militiamen. Regular troops in three New York garrisons, and garrisons in Nova Scotia and Newfoundland, repeatedly essayed soldier-colonization on the Roman model from 1696 until the eve of the Revolution. Such units manifested the army's social, political, and profoundly imperial influence in colonial America.[30]

"Force gives the rule to law." The laws of trade, of politics, of religion, unquestionably important as they were to the shape of empire, received the color of authority from the palette of physical force. Symbolically as well as actually, the army supported executive authority everywhere in the empire. Whether in Carlisle, England, or in Port Royal, Jamaica, the earl of Carlisle

[29] *Calendar of State Papers, Dom. Ser., 1677-1678,* 535; *Calendar of State Papers Col. Ser., 1677-1680,* 177, no. 479; 182, no. 496; 231, no. 643, 381-383, nos. 1036-1038; 624, no. 1569. The relation of colonial officers' fiscal reliance on England and their political control by England is insisted on in "Overtures touching the Council to be erected for foreigne plantations," Egerton MS, 2395, 271, and exemplified in "the petition for his salary as governor general of Barbados by Lord Willoughby to the king" [Nov. 1672], *ibid.,* 485-486, and in the royal warrants of Nov. 13, 28, 1677, for the armaments of the earl of Carlisle's government of Jamaica, C.O. 3/138, 165-168, 175-176, Public Records Office. See also Ella Lonn, *The Colonial Agents of the Southern Colonies* (Chapel Hill, N.C., 1945), 22; *Calendar of State Papers, Col. Ser., 1661-1668,* 126, no. 428; 256, no. 855; 290-291, no. 975; 318, no. 1037; 380, no. 1194; 513, no. 1618; *ibid., 1669-1674,* 24, no. 71; 62-63, no. 195; W. L. Grant and James Munro, eds., *Acts of the Privy Council of England, Colonial Series, 1613-1680* (London, 1908), 695; Wilcomb E. Washburn, "The Effect of Bacon's Rebellion on Government in England and Virginia," United States National Museum *Bulletin* (Washington, D.C., 1962), 225; J. R. Tanner, ed., *A Descriptive Catalogue of the Naval Manuscripts in the Pepysian Library* . . . ([London], 1903-1923), III, 296, 301-303, 307, 308-309, 310, 312, 314-316, 355, 411, 416, 435, 458, IV, 349, 356, 377; *Calendar of State Papers, Col. Ser., 1675-1676,* 458, no. 1043; 462, no. 1063, 460, no. 1053; 461, nos. 1057-1058; 462, no. 1062; 484, no. 1114. See also the military establishments in Auditor General and Secretary at War William Blathwayt's Letter Book, T. 64/88-89, Public Record Office.

[30] On Jamaica see nn. 24 and 28 above. The work of the Guards in Virginia appears at large in the MSS of Henry Coventry at Longleat House, Warminster,

took coach to church surrounded by his life guard of cavalry. He took his seat in a canopied chair of state, the altar at his left hand and the redcoated files of his garrison at his right. He heard a sermon on the holy duty of obedience to governors preached by the garrison chaplain. Carlisle's garrison governments thus manifested the authoritarian marriage of the military and the ministry in the service of the state. In Portsmouth or New York, Col. Richard Nicolls found little fighting for his soldiers, but they enforced the embargoes by which he kept wheat in the port in famine times. They manned patrol boats and (rather roughly) collected the customs duties from merchants. Even by their impact on the local labor supply Nicolls's garrisons helped show how much the economic authority of the English government was a function of force. The corporation of York and the council of Virginia both suffered as Col. Herbert Jeffreys turned from a civil war career of fighting English and French rebels against royal authority to a peacetime occupation of punishing English and American opponents of the crown's control. The elements of the royal guards which composed Jeffreys's garrisons chopped up defiant Yorkshiremen and hanged Baconians. Hearing of the obduracy of some Virginia councilors, rather more provincial-minded than the rest, the Guards asked leave of the colonel to hang them too. The

Wilts., Eng., LXXVII-LXXVIII, microfilm copy in the Library of Congress cited by permission of Lord Bath, and in Samuel Wiseman's Book of Record, Pepysian Manuscripts 2582, Magdalene College, Cambridge, cited by permission of the Pepysian Librarian and published from "A True Narrative of the Rise, Progresse, and Cessation of the Late Rebellion in Virginia . . . ," C.O. 5/1371, in Charles M. Andrews, ed., *Narratives of the Insurrections, 1675-1690*, Original Narratives of Early American History (New York, 1915), 99-141. The crucial entry book is "Entries of Virginia," C.O. 5/1355. On New York See Stanley McCrory Pargellis, "The Four Independent Companies of New York," *Essays in Colonial American History Presented to Charles McLean Andrews by his Students* (New Haven, Conn., 1931), 96-123. The survey of garrisons by John Shy, *Toward Lexington: The Role of the British Army in the Coming of the American Revolution* (Princeton, N.J., 1965), 3-44, is unequalled. Note, however, Shy's emphasis as indicated in the title of his second chapter, "The Decision of 1763." The other broad treatment of the 18th-century garrisons is the opening chapter of Stanley McCrory Pargellis, *Lord Loudoun in North America* (New Haven, Conn., 1933), in which Andrews's prize student (1929) and junior colleague asserts that "the real problem of colonial defense, before Pitt's time, had nothing to do with empire" (p. 3), and that the words "Enlarged the Dominion, And upheld the Majesty of these Kingdoms" on a monument commemorating Ticonderoga (1759) "strike a new note in British history; through them breathes for the first time the spirit of Empire" (p. 1). On the 18th-century garrisons see also D. W. Prowse, *A History of Newfoundland from the English, Colonial, and Foreign Records*, 2d rev. ed. (London, 1896). On the role of the military in Nova Scotia see R. H. Raymond Smythies, *Historical Records of the 40th (2nd Somersetshire) Regiment* (Devonport, Eng., 1894). On the military plantations of New York see Guzzardo, "Sir William Johnson's Official Family."

ultimate identity of military force and monarchical—imperial—politics was apparent to all.[31]

There are questions about the efficacy of English soldiers as the physical basis of garrison government in America. The garrisons were diseased, dispersed, and undisciplined, and their numbers were small. In the seventeenth century there were seldom more than one thousand regular soldiers on the North American continent. Often there were no more than three hundred. Both numbers were doubled in the English West Indies. These deficiencies, however, were at least partly offset by the physical debility and the small numbers of the colonists themselves. In proportion to population the garrisons were larger than the armies commanded by present-day authoritarian regimes. Moreover, the garrisons' domestic effect was multiplied many times, both in British and American provinces, by the militarily weak but politically puissant select militias. The garrisons' greatest reinforcement was psychological. A widespread desire for local peace and social order placed much of the populace of almost every province on the side of the armed agents of imperial authority. In addition, when provincials felt exposed to the attacks of hostile natives or alien empires, as was often the case in much of the Atlantic world, the exchange of popular acquiescence, and often ready obedience, to royal rule in return for the protection of garrison government or the leadership offered by the governors-general was especially easy and natural.[32]

[31] The duke of Newcastle's reminder to the king is quoted in David Ogg, *England in the Reign of Charles II*, I (Oxford, 1934), 145. On Carlisle see nn. 24, 28, 29 above, and C. Roy Hudleston, ed., *Naworth Estate and Household Accounts, 1648-1660*, Surtees Society, CLXVIII (London, 1958); John Clough Nichols, ed., *Lady Anne Halkett, Autobiography*, Camden Society, N.S. XIII (London, 1875), 36ff; *The Manuscripts of S. H. le Fleming, Esq. of Rydal Hall* (Hist. MSS Comm., *Twelfth Report*, Appendix [London, 1890], Pt. VII), hereafter cited as *le Fleming MSS;* M. Creighton, *Carlisle*, in E. A. Freeman and William Hunt, eds., *Historic Towns* (London, 1889); R. S. Ferguson, ed., *The Royal Charters of the City of Carlisle* (Carlisle, 1894), xxvi. The activities of Nicolls's troops are recorded in E. B. O'Callaghan and B. Fernow, eds., *Documents Relative to the Colonial History of the State of New York*, III (Albany, N.Y., 1859). Some hints of Nicolls's imperial role appear in Robert C. Ritchie, "The Duke of York's Commission of Revenue," *New-York Historical Society Quarterly*, LVIII (1974), 177-187, and in Stephen Saunders Webb, " 'Brave Men and Servants to His Royal Highness": The Household of James Stuart in the Evolution of English Imperialism," *Perspectives in American History*, VIII (1974), 55-80. On Jeffreys see n. 29 above.

[32] On select militias in England see particularly Abbott, "English Conspiracy," *AHR*, XIV (1909), 521; *Calendar of State Papers, Dom. Ser., 1661-1662*, 27, 603; *le Fleming MSS*, 6, 29, 32; Andrew Browning, ed., *English Historical Documents, 1660-1714*, VIII (New York, 1958), 775-796; and J. R. Western, *The English Militia in the Eighteenth Century: The Story of a Political Issue, 1660-1802* (Toronto, 1965), 8, 12-15, 44-47.

Fear of alien attack and desire for domestic order produced provincial political successes for the party of monarchical and military authority, while arousing metropolitan criticism. The crown's crippling of the Jamaica and Virginia assemblies, for example, helped alert English parliamentary enemies of executive power to the menace that garrison government posed to legislative and statutory rule. American elites' apprehensions that "we shall be governed as an army," rather than by legislature and law, were validated in English opinion as the crown enhanced its influence by regarrisoning Cromwellian citadels and "reforming" corporate charters. Their power enhanced physically and politically, the local governors grew increasingly aggressive in England as well as overseas.[33]

As the imperial executive verged on absolutism, political moderates or "trimmers" such as the earl of Halifax moved to strengthen their position midway between monarchical militarism and legislative republicanism. Rejecting the exclusion from the royal succession of James, duke of York, and accepting the argument that James's supporters in Ireland, Scotland, "and the Plantations" would react to exclusion with civil war, Halifax joined the garrison government elements that upheld the crown—"Well, if it come to a war," he said to the governor of York, "you and I must go together"—and denounced the "popular" program of Shaftesbury and the Commons majority.[34]

Halifax's forum was as much the Privy Council as it was the House of Lords, and he was as much concerned for the survival of colonial representative assemblies as he was to preserve an effective executive for the empire. The imperial debate of 1680-1681 was a part of the Exclusion Crisis. That

[33] On colonial fears see Thornton, *West India Policy*, 251. The quotation is in Collection of Tracts Relating to Jamaica 1503-1693, Add. MSS 12429, 98, 99b. On the reestablishment of the Cromwellian network see Firth and Davies, *Regimental History*, 522, and Gardiner, *Commonwealth and Protectorate*, III, map, for the original plan, and compare *Calendar of State Papers, Dom. Ser., 1660-1661*, 303-304, *1662-1663*, 205, *1666-1667*, 282-283, *1671-1672*, 294-295, *1677-1678*, 573-574; Dalton, ed., *English Army Lists*, I, 10-16, 59-62, 76-77. See also Western, *English Militia*, 11-13, 48-49, 50-51; Clarke, ed., *Life of James the Second*, 434, 443, 446-447, 495-496; Haley, *First Earl of Shaftesbury*, 361-362; and Browning, *Thomas Earl of Danby*, II, 68-69, 89-91. On charter revision see B. L. K. Henderson, "The Commonwealth Charters," Royal Hist. Soc., *Trans.*, 3d Ser., VI (1912), 139-142, and J. H. Sacret, "The Restoration Government and Municipal Corporations," *Eng. Hist. Rev.*, XLV (1930), 232-259.

[34] J. P. Kenyon, *Robert Spencer Earl of Sunderland, 1641-1702* (London, 1958), 48-60; Airy, ed., *Burnet's History*, I, 281n; H. C. Foxcroft, *The Life and Letters of Sir George Savile, Bart.: First Marquis of Halifax . . .*, I (London, 1898), 225-228. See also the effective, abbreviated treatment in Foxcroft, *A Character of the Trimmer: Being a Short Life of the First Marquis of Halifax* (Cambridge, 1946), 116-117. The remark to the governor, Sir John Reresby, is noted in his *Memoirs*, ed. James Cartwright (London, 1875), Dec. 29, 1680, 197.

debate shaped the constitution of the English empire to, and indeed far beyond, the American Revolution. Its decisive moment occurred in two dramatic Privy Council sessions. There the earl of Halifax helped persuade Charles II to partially re-empower provincial legislatures and to excuse the leaders of their opposition parties from prosecution as enemies of the crown. The royal return of the power of legislative initiative and amendment to the assemblies of Jamaica and Virginia was soon followed by the duke of York's grant of a representative body to New York. Excusing political opposition and confirming assembly authority (once the assemblies agreed to raise revenues for royal use) was a victory for political moderation. These acts went far to establish the governmental structure of the empire and also helped to define the conduct of Anglo-American politics for a century to come.[35]

Resolution of the imperial crisis was facilitated by an available and proven compromise between the extreme opinions of "court" and "country." Lord Culpeper had worked out such a compromise while in command of Virginia. He had actually preserved the colonial legislature's powers of initiative and amendment, despite royal orders to the contrary. But in return Culpeper had exacted a high price in prerogative power: the Virginia assembly accepted a bill, written in the Privy Council, that provided for a permanent provincial tax to support imperial authority. Equally important to the reduction of local autonomy and to the increase of imperial influence was the acquiescence of the Virginia burgesses in the division of legislative authority among the governor, the council, and themselves. Unwillingly, the lower house had also adopted parliamentary practices and public records, both of which opened legislative proceedings to prerogative influence, and accepted regular royal review, revision, and rejection of provincial laws. Finally, and most important, the assembly formally acknowledged as law the absolute military authority of the king's governor-general.[36]

[35] *Calendar of State Papers, Col. Ser., 1677-1680*, 613-614, no. 1540; 616, nos. 1550-1552; 621-622, no. 1559; 662, nos. 1561-1562; 623-625, nos. 1566-1572; 636, no. 1612; Bryan Edwards, *The History, Civil and Commercial, of the British Colonies in the West Indies*, I (London, 1801), 171-174, 310-316; Agnes M. Whitson, *The Constitutional Development of Jamaica—1660 to 1729* (Manchester, Eng., 1929), 107-108.

[36] The major sources on Culpeper's compromise are William Waller Hening, ed., *The Statutes at Large; Being a Collection of All the Laws of Virginia . . .* (Richmond, 1819-1823); H. R. McIlwaine, ed., *Legislative Journals of the Council of Colonial Virginia*, I (Richmond, 1918), and McIlwaine, ed., *Journals of the House of Burgesses of Virginia, 1659/60-1693* (Richmond, 1925); "Instructions to Lord Culpeper Together with an Account of his Lordships Compliance Therewith," in the Papers of Francis Baron Howard of Effingham, IV, Library of Congress, cited by permission of the owner. Commission to Lord Culpeper as governor general of Virginia, Dec. 6, 1679, C.O. 5/1355, 313-326.

Utilizing the Virginia model, Charles II quickly extended the constitutional settlement of 1681 to all the crown colonies. Limited local legislative authority, provincial taxes for imperial use, and an unfettered military prerogative characterized the 1681 settlement.[37] This imposition on American provinces of the Civil War formula of governor, council, and martial law testified to the great growth of executive authority in the empire in the generation after 1653, while the survival of the provincial assemblies and courts preserved elements of corporate privilege, provincial autonomy, and individual liberty. The imperial balance struck in 1681 between metropolis and provinces, coercion and consultation, military-imperial executive and civilian-localist legislature endured for the greater part of a century as the constitution of the first English empire. Thus Anglo-American relations were not shaped by an exclusively "commercial and colonial system," in which the strongest political element was "colonial self-government." Rather, they were predominantly directed by a military and provincial system the strongest political element of which was Anglo-American *imperial* government.

Imperialism and its leader, James Stuart, prevailed in 1681 only because of the support of such moderates as Halifax, many of them powerfully placed in the army and in James's own household, where, as members of his "shadow cabinet," they greatly influenced imperial administration. The moderates had not dared let James, the personification of monarchical order and social stability, fall before the levelling, republican, and localist forces led by Shaftesbury. So, too, in the garrisoned provinces of Britain and America the party of authority had succeeded with the aid of imperially ambitious, but not authoritarian, councilor-administrators.[38]

The character and authority of the councilors themselves had been, and would continue to be, a precise measure of the influence of the "court" or of the "country" in each royal colony. Acting on their garrison government principles, the governors-general regarded their colonial councils as advisory and executive groups of subordinate officers. In this view each of the councilors, if only as colonel of the royal militia, was bound by martial law, first to advise the provincial captain general and governor-in-chief and then "to express his obedience to his *General,* although it be a service that corresponded not with his own opinion at the first." Opposite expectations of the council model and the councilors' role were held by "country" politi-

[37] The Papers of William Blathwayt, I, no. 4, XXVII, no. 3, XXXVIII, no. 3, Colonial Williamsburg, Williamsburg, Va.; *Calendar of State Papers, Col. Ser., 1681-1685*, 83, no. 161; Governor-General Sir Thomas Lynch to the Jamaica Assembly, Add. MSS 12429, 136.

[38] Webb, " 'Brave Men and Servants,' " *Perspectives in Am. Hist.*, VIII (1974), 55-80.

cians. When in 1674 Shaftesbury and Locke sought to limit the governors' power to suspend councilors and to declare martial law without council consent, they made their social and political purposes plain. Councilors were to be chosen by Shaftesbury and his "city" merchant allies from colonial candidates who combined "country" principles with wealth. The councilors were to possess freedom to debate and to oppose governors' proposals. The governors' colonial councils were to be remodeled on the king's Privy Council, as it was idealized in "country" opinion. That is, the council was to represent the various elements of oligarchy in the provincial society. So composed, it would check the authority of the royal executive.[39]

By the mid-1680s the upshot of the struggle to shape the colonial councils was not so much a compromise between the opposed views as it was a division of each royal council into two parties. The majority was composed of men powerful in their communities, possessed of administrative talent, and loyal to the prerogative. The minority was made up of oligarchs who devoted their personal force, economic advantage, and "country" opinions to the leadership of legislative and localist opposition to the executive and to imperialism. Combined in the colonial councils, these opposed elements both effectively administered prerogative programs and criticized executive excesses, either directly or, more commonly, through their English correspondents.[40]

These correspondents were increasingly sympathetic to complaints of absolutism. During the seven years after 1681, metropolitan as well as provincial moderates slowly and reluctantly were driven to join James Stuart's opponents as he pushed autocratic government (and religious change) to counterproductive extremes. He executed the leading whigs in 1683; massacred the Monmouth rebels in 1685; subverted both the most and the least imperial of the colonial constitutions, those of Jamaica and New England, in 1686; and in 1687 attacked the status of that sanctuary of social order, the Church of England. The antagonisms thus accumulated gave social and ideological focus to the army's dislike of stricter discipline and the admission of Irish and Catholics to military service. There followed the military coup (called "the Glorious Revolution") against James in 1688 and against his governors-general in America in 1689. By 1692, William III, the soldier-king who displaced James, had rebuffed whig-commercialist efforts to return

[39] See nn. 19, 20, and 25 above on the formation of the opposed views of council status and function. The quotation is from Maj. Richard Elton, *The Compleat Body of the Art Military compiled for the foot soldier* . . . (London, 1659), 185.

[40] An accessible example is the Virginia council, as evidenced in H. R. McIlwaine and Wilbur M. Hall, eds., *Executive Journals of the Council of Colonial Virginia*, I (Richmond, 1925-1945); Account of the Government from the Council [May 4, 1683], received Sept. 9, 1683, C.O. 5/1356, 175-187; *Calendar of State Papers, Col. Ser., 1681-1685*, 423-426, no. 1063; 517, no. 1309; and the sources cited in n. 36 above.

to the status quo ante 1675 and, instead, had restored the 1681 imperial settlement, which balanced military, imperial, and executive dictates with civilian, localist, and legislative demands.[41]

The reestablished imperial constitution proved its worth in inspiring and organizing provincial defenses as far apart as Newfoundland and Jamaica during the first round of England's war with France for Atlantic empire. The truce in that conflict, from 1697 to 1702, offered whigs and commercialists a chance to reassert the Shaftesbury-Locke program of 1674. In England they forced William III to constitute a board of trade and to appoint John Locke to it. In America they tried to re-enfranchise the colonial elites in council and assembly, to reinforce the rule of law in the provinces, and to reduce the imperial authority of the governors-general, especially by attacking their military power. By 1705 this whig effort had failed, for further war with France had once again mandated executive authority and military discipline throughout the empire.[42]

The North American colonies soon shared more directly than ever before in the political as well as the military outcome of England's conflict with her

[41] Even as the imperial compromise was effected in 1681, moderates in James's own household recognized that, because of his religion, "sooner or later we must all be undone." Col. John Churchill to Col. George Legge, Sept. 12, 1681, in Keith Feiling, *A History of the Tory Party, 1640-1714* (Oxford, 1924), 181. See also William Coxe, *Memoirs of the Duke of Marlborough, with His Original Correspondence* . . . , I (London, 1872), iii. Besides Feiling's fundamental analysis and the sources named above, particular use has been made here of J. R. Western, *Monarchy and Revolution: The English State in the 1680s* (London, 1972); John Miller, *Popery and Politics in England, 1660-1688* (Cambridge, 1973); J. R. Jones, *The First Whigs: The Politics of the Exclusion Crisis, 1678-1683* (London, 1961); and Jones, *The Revolution of 1688 in England* (New York, 1972). On the motivation of colonial court parties see Olson, *Anglo-American Politics,* 74. The reversionary political impact of the coup in the colonies is discussed in Webb, "William Blathwayt," *WMQ,* 3d Ser., XXVI (1969), 373-374, 377-378; Webb, "The Strange Career of Francis Nicholson," *WMQ,* 3d Ser., XXIII (1966), 523-525; and James Kirby Martin, ed., *The Human Dimensions of Nation Making* (Madison, Wis., 1976), 42-45. See also Olson, *Anglo-American Politics,* 75-78, and J. H. Plumb, *The Origins of Political Stability: England, 1675-1725* (Boston, 1967).

[42] On the whig interlude see Maurice Cranston, *John Locke* . . . (London, 1957); Peter Laslett, "John Locke, The Great Recoinage, and the Origins of the Board of Trade: 1695-1698," *WMQ,* 3rd Ser., XIV (1957), 370-402; Gertrude Ann Jacobsen, *William Blathwayt: A Late Seventeenth-Century English Administrator* (New Haven, Conn., 1932); and I. K. Steele, *Politics of Colonial Policy: The Board of Trade in Colonial Administration, 1696-1720* (Oxford, 1968), esp. Appendix B. For an application of whig/mercantilism see the attitudes of the Board of Trade (without Blathwayt but including Locke) toward Virginia, exemplified in instructions to Col. Nicholson as Governor of Virginia, Sept. 13, 1698; representation of the Board to the Lords Justice, Aug. 23, 1698; additional instructions to Nicholson, May 18, 1699; Circular Letter to the Governors, June 26, 1699; Board to Nicholson, June 28, 1699, C.O. 5/1359, 226ff., 252-259, 314-315, 330-332, 333-334.

European rivals. During the five years after the battle of Blenheim, from 1705 to 1710, officers who had trained under England's greatest general and chief minister, John Churchill, duke of Marlborough, went out to govern Virginia, New York, Massachusetts, Newfoundland and Nova Scotia, Jamaica, and the Leeward Islands. The decade that followed marked the acme of the "old empire." Two thousand regular troops in North America and large garrisons in the West Indies carried out the orders of professional officers deeply imbued with the precepts of garrison government. Marlborough's governors-general gave a momentum to imperial administration and a shape to provincial politics and society that were not overtly challenged until the mid-1760s, when an overdecisive imperial victory permitted and inspired the Revolutionary generation to enter politics.[43]

Yet, in their own eyes, the imperialists suffered decisive defeat as early as 1722. In the previous year the Board of Trade (headed by a colonel whose particular qualification for imperial office seems to have been his translation of Caesar's *Commentaries* into English and its dedication to the duke of Marlborough) had urged on the king-in-council a program of American government prepared by Marlborough's governors-general. This plan proposed the coordination of American commands under a captain-general. It would set limits to the colonies, and defend them against France, by fortifying and garrisoning the inland frontiers. Eight additional regiments would control the Atlantic coast and its population centers. But this summary of imperial aspirations was filed away for a generation when the entire imperialist leadership—Marlborough, Sunderland, and Stanhope—died in 1722.[44]

In their places the whiggish and commercialist Walpole regime came to power. That regime—the partisans of merchants and aristocrats—took advantage of an abnormally peaceful period to debase the administration of the

[43] Himself the key to imperial administration of 1704-1710, and exercising an indirect but pervasive influence through his former officers for decades afterwards, the duke of Marlborough can be pictured in part from published sources, chiefly Sir George Murray, ed., *The Letters and Despatches of John Churchill . . . , 1702-1712* (London, 1845); Coxe, *Memoirs of Marlborough;* Winston Churchill, *Marlborough: His Life and His Times,* 4 vols. (New York, 1933-1938). Further references are assembled by R. E. Scouller, *The Armies of Queen Anne* (Oxford, 1966).

[44] Alexander Spotswood to the Board of Trade, Jan., 16, 1720/1; Mr. Auditor Walpole's objections; order of the Privy Council, Aug. 17, 1723; Hugh Drysdale to the Board, Nov. 17, 1725; the earl of Orkney to the Board, Dec. 30, 1725, C.O. 5/1319, 3, 35, 52, 91, 92; the case and petition of Colonel Spotswood, C.O. 5/1344, 1, 7; Board to Secretary Carteret, July 17, 1721, C.O. 5/1365, 229-236; Board to the king, "In regard to the Government of the Plantation," Sept. 8, 1721, Add. MSS 35907; *Journals of the Commissioners for Trade and Plantations from November 1718 to December 1722* (London, 1925), 279-280; Steele, *Politics of Colonial Policy,* 167-170; *DNB,* s.v. "Bladen, Martin."

empire into an uncoordinated assortment of patronage posts, reserved for the well-connected and the unqualified. Peace reduced the imperatives of authoritarian politics and substituted the politics of autonomy. Provincial societies became far more concerned with civil profit than with military security. The government of the increasingly autonomous dependencies was gradually assumed by enriched provincial elites, venial English placemen, and, after 1736, aggrandizing assemblies. At last Shaftesbury's alliance of the ambitious classes in the "country," the "city," and the colonies was fully realized. Commonwealthmen, commercialists, and colonists dominated Anglo-American relations as they had not since the 1640s.[45]

The return of war to English America in the decade 1739-1748 meant that, on much evener terms than had prevailed before 1722, the ancient debate between armed authority and moneyed autonomy was resumed. War made its inevitable demands for forcefulness and order even on the most pacifist and oligarchical of English administrations. Indeed, on the frontiers of empire, in South Carolina, Georgia, Nova Scotia, and in Maroon-menaced Jamaica, the physical imperatives of empire produced a doubling of regular forces and the appointment of militant governors-general by 1748. By that date, however, despite the imperialist resurgence, it appeared that the administrative excellence, the political assurance, and the social relevance of the governors-general during the first century of English colonization would not be equaled again. Instead, the anti-imperial forces of acquisitive capitalism, individual liberty, provincial autonomy, and Anglo-American oligarchy had won an irreducible social and political status for their beneficiaries, the eventual authors of the American Revolution.

The final confrontation of empire with autonomy began when four imperial regiments were destroyed or captured on the Ohio and Ontario frontiers in 1754. "The great war for the empire" poured thirty thousand regulars into England's American provinces by 1759.[46] Conquering vast territories, subjugating both natives and planters to England (a subjugation symbolized by American service in the English army and by colonial taxes for the army's support), the army achieved at last the imperial ambition coeval with colonization itself.

Undersecretary William Knox's memorandum of February 1763 has been called the fullest expression of the "new" imperialism. Knox antici-

[45] J. H. Plumb, *Sir Robert Walpole: The Making of a Stateman* (London, 1956), 262, 263, 270, 363-389; Olson, *Anglo-American Politics*, 106-141; Alfred James Henderson, *London and the National Government, 1721-1742* (Durham, Eng., 1945), 92, 109-111, 127-130; James A. Henretta, *"Salutary Neglect": Colonial Administration under the Duke of Newcastle*, I (Princeton, N.J., 1972), esp. 260-263.

[46] Lawrence Henry Gipson, *The British Empire before the American Revolution* (New York, 1936-1969); Shy, *Toward Lexington*; Pargellis, *Lord Loudoun*.

pated that protection would be offered and obedience enforced by frontier and urban garrisons, "to secure the Dependence of the Colonys on Great Britain."[47] This was imperialism, but it was not new. The Knox memorandum of 1763 marked the return to Anglo-American political preeminence of coerciveness and power-hunger, paternalism and militarism. These forces had woven an imperial pattern throughout the fabric we habitually call "the colonial period of American history," but which was really the period of Anglo-American empire.

[47] Knox, as quoted in Shy, *Toward Lexington*, 64-65.

10

Governors or Generals? A Note on Martial Law and the Revolution of 1689 in English America

Ian Steele

CLAIMS that the first British empire was essentially military, rather than commercial or political, have rightly centered on James II, particularly as duke of York. His influence on his royal brother, as well as his own experience, style of government, choice of colonial governors, and imperial preoccupations, is said to have reflected an essentially military perspective.[1] This view is compatible with some of the fears, claims, and experiences of Englishmen on both sides of the Atlantic before and during his short, unhappy reign. Yet suggestions that his imperial administration was primarily military need further examination, especially since no written plan of "garrison government" has survived, contrary opinion abounds, and the theory has not been applied to the study of the English empire while James II was king.

James's empire was never more fully developed, in personnel and policies, than in the last year of his reign. Then came a strenuous test of how that empire was perceived, when his royal governors were forced to respond to the long crisis that ended the reign in 1688-1689. Amid uncertainties that lasted as long as eight months and prompted dissidents

[1] See the work of Stephen Saunders Webb, especially "'Brave Men and Servants to his Royal Highness': The Household of James Stuart in the Evolution of English Imperialism," *Perspectives in American History,* VIII (1974), 55-80, *The Governors-General: The English Army and the Definition of Empire, 1569-1681* (Chapel Hill, N.C., 1979), and his exchange with Richard R. Johnson in the *William and Mary Quarterly,* 3d Ser., XLIII (1986), 408-459.

to various levels of resistance,[2] did the royal governors react in ways that suggested the primacy of military, or civilian, perceptions of their positions?

Although reluctant to use martial law in England, James II had given one stunning demonstration of thoroughly military power in the brutal destruction of the duke of Monmouth's rising in 1685.[3] For weeks after their victory, his troops exercised what proved to be the last instance of unfettered martial law in England. Two of James's colonial governors of 1689, Edmund Andros and Francis Nicholson, had been army officers involved in suppressing Monmouth's followers, as had others who became military officers in the colonies in the interim.[4] Formal colonial addresses congratulated James on his success. Shiploads of convicted rebels were transported to the West Indian colonies. Leaders of all the royal colonies in 1689 should have recalled James's own military model for crushing a challenge to the throne.

Not only was the wide use of martial law exemplified by the royal response to Monmouth, but it was also clear that the military had much more freedom of action outside England than was allowed within. In Ireland, Scotland, Tangier, or America the imposition of martial law, which effectively suspended the operation of civil authority, met no resistance in English law. Later distinctions, between the disciplining of the military through the Articles of War and the power of martial law over civilians, were unclear in England before 1689 and even less clear in the overseas garrisons and colonies of the restored Stuarts.[5]

[2] Communications aspects of this situation are discussed in Ian Steele, *The English Atlantic, 1675-1740: An Exploration of Communications and Community* (New York, 1986), chap. 6.

[3] John Childs, *The Army, James II, and the Glorious Revolution* (London, 1980), 92-93. Martial law was never brought into England under Charles II, according to John Childs, *The Army of Charles II* (London, 1976), 76-77.

[4] Bruce T. McCully, "From the North Riding to Morocco: The Early Years of Governor Francis Nicholson, 1655-1686," *WMQ*, 3d Ser., XIX (1962), 534-556; Stephen Saunders Webb, "The Trials of Sir Edmund Andros," in James Kirby Martin, ed., *The Human Dimensions of Nation Making: Essays on Colonial and Revolutionary America* (Madison, Wis., 1976), 41-42. In recruiting their two new companies for New England in 1686, it seems likely that Andros and Nicholson drew on men of their own. Regarding Lt. John Jordan, see below, n. 30. Gov. Nathaniel Johnson promoted to lieutenant Francis Overton, who served in the Guards in suppressing Monmouth's rising. W. Noël Sainsbury *et al.*, eds., *Calendar of State Papers, Colonial Series*, 43 vols. (London, 1860-1963) *1685-1688*, no. 1387, hereafter cited as *Cal. State Papers*. Although numerous officers who served against the Monmouth rebels eventually became royal governors, only two of them were James II's governors. Cf. Webb, "Household," *Perspectives Am. Hist.*, VIII (1974), 74.

[5] See W. S. Holdsworth, "Martial Law Historically Considered," *Law Quarterly Review*, XVIII (1902), 117-132; H. Earle Richardson, "Martial Law," *ibid.*, 133-142; Charles M. Clode, *The Administration of Justice under Military and Martial Law*, 2d ed. (London, 1874), chap. 1; Clifford Walton, *History of the*

Sir Francis Watson, acting governor of Jamaica, can provide the model of an essentially military response to the rising tensions of 1689. A career soldier, Watson had been quartermaster of Sir Philip Howard's troop in the Royal Horse Guards and major general in Jamaica under Charles Howard, earl of Carlisle.[6] When Carlisle became governor of Jamaica in 1678, Major General Watson served on his council and commanded the militia. In 1679 he had returned to England to participate in a full-scale debate on the role of the military in governing Jamaica, and in the next decade martial law was rather routinely used in Jamaica to respond to invasion scares or to suppress Negro uprisings.[7]

Watson became acting governor in October 1688 on the death of Christopher Monck, second duke of Albemarle. He continued the pro-buccaneer appointments and policies of Albemarle that had provoked political retaliation in London by the planters and their merchant allies. In February 1689, as rumors of William III's Torbay landing reached Jamaica, so did orders from James II to restore the council to its composition at the duke's arrival. Watson found these orders, and news that Lt. Gov. Hender Molesworth was hurrying back to the island, very unpalatable. He delayed implementation of his orders and insulated his colony from confusion by declaring martial law. Martial law was enforced entirely by the militia, as there were no regular troops on the island.[8] Weekly courts martial were held in each parish, and martial law remained in force for nearly four months before formal orders to proclaim William and Mary were received.[9]

In declaring martial law, Watson asserted tighter control over the militia and successfully silenced local opposition. Despite severe local political factionalism, an unaristocratic soldier with inadequate information was able to use the militia to control his jurisdiction through a confusing hiatus in imperial power that lasted for six months. In justifying his behavior to London authorities, Watson cited King James's proclamation of Septem-

British Standing Army, 1660-1700 (London, 1894), chap. 26, app. 53. James was developing the military legal system as the exclusive method to discipline soldiers (Childs, *Army, James II*, 92-95, 102).

[6] *Cal. State Papers, 1677-1680*, nos. 573, 1370.1; Webb, *Governors-General*, 81, 69-100.

[7] *Cal. State Papers, 1677-1680*, nos. 975, 1059, 1141. Gov. John Vaughan had done the same from Apr. 5 to June 10, 1678, apparently to obtain labor for fortifications (*ibid.*, 649, 682, *1685-1688*, nos. 299, 311, 330, 339, 372, 883).

[8] There had been two foot companies of regulars, along with some 4,000 militia, in Jamaica in 1679 (*ibid., 1677-1680*, nos. 1118, 1238, 1243). There were no regulars there during the reign of James II (*ibid., 1685-1688*, no. 759, *1689-1692*, no. 204).

[9] *Ibid., 1685-1688*, nos. 1940, 1941, 1943, *1689-1692*, nos. 50, 51; Smyth Kelly to William Blathwayt, May 27 and June 5, 1689, Blathwayt Papers, Vol. XXII, Colonial Williamsburg Foundation Library, Williamsburg, Va., 23185. See also Agnes M. Whitson, *The Constitutional Development of Jamaica, 1660-1729* (Manchester, 1929), 131-132.

ber 28, 1688, warning of a Dutch invasion in one instance[10] and legitimate public fear of French and Spanish hostility in another.[11]

Maj. Gen. Francis Watson was a soldier acting as governor of a royal colony of conquest; nevertheless, his solution to the confusing time between kings should have occurred to other governors if they perceived the administration of the empire as essentially military. All royal governors had the legal power to impose martial law, both over soldiers under their command and, in an emergency, over militia and civilians.[12] This power could suspend all laws, sanction whatever actions the commander took, and leave him subject to no authority beyond a military review. Watson's justifications for imposing martial law were usable by all other royal governors that winter. Jamaica's Watson provides the military model for keeping the peace through the Revolution of 1688-1689; the governors of the other five royal colonies can fruitfully be studied against that example, in ascending order of their military experience.

Barbados, the premier English colony in 1688, had a longer tradition of civil government than the conquered colony of Jamaica.[13] It was ruled by the unmilitary and unpopular Edwin Stede, an English placeman who had arrived in 1670 to take up his post of provost marshal and ex officio councillor. Stede went on to become receiver of royal revenues, agent for the Royal African Company, colonel of militia, secretary of the colony, and collector of customs before governing the colony as lieutenant governor from 1685 to 1690.[14] Informed of English developments regularly, he shifted from lavish public celebration of the birth of a Catholic Prince of Wales in August 1688, to an exclusion of Catholics from military and civil posts by the following February, and then to grand festivities accompanying the proclamation of William and Mary three months later. This industrious and well-informed civilian opportunist had been entrusted with the government of a vital colony. Although James II appointed the veteran soldier-administrator Thomas Dongan as governor

[10] *Cal. State Papers, 1685-1688,* no. 1910; Watson to Blathwayt, June 6, 1689, Blathwayt Papers, Vol. XXVII.

[11] *Cal. State Papers, 1689-1692,* no. 52. Although Hender Molesworth represented the revolution against Francis Watson, he was careful to insist that the power to execute martial law was continued in his own commission (*ibid.,* nos. 204, 222).

[12] Holdsworth, "Martial Law," *Law Qtly. Rev.*, XVIII (1902), 117-132; Leonard Woods Labaree, ed., *Royal Instructions to British Colonial Governors 1670-1776,* 2 vols. (New York, 1935), I, 392-397.

[13] Barbados was the only colony in which, between 1674 and 1680, martial law could be proclaimed only with the consent of both the council and the assembly (Labaree, ed., *Royal Instructions,* I, 396). This concession followed the appointment of soldier-governor Sir Jonathan Atkins (Vincent T. Harlow, *A History of Barbados, 1625-1685* [Oxford, 1926], chap. 5).

[14] On colonelcy in the Royal Regiment of Foot, see Stede to Blathwayt, January 31, 1681/2 in Blathwayt Papers, Vol. XXXIV. A. P. Thornton, *West-India Policy under the Restoration* (Oxford, 1956), 182, 206; K. G. Davies, *The Royal African Company* (London, 1957), 297; Harlow, *Barbados,* 216-217, 321, 323.

of Barbados in the spring of 1688, Dongan was allowed to remain in New York, and a more military government of James II's Barbados was neither accomplished nor needed.[15]

The recently rebellious and fiscally important colony of Virginia was formally governed by Francis Howard, fifth baron Howard of Effingham, from 1683 to 1692. This Catholic courtier, whose only claim to be among the garrison governors of England's empire may have been a brief captaincy in the unprofessional Buckingham's foot regiment,[16] was a very effective governor who extended royal prerogative in Virginia by determined assertion of the legal powers of the crown.[17] In February 1689 he left his colony (with formal permission granted ten months earlier),[18] and the senior councillor, Nathaniel Bacon, Sr., became acting governor.

Nathaniel Bacon, Sr., settled in Virginia in the 1650s and became a J.P., member of the Burgesses, and councillor before 1660. After the Restoration this plantation owner became a loyal member of Sir William Berkeley's council, militia colonel and, in 1676, the embarrassed relative and opponent of his young cousin, Nathaniel Bacon, Jr. In the twelve years after witnessing that rebellion and the use of martial law in its suppression,[19] Nathaniel Bacon, Sr., went on to be William Blathwayt's auditor general of royal revenues in Virginia, president of the council, and acting governor.

[15] Blathwayt Papers, Vols. XXIII, XXXII; *Cal. State Papers, 1685-1688,* no. 1876, *1689-1692,* nos. 34, 35, 47, 158. See also "The Diary of Samuel Sewall, 1674-1729," Massachusetts Historical Society, *Collections,* 5th Ser., V (Boston, 1878), 213. Dongan had been lieutenant colonel of the Tangier regiment, lieutenant governor of Tangier, and governor of New York.

[16] Webb, *Governors-General,* 510. Howard's fellow captains would have included dramatist William Wycherley and "Swift Nix," formerly an infamous highwayman. The unit served as marines through its two-year existence, and Howard may have held a captaincy during the year before it was disbanded in 1674. Childs, *Army of Charles II,* 41, 43, 216, 234. In his forthcoming *Their Majesties' Governor and Captain General of Virginia: The Life and Times of Francis Howard, Fifth Baron Howard of Effingham,* Warren M. Billings argues that Howard had no military affiliation whatever before becoming governor. The only Francis Howard listed in Charles Dalton, ed., *The English Army Lists and Commission Registers, 1661-1714,* 6 vols. (London, 1892-1904), is a much older Francis Howard of Corby Castle, lieutenant in Berwick-on-Tweed garrison in 1661, and captain in the earl of Carlisle's regiment in 1673 (I, 15, 135).

[17] On the strength of this legal resurgence of the crown see Howard Nenner, *By Colour of Law: Legal Culture and Constitutional Politics in England, 1660-1689* (Chicago, 1977), and Michael Landon, *The Triumph of the Lawyers: Their Role in English Politics, 1678-1689* (University, Ala., 1970).

[18] *Cal. State Papers, 1685-1688,* no. 1786; W. L. Grant and James Munro, eds., *Acts of the Privy Council of England, Colonial Series,* 6 vols. (London, 1908-1912), II, 109.

[19] Berkeley used martial law, and Lt. Gov. Herbert Jeffreys had special instructions to do so in accordance with the 1673 Articles of War for English troops abroad (*Cal. State Papers, 1675-1676,* nos. 940, 1032, 1074, 1118, 1140).

Virginia lived in blissful ignorance of the English turmoil until the end of February 1689, when news of William of Orange's Torbay landing began circulating. Disturbances in Stafford County, Virginia, were initially roused by locally generated fears of a papist and Indian plot, reminiscent of problems in the same county thirteen years earlier. By early April, dissidents claimed that there "was neither King, Law nor Government" in England, and no need to obey local authorities. Bacon and his council hesitated until the arrival of orders to proclaim William and Mary cleared the legal confusion at the end of the month; then the leaders of the Stafford County disturbances were arrested.[20] Although the trouble did not end immediately, Virginia had the shortest period of legal uncertainty of any English colony, and Acting Governor Bacon and his nervous council left no indication that they were tempted to impose martial law.

Capt. Robert Robinson of the Royal Navy had the dubious honor of becoming James II's governor of Bermuda in 1687. Bermuda had become a royal colony almost accidentally in 1684, while maintaining its reputation as virtually unmanageable.[21] One of Robinson's first concerns was to organize the island's militia of more than 800 men.[22] He quickly found both the locals and the royally appointed chief justice politically intractable and as avaricious as himself. In keeping with the island's position as a metropole for rumor and a desert for news, the confusion of 1689 lasted from the end of January until October.[23] Despite Robinson's penchant to treat his colony as though it were his ship, and his persistent frustration in dealing with policies or people, his enemies never accused him of threatening martial law, or arrests for mutiny, at any time during the crisis.[24]

James II's most visibly loyal governor-general in 1688 was Sir Nathaniel Johnson of the strategically and culturally vulnerable Leeward Islands. Johnson described himself "as an Englishman, a Protestant, a man of honor and a soldier." He had also been a tax farmer, mayor of Newcastle-upon-

[20] H. R. McIlwaine *et al.*, eds. *Executive Journals of the Council of Colonial Virginia*, 5 vols. (Richmond, Va., 1925-1945), I, 104-107; N. Spencer to Blathwayt, Apr. 27, June 10, 1689, Blathwayt Papers, Vols. XVI, XVII; *Cal. State Papers, 1689-1692*, no. 93.

[21] On the dissolution of the Bermuda company see Richard S. Dunn, "The Downfall of the Bermuda Company: A Restoration Farce," *WMQ*, 3d Ser., XX (1963), 487-512, and Charles M. Andrews, *The Colonial Period of American History*, 4 vols. (New Haven, Conn., 1934-1938), I, chap. 12.

[22] René Chartrand, "Notes on Bermuda Military Forces, 1687-1815," *Military Collector and Historian*, XXII (1970), 73-79; *Cal. State Papers, 1685-1688*, no. 1341 vii. For his request for regulars, May 10, 1689, see *ibid., 1689-1692*, no. 114.

[23] *Cal. State Papers, 1685-1688*, no. 2033, *1689-1692*, nos. 32, 945.

[24] *Ibid., 1689-1692*, nos. 31, 32, 114, 137, 472. His predecessor, Lt. Gov. Richard Cony, arrested opponents linked to Monmouth's rising on charges of mutiny, which were dismissed in England. *Ibid., 1685-1688*, nos. 533, 1533; Blathwayt Papers, Vol. XXXVI.

Tyne, and M.P. for that town from 1680 to 1685.[25] Upon becoming governor of the Leeward Islands in 1686, Johnson showed particular concern for the two companies of regulars on St. Christopher's, one of which was his own.[26] As soon as he heard of William's invasion, he offered to return to England to help defend James, and this offer was also sent to France once Johnson knew that James was there. This forthright, if unique, response did not preclude Johnson's dutiful proclamation of William and Mary when the orders to do so arrived early in May.[27] The intervening months of uncertainty were of particular concern in a colony that shared the island of St. Kitt's with the French and contained more Irish Catholic servants than English Protestants on the island of Montserrat.[28] Johnson's self-proclaimed military bias, his loyalty to James II, his two companies of regulars, and his fear of local revolt did not lead him to invoke martial law on the basis of James's warning of a Dutch invasion. The martial element of royal governorship was not paramount on this vulnerable Caribbean frontier.

The centerpiece of James II's empire was the Dominion of New England, which, at its largest, incorporated the colonies of Massachusetts, Rhode Island, Connecticut, the Jerseys, and James's own province of New York. Here was the nearest thing to a blueprint of empire under James II, and by 1688 it was entrusted to that epitome of military governorship, Sir Edmund Andros, with the equally military Francis Nicholson as lieutenant governor.

Andros had arrived in December 1686, accompanied by sixty regulars, to establish a regime characterized by imprisonment without bail, trial without jury, and government without assembly. He had been a professional soldier for twenty-four years, mostly with the Barbados regiment in America, and had served as the duke of York's lieutenant governor of New York from 1674 to 1681. He had participated in the imposition of martial law upon civilians during that career,[29] and his support for

[25] See *Dictionary of American Biography*, s.v. "Johnson, Nathaniel"; Robert P. Sherman, *Robert Johnson, Proprietary and Royal Governor of South Carolina* (Columbia, S.C., 1966), 5-6; and Webb, *Governors-General*, 484-485. In November 1687 Johnson responded to a Catholic petition by ending treasury support for all clergy (*Cal. State Papers, 1685-1688*, no. 1527). In resigning, he sounded like an Anglican non-juror (*ibid., 1689-1692*, no. 143).

[26] *Cal. State Papers, 1685-1688*, nos. 905, 906, 1387. In April 1685 a "council of war" composed of 18 officers of these two companies tried two sergeants for mutiny and had them shot (*ibid.*, no. 134, *1689-1692*, nos. 4, 65, 83). Although initially ordered disbanded in May 1688, they were finally disbanded a year later, when their 162 men were incorporated into a regiment of 780 men (*ibid.*, no. 113).

[27] *Ibid., 1689-1692*, nos. 88, 143.

[28] The feared rebellion of Irish servants on St. Kitt's did not come until after the declaration of war with France (*ibid.*, nos. 212, 237, 256, 312, 345).

[29] Webb, "Trials of Andros," in Martin, ed., *Human Dimensions of Nation Making*, 25, 41-42.

arbitrary government was legendary.

During the winter of 1688-1689 Andros was conducting an exhausting and unpopular campaign against Indians in Maine.[30] Early in January he received and promulgated King James's warning of a threatened Dutch invasion.[31] The next month Andros received news of William of Orange's landing at Torbay, and members of his Council of the Dominion of New England made some arrests for "scattering & publishing seditious & rebellious libells."[32] No further action was taken by either side, and Andros did not leave Pemaquid for Boston until March 16. News that William of Orange had command of the English government was current in Boston a few days later and was made public on April 4 by John Winslow, a young traveler returned from Nevis. Andros, who had not taken any measures in response to the situation as yet, questioned Winslow and imprisoned him briefly.

The news that upset Andros was current, but he had no official orders on which to proceed, and he had many resentful and unhappy subjects with whom to contend. During the next two weeks the militia at Pemaquid mutinied; their predictable return to Boston would prompt additional trouble. Andros ordered all justices, sheriffs, and constables to help officers compel the mutineers to their duty.[33] Although he was back in Boston for four weeks before the revolution erupted there, he did not declare martial law. On April 18, when Boston rose to join the returning militia mutineers, it was too late; Andros and members of his government were imprisoned by the Council of Safety. It is worth noting that four regular army officers were taken prisoner by the revolutionaries, as were several militia officers, including two lieutenant colonels.[34]

Martial law would have improved Andros's position markedly, had it been enforced late in March or early in April. It would have given him absolute power over life and limb in a divided militia and unchallengeable legal dominance over his civil opponents. Andros had sufficient warning of

[30] The imposition of military brutality on frontier militia was evident in the charges against Lt. John Jordan (*Cal. State Papers, 1689-1692*, nos. 207, 208). See also W. H. Whitmore, ed., *The Andros Tracts . . . .* 3 vols. (Boston, 1868-1874), I, 171-173. Jordan's apparent use of a cavalry torture called picquet may be its first use by the English army, and evidence that he had served in Tangier (Walton, *British Standing Army*, 571).

[31] Whitmore, ed., *Andros Tracts*, I, 75n-76n.

[32] John West to Fitz-John Winthrop, Boston, Feb. 23, 1688/9, "The Winthrop Papers," Mass. Hist. Soc., *Colls.*, 6th Ser., III (Boston, 1889), 496-497.

[33] Massachusetts Archives, CXXIX, 368-370, Boston.

[34] Whitmore, ed., *Andros Tracts*, I, xxxii. The regulars were: Capt. Anthony Brockholls and Lt. John Jordan of a new independent company commissioned in 1688; Lt. Thomas Trefry of Andros's own company; and Ens. Joshua Pipon of Francis Nicholson's company. See Dalton, ed., *Army Lists*, II, 82-83, 159. The senior militia officers imprisoned with Andros were Lt. Col. Charles Lidgett, Lt. Col. Macgregry, Capt. William White, and Capt. Samuel Ravenscroft. See "Sewall's Diary," Mass. Hist. Soc., *Colls.*, 5th Ser., V, 168, 190.

serious trouble but did not redeploy his regulars or impose martial law as an interim defense of himself and public order. His actions suggest that this soldier saw his role as governor general of the Dominion of New England to be fundamentally political rather than military.

Imprisonment of Governor Andros disrupted the Dominion of New England and brought challenges to the power of his lieutenant governor in New York, Capt. Francis Nicholson. Commissioned ensign a decade earlier, Nicholson had served as lieutenant in the Tangier garrison from 1680 to 1684, subject to the most elaborate Articles of War prepared in Restoration England. He was involved in suppressing Monmouth's rebellion, and his loyalty to the Stuarts had been rewarded with bounties four times in as many years.[35] He came to New England in 1686 as captain of a company of soldiers attending Andros and received his first civil post when he became lieutenant governor in 1688. With the incorporation of New York into the Dominion of New England, Nicholson succeeded Thomas Dongan, his old superior officer in the Tangier garrison. Although assigned the Barbados governorship, Dongan remained in New York as Nicholson's friend, military-minded adviser, and suspected éminence grise throughout the crisis that followed.[36]

Although Nicholson was one of James II's committed military servants, he handled the crisis in New York with so much caution as to appear militarily inept. The Torbay landing was known in New York by February; by mid-March it was clear that "there is a total Revolution att home."[37] On April 26 New York heard of the Boston revolution of eight days earlier, and the next day brought unconfirmed reports of war with France. The governor had twenty-two regulars and four companies of militia in New York City, which was quiet, if tense.[38] Inhabitants of Suffolk County on Long Island followed the rebellious example of Boston, reorganizing their own militia and threatening to take control of the fort in New York City. During the next three weeks, the militias of Queen's and Westchester counties and the town of Albany did likewise.

Nicholson reacted minimally to rumors of war with France and the rebellion of county militias. He worked with local members of the council

[35] See McCully, "Nicholson," *WMQ*, 3d Ser., XIX (1962), 534-556, and Stephen Saunders Webb, "The Strange Career of Francis Nicholson," *ibid.*, XXIII (1966), 513-548.

[36] E. B. O'Callaghan and J. R. Brodhead, eds., *Documents Relative to the Colonial History of the State of New-York*, 15 vols. (Albany, N.Y., 1856-1883), III, 590-597, hereafter cited as *N.-Y. Col. Docs.*

[37] Robert Livingston to Edward Randolph, Mar. 22, 1688/9, in *Edward Randolph . . . Including His Letters and Official Papers, 1676-1703 . . . .* 7 vols. (Boston, 1898-1909), IV, 262.

[38] See Robert C. Ritchie, *The Duke's Province: A Study of New York Politics and Society, 1664-1691* (Chapel Hill, N.C., 1977), chap. 9. James II had ordered the establishment of two regular companies, of 3 officers, 5 noncommissioned officers, a drummer, and 50 privates in each, as of Aug. 1, 1688, but they were not commissioned (*Cal. State Papers, 1685-1688*, no. 1853).

of the Dominion, New York City officials, and militia officers including Jacob Leisler. It was another month before the remnants of royal authority evaporated completely and a minor dispute between regulars and militia led to revolt by part of the city militia and their seizure of the fort.[39] Nicholson, whose temper was notorious, only then threatened to shoot the militia officers and fire on the city.[40] By then he had lost control of himself and his government. Despite his personality, his military background, and his lack of political experience, Nicholson did not attempt to use martial law in those weeks when it could have strengthened his control over the militia that would eventually overthrow him, as the Massachusetts militia overthrew Andros.

The soldier-governors of James II's royal colonies (Edmund Andros, Nathaniel Johnson, and Francis Nicholson) displayed military habits of thought but apparently saw clear distinctions between being governors and being soldiers. Their military experience was part of their qualifications for the task, representing administrative experience, presumed loyalty to the crown, and skills that might be necessary to defend the colonies against attack. Yet soldiers were not the only governors appointed by James: witness Edwin Stede, Francis Howard of Effingham, and Hender Molesworth, whom James sent back to retrieve Jamaica from Francis Watson. Watson's use of martial law was acceptable within the recent history of the conquered colony of Jamaica, but the rest of the empire did not follow Jamaica's example. It is also noteworthy that James II put little priority on supporting his governors with regular troops. His growing army was kept much closer to home, even though regiments were rented to rival powers, including the Netherlands.[41] The whole English empire in America was garrisoned by only five independent companies of regulars, representing slightly more than one percent of James's peacetime army.[42] It was the colonial militias that were the sword of the civil power, and they defended James's government in Jamaica and overthrew it in

[39] See Ritchie, *Duke's Province*, chap. 9; Thomas J. Archdeacon, *New York City, 1664-1710: Conquest and Change* (Ithaca, N.Y., 1976); David S. Lovejoy, *The Glorious Revolution in America* (New York, 1972), chaps. 6, 11, 14; and Jerome R. Reich, *Leisler's Rebellion: A Study of Democracy in New York, 1664-1720* (Chicago, 1953).

[40] *N.-Y. Col. Docs.*, III, 577, 584; "Documents Relating to the Administration of Leisler," New-York Historical Society, *Collections*, I (1868), 292-293.

[41] On James's inability to recover these regiments in 1688 see Childs, *Army, James II*, 119-137.

[42] Two of the companies were in St. Kitt's, captained by Nathaniel Johnson and Thomas Hill, and numbering 162 officers and men (*Cal. State Papers, 1685-1688*, no. 1387). The other three companies, captained by Andros, Nicholson, and Brockhalls, were largely integrated into the New England militia, though there were 24 regulars in Boston and 22 others at New York City when the revolution occurred. Three other regular companies were planned for early in 1688 but did not materialize. *Ibid.*, no. 1709. For the size of the army see Childs, *Army, James II*, 1-5.

Boston and New York. None of the officiating governors or lieutenant governors, or Acting Governor Bacon, followed the Jamaican path through the confusion of 1688-1689. Despite their experience as soldiers or their legitimate powers and provocations, the royal governors of James II's empire recognized that their authority was ultimately civilian and political in nature.

11

Sir Thomas Lawrence, Secretary of Maryland: A Royal Placeman's Fortunes in America

David W. Jordan

SIR THOMAS LAWRENCE OF CHELSEA, ENGLAND, GAINED APPOINTMENT as royal secretary of Maryland in 1692, a post he would hold for most of the period until his death in 1714. Lawrence was a controversial placeman, but like most of the contemporary imperial bureaucracy, he remains largely an unknown figure. Secretaries, customs collectors and naval officers as well as governors arrived in North American colonies in unprecedented numbers in the latter decades of the seventeenth century, as the mother country sought to extend her control over colonial affairs. Only the governors among these special immigrants, and not even all of them, or an occasional figure like Edward Randolph whose jurisdiction spanned several colonies, have received extended study. Yet individually and collectively, this burgeoning bureaucracy exerted an extraordinary influence greater than the impact of many more famous figures in England or America.[1]

Lesser placemen constitute a category of officials particularly distinct from their better known superiors, the governors. These more numerous subordinates were involved with place and patronage rather than with administration. They engaged in less of the necessary give and take which preoccupied the successful governor; armed with a commission from the crown, lesser placemen usually focused on extracting as much wealth as possible from their positions with slight regard for local sentiment or for the most effective, judicious execution of business. These men rarely intended to settle permanently in the colonies and they always looked to English officials, not local residents, for their ultimate source of identity and support. The governors often lent support and encouragement to lower ranking royal officials, but the chief executives were also likely to sacrifice their subordinates as expendable pawns in the continuing struggles between themselves and local politicians.

The following account of Sir Thomas Lawrence in the New World illuminates the career of one such placeman and suggests the critical impact these often neglected imperial bureaucrats could and did have in the colonies. Lawrence's involvement with Maryland lasted 23 years and extended through the tenures of four different royal governors and several temporary chief executives. No other

---

The co-author of *Maryland's Revolution of Government, 1689-1692*, Professor Jordan has also published numerous articles about Maryland's early development.

single individual, immigrant or native, had a more continuing role during the royal period of the colony's history from 1692 to 1715.

Before 1692, as a proprietary colony Maryland had relatively little experience with imperial bureaucrats. Most patronage resided in Lord Baltimore's control, except for the revenue and inspection officials appointed after passage of the Navigation Acts. Even these initial customs collectors, like Christopher Rousby, collector of Patuxent, owed their appointments to the recommendations received from Charles Calvert. Patronage went primarily to promising men who had settled in the colony. Increasingly, however, by the 1680s, these men came into conflict with the proprietary government and dispatched letters with their complaints to Whitehall officials in England. These negative reports had spurred moves to revoke Lord Baltimore's charter.[2]

The Glorious Revolution of 1688 in England brought in its wake a successful overthrow of the proprietary government in Maryland. The crown assumed control of the colony and thereby also acquired numerous additional positions to fill with royal appointees. One of these posts was the secretaryship of the province. Lawrence received his appointment as secretary in July of 1691, and by late September, he had also been commissioned as a councillor.[3]

Like a growing number of lesser English gentry, Lawrence hoped to increase his modest fortunes through the expanding imperial bureaucracy. The Lawrence family resided in Chelsea, Middlesex, and had proudly possessed its baronetcy since 1628. Lawrence, born about 1645, had matriculated at St. John's College, Oxford in 1661 and received his B.A. degree in February 1664/65. He may be the same Thomas Lawrence who returned to University College for a M.A. degree in 1668, but there is no doubt of his admittance to Middle Temple in 1664. There he surely made the acquaintance of William Blathwayt who became in the last quarter of the century the most influential dispenser of colonial favors and patronage. Little is known of Lawrence between his study at the Inns of Court and his Maryland appointment. He married Anne English of St. Clement's Dane in 1674 and they had at least two sons and a daughter. He probably served in some minor government post on the continent.[4]

The position which Lawrence acquired in 1691 was an extremely desirable office in the Maryland government, second only to the governorship in potential influence and profit, although a number of powers had been gradually whittled from the office during the course of the century. It was natural that the position drew the attention of non-colonists as well as Marylanders. Initially, the secretaryship had included "all functions not definitely assignable to the Governor or Chancellor." The secretary kept most of the provincial records, was the notary public, and appointed the clerks of the secretary's office, the provincial court and the county courts. He was always a councillor, and as such sat also in the upper house of the assembly. The income from the office, both substantial and complicated, arose from fees controlled by legislation and revenues bestowed as gifts from the proprietor. Most of the income accrued through the incumbent's control of official records and his position as notary, but after 1676 the secretary also received the lucrative license fees for ordinaries. He traditionally received a share of the profits of those clerks and deputies whom he appointed, and as the colony expanded after mid-century with the creation of several new counties, this revenue became more substantial. From this varied income, the secretary was expected to pay the expenses of his office. It has been estimated that the office was worth at least £ 400 sterling annually in 1672 and probably £ 1,000 in 1725. Now at the disposal of the crown, it was certainly an office to be prized.[5]

Even before leaving England, Lawrence learned just how much this office was valued by others. He had successfully edged out any Maryland claimants for the position, but Sir Lionel Copley, the new royal governor of Maryland, was a more formidable rival. Copley shared with Lawrence a greater interest in the possible profits of Maryland officeholding than in any obligations to the colonists there; it was to be perhaps the only thing they would share in their new world ventures. Avariciously eyeing Lawrence's lucrative power to appoint county clerks, Copley learned that this power was once exercised by the governor, and he sought its return to his office. A vigilant Lawrence incurred his new superior's lasting enmity by battling successfully to retain these appointments and the revenue they generated. Whitehall officials, however, did forbid Lawrence to sell the clerkships, a controversial practice of his predecessors. His instructions entitled him to "receive yearly a fee or Gratuity of the tenth part of one year's value . . . of each place from such clerks as shall be nominated by him, the said Value to be estimated by the Governour and Council upon a vacancy." Copley, though obviously resentful of Lawrence's victory, made a public gesture of promising never to infringe "any law of Maryland to hurt Sir Thomas."[6]

Nonetheless, the ill-feeling between these two ranking royal officials of the colony was so explosive, Lawrence made a last minute change of plans in the early spring of 1692 to avoid sailing on the same vessel with Copley to Maryland.[7] The postponement cost Lawrence dearly; before the secretary arrived some months later, Copley had established an alliance with local leaders and had set in motion a vigorous campaign against Lawrence.[8]

Copley had found the elected representatives of the first royal assembly particularly anxious to strike at plural officeholding and high fees, grievances voiced during the revolution which had overthrown the proprietor three years earlier. Less anxious were the leaders of that revolt, now sitting in the upper house and enjoying many of these multiple offices and revenues. The burgesses insisted, however, on specifying each fee in an Act for Limitation of Officers' Fees. Copley, who was shrewdly seeking mutually advantageous compromises on all disputed issues, allowed the legislation to pass and took much satisfaction in the assembly's subsequently awarding him the 14 pence per ton port duty which Whitehall officials had explicitly denied him and had left in the proprietor's domain; Copley also received through the legislation half of the two shillings per hogshead export duty, an additional three pence per hogshead tax, a four pence per gallon liquor duty, and a special gift of 100,000 pounds of tobacco. He further succeeded in exacting vengeance on the absent Lawrence by approving a transfer from the secretary to the governor of revenue arising from the fees for ordinary licenses, and he cooperated in the assembly's stripping the secretary's office of other sources of income as well, some of which now went to Nehemiah Blakiston, Copley's primary confidante and co-conspirator on the council, and himself a minor royal placeman as customs collector of North Potomac River.[9]

When royal officials did not stand together, trouble inevitably ensued. The assembly had quickly observed that the new secretary did not enjoy the support of the governor and was therefore quite vulnerable. Local leaders were rapidly learning how to discriminate between royal placemen and how to pit them against each other. At the moment, Lawrence seemed even less threatening than the arrogant Edward Randolph, surveyor general of customs, who visited Maryland in May of 1692 and initiated numerous actions against colonists for violations of the trade and navigation acts. This royal official posed a distinct problem, especially for several members of the council, and Copley further cemented his profitable alliance by staunchly supporting the local leadership in its battle against Randolph, a man whose authority the governor was sworn to uphold. In turn, the Marylanders actively defended the governor against Randolph's charges of extensive misconduct of office with respect to collection of customs duties and prosecution of alleged offenses. Most colonists came to view Copley as the best line of defense against Randolph and thus automatically took the governor's side against Lawrence as well.[10]

When Lawrence finally arrived the last week of September, the governor appeared firmly entrenched in power. Lawrence was accompanied by Lt. Governor Francis Nicholson, another royal official but one predisposed to oppose Copley and his clique and to support Randolph and Lawrence in any disputes, and many were immediately forthcoming.[11]

Lawrence was incensed to find his office stripped of many revenues and two locals—William Taylard and John Lewellin—enjoying full possession of the remaining profits in their performance of the secretary's duties. The two clerks resolutely declined to share with Sir Thomas the revenues accruing between the date of his commission and his arrival in Maryland. Acting in tandem with the governor, they made it very difficult for Lawrence to obtain full documentation of the actions taken against him in the previous six months. Copley, in preparing his own defense against the charges Randolph had dispatched to England, had of necessity relied heavily upon Lewellin and Taylard for doctoring of records. As a reward, the two men now occupied the clerkships of the council, the upper house, the secretary's office, the prerogative court, the provincial court, the land office and St. Mary's and Talbot counties. Questionable characters each, they could obligingly guarantee the governor that all of the various journals were in agreement and would contain nothing prejudicial to his position.[12]

When Lawrence appeared before the governor and council to take the oaths of his office, Copley demanded security of £ 2,000 before Lawrence could begin serving or even obtain custody of the records. Furthermore, Copley ruled that Lawrence's own bond for such security was not sufficient. The governor's mastery of the council became clear when each man in turn refused to stand security for Lawrence, who "being a meer Stranger and unacquainted in the Country" could not easily find security anywhere. The council finally agreed to allow Lawrence to execute his duties provisionally until the next meeting of the assembly, but also ruled that he would gain custody of the records only after they "can conveniently be perfected." Nor was Lawrence entitled, the council argued, to any of the profits of the office which accrued prior to his actual arrival in the colony. Copley endorsed this ruling, even though he himself was claiming gubernatorial revenues since the date of his appointment, not his arrival in Maryland.[13]

Lawrence nursed a legitimate grievance over his brusque treatment, but like

Randolph and other royal placemen, he found his reception very contingent on the governor's signals. Moreover, like most of his fellow bureaucrats, a seemingly single-minded pursuit of money—what the council called his "avaritious and greedy appetite" and "Ravenous Expectations"—and an arrogantly blind disregard of local attitudes quickly alienated the very colonists upon whom he must depend for any assistance. Extraordinary tact and diplomacy were required when interacting with these men who were seeing local positions of importance going to strangers. Lawrence demonstrated little if any sensitivity for their feelings, for their opinions about his responsibilities, or even for an impartial interpretation of the laws affecting his post. For example, while declaiming almost endlessly on the necessity of obeying the letter of the law or royal instructions when they were in his favor, Lawrence would conveniently ignore the text when it was to his detriment, as in his disregard of the clause in his commission requiring "the residence of the said Sir Thomas Lawrence in the said province." Technically, Lawrence was not entitled to the fees "from the date of his commission," as he greedily asserted.[14]

More illustrative of his avarice and contempt for local sentiment was the retaliatory course Sir Thomas quickly pursued. His most lucrative power still untouched by the assembly or council was the authority to appoint county clerks. Ignoring the special wording of the Whitehall instructions—"upon a Vacancy"—Lawrence busily proceeded in October of 1692 to dismiss the incumbents in the five most profitable county clerkships, two of the men being Taylard and Lewellin, and then to fill those vacancies with men who stood indebted to him for one-tenth of their profits, and, according to some observers, also for a considerable price for purchase of the new appointments. In some instances, Lawrence's appointees were qualified neither by age nor experience, and they had to subcontract for deputy clerks. These new officeholders included Lawrence's own dependent Thomas Briscoe, a minor; Thomas Gladman, who had come from England in Lawrence's entourage; and Charles Hynson, the son of a disaffected proprietary supporter and perhaps some distant relation of the secretary.[15]

One of the five clerks whom Lawrence continued in office, Cleborne Lomax in Charles county, swore later that a stipulation for retention had been that he pay the secretary one-tenth of the fees earned since the date of Lawrence's own commission and that the secretary would henceforth share fully one-half of the profits. It is unclear how much to believe of the testimony of Lomax and others who spoke against Lawrence; they were all men dependent on Copley, who was in a position to make such testimony profitable for them. Nonetheless, it is clear that Lawrence was indisputably driving difficult, and most likely illegal, bargains with the incumbent clerks. The justices "and other their good People of Ann Arundell County" petitioned in October against Lawrence's intention to remove a man who had faithfully served for many years in order to "impose a Stranger upon us for Clerk of this County a person altogether unacquainted with the same and in whome we dare not repose so great a trust." The council easily gathered incriminating depositions detailing the complaints of clerks and other irate county officials. Informing Lawrence of "the resentment this Board had taken at his proceeding so far," the council bundled the evidence together and dispatched it to England. They formally charged that Lawrence had ignored the provision that offices were not to be sold and that he was supposed to receive one-tenth of the fees only upon natural vacancies, not forced ones, and the councillors reminded English officials that the value of the offices was to be set by the governor and council. They noted also that Sir Thomas was operating without security.[16]

These actions soon threw Lawrence into an unnatural alliance with other Marylanders disgruntled about the new government. Most of them had opposed the recent revolution and remained loyal at heart to the proprietor. Finding no solace in the actions of Copley, who had embraced the rebels, these displaced colonists turned to Lawrence, the next ranking official and a man clearly at odds with the governor, as someone who might lend comfort and support to their grievances. The council hastened to cite these very associations as additional evidence to discredit Lawrence for "associating caballing & advising and indeed conversing with none but the Kings open professed Enemies and Malignants to the present Government."[17]

That present government had a very loose definition for "professed Enemies and Malignants." It compassed anyone who challenged the status quo, which included some flagrant self-enrichment and disregard of the law by the governor and his intimate circle. Branded together were Lawrence, Randolph, Nicholson, Blathwayt, and Lord Baltimore in England, and locals who voiced any displeasure with the ruling clique. Two members of the council who declined to cooperate lost their positions. One, James Frisby, had openly opposed the revolution which made him suspect from the start, but Henry Jowles had been probably the most respected leader of the revolution. Finding himself edged aside in Copley's new circle, Jowles declined to accept the passive role of cipher which most of the councillors were assuming. He alone from the council extended support to Lawrence, whom he had almost certainly known as a fellow student at the Inns of Court. Lawrence now represented the only viable challenge to Copley, however weak that challenge might initially appear, and Jowles attached himself to the secretary. For unspecified reasons, Copley dismissed Jowles as chief military officer of Calvert on October 29, but the motivation was clearly Jowles' relationship with Lawrence, from whom the former now accepted appointment as clerk of Calvert. That immediately provoked Jowles' suspension from the council and from all other public offices for his "basely deserting" his commission.[18]

Lawrence himself was no less vulnerable, and a few months later came his dismissal from all offices. The charge was "several high crimes and misdemeanours," primarily dependent on testimony from Taylard and Lewellin. By the end of March, Lawrence was under the prison custody of the sheriff of Charles County with open disregard of judicial process and of the prisoner's personal rights. Once again, Taylard and Lewellin enjoyed possession of the secretary's office.[19]

Lawrence was still languishing in prison, under watchful eyes that almost precluded any visitors, when Copley died suddenly on September 9, 1693. A power struggle promptly ensued. Blakiston hastened to the capital and soon dispatched a faithful subordinate to arrest Jowles, the most serious potential rival still free in the colony. No one on the council dared to oppose Blakiston, but he carelessly misjudged the alienation of some other Marylanders, especially other former rebels in arms who had not shared so munificiently in spoils dispensed by the governor. Among these was Blakiston's brother-in-law John Coode, the ostensible leader of the revolution, who had been completely excluded from office in the new royal government. Coode quickly gathered some neighbors and forced the release of Lawrence, no particular friend of Coode's but a royal appointee who might stop Blakiston.[20]

Lawrence and Blakiston were contending for control when delegates to the previously scheduled assembly convened in St. Mary's City in late September. The lower house addressed the dispute and ruled "nemine contradicente" that Lawrence's arrest had been illegal and the governor's actions improper, and it passed a vote of censure on Blakiston for illegal conduct as well. Just when Sir Thomas had apparently persuaded the reluctant council to recognize him as president through vitrue of his being first named in the council commission of 1691, Governor Edmund Andros of Virginia arrived to claim the post of chief executive. Andros' commission empowered him to succeed to the governorship of Maryland upon the death of Lt. Governor Nicholson and in the absence of Copley. Lawrence abruptly challenged that the wording was inappropriate, given Nicholson's absence and Copley's death. Most of the other councillors seized this opportunity to side with Andros and to avoid Lawrence's leadership; they later gratefully accepted patronage which Andros generously bestowed.[21]

Again, Lawrence in his eagerness and self-righteousness had antagonized a royal superior who might have helped him, and the secretary had given leading Marylanders further excuse to ignore his cause. Andros made Lawrence painfully conscious of his mistake. The secretary had just received the crown's ruling which disallowed the disputed legislation of 1692 denying ordinary license fees to him. The ruling had gone on to order restoration to Lawrence of those fees and of some others which had been transferred to Blakiston. Lawrence was to give only £ 1,000 as security, half the amount originally demanded. It was almost a complete vindication of Lawrence's position, but Governor Andros in council still declined to reinstate Lawrence fully. No public announcement was forthcoming of the crown's ruling, and Andros ignored both Lawrence and Jowles in the new commission for provincial court justives, nor did he allow either man salaries as councillors. The ultimate insult came October 2, when, in preparation for returning to Virginia, Andros passed over both men, the two senior councillors, to bestow the presidency of the council and responsibility as acting chief executive, on Nicholas Greenberry.[22]

The crown's order in council of September 18, 1693, completely restoring Lawrence to all offices and perquisites, reached the Chesapeake colonies by February, but Andros delayed until May the secretary's full reinstatement as secretary, president of the council, and chief justice of the provincial court. Lawrence had sufficiently learned the lesson of acquiescing quietly and accommodating a governor, at least for the moment. He did not raise immediate objection when Andros appropriated from the Maryland treasury £ 500 as reimbursement for his own very limited services as commander-in-chief over the previous seven months and £ 150 to Greenberry "upon Account as President." However, Lawrence soon registered protests in his letters to England, and he set about gathering complete and unaltered copies of council journals for mailing home. He had earlier refused to send the altered versions which Copley had ordered him to post without perusal. Now, in cooperation with Randolph who was back in the colony, Lawrence speedily gathered documentation for their own extensive charges against the Copley regime.[23]

Lawrence entered in the summer of 1694 an unusual and brief period of cooperation with Maryland's executive authorities, a course rendered somewhat easier by the arrival of Francis Nicholson as the new governor. Still, neither a new superior nor a more accommodating tact could fully quell the distrust, suspicion and even outright opposition frequently directed at Lawrence by lesser officials, particularly justices and clerks and increasingly by members of the lower house. They could acknowledge injustices done to Sir Thomas in his arrest and imprisonment, they could even endorse some of Lawrence's claims to certain fees, and juries could decide cases in his favor against Taylard regarding allocation of revenues.[24] However, no governor or royal order could automatically rally these colonists to like the secretary and his patronage policies or to bestow on him any revenues which they wished to dispose of otherwise.

Lawrence was either unaware of this widespread hostility in 1694, or more likely, he was callously confident that he could successfully disregard it. Nicholson had wholeheartedly endorsed Lawrence's cause, sought his close counsel, and the two senior royal officers in Maryland wasted no time in demonstrating which side now had the upper hand. Patronage was always the most dramatic and visible weapon of reward or punishment; Nicholson relied heavily on Lawrence's advice and the secretary's allies soon replaced most of his enemies in new commissions, with even John Coode finally gaining preferment again for his role in securing Lawrence's release from prison. Special vengeance was reserved for nemeses Lewellin and Taylard who lost all of their posts.[25]

While Nicholson's diligence in recruiting able and honest officials and in punishing and discharging incompetent or dishonest men worked essentially to reward the secretary's friends and punish his enemies, Nicholson was more astute than Lawrence and always had higher goals of responsible government than did the secretary. Indeed during Nicholson's sojourn in Maryland, he often forsook possible revenues and contributed generously from his own pocket in his efforts to encourage the development of schools and churches. While dedicated absolutely to the royal prerogative and its defense, Nicholson was also keenly aware of local grievances and needs. Here as in Virginia, his efforts at reform often found support more among the less fortunate majority than among the rising elite which was benefitting most from the status quo.[26] Lawrence, in contrast, could usually muster support in Maryland only among those local men dedicated blindly to upholding royal appointees, from those beholden in some way to the secretary, or from men who saw an opportunity to use Lawrence for their own purposes.

The assembly which gathered in September of 1694 reflected particularly this last attitude while continuing an uneasiness about royal placemen in general and Lawrence in particular. Expressing the obligation to "doe Equall Right to all their Majesties good & faithful Subjects," the lower house again declared Copley's proceedings against the secretary to have been "both Arbitrary & illegal." The delegates described Lawrence as "a protestant, a Loyal subject to their Majestys of great & good Service to the Country & both liberall and Generous in promoteing & Contributeing to what may tend to the good & wellfare of the publick." This overly fulsome praise arose in part from the influential role in this assembly of several of Lawrence's most ardent supporters, especially William Dent. More important, however, was the widespread awareness of the possible services Lawrence might render on his announced return to England. The secretary's influence in Whitehall had not been lost on the assembly, which desired effective representation with respect to several critical pieces of legislation before the Privy Council, particularly a new act establishing the Church of England in the colony and another founding a school in the province. The assembly also wanted Lawrence to attempt recovery of the £ 500 Andros had awarded himself, no small amount for a colony presently in debt. Lawrence had further curried their favor with contributions of 5,000 pounds of tobacco toward building a free school and 2,000 pounds of tobacco promised as an annual gift toward maintaining school masters as long as Lawrence remained as secretary. These gifts had followed Nicholson's example, as did a further pledge of 1,000 pounds of tobacco to each county toward the building of houses for the ministers whom the colony hoped to attract. The assembly, in turn, could afford to be generous in its language and partially to vindicate Lawrence by passing a bill restoring to the secretary's office fees for ordinary licenses, as the crown had instructed. Significantly, however, the assembly made this a temporary act only, to "endure for three years or to the end of the next Session of Assembly which shall first happen." Lawrence's other fees reduced by law in 1692 were not restored to their former levels, and the upper house declined to support his pleas for payment of search fees by Lord Baltimore's agents seeking access to land records. Finally, angered by Lawrence's patronage practices and the mounting intrusion of immigrant officeseekers, this assembly also passed the Act for Incouragement of Learning and Advancement of the Natives which established a three-year residence as prerequisite to holding most positions of profit not awarded directly by the crown. This act should clearly have conveyed to Lawrence the burgesses' response to his appointments of dependents and outsiders to the clerkships.[27]

For the time being, Sir Thomas was in an uneasy accommodation of sorts with Marylanders, but the truce owed much to the strong backing of the new governor in his own "honeymoon" period, to the assembly's awareness it could temporarily use the secretary for its own purposes, and to Lawrence's temporary strategy of cooperation. But Lawrence and other minor royal placemen rarely pursued conciliatory tactics for any extended period, nor could they always count on governors or local support being automatic. These placemen invariably worked more assiduously on maintaining and currying support in England, usually in hopes of obtaining an even better position with more income. They were royal officials foremost and not officers in a colonial government with which they identified. Lawrence's proposed trip to England was characteristic. He wanted to renew important contacts and through the auspices of new allies Randolph and Nicholson to establish valuable new connections.

By mid-November, Lawrence had sufficiently arranged his affairs to depart for the mother country. With his colleagues' approval, he left Councillor Thomas Brooke as his deputy secretary and notary. Less popular was Lawrence's last minute appointment of his son, Thomas, Jr., as clerk of Talbot. This youth was not of age, had not been a resident for three years, and may not have even been in the colony at the time. The appointment flagrantly ignored the new legislation. In turn, the Talbot justices, who had never accepted Lawrence's appointment of Thomas Gladman in 1692, ignored this new commission and continued John Valiant, the clerk whom they had illegally appointed themselves two years before. The dispute over the rightful clerk continued for three years and kept Lawrence's name unfavorably before the colonists even while he was away from Maryland.[28]

Meanwhile, Sir Thomas could not escape personal difficulties simply by departing from the colony. French seamen seized the ship on which Lawrence was traveling, and they detained him in prison for some months.[29] The pirates apparently released him sometime before July, 1695, when Lawrence was in London soliciting the colony's affairs and his own interests. The first order of business was to present evidence in his behalf to the court at Whitehall which subsequently dismissed all outstanding complaints and accusations against him. Lawrence also obtained a ruling entitling him to a half-share in any fees arising from searches in the land records.[30]

Sir Thomas was to remain in England for approximately six months. His duties as colonial agent had more mixed results. To his sincere regret, he was unable to obtain royal approval for the legislation establishing the Church of England and the free school at Annapolis. An unfortunate reference to the application of English law in the province, some objectionable details of the organizations of church vestries and the school's governing board, and the active lobbying of English Quakers before the Privy Council combined to bring vetoes in early January of 1695/96 of all bills involved. Lawrence was more successful, however, in his cooperative efforts with Henry Compton, Bishop of London, and Thomas Tenison, the Archbishop of Canterbury, to raise funds for the Maryland church, to acquire parish libraries, and to recruit ministers. His efforts were also quite salutary in the appointment of Thomas Bray as commissary for the church in Maryland. Furthermore, with the assistance of Tenison and of Lord Lonsdale, Lawrence had succeeded in gaining an order in council for Edmund Andros to return £ 300 or the £ 500 he had appropriated for his services in 1693–94.[31]

Lawrence had returned to Maryland by early August of 1696. Nicholson now enjoyed much less widespread support in the colony, as his attempted reforms and general administration had begun to chafe many local political leaders.[32] This should have been a clear warning to Sir Thomas. Instead, he plowed ahead in his usual fashion and quickly squandered any good will generated by his activities as agent in England. Abandoning any strategy of compromise or humility, Lawrence presented the assembly with claims for reimbursement for the time he had served as president of the council from May 8 to July 26, 1694. Their first encounter with him upon his return, then, was to see the avaricious aspect of his tenure. The burgesses awarded him £ 50 from the £ 300 he had retrieved for them from Andros. Lawrence was not satisfied and demanded money then for his services in England. Upon his appointment as agent in 1694, the assembly had voted him £ 60 as an "Encouragement." This would have been a normal salary for two years as a councillor, but since Lawrence held a separate office of profit, he did not qualify for a regular council salary. Lawrence's careful scrutiny of past records had disclosed that Blakiston had received £ 30 per annum despite holding another office of profit, and Sir Thomas, instead of denouncing this illegality, now argued that he was similarly entitled to double income. He complained that he had "received nothing from the Country for all the Services he had done them." The lower house, decidedly unimpressed, responded that it had already sufficiently gratified him. Lawrence snidely derided the assembly's low opinion of his services and declined a conditional £ 50 promised him if he obtained passage of three controversial bills then pending royal approval.[33]

A few weeks later, Lawrence appealed unsuccessfully to the governor and council for enlargement of his fees, and he subsequently registered his appeals in England also. Maryland looked no better now that it had on his first arrival four years previously, and he was acting no differently himself. He wrote home that "these ill bred and ungratefull people" would give him nothing for his troubles for them in England, that he could never get over half of his yearly profits from people in the colony, and that if a vacancy occurred in the agency in Portugal, he would welcome an appointment there.[34]

By June of 1697, Sir Thomas was already planning his return to England, a trip he did not receive permission to make for another year. It was an unpleasant period, during which Lawrence almost died from a distemper. The provincial court threw out his ill-considered suit against Greenberry for complicity in the 1692–92 actions against the secretary and for accepting the £ 150 salary as president of the council which Lawrence was claiming should rightfully have been his; the council denied Lawrence's subsequent appeal. Further efforts to increase his revenues also failed miserably, and the assembly even declined to reappoint him as its agent in England.[35]

Despite this unpleasant situation, the governor still sent fulsome praise of Lawrence to influential Englishmen. Both Nicholson and Sir Thomas always professed the highest regard for each other and fostered each other's career. The secretary was obliged, Nicholson wrote in numerous letters, for reasons of health to move where winters were shorter and more moderate. He characterized Lawrence as a pious and zealous son of the church, a constant asserter of monarchy and wholly devoted to His Majesty's interests. The governor failed to mention how hostile Marylanders were to the secretary or how devoted Sir Thomas was to his own enrichment, noting only that the secretary had often suffered in estate as well as in health.[36]

Lawrence clearly intended this to be a permanent departure from Maryland. He always felt more at home and encountered more favorable support in London than in Annapolis, and by early November he had even obtained a favorable order in council regarding his claims to Greenberry's £ 150. But having tendered his resignation as secretary of Maryland, he encountered less success in his efforts over the next two years to receive a more lucrative appointment where the climate would be more congenial and the locals less antagonistic to his schemes.[37] He had managed, however, to keep the Maryland secretaryship in the family, securing it for his younger son Thomas, who was commissioned by the crown September 5, 1698 and served until his death April 15, 1701.[38]

Lawrence's personal fortunes had not improved when word reached London by June 12, 1701 of his son's death. Undoubtedly with some sense of despair and necessity, Lawrence petitioned to be reappointed as secretary of Maryland to succeed his son; the commission, dated July 11, 1701, explicitly required that he return to Maryland within four months or the appointment would be void. Furthermore, he was not reappointed to the council; Lawrence would return to the colony with less stature and power than during his previous term. Nonetheless, he met the conditions and left England September 10.[39]

Nathaniel Blakiston, the nephew of Lawrence's old nemesis Nehemiah Blakiston, was now the governor of Maryland, since Nicholson had been transferred to the more prestigous post of chief executive of Virginia. Blakiston was a more pliable individual who had reached a comfortable accommodation with the local leaders. Without completely sacrificing the royal prerogative, Blakiston interfered less in the governance of Maryland and allowed the colonists greater discretion in the conduct of local government. He understood their sensitivity regarding non-local officers. For example, when the council had considered Lawrence's appeal in July, 1699, for reimbursement of the £ 150 which Whitehall had endorsed, Blakiston had not opposed the decision to award Lawrence only £ 50 while allowing the remaining £ 100 to stay in the estate of Greenberry, now deceased. That same month, Blakiston had also approved a new act of assembly limiting officers' fees, which had slightly reduced the income of the secretary's office. Furthermore, the assembly in 1699 with Blakiston's concurrence had rescinded the "permanent" act of 1695 which Nicholson had skillfully achieved to guarantee the secretary's rights to ordinary license fees; once again, the statute became a temporary law, limited to three-years duration.[40]

No one in power in 1701 was likely to champion Sir Thomas' cause upon his arrival in November. Indeed, many were well disposed to attack him. Once again, William Taylard, now married to John Lewellin's widow, was ensconced in the powerful clerkships of the lower house, the secretary's office, the provincial court, the prerogative office and of Anne Arundel county, where Lawrence's former protege Henry Denton had died. Lawrence was reluctantly obliged to continue Taylard in all of these posts.[41] A more serious opponent was William Bladen, the clerk of the council who had made a dramatic rise in the colony since his arrival in 1691. Now, as a wealthy, permanent resident of the colony, he enjoyed the respect and support of most Marylanders; moreover, he still commanded significant influence in England through his well placed family.[42] When Lawrence, Jr., had died, Bladen had received from Blakiston an appointment as temporary secretary; Blakiston had also strongly recommended his close ally Bladen to English authorities for the permanent appointment. Lawrence's return incurred Bladen's deep-seated resentment, and the two men became formidable rivals.[43]

Circumstances clearly dictated that Lawrence assume a more cautious and less aggressive posture in Maryland, and he accordingly raised little stir over the next two years, except for his conflicts with proprietary agents Charles Carroll and Henry Darnall over a half share of land office fees.[44] It was during these years that the emerging native elite first achieved dominance in the assembly. These Marylanders evidenced a keener suspicion of outsiders and a greater jealousy over local rights and access to positions of power and profit than had their predecessors of the 1690s. New immigrants intending to settle permanently as well as placemen like Lawrence confronted a stiffening in attitude and a greater difficulty in mobility. Interactions between governors and colonists and especially battles over lesser royal officials increasingly reflected the presence of different world views. Francis Nicholson had astutely detected the beginnings of this phenomenon during his tenure. A prophetic letter of July 1, 1699 to the Board of Trade had brought Whitehall's attention to the diverging interests of mother country and colony. Nicholson warned that the new local orientation of the assembly would lead to passage of acts which Marylanders "will imagine for the good of their Country, and made and serve an Interest with the People. But their doing one or more of these things may be very prejudicial to his Majesty's Interest and Service." Henceforth, Nicholson predicted, any royal governor must "be esteemed by the people to be a lover of them and their Country, and not that he be sent, or come, to make or retrieve a fortune."[45]

Nicholson might well have extended his observations to cover other royal appointees, for Sir Thomas Lawrence, already a major contributor to that local suspicion, became the subject of the first major clash along the lines which the retiring governor had shrewdly forecast. Lawrence had never been esteemed by Marylanders to be a lover of them or their country, as indeed he was not; furthermore, colonists had ample reason for regarding him as obsessed with making or retrieving a fortune. His two years back in Maryland, even with a lower profile, had sufficiently reacquainted the colonists with Lawrence's avarice and his disdain for them. The emerging native or country party made ready to challenge this most vulnerable officeholder.

The assault began in earnest in the fall of 1703. Blakiston, himself with sights higher than the Maryland governorship, had returned to England. Thomas Tench, president of the council, summoned a session of the assembly to lay the public levy. The Act for Regulating Ordinaries was due to expire at the end of the session, and the lower house seized this opportunity, in the absence of a governor, to draft a bill transferring the license fees from the secretary to the justices of each county court who would apply the revenue toward defraying the public charges. To the regret of the burgesses, Tench dissassented to the bill.[46]

A new governor, John Seymour, arrived the following spring and summoned the assembly to convene April 26. It was to be a brief session, since to Seymour's surprise, this assembly had been sitting for over three years and it had been elected in the name of the now deceased King William. Still, the delegates were anxious to pass a revision of the statute on ordinaries. Lawrence vigorously protested that the fees were a perquisite of his office and constituted one-third of his profits. A joint committee of the two houses argued persuasively that these revenues did not inherently belong to the crown, but could be appropriated as the assembly saw fit. The men considered their designation of the fees "to be more to the advantage and interest of the Province," than if the money went to the secretary. Seymour was uneasy about acting until he had studied the matter further, and after efforts failed to pass a bill with a suspension clause, he finally convinced the burgesses to defer the issue until a new assembly met in the fall. Meanwhile, in the absence of any legislation, Lawrence had no authority to collect the fees for 1703 or 1704.[47]

Clearly, no Maryland assembly was likely ever again to bestow the license fees on Lawrence or any outsider. Whether this realization was the stimulus or not, Lawrence again made plans to return to England where he could expect a more sympathetic hearing. On May 22, three weeks after the close of the assembly session, he applied to Seymour for leave to depart. Lawrence stressed that "his office was of late much lessened and Impaired as likewise his health." After examining Lawrence's commission and learning that the office could be exercised temporarily by a deputy, Seymour extended approval for the leave.[48]

Before actually departing in June, Lawrence attempted to settle some of his affairs. To avoid prosecution for a debt he was unable to pay at that time, he signed over to Bladen, under pressure, claims in excess of £ 400 which the secretary held against various Marylanders, as well as signing over all anticipated profits from his office to Bladen as security for the debt. Lawrence appointed his close friend William Dent as his personal attorney and agent to supervise collection of the money and settlement of the debt. Dent died within four months, however, and Bladen, with the governor's backing, assumed management of Lawrence's affairs, a control Bladen would exercise for two years despite Lawrence's subsequent empowering of other agents. During these years, Bladen enjoyed unhampered authority to collect and dispose of the secretary's revenues. Lawrence later estimated that he suffered a loss of nearly £ 1,000 for the years 1703-1705.[49]

Lawrence's vulnerability became even clearer in September when the new assembly convened. The lower house succeeded in obtaining Seymour's consent to "An Act for regulating of Ordinarys," without a suspension clause, which vested the revenues in county justices to defray public costs. The statute was to be in effect for three years.[50] In the next session, the burgesses struck again at the secretary's revenues. They revised the table of fees allowed the primary offices of profit in the colony, with the secretary's office probably the hardest hit. This session also reenacted the lapsed Act for Advancement of Natives.[51]

Lawrence's claims to part of the land office income also came under scrutiny. According to the royal order of 1695/96, he was entitled to receive half of all fees accruing from searches of land records for warrants and patents. The ruling did not resolve the disagreement between the proprietor and the secretary about access to land records, nor did it please the colonists who blamed Lawrence, rightly or wrongly, for the recent increase in the purchase price of land from an original 50 or 100 pounds of tobacco for every 50 acres, according to the location of the land, to 480 pounds for every 100 acres. In 1704, Charles Carroll, clerk of the land office, defended the increase as necessary because of the allotment of half of the fees to the secretary. If free access to land records were restored to proprietary agents, Carroll promised, then 240 pounds of the tobacco cost of land would be dropped. The assembly, with whom the secretary was no favorite, was eager to strike a bargain and did so.[52]

While matters could scarcely have been proceeding any worse for Lawrence in Maryland, he was finding his customary solace in England. After fully hearing Sir Thomas' case, the Board of Trade endorsed his position and wrote to Seymour not to pass any act whereby the "just and usual" fees of a patent officer would be diminished and to justify promptly his earlier acquiescence in such an action. Lawrence's requests were to receive "all due encouragement" from the governor.[53] The crown extended the secretary's leave of absence from 18 months to an indefinite period as one slight compensation for his hardships, and he continued to petition in Whitehall and to write Maryland officials in frustrated efforts to collect the money he was convinced was due him.[54]

The more adamant and shrill Lawrence became, the more entrenched became attitudes in the colony against him. The council, influenced by Seymour and Bladen, expressed resentment in September of 1706 about Lawrence's "unjust Reflections" and "very ungratefull Return" against the governor, clerk and themselves. They spoke of "a colourable pretense of some hardship done to Sir Thomas when indeede there is not any," and in carefully constructed prose they presented their own case. An even stronger defense a short time later concluded "We cannot but wonder why any Gentleman should use such base means to move Commiseration, and are Extreamly Sorry Sir Thomas Lawrence's [unworthy] Calumny on our Governor has obliged this our just Refutation."[55]

The lower house made no concessions when Seymour passed along the royal request for reinstatement of Lawrence's former revenues. Indeed, with each session the burgesses became more confident and assertive that the ordinary license fees were not historically a part of the royal revenue, but went to the secretary because the assembly had voted them so, and if the assembly decided to direct them otherwise, it could.

We have, they asserted in April, 1706, no

> "Reason to believe our most gracious Queene will deny her royal Assent to any Law Enacted here for the good of this Province upon the bare Insinuation of private or particular persons whose Interest leads them to think or say the Contrary Especially where they do not (as the Act for Ordinary Lycenses does not) lessen her Majestys Officers Just Fee they being limmitted by another Act of Assembly for that purpose."[56]

Seymour himself was trapped in a delicate position. While committed to upholding the royal prerogative, the governor was not exerting the full power of his office to redress Lawrence's grievances. Seymour was not convinced of the secretary's position, and his own relations with Lawrence were strained. Furthermore, he was reluctant to alienate the assembly and to jeopardize his own ambitious program to reform the colony's judicial system, which carried for him a higher priority and was already generating enough opposition as it was. Seymour remained content to deliver to each assembly the latest petitions from Lawrence and requests from royal officials, accompanied only by perfunctory admonitions. Seymour allowed the burgesses and councillors to voice their own strong objections to Lawrence, while excusing himself, except occasionally to rally the council to endorse officially the integrity of his own endeavors in Sir Thomas' behalf. "Because I would not lye under the Imputation of any ill natured person," he wrote on March 6, 1706/07, "I begg your Lordshipps will excuse the trouble of the Inclosed Representation from the Council here, who having been upon the Spott are best Sencible how well or ill I have deserved from that Gentleman." Seymour warned his superiors that with the Act of 1704 on Ordinaries due to expire in 1707, "The Assembly will be very unwilling to anex that perquisite to Sir Thomas Lawrences, Her Majestys Secretarys Office without Some Order to oblige them So to do."[57]

Not even such an order was sufficient. By the fall of 1707, Lawrence had convinced Whitehall officials to recommend that the crown disallow the act of 1704 and that a permanent act be passed bestowing the benefit of license fees on the secretary. It had taken so long for Lawrence to obtain this decision in the byzantine colonial bureaucracy, however, that the Privy Council addressed the attorney general's recommendation only after the three-year statute had already expired. The Lords consequently decided to recommend to Seymour their dislike of that previous law and to convey the royal wish that he not approve passage of any other such law. If possible, Seymour was to push for restoration of the fees to the secretary, and meanwhile the Lords would examine Lawrence's allegations about claims of over £ 600 denied him. In the typically slow fashion of transacting colonial business, the letter to Seymour was not dispatched until January 15, 1707/08, three months after the decision to send it, and it appears that Lawrence himself was finally serving as a bearer of messages between offices in an effort to speed up the process.[58]

Even this instrument of royal pleasure and displeasure had little effect in Maryland. Seymour's relations with the assembly had deteriorated badly. Voters had returned to two successive assemblies "Stiffnecked" men, "very backward" and "Country borne," according to the governor; in any event, they resolutely opposed Seymour on all the issues he espoused, and retribution for Lawrence was not even that high on the chief executive's agenda. The burgesses insisted on passing an ordinance which continued to vest the fees in the county justices "until her Majesty's Pleasure be further known." The local leaders addressed the Queen with still another explanation of their position and noted that since "the Fees of the Secretary's Office is vastly increased of late through the Multitude of Business therein," Lawrence should not complain.[59]

Seymour filled his next letters to the Board of Trade with apologies, excuses and attacks on the "restless and pernicious Crew" who were behind the assembly's general obstinancy. He bewailed the absence of "any person of liberall Education" in the assembly and lamented "it was too difficult a Taske for me, to graft good manners on so barren a Stock." He especially lashed out at the "Specious pretence of the Encouragement of Learning," the act for advancement of natives, which barred newly settled English subjects from holding offices of trust and profit. Seymour even supplied figures on a number of talented men who had been unwilling to settle under these conditions. With such unfortunate discrimination and catering to "the Country borne (as they call 'em)," Seymour noted "no Ingenious Men capable of serving her Majesty of the Province will come here to Starve So Long a Terme."[60]

The problem was much more complicated. Lawrence, for example, was not just an "Ingenious" man and he was scarcely starving. He and others had no pretense of settling in Maryland, nor was he seeking merely a reasonable income or advantage. The income of few individuals in the colony equalled the legitimate profits of his posts. Locals knew this and were also aware that Lawrence never initiated any particular improvements in the administrative system he oversaw; to the contrary, he often introduced greater confusion by his appointments and his frequent absences. Sir Thomas was the primary example Marylanders saw of outside office-seekers, and if he was the wave of the future, a maturing local polity wanted little part of it.

Lawrence would have joined in rare agreement with Seymour who lamented in 1708/09 that "the Natives who are ignorant and raw in business and naturally proude and obstinate, are not only the Representatives in Assembly but the Justices of the County Courts; and by the name of Country Borne distinguish themselves from the rest of her Majestys' Subjects.... They know little of the laws and good manners they practice less."[61] Clearly both men, in their anger and smugness, underestimated the talents of their Maryland opponents, and that miscalculation proved their mutual undoing.

Seymour eventually acknowledged that Lawrence could receive justice only through an act of Parliament or through some other legal power in Britain, for the assembly showed not the slightest inclination to heed the royal directive. Lawrence seemed the last person the burgesses were willing to oblige, Seymour reported, and the assembly was so suspicious of Lawrence's ability to obtain his way in England, it would approve of nothing which left any possibility of his attaining access to the revenues.[62]

Indeed, Lawrence was the last person the assemblymen would gratify. After Seymour's death and in the absence of another governor in residence for five years, the council's dutiful obedience to royal requests to restore the fees went nowhere, as the lower house steadfastly refused to cooperate. "It was high crime for any man to act as attorney or appear as friend to Lawrence," reported Philemon Lloyd, whom Seymour had appointed as Lawrence's deputy in the colony; Lloyd even begged to be discharged, claiming that hostility toward Lawrence and the office were leading colonists to look upon Lloyd himself with an "evil eye" and that other profits of the office would be attacked next. Anyone who spoke in behalf of Lawrence or the office was seen as an "enemy to the country." Lawrence's opponents, led by Bladen, were now even denying that Sir Thomas was legally the secretary.[63]

Lawrence, by now surely a weary man, continued to roam the corridors of Whitehall and to petition regularly to the Lords of Trade. He had sheafs of paper covered with figures which allegedly substantiated his claims to lost revenues, although the Maryland council, the governor, and according to Seymour, even Lawrence's own agents in the colony had disputed the calculations as "soe Extravagant that it [£ 600] is almost two-thirds more than what they truly amount to." Beyond the tabulations, Lawrence had letters from Seymour's own people and from the secretary's few supporters which accused the governor of laxity in Sir Thomas' behalf, charged the assembly with deviously and deliberately not forwarding its ordinance of December 1708 to England, and finally attacked Bladen for conspiring to have Lawrence's commission declared void. Robert Quarry, the royal surveyor of customs who held appointment to the Maryland council, had informed Lawrence that Maryland juries, with much encouragement to do so, were now resolved always to render verdicts against the secretary, rightly or wrongly.[64] Sir Thomas had carefully detailed the entire controversy in a four-page printed tract, "The Case of Sir Thomas Lawrence, Bart., Secretary of her Majesty's Province of Maryland." In its conclusion, he had appealed for an investigating commission, to include either Quarry or Nicholson, to examine the case in Maryland.[65]

For the limited good it did Lawrence, he was again vindicated by colonial officials and the crown. An order of the Queen in Council, dated March 30, 1710, declared the ordinance of 1708 illegal, restated support of Lawrence's case, and directed the new governor to obtain a law restoring the fees to the secretary's office.[66] But a new governor would not go out for another four years as the Board of Trade, in exceedingly leisurely fashion, disregarded the urgent pleas of Quarry and others that a governor be sent immediately to uphold the royal prerogative. Lawrence found himself in the familiar pattern of petitioning and waiting. Earlier royal orders were not producing the money he needed, and he asked again and again for satisfaction. In October, 1712, still another letter from the Queen in his behalf was sent to Maryland.[67]

Meanwhile, the assembly in November of 1711 had fulfilled Lloyd's prophecy of 1709 in lashing out at other aspects of the secretary's office. Lloyd's brother was acting chief executive as president of the council and managed to forestall most of the attacks.[68] In 1713 after receipt of the Queen's commands of 1710 and 1712, the delegates brazenly declined to concur. They claimed that Lawrence was not meeting the terms of his commission and charged that he and his deputy were receiving over one-third, rather than just one-tenth, of the yearly profits of some of the clerkships and that Lawrence had rented out his offices against instructions. The burgesses strongly voiced their position in an address to the Queen.[69]

"When can you think there will be an End of It whilst the Secretary continues to make his Clamour," the upper house had asked the burgesses during the debate. Certainly not as long as Sir Thomas had breath to speak. He busily lobbied all the winter of 1713-14 particularly since a new governor, John Hart, would soon depart for the colony. But the end finally did come April 25, 1714 with Lawrence's death.[70]

Apparently Lawrence's personal claims were soon dropped and never officially settled. He left no known heirs and the baronetcy became extinct. Interesting developments did ensue with respect to the office. Hart, before leaving England, conferred with Lord Baltimore who confessed he had bestowed the license fees on the secretary "not as secretary but purely as his Relation and that if ever he had the Government again He would reassume those Fines." Hart therefore concluded that under the royal government, the "Right of them was in the crown." Accordingly, he asked the assembly to pass a law determining what the fees should be and positing them in the crown; he indicated his desire that during his tenure the revenues be applied toward building a house for the governor, a project long delayed for lack of funds. The burgesses sensed a partial victory over the previous claims of Lawrence and the current objections of Lloyd; the assembly accepted Hart's proposal, but for unexplained reasons, no law was passed.[71]

Within the year, Charles Lord Baltimore died, and when his Protestant son Benedict Leonard Calvert succeeded him, the colony was restored to proprietary control. The secretaryship became a proprietary rather than royal appointment. Baltimore's spokesmen and the assembly disagreed for several years on resolution of the fees dispute. In a cleverly worded compromise in 1717, legislation passed which bestowed the fees on Lord Baltimore without affirming or denying the "undoubted right" the proprietor had claimed. Half of the revenues arising from any forfeitures under the Act for Regulating Ordinaries were to go for the use of public schools in each county. Without a clear title to the funds, by mid-century the proprietor had abandoned his claims on them as a right. The revenue was generally applied to defraying the public charges.[72]

Most historians have paid little attention to this lengthy confrontation in the colony's history, or like Donnell M. Owings, the foremost student of patronage in Maryland, have considered the struggle a "long and singularly tiresome dispute."[73] Such a view misses the importance of this conflict in the broader history of Maryland and particularly slights the significance of Sir Thomas Lawrence. Tiresome the battle may have been, but for the colonists and for upholders of the royal prerogative the conflict was most serious, immediate and far-reaching. The struggle over the ordinary license fees was but the most salient of the critical issues which this royal placeman posed for this colony from 1691 to 1714, just a few months short of encompassing the entire royal period of the colony's history.

At a time when a native elite was emerging in the colony, Sir Thomas Lawrence provided the most clearly defined symbol of what these men were not. His title, a reminder itself of the earlier unsuccessful attempt to implant a titled aristocracy in Maryland, his haughty manner, doubtless his dress, and certainly his refusal even to consider himself a Marylander or to appreciate the perspective of the "natives," all served to set him apart. Other men might also greedily seek profits from office and might neglect the general interest of the entire colony, but at least they were usually from the colony's own population. Not surprisingly the new country-born leadership first coalesced in its opposition to him and measured its increasing strength over two decades by the victories it scored over the secretary and his often impressive allies.

Lawrence's aspirations, his attitudes toward Marylanders, and his difficulties in interacting with the colonists had parallels in the experiences of lesser royal placemen in other colonies. The careers of these men demonstrate that a placeman's first concern was place, not administration, that the scramble for patronage and perquisites usually involved much less than the best interests of the colonists themselves, and that the scramble would almost certainly antagonize them. An intelligent, shrewd governor, with more powers at his disposal, like Francis Nicholson, might for a brief period manipulate local factionalism in his own or the crown's or the colony's interest, but lesser, more ordinary imperial bureaucrats were more likely to be caught in the crossfire of local disputes, to provide a focus for common opposition among otherwise disparate colonists, and often to find themselves without any viable support in the respective colony except for uncertain backing from the governor. With varying priorities and styles and personalities, odds remained high that not even the governor would remain in one's camp for long. His goals were different, and a subordinate royal appointee with independent ties to London was always a serious potential rival. A commission from the crown and continuing gestures of support from Whitehall counted for little in the face of entrenched colonial opposition, and few men enjoyed sufficient patronage or standing at home to gain preferment to another post. Lawrence sadly learned that lesson.

In the old parish church in Chelsea, where Lawrence was buried, there remain today mementoes of the Lawrence family and especially of Sir Thomas' sojourn in Maryland. Several embroidered kneelers commemorate Maryland and Lawrence's motto *Deo Non Fortuna Fretus*, "Trust in God and Not in Fortune."[74] Had Lawrence been more mindful of that admonition or had displayed in his own lifetime less fascination with material gain, his association with Maryland might have been less frustrating and unpleasant.

References

1. The best study to date of such a figure is Michael Garibaldi Hall's *Edward Randolph and the American Colonies 1676–1703* (Chapel Hill, 1960). While scholars have mined the voluminous correspondence of these officeholders for commentary on particular events, the men themselves, like Robert Quarry, Randolph's successor, remain relatively obscure figures. They deserve prosopographical study of the calibre which Stephen Saunders Webb has recently given to the royal governors, with whom these colonial bureaucrats worked closely. See Webb's " 'Brave Men and Servants to his Royal Highness': The Household of James Stuart in the Evolution of English Imperialism," *Perspectives in American History* 7 (1974): 55–82; "Army and Empire: English Garrison Government in Britain and America, 1569 to 1763," *William and Mary Quarterly* 34 (1977): 1–31; and *The Governors-General: The British Army and the Definition of Empire, 1569–1681* (Chapel Hill, 1979).
2. Donnell M. Owings, *His Lordship's Patronage: Offices of Profit in Colonial Maryland* (Baltimore, 1953), pp. 92–101, 179–180; Newton D. Mereness, *Maryland As A Proprietary Province* (New York, 1901), pp. 460–464.
3. Board of Trade Journal, 1691–1695, July 29, 1691, f. 40, Pennsylvania Historical Society (transcription of original in Public Record Office, London); William Hand Browne *et al.*, eds., *Archives of Maryland* (72 vols. to date: Baltimore, 1883–), 8: 283.
4. G.E. Cockayne, *Complete Baronetage 1611–1800* (5 vols., Exeter, 1900–1906), 2: 61; Chelsea Parish Register 1653–1704, P74/LUK/162, Greater London Record Office; Alfred Beaver, *Memorials of Old Chelsea* (London, 1892), p. 89; n.a., "Chelsea Old Church—Kneelers," Chelsea Old Church Library, London. Lawrence was quite familiar with Portugal and may have served there earlier in his career. Lawrence to John Ellis, March 25, 1697, Add. Mss. 28,881, British Museum. On Blathwayt, see Gertrude Jacobsen, *William Blathwayt: A Late Seventeenth Century Administrator* (New Haven, 1932) and Stephen Saunders Webb, "William Blathwayt, Imperial Fixer: From Popish Plot to Glorious Revolution," *William and Mary Quarterly* 25 (1968): 3–21.
5. Owings, *His Lordship's Patronage*, pp. 6, 30–34. County clerkships were generally worth £ 80+ in the early 1690s and more by the end of the decade. Lois Green Carr, "County Government in Maryland, 1689–1709" (unpubl. Ph.D. diss., Harvard University, 1968), pp. 490–495.
6. Lois Green Carr and David William Jordan, *Maryland's Revolution of Government, 1689–1692* (Ithaca, N.Y., 1974), pp. 173–175.
7. *Ibid.*, 175–176.
8. David W. Jordan, "The Royal Period of Colonial Maryland, 1689–1715" (Ph. D. diss., Princeton University, 1966), pp. 73–130 provides the fullest discussion of Copley's tenure as governor and especially his success in forging local alliances.
9. *Archives of Maryland*, 13: 249–561 presents the journal of this assembly. See also Copley to Wm. Blathwayt, June 30, 1692, Blathwayt Papers, Research Library, Colonial Williamsburg; Edward Randolph to Blathwayt, June 28, 1692, in Robert Noxon Toppan and Alfred T.S. Goodrick, eds., *Edward Randolph: Including His Letters and Official Papers . . . 1676–1703* (7 vols.; Boston, 1898–1909), 7: 373–385 (hereafter cited as *Randolph Letters*). Blakiston had been a royal placeman since 1685. Owings, *His Lordship's Patronage*, p. 180.
10. Hall, *Edward Randolph*, pp. 138–140. Randolph's extensive correspondence presents his version of the Maryland scene, especially Copley's liaison with Blakiston and their misdeeds. *Randolph Letters*, 7: 347–385, 392–394, 397–398. For Copley's defense, see *Archives of Maryland*, 8: 335–337, and his letter to Blathwayt, cited in n. 9.
11. Nicholson's and Copley's paths may have crossed earlier in their military careers, but as contemporary chief executives in Maryland and Virginia they pursued quite different paths. Copley's actions since arriving had bothered Nicholson, particularly the hostile reception to

Randolph. Hall, *Edward Randolph*, pp. 138–139, 144; *Archives of Maryland*, 8: 442; and Stephen Saunders Webb, "The Strange Career of Francis Nicholson," *William and Mary Quarterly* 23 (1966): 513–548.

12. *Archives of Maryland*, 8: 365–366, 383–384, 494; Owings, *His Lordship's Patronage*, pp. 136, 140, 142, 145, 152, 169.
13. *Archives of Maryland*, 8: 384–388; George Plater to Blathwayt, June 26, 1695, Blathwayt Papers.
14. *Archives of Maryland*, 8: 408, 416.
15. Owings, *His Lordship's Patronage*, pp. 145, 147, 148, 149, 152.
16. *Archives of Maryland*, 8: 398–399 (quote, 398), 401–403, 410–412 (quote, 411), 414–420. Lawrence later claimed that some of the petitions against him contained forged signatures, which the council never convincingly disproved. *Ibid.*, p. 425. For one of Lawrence's many personal defenses, see his appeal to the Privy Council, *ibid.*, pp. 450–452.
17. *Ibid.*, p. 416.
18. *Ibid.*, pp. 331–333, 410, 424–425; Owings, *His Lordship's Patronage*, pp. 148–149; Carr and Jordan, *Maryland's Revolution of Government*, pp. 98, 130, 266–268.
19. *Archives of Maryland*, 8: 438–440, 482–486, 487–489, 493–495, 497–502, 508–511.
20. *Ibid.*, p. 544: 19: 15; 20: 127; Richard Lee to Virginia Council, Sept. 18, 1693, in H.R. McIlwaine, ed., *Executive Journals of the Council of Colonial Virginia* (5 vols.; Richmond, 1925–1945), 1: 298; *Randolph Letters*, 7: 451–453. On Coode, see David W. Jordan, "John Coode, Perennial Rebel," *Maryland Historical Magazine* 70 (1975-): 1–28.
21. *Archives of Maryland*, 19: 8–10, 62–63, 66; 20: 6–8.
22. *Ibid.*, 8: 456–457; 20: 11, 13, 22, 27–30; Provincial Court Judgments, DSC, ff. 323–325, Hall of Records, Annapolis; *Randolph Letters*, 7: 454–455. Jeanne G. Bloom, "Sir Edmund Andros-A Study in Seventeenth Century Colonial Administration" (Ph. D. diss., Yale University, 1962) is a sympathetic portrayal of Andros which finds no fault with any of his actions in Maryland. My research does not support this view. For Andros' own accounts, see W. Noel Sainsbury *et al.*, eds., *Calendar of State Papers, Colonial Series, America and West Indies, 1693–1696* (44 vols. to date; London, 1860-), nos. 637, 639 (hereafter cited as *Calendar of State Papers, Col. Ser.*).
23. *Archives of Maryland*, 8: 564–565; 20: 53–57, 58, 156–159; Lawrence to Blathwayt, May 7 and 22 and June 22, 1694, and Andros to Blathwayt, May 4, 1694, all in Blathwayt Papers; Provincial Court Judgments, TL No. 1, ff. 1-9. Andros' expenses for the two trips totaled £ 100.18.6, and as later investigations showed, he had not performed his full duties nor paid for arms and ammunition out of his salary, which was required by law. See also *Randolph Letters*, 7: 461–462, and *Calendar of State Papers, Col. Ser., 1693–1696*, nos. 1037, 1041.
24. See, for example, Provinicial Court Judgments, TL No. 1, ff. 486–488.
25. *Archives of Maryland*, 20: 64, 77, 99, 106–111; Provincial Court Judgments, TL No. 1, f. 3; Owings, *His Lordship's Patronage*, p. 140.
26. Jordan, "Royal Period," pp. 131–200; Webb, "The Strange Career of Francis Nicholson"; Edmund S. Morgan, *American Slavery-American Freedom, The Ordeal of Colonial Virginia* (New York, 1975), pp. 351–358.
27. *Archives of Maryland*, 19: 23–116, especially 35–36, 55–59, 87, 89–90 (quote); 20: 157–159; 38: 13–15.
28. Thomas Lawrence, Jr. was at most 18. The justices still balked in February 1695/96, when the appointment was pressed by Robert Smith, a Nicholson-Lawrence ally who was chief justice of the Provincial Court and a Talbot resident. Nicholson instituted proceedings against the justices, had Valiant arrested, and appointed new justices to the Talbot bench. Ironically, having finally acquired the post, Lawrence, Jr., became an absentee officeholder. From 1696 to 1698 he was reportedly engaged in the crown's service "by sea" and had a deputy serve in his absence. *Archives of Maryland*, 19: 99; 20: 180, 255–256, 365; Owings, *His Lordship's Patronage*, p. 152; Talbot Judgments, 1692–1698, f. 244, Hall of Records.
29. Nicholson to Blathwayt, June 15, 1695, Blathwayt Papers; *Calendar of State Papers, Col.Ser., 1693–1696*, nos. 1896, 1897, 1898. Lawrence lost to his captors the furs and other gifts he was bringing from Nicholson to influence English officials. See James Vernon to Nicholson, Jan. 10, 1695/96, Fulham Palace Papers, II, f. 50, Lambeth Palace Library, London.
30. *Archives of Maryland*, 20: 272, 434–436; on Lawrence's testimony, see Colonial Office Papers 5/713/III, no. 113, Public Record Office, London.
31. *Archives of Maryland*, 19: 309; *Calendar of State Papers, Col. Ser., 1693–1696*, nos. 2190, 2230; *1696–1697*, nos. 856, 857, 858; Lawrence to Archbishop Tenison, Feb. 20, 1696/97, Fulham Palace Papers, II, ff. 85–86; Kenneth L. Carroll, "Quaker Opposition to the Establishment of a State Church in Maryland," *Maryland Historical Magazine* 65 (1970-): 149–170. During this period, Lawrence probably wrote for Thomas Bray the pamphlet entitled The Present State of the Protestant Religion in Maryland. Joseph Wheeler, "Thomas Bray and the Maryland Parochial Libraries," *Maryland Historical Magazine* 34 (1939-): 250.

32. Jordan, "Royal Period," pp. 131-200.
33. *Archives of Maryland*, 19: 454, 459, 463 (quote), 466, 468.
34. *Ibid.*, 20: 586-588; *Calendar of State Papers, Col. Ser., 1696-1697*, no. 747; Lawrence to Vernon, March 25, 1697, C.O.5/719/V (quote). See also, David W. Jordan, "'Maryland Hoggs and Hyde Park Dutchesses': A Brief Account of Maryland in 1697," *Maryland Historical Magazine* 73 (1978-): 87-91.
35. *Archives of Maryland*, 22: 60; 23: 96-98, 119-120, 345, 423; Nicholson to Archbishop Tenison, May 26, 1698, Fulham Palace Papers, II, ff. 110-111; Nicholson to Lords of Trade, May 28, 1698, *Calendar of State Papers, Col. Ser., 1697-1698*, no. 517.
36. Nicholson to James Vernon, May 26, 1698, C.O.5/719/VI, to Archbishop Tenison, May 26, 1698, Fulham Palace Papers, II, ff. 110-111, and to Blathwayt, May 28, 1698, Blathwayt Papers. See also John Locke to Nicholson, Oct. 10, 1699, Nicholson Papers, Research Library, Colonial Williamsburg.
37. *Calendar of State Papers, Col. Ser., 1697-1698*, nos. 863, 874, 885, 935, 968; *1699*, nos. 468, 471, 475; *1700*, nos. 87, 127, 131; *Archives of Maryland*, 25: 59.
38. Owings, *His Lordship's Patronage*, p. 127. Lawrence, Jr. was subsequently appointed to fill a vacancy on the council, but he died before his commission reached Maryland. *Archives of Maryland*, 25: 10-11, 58.
39. W. L. Grant and James Munro, eds., *Acts of the Privy Council of England, Colonial Series, 1680-1720* (Hereford, 1910), p. 828; James Vernon to Lords of Trade, June 10, 1701, C.O.5/715/IV; *Archives of Maryland*, 25: 106-107, 118; Lawrence to Lords of Trade, Dec. 8, 1701, C.O.5/715/V; *Calendar of State Papers, Col. Ser., 1701*, nos. 529, 530, 532.
40. *Archives of Maryland*, 22: 302-307, 518-522, 570-580; 38: 44-48.
41. Owings, *His Lordship's Patronage*, pp. 136, 138, 140, 143, 145, 148.
42. See file on William Bladen, Legislative History Project, Hall of Records.
43. Blakiston to Lords of Trade, April 15, 1701, C.O.5/713/III; Owings, *His Lordship's Patronage*, p. 127.
44. *Archives of Maryland*, 25: 130, 137-139, 161-162.
45. See David W. Jordan, "Political Stability and the Emergence of a Native Elite in Maryland, 1660 to 1715," in Thad W. Tate and David L. Ammerman, eds., *The Chesapeake in the Seventeenth Century* (Chapel Hill, 1979), pp. 243-273; Nicholson to Lords of Trade, July 1, 1699, C.O. 5/1310, 2.
46. *Archives of Maryland*, 24: 379.
47. *Ibid.*, pp. 341-343, 350, 378-380 (quote, 380), 403-407; Seymour to Lords of Trade, May 23, 1704, C.O.5/715/VI. The Upper House had split 3-3 on the issue. On Seymour's governorship, see Charles Branch Clark, "The Career of John Seymour, Governor of Maryland, 1704-1709," *Maryland Historical Magazine* 48 (1953-): 134-159, and Jordan, "Royal Period," pp. 201-315.
48. *Archives of Maryland*, 25: 175.
49. *Ibid.*, 26: 377-378; "Case of Sir Thomas Lawrence," in William Stevens Perry, ed., *Historical Collections Relating to the American Colonial Church* (4 vols.; Hartford, 1870-1878), 4: 68-69. Lawrence's figures are not out of line with Owings' estimate of the office's worth. *His Lordship's Patronage*, pp. 32-34. See also Lawrence to Thomas Bordley, Feb. 4, 1705/06, Bordley-Calvert Papers, Maryland Historical Society, Baltimore.
50. *Archives of Maryland*, 26: 46, 48, 62-65, 304-309 (act). In a later defense of his position, Lawrence mistakenly collapsed this and the previous assembly and had Seymour signing the act in April, 1704 in exchange for a bill which bestowed on the governor a revenue of 3 pence per hogshead of exported tobacco. See Perry, *Historical Collections*, 4: 65-66. The session of the subsequent fall did extend that traditional gubernatorial revenue to Seymour, *Archives of Maryland*, 26: 312-314, 360.
51. *Ibid.*, pp. 413-423, 429-430.
52. *Ibid.*, pp. 143-144, 166-167. The assembly in December did reduce the search fees and the price of land seems to have fallen soon after. *Ibid.*, XXV, 206. The best guide to the history of land issues in John Kilty, *The Landholder's Assistant* (Baltimore, 1808).
53. *Calendar of State Papers, Col. Ser., 1704-1705*, nos. 758, 1030.
54. Queen's Warrant, Dec. 31, 1705, C.O.5/716/I; Lawrence to Lords of Trade, Jan. 18 and 28, 1705/06, May 5, 1707, and Aug. 5, 1707, C.O.5/716/I; Lawrence to Bordley, Feb. 4, 1705/06, Bordley-Calvert Papers; *Archives of Maryland*, 25: 204. Lawrence was seeking £ 600 in lost profits, repeal of the act of 1704 on ordinaries, and chastizement of Seymour for not fully defending the secretary's rights.
55. *Archives of Maryland*, 25: 204-206; Seymour to Lords of Trade, March 6, 1706 and enclosure (quote), C.O.5/716/II.
56. *Archives of Maryland*, 26: 535-537; 27: 15-16.

57. Seymour to Lords of Trade, March 6, 1706/07, C.O.5/716/II; *Archives of Maryland*, 25: 265.
58. *Calendar of State Papers, Col. Ser., 1706–1708*, nos. 885, 929, 1072, 1086, 1151, 1269, 1280, 1292, 1326, 1337.
59. *Archives of Maryland*, 25: 262–267; 27: 178–374, especially 280 (quote).
60. Ibid., 25: 262-267 (quote, 263) 267–270 (quote, 269), and *Calendar of State Papers, Col. Ser., 1708–1709*, no. 290. In the past 14 years, Seymour noted, "there are scarce fourteen men who have undergone that tedious disability." *Archives of Maryland*, 25: 269.
61. *Ibid.*
62. Seymour to Lords of Trade, June 23, 1708, C.O.5/716/III, and same to same, Jan. 10, 1708/09, C.O. 5/716/IV.
63. *Archives of Maryland*, 27: 378–380, 440–442, 467–468. Lloyd's comments were included in Lawrence's letter to Lords of Trade, Feb. 24, 1709/10, C.O.5/717/I.
64. Lawrence to Lords of Trade, Dec. 27, 1708 and enclosures, and Seymour to same, Sept. 7, 1708, C.O.5/716/III; Lawrence to Lords of Trade, Feb. 24, 1709/10 and enclosures, March 13, 1709/10, and Queen's Order in Council, Jan. 26, 1709/10, and enclosures, all in C.O.5/717/I.
65. C.O.5/717/I and printed in full in Perry, *Historical Collections*, 4: 64–72.
66. *Calendar of State Papers, Col. Ser., 1710–1711*, nos. 156, 173.
67. Lawrence to Lords of Trade, Jan. 2, 1710/11, Feb. 15, 1710/11, both in C.O.5/717/II; *Calendar of State Papers, Col. Ser., 1712–1714*, no. 112.
68. *Archives of Maryland*, 29: 24–25, 64–65; Edward Lloyd to Viscount Bolingbroke, Feb. 20, 1713/14, C.O.5/720/III.
69. For the address, dated Nov. 20, 1713, see C.O.5/717/IV. *Archives of Maryland*, 29: 203–328 covers this session but see especially 209 (quote), 236, 243–244, 249, 254, 262–263.
70. *Archives of Maryland*, 29: 249 (quote); Petition to Lords of Trade, Jan. 15, 1713/14, C.O.5/717/III; Chelsea Parish Register, 1704–1747, P74/LUK/163, Greater London Record Office.
71. *Archives of Maryland*, 30: 54–56, 68, 162, 189.
72. *Ibid.*, pp. 434, 444, 448; 23: 19–20, 34–37, 70–71, 84–88; 36: 503–507 (text of act of 1717); Owings, *His Lordship's Patronage*, pp. 37–38, 127.
73. *Ibid.*, p. 37.
74. "Chelsea Old Church-Kneelers," Chelsea Old Church Library, London.

12

Politics in New Hampshire under Governor Benning Wentworth, 1741–1767

Jere R. Daniell

WHEN John Wentworth arrived at Portsmouth in the summer of 1767 to assume the governorship of New Hampshire, the selectmen of the second largest provincial town, Londonderry, published a welcoming address in which they noted the "kind patronage" of Wentworth's grandfather, John, and of his uncle, Benning, who had preceded him in office. They thought it "a hopeful presage of much future good" that "an amiable branch, sprung from such ancestors," had "come to fill the chief seat in the government," and concluded with a prayer "that the name of Wentworth" be made "hereditary." Others in the province were less pleased with Wentworth's appointment, for it perpetuated an administration which a bitter opponent had once accused of leaving the province like "a field of battle after the fight is ended; the common people being compared to the carcasses, and those who are the chief in power to the vultures and ravens glutting on the carnage."[1] Whatever his reaction to the new Governor, the individual inhabitant knew that the Wentworths, their relatives, and their friends had monopolized the key positions of political authority in New Hampshire since Benning Wentworth became governor in 1741.[2]

The rewards of political preference were most apparent to inhabitants of the provincial capital, Portsmouth. There the wealthy and inter-

[1] *New Hampshire Gazette* (Portsmouth), July 10, 1767; Richard Waldron to Jonathan Belcher, Sept. 24, 1747, in Nathaniel Bouton, ed., *Documents and Records relating to the Province of New Hampshire* (Manchester, 1872-1943), VI, 41. Titles, editors, and places of publication vary in this 40 volume series; hereafter all volumes will be cited *NHPP*. I have modernized the spelling and punctuation of quotations in this article.

[2] Benning's father John had been lieutenant governor during the 1720's; but during the thirties Governor Belcher had kept the Wentworth influence in check. See Jeremy Belknap, *The History of New Hampshire* (Philadelphia, 1784-92), II, 1-157. As one of 14 children, Benning Wentworth had no trouble finding relatives to reward. John Wentworth, *The Wentworth Genealogy: English and American* (Boston, 1878), I, 99-101.

married Atkinson, Jaffrey, Peirce, Rindge, Warner, and Wentworth families led an exclusive social life, met weekly in their own Anglican chapel, and occupied most provincial offices of profit and honor. Just south of the capital Benning Wentworth resided in a fifty-two room mansion built with the rewards of his governorship. Members of the provincial government—many of them wardens or vestrymen in Queens Chapel—traveled regularly to the Governor's mansion where until 1758 the Council held its meetings, conveniently near the gaming and billiard rooms.[3]

Even those who lived elsewhere in the colony witnessed the authority and wealth of the provincial aristocracy. As most of settled New Hampshire lay within a day's travel of Portsmouth, many had seen the bustling port themselves. The capital was the commercial center of New Hampshire and the only place where provincial courts met. Inhabitants who did not travel had indirect contact with the "clan," as its critics labeled the family group. Large sections of virtually every township in the province were owned by members of the oligarchy. Governor Wentworth exercised special authority in the interior as Surveyor of the King's Woods, charged with the responsibility of preserving provincial forests from wasteful lumbering.

The Wentworth family maintained its political power from 1741 until the outbreak of revolution; between 1752 and the early 1770's it reigned unchallenged.[4] A complex pattern of personal, social, economic, and constitutional relationships linked the family interests to the interests of others concerned with provincial government. The Crown, individual British administrators, Assembly representatives and their fellow townsmen, even the inhabitants of unrepresented communities, felt, for the most part, satisfied with the existing political structure. From an im-

[3] For a description of Portsmouth society see Mary C. Rogers, *Glimpses of an Old Social Capital* (Boston, 1923), and "Benning Wentworth" in Clifford K. Shipton, *Sibley's Harvard Graduates . . .* (Boston, 1873—), VI, 114. Of the seven wardens and vestrymen in 1762, five were Councilors, another was soon to become one, and the seventh was the Governor's brother: Society for the Propagation of the Gospel Papers, transcript volume, 79, New Hampshire Historical Society, Concord, New Hampshire, hereafter cited as SPG Papers; Belknap, *History,* II, 487. The Governor's mansion is described in Charles W. Brewster, *Rambles about Portsmouth . . .* (Portsmouth, 1859), I, 99.

[4] John Wentworth remained governor until the Revolution, but the family had begun to lose control of provincial politics before the collapse of royal government. See Jere R. Daniell, New Hampshire Politics and the American Revolution, 1741-1790 (unpubl. Ph.D. diss., Harvard University, 1964), 53-105.

perial point of view, the administration operated as effectively as any in pre-Revolutionary America.

Few provincial administrations could remain long in power without dependable and influential friends in England to see that the right people were appointed to the governorship and to other imperial offices. The Wentworths were represented at court by John Thomlinson—merchant, mast contractor, deputy paymaster of His Majesty's troops in North America, and political associate of Thomas Pelham-Holles, Duke of Newcastle.[5] As a young and aggressive London merchant in the 1730's Thomlinson had developed a trade with many leading Piscataqua merchants, among them Theodore Atkinson and the Wentworth brothers, Benning and Mark.[6] Familiar with the commerce of the province, he obtained near the end of the decade his first mast contract from the Navy Board; and from then until the mid-sixties he and his merchant friends conducted a lucrative mast trade with Mark Wentworth and Theodore Atkinson—the Governor's brother-in-law and the provincial secretary—acting as their New England subcontractors.[7] Thomlinson was also the Assembly-appointed agent for the province of New Hampshire, a remunerative position he obtained in the 1730's while Atkinson and Wentworth were members of the House. His association with the province provided an opportunity for him to assist the growth of Anglicanism; as a devoted member of the Society for the Propagation of the Gospel, the provincial Agent manifested an almost paternal concern for the welfare of Queen's Chapel and its "missionary" minister, the Reverend Arthur Browne.[8]

Thomlinson obtained leverage to serve his adopted province through extensive political relationships. By the 1750's he had become friendly

[5] See Robert M. Howard, ed., *Records and Letters of the Family of the Longs of Longville, Jamaica, and Hampton Lodge, Surrey* (London, 1925), I.

[6] Joshua Peirce Letter book and Daniel Rindge Letter book, Wendell Collection, Baker Library, Cambridge, Mass.; Thomlinson to Moffatt, Oct. 16, 1745, Moffatt, Whipple, and Mason Papers, New Hamp. Hist. Soc.; Thomlinson-Atkinson correspondence, *NHPP,* XVIII, passim; and Belknap Papers, New Hamp. Hist. Soc.

[7] Atkinson to Thomlinson, Nov. 26 and Dec. 20, 1740, *NHPP,* XVIII, 165, 166; Joseph J. Malone, *Pine Trees and Politics: The Naval Stores and Forest Policy in Colonial New England, 1691-1775* (Seattle, 1964), 124-133; Peter Livius to Henry Muilman, Feb. 6, 1764, Livius Letter book, 19, New Hamp. Hist. Soc.

[8] See Atkinson to Thomlinson, May 19, 1742, *NHPP,* XVIII, 175; and *SPG* Papers, 39-85.

enough with the Duke of Newcastle to write him directly when he wanted favors more rapidly than the Privy Council and Board of Trade could provide. Earlier he was supported by a member of the Board of Trade itself, Martin Bladen, who handled such a large portion of its business that he was referred to as "trade" while the other members were only "board."[9] After Bladen's death in 1746 Thomlinson relied on the Board's powerful secretary, John Pownall; in 1753, when Thomlinson began to tire of his work as agent, it was Pownall whom he recommended to the Governor and Assembly as his replacement.[10] Thomlinson had worked with Ferdinand John Paris, one of the most successful solicitors in England and a skilled and powerful colonial agent, to obtain a separate governor for New Hampshire after Jonathan Belcher's removal from the joint governorship of Massachusetts and New Hampshire in 1741, and Paris continued to represent provincial interests at Whitehall.[11] Furthermore, the New Hampshire Agent was an important member of the group which had supported William Shirley as Belcher's replacement in Massachusetts. Thomlinson lent Shirley £1,000 on condition that Shirley ask his patron Newcastle to seek Wentworth's appointment; shortly thereafter Newcastle announced that Benning Wentworth would be appointed governor. Elsewhere, in Parliament, at the Treasury, the Navy Board, and the Board of Ordinance, the ubiquitous merchant had his contacts. Robert Morris wrote of Thomlinson and John Hanbury, Thomlinson's partner in the business of supplying specie

[9] Thomlinson to Newcastle, Colonial Office Papers, Class 5, X, 143 (73), Public Record Office, London (available on microfilm at the Library of Congress, Washington, D. C.); Jack P. Greene, "Martin Bladen's Blueprint for a Colonial Union," *William and Mary Quarterly*, 3d Ser., XVII (1960), 517. See also, John A. Schutz, *William Shirley: King's Governor of Massachusetts* (Chapel Hill, 1961), 34; Atkinson to Thomlinson, May 19, 1744, *NHPP*, XVIII, 187.

[10] James Nevin to Atkinson, Nov. 14, 1761, *NHPP*, XVIII, 543; Thomlinson to Atkinson and others, Mar. 3, 1753, New Hampshire Miscellaneous Manuscripts, Lib. Cong.; *NHPP*, VI, 219; Thomlinson to Assembly, Oct. 9, 1753, Belknap Papers. Franklin B. Wickwire, "John Pownall and British Colonial Policy," *Wm. and Mary Qtly.*, 3d Ser., XX (1963), 543-554, discusses Pownall's influence with the Board of Trade.

[11] John A. Schutz, "Succession Politics in Massachusetts, 1730-1741," *Wm. and Mary Qtly.*, 3d Ser., XV (1958), 508-520; *NHPP*, XVIII, 64-115, 151-162; Thomlinson to Atkinson and others, Mar. 3, 1753, New Hamp. Misc. MSS.; same to same, May 21, 1754, Miscellaneous Bound, XII, Massachusetts Historical Society, Boston. For details on Paris see Mabel P. Wolff, *The Colonial Agency of Pennsylvania, 1712-1757* (Philadelphia, 1933), 39-40 et passim.

to the British Army in America, that he "knew of no two merchants in London that have such personal weight and interest with the ministry."[12]

Thomlinson's service to Wentworth, Atkinson, and their merchant friends was continuous and varied. He obtained the mandamuses placing them and their children in office and advised them what they should do to maintain those offices; any criticism of the governor and his officers heard in London coffeehouses or the ministry he relayed to Wentworth without delay. Acting as their commercial agent, Thomlinson and his business partners sold their shipments and forwarded English goods for sale and use in New Hampshire. At Whitehall, the center of political activity, he represented the interests of the Piscataqua merchants, as well as the entire merchant community of New England, in disputes with West Indian planters. So intimate were his relations with at least two New Hampshire merchants, Atkinson and George Jaffrey, that Thomlinson selected some of their clothing.[13]

Thomlinson's influence and his understanding of imperial politics were particularly important to the Governor. Before 1752 frequent disputes marked Governor Wentworth's relationship with the House of Representatives. Sometimes Wentworth sympathized with Assembly demands but hesitated to disobey royal instructions which ordered him not to conform to those demands; on such occasions he sought the aid of Thomlinson or Governor Shirley in obtaining from the ministry either formal or informal permission to make concessions to the Assembly. When, on the other hand, Wentworth disapproved of demands by the House or felt they would infringe upon royal prerogative, he asked Thomlinson to obtain an additional instruction to support him in his resistance to House action. If internal disputes threatened to embarrass the Governor at Whitehall, Thomlinson either defended the Governor or

[12] Schutz, *William Shirley*, 34-35, 56-57, 71-73; Thomlinson to Atkinson, Feb. 6, 1740/1, *NHPP*, XVIII, 169; *NHPP*, V, 255; Henry W. Foote and others, eds., *Annals of King's Chapel from the Puritan Age of New England to the Present Day* (Boston, 1882-1940), II, 143; Robert Morris to P.V.B. Livingston and [John] Stevens, Apr. 12, 1756, Boggs Papers, Rutgers University Library, New Brunswick, N. J., quoted in Beverly McAnear, ed., "An American in London, 1735-1736: The Diary of Robert Hunter Morris," *Pennsylvania Magazine of History and Biography*, LXIV (1940), 358*n*.

[13] Thomlinson-Atkinson correspondence, *NHPP*, XVIII, 161-164, 174-182, 312, 385, 549, and Misc. Bound, XII; Nevin to Atkinson, Nov. 14, 1761, *NHPP*, XVIII, 543; Daniel Rindge Letter book, Wendell Collection, passim.

used his "interests" to keep the matter from being heard before the Privy Council or the Board of Trade.[14]

But Thomlinson did not confine his support to Wentworth and the "clan." As Assembly-appointed agent for the province and a business associate of numerous Portsmouth merchants, he could not play favorites. Through the years of intense struggles between Governor and House he did everything in his power, as he told Atkinson, "to reconcile things for the benefit of the province." He scolded Wentworth after the Governor had arbitrarily reduced in militia rank certain of his personal enemies, and saw to the restoration of their commissions. The only time House members formally requested Wentworth's dismissal, Thomlinson, so he claimed, presented their complaint to ministry officials. When he reported his action to Henry Sherburne, Jr., he explained that he was as much a friend "to you and every other gentleman in the province" as to the Governor. Although Sherburne may not have been convinced—his brother later led an unsuccessful effort to appoint a different agent—others were: Thomlinson retained both the agency and the confidence of provincial inhabitants until his death in 1767.[15]

Most of the time apologies were unnecessary, for Thomlinson's efforts on behalf of New Hampshire benefited both Governor and Assembly. The appointment of Benning Wentworth as governor in 1741 was only one part of an elaborate scheme which among other things resulted in the settlement in New Hampshire's favor of its long-standing boundary dispute with Massachusetts.[16] In imperial eyes the settlement saved valuable naval stores in the contested areas from the unruly citizens of the Massachusetts charter government; but Massachusetts men saw their dreams of landed wealth evaporate in an instant and immediately dispatched Thomas Hutchinson to present their grievances. The New Hampshire agent helped ensure the failure of Hutchinson's mission.

[14] *NHPP*, V, 238-242, 336, 654; Albert S. Batchellor and Henry H. Metcalf, eds., *Laws of New Hampshire* (Manchester, 1904-16), III, 631-634; Atkinson to Thomlinson, June 28, 1758, *NHPP*, XVIII, 472; Shirley to Wentworth, Sept. 25, 1744, *NHPP*, XVIII, 210; Thomlinson to Atkinson and others, Mar. 3, 1753, New Hamp. Misc. MSS.; Wentworth to Thomlinson, Oct. 21, 1743, in Howard, ed., *Records*, I, 207.

[15] Thomlinson to Atkinson, Aug. 10, 1749, *NHPP*, VI, 887; *NHPP*, XVIII, 332-335; Thomlinson to Henry Sherburne, Jr., Nov. 13, 1749, *NHPP*, VI, 888; John Sherburne to John Huske, Feb. 9 and Aug. 20, 1754, New Hamp. Misc. MSS.

[16] So effective were Thomlinson and his aids that the decision gave New Hampshire even more than it had claimed. Most of the documents pertaining to the boundary controversy are in *NHPP*, XVIII, 42-171, and XIX, 177-646.

Later, in both 1753 and 1761, when settlers under a Massachusetts charter in Rumford (now Concord) appealed to the Privy Council for reversal of a decision in New Hampshire courts awarding land they had settled to a group of New Hampshire proprietors, Thomlinson argued against the appeal. Throughout the period of his agency, he collected and invested specie due the province from the Treasury.[17]

The actions of Benning Wentworth himself reinforced the influence stemming from Thomlinson's political interests; stubborn, at times vindictive, but neither aloof nor uncompromising, the Governor was well suited to the task of maintaining internal political harmony while presenting a picture of administrative competence to his English superiors. As surveyor general he did almost nothing to enforce the laws for preserving mast trees, yet wrote to London convincingly of efforts to prevent wanton destruction of the American forests. He informed the Board of Trade that no illegal commerce existed in New Hampshire; "the place of my residence is within a mile of . . . the harbour," he wrote, "and no vessel can come into port without coming within my sight, which . . . has contributed in a great measure to the chastity of the port" —at a time when Piscataqua was notorious for smuggling.[18] He continuously asked the Duke of Newcastle's colonial favorite, Governor Shirley, for advice and treated the Massachusetts magistrate with a deference reports of which undoubtedly reached the minister's ears. When New Hampshire troops performed well and willingly in both the Louisbourg expedition and later campaigns, the Governor made certain that his part in such operations became known to military leaders in America and to officials in England. In all his official correspondence, Wentworth gave the impression that his devotion to the royal prerogative and his gubernatorial instructions was absolute and inflexible, and that primarily through his stubborn loyalty to the Crown, New Hampshire had become a productive and peaceful part of the British Empire.[19]

The Governor went even further in his efforts to please those whose

[17] *Ibid.*, V, 180 and 846, VI, 144 and 544, XVIII, 135, XIX, 475, 510-536.

[18] Malone, *Pine Trees and Politics*, 128-134. The quotation is from Wentworth to Board of Trade, Mar. 4, 1764, Sparks Manuscripts, #43, IV, 2, Houghton Library, Cambridge, Mass. Byron Fairchild, *Messrs. William Pepperrell: Merchants at Piscataqua* (Ithaca, 1954), 190 et passim, describes smuggling in the Portsmouth area.

[19] Schutz, *William Shirley*, 64-66; *NHPP*, V, 933-950; Wentworth-Amherst correspondence, War Office Papers, 34, XXIV, passim, Public Record Office (photostats available in Lib. Cong.); Robinson to Wentworth, Nov. 11, 1757, New Hamp. Misc. MSS.; Wentworth to Lords of Trade, Mar. 23, 1750/1, *NHPP*, XVIII, 396.

pleasure would be of use to him. He supported Anglicanism, recommended the creation of an American Bishopric, and offered to grant land for its financial support. In each new township he set aside a lot for the Society for the Propagation of the Gospel, and after 1760, an additional one for the first settled Anglican minister. Furthermore, Wentworth courted the interest of the Earl of Strafford, Lord Rockingham, Baron Monson, the Duke of Grafton, Admiral Boscawen, Thomas and John Pownall, and dozens of other important civil and military officials by naming townships after them. The men so honored were frequently presented with grants of land, sometimes without having to bear any of the proprietary fees.[20]

Jonathan Belcher once wrote of Wentworth, "guts sometimes can do more than brains." Belcher without doubt underestimated his antagonist's political wisdom; but he did understand the Governor's political technique. How much actual support Wentworth gained through his actions and how seriously English officials took the Governor's image of himself is impossible to measure. Yet with Thomlinson as the ministry's primary source of information about the province, those whose responsibility it was to judge the effectiveness of New Hampshire's provincial government remained ignorant of much that went on in the colony. Since the Thomlinson-Wentworth team functioned smoothly until the early 1760's, it is not difficult to understand how Benning Wentworth retained his governorship for twenty-five years—longer than any other colonial governor in British North America.[21]

The trade in masts ensured Thomlinson's continued political co-

[20] Wentworth to the Secretary of the SPG, Additional Manuscripts #32704, fol. 135, British Museum, London (transcript available in Lib. Cong.); Arthur Browne correspondence, SPG Papers, passim; John F. Looney, The King's Representative: Benning Wentworth, Colonial Governor 1741-1767 (unpubl. Ph.D. diss., Lehigh University, 1961), 105; Elmer Hunt and Robert A. Smith, "The English Background of some of the Wentworth Town Grants," *Historical New Hampshire,* VI (1950), 2-52; C.O. 5/925, passim. Both Browne and Wentworth felt that support of the Church of England played an important role in keeping the Governor in office.

[21] Belcher to Waldron, Jan. 13, 1741/2, Belcher Papers, III, #112, New Hamp. Hist. Soc. Thomlinson lost his influence in the early 1760's after Newcastle fell from power. Proceedings then were initiated against Wentworth at the Board of Trade. The New Hampshire Governor escaped removal only because Lord Rockingham (an English Wentworth who had become devoted to the Governor's nephew John) became first lord of the treasury. Rockingham quashed the proceedings and let Benning Wentworth resign in favor of his nephew. Daniell, New Hampshire Politics, 53-59.

operation with the Wentworths. The successful English mast contractor needed widespread political connections in both England and the colonies. He had to purchase a license from the Privy Council before contracting with the Admiralty, obtain affidavits from the Surveyor General, Governor, and naval officer of the province where he procured his masts, get certificates from customs commissioners and dockyard officials attesting that his masts met contract specifications and qualified for premium payments, and have connections in the Treasury to hasten the notoriously slow process of payment for masts delivered to the Admiralty. In addition he needed dependable colonial agents to purchase masts of the quality to meet rigid naval standards.[22] Politically well connected in England and New Hampshire, wealthy enough to participate in a business requiring heavy initial capital outlay, and certain of his colonial subcontractors, Thomlinson enjoyed a secure and profitable situation: no one could seriously challenge his control of the mast trade from New Hampshire while Wentworth remained in power.[23]

Thomlinson's control of this trade was highly satisfactory from the Wentworths' point of view. As long as Thomlinson continued to deliver masts, Admiralty and Board of Trade officials were apt to remain satisfied with the provincial government. Moreover, the existing arrangement ensured family domination of the mast business in New Hampshire. Peter Livius, a well-to-do Englishman who came to Portsmouth in the sixties to manage the American estate of his father-in-law John Tufton Mason, was obviously disappointed to discover that masting was "in the hands of a few associated gentlemen of very large fortunes," who had the Surveyor General "entirely at their devotion," and opposed any interference in their affairs.[24]

Livius had good cause to lament that such conditions made masting

[22] Malone, *Pine Trees and Politics*, 47-51.

[23] There may have been some competition between Thomlinson and the powerful mast contractor Joseph Gulston in the early forties, but I have encountered no evidence of any after that. The other leading contractor was John Henniker who worked in close co-operation with Thomlinson. See Atkinson to Thomlinson, Dec. 20, 1740, *NHPP*, XVIII, 167; unsigned note, Dec. 1, 1757, Wentworth Papers, Box II, New Hamp. Hist. Soc.; Peter Livius to Henry Muilman, Feb. 6, 1764, Livius Letter book, 19; Robert G. Albion, *Forests and Sea Power: The Timber Problem of the Royal Navy, 1652-1862* (Cambridge, Mass., 1926), 56, 235.

[24] Livius to John Raymond, June 18, 1765, Livius Letter book, 59. For biographical details on Livius see *ibid.*, passim, and Langdon Papers, 23, Historical Society of Pennsylvania, Philadelphia.

"too perilous" for him to attempt, for he had some idea how profitable the trade could be. The exact terms of the naval contracts, he found, were "kept profound secrets" in Portsmouth "in order to deter anyone from attempting the contract"; nevertheless, even those who wanted "to diminish any opinion of their being very large" acknowledged the profits exceeded 100 per cent. Livius was not exaggerating. In 1764 a mast of twenty-four inches in diameter which cost a Portsmouth agent £6 5s was worth about £35 to the contractor in England; a thirty-inch mast cost £25 10s and sold for about £75; and a thirty-six-inch mast could be obtained for less than £100 while selling for about £180.[25] Benning Wentworth was bankrupt when he was appointed governor—indeed his appointment was largely a product of the political influence of his creditors—and his cut in the mast trade combined with his salary and his fees as governor and surveyor general made him in time a wealthy man. The mast agent Mark Hunking Wentworth in 1754 was by far the largest taxpayer in Portsmouth, paying 3 per cent of the town's entire tax. Masting was without doubt, as Livius concluded, "a business where the profits are very great, morally certain and attended with very little trouble."[26]

The Wentworths' influence in England gave them control over royal appointments in New Hampshire and allowed them to dominate the mast trade. It did not, however, guarantee them the co-operation and approval of their fellow provincial inhabitants. To be sure, men who lived in mid-eighteenth-century America expected that wealth, social superiority, and political preferment would go hand in hand, and thus were conditioned to respect any governing aristocracy. But in some colonies royal officials commanded little allegiance. They found their effective authority undermined by their inability to reward those whose political support was necessary to the successful conduct of everyday governmental affairs. The oligarchy in New Hampshire, however, suffered from no such inability. Circumstances in the province gave the Wentworths opportunity to construct a broad economic and political founda-

[25] Livius to Raymond, June 18, 1765, and Livius to Henry Muilman, May 14, 1764, Livius Letter book, 38, 59; Malone, *Pine Trees and Politics,* 147. In his letter to Muilman, Livius reports mast costs to colonial agents; Malone has charted mast prices (Appendix B) from information in Admiralty ledgers. Prices in general doubled between 1740 and 1758, then began to decline.

[26] Portsmouth Tax Records, City Hall, Portsmouth, New Hampshire; Livius to Muilman, May 14, 1764, Livius Letter book, 36.

tion on which their provincial authority could rest. They took every advantage of their opportunity.

Pre-Revolutionary New Hampshire depended economically on the export of masts, ships, and lumber which were marketed in England, Spain, Newfoundland, and the West Indies in exchange for specie, raw materials, or finished goods. All of settled New Hampshire engaged in the trade. In the Great Bay area and up what is now Salmon Falls River, hundreds of lumbermen provided the raw materials for building vessels near Portsmouth and for their future cargoes; along the Merrimack, woodsmen worked to supply ships at Newburyport. Indeed, so many men were engaged in lumbering that provincial merchants had to import grain and other foodstuffs. And there was little reason to think the trade would decline; even in the 1750's the forests of New Hampshire seemed to provide an endless supply of timber.[27]

But one threat to the lumber trade did exist. The imperial government considered New Hampshire an important source of naval stores. Fearful that colonists would destroy American forests in their eagerness to build up trade, the Admiralty had urged Parliament and the ministry to enact regulations protecting American forests from waste, and by the time Wentworth became governor of New Hampshire, Parliament had prohibited the cutting of any white pine trees on public property and pines on private property which were twenty-four inches or more in diameter two feet from the base.[28] Had the colonists been forced to obey the regulations, their trade might well have been destroyed. White pine boards constituted nearly all their export shipments.

As surveyor general charged with the enforcement of the white pine policy, Benning Wentworth made certain that nothing disturbed the lumber trade. Richard Waldron, searching in 1748 for a way to undermine the ministry's good opinion of Wentworth, wrote that there was "one thing, which if rightly represented . . . would break the Don[29] in

[27] Fairchild, *William Pepperrell*, 61-66; Samuel J. McKinley, Economic History of Portsmouth (unpubl. Ph.D. diss., Harvard University, 1931), passim; Livius to Muilman, Jan. 9, 1764, Livius Letter book, 6; Nathaniel Adams, *Annals of Portsmouth* . . . (Portsmouth, 1825), 258; Belknap, *History*, III, 203-212.

[28] Malone, *Pine Trees and Politics*, chaps. 5, 6; Bernhard Knollenberg, *Origin of the American Revolution: 1759-1766* (New York, 1960), 127-128; Albion, *Forests and Sea Power*, 241-256.

[29] Waldron had a variety of names for Governor Wentworth who often boasted of his former exploits in Spain.

pieces; that is the waste of the King's timber." But Waldron knew that "hardly a man in the province would mention it, either as a complaint or a witness, as most of the people" made "earnings out of the unrighteous indulgence." They made their earnings because the mast agent agreed to accept all good quality masts tendered to him, regardless of current contract demands, and the surveyor licensed all who supplied masts to the agent. The arrangement meant that Mark Wentworth had a "dock of masts always ready to supply the wants of those . . . in need, at his own price . . . and the countrymen cut what trees they please, making masts of the best . . . and converting the rest into mill logs for their own use." Only a court of inquiry, Waldron lamented, could expose the "affair . . . and moving in it would be one of the most unpopular things in the world." During Wentworth's governorship there were about a dozen seizures of illegally cut timber—the logs were sometimes bought back at auctions by the same people from whom they had been seized—and no successful prosecutions of millmen.[30] No wonder Richard Waldron had difficulty exciting the inhabitants of the colony about the iniquities of Wentworth's administration.

There were other reasons for acquiescence in family rule. The ambitious colonist identified wealth with land ownership, and when he needed land for lumbering, farming, settlement, or speculation, he wanted to get it cheaply. Land was plentiful in New Hampshire and its cost reasonable. But if a man co-operated with those in power, he might acquire a huge estate with little expense at all, for the members of the clan had absolute control over vast areas of ungranted territory in the province.

The Wentworths exercised control in part through the Masonian proprietorship. Late in the 1730's John Thomlinson had arranged for the New Hampshire Assembly to purchase John Tufton Mason's claim to ownership of all wastelands within ninety miles of New Hampshire's coast. But the House members in 1744 balked at payment unless disposal of the lands was left to them—a demand to which neither Governor nor Council would agree. While the Assembly bickered, a group of twelve Portsmouth merchants led by Atkinson and Mark Wentworth secretly paid Thomlinson for the purchase and began to organize their proprie-

[30] Waldron to Belcher, Sept. 16, 1748, in John Farmer and Jacob B. Moore, eds., *Collections, Historical and Miscellaneous . . .*, III (Concord, 1824), 256; Malone, *Pine Trees and Politics*, 131-132.

torship.[31] Their move astounded even the Governor: he contemplated instituting proceedings against the proprietors to recover the land for the Crown and informed his ministerial superiors that he felt the proprietors' power should be contained.[32] But when officials at Whitehall said nothing Wentworth pursued the matter no further.

Although the legality of the purchase and the validity of Mason's title were both questionable, provincial inhabitants made little complaint against the proceedings. The Masonian proprietors were quick to confirm all actual settlers in their possessions and to issue quit claim deeds to the existing towns in the purchase. Furthermore, it soon became evident that the proprietors' terms for granting unsettled lands were so generous that objection would have been ridiculous. Rather than attempting direct sale in a province where money was scarce and liquid capital mostly in their own hands, the proprietors simply gave town charters to those who met with their approval, offered an additional one hundred acres for each settled European immigrant, and reserved plots in each township for themselves. Their profits came from the increase in value of their own plots resulting from the settlement they encouraged.[33]

Those who sought land grants outside the Masonian Patent had to deal with a Governor and Council they found equally accommodating. Wentworth had a seemingly endless supply of townships at his disposal. As far as he was concerned the settlement of the boundary dispute with Massachusetts gave New Hampshire jurisdiction over all land north of the boundary as far west as what is now New York. Much of the territory which before settlement of the boundary dispute had been granted to influential Massachusetts men he regranted to the same men. They and new grantees found quit rents nominal and fees moderate; in some cases Wentworth may have asked no fees at all.[34] And although the

[31] *NHPP*, V, 409-470. The family relationship of the various proprietors has been tabulated by Otis G. Hammond, "The Mason Title and Its Relations to New Hampshire and Massachusetts," in American Antiquarian Society, *Proceedings*, XXVII (Worcester, 1916), 256-257. It provides an excellent history of the proprietorship.

[32] Wentworth to Board of Trade, Mar. 23, 1750/1, *NHPP*, XVIII, 390-400; Looney, The King's Representative, 76-81.

[33] *NHPP*, VI, 896-904; Hammond, "The Mason Title," 258-262.

[34] George P. Anderson's paper on land grants made in New Hampshire by Governor Benning Wentworth to Boston men, in Colonial Society of Massachusetts, *Publications*, XXV (Boston, 1924), 33-38; Atkinson to Thomlinson, Nov. 19, 1752, *NHPP*, VI, 161; Charles B. Kinney, Jr., *Church and State: The Struggle for Separa-*

Governor did require that some of his friends be included as proprietors of townships; that schools, the first settled minister, the Society for the Propagation of the Gospel, and the Church of England be reserved one share each; and that a large plot, usually 500 acres but sometimes as much as 800 acres, be reserved for His Majesty's Royal Governor, no one complained.[35] There was land enough for all. By 1765 Wentworth had granted 124 townships and few men of means and ambition in New Hampshire had failed to increase their estate.[36]

Wentworth had still another way of repaying the faithful or punishing the recalcitrant; as governor of New Hampshire he had no trouble finding offices to distribute or to withhold. Richard Waldron informed Isaac Royall, when encouraging him in 1748 to seek the governorship, that as chief magistrate he would appoint "Judges and Justices . . . the Secretary, Treasurer, Sheriff, Register of Probate and the military officers" and recommend appointment of clerks to the courts. Waldron knew how effective patronage could be. Under Belcher he had been secretary of the province, judge of the Inferior and Probate Courts, councilor, justice of the peace, and for nearly a decade the Governor's unofficial lieutenant in charge of New Hampshire; by 1743 Wentworth had stripped him of every office and Belcher was surprised that the treasurer, the sheriff, and the clerk of courts had "stood so long."[37] But the Governor showed more interest in courting friends than in punishing enemies. Wentworth bestowed justice of the peace commissions so

tion in New Hampshire, 1630-1900 (New York, 1955), 69; William H. Fry, *New Hampshire as a Royal Province* (New York, 1908), 290-324; *NHPP,* XXIV-XXVI, passim; Matt B. Jones, *Vermont in the Making, 1750-1777* (Cambridge, Mass., 1939), 52-53.

[35] Some astounding paper fortunes were accumulated in this way. Wentworth himself owned close to 100,000 acres. Friends John Nelson, John Temple, and James Nevin had shares in from 19 to 46 townships; brothers Mark and John and cousin Theodore were equally well treated. See Roy H. Akagi, *Town Proprietors of the New England Colonies: A Study of Their Development, Organization, Activities and Controversies, 1620-1770* (Philadelphia, 1924), 212; Joseph B. Walker, "The Controversy between the Proprietors of Bow and Those of Penny Cook, 1727-1789," in New Hamp. Hist. Soc., *Proceedings,* III (Concord, 1895-99), 269; *NHPP,* XXIV-XXVI, passim.

[36] For a typical example, see William H. Brown, *Colonel John Goffe* (Manchester, 1950).

[37] Waldron to Royall, Sept. 16, 1748, *NHPP,* VI, 60; "Richard Waldron," in Shipton, *Harvard Graduates,* V, 655-656; Wentworth to Board of Trade, Mar. 23, 1750/1, *NHPP,* XVIII, 397; Belcher to Waldron, Apr. 3, 1742, New Hamp. Hist. Soc., *Collections* (Concord, 1824-1915), IV, 99.

prodigally that by the sixties they had become objects of ridicule. If Jeremy Belknap's information was correct, there were but twenty-five justices in the entire province when Wentworth arrived, and he appointed that many again from Portsmouth alone. In 1765 a local wag described Wentworth's administration as "the happy silver age/ When magistrates, profoundly sage/ O'erspread the land; and made it seems/ Justice run down the streets in streams."[38]

If the Governor ran out of civil commissions, there were always military honors to bestow. Atkinson was a full colonel in the militia, as were Nathaniel Meserve of Portsmouth and Thomas Wallingford of Dover (both Masonian proprietors), Joseph Blanchard of Dunstable (surveyor for the Masonian proprietors), John Goffe of Bedford, and Meshech Weare of Hampton Falls. Most of these and other appointees were capable and effective military leaders, but Wentworth's selection of his own young sons and a ten-year-old nephew as officers can hardly have improved the military efficiency of the province. Such appointments irritated his enemies, particularly since Wentworth simultaneously cashiered or failed to promote Waldron's son Thomas and others, like John Sherburne and Peter Gilman of the Exeter family which had strongly supported Belcher, whom he felt he could not trust. Wentworth had been serious in his observation when extending commissions that "as the power is absolutely in me, I can remove at pleasure if there is any occasion."[39]

Most royal governors in colonial America possessed the same official powers as did Benning Wentworth, yet found themselves unable to control the behavior of provincial judicial and legislative officials. The effectiveness of royal government in New Hampshire, however, was never seriously compromised during Wentworth's administration. Councilors, judges, and House representatives remained for the most part loyal to their appointed ruler; and the one serious challenge to family and royal government, which came in the late 1740's, met with de-

[38] Belknap, *History,* II, 340; *Portsmouth Mercury,* Oct. 7, 1765, printed in Belknap, *History,* II, 341.

[39] Weare Papers, II, 82, New Hamp. Hist. Soc.; Batchellor and Metcalf, eds., *Laws of New Hamp.,* II, 595; Waldron to Belcher, Sept. 24, 1747, *NHPP,* VI, 40; Waldron to Royall, Apr. 22, 1748, *NHPP,* VI, 48; Waldron to Belcher, July 1, 1748, in Farmer and Moore, eds., *Collections,* III, 228; Wentworth to Thomlinson, Oct. 21. 1743, Howard, ed., *Records,* I, 207.

cisive defeat. In fact, the pattern of influence which the merchant oligarchy developed through their extensive connections in England and their distribution of political and economic rewards made Wentworth's management of provincial political institutions a relatively easy task.

The Council presented no problems at all. Wentworth's dismissal of Waldron warned those already on the Council that if they wished to retain the social prestige and influence over land grants and political patronage that membership provided, they had better co-operate with the Governor. Furthermore, the support of Thomlinson and Wentworth at Whitehall was necessary before any candidate for appointment could obtain his mandamus; when vacancies occurred, friends and relatives of the Governor found themselves in an enviable position. Of the twelve councilors chosen between 1741 and 1764, all except William Temple—a nonresident friend of the Governor—were Portsmouth merchants, and most were Anglicans. In 1753 a Congregational minister complained that the Council had become an Anglican stronghold; a decade later the Reverend Arthur Browne as chaplain of the Council offered prayers with a group which included a brother, a brother-in-law, a nephew, and five other relatives of the Governor.[40]

Once the Belcher men had been weeded out or silenced, the Council had no reason to disagree with its Governor except for the rare cases when Wentworth's vindictiveness seemed insupportable even to his merchant associates. As the members of the upper house of the legislature, the councilors consistently backed their benefactor in disputes with the lower house. They voted against taxes on unimproved lands, supported Wentworth's financial and military plans, and helped persuade reluctant representatives to comply with the Governor's legislative requests. When the House and Governor came to such an impasse that the Assembly went without meeting for more than three years, the councilors continued to assist Wentworth in his administration.[41] As his sworn advisers it was their legal duty; as his friends and relatives it was their inclination.

Co-operation between Governor and Council meant family domination of the court system. Not only were judicial appointments made by

[40] Wentworth to Board of Trade, Mar. 23, 1750/1, and Atkinson to Thomlinson, Jan. 28, 1758, *NHPP*, XVIII, 398, 473; John Odlin to Dr. Avery, June 1753, in New Hamp. Hist. Soc., *Colls.*, IX, 22. Councilors are listed in Belknap, *History*, II, 487. Brewster, *Rambles*, and Wentworth, *Wentworth Genealogy*, I, contain scattered information on most colonial council members.

[41] *NHPP*, V, 126, 458, et passim, and VI, 341, 448-486.

Wentworth and the councilors, but together they acted without jury as a final Court of Appeals on matters both civil and criminal. Understandably the Court of Appeals alienated some people. Belknap, who moved to New Hampshire in the mid-sixties, reported that "frequent complaints were made of partiality," particularly in cases where Council members had earlier sat as judges in the decisions being appealed. John Sherburne, son of a prominent Congregational merchant, became enraged at the situation: as primary legatee of his father's will he saw the will disallowed because the Court of Appeals would not accept the testimony of Portsmouth's leading Congregational ministers, Samuel Haven and Samuel Langdon. Sherburne possessed the wealth and patience to seek a reversal in England. But few others could afford to fight decisions of the Court of Appeals.[42]

Family influence in the Superior, Inferior, and Probate Courts was no less obvious. As Belknap noted, "members of the Council" and others "devoted to the interest of the governor or personally related to him" filled court offices. When Wentworth became Governor the situation had been different. Actually he made no wholesale purge; but he was determined to see that judges remained loyal to his personal rule. In 1754 he forced the resignation of Chief Justice Ellis Huske, who a few years before had been an accomplice of Waldron in the attempt to oust Wentworth from the governorship, and replaced him with Atkinson. When the House refused to vote Atkinson a salary, Wentworth agreed to pay it himself. And as other judges resigned or died, Wentworth put friends and relatives in office.[43]

The influence of the merchant oligarchy reached even deeper into the judicial system. Those who had interest with court officials could sometimes obtain a hearing out of court. The practice of "watering the jury" —the phrase is Belknap's—was familiar, and since all courts met in Portsmouth, it was not difficult to find jurors sympathetic to royal government. Wentworth had no intention of disturbing the situation. In 1737 the Privy Council had disallowed a law locating courts in Exeter, on the grounds that inland juries would be biased in cases involving illegal

[42] Fry, *New Hampshire*, 119-127, 458; Belknap, *History*, III, 256; Add. MSS. #36218, foll. 147-150 (transcripts in Lib. Cong.); John Huske to [John Sherburne], Apr. 11, 1765, New Hamp. Misc. MSS.; Joseph H. Smith, *Appeals to the Privy Council from the American Plantations* (New York, 1950), 667-670.

[43] Belknap, *History*, III, 256; *NHPP*, VI, 339, 418, 721, and XVIII, 496; Charles H. Bell, *The Bench and Bar of New Hampshire . . .* (Boston, 1894), 18.

lumbering. The argument seemed so sound Wentworth used it to justify his refusal in 1760 to go along with an Assembly plan to divide the province into counties and organize a county court system. "I hope your lordships will think I am as well qualified to judge" as the Assembly when such a division should be made, he wrote to the Board of Trade, "and my sentiments are fixed that this is the most improper time to make any alteration."[44]

Yet in spite of family influence in the courts, there was no widespread disapproval of the judicial system. Wentworth's associates were better educated and more qualified for judicial posts than all but a few men in the province. And the Governor did not restrict judicial appointments to his merchant relatives. Meshech Weare, for example, a Harvard graduate whose father and grandfather had been provincial political leaders and who himself had become town moderator of Hampton Falls early in his twenties, had no particular family connection with the Governor and was not a merchant; yet he was a permanent justice of the Superior Court of Common Pleas from 1747 to 1776 as well as a trusted militia leader.[45] In an age when it was generally assumed that justice would be meted out by "the better sort of people," exclusiveness on the bench did not trouble the ordinary citizen who, in any case, rarely carried legal matters further than the local justice of the peace.

One specific legal problem in which the interests of New Hampshire as a whole were involved made family influence in the court system seem to some a positive good. The problem involved a controversy between the proprietors of the township of Rumford and the proprietors of the township of Bow. Years before settlement of the Massachusetts–New Hampshire boundary dispute, a group of Bay State Congregationalists under the leadership of their minister, Timothy Walker, had created a prospering agricultural community near the junction of the Contookook and Merrimack rivers. The deed to their township of Rumford had been granted by Massachusetts in 1727, but much of the same land was shortly thereafter granted as the township of Bow by Lieutenant

[44] Belknap, *History*, III, 256; James Munro, ed., *Acts of the Privy Council of England, Colonial Series* (London, 1908—), III, 453; *NHPP*, VI, 454, 722-726, 749, 766; Wentworth to Board of Trade, Aug. 13, 1760, C.O.5/928.

[45] "Theodore Atkinson," in Shipton, *Harvard Graduates*, VI, 221-231, and "Meshech Weare," IX, 590-596. A more recent study of Weare is Avery J. Butters, New Hampshire History and the Public Career of Meshech Weare, 1713-1786 (unpubl. Ph.D. diss., Fordham University, 1961).

Governor John Wentworth. During the 1740's Walker and his congregation were allowed to run their affairs as a district of New Hampshire and were even sent a precept for the Assembly election of 1748. In 1749, however, the Bow proprietors, who included Wentworth, three of his brothers, Atkinson, and Jaffrey, brought suit in the New Hampshire courts against settlers under the Rumford deed, and the courts decided in their favor. Walker, armed with a grant from the Massachusetts General Court and letters of introduction from Jonathan Mayhew and the New Hampshire convention of ministers, sailed to England with a petition for redress.[46]

The Rumford proprietors sent Walker because they had no hope of redress in New Hampshire courts. The fact that "the Governor and most of the Council" were "proprietors of Bow" and responsible for appointing judges was only part of the trouble. The petitioners felt that any New Hampshire jury would manifest "prejudices by reason of relations, favor or interest in similar causes." The people of New Hampshire, they lamented, are "generally disaffected to your petitioners on account of their deriving their titles from the Massachusetts." The proprietors described the situation accurately, for a determination in favor of the Rumford claim would have threatened anyone holding title in New Hampshire to land also claimed under a Massachusetts deed. Waldron, the Exeter Gilmans, and hundreds of others held such titles. When the New Hampshire Assembly learned of Walker's departure, they voted to lend the Bow proprietors £100 to finance Thomlinson's defense against Walker's appeal. The Rumford-Bow case helps explain why the provincial Assembly in 1767 made a point of thanking Benning Wentworth particularly for his "steady administration of justice."[47]

Prevailing economic conditions, the kinship structure of Portsmouth's merchant community, and the accepted constitutional framework of provincial government made it possible for Benning Wentworth

[46] Two competent summaries are Walker, "The Controversy," 261-292, and Akagi, *Town Proprietors,* 165-174. Documents concerning the dispute are scattered: see Add. MSS. #36218, foll. 181-192 (transcripts in Lib. Cong.); Walker Papers, I, New Hamp. Hist. Soc.; New Hampshire Miscellaneous, Box I, New York Public Library, New York City; *NHPP,* IX, 134-139, 349-358, and XVIII, 354; Waldron to Belcher, Feb. 9, 1753, Waldron Papers, II, #115, New Hamp. Hist. Soc.

[47] Walker Papers, I, 27, printed in Walker, "The Controversy," 278-281; "A State of a Case . . . ," New Hamp. Misc., Box I, N. Y. Pub. Lib.; *NHPP,* VI, 294, IX, 67-68, and VII, 116.

and his associates to maintain control of New Hampshire's executive and judicial institutions, as long as they retained their influence in England. Different circumstances prevailed in the lower house of the legislature. Members of the House of Representatives were elected in town meetings by freeholders over whom the Wentworths had little direct influence. As elected representatives they customarily felt more responsible to their local constituents than to imperial interests or the needs of the merchant aristocracy. In the House, therefore, the Wentworths could not expect to dominate as they did in the Council and courts.

The goal of the Wentworths in the House, however, was not complete political domination. Quite to the contrary, they expected House members to assume independent responsibility for many of New Hampshire's internal affairs. The House appointed excise collectors, handled petitions from individuals and communities, and determined the outcome of disputes between the units of local government. In addition the Governor and councilors depended often on representatives to make recommendations for local judicial and military posts. The arrangements satisfied most elected representatives. They had sought or accepted election in part because membership gave them access to those sources of authority over local affairs lodged in the provincial government. Many representatives, an observer noted, were so limited in their concerns that they "never find they have anything to do in the House when there is nothing on the tapis in which the town or borough which chose them is not immediately concerned."[48] The Governor and his advisers had neither the need nor the desire to become involved in such local business.

What Benning Wentworth did expect from the House was that it help him fulfill his responsibilities as New Hampshire's royal governor. If the House threatened in any way to prevent him from obeying what he considered to be his duty, or from pleasing those who at any time could remove him from his offices, then Wentworth could no longer afford to let its members act without interference. Furthermore, the Governor understood that the House of Representatives provided those with wealth and ambition a convenient place for maneuvering in the game of imperial politics. During the 1740's the House contained only twenty

[48] *New Hampshire Gazette,* Nov. 3, 1758. Volumes IX and XI-XIII of *NHPP* contain records of petitions handled in the Assembly.

members. Since most of these members, Wentworth explained to his superiors at Whitehall, "were very little acquainted with men of the world," any House member with education and acknowledged social superiority—including the Governor's personal enemies—automatically commanded great influence. Such circumstances, Wentworth continued, made it possible for "two or three designing persons, under pretence of defending the liberties of the people and opposing the King's Governor, to obtain followers." He wrote from experience: in the 1730's he and Atkinson as House Representatives had been able to harness resentment against royal authority in their efforts to embarrass Governor Belcher.[49] From the beginning of his administration, then, Wentworth acted upon his knowledge that House opposition was most dangerous when led by those capable of replacing him in his position of political authority.

As governor, Wentworth could utilize both the prerogative and his royal instructions as constitutional weapons in disagreements with his House. He had the right to convene, adjourn, prorogue, or dissolve the Assembly at any time. He could veto legislation, negative the choice of House Speaker, and if necessary attempt to change personnel in the House by calling for new elections. Existing laws worked to the advantage of the governor in such elections. In the first place, representatives were required to have £300 of rateable estate: men of such wealth, particularly in frontier communities, were apt to have gained their wealth through dealing with the Wentworths in the masting business, or through receiving land grants from the Governor. In addition the Governor claimed the right to issue precepts to previously unrepresented communities, many of which he could be reasonably certain would return representatives friendly to his administration. The House members naturally claimed the right to control their own representation and challenged Wentworth's use of his other constitutional powers. But they were unsuccessful.[50]

The general circumstances of Wentworth's administration helped him in his efforts to prevent the House from obstructing his exercise of royal authority. He held office during wartime in a province continuously threatened by encroachments from the French and Indians. When he de-

[49] Wentworth to Board of Trade, Mar. 23, 1750/1, *NHPP*, XVIII, 396; same to same, Nov. 8, 1747, C.O.5/926; *NHPP*, IV, 794, 802. The struggles between Governor Belcher and the House of Representatives are described in Belknap, *History*, II, 101-157.

[50] *NHPP*, VI, 94; Fry, *New Hampshire*, 66-208.

manded appropriations to support British military policy in America, the Assembly usually complied with his requests; as individuals they benefited from supply contracts and as representatives of the people they sought protection of the frontiers. Moreover, the only way to finance war was to issue paper money backed by future taxes. Since provincial residents and their elected representatives found business easier to conduct with paper currency than without, they encouraged their chief magistrate to permit emissions and applauded his success in obtaining royal permission for what in peacetime would not have been allowed.[51]

The financial independence of the Governor further strengthened his hand in dealing with the House. To be sure, Wentworth did not hesitate to seek an adequate salary; and in the early part of his administration he needed the money to pay debts.[52] But as his fortune accumulated, his dependence on the Assembly decreased. By the time organized resistance to his rule had developed in the House, Wentworth had sufficient wealth to go without salary for nearly four years. He could afford, a few years later, to pay Atkinson's salary as Chief Justice of the Superior Court when the House refused to make an appropriation for his salary.

Wentworth and the Council could, in addition, reward co-operative House members directly. "I suppose," wrote Waldron in 1742 after the Governor had been voted a salary even he considered adequate, "our Assembly expect to be landlords of thousands and thousands of acres, esteeming but reasonable, for generous grants of money, to have a return of as generous grants of land, *huzza, huzza, huzza*." Wentworth did not disappoint them. His generosity, particularly in the fifties, became so lavish that of the thirty-one representatives in the House which met in 1764, all but three new members had been granted land in from one to eleven towns. The next year, during the Stamp Act crisis, he granted an entire township to the House members. The distribution of political patronage and military supply contracts could be used to serve the same purpose.[53] And the possibility that Wentworth might as surveyor general institute proceedings against those who were engaged in illegal lumber-

[51] *NHPP*, V and VI, passim; *New Hampshire Gazette*, Jan. 21, 1757, and Mar. 23, 1758.

[52] For a typical salary controversy see *NHPP*, V, 136-153.

[53] Waldron to Pepperrell, Mar. 26, 1742, *New England Historical and Genealogical Register*, XIX (1865), 223; Looney, The King's Representative, 141; *NHPP*, VII, 56; "Meshech Weare," in Shipton, *Harvard Graduates*, IX, 593; Belknap, *History*, II, 277.

ing may also have deterred some representatives from opposing their royal Governor.

The normal activity of the Assembly reflected the degree to which the political management of New Hampshire was in the hands of Governor Wentworth. Except in times of military crisis, there was little for the House to do. Sometimes it went six months without meeting and when it did meet, it often lacked a quorum. Those members who attended worked in small committees appointed to consider local and personal petitions. When they met as a House it was not for general debate, but rather to listen to the Governor speak or to hear a bill which had been prepared by Wentworth, Atkinson, and their associates in the Assembly. House leaders worked closely with their executive; as a result political disagreements often were compromised before reaching the floor of the House. Wentworth contributed to this harmony by omitting sessions during planting and harvesting, and by inviting representatives to Little Harbour to drink the King's health.[54]

It is not surprising then that for much of Wentworth's administration relations between the Governor and House remained relatively amicable. The terms of the boundary settlement, the establishment of an independent governorship, and the redistribution of patronage and land grants all helped to prevent serious conflicts during the first few years of Wentworth's administration. Between 1752 and Wentworth's resignation fifteen years later the House and Governor got along equally as well. The usual disputes concerning salary, the sources of tax revenue, the raising of troops and supplies for war all were compromised, although Wentworth, like other colonial governors, complained constantly about House control of financial appropriations. The controversy over judges' salaries and the proposed division into counties was dropped before animosities became intense. Even during the Stamp Act crisis the royal Governor and his Assembly reached agreement on what should be done: the House forwarded a protest to Thomlinson, but it refused to send a representative to the Stamp Act Congress.[55]

One major struggle, however, did take place between the Governor and House. Trouble first appeared in 1744 and four years later exploded

[54] *NHPP*, VI, 158, 169, 248, 321, 790, 830, and VII, 49-50; Wentworth to Amherst, Mar. 27, 1761, and June 18, 1762, War Office, 34, XXVII (photostats in Lib. Cong.).

[55] John Sherburne to John Huske, Feb. 9 and Aug. 20, 1754, New Hamp. Misc. MSS.; *NHPP*, VI, passim; Belknap, *History*, II, 277; Looney, The King's Representative, 131-141.

with such intensity that Wentworth and the legislature remained at loggerheads until 1752. The issues which precipitated the conflict were both constitutional and personal. When it was all over, Wentworth had succeeded in defending royal prerogative, had completely eliminated the immediate threat to family government, and had demonstrated the basic strength of his administration so plainly that no one in New Hampshire dared challenge his authority again.

The original dispute in 1744 arose when the House, led by former supporters of Governor Belcher, refused to vote supplies for Fort Dummer, a Connecticut Valley outpost so distant from existing provincial settlements that representatives felt it offered no military protection to New Hampshire residents. The opposition justified its conduct in constitutional terms. "We think ourselves at liberty," they explained, "fully and freely to remonstrate against any part of your Excellency's public conduct, which we apprehend affects the privileges of the House or the people we represent." As free men and representatives of free men they argued that the King's Governor, "however much he may be exalted above us by the honor he receives from His Majesty's commission, is yet liable to mistakes and errors in his conduct, and may do wrong though his royal master cannot." Wentworth defended his conduct as defense of the royal prerogative—he had been given specific instructions to have Fort Dummer supplied—and then dissolved the Assembly and called for new elections.[56]

Wentworth did not leave the results of the new elections to chance. He issued election precepts to several communities in the Merrimack Valley where he knew men supporting his legislative demands would be elected. At the same time he used what influence he had in communities already represented in the legislature to obtain the election of sympathetic candidates. In Dover, Thomas Wallingford, a Masonian proprietor and local selectman, engineered the election of a delegation favorable to Wentworth; the Governor undoubtedly received similar assistance elsewhere. The disputed issue itself tended to help the Governor, for the threat of war with France made Wentworth's argument for protecting the frontier difficult for voters to resist. Of the twenty Assembly members returned, nine were new; eight of these voted to supply Fort Dummer. When the House refused to seat members elected in newly represented

[56] Documents concerning the Fort Dummer controversy are in *NHPP,* V, 226-339, especially 301-339; the quotation is from 307.

communities, Wentworth did not press the issue. He had gained his main objective and did not want to run the risk of alienating a House which continued to support him when he asked for troops and supplies for the attack on Louisbourg and defense of the province.[57]

By 1748, when the Governor was required by the provincial triennial act to call for new elections, antagonism to Wentworth and his associates had increased. Many had been angered by the Governor's military appointments. Those whose political co-operation with Wentworth during the war had resulted more from the military threat than from any fondness for their executive again questioned the wisdom of supplying Fort Dummer. Most important, the opposition now had an effective leader, Richard Waldron, who planned to use the Assembly elections in furthering his plans "to oust Diego" from the governorship.[58]

Ever since Wentworth's appointment Waldron had yearned to rid the province of those who were responsible for his political ruin. His correspondence with Belcher included frequent suggestions on the strategy he and his kinsman might employ to turn the tables on the Wentworth clan. Belcher's interest waned after his appointment as governor of New Jersey; but throughout the forties Waldron's increased. A New Light Congregationalist, he felt that Anglican officials who scorned Puritanism (the Wentworths had taken no part in the religious revival inspired by George Whitefield) and flaunted traditional standards of public morality by conducting "balls," "parties," and "other gay scenes of life," were corrupting his native province.[59] A series of personal misfortunes, capped by the accidental death of his eldest son, further embittered the former councilor. After Wentworth blocked the military and political advancement of Thomas, the new family scion, Waldron could contain himself no longer. Destruction of family government became the consuming ambition of his life.[60]

[57] *NHPP*, V, 260-265, 304-339, and XI, 515-516.

[58] *NHPP*, V, 478-480, and XVIII, 332, 353; Waldron to Belcher, July 1, 1748, in Farmer and Moore, eds., *Collections*, III, 227. Much correspondence from Waldron's plot has been preserved in the Waldron Papers and Belcher Papers, III. Some of the letters have been printed in *NHPP*, VI, 39-68, and Farmer and Moore, eds., *Collections*, III.

[59] Belcher-Waldron letters, Belcher Papers, III, #112 to 141; Arthur Browne to SPG, July 24, 1742, in Rogers, *Glimpses*, 23; Waldron to Nicholas Gilman, Aug. 3, 1733, and Waldron to Greenwood, 1752, *NHPP*, XVIII, 50, 406; William Vaughn to Waldron, Jan. 1744/5, in Farmer and Moore, eds., *Collections*, III, 35.

[60] Waldron to Belcher, Sept. 24, 1747, and Apr. 15, 1748, *NHPP*, VI, 39, 47; letters from Richard Waldron to Thomas Waldron, Miscellaneous Manuscripts,

Waldron found others prepared to join in his scheme. In Portsmouth, fellow New Lights Ellis Huske and Henry Sherburne disliked the religious and political orientation of their rulers. Malcontents in Exeter—where Whitefield had been surprised to find that the "power of God" was manifest "chiefly among the rich"—were even easier for Waldron to locate, for Wentworth had alienated the politically prominent Gilman family. Similarly, Dover and Hampton contained men of sufficient wealth and prestige to feel the loss of patronage Belcher's dismissal had meant. Waldron was doubtless aware that these four towns supplied eleven of the twenty House members.[61]

For support outside the Assembly, Wentworth's antagonist sought help from a number of sources. Ellis Huske aspired to the governorship and possessed some influence through his brother, a lieutenant general in the British army. Waldron felt that Isaac Royall, a wealthy and ambitious Massachusetts merchant, would prove a better replacement for Wentworth, mostly because Royall expressed willingness to contribute £600 to the cause. Excited at the possibility of preferment, Royall obtained the services of Slingsby Bethell, a Member of Parliament from London, and offered to enlist the aid of Admiral Peter Warren, Admiral Edward Hawke, and George Whitefield himself. Governor Belcher refused to take an active part but contributed constant advice. Belcher considered the Kittery merchant William Pepperrell, hero of the Louisbourg expedition and an old merchant rival of the Wentworths, a stronger gubernatorial candidate than either Huske or Royall; Pepperrell seemed willing to replace Wentworth who had accused him of military mismanagement. Pepperrell's son-in-law Nathaniel Sparhawk encouraged him and offered up to £12,000 for the surveyorship should he succeed. A few of Belcher's friends in Massachusetts joined forces as opposition to Wentworth grew.[62]

New York Historical Society, New York City; Waldron-Belcher letters in Waldron Papers and Belcher Papers.

[61] Earnest E. Ells, "An Unpublished Journal of George Whitefield," *Church History*, VII (1938), 312, 338, 341; "Nicholas Gilman," in Shipton, *Harvard Graduates*, VII, 338-344; *NHPP*, V, 322, 330.

[62] Belcher-Waldron and Royall-Waldron letters, *NHPP*, VI, 41-52, and Farmer and Moore, eds., *Collections*, III, 226, 254, 323; Waldron letters to Pepperrell, Waldron Papers, I, #133, 136, 137; Sparhawk to Pepperrell, Sept. 24, 1749, and Mar. 8, 1750/1, in Usher Parsons, *Life of Sir William Pepperrell, Bart., The Only Native of New England Who Was Created a Baronet During Our Connection with the Mother Country* (Boston, 1855), 214-219; Fairchild, *William Pepperrell*, 179.

The members of Waldron's party close to the situation in New Hampshire expected that the impending Assembly dissolution and elections would, as Royall commented, "prove great helps toward effecting our scheme." They knew that Wentworth had lost support among provincial voters, and that the Governor had been unable to force House acceptance of members elected from communities to which he had sent election precepts. What they did not know, however, was that since the election of 1745 Wentworth had obtained through Thomlinson an additional instruction confirming his right to extend representation to deserving communities. Six new groups of towns received precepts for the 1748 election; they returned, among others, Thomas Packer who was the Governor's brother-in-law and the provincial Sheriff, and Joseph Blanchard, the surveyor of the Masonian proprietors. When the Assembly convened, Wentworth and Waldron—now the Hampton representative—clashed openly. Waldron controlled a majority of delegates from the old towns. Packer, Blanchard, and the other new representatives were refused House membership on the grounds that only the House could extend its own representation; the old members then elected Waldron Speaker. Wentworth in turn disallowed the House's choice of Speaker because delegates from the new towns had not been allowed to vote.[63]

Following the initial confrontation Waldron organized a massive assault on the Wentworth administration. His associates described the political crisis to the Massachusetts Assembly agent, Richard Partridge, and asked his help in obtaining redress. Henry Sherburne, Jr., and perhaps Waldron himself, wrote directly to Thomlinson—they had no idea that Wentworth and the House agent were so intimate—and pleaded with him to do something. An Assembly address to the citizens of New Hampshire exposing the need for a change in government was prepared. Meanwhile, as chairman of a House committee to present grievances to the Crown, Waldron readied a formal petition of protest and sent it to Slingsby Bethell in London.[64]

The formal petition included only a statement of the malcontents' constitutional argument. The Assembly possessed, it asserted, the privi-

[63] Royall to Waldron, Apr. 11, 1748, *NHPP*, VI, 46; *ibid.*, 69-126, and XVIII, 339; Batchellor and Metcalf, eds., *Laws of New Hamp.*, II, 653; Thomlinson to Atkinson, Mar. 2, 1752, *NHPP*, XVIII, 403.

[64] Thomlinson to Henry Sherburne, Jr., Nov. 13, 1749, *NHPP*, VI, 889; Waldron to Thomlinson, undated draft, Waldron Papers, II, #155; *NHPP*, VI, 63-64, 89-93, 99. Thomlinson told Sherburne he had nothing to do with the additional instruction.

lege of determining its own representation and its own speaker; the Governor had denied these rights by issuing election precepts and by rejecting Waldron as speaker; the normal political processes of the province had been brought to a standstill by the Governor's actions. In a letter to Bethell, Waldron exhibited no such restraint. The iniquities and depredations of the Governor he described in detail. Wentworth had made "arbitrary attempts on our civil and religious privileges" and had been disrespectful to Congregational ministers; he had flaunted the Assembly and threatened it with the prerogative; he had misused funds and made unjust civil and military appointments which favored those related to him. In short, the inhabitants of New Hampshire could be redeemed from what Waldron had earlier labeled their "Spanish bondage" only if His Majesty would "place a gentleman of better abilities, and a different disposition" in the Governor's chair.[65]

Even as those complaints were sent, Waldron must have suspected there would be no redemption. Wentworth had made known his possession of the additional instruction just at the time the House felt it had gained the upper hand. If Waldron remained hopeful in spite of the instruction, the reaction of those in England undoubtedly sobered his enthusiasm. Thomlinson read the petition and wrote back that if the "address was calculated and designed to turn out the Governor . . . in favor of a Massachusetts man," as he had been told, "it would not have been in your power, or in the power of the most sanguine of his enemies to remove him." If the controversy had taken place when New Hampshire was under the Massachusetts governor, Thomlinson pointed out, the Assembly "might have been indulged." But one reason for separating the two had been to strengthen royal government where the Crown's best supply of mast trees grew, and the Lords of Trade were in no mood to support the provincial Assembly. In any case the Assembly's constitutional position was weak. Why should New Hampshire demand fewer representatives when all the other provinces sought more? Thomlinson was not the only one to criticize the petition. John Thorpe informed Bethell that if anything the Assembly petition would fix Wentworth "firmer in his seat" since he was acting in accordance with specific instructions. Another contact in London, Samuel Storke, wrote that Ferdinand Paris advised the Assembly to draw up "a new petition against

[65] *NHPP*, VI, 63-64, 89-93; Waldron to Belcher, Mar. 10, 1748/9, in Farmer and Moore, eds., *Collections*, III, 226.

the Governor for illegal acts he may have committed" as it was the Chancellor's opinion that Wentworth had power to negative its choice of speaker.[66]

Wentworth's enemies, however, were not convinced that constitutional issues would determine the outcome of their campaign. "Wishers and woulders are but poor house builders," Waldron was advised by Belcher; "a good soliciter at home with a pocket full of yellow dust might do something; but alas, where is such a one to be found?" Waldron thought he knew. An influential candidate for the governorship might obtain such a solicitor and, as Belcher recognized, Royall did not have the necessary interest; Sir William Pepperrell, still basking in the prestige of his Louisbourg victory, was far more powerful. After the fruitlessness of pushing Royall became evident, Waldron obtained a House address asking Sir William to seek the appointment. For a time it appeared he would accept and the Assemblymen warned their English supporters to prepare for a second assault. But late in 1750 Pepperrell informed Waldron he was not qualified to fill "the breach made in your state affairs."[67]

Pepperrell's refusal to seek the governorship meant the disintegration of Waldron's party. Belcher had once written that "the body [of New Hampshire] merchants are such a divided herd that it is to be feared they'll not be enough united to withstand the torrent that's going to be let loose from your province." In 1748 enough Portsmouth merchants had backed Waldron to return sympathetic candidates to the Assembly. But their enthusiasm for his cause waned as Wentworth's strength became apparent. Henry Sherburne announced in February 1750 that he could no longer see his "way clear to be concerned"; and others like Daniel Warner became "very cool in the affair." Elsewhere those who had participated in the scheme to rid New Hampshire of Wentworth domination decided to come to terms with the Governor.[68]

[66] *NHPP*, XVIII, 339; Thomlinson to Henry Sherburne, Jr., Nov. 13, 1749, *NHPP*, VI, 888-893; John Thorpe to Slingsby Bethell, July 5, 1749, *NHPP*, VI, 65; letter from Samuel Storke, Mar. 9, 1750/1, Weare Papers, II.

[67] Belcher to Waldron, Aug. 7, 1749, in Farmer and Moore, eds., *Collections*, III, 324; Assembly to Pepperrell, Dec. 19, 1749, Belknap Papers, 61.C.96, Mass. Hist. Soc.; letter from Samuel Storke, Mar. 9, 1750/1, Weare Papers, II; Pepperrell to Waldron, Nov. 29, 1750, in Parsons, *Life of Pepperrell*, 231.

[68] Belcher to Waldron, Sept. 10, 1743, Belcher Papers, III, #141; Waldron to Belcher, Apr. 15, 1748, *NHPP*, VI, 46; Henry Sherburne to Waldron, Feb. 13, 1750/1, Dreer Collection, Albany Convention, Hist. Soc. of Pa.; *NHPP*, VI, 127.

As soon as Wentworth sensed victory, he called for new elections and issued precepts to the same six groups of towns whose representatives the House had rejected before. This time there was little serious trouble. Although all but four of the rebellious representatives elected in 1748 returned to the new Assembly, when it met the House voted to admit the new members and then elected a speaker—Meshech Weare—acceptable to the Governor. Wentworth celebrated the House action, Belknap commented later, by making "a liberal distribution of commissions, civil and military," which inaugurated "an era of domestic reconciliation." The possibility of further disputes was reduced when Waldron resigned early in 1753 and died a few months later. Soon thereafter Waldron's political associate John Sherburne lamented that the House would make "no complaints at the Governor, do what he will." Wentworth had completely repulsed the legislative threat to his government.[69]

Benning Wentworth and his relatives and friends dominated New Hampshire politics from 1741 to 1767. Not only did they occupy most important appointive offices because they possessed "interest" in England, but through control of the Council and effective use of their constitutional powers, they also influenced the behavior of elected officials. They even interfered successfully in local elections when such interference seemed necessary to prevent the weakening of their authority.

The success of the Wentworths in maintaining their political ascendancy provided New Hampshire with both stable and effective government. Family control inhibited development of the type of factionalism which in many colonies undermined royal authority. It provided a system of personal influence which reinforced the formal constitutional structure. Furthermore, family government pleased the vast majority of provincial inhabitants, who shared with their rulers the benefits of existing economic and political conditions. When Benning Wentworth resigned his commission as governor, the Assembly of New Hampshire thanked him for "the steady administration of justice, the quiet enjoyment of property, the civil and religious liberties and privileges his Majesty's good subjects of this province have experienced and possessed during this period."[70]

[69] *NHPP*, VI, 127-130, 178-181; Belknap, *History*, II, 277; Sherburne to Huske, Aug. 20, 1754, New Hamp. Misc. MSS.
[70] *NHPP*, VII, 116.

13

Customs and Contentions: John Hatton of Salem and Cohansey, 1764–1776

Larry R. Gerlach

Given its proximity to two of the major ports in British North America and the numerous coves, inlets, and rivers which permeate its shore line, colonial New Jersey was not surprisingly the scene of considerable, albeit indeterminable, illicit trade. The combination of geographical realities and inefficient customs machinery served both to facilitate smuggling and inhibit the enforcement of imperial trade regulations; many New York and Philadelphia merchants as well as Jersey shippers regularly circumvented the navigation laws as a routine, if risky, part of normal business enterprise.[1] To a large extent the widespread violation of the commercial codes is traceable to the fact that revenue officers normally were stationed only at designated ports of entry and, in the words of Governor Jonathan Belcher, "as there are many Creeks and Rivers at distances from them, illegal trade may be carried on beyond their power to prevent it."[2] Moreover, the duplicity and venality of some members of the customs service often exacerbated the problem. For example, Acting Governor Cadwal-

1. Virginia D. Harrington, *The New York Merchant on the Eve of the Revolution* (New York, 1935); Arthur L. Jensen, *The Maritime Commerce of Colonial Philadelphia* (Madison, 1963); Mary A. Hanna, *The Trade of the Delaware District before the Revolution* (Northhampton, 1917); Frederick Tolles, *Meeting House and Counting House: The Quaker Merchants of Colonial Philadelphia, 1682–1763* (Chapel Hill, 1948). On the operation and enforcement of the acts of trade, consult Lawrence A. Harper, *The English Navigation Laws: A Seventeenth-Century Experiment in Social Engineering* (New York, 1939); Oliver Morton Dickerson, *The Navigation Acts and the American Revolution* (Philadelphia, 1951); Dora Mae Clark, *The Rise of the British Treasury: Colonial Administration in the Eighteenth Century* (New Haven, 1960) and "The American Board of Customs, 1767–1783," *American Historical Review*, XLV (July, 1940), 777–806; Thomas C. Barrow, *Trade and Empire: The British Customs Service in Colonial America. 1660–1775* (Cambridge, 1967); Alfred S. Martin, "The King's Customs: Philadelphia, 1763–1774," *William and Mary Quarterly*, 3d ser., V (April, 1948), 201–16; and William S. McClellan, *Smuggling in the American Colonies at the Outbreak of the Revolution with Special Reference to the West Indies Trade* (New York, 1912).

2. Quoted in Barrow, 153.

lader Colden of New York in 1760 implicated as accomplices in the extensive smuggling operations in New York and Pennsylvania the customs officers of New Jersey who, he claimed, frequently issued false papers to unscrupulous shippers.[3] Then, too, the laxity of collectors over the years resulted in a tradition of unofficial toleration of sundry illegal practices due to the impracticality of adhering to the letter of cumbersome, often archaic, trade regulations and the impossibility of preventing certain kinds of clandestine commerce. William Alexander, the self-styled Lord Stirling, succinctly summarized the smuggling quandary: "The attempts of the Custom House Officers to suppress it are sometimes feeble & generally in Vain from the Great Number of Small Harbours our Coasts abound with, there they land their Cargoes unnoticed."[4]

Compounded by extensive wartime trade with the enemy, smuggling reached unprecedented proportions in New Jersey during the Anglo-French conflict of 1754–63, necessitating a brief blockade of the colony by the royal navy. To be sure, measures instituted from 1762 to 1764 designed to augment the customs service, tighten enforcement of the acts of trade, and raise revenue to finance the post-war settlement did curtail the more blatant commercial violations and sharply reduce the illegal traffic in West Indian sugar and molasses. Yet Governor William Franklin's claim that customs officials in Jersey had by late 1764 "put a Stop to the greatest Part, if not the whole, of the illicit Trade within this District" was unwarranted.[5] For it was simply impossible to terminate all clandestine commerce; smuggling in New Jersey continued to vex provincial and imperial authorities until 1776.

3. Colden to William Pitt, Oct. 27 and Nov. 11, 1760, "The Letters and Papers of Cadwallader Colden," New York Historical Society, *Collections* (9 vols., New York, 1918–37), I, 27, 36–37. The Jersey customs collectors were Andrew Dewar at Salem-Cohansey, Charles Read at Burlington, and John Barbarie at Perth Amboy.

4. Alexander to Lord Shelburne, Stirling Mss., III, 43, New York Historical Society. See also Cadwallader Colden to the Earl of Hillsborough, Oct. 9, 1764, "Colden Papers," I, 375, and Archibald Kennedy to Philip Stephens, Nov. 20, 1764, Admiralty Papers, 1/2012:1, British Public Record Office, London.

5. Larry R. Gerlach, "Revolution or Independence? New Jersey, 1760–1776," (Ph.D. dissertation, Rutgers University, 1968), 60–63; Lawrence Henry Gipson, *The British Empire before the American Revolution* (14 vols. to date, Caldwell and New York, 1936–), X, *The Triumphant Empire: Thunder-Clouds Gather in the West, 1763–1766*, 200–45; Franklin to the Earl of Halifax, Nov. 9, 1764, Frederick W. Ricord, *et al.*, eds., *Archives of the State of New Jersey* (30 vols., Newark, 1880–1906), IX, 484. The *Archives* are hereafter cited as *N.J.A.*

On the eve of the Revolution New Jersey was divided into three customs districts, each with a single port of entry: Burlington (or Bridlington), Perth Amboy, and Salem and Cohansey. Encompassing the area from the head of navigation on the Delaware River to the southern boundary of Gloucester County, Burlington had experienced a drastic decline as a port during the course of the eighteenth century. Overshadowed by the burgeoning Quaker metropolis a short distance downriver, Burlington's maritime traffic by mid-century consisted almost exclusively of local trade. Perth Amboy, located at the mouth of Raritan Bay and adjacent to New York harbor, serviced the entire Eastern Division of the colony. Predictably, extensive smuggling was carried on in this elongated district. Officials charged with making a comprehensive survey of customs operations in America during the period 1769–70 noted considerable illicit trade in the Perth Amboy area, noting "Large quantities of Tea, etc. brought in Small Boats." Although customs regulations were evaded or ignored at all three Jersey ports, such activity at Perth Amboy and Burlington paled when compared to the volume of illegal commerce which passed through Salem and Cohansey. (The designation "Salem and Cohansey" is misleading; the town of Salem was the only official port for the district, Cohansey being a geographical reference to the river in Cumberland County.) Comprising Salem County above the Cohansey River and the Counties of Cumberland and Cape May for a distance of 130 miles along the Delaware, Salem-Cohansey, despite relatively heavy traffic, was one of five North American ports which recorded no revenue for the fiscal year 1766–67.[6] Strategically located on Delaware Bay comfortably downstream from the bustling port of Philadelphia and laced with myriad estuaries and navigable creeks, the region deserved its reputation as a haven for smugglers.

Under the best of circumstances customs officers faced a formidable task in superintending the enforcement of the navigation laws in these unwieldy

6. Barrow, 241, Appendix D, 269–72; An index to the amount of smuggling in the Delaware region is the table of duties, fines, and forfeitures taken in by North American customs districts from October 10, 1766 to October 17, 1767. Two of the four ports which recorded no revenue in any category were situated in West Jersey: Burlington, which was nearly defunct as an operative port, and Salem and Cohansey. The others, Lewis (Lewes) and Chester-Petapsco, were in Delaware. The third Jersey port, Perth Amboy, took in £154:18:0 in duties, but no fines or forfeitures. P.R.O. Treasury Papers, 1/452:47.

Portion of a navigation map of "Virginia, Maryland, Pennsilvania, East and West Jersey" from The English Pilot, The Fourth Book, *printed for J. Mount, T. Page, W. Mount, and T. Page, on Tower-Hill, London, 1780. Collections of The New Jersey Historical Society.*

districts. Yet the successful implementation of the commercial regulations and the reputation of the revenue service turned in large measure upon the individual entrusted with the post of customs collector. Unfortunately for the customs service, the residents of southern Jersey, and the provincial government, John Hatton was a man of mediocre ability, questionable integrity, and irascible temperament. Virtually nothing is known of him prior to his entry into the customs service in 1764, other than that he was the brother of the Reverend Thomas Hatton of Waters Upton, Shropshire, England and that he emigrated to America at the age of sixteen with a modest fortune inherited from an uncle. Nor are the circumstances surrounding his appointment as collector known.[7]

The lack of personal qualifications and experience aside, Hatton assumed direction of the customs service in the summer of 1764 at an

7. For a brief biographical sketch of Hatton and his son, see E. Alfred Jones, *The Loyalists of New Jersey in the Revolution* (Newark, 1927), 92–94. Because no copy of his commission is extant and the first published reference to Hatton as collector occurs in the *Pennsylvania Gazette* for November 26, 1767, it has been erroneously assumed that he obtained the post in or about 1767. See Jones, 92, and Arthur D. Pierce, *Smuggler's Woods: Jaunts and Journeys in Colonial and Revolutionary New Jersey* (New Brunswick, 1960), 22.

inauspicious time. In the first place, any attempt to contravene the traditional freewheeling brand of maritime commerce that obtained in the district would encounter determined resistance from a considerable segment of the population. Succumbing to convention like their counterparts elsewhere, the revenue officers in Salem-Cohansey had never been distinguished for assiduity in enforcing the acts of trade; neither Francis Hopkinson nor Andrew Dewar, Hatton's predecessors during the previous year, had been especially attentive to their duties.[8] Furthermore, some colonials took strong exception to certain aspects of the Parliamentary program for the post-war reorganization of the Empire. Provincial Deputy Secretary Charles Pettit, whose father was a partner in the Philadelphia mercantile house of Pettit and Reed, complained of the excessive "Impost & Duties with which we are loaded," while Daniel Coxe of Trenton interpreted the reform of the customs service as a plot on the part of the British government "to send over Among Us a lott of Rascals for Duty Officers, who will knaw upon our Vitals, by depriving Us of our Sustance." Governor Franklin opined that the Revenue Act of 1764, which lowered the duty on foreign molasses 50 per cent, would simultaneously reduce smuggling and engender opposition from certain traders. Finally, the zealous implementation of various aspects of the navigation laws—specifically the execution of the intricate system of bonds and cockets—worked an unnecessary hardship on routine coastal shipping. Pennsylvania Chief Justice William Allen observed from Philadelphia that enforcement in the Delaware Valley was so stringent that

> even the Intercourse between here & New Jersey is, in a great Measure interrupted, which was carried on in Flats & small Boats, and the produce of the Western part of that Colony shipped off from this City, But now, one of those poor fellows cannot take in a few Staves, or Pig Iron, or Bar Iron, or Tar &c., but they must go thirty or forty Miles, or more to give

8. Hopkinson, who replaced Dewar on November 3, 1763 when the latter was transferred to Dominica, less than a year later assumed the post of collector at Newcastle, Del. *Pennsylvania Gazette*, Nov. 17, 1763. Dewar apparently was guilty of complicity as well as laxity, for a fellow revenue officer indicated that he had been "very much imposed on" by certain Philadelphia merchants in order to "conceal some Fraud." John Swift to [Dewar], Sept. 19, 1763, Philadelphia Customs House Papers, II, 148, Historical Society of Pennsylvania.

> Bond, the Charge of which & his travelling, make the Burthen intolerable.[9]

In short, the times boded ill for any substantial reform of the revenue service in South Jersey.

To complicate matters, Hatton fell under the influence of illicit traders almost immediately upon being appointed to the post of collector. Philadelphia merchants engaged in the West Indian trade were responsible for most of the endemic smuggling in the Delaware region, and they lost no time in protecting their lucrative enterprise by drawing the new customs officer into the vortex of illegal commerce. For example, the notorious smuggler Thomas Riche, acting upon the advice of fellow merchant Jacobus Van Zandt, lavishly entertained the Hattons at Philadelphia in August, 1764 and, when the collector found it necessary to remain behind on business, personally conveyed Mrs. Hatton to Salem in his luxurious carriage. After that, Riche regularly instructed his captains to secure entrance and clearance papers from Salem instead of Newcastle or Philadelphia, forewarned Hatton of impending investigations by customs inspectors, and apprised the inexperienced officer of ways and means of circumventing the navigation laws.[10]

Tacit agreements with certain smugglers notwithstanding, Hatton assumed his duties intent upon implementing generally the acts of trade. However, from the outset he encountered considerable resistance from subordinates, not to mention merchants who had become accustomed to haphazard enforcement. No less a personage than Jacob Spicer, a veteran of twenty-one years in the provincial assembly and one of the foremost political figures in the colony, strongly opposed Hatton's determination to abide by his instructions to seal and sign personally all clearances and permits. During nearly thirty years as Deputy Collector of Salem-Cohansey charged with supervising shipping in the Cape May region, Spicer had

9. Pettit to Joseph Reed, Mar. 14 and June 22, 1764; Coxe to Reed, Apr. 12, 1764; see also Moores Furman to Reed, June 23, 1764, all in Reed Papers, I, 12, 28, 16, 29, New York Historical Society; Franklin to the Board of Trade, Feb. 8, 1764, *N.J.A.*, IX, 404; Allen to D. Barclay & Sons, Nov. 20, 1764, in Lewis B. Walker, ed., *The Burd Papers: Extracts from Chief Justice William Allen's Letter Book. . . .* (Pottsville, Pa., 1897), 65.

10. Riche to Van Zandt, Aug. 19, 1764; to Captain Wheaton, Feb. 19, 1765; to Hatton, July 29, Aug. 25, Nov. 16, 1765; to John Riche, Nov. 7, 1765, Riche Letter Book, II, 85, 188, 202, 211, 255, Historical Society of Pennsylvania.

found it both practical and prudent to eschew strict enforcement of the system of bonds and cockets affecting coastal commerce. He candidly admitted that the "Great Neglect" with which coastwise traders treated his office made it impossible to fashion a comprehensive record of the maritime traffic channeled through his district and, even more incredible, that he had not been charging any duties or fees because his copies of rates and regulations had been consumed "some years past" in a fire at his home. He also pointed out that because calling at Salem to take out proper papers would constitute "a hardship almost insurmountable" for individuals engaged in local trade, statutory procedures regarding registration and payment of fees had long been ignored in the Cape May district and warned that any substantive alteration of the informal practice "will Occasion great Murmuring." Should Hatton persist in his scheme to alter the "Accustomed mode" of shipping in the area, Spicer requested that his superior officer "Notify the publick that you Insist on & have directed me to take those Bonds . . . least I should otherwise Incur the Displeasure of the populace while I am attempting to Service the Office & Ease the navigation."[11] Thus cajoled by smugglers, pressured by the public, and frustrated by subordinates, it is small wonder that Hatton, already given to avariciousness and venality, became derelict in his duties.

It soon became common knowledge that Hatton neglected to enforce the acts of trade and was intimately involved with known smugglers. By September, 1766 customs violations in the Salem-Cohansey district had become so flagrant that the Deputy Collector of Philadelphia, John Swift, felt obliged to file a lengthy report with the American Board of Customs Commissioners in Boston exposing the irregularities prevalent in the port and charging Hatton with duplicity and dishonesty. According to Swift, vessels bound for Philadelphia—especially those laden with foreign sugar, molasses, and wine—in increasing numbers anchored below Philadelphia at Renshaw's Point opposite Gloucester, obtained fraudulent entry papers from Salem, and then either transferred commodities to smaller vessels for immediate shipment to the Pennsylvania port or landed them at Gloucester for later transshipment. Noting that the process was "attended with considerable expence" which would be obviated by direct entry at Phila-

11. Spicer to Hatton, Sept. 11, Nov. 7 and 19, 1764, Spicer Papers, New Jersey Historical Society.

"The East Prospect of the City of Philadelphia, in the Province of Pennsylvania," London Magazine, *October, 1761. This view of Philadelphia from the Jersey shore shows the variety of vessels on the Delaware River in the mid-eighteenth century.*
The Edwin A. Ely Collection, The New Jersey Historical Society.

delphia, he felt it "reasonable to suppose that some illegal Advantages are obtained by Entering at Salem." Lest his complaint be viewed as sour grapes motivated by the loss of entry fees, he substantiated the allegation by providing a detailed account of a recent incident involving the brigantine *Endeavour*. Not only did the captain of the brig and Hatton obdurately refuse to cooperate with agents of the revenue service sent to inspect the vessel, but the Salem officer also issued a permit to land fifty-four hogsheads of molasses when in reality one hundred fifty-four hogsheads and fifty tierces were landed. Unless halted, Swift opined, the questionable practices prevailing at Salem-Cohansey "will be attended with great Prejudice to the Revenue."[12] The Commissioners, however, ignored the warning and took no action at the time.

As an agent of the imperial revenue service Hatton, for obvious reasons, could not be expected to rank among the most popular personages in West Jersey. But his disagreeable character and exceptionable conduct soon unnecessarily antagonized many residents of Salem, Cumberland, and Cape May Counties. To begin with, the application of dual standards in his official capacity as collector—aiding and abetting some shippers in evading regulations while demanding strict compliance from others—understandably aroused the ire of interested and disinterested parties alike. Moreover,

12. Swift to Charles Steuart, Sept. 7, 1766, Philadelphia Customs House Papers, V, 614. Unfortunately, Hatton's rebuttal is so mutilated as to be undecipherable. Hatton to Steuart, Nov. 4, 1766, *ibid.*, VI, 657.

during the Stamp Act controversy he had, deservedly or not, become the object of popular resentment when it was rumored that he was actively seeking the office of provincial stamp distributor in place of John Hughes, who had resigned in September. While the veracity of the story cannot be ascertained, a large group of Salem residents assembled at the court of quarter sessions early in November believed it possible, for they dispatched a four-man delegation to call upon the collector "in order to know the Truth of the Report." Hatton readily signed a statement declaring that he would neither solicit the post nor attempt to implement the act in his district. Quarrelsome and overbearing, he also became embroiled in numerous private contentions which carried over into his public life. One such incident, involving the allegedly fraudulent sale of an epileptic Negro slave to Jacob Scroggin of Alloways Creek, was debated in the Philadelphia press during the fall and winter of 1767–68.[13] The vituperative and *ad hominem* nature of the exchange served to cast the office as well as the man into disrepute.

During the spring of 1768 the choleric collector became involved in the first of two altercations with the citizenry and magistracy of his district which eventually involved the provincial government and the American Board of Customs. In March he filed complaints with Governor Franklin and the Customs Commissioners alleging that the sheriff and a justice of the peace of Salem County, Edward Test and Grant Gibbon respectively, had refused to assist him and his deputy, John Clark, in the performance of their duties. Specifically, Hatton charged that upon presenting a writ of assistance and his credentials to Test, the latter "with great Contempt struck at them, damned the Collector & his Commission," and adamantly refused to cooperate with the revenue officers. Although not personally acquainted with either of the magistrates, Franklin was "inclined" to think "from the general good Character they sustain" that Hatton had "exaggerated the Affair." "He appears to be of such an unhappy Temper," the

13. *Pennsylvania Gazette*, Dec. 12, 1765. On the Stamp Act crisis in New Jersey, see Gerlach, "Revolution or Independence," Ch. 5; *Pennsylvania Gazette*, Nov. 26, 1767; *Pennsylvania Chronicle*, Dec. 14, 1767, and Feb. 22, 1768. Denying Hatton's charge that he was "a contentious man," Scroggin averred the opposite: "if a perpetual state of litigious cavilling, or the universal voice of a people can give a just title to that character, I am sure no man can, with equal demerit, claim it as JOHN HATTON, Esquire, Collector of his Majesty's Customs, in the port of Salem."

Governor observed, "that it is scarce possible he can live long in any Place without involving himself in Squabbles with his Neighbors." Nonetheless, Franklin promised to investigate the allegations and summarily remove any officer found guilty of misconduct. However, from the distant perspective of Castle William in Boston Harbor, the fracas took on a decidedly more serious appearance to the Commissioners than it had to provincial authorities. Acutely aware of the adverse effect recalcitrant and uncooperative magistrates had had upon the operation of the customs service in New England, the members of the Board were understandably apprehensive about the appearance of similar occurrences in other colonies. Therefore, forthrightly reminding Franklin that the successful enforcement of the acts of trade turned largely upon the assistance rendered by civil officials, they directed him not only to see to it that all customs personnel in New Jersey received "the most effectual Aid & Protection" possible, but also to "make an Example of such of your Officers as may be found in any respect delinquent."[14]

The dispute was brought before the Council on May 16. Chief Justice Frederick Smyth reported that as the result of Hatton's complaints of "frequent opposition to the discharge of his Duty . . . from several Persons Magistrates and others, with so much insult and Contempt that he conceived the safety of his Person indangered," he had earlier laid the grievances before a Salem County grand jury on April 28. But when no one—not even Hatton—appeared before the panel to corroborate the charges, the matter was dropped. The councillors then advised Franklin to hold a formal hearing attended by all interested parties.[15]

The inquiry commenced on July 14. In addition to the charges against Test and Gibbon, Hatton now alleged that justices of the peace Robert Johnston, Preston Carpenter, and George Trenchard, had refused to take action on a complaint filed by him against one William Pike for "obstructing him in the Execution of His Office, and cursing the King." After all depositions had been read and testimonies heard, the councilmen were of one mind that "the Charges against the Persons Complained of, are by no

14. Franklin to the American Board of Customs, Mar. 29, 1768; American Board to Franklin, July 8, 1768, Franklin Papers, XLVIII, 135, American Philosophical Society Library.

15. "Journal of Governor and Council," *N.J.A.*, XVII, 513–14.

"A Representation of Mooring Chains," an engraving by P. Maverick, New-ark, N. J., 1811, for Seamanship, Both in Theory and Practice, *a manual printed and sold by Edmund M. Blunt, New York, 1813, "The whole forming a useful compendium to the officer, to instruct him when young, and to remind him when old." Collections of The New Jersey Historical Society.*

means supported." On the contrary, they determined that the quarrels between Hatton and the civil officers had no relation whatever to his duties as customs collector, but rather were "entirely of a private Nature" in which he had been "both the first & greater Aggressor." In apprising the Customs Board of his wholehearted concurrence with the verdict, Franklin observed that Hatton's behavior during the hearing "in several Instances" led to the suspicion that he was "at Time some what out of his Senses" and noted that the Council, save for "Compassion to his Family," was disposed to advise his dismissal because of the "rude, indecent, & over-bearing Treatment" accorded the magistrates! He warned the Commissioners that unless Hatton changed his attitude and conduct "the Revenue must suffer; for his violent Temper frequently disqualifies him for the due Execution of his Office."[16] Governor and Council considered the matter ended.

But the case was far from closed. Hatton promptly appealed to the American Board, reiterating complaints of the "Abuse & Insult . . . and the Danger he is expos'd to both in Person & Character as an Officer of the Customs." The claim that he was the victim of "combinations formed

16. "Journal of Governor and Council," *N.J.A.*, XVII, 517–18; Franklin to the American Board, July 30, 1768, Franklin Papers, XLVIII, 135, APS. The nature of the alleged private dispute between Hatton and the magistrates remains a mystery, but some of the ill-feeling between the sheriff and the collector may have arisen when Scroggin secured the assistance of Test on several occasions during the row over the sale of the slave a few months earlier. Governor Franklin informed the Secretary of the American Department, the Earl of Hillsborough, that Hatton was "a Man of a most unhappy Temper" who had "exceedingly misbehaved himself; and had no just Foundation for his Complaint." Franklin to Hillsborough, Aug. 25, 1768, *N.J.A.*, X, 53–54.

against him by People in Power & Office who carry on and countenance illicit Trade" was not without foundation and constituted an oblique censure of local and provincial authorities.[17] Acting upon the appeal, the Customs Commissioners instructed Governor Franklin to forward for their perusal copies of the affidavits and testimonies relating to the altercation. However, Franklin was unable to produce all germane evidence because Hatton had voluntarily withdrawn his written charges and, as the Governor readily admitted, "many Matters concerning the Merits of the Dispute appeared on the Examination of the Parties face to face, which were not taken down in writing tho' they in Part occasioned the Opinion" of the Council. Nor could Franklin refrain from expressing his consternation at what he regarded as the Board's excessive concern with the incident, considering it "somewhat extraordinary," given Hatton's known character and the fact that the Council had already examined "very particularly" into the matter.[18]

But the Commissioners, unwilling to base any substantive action upon the complaints filed by Hatton and the fragmentary report submitted by the Governor, determined to hold the matter in abeyance pending the receipt

17. There is reason to suspect that Hatton's charge of official collusion had some validity. In the first place, the only councillors present at the hearing of July 14 were Charles Read and Joseph and Samuel Smith—prominent Burlington merchants closely associated with the Philadelphia mercantile community. Read was also collector of the port of Burlington. Although there is no tangible evidence that any of these men were either directly or indirectly engaged in extra-legal commerce, their conclusion that except for "some instances of irregularities" such as the failure of shipmasters plying the waters between Salem and Philadelphia to take out proper papers, "there is not any Contraband or Illicit Trade carried on the District of Salem" is incredulous. Each was fully cognizant of the rampant smuggling in the area, and circumstantial evidence suggests that they were not entirely free of complicity (especially Read). Seemingly Hatton applied different standards to Pennsylvania and New Jersey smugglers, cracking down only on the latter. "Journal of Governor and Council," *N.J.A.*, XVII, 517. See also Hatton's later animadversion of Read's conduct in a letter to the American Board, December 25, 1770, *N.J.A.*, X, 215.

18. The American Board to Franklin, Oct. 13, 1768, and reply [Oct.-Nov., 1768], Franklin Papers, XLVIII, 135. The Governor also took exception to the Commissioners' pointed remark that they hoped Hatton would receive the backing of the provincial government during impending condemnation proceedings against the *Speedwell*. Franklin noted somewhat caustically that the vessel in question was a flat, not a sloop as claimed by Hatton, and assured them that "notwithstanding Mr. Hatton's pompous Accounts of its Importance, you would, if you knew all the Circumstances, think it a very trifling Affair, scarce worth Attention." Nonetheless, he assured the Board that Attorney General Cortlandt Skinner had and would continue to render unqualified assistance in prosecuting the case. To complicate matters, the affair was colored by personal antipathies between Franklin and Hatton. The former was convinced that a letter highly critical of his performance as chief executive, purportedly written by one Murch and forwarded to the Board by Hatton, was a patent fraud and a low expression of the collector's desire "to do me a Prejudice." Franklin to John Williams, Apr. 10, 1769, Franklin Papers, XLVIII, 135.

of additional, independent information. In order to secure such intelligence, John Williams, Inspector General of the Customs in America, was promptly dispatched to New Jersey. As if to allay any uneasiness which might be created in Jersey officialdom by the investigation, Commissioner John Temple apprised the Governor that the Board had not and would not call the matter to the attention of superiors in England and advised him "in the mean Time treat the Affair with Neglect, & as below your Notice." Williams arrived in the province early in April of 1769 and was furnished by the Governor with letters of identification and orders directing local magistrates to cooperate fully with the investigation.[19]

Upon the conclusion of his inquiry in June, Williams filed a lengthy report that was nothing less than a resounding condemnation of Hatton's behavior as a customs officer. An examination of the Salem customshouse ledger revealed that the only vessels to register at the port were those belonging to "noted Smugglers," that from April, 1765 to May, 1766 every ship bound from the West Indies not inspected by a man-of-war was entered "in ballast," that no duties whatsoever had been collected since September 1767, and that shippers had been "indulged" to "a very great Degree" including the distribution of "blank Certificates and blank Permits to be filled up by themselves." Moreover, it was physically impossible for Hatton to superintend effectively the district, since he now resided in Cold Spring in Cape May County—some ninety miles below the port of entry and "out of the way of all business." "Every Smuggler speaks well of him as a Collector," the Inspector noted, "but in his private Conduct as a peevish, fretfull, and not a very good natured Person." While it was likely that Hatton had on occasion been "ill used," Williams had "little Doubt" that it was due to "an unwise Deportment in his private Station." In fact, he concurred with the opinion of the Council that the disputes between the collector and the Salem magistrates had been "of a private Nature, and arose from trifling Matters." While conceding that having to support a family "with a narrow Income might Account for some of the irregular Appearances" in Hatton's conduct as an officer (he received an annual salary of £40 plus fees), the Inspector General was cognizant of the

19. Temple to Franklin, Apr. 6, 1769; Franklin to Williams, and to George Trenchard and Grant Gibbon, Apr. 10, 1769, in Franklin Papers, XLVIII, 135–36.

damage an unscrupulous and unpopular officer could do to the entire revenue service. Therefore, he concluded his report with the recommendation that the Board admonish Hatton to upgrade his private as well as public behavior.[20]

Apparently the report convinced the Commissioners that the provincial government had handled the affair in a just and equitable manner, for they took no further action at the time. Neither, however, did they act upon the advice of Inspector Williams and officially censure Hatton. They would later regret the omission; the last had not yet been heard from the cantankerous collector.

Whether to escape from the troublesome neighborhood of Salem or superintend the customs service in the most loosely-administered region of the district, Hatton removed to Cape May County in the spring of 1769. There he was probably neither more assiduous in enforcing the navigation laws nor less adept at accommodating shippers than he had been in Salem. For nearly a year and a half the collector resided in a center of extensive smuggling operations without becoming embroiled in any personal or public imbroglios. Then, suddenly, in the fall of 1770 he once again became the object of extended controversy involving local, provincial, and imperial authorities when in the course of performing official duties he was subjected to physical violence.

The episode began on November 8 when Hatton, accompanied by his son, slave, and a half-dozen other men, set out to investigate reports that the cargo of the recently arrived *Prince of Wales*, Captain Patrick Crawford from Liverpool, at anchor some ten miles off shore near the entrance to Delaware Bay, was being surreptitiously transferred to pilot boats for transshipment to Philadelphia. According to Hatton, the crew of the ship upon sighting the search party cast overboard "a great quantity of Bales and casks of Clarett" and then manned the rails armed with "Swivels, Guns, Peteraroes, Blunderbusses & Musketts."

Unable to board the floating fortress or obtain any information concerning her cargo and consignment, the collector decided to seize one of the pilot boats. After successfully boarding and impounding one of the smaller

20. Williams to the American Board, June 17, 1769, *N.J.A.*, X, 295–97.

View of the Delaware River from "Fancy Hill," the home of Samuel Ladd Howell in Gloucester, New Jersey. Painted by an unknown American artist in oil on a wooden panel over the mantel after "Fancy Hill's" 1805 construction and now preserved in the Hampton Room of the Winterthur Museum.
Courtesy, The Henry Francis du Pont Winterthur Museum.

craft laden with contraband, the Hattons and their slave hurriedly set sail for the safety of the shore with their prize, hotly pursued by a barge bearing nine men from the ship. The four-mile chase ended when, becalmed, the customs officers were easily overtaken, boarded after a lengthy skirmish, mercilessly beaten, and robbed by the smugglers, who triumphantly departed with the confiscated vessel.[21]

Perhaps actuated as much by a desire for revenge as dedication to duty, Hatton resolved not to let the attackers escape with impunity. Bruised and battered, he commenced at once a search for any illicit goods which might have been landed in the vicinity of the Capes, while his son set out for Philadelphia to inform the revenue officials there of the assault and to recapture the pilot boat which reportedly had headed for the Pennsylvania capital. Arriving in Philadelphia on the 12th still suffering from multiple lacerations, young Hatton promptly secured the assistance of Deputy Collector John Swift and his men in seeking out the vessel. A diligent search of the waterfront by waiters located the boat at Carpenter's Wharf two days later. But en route to identify and secure the craft, Hatton and Swift's son were "artfully engaged" in conversation by the owner who, pretending to be "very sorry for what had pass'd," detained them until the arrival of "seven or eight Sailors arm'd with Clubbs." Swift escaped by obtaining refuge in a private home, but when Hatton attempted to do likewise

> the Sailors follow'd & dragg'd him out, and drove him about from place to place and with more than savage barbarity tore off the dressings from

21. Hatton to John Swift, Nov. 9, 1770, and to John Tabor Kempe, [Dec.] 8, 1770, Philadelphia Customs House Papers, X, 1285, 1288.

> the Wounds on his head and Arm, and pour'd a pot of Tar upon his Head, and then feather'd him. The Mob gather'd as they drove him with sticks from Street to Street they had a rope round his body, and when he would not walk or run they drag'd him; they put him in the Pillory, and when they tired of that, they drove him to the River and duck'd him. . . .

After "an hour or more" of such sport, the tars rowed their semi-conscious victim to the Jersey side of the Delaware and dumped him more dead than alive at Cooper's Ferry.[22]

This time there could be no question that Hatton and his assistants had been maliciously prevented from performing their official duties. Yet the circumstances surrounding the incident are shrouded in uncertainty. The altercations in Cape May and Philadelphia were not reported in the newspapers; the lone description of the former is by Hatton himself and of the latter by Swift, who admitted that he was "in a different quarter of the town [and] heard nothing of it till it was all over." And while there is no reason to challenge the essential veracity of the account rendered by the Philadelphia collector, the same confidence most assuredly cannot be placed in that of his Jersey counterpart. In fact, the only other known commentary on the Philadelphia fracas offers a decidedly different tale from that told by the customs officers. Eyewitness William Logan, a prominent Quaker merchant, wrote the following to religious and business associate John Smith of Burlington:

> A Large Mob of People consistg. chiefly of Sailors & such like passed my door this afternoon with a poor young fellow in tow with a rope round his middle & tard. I know not ye Particular Cause . . . but I hear he is the Collectors son of your Salem who seized ye Irish Vessel, & Greatly misbehaved to some Captn. & others when he could find nothing to seize.

22. Hatton to John Swift, Nov. 9, 1770, and to John Tabor Kempe, [Dec.] 8, 1770, Philadelphia Customs House Papers, X, 1285, 1288. Swift penned the following description of Hatton: "He was in a sad condition, he has one cut on the inside of his wrist an inch & half long & very deep, but the Sinews are not cut; and two cuts on his head, one of two inches long & the other an inch & half, & both to the bone." Swift felt that, despite professions of the citizenry to the contrary, "most in their hearts approve" of the vicious assault, and had "no doubt" that the action could be traced to an Irish merchant named Caldwell, the consignee of the *Prince of Wales*, and to the presence in the port of nearly a thousand seamen who were "always ready to do any mischief that their captains or Owners set them upon." Swift to the American Board, Nov. 15, 1770, Philadelphia Customs House Papers, X, 1292.

> They say [he was] much too forward & beyond his Authority, & being met with to day They thus rewarded him. . . .[23]

Thus it was certain only that a violent altercation had taken place involving the revenue officers of Salem-Cohansey; the determination of the causes and circumstances of the incident would await an official investigation.

The elder Hatton now confidently applied to civil authorities for a legal redress of grievances against his assailants. After all, he had positively identified Memucan Hughes and one Smith as the leaders of the gang of smugglers who had forcibly liberated the seized pilot boat owned by Jedediah Mills (who had remained aboard the *Prince of Wales*) and had secured six depositions supporting his account of the incident. Local officials responded to the charges by committing Hughes to the county jail, while Governor Franklin issued a proclamation condemning the flagrant obstruction of the customs service and calling for the speedy apprehension of those responsible for the audacious act. (Franklin also advised Hatton to seek a similar proclamation from the governor of Pennsylvania and obtain a warrant for the arrest of his son's attackers; he did neither.[24])

However, the only subsequent punitive legal action to be taken was directed against the collector! On November 12, five Cape May justices of the peace, acting upon the complaint of the incarcerated Hughes, issued a warrant for Hatton's arrest on the grounds that he had wounded an unnamed person and assaulted "divers others" during the battle for possession of the impounded pilot boat. And, at the behest of Mills, warrants were signed on December 6 requiring Hatton and his slave, Ned, to post

23. Swift to the American Board, Nov. 15, 1770, Philadelphia Customs House Papers, X, 1292; Logan to Smith, Nov. 14, 1770, Smith Correspondence, 222, Historical Society of Pennsylvania. The date appearing on the latter manuscript (Sept. 14, 1766) is incorrect, an archivist misreading the month and mistaking the year. Logan noted that young Hatton had been "so much abused as some think it may endanger his Life."

24. The affidavits were obtained from Christopher and Nathaniel Foster (business associates of Mills), Tristam Hedges, Enos Buck, Robert Parsons, and John Hatton, Jr. No statement was taken from the slave, Ned, presumably because the testimony of slaves was inadmissible as legal evidence. Hatton to John Swift, Nov. 9, 1770, and to John Tabor Kempe, [Dec.] 8, 1770, Philadelphia Customs House Papers, X, 1285, 1288; Proclamation of Governor Franklin, November 7, 1770, *N.J.A.*, X, 205–06. The date of the proclamation, reprinted from Samuel Hazard, *et al.*, eds., *Pennsylvania Archives* . . . (138 vols., 9 ser., Harrisburg and Philadelphia, 1852–1935), 1st ser., IV, 381–82, is obviously incorrect since the incident in question occurred on the 8th. A copy of the original proclamation has not been found; therefore, it has not been possible to ascertain the exact date; Franklin to the American Board, Apr. 10, 1771, *N.J.A.*, X, 288.

peace bonds.[25] Hatton was confined but a short while before being released on his own recognizance, but his servant was held without bail. His request that like proceedings be instituted against Mills was denied by local officers. Notwithstanding the fact that the identity of several participants in the fray was common knowledge, no arrests or interrogations were made. And the lone culprit to have been jailed, Hughes, was released without security to seek bail; it was finally posted by Charles Read, councilman, assistant justice of the supreme court, and collector of the port of Burlington.[26]

The action of the Cape May magistrates added a new dimension to the affair. Not only had the customs collector been physically prevented from performing his duties, but it also appeared as if local law enforcement officers had assisted the lawbreakers by a series of acts of commission as well as omission. On December 7 Hatton wrote to Governor Franklin animadverting at length upon the behavior of Cape May justices of the peace Thomas Leaming, Sr., John Leonard, and James Whilden. He described in great detail the ill-treatment and threats to his person and property received from residents of the county, the collusion between the justices and Mills, and the open smuggling conducted in the region by armed men who, not fearing action by civil authorities, dared him to intervene.[27] But when the complaint failed to elicit any response from the Governor and an appeal to the Customs Commissioners in Boston resulted only in a recommendation to seek the legal opinion of the Attorney General, Hatton set out on a late December journey to Burlington and Perth Amboy in order to present his case personally to Franklin and Cort-

25. Thomas Leaming, Daniel Swain, John Leonard, James Whilden, and Henry Hand issued the warrant. Philadelphia Customs House Papers, X, 1289. The warrants were signed by Leaming, Leonard, and Whilden. *N.J.A.*, X, 207–09; P.R.O. C.O. 5/72:555–62.

26. Hatton to William Franklin, Dec. 7, 1770, *N.J.A.*, X, 209–10 and P.R.O. C.O. 5/72:541–46; to John Tabor Kempe, [Dec.] 8, 1770, Philadelphia Customs House Papers, X, 1285; to the American Board, Dec. 25, 1770, *N.J.A.*, X, 215 and P.R.O. C.O. 5/72:537–40. Hatton was not surprised by Read's action, deeming it consistent with previous efforts "to distress me and the Service of the Revenue all He can."

27. As justices of the peace, the trio ranked among the most respected and influential citizens of Cape May. Leaming was the uncle of Aaron Leaming, who along with Jacob Spicer dominated county politics for a quarter-century. An elder in the Cold Spring Presbyterian Church from 1754 until his death in 1780, Whilden had served as j.p. since 1753. Leonard, a wealthy farmer, occupied a number of posts in county and local government. Hatton to Franklin, Dec. 7, 1770, *N.J.A.*, X, 209–13 and P.R.O. C.O. 5/72:541–46.

landt Skinner respectively. Convinced that Hatton had been "sadly harass'd" by Cape May magistrates "who have done every thing in their powers to perplex & plague Him," the Deputy Collector and Comptroller of Philadelphia were nonetheless pessimistic about the efficacy of an appeal to civil authorities, fearing that he "would have done just as well, if he had stay'd at Home & whistled to the wind."[28]

The prediction of the Pennsylvania revenue officers was only partially correct. After reviewing the evidence, Attorney General Skinner was of the opinion that New Jersey had no jurisdiction over the affair because the "transaction" had taken place on the high seas. Consequently, Hatton would have to seek recourse from the Admiralty courts. This being the case, it followed that the Cape May justices had been "forward in taking upon them any Enquiry" into the matter; if Hatton's allegations were true, ample grounds existed for their dismissal. He therefore advised Franklin to summon the contending parties posthaste to a formal hearing before Governor and Council.[29]

Hatton was less than enthusiastic about the decision to hold an official inquiry. Recalling the adverse decision of July, 1768, during which his private character and public performance had been impugned and the recent involvement of Councillor Charles Read in the affair, he was highly dubious about the prospect of receiving satisfaction from the New Jersey government. Earlier he had gone beyond the legal hierarchy of the province and sent a deposition to John Tabor Kempe, Attorney General of New York, describing the incident and requesting legal advice on the actions instituted against him by the Cape May officials as well as how best to proceed against the "Audacious Offenders so that they may be brought to Speedy Justice and receive punishment due to their demerits." Despairing the outcome of a local investigation, he once again pleaded with the Customs Commissioners to "interpose so as to get the Magistrates

28. John Swift and Alexander Barclay to the American Board, Dec. 20, 1770, P.R.O. C.O. 5/71:533–35; Philadelphia Customs House Papers, XII, 1517. Hatton had visited Philadelphia en route to the West Jersey capital.

29. John Swift to the American Board, Nov. 15, 1770, Philadelphia Customs House Papers, X, 1291; Skinner to Charles Pettit, and to Hatton, Dec. 25, 1770, *N.J.A.*, X, 216–18, and P.R.O., C.O. 5/72:547–50. The accuracy of Skinner's legal opinion was attested to by the Deputy Collector of Philadelphia, who from the beginning had doubted Hatton could obtain any redress for an offence committed "upon the high Seas."

punished according to their deserts."[30] But the American Board, exercising prudent discretion, decided to postpone any consideration of the collector's presentment pending completion of the Jersey inquiry.

The hearing opened in Burlington on February 21, 1771, with the bulk of the ensuing three-day session being devoted to the conduct of the Cape May justices.[31] Although it was clear that Hatton and his assistants had been physically attacked by persons engaged in smuggling, it was equally certain that no legal redress was obtainable from the provincial government for want of jurisdiction in the matter. Similarly, New Jersey officials were unable to take any action on the brutal beating administered to the younger Hatton in Pennsylvania. And the attempt by Hatton either to broaden the scope of the inquiry or obfuscate matters by charging that "the greatest Part of the People of the County" were "Smugglers, boasting the Sweets of an illicit Trade, and depending on the Magistrates for Support in their Villany," was rejected for want of evidence. As to the question at hand—the behavior of local law enforcement officers—the councillors were unanimously of the opinion that there was no just foundation for Hatton's complaints. To their collective mind there was no question but that his professed fears of personal injury were "chimerical and without Foundation;" that he had made false and distorted accusations against the three

30. "A State of the Case of one John Hatton . . . referred to the Consideration of John Tabor Kempe . . .," [Dec.] 8, 1770, Philadelphia Customs House Papers, X, 1285; Hatton to the American Board, Dec. 25 and 30, 1770, *N.J.A.*, X, 215–19; P.R.O. C.O. 6/71:537–50, 563–66. Internal evidence demonstrates that Hatton's deposition to Kempe was written in December, not November as added to the manuscript by an archivist. Several relatively minor yet important discrepancies between Hatton's account of the altercation of November 8 and his earlier versions exist in his memorandum to Kempe. In his letter to the Board, Hatton attempted to heighten the interest of the Commissioners in the cases by dwelling upon smuggling operations in Cape May and the dire threats engendered by his indefatigable attempts to halt clandestine commerce. Noting that five more vessels had unloaded illicit merchandise in the area since November 5, he reported that he had been "credibly informed that a Set of Merchants at Philadelphia have remitted a Quantity of money to this Province in Order to gain any Point they want and likewise make this Cape their STANCH Store, as they say they can not do without It for their contraband Trade."

31. Unfortunately, the paucity of documentary material makes it impossible either to reconstruct the events of the investigation or to analyze in depth the testimony and evidence submitted. The Council minutes from January 8 to March 26, 1771, containing the proceedings of the hearing as well as other germane information have been lost. See "Journal of Governor and Council," *N.J.A.*, XVIII, *passim*. The only extant information concerning the inquiry—notes compiled by Deputy Secretary Charles Pettit and two reports prepared by Governor Franklin—consist largely of comments upon Hatton's charges and and rationale behind the Council's verdict. Nevertheless, there is every indication that the available sources constitute an accurate representation of the substance of the arguments presented by the contending parties and the views of the Council.

justices; that on the basis of his son's testimony he had perjured himself; and that he had been remiss in the performance of his duty as collector. All twelve affidavits presented by Hatton in support of his charges were either in his hand or that of his son and gave every indication of having been "doctored." Deputy Secretary Charles Pettit may well have expressed the consensus of the Council when he opined:

> The Truth I believe is, that Mr. Hatton being disappointed of the Prize he had taken, was determined to turn his Wounds to some Account another Way. He seems to have had it in View, from the Beginning of his Quarrel, to provoke the Magistrates into Acts of Indiscretion, that might wear the Appearance of Persecution; and strives to ground all their Transactions against him, on a Settled Dislike to his Office, as one that the People wish to be entirely rid of. He wants to induce a Belief in his Superiors that he is persecuted for a strict Adherence to his Duty, which he doubts not will procure him Preferment. It is not the *Office* but the *Officer* that is unpopular in the Province.[32]

Disgruntled but undaunted by the decision, Hatton renewed his efforts to bring about the intercession of the American Board. Opportunely failing to mention the outcome of the inquiry, he once again complained to the Board of the mistreatment and abuse suffered in the performance of his duties at the hands of government officials, private citizens, and smugglers alike. Still hesitating to act without prior knowledge of the determination of the hearing and suspecting that Hatton's tales of "Distresses & Embarrasments" were "most extraordinary and in some Instances improbable," the Commissioners once again instructed Franklin to forward a full report of the proceedings relative to the case.[33]

In sending a comprehensive account of the inquiry along with copies of germane documentation to the Board on April 10, the Governor signified his concurrence with the Council that Hatton's charges against the justices were "entirely false and malicious," adding that "the Facts in favour of the Justices were, indeed, too evident to admit of any Hesitation in the Mat-

32. Pettit, "Notes and Observations," *N.J.A.*, X, 276–85. The notes, the only extant first-hand account of the proceedings, are not comprehensive but are supplementary, and consist largely of "several Matters omitted or but slightly mentd. in the Minutes. . . ."

33. The American Board to Franklin, Mar. 26, 1771, *N.J.A.*, X, 286–87.

ter." He went on to characterize Hatton as "a Man of a very unhappy, violent Temper, sometimes bordering on Madness," and implied that the recurrent difficulties were due in part to the fact that Hatton had such "extravagant Notions of his Power and Importance as Collector of the Customs" that he "insists upon great Homage and Deference being paid him by the County Magistrates." Again pointing out that Hatton was "strongly connected with some of the most noted Smugglers in Philadelphia," Franklin caustically commented that he had not "the least doubt, if the People on board the Ship and Pilot Boat had offered him Money instead of blows . . . he would readily have accepted of it, and left them to pursue their Measures without any Disturbance from him whatever." He too interpreted Hatton's exaggerated and fanciful professions of zealous devotion to duty as nothing more than an attempt to "make himself a Man of Consequence" and "get preferred to a better Collectorship." "In short," the Governor concluded, "there is nothing so absurd & outrageous, that he has not shown himself capable of saying or doing, on which Account I have had more Trouble with him than with all the other People in New Jersey."[34]

As before, Franklin interpreted the request for a formal report as a personal affront and an implicit challenge to the integrity of the Council, the equity of the decision reached, or both. Expressing doubt that the report would have "much Weight" because the Board had paid "so little Regard" to either the previous decision reached under strikingly similar circumstances in 1768 or the findings of Inspector General Williams a year later, he chastised the Commissioners for their attitude toward the activities of the collector over the past several years. To his mind, the Board had been greatly remiss in its responsibilities in failing to remove or rebuke Hatton. Furthermore, Franklin was "alarm'd" as well as angered upon learning that several of Hatton's complaints (presumably including a scurrilous criticism of his performance as chief executive) had been forwarded to the Commissioners of the Treasury in London without any effort to ascertain the validity of the allegations, and did not hesitate to voice his indignation in the strongest possible terms.[35]

34. Franklin to the American Board, Apr. 10, 1771, *ibid.*, 287–90.
35. Franklin to the American Board, Apr. 10, 1771, *N.J.A.*, 290–95.

When no reply was forthcoming from Boston, the Governor sent his version of the case along with supporting material to Lord Hillsborough. He also took the opportunity to comment upon the failure of the Commissioners to dismiss Hatton from office despite "the strongest Proofs of his Unfaithfulness in the Execution of it." The Secretary of State was completely satisfied that the New Jersey government had conducted the investigation "with great Attention and Impartiality" and assured Franklin that he would so inform his superiors. Since no further action was taken by either the Treasury Board or the Commissioners in America, imperial authorities apparently considered the case closed.[36] And so it was. For while Hatton continued to serve as collector until the outbreak of the Revolution, he became involved in no further public or private altercations —presumably because the navigation acts were a dead letter in New Jersey after 1773.[37]

Yet irreparable damage had already been done. Occurring at a time when relations between the mother country and the colonies were on the decline, the several incidents involving Hatton called imperial authority as well as the customs service into further disrepute. The actions of petty officials resident in the colonies undoubtedly had considerably more influence upon the lives of Americans than the decisions made in Whitehall and Westminster. And for the numerous residents of South Jersey whose only direct contact with the empire was through contact with such local

36. Franklin to Hillsborough, May 19, 1771; Hillsborough to Franklin, July 19, 1771, both in Franklin Papers, XLVII, 135, 304. See also John Robinson to John Pownall, July 13, 1771, P.R.O. C.O. 5/72:507; Pownall to Robinson, July 19, 1771, and Franklin to Hillsborough, Oct. 21, 1771, *N.J.A.*, X, 305–06, 314. Franklin in the latter item reported that he had been "credibly informed" that the Customs Commissioners had sent another investigator into Jersey who, like Williams, "openly declared that he found [Hatton] had been guilty of many undue Practices, and was every way unfit to be a Collector of His Majesty's Customs."

37. As might be expected, the Hattons remained loyal to the crown during the Revolution. The elder Hatton purportedly earned the epithet "King of the Tories" for maintaining an "open house for all the King's friends" during the early stages of the war, while his son left the province to take up arms in defense of the royal standard. In early August, 1776, the Pennsylvania Council of Safety issued a warrant for the arrest of the Hattons for complicity in the escape of one Colonel Kirkland from a Philadelphia jail. The Salem County Committee of Inspection readily agreed to the extradition of the senior Hatton, and on August 5 he was committed to the Pennsylvania state prison. Upon examination, he was subsequently released fifteen days later after posting a £500 bond for good behavior. *Pennsylvania Archives*, 1st .ser., X, 666, 670, 694–95; 2nd ser., V, 7. Hatton eventually emigrated to London, where he received from the British government an annual pension of £90 and a grant of £1,534 as compensation for the financial loss incurred by the confiscation of his property in Jersey and the interruption of his salary as collector. Young Hatton also removed to England and pursued a military career. Jones, 92–94.

officers, the exceptionable behavior of a man like John Hatton, a visible symbol of royal authority, was likely a greater source of alienation from Great Britain than either the exactions of the Stamp Act and Townshend duties or the more glamorous intercolonial manifestations of the protest-independence movement. Furthermore, the controversies involving the collector also served to strain relations between imperial and provincial authorities and in the process exposed some of the defects in the colonial administrative machinery and the weaknesses of the civil government. The Customs Commissioners in Boston, their influence and effectiveness almost completely obviated by intransigent colonial opposition while simultaneously under increasing pressures from superiors in England to implement the navigation laws, tended to pay inordinate attention to minor rows such as those involving Hatton. For their part, New Jersey officials resented what appeared to be an overreaction and unwarranted interference in local affairs. Wholesale violations of the acts of trade had become part and parcel of everyday commercial enterprise in colonial America; the authority of Great Britain was openly flaunted while local, provincial, and imperial officials alike stood by unable or unwilling to act. Notwithstanding the scurrilous nature of many of Hatton's accusations, the fact remains that imperial authorities could not and local magistrates all too often would not reinforce the revenue service for fear of incurring the wrath of a considerable segment of the populace. As the customs officials in Philadelphia so cogently observed:

> . . . the truth of the matter is, the hands of Government are not strong enough to oppose the numerous body of people who wish well the cause of smuggling. . . . What can a Governor do, without the assistance of the Governed? What can the Magistrates do, unless they are supported by their fellow citizens? What can the King's Officers do, if they make themselves obnoxious to the people amongst whom they reside?[38]

In its essential characteristics the career of John Hatton as collector of Salem and Cohansey was not singular but rather symptomatic of the conditions which contributed to, if not caused, the disruption of the First British Empire.

38. John Swift and Alexander Barclay to the American Board, Dec. 20, 1770, P.R.O. C.O. 5/71:533–35; Philadelphia Customs House Papers, XII, 1517.

14
Colonial Civil Servant and Counter-revolutionary: Thomas Irving (1738?–1800) in Boston, Charleston, and London

John J. McCusker

For the last two decades of the eighteenth century almost every officially compiled account of the trade of Great Britain and its empire bore the signature of Thomas Irving (1738?–1800).[1] A careful, astute, efficient administrator, Irving was one of many Scots employed in the British civil service. (See figure 9.1.) Since his early years included experience in Great Britain's North American colonies, aspects of his career offer considerable insight into a significant period of Anglo-American history. Among his many activities were an attempt at forestalling the American revolutionary movement from the vantage point of the customhouse in Boston and, later, at thwarting the emerging, post-war economic independence of the United States from a strategic post within the customhouse in London. His failure in the first enterprise fueled his ardor for the second, an effort in which he was indeed more successful.

♦ ♦ ♦ ♦ ♦

The surviving personal details of Irving's life are sparse. He was the fourth son of William Irving of Gribton (ca. 1690–1774), a member of a strongly Jacobite strain of the Irvings of Dumfriesshire, and Katherine Menzies of Enoch; they had twelve children in all. The family estate, where Thomas Irving was presumably born, consisted of several hundred acres in the parish of Hollywood, about four miles northwest of the burgh of Dumfries.[2]

1 The original version of this chapter was published in *Perspectives in American History*, XII (1979), 313–350. This revision is presented here with thanks to the original publishers and to the President and Fellows of Harvard College.

I continue to be grateful for the help and support given me by the American Council of Learned Societies, National Endowment for the Humanities Research Fellowship at the American Enterprise Institute Center for Advanced Study, Washington, DC, and the Institute of Early American History and Culture, Williamsburg, Virginia.

2 All that we are ever likely to know about Thomas Irving of Gribton and the Irving family has been assembled by Alastair M. T. Maxwell-Irving of Stirlingshire, Scotland, in a model

THOMAS IRVING: LOYALIST AND CIVIL SERVANT

Figure 9.1 Thomas Irving (1738?–1800). Small monochrome drawing. Done just before his death on 13 July 1800.
Formerly in the possession of Mrs Isobel Irving of Wellwick, Wendover, Buckinghamshire, England. Courtesy of A. M. T. Maxwell-Irving, Stirlingshire, Scotland.

of genealogical research. He has been both kind and generous in placing the results of his efforts at the author's disposal and I am grateful for his help. Maxwell-Irving's study, "The Irvings of Dumfries (Senior Cadets of the Irvings of Bonshaw)" (unpublished typescript, 1968), is on deposit in the National Library of Scotland, Edinburgh, and Ewart Public Library, Dumfries. It is founded largely on family papers still in private hands and is itself the basis of the entry in [John] Bernard Burke, *Burke's Genealogical and Heraldic History of the Landed Gentry*, ed. Peter Townend, 18th edn, 3 vols (London, 1965–1969), II, 338–340. See also Maxwell-Irving's *The Irvings of Bonshaw: Chiefs of the Noble and Ancient Scots Border Family of Irving* (Bletchley, 1968), p. 32. His efforts, and some of my own – directed largely by the suggestions of Jacob M. Price of the University of Michigan – are the foundation of most of what is said in this chapter about Irving's family. See also John Beaufin Irving, *The Irvings, Irwins, Irvines, or Erinveines, or Any Other Spelling of the Name: An Old Scots Border Clan* (Aberdeen, 1907), pp. 84–86, 220, based in part on an article in the *Dumfries Courier*, 5 June 1877; and Burke, *Genealogical and Heraldic History of the Landed Gentry*, 6th edn, 2 vols (London, 1879), I, 856. For Gribton, see Francis H. Groome, *Ordnance Gazetteer of Scotland: A Survey of Scottish Topography, Statistical, Biographical, and Historical* (Edinburgh, 1886), II, 228, 273–274.

The miniature of Thomas Irving illustrated here as fig. 9.1 was supplied to me by Mrs Isobel Stuart Irving of Wellwick, Wendover, Buckinghamshire, England, the wife of Charles Maxwell Trelawny Irving. The inscription on the back of the miniature, said to be in the handwriting of Thomas's grandson James Corbet Irving, reads: "Thos. Irving, Esqr., taken a few hours before his death 13th July, 1800." Letter from C. M. Trelawny Irving, at Wellwick, to [A. M. T.] Maxwell-Irving, 6 Nov. 1962. Copy in the author's possession.

THOMAS IRVING: LOYALIST AND CIVIL SERVANT

Thomas Irving's father and Thomas's brother James were among a handful of people in Dumfries who were cited as active supporters of Bonnie Prince Charlie in the rebellion of 1745.[3] Another brother, Charles, a naval doctor and something of an inventor, demonstrated a practical method for the desalination of sea water for which in 1772 Parliament granted him the rather spectacular sum of £5,000, the modern equivalent (in 1997) of roughly £320,000, more than $530,000.[4] In later life Thomas Irving frequently visited Edinburgh, on 3 April 1774 he and Marion Corbet, the daughter of a merchant and Provost of Dumfries burgh were married there, and it is possible that he attended school or worked there or at Glasgow while a young man.[5] Irving acquired learning

3 For father and son in The '45, see Herbert Maxwell, *A History of Dumfries and Galloway*, 2nd edn (Edinburgh, 1900), pp. 360–361; *A List of Persons Concerned in the Rebellion, Transmitted to the Commissioners of the Excise by the Several Supervisors in Scotland, in Obedience to a General Letter of the 7th May 1746 with a Supplementary List with Evidences to Prove the Same*, ed. Walter Macleod, Publications of the Scottish History Society, [1st ser.], vol. 8 (Edinburgh, 1890), pp. 142–145; and letter from W. C. at Dumfries to George Clerk at Durham, in W[illiam] A. J. Prevost, "Letters from Dumfries during the Jacobite Rebellion in 1745," Dumfriesshire and Galloway Natural History and Antiquarian Society, *Transactions and Journal of Proceedings*, 3rd ser., XL (1961–1962), 178 and n. 25.

4 The Admiralty had already granted him £300 in 1771. Secretary to the Admiralty to Charles Irving, 9 Oct. 1771, Adm. 2/731, PRO; [GB, Parl., Commons], *Journals of the House of Commons*, in progress ([London, 1742 to date]), XXXIII, 534, 600, 661–664, 714, 717, 740–741, 745; *The Annual Register . . . for the Year 1772* (London, 1773), "Chronicle," pp. 98, 212; Thomas Irving, at London, to Dr William Smibert, at Boston, 3 Mar. 1772, as referred to in Smibert to Dr Thomas Moffat, 8 Apr. 1772, in the papers of Dr Thomas Moffat, bundle labeled "Smibert to Moffat . . . 1767–1773," *Curgenven* v. *Peters*, C 106/193, pt i, PRO – hereafter cited as "Moffat Papers" (both physicians were friends of Irving; Moffat held the position of Comptroller of Customs at New London, Conn.); *Virginia Gazette* (Williamsburg), ed. Alexander Purdie and John Dixon, 20 May 1773; Constantine John Phipps, *A Voyage Towards the North Pole Undertaken by His Majesty's Command, 1773* (London, 1774), pp. 11, 28, 205–221; James Lind, *An Essay on the Most Effectual Means of Preserving the Health of Seamen in the Royal Navy*, new edn, enl. (London, 1774), pp. iv, 97–130; John Sinclair, *The Statistical Account of Scotland. Drawn Up from the Communications of the Ministers of the Different Parishes*, 21 vols (Edinburgh, 1791–1799), I, 35; Christopher [C.] Lloyd and Jack L. S. Coulter, *Medicine and the Navy . . . 1714–1815*, vol. III of J[ohn] J. Keevil, Christopher [C.] Lloyd and Jack L. S. Coulter, *Medicine and the Navy, 1200–1900* (Edinburgh and London, 1961), pp. 90–92, 313; *The Journals of Captain James Cook on His Voyages of Discovery*, ed. J[ohn] C. Beaglehole, 5 vols in 6 pts (Cambridge, Eng., 1955–1974), II, 10; P[atricia] K. Crimmin, "A Distilling Machine of 1772," *MM*, LII (Nov. 1966), 392; J. E. Roberts, "Distillation of Water at Sea," *MM*, LXIV (Nov. 1978), 299–300; J. A. Sulivan, "The Distillation and Purification of Water at Sea," *MM*, LXV (May, 1979), 161–162; and Ann Savours, "The Parliamentary Award of 1772 to Dr. Charles Irving for Salt Water Distillation at Sea," *MM*, LXXVI (Nov. 1990), 362–365.

5 Maxwell-Irving, "Irvings of Dumfries," pp. 72–73; *Register of Marriages of the City of Edinburgh, 1751–1800*, ed. Francis J. Grant, Publications of the Scottish Record Society, [o.s.], vol. 53, 1 vol. in 11 pts (Edinburgh, 1917–1922), p. 374. James Corbet (1709?–1762) was Provost of Dumfries, 1758–1760. William McDowall, *History of the Burgh of Dumfries, with Notices of Nithsdale, Annadale, and the Western Border*, 3rd edn (Dumfries, 1906), pp. 607–619, 868–869, and elsewhere. See also McDowall, *Memorials of St. Michael's, the Old Parish Churchyard of Dumfries* (Edinburgh, 1876), pp. 65–66. Marion Corbet Irving's father and her uncle Thomas Corbet were merchants and shipowners of Dumfries engaged in the Virginia trade. Some of their business papers, from the years

and sophistication somewhere and one might plausibly conjecture that this exemplar of the new, rationalized bureaucracy was early exposed to the ideas of Adam Smith but there is no direct evidence of this.[6]

Ties of blood and kinship were important to Thomas Irving.[7] His country credentials as a member of an ancient and noble landed family greatly assisted his early career. Through his mother's family, the Menzies of Enoch and Stenhouse, Irving was related to Charles Douglas, the third Duke of Queensberry, a favorite of King George III, and to others in Queensberry's political circle in Dumfries. John Douglas of Kelhead, a second cousin of Thomas's mother, was the Member of Parliament for Dumfries from 1741 to 1747, on Queensberry's interest. One observer called him "the chief director of his friend the Duke of Queensberry's country affairs and parliamentary interest in the county of Dumfries." Imprisoned in the Tower of London for two years because of his involvement in The '45, John Douglas was doubtless willing to look after the son and brother of like-thinking men and to recommend Thomas to Queensberry. In 1770 a colleague of Irving's in the Customs pointedly informed the Treasury, the fountain of patronage, that "the Duke of Queensberry is a friend of Mr. Irvings family and will probably make some appl[icatio]n on his behalf."[8]

1745 to 1762, are in the James Corbet Papers, 1745–1762, Court of Sessions Productions, CS 96/2147–2162, 4912–4193, Scottish Record Office, Edinburgh.

6 Smith was part of the same Douglas–Queensberry clientage network to which Irving belonged (see n. 8 of this chapter) and accompanied Henry Scott (1746–1812), later the fifth Duke of Queensberry, as his tutor on the Grand Tour; see *Dictionary of National Biography*, ed. Leslie Stephen and Sidney Lee, 63 vols (London, 1885–1901), s.v. One author has identified some of Irving's ideas as "Smithian." John Ehrman, *The Younger Pitt: The Years of Acclaim* (London, 1969), p. 503. And Adam Smith and Thomas's eldest brother and namesake were in the same class at the University of Glasgow, Smith having matriculated in his third year in 1737 and Irving in his fourth year in 1738. W[illiam] Innes Addison, ed., *The Matriculation Albums of the University of Glasgow from 1728 to 1858* (Glasgow, 1913), pp. xx, 18, 20. The first Thomas died soon thereafter and, as happened, William and Katherine named their next baby boy after their dead first son. Since Thomas's younger brother Joseph Irving of Borran, Kirkbean, was also born in the 1730s, our Thomas, arriving between the death of his eldest brother and the birth of this younger one, had to have been born in 1738 or very early in 1739. Maxwell-Irving, "Irvings of Dumfries," pp. 51, 92–93.

7 Unfortunately there is little about his early life or family in the single most important collection of materials relating to Irving, the various papers he prepared in support of his claim for compensation as a Loyalist *émigré*. See the Memorials and Supporting Documents Presented by Thomas Irving to the Loyalist Claims Commission, ser. I, 1786–1788, AO 12/51, fols 152v–164v, PRO. There are copies of the materials in Series I in the Transcripts of the Manuscript Books and Papers of the Commission of Enquiry into the Losses and Services of the American Loyalists, 1783–1790, New York Public Library, New York City. For related documents concerning Irving, see AO 13/130, fols 24–56, PRO. For a summary of his earlier case and the determinations made, under dates 27 May and 11 June 1783, see AO 12/99, fols 282r–283v, PRO. There is no other known collection of "Thomas Irving Papers." Compare, John Ehrman, *The British Government and Commercial Negotiations with Europe, 1783–1793* (Cambridge, Eng., 1962), pp. 12n.

8 For Irving's place in the Douglas–Queensberry patronage system, the establishment of which I owe in great measure to Jacob M. Price, see [John Anderson], "Douglas, Duke of Queensbury," in *The Scots Peerage*, ed. James Balfour Paul, 9 vols (Edinburgh,

THOMAS IRVING: LOYALIST AND CIVIL SERVANT

Personal friendships, as well as family connections, played an influential role in Irving's life. At Boston, during his service in the colonies, he fell in with Charles Steuart, the Surveyor-General of the Customs in the Eastern-Middle District of America and later Cashier and Paymaster-General of the Customs in North America. Steuart had himself come out from Scotland in 1742 and had worked as a merchant at Norfolk until his diplomatic handling there of the potentially explosive "Spanish Affair" in 1762, during the Seven Years War, earned him his Surveyor-Generalship in 1765. Two years later he became the Cashier and Paymaster-General: offices that, after he returned home in 1769, he exercised through his deputy, Nathaniel Coffin.[9] By way

1904–1914), VII, 143–147, 150–151; Craufurd Tait Ramage, *Drumlanrig Castle and the Douglases: with the Early History and Ancient Remains of Durisdeer, Closeburn, and Morton* (Dumfries, 1876), pp. 93–94; and R[obert] C. Reid, "The Baronies of Enoch and Durisdeer," Dumfriesshire and Galloway Natural History and Antiquarian Society, *Transactions and Journal of Proceedings*, 3rd ser., VIII (1923), 153–171. For John Douglas (ca. 1708–1778), see Romney Sedgwick, *The History of Parliament: The House of Commons, 1715–1754*, 2 vols (London, 1970), I, 384, 618. The quotation about him is from a memorandum by Alexander Dick in *Curiosities of a Scots Charta Chest, 1600–1800, with the Travels and Memoranda of Sir Alexander Dick, Baronet, of Prestonfield, Midlothian Written by Himself*, ed. Margaret Alice Forbes (Edinburgh, 1897), p. 223. The quotation about Irving is in a letter from Joseph Harrison, [at London?], to Grey Cooper, at London, [1770], AO 12/51, fol. 161r, PRO, and AO 13/130, fol. 34v, PRO. Harrison, Collector of Customs at Boston, wrote this letter to Cooper, one of the joint Secretaries to the Treasury (1765–1782), soon after Harrison arrived back in England in 1770. See Harrison, at "Bawtry," to Irving, 7 Nov. 1783, AO 12/51, fol. 160r, PRO, and AO 13/130, fol. 28v, PRO. Irving's family, headed by his brother James, who became Laird of Gribton in 1773, was still considered to be firmly in the Queensberry camp fifteen years later. *View of the Political State of Scotland in the Last Century: A Confidential Report of the Political Opinions, Family Connections, or Personal Circumstances of the 2662 County Voters in 1788*, ed. Charles Elphinstone Adam (Edinburgh, 1887), pp. 97, 102. See also Lewis [B.] Namier and John Brooke, *The History of Parliament: The House of Commons, 1754–1790*, 3 vols (London, 1964), I, 476, II, 329, 332–333. Presumably it was the Duke of Queensberry to whom John Pownall, the Undersecretary of State for the Colonies, referred in his letter of introduction for Irving that he sent to Gov. Francis Bernard of Massachusetts: "Mr. Irving . . . who will wait upon you with this, has been particularly recommended to me by a friend." Letter, dated London, 23 Oct. 1767, Bernard Papers, vol. XI, p. 99, Jared Sparks Manuscripts, pt IV, Houghton Library, Harvard University, Cambridge, Mass. Given Pownall's own remarkable career, his recommendation was impressive in itself. For Pownall (1720–1795), in the words of Edmund Burke, "an able, intelligent, honest man, of remarkable probity," see Namier and Brooke, *House of Commons*, III, 315–316.

The Duke of Queensberry's patronage extended to writing the Loyalist Claims Commission on behalf of Alexander Irving, Thomas's younger brother, who accompanied him out to Boston in 1768, worked with him for a while there, and then moved to South Carolina where he set himself up as a planter in the vicinity of Georgetown, presumably near to his sister and brother-in-law, Winifred and Archibald Baird. Alexander, like his brother Thomas, was forced to leave the state in 1777. See his memorials to the commission dated 26 Dec. 1778 and 14 Feb. 1780, AO 13/70B, pt ii, fols 298r, 300r, 302r, PRO. See also nn. 10 and 63 of this chapter.

9 Steuart (1725–1797) deserves a full biography, the sources for which are readily available. See the Charles Steuart Papers, 1758–1798, MSS 5025–5046, Charters 3887, 4006, National Library of Scotland, Edinburgh; the Charles Steuart Letter Books, 1751–1763, HSP; the Charles Steuart Papers, 1762–1789, Colonial Williamsburg Foundation Library, Williamsburg, Va.; Steuart's memorial to the Loyalist Claims Commission, 26 Aug. 1789, AO 13/48, PRO; and the accounts of his office in AO 1/844/1137–1140, PRO, and AO

of Steuart, Thomas Irving not only had ties in the colonies to others like Coffin in the Customs bureaucracy but also to Steuart's Scottish merchant friends at Norfolk and elsewhere.[10] The two men maintained contact once Steuart was back in London, where he also proved helpful to Irving. Their friendship ended only with Steuart's death in 1797. Others among Irving's circle of acquaintances in London later in his life were John Baker Holroyd, Earl of Sheffield, the friend and editor of Edward Gibbon, and John Sinclair, Scottish MP, organizer and President of the Scottish Board of Agriculture, and the man who in the 1790s compiled the famous *Statistical Account of Scotland*.[11]

♦ ♦ ♦ ♦ ♦

3/305, PRO. See also [George Chalmers], ["Biographical Account of Charles Steuart, Esqr."], *Gentleman's Magazine*, LXVIII (May 1798), 442–444. The title supplied for this obituary is the one that Chalmers used to identify it in his own set of his collected works. George Chalmers, [*Works*], 26 vols in 8 pts ([London, 1777–1799]), III, [item 2], Division of Rare Books and Special Collections, LC. When Steuart arrived in England from Virginia in Nov. 1769, he had with him his black slave, James Somerset. Somerset later sued for his freedom, which was the occasion of the famous decision of Lord Chief Justice Mansfield in 1772. James Walvin, *Black and White: The Negro and English Society, 1555–1945* (London, 1973), pp. 117–131.

10 Thomas Irving was also associated by marriage with others in the Customs service. His youngest sister Winifred's first husband was Archibald Baird, Collector of Customs at Georgetown, SC, from 1740 until his death in 1777. Baird's memorial, 5 Mar. 1774, T 1/511, fols 204–205, PRO; Irving, *The Irvings*, p. 86; Maxwell-Irving, "Irvings of Dumfries," p. 52; Caroline T. Moore and Agatha Aimar Simmons, *Abstracts of the Wills of the State of South Carolina, 1670–1784*, 3 vols (Columbia, SC, 1960–1969), III, 264; George C. Rogers, Jr, *The History of Georgetown County, South Carolina* (Columbia, SC, [1970]), pp. 37–38, 48; Winifred [Irving] Baird, at Georgetown, SC, to Charles Steuart, 1 June 1778, in A[rchibald] Francis Steuart, "Letters from Virginia, 1774–1781," *Magazine of History*, III (Apr. 1906), 212–213; Steuart Papers, National Library of Scotland. His second cousin Ann Irving (1729?–1819) married David Blair (d. 1784), the Collector at Dumfries. Burke, *Landed Gentry*, ed. Townend, 18th edn, II, 338. Most importantly, Thomas Irving seems to have been related to Robert Menzies of Culterallers (d. 1769), the Inspector-General of Imports and Exports of Scotland, 1764–1769, whose family also came from Dumfries. Robert Menzies' father was Dr John Menzies, a physician there. Since it is likely that Irving had had some training and experience in the Customs service before 1767, we can speculate whether or not he might have worked as an assistant clerk in the Edinburgh office of his kinsman, the Scottish Inspector-General. (As such he would not have been carried upon the establishment.) This speculation has been provoked by Jacob M. Price, who also established the Dumfries connection of Robert Menzies. Personal communication, 31 July 1978, citing Robert Menzies Papers, Register House Records, Miscellaneous Bundles, RH 15/92/13, and Lanark Commissary Court Records, CC 14/5/18, Scottish Record Office, Edinburgh, and *The Register of Marriages for the Parish of Edinburgh, 1585–1750*, ed. Henry Paton, Publications of the Scottish Record Society, [o.s.], vols 27, 35, 2 vols in 11 pts (Edinburgh, 1905–1908), II, 330, 370.

11 For Sheffield (1735–1821), see n. 69 of this chapter. For Sinclair (1754–1835) – author of *The Statistical Account of Scotland*, 21 vols (Edinburgh, 1791–1799), see *The Correspondence of the Right Honourable Sir John Sinclair, Bart., with Reminiscences of the Most Distinguished Characters Who Have Appeared in Great Britain, and in Foreign Countries, during the Last Fifty Years*, [ed. John Sinclair], 2 vols (London, 1831), I, xvii–xxxiv; Rosalind Mitchison, *Agricultural Sir John: The Life of Sir John Sinclair of Ulbster, 1754–1835* (London, 1962); Namier and Brooke, *House of Commons*, III, 440–441; and n. 81 of this chapter. It was at a dinner party at John Sinclair's in Apr. 1790 that the brilliant American

THOMAS IRVING: LOYALIST AND CIVIL SERVANT

The narrative of Thomas Irving's public life begins on 9 September 1767, the date of the warrant that appointed him Inspector-General of Imports and Exports and Register of Shipping of North America. This office had been established as part of the effort to tighten British control of the Thirteen Continental Colonies by reproducing in miniature at Boston the Customs establishment in London. Irving was thus part of the bureaucracy supervised by the Commissioners of the American Board of Customs. His job combined for the North American colonies two posts that were separate in London, the Inspector-General of Imports and Exports and the Register of Shipping. The former office oversaw the collection and compilation of the statistics of imperial trade, the latter supervised the registration of British vessels and compiled statistics concerning their employment.[12]

At Boston, Irving had to create the job from scratch. The Commissioners of Customs in London had sought to instruct him in his duties before he went out and even prepared samples of the required forms for his education.[13] But Irving altered both the forms and the substance of his position after he

diplomat Gouverneur Morris took Irving's measure and pronounced him "a statesman," although one "decidedly opposed to America." *The Diary and Letters of Gouverneur Morris, Minister of the United States to France* . . ., ed. Anne Cary Morris, 2 vols (New York, 1888), I, 315. Compare Charles R. Ritcheson, *Aftermath of Revolution: British Policy toward the United States, 1783–1795* (Dallas, 1969), p. 13.

12 Warrant, 9 Sept. 1767, T 28/1, p. 303, PRO. See also Treasury Board, meeting of 27 Aug. 1767, Minute Books, T 29/38, p. 459, PRO; and Thomas Bradshaw to Commissioners of the Customs, 28 Aug. 1767, announcing Irving's appointment, T 11/28, p. 145, PRO. For the establishment at Boston, reference should be had to Dora Mae Clark, "The American Board of Customs, 1767–1783," *AHR*, XLV (July 1940), 777–806. At one time Joseph R. Frese was at work on a book-length study of this body; I am in his debt for sharing with me some of the fruits of his research. The fullest discussion of the two London offices is still G[eorge] N. Clark, *Guide to English Commercial Statistics, 1696–1782*, Royal Historical Society, Guides and Handbooks, no. 1 (London, 1938), pp. 1–42, 45–51. See also Elizabeth Evelynola Hoon, *The Organization of the English Customs System, 1696–1786* (New York, 1938), pp. 116–119. Both positions were parts of the operations of the Customs which was itself part of the Treasury. The office of the Inspector-General was the antecedent of the modern Statistical Office of HM Customs and Excise. See Rupert C. Jarvis, "The Archival History of the Customs Records," *Journal of the Society of Archivists*, I (Apr. 1959), 245. We have no consolidated collection of Customs papers for this era, largely because of their destruction in the fire in the London customhouse in Feb. 1814. Edward [A.] Carson, *The Ancient and Rightful Customs: A History of the English Customs Service* (London, 1972), pp. 131–132. With minor exceptions, what papers do survive are now in the PRO. See nn. 16 and 24 of this chapter.

13 Commissioners of the Customs, at Custom House, London, to Lords of the Treasury, 26 Aug. 1767, T 1/459, fol. 140r, PRO. See also Treasury Board meeting of 26 Aug. 1767, T 29/38, p. 459, PRO. Some of their instructions might well have been based on a memorandum prepared by Henry Hulton, plantation clerk to the Customs Commissioners, 16 May 1765, about which the Commissioners thought highly enough to send it on to the Lords of the Treasury. T 1/442 fols 333–334, PRO. Hulton was later named as one of the Commissioners of the American Board of Customs. See *Letters of a Loyalist Lady: Being the Letters of Ann Hulton, Sister of Henry Hulton Commissioner of Customs at Boston, 1767–1776* (Cambridge, Mass., 1927); and "An Englishman Views the American Revolution: The Letters of Henry Hulton, 1769–1776," ed. Wallace Brown, *Huntington Library Quarterly*, XXXVI (Nov. 1972, Feb. 1973), 1–26, 139–151.

arrived. He was uniquely successful in bringing order and efficiency to the collection of American commercial statistics. Moreover, under his direction, these dispread data were consolidated into the first composite view of colonial commerce, a document that survives as the one-volume ledger of imports and exports of the North American colonies for the five years 1768–1772, known best by its classification in the Public Record Office, London: "Customs 16/1."

In 1770, in a report to the Commissioners of the American Board of Customs, Irving reflected on the state of the records before he had begun his reforms. Until he had reorganized things,

> accounts of imports and exports . . . were drawn out in a very confused, imperfect and inaccurate manner, the accounts of imports from Great Britain being entirely omitted by reason of the multiplicity of articles of which such cargoes generally consist, and the imports and exports to and from the neighbouring colonies (which commonly pass under the denomination of coasting trade) being seldom or ever inserted in the accounts and even such goods and commodities as were brought into account were not arranged in any order or method nor were the real quantity thereof ascertained with proper precision.[14]

After he had taken matters in hand, not only did he right all these wrongs, but he also introduced many innovations.

One of Irving's innovations involved the more systematic collection of information. The gathering of colonial trade data had started in the seventeenth century when Customs officials were first installed in each colonial "port" (i.e., Customs district or port of entry [POE]).[15] One of their responsibilities was to check the registry and the cargo of the vessels that cleared into and out of their ports in order to insure conformity with the Acts of Trade.[16] Each time a vessel came or went, the clerk of the Naval Office copied down the details of the ship and its cargo based on its registry certificate and manifests. He assembled the information quarterly and passed the completed compilation – the Naval Office shipping lists (NOSL) – to the colony's Governor who then sent them on to London. Sometime after Irving's assumption of office in May 1768, he directed the clerks of the Naval Office in all the colonial ports to dispatch them directly to his Boston office

14 Report, enclosed in Irving to American Board of Customs, Boston, 31 Jan. 1770, T 1/476, fol. 47r, PRO. Part of this report has been printed in Mary Alice Hanna, *Trade of the Delaware District before the Revolution* (Northampton, Mass., 1917), p. 285.

15 The best summary of the origins and functions of the clerks of the colonial Naval Offices is in Charles M. Andrews, *The Colonial Period of American History*, 4 vols (New Haven, Conn., 1934–1938), IV, passim. See also my own forthcoming study, *An Introduction to the Naval Office Shipping Lists* (in progress).

16 See, especially, the Acts of 12 Charles II, c. 4, and 14 Charles II, c. 11. Compare Lawrence A. Harper, *The English Navigation Laws: A Seventeenth-Century Experiment in Social Engineering* (New York, 1939), pp. 321–364.

in the customhouse.[17] Similar instructions were given to the Customs officers in those ports; he also told them to send him the duplicates of the ship registers issued in their ports.

With all of this information at hand, Irving and his assistants had the basis for producing their own yearly summaries of colonial trade. Before setting to work, however, they carefully scrutinized the shipping lists. One of Irving's office letter books survives; it testifies to his efforts to insure that these records were as complete and as accurate as could be. He badgered and threatened any who were recalcitrant and he questioned and cross-checked everything he found sloppy or suspect.[18] Such labors required his writing 700 letters in 1769 alone and the keeping of 250 ledgers.[19] Little if anything escaped his attention.

17 This is the date of "General Letter (No. 1)" over Irving's name in the Letter Book of the Inspectors-General of Imports and Exports and Register of Shipping in North America, 1768–1775, Customs 21/16, PRO.

Irving had arrived at the end of Jan. *Massachusetts Gazette. And Boston News-Letter*, 4 Feb. 1768. The reference is to "Robert Irvine, the inspector of imports and exports" on board the brig *Abigail* after a cold passage of fourteen weeks; this suggests a departure from London the last week of Oct. 1767. (Irving carried with him a letter of introduction to Gov. Bernard dated 23 Oct.; it was endorsed as having been received 30 Jan. 1768 [see n. 8 of this chapter].) By contrast the Commissioners and some members of their staff, about twenty men altogether, had left London in mid-Sept. on board the ship *Thames* and arrived after a passage of six weeks on 4 Nov. 1767. They were greeted next day during the Bostonians' annual "Pope's Day" (Guy Fawkes Day) fête by signs pinned to twenty holiday dummies labeled "Liberty and Property and No Commissioners." [Hulton], *Letters of a Loyalist Lady*, p. 8; *Letters and Diary of John Rowe, Boston Merchant, 1759–1762, 1764–1779*, ed. Anne Rowe Cunningham (Boston, 1903), p. 145. See also the report of that day's events in [George Sackville], at London, to [John] Irwine, at Bath, 29 Dec. 1767, Germain Papers, 1683–1785, vol. 3, no. 64, fol. 136v, William L. Clements Library, University of Michigan, Ann Arbor, Mich.

18 See, e.g., Irving, at Boston, to Collector and Comptroller, at New York, 20 Jan. 1772, Customs 21/16, fols 28–29, PRO, in which he faults their carelessness. (Andrew Elliott was the Collector and Lambert Moore was the Comptroller.) Upon comparing the record of the clearance of the sloop *Sally* from the port of Philadelphia with the record of its entry in New York, Irving noted that the 28 hogsheads of rum and 2 casks of flour had been mistakenly entered as 28 hogsheads and 2 casks of flour. Irving did not imply fraud, though that may have been the case; rather he complained about a lack of due care.

19 Irving to American Board of Customs, 31 Jan. 1770, T 1/476, fols 46r–v, PRO. Very little of this material has come down to us. See Winslow Warren ["Loss of Boston Customs Records, 1776"], *Proceedings of the Massachusetts Historical Society*, XLIII (1909–1910), 423–428. Other than Customs 16/1, PRO, and the Letter-Book of the Inspectors-General, Customs 21/16, PRO, referred to above, there is not much else. Eleven miscellaneous accounts compiled in the Inspector-General's office survive as GB, Commissioners of the Customs in America, Customs Papers, 1765–1774, Massachusetts Historical Society, Boston. Three of them, nos 5, 6, and 7, are extracts from or duplicate parts of Customs 16/1, PRO. See also n. 27 of this chapter. There are also some of Irving's letters to the Collector of Customs at Philadelphia, John Swift, and some of Swift's responses, in Custom House Papers, 1750–1774, IX, fols 1084, 1101, 1102, 1104, and X, fols 1184, 1229, 1236, 1259, Custom House Papers, 1704–1789, HSP. See especially the "Directions in order to keep your books agreeable to the annex'd plan." It appears to have been an enclosure in Irving to the Collector and Comptroller of the Customs at Philadelphia, Boston, 26 Aug. 1768, Custom House Papers, IX, fols 1084, 1104, HSP. See also Alfred S. Martin, "The King's Customs: Philadelphia, 1703–1774," *W&MQ*, 3rd ser., V (Apr.

THOMAS IRVING: LOYALIST AND CIVIL SERVANT

This is not to say that his data, as compiled in the Customs 16/1 ledger or preserved elsewhere, have no defects. For instance, despite all his letters, Irving never did get the officers at Port Royal, South Carolina, to send him even one of the quarterly reports that they were supposed to prepare. But according to Irving, this was "the only delinquent port in the continent."[20] There were other problems with the shipping lists and, therefore, with the ledger.[21] Since they recorded only the legally permitted trade, goods smuggled in or out did not appear in their pages. Sugar, molasses, and rum were the major smuggled imports and the quantities of these items recorded in the ledger are only a fraction of what really entered North American markets. Some tobacco was smuggled out.[22] Irving and other Customs authorities were

1948), 201–216. There are references to Irving and his reforms in the letters from William Smibert to Thomas Moffat, "Moffat Papers."

In addition to the reasons Warren offered (above), there is another explanation for the disappearance of these records. The London Custom House fire of 1814 mentioned in nn. 12 and 72 of this chapter destroyed not only all of the records generated in London that were stored there but also any from other ports that had been returned there, such as those brought home or sent home from abroad by Customs officers. Irving did just that; he brought home from Boston many such records. See his statement, in reference to his term as Inspector-General of Imports and Exports of North America, that "the books and papers of that office are still in my possession." Testimony, 5 Apr. 1791, [GB, Parl., Commons], *Minutes of the Evidence . . . Respecting the African Slave Trade*, HC Sessional Papers to 1801, Accounts and Papers, vol. XXXIV, no. 747 (3) [Lambert 4281] ([London], 1791), p. 265. Where they were when he spoke of them and what happened to them afterwards is not known but, if he or his son and successor, William Irving, deposited them with the Customs authorities prior to 1814, then they could have been lost in the fire.

20 Irving, at Boston, to Richard Halloway, Collector at Port Royal, SC, 16 Sept., 1769, Customs 21/16, fol. 11v, PRO; James Murray, at Boston, to Collector and Comptroller at Port Royal, SC, 12 Oct. 1774, Customs 21/16, fol. 32v, PRO. (Murray was Irving's successor; he took over in 1774. See n. 57 of this chapter.) Irving, at Boston, wrote the same thing to the Benedict Calvert, Collector at Patuxent, Maryland, 7 May 1770, Customs 21/16, fol. 20, PRO.

21 There are no figures for imports into any of the colonies from Great Britain for 1768 or 1772, for instance, and the data for Philadelphia are defective.

22 For the extent of the smuggling of sugar, molasses, and rum, see John J. McCusker, *Rum and the American Revolution: The Rum Trade and the Balance of Payments of the Thirteen Continental Colonies, 1650–1775*, 2 vols (New York, 1989 [Ph.D. diss., University of Pittsburgh, 1970]), passim. Concerning tobacco, in 1770 John Williams, the Inspector-General of the Customs in North America, estimated that about 80,000 hogsheads were grown annually in Maryland and Virginia, of which only about 63,000 were legally exported. "The deficiency (being about 17,000 hogsheads) can be accounted for in no other way than that it is clandestinely carried away." Williams, at Boston, to American Board of Customs, 28 July 1770, T 1/476, fol. 259r, PRO, and as printed in Joseph R. Frese, "The Royal Customs Service in the Chesapeake, 1770: The Reports of John Williams, Inspector General," *Virginia Magazine of History and Biography*, LXXXI (July 1973), 315. Not only can one be skeptical of his estimate because of the recognized propensity of Customs officials to imagine smugglers behind every rock and tree, but also because he seems not to have allowed for any domestic consumption. In this regard, see Harper, *English Navigation Laws*, pp. 246–274 (esp. p. 262). Compare Andrews, *Colonial Period of American History*, IV, 240, n. 1: "Present-day conclusions are favorable to the idea that the colonists were not the inveterate smugglers that older writers, as well as some modern ones, have thought." See also n. 38 in chapter three of this book.

aware of these gaps, which they tried to repair and, more importantly for our purposes, for which they sought to compensate when compiling their data and basing arguments upon those compilations.[23] Modern historians, often following some of Irving's own suggestions, have continued these attempts.[24] As a result of Irving's efforts, eighteenth-century civil servants who collected and compiled the data were better able to understand the nature of their defects and thereby to correct for them. Twentieth-century scholars have been equivalently empowered.

We may well ask what it was that spurred Irving to reorganize on his own the collection and compilation of colonial trade data. He was later to do similar things as Receiver-General of the quit rents in South Carolina and, still later, on a grander scale, during a long career in London. His activity at Boston thus fitted a lifelong pattern of innovative assembly and analysis of financial and commercial information. More broadly, his behavior was characteristic of many Scots who joined the imperial civil service in the eighteenth century. Loyal, efficient, vigorous, industrious, public spirited, they worked hard at their jobs to please and impress their superiors. The reward sought and expected was advancement through the ranks to a higher position, larger salary, and greater prestige. Firm in their belief that they could serve the good of the public as well as their own through public office, many found that a term of service in the colonies moved their careers along more quickly. Yet the colonials, in North America at least, cared little for these professional administrators whose loyalties were clearly lodged in London just as the bureaucrats themselves someday expected to be. In the years after mid-century, especially in the colonial Customs service, this new type of professional civil servant came to predominate. Colonial and bureaucrat were bound to collide.[25]

23 See, e.g., Irving's testimony before the Commissioners for Trade and Plantations early in 1784, BT 5/1, PRO. There is a copy of this volume in the Liverpool Papers, Add. MS 38388, BL.

24 As one example, Irving appreciated that the colonists consistently registered their vessels at less than the full measured tonnage in order to diminish the impact of tonnage duties. He not only estimated how much the difference was, but also added it back when appropriate, in order to insure the comparability of data or the validity of an argument. See the account, dated Boston, May 11, 1771 [*sic*; 1772?], in John [Baker Holroyd], Lord Sheffield, *Observations on the Commerce of the American States*, 6th edn, enl. (London, 1784), p. 96; his testimony before the Commissioners for Trade and Plantations in 1784 in BT 5/1, p.165, PRO; and his letter to the Commissioners of the Land Revenues, London, Jan. 7, 1792, in [GB, Parl., Commons], *Journals of the House of Commons*, LXVII, 272–273, 356–357. See also John J. McCusker, "The Tonnage of Ships Engaged in British Colonial Trade during the Eighteenth Century," *Research in Economic History*, VI (1981), 73–105 – revised as chapter three of the present book.

25 For the Scots who ventured to the colonies, see Gordon Donaldson, *The Scots Overseas* (London, 1966); William R. Brock, *Scotus Americanus: A Survey of the Sources for Links between Scotland and America in the Eighteenth Century* (Edinburgh, 1982); and Alan L. Karras, *Sojourners in the Sun: Scottish Migrants in Jamaica and the Chesapeake, 1740–1800* (Ithaca, NY, [1992]). Stanley H. Palmer, *Economic Arithmetic: A Guide to the Statistical Sources of English Commerce, Industry, and Finance, 1700–1850* (New York, 1977), pp. 180, noted

THOMAS IRVING: LOYALIST AND CIVIL SERVANT

Thomas Irving's efforts soon attracted considerable attention, both in the colonies and at home. His reforms pleased the Commissioners of the American Board of Customs, who wrote to London praising his work. In March 1770 they recommended him to the Lords of the Treasury, calling him "in all respects a good officer," and suggested that his salary be increased.[26] To demonstrate his abilities, the Commissioners sent along an early version of the ledger of imports and exports. Frederick, Lord North, First Lord of the Treasury and Prime Minister, was sufficiently impressed to keep it for himself; the volume remains among his papers to this day.[27]

It was not only in London that people were becoming aware of Irving's achievements. Each of his reforms served to tighten the control of the British government over American trade. Irving, as an efficient representative of the new Customs bureaucracy in North America, was helping to shape a pattern of administrative reform that many colonists perceived as an attempt to alter or annul their traditional privileges and rights. Some of the Customs men went even further and found in the stricter enforcement of legal minutiae an opportunity to make money from fees and fines. Oliver M. Dickerson has aptly described this last practice as "Customs racketeering."[28] Yet, just as all colonial merchants were not smugglers, neither were all Customs men racketeers. Such subtleties were lost upon both sides in the inflamed atmosphere of Boston during the crisis occasioned by the Townshend Revenue Act and the subsequent non-importation movement.[29]

the prominence of Scotsmen at this time in the collection and compilation of economic statistics, "whether because of the religious training or strong morality, the strenuous work-ethic or the educational system . . ." he confesses not to be able to discern. Compare Donaldson, op cit., p. 20, on the importance and quality of local education in Scotland.

26 American Board of Customs, at Boston, to Lords of the Treasury, 9 Mar. 1770, T 1/476, fols 45r–v, PRO. The Treasury increased his salary by £50 sterling, only half the recommended raise. Warrant, 16 July 1771, T 28/1, p. 370, PRO. The American Board of Customs did allow Irving the occasional extra sum for the hire of clerks. "List of Warrants issued by the Commissioners of His Majesty's Customs in America on Account of Incidental Expenses attending the Service," 10 Oct. 1769–10 Oct. 1770, T 1/471, fols 337–338, PRO.

27 Account of the Goods Imported into North America from Great Britain and Ireland, 1769, MS North c. 83 (SC 49488), Papers of Frederick, Lord North, 2nd Earl of Guildford, North Family Papers, Bodleian Library, Department of Western Manuscripts, University of Oxford. See also the Imports and Exports of North America, 1770, MS 1030, Department of Special Collections, Joseph Regenstein Library, University of Chicago, Chicago, Illinois. Both were signed by Thomas Irving.

28 Oliver M. Dickerson, *The Navigation Acts and the American Revolution* (Philadelphia, 1951). Joseph R. Frese has shown how the attempts by the American Board of Customs to "tidy up" two areas of customhouse administration – enforcing the payments of fees both for Customs certificates and for the support of the Royal Hospital for Seamen – caused considerable annoyance. Frese, "Some Observations on the American Board of Customs Commissioners," Massachusetts Historical Society, *Proceedings*, LXXXI (1969), 3–30; "The Greenwich Hospital Tax, Continued," *Essex Institute Historical Collections*, CVI (Jan. 1970), 46–53; and "Henry Hutton and the Greenwich Hospital Tax," *American Neptune*, XXXI (July 1971), 192–216.

29 Act of 7 George III, c. 46. The most convenient and authoritative overview of these events can be found in Merrill Jensen, *The Founding of a Nation: A History of the American*

THOMAS IRVING: LOYALIST AND CIVIL SERVANT

Thomas Irving played an important if hitherto unappreciated role in the pre-Revolutionary crisis in the Thirteen Continental Colonies. A closer look at his actions shows him to have been one of the leaders in the drive by the Customs bureaucracy in Boston to discredit and destroy the non-importation movement. He may well have been motivated more by a positive regard for the laws of Parliament than by any strong negative reaction to the "patriots" of Boston. Still, his feelings about Bostonians must have been affected by the fact that they twice tried to do him bodily harm. In April 1768 and again the following June, the mob set upon him. The first time, a crowd of 200 people stoned and nearly sank a boat in which he and others had just departed from Long Wharf; the second time, again on Long Wharf, the mob attacked him, beat him, and dragged him through the streets.[30] Irving's clandestine scheme to discredit non-importation and, with it, the patriots' cause began soon thereafter and involved much of the Customs bureaucracy and loyalist Boston. The actions of Irving and his colleagues come close to being identifiable as a conspiracy, one that was supported at least after the fact by Lord North's government and that resulted in substantial rewards for the men involved, Irving included.[31]

Someone in the loyalist community in Boston hit upon the notion that the best way to disrupt non-importation was to show that the leading patriot merchants were cheating on their fellows and continuing to import goods from Great Britain. John Mein is usually given the credit for this scheme. Certainly he was the most visible participant. A Scot who came to Boston from Edinburgh in the fall of 1764, Mein and another Scot, John Fleeming, were the publishers of the *Boston Chronicle*, the largest newspaper in Boston,

Revolution, 1763–1776 (New York, 1968), pp. 334–372. See also Arthur Meier Schlesinger, *The Colonial Merchants and the American Revolution, 1763–1776*, Columbia University Studies in History, Economics and Public Law, vol. LXXVIII, no. 182 (New York, 1918), pp. 104–239.

30 Richard Reeve and Irving, at Boston, to American Board of Customs, at Boston, 18 Apr. 1768, T 1/465, fol. 72, PRO; Irving, at Boston, to American Board of Customs, 11 June 1768, T 1/465, fol. 130, PRO. There are copies of these depositions in the Liverpool Papers, Add. MS 38340, fols 214, 255, BL.

31 Isaiah Thomas, *The History of Printing in America* (1810), new edn, ed. Marcus A. McCorison (New York, 1970), p. 152, argued that a key figure, John Mein, "had unquestionably been encouraged, in Boston, as a partisan and an advocate for the measures of government." Schlesinger, *Colonial Merchants*, p. 160n., reads this as an inclination by Thomas toward "the contemporary opinion that Mein was in the pay of the government." Mein was indeed "in the pay of the government," but not directly, in the way Schlesinger's phrase would suggest. In other words, I do not think that the American Board of Customs Commissioners did anything more than take advantage of opportunities offered them to stir up trouble for the leaders of non-importation. Mein was in their pay as stationer and printer from spring 1769 and, I think, as nothing more – even if, after the fact, the Treasury did reimburse him for his costs (see n. 34 of this chapter). See John Mein, [at London], to the Lords of the Treasury, received 21 Mar. 1770, T 1/478, fol. 478r, PRO; "List of Warrants issued by the Commissioners of His Majesty's Customs in America on Account of Incidental Expenses attending the Service," 5 Apr.–10 Oct. 1771, T 1/482, fols 225–226, PRO. For what Dickerson makes of all this, see his *Navigation Acts*, p. 263, n. 81. I have been unable to trace his reference to "Mr. Irving from Scotland."

from December 1767 until its demise in June 1770. Beginning in August 1769, the *Boston Chronicle* published detailed copies of the manifests of cargoes imported by the leaders of the non-importers. John Hancock headed the list. Mein added an invective commentary upon the lives and habits of these men, only lightly screening their identities behind caustic pseudonyms. Hancock became "Johnny Dupe, a young man with long ears [and] a silly grin"; John Otis was "Counsellor Muddlehead"; and Sam Adams, "Samuel the Publican." Neither the name-calling nor the embarrassing revelations of their inconstancy was tolerated for long, and the mob was quickly unleashed upon Mein. He left town shooting – quite literally – on 17 November 1769, and was rewarded in London with a job writing propaganda for the North Ministry and a government pension.[32]

The newspaper pieces, both the cargo manifests and the satire, were soon reprinted in a book titled *A State of the Importations from Great-Britain into the Port of Boston, From the beginning of Jan. 1769 to Aug. 17th 1769* (Boston:

32 Mein's story has been told frequently. See Thomas, *History of Printing in America*, pp. 151–152; Schlesinger, Colonial Merchants, pp. 159–170; Charles M. Andrews, "The Boston Merchants and the Non-Importation Movement," *Publications of the Colonial Society of Massachusetts*, XIX (*Transactions*, 1916–1917), 227–230, 250–252; Arthur M. Schlesinger, "Propaganda and the Boston Newspaper Press, 1767–1770," *Publications of the Colonial Society of Massachusetts*, XXXII (*Transactions* 1933–1937), 411–416; John Eliot Alden, "John Mein, Publisher: An Essay in Bibliographic Detection," *Papers of the Bibliographical Society of America*, XXVI (1942), 199–214; and Alden, "John Mein: Scourge of Patriots," *Publications of the Colonial Society of Massachusetts*, XXXVI (*Transactions*, 1937–1942), 571–599. For another instance of Mein's contentiousness, see Catherine [S.] Menand, "Juries, Judges, and the Politics of Justice in Pre-Revolutionary Boston," in *The Law in America, 1607–1861*, ed. William Pencak and Wythe W. Holt, Jr. ([New York, 1989]), pp. 155–185.

Alden's second essay emphasized Mein's later career as a paid propagandist for the North ministry – he authored the "Sagittarius" letters – and ends the speculation about whether he ever returned to Boston. He did not. The chief reason for believing that Mein stayed on at, or later returned to Boston, is the continued appearance of the tracts associated with his name. Schlesinger, *Colonial Merchants*, p. 160n. See also Mein to Treasury, received 21 Mar. 1770, T 1/478, fols 478–479, PRO; "Extracts of a Letter from Mr Fleeming Printer at Boston to his Partner Mr John Mein now in London. Dated Castle William near Boston. July 1st 1770," Papers Relating to New England, vol. IV, fol. 5, Sparks Manuscripts, pt X; and John Mein, at London, to Lords of the Treasury, 1 July 1771, T 1/481, fols 62–63, PRO. Dickerson, *Navigation Acts*, p. 263, n. 81, inferred that Mein's inclusion in Lord North's list of those who received pensions (at £200 per year) was a reward for Mein's activities at Boston. The list included all those added between 1770 and 1782, however, and Mein's reward might just as easily have been for his later activities in London as for his earlier ones at Boston. *The Correspondence of King George the Third from 1760 to December 1783*, ed. John [W.] Fortescue, 6 vols (London, 1927–1928), V, 468.

The *Chronicle* ceased publication largely because, reacting to Mein's publishing of the manifests, some 700–800 subscribers canceled their orders for the newspaper. Mein to Treasury, received 21 Mar. 1770, T 1/478, fol. 478r, PRO. Among them was Nicholas Brown and Co. of Providence, RI. See Nicholas Brown and Co., at Providence, to Mein and Fleeming, at Boston, 16 Oct. 1769, Brown Papers, Correspondence-Miscellaneous, 1768–1769, John Carter Brown Library, Brown University, Providence, RI. I benefited in my understanding of Mein from a conversation with John Eliot Alden at Brown University in July 1975. I am grateful for his help.

Printed by Mein and Fleeming, 1769).[33] At least three and probably four further editions were printed in 1770. Only three of them survive in known copies, two of which are unique.[34] The 1770 editions all bore the same basic title, *A State of Importations From Great-Britain, Into the Port of Boston, From the beginning of January, 1770*; they differed only in their length. They all printed merely the cargo manifests: the first 1770 edition listed goods imported from 8 January through 5 May 1770; the second added an account of goods re-exported after January 1769; and the third added further manifests from the period 24 May through 29 June 1770.[35] There seems also to have been a fourth 1770 edition, judging from a reference to it in the *New-York Gazette and the Weekly Mercury* for 15 October 1770. The writer spoke of having "received [it] from the same authority"; it listed entries inward for 7 July through 14 August; there is no known extant copy of this edition. The three 1770 editions of which we have copies all used the same typeface as the 1769 edition, indicating that John Fleeming had continued to have a hand in publishing them after Mein had fled for his life.[36] But, as we might

33 John Mein signed the foreword. This is entry number 71 in Thomas R. Adams, *American Independence, the Growth of an Idea: A Bibliographic Study of the American Political Pamphlets Printed between 1764 and 1776 Dealing with the Dispute between Great Britain and Her Colonies* (Providence, RI, 1965), p. 54. The tract appears to have been published on 20 Nov. 1769. *Boston Chronicle*, 20 Nov. 1769. But see Cunningham, *Letters and Diaries of John Rowe*, p. 194. Mein stated that he "printed upwards of 4000 sheets of the principal importations and circulated them, gratis, over all America, from Florida to Nova Scotia; besides printing 500 copies of the whole, in a quarto pamphlet, one half of which he has, already, given away." Mein to Treasury, received 21 Mar. 1770, T 1/478, fol. 478v, PRO. There seem to be no surviving copies of the "4000 sheets," presumably a broadside printing of just the cargo manifests. Adams found only 9 copies of the tract in the 30 libraries he surveyed. Andrews, "Boston Merchants," p. 228n., appears to have seen a copy of the booklet "with an appendix of importations to January 1, 1770." Such an appendix was indeed advertised in the *Boston Chronicle* as forthcoming over about a ten-week period beginning 11 Dec. 1769, but there are no known copies. The copy of the pamphlet in Houghton Library (*AC7.M4771.769s), Harvard University, has this appendix, not printed, however, but handwritten.

34 Adams, *American Independence*, p. 64. The American Board of Customs paid Mein £28 14s. 3rd. (£28.71) "for paper and printing a state of the Importations for 1770 and Postage of Letters." T 1/482, fol. 225r, PRO.

35 For the complete titles and fuller bibliographical details, see entries 83a, 83b, and 83c in Adams, *American Independence*, p. 64. Compare entry number 11744 in Charles Evans, *American Bibliography: A Chronological Dictionary of all Books, Pamphlets and Periodical Publications Printed in the United States of America, 1639–1800*, 14 vols (Chicago, New York, and Worcester, Mass., 1903–1959), VI, 240. Evans's title appears to be a confused composite of the titles of the three 1770 editions. He added without attribution: "One hundred fifty copies of this pamphlet [*sic*] was distributed in Philadelphia." The *Pennsylvania Journal, and the Weekly Advertiser* (Philadelphia), June 28, 1770, reported the same information. The version referred to was probably the first 1770 edition which, given an appearance at Philadelphia late in June, was probably published at Boston in late May. The second 1770 edition seems to have been published on June 29 or 30 (see n. 36 of this chapter). Extracts from the third 1770 edition were printed in the *New-York Gazette and the Weekly Mercury*, 27 Aug. 1770, arguing for a publication date late in July or early in Aug.

36 Adams, *American Independence*, p. 64. On Sunday, 1 July 1770, Fleeming wrote to Mein (in London) telling him that the mob was so furious over the appearance of the latest

expect, the publisher's name did not appear on the title page, nor is there any claim to authorship anywhere in any of them, first to last.

The 1769 edition is commonly ascribed to Mein; for the others there is no acknowledged author. Mein was thought to have had some aid with his pieces of invective; it is certain that someone in the customhouse helped him out with the basic information.[37] Since there were apparently four more editions published after Mein left the country, someone else continued the project, perhaps his original collaborator. And since these later editions published cargo manifests, that collaborator must have had continued access to the Customs records. In fact, it seems likely that it was this individual who originated the whole scheme, since only someone familiar with the Customs records in the first place could have known that there was cheating going on. All such records passed through Thomas Irving's office as a matter of course.

One contemporary actually accused Irving of complicity in the affair. On 24 August 1769, soon after Mein began publishing the cargo manifests, John Hancock's store manager, William Palfrey, tried to defend his employer in a letter in the *Massachusetts Gazette.* Not only were reports of Hancock's importing forbidden goods spurious, he charged, but they were being "industriously propagated by the Inspector of Exports and Imports and his emissaries." In what can only have been a charade staged to mislead the Sons of Liberty, Irving sought to protect his innocence by berating the *Gazette*'s printer, Richard Draper, for publishing Palfrey's letter. Draper, a good Loyalist himself, played his part by then swearing the peace against Irving.

> When Irving made his appearance before the justices a vast number of the true sons collected themselves who when he came out of the [court] house, his'd laughed shouted and gave three huzzas to the hero, who had the resolution to attack a poor sick disabled printer.[38]

edition (probably the second 1770 edition) that the day before he had fled for safety to Castle William in Boston harbor. Fleeming to Mein, 1 July 1770, Papers Relating to New England, vol. IV, fol. 5, Sparks Manuscripts, pt X. See also Mein to Treasury, 1 July 1771, T 1/481, fol. 62v, PRO. The first 1770 edition, said the *Pennsylvania Journal, and the Weekly Advertiser* (Philadelphia), 28 June 1770, "is the work of the detestable Board of Commissioners [because] it is plain [that] it is printed by Mein and Fle[e]ming, their printers in Boston."

37 Schlesinger, "Propaganda and the Boston Newspaper Press," p. 415n., repeated allegations that "Mein was aided in his editorial labors by Samuel Waterhouse, a customs officer, and Joseph Green, a Boston wit of repute. He may also have had other helpers . . . [including] William Burch, one of the customs commissioners. . . ." The last was based on a statement implicating Burch in *Boston-Gazette, and Country Journal,* 11 Sept. 1769. See also *Boston Chronicle,* 1 June 1769.

38 Nathaniel Coffin, at Boston, to Charles Steuart, 11 Sept. 1769, Steuart Papers, MS 5025, fols 185–186, National Library of Scotland. For Draper, see Thomas, *History of Printing in America,* esp. pp. 143–145, 228–231. For Coffin, see the discussion of him earlier in this chapter. For the court case, see Menand, "Juries, Judges, and the Politics of Justice," p. 180, n. 8, and her reference to the case papers among the records of the Inferior Court of Common Pleas, Suffolk, in the Judicial Archives, Archives of the Commonwealth of

THOMAS IRVING: LOYALIST AND CIVIL SERVANT

Although the ruse seems to have diverted the mob's attention from Irving, we now know that Palfrey was right. Irving was the originator of the scheme, the author of the first tract, with or without any help, and the sole author of the four subsequent editions. We have this on the best authority: Irving himself and a colleague at Boston in the customhouse. Joseph Harrison, the Collector of Customs of the Port of Boston, wrote Grey Cooper at the Treasury in 1770 giving Irving full credit for the whole affair. While "Mr. Mein (as the publisher) is highly deserving of the favour and protection of government" because of his part in the publication, Irving was the one behind it all.

> . . . as I was knowing to the forming of this plan of communicat[in]g to the public the true state of the Boston import[atio]ns I think it a piece of justice due to an absent person to inform you, and to desire the same may be communicated to my Lord North, that another gentleman Mr. Tho[ma]s Irving Inspector Gen[era]l of the Imports and Exports of America and Register of Shipping had *the prin[cipa]l hand in projecting and executing that useful plan* he being the person who with much labour and industry collected from the cocketts all the articles imported from Great Britain and by means of the entries at the Custom House *formed and digested a state of those accounts in a pamph[le]t* which he distributed at a very great risk over the Continent.[39]

Later, in 1779, Irving said the same things himself in a letter to the Secretary of State for the Colonies, Lord George Germain, and still later, in 1786, in a petition to the Loyalist Claims Commission, though by then this had become only one of many accomplishments in a long career. His 1786 statement that while at Boston he "undertook and at the hazard of his life executed a publication formed chiefly from the books of the customs" is sufficiently obscure to have passed unnoticed even in an era of increased interest in the Loyalists and their papers.[40]

The activities of Irving – and probably others – did not stop with Mein's flight nor did their antagonists retire quietly from the field. The efforts of the patriot party to maintain non-importation intensified in the fall of 1769

Massachusetts, State Archives Facility, Boston. The plaintiff was Thomas Irving and not "John Erving."

39 Emphasis added. Harrison, [at London?], to Cooper, at London, [1770], AO 12/51, fols 160v–161r, PRO, and AO 13/130, fol. 34v, PRO. Harrison sent Irving a copy of his letter in 1783 at which time he said that he had written it to Cooper "to inform him of the prin[cipa]l share you had in that publication." Harrison to Irving, 7 Nov. 1783, AO 12/51, fol. 160v, PRO.

40 Irving's memorial, Mar. 1786, AO 12/51, fol. 153r, PRO. The statement in Irving to Germain, London, 12 Aug. 1779, CO 5/176, fols 46–47, PRO, was more explicit:

> The nature of my office furnishing me with the best information on the subject, I made out a state of the imports &c into the different provinces which I caused to be secretly printed in a pamphlet, and distributed over the whole continent. This pamphlet by exposing the duplicity of the Bostonians, created a suspicion in the southern and middle provinces and soon broke up the whole scheme.

and the following winter and spring. But Boston could not hold the wall alone. Just as the Boston merchants had worked to secure New York City's and Philadelphia's cooperation in the non-importation movement, so did Irving seek to undermine it. As Inspector-General of Imports and Exports, he was in regular communication with Customs officials at both places. In letters to John Swift, the Collector at Philadelphia, he argued that the Boston non-importers were continuing to import considerable quantities of goods.[41] He also sent Swift copies of the various booklets to distribute there.[42] Two key communications discussed in the New York City press probably came from Irving.[43] It seems highly likely that he wrote to other places, too.

These letters and booklets had their effect. New York fell out first, early in June 1770. Arthur Schlesinger, Sr, has called attention to the impact of the "timely pamphlet" – Irving's second 1770 edition – on the vote taken there. Philadelphia broke next, in September, and the Boston merchants thereupon caved in as well. A meeting in Boston on 12 October 1770 ended non-importation. Though we would be wrong to attribute the outcome entirely to Irving, his demonstrations of the duplicity of leading Boston merchants did much to play upon the fears and jealousies of other merchants there and in the other Thirteen Continental Colonies. The cracks in the patriots' wall were not of his making, but Irving's paper wedges did split them wider and helped to bring it down.[44]

His contemporaries certainly believed that Thomas Irving deserved credit for ending non-importation. Joseph Harrison later wrote that he felt that "the principle share" Irving had "in that publication . . . which in a great measure rendered abortive the intentions of the famous non-importation agreements."[45] In his earlier letter of 1770, he had told Grey Cooper that Irving's "publications respecting the importation at Boston were undoubtedly the occasion of disuniting the colonies."[46] If some Bostonians would have had their rebellion in 1770, and Irving helped to stop them, he had a hand in delaying the American Revolution.

41 See especially Irving, at Boston, to Swift, 5 June 1770, Custom House Papers, X, 1256-a, HSP.

42 Irving to Swift, 5 June 1770, ibid.; *Pennsylvania Journal and the Weekly Advertiser*, 28 June 1770. The "pamphlets are said to be brought here by one—M'D—n—d, third clerk of the board." The man seems to have been Thomas MacDonogh of New Hampshire who was the third clerk to the American Board of Customs. I am indebted to Joseph R. Frese for this identification.

43 *New-York Gazette and the Weekly Mercury*, 27 Aug., 15 Oct. 1770.

44 Schlesinger, *Colonial Merchants*, p. 225. Jensen, *Founding of a Nation*, pp. 362, 372, joins numerous others in ascribing the loss of Boston's leadership role to the confirmation of "the suspicion long held in other colonies that Bostonians were cheats and canting hypocrites" and the ending of non-importation to "the widespread conviction that the Bostonians were cheaters." Irving was the one who confirmed that suspicion and established that conviction. Even though his role has heretofore not been appreciated, it is Irving, not Mein, to whom is due whatever recognition those actions earned.

45 Harrison to Irving, 7 Nov. 1783, AO 12/51, fol. 160v, PRO.

46 Harrison to Cooper, [1770], AO 12/51, fol. 160v, PRO.

THOMAS IRVING: LOYALIST AND CIVIL SERVANT

Irving's actions, however unrecognized by historians, did not go unrewarded by the North government. Although Irving continued at Boston for another year, his situation there grew increasingly precarious. He felt his life to be in danger.[47] By November 1771 he had determined to go home and was in the process of leaving Boston.[48] On 10 January 1772, the Treasury granted him a six months' leave of absence with salary, a leave later extended through the following eighteen months.[49] His next employment did not begin until January 1774.[50] In recognition of his efforts in Boston, he was appointed Receiver-General of the Quit Rents of South Carolina.[51]

While in London, Irving, ever the organizer, argued that imperial revenues could be increased if land rents were more efficiently collected in those colonies where they were due.[52] The key to such a plan was an accurate and

47 Irving's memorial, Mar. 1786, AO 12/51, fol. 153r, PRO.

48 Irving appointed William Barrell to act as his deputy while he was away. Charter 3887, [Boston], 13 Nov. 1771, Steuart Papers, National Library of Scotland. William Smibert wrote Thomas Moffat from Boston on 11 Nov. 1771, that Irving "is hastening for embarkation in a very short time – a week – I shall miss him much as a warm hearted friend." "Moffat Papers." Nathaniel Coffin wrote from Boston to Charles Steuart in London, 20 Nov. 1771, that "you'l receive this by my worthy friend Mr. Irving . . . as Irving is going home." Steuart Papers, MS 5027, fols 57r, 58r. The letters in the "Moffat Papers" further reveal that Irving had arrived in London by 3 Mar. 1772, when he wrote Smibert that a spate of poor health ("rheumatic fever, which threatened his lungs, but turned to diarrhea and inflammation of his bowels that had well nigh finished him," Smibert to Moffat, 8 Apr. 1772) had forced him to go to Scotland (Smibert to Moffat, 23 Nov. 1772); to Gribton, one imagines. Irving was indeed staying at Gribton again in 1773 for he conducted some family business at that time; his father was to die there the next year. Maxwell-Irving, "Irvings of Dumfries," pp. 52, 72. Later in 1773 he returned to London; he appeared before the Treasury Board at their meeting on 10 Dec. 1773, T 29/43, fol. 119v, PRO.

49 Warrants, 10 Jan. 1772, 5 Aug. 1772, T 28/1, pp. 309, 380, PRO.

50 Smibert wrote Moffat on 23 Aug. 1773, presumably having had another letter from Irving, that he "is still unsuccessful in his application for an encreas'd salary or further promotion, and it is thought [he] will return to us. It is a pity his merit is not sufficiently known and rewarded." "Moffat Papers."

51 Irving later wrote to the Loyalist Claims Commission that upon his return home "Lord North [had expressed] . . . to his friends his approbat[io]n of his conduct and his wish to provide for him in some other part of the world" and that "his appointment to the office of Receiver General of South Carolina . . . was meant by [the North] administration as a reward for his services." Irving's memorial, Mar. 1786, AO 12/51, fols 153r, 156v, PRO.

52 Irving's case, 27 May and 1 June 1783, AO 12/99, fol. 282r, PRO; and Irving's supplementary memorial, 9 Oct. 1787, AO 12/51, fol. 158r, PRO. In the latter he claimed that the idea had been given him by one of the joint secretaries to the Treasury (perhaps Grey Cooper). The quit rents of South Carolina were particularly known to be in need of reform. See Robert K. Ackerman, *South Carolina Land Policies* (Columbia, SC, 1977); Alan D. Watson, "The Quitrent System in Royal South Carolina" (Ph.D. dissertation, University of South Carolina, 1971); and Watson, "Placemen in South Carolina: The Receiver Generals [*sic*] of the Quitrents," *South Carolina Historical Magazine*, LXXIV (Jan. 1973), 18–30. See also Beverley W. Bond, Jr, *The Quit-Rent System in the American Colonies* (New Haven, Conn., 1919).

For rumors of Irving's appointment to various other posts during this period, see *Virginia Gazette* (Williamsburg), ed. William Rind, 12 Dec. 1772, and *Virginia Gazette* (Williamsburg), ed. Purdie and Dixon, 20 May 1773. He is also at this time supposed

complete rent roll. Irving drew up a detailed manual incorporating his plan and presented it to government where it was well received. Promised the next available position as Receiver-General, he preferred to hurry the process a bit by buying his office from an incumbent, George Saxby, Receiver-General of South Carolina, for a one-time payment of £500 sterling and an annuity of £40 sterling.[53] On 1 February 1774, Irving received the usual appointment allowing him £70 sterling per year for expenses and 10 percent of all moneys collected.[54] The office was considered to be worth £500 sterling a year.[55] The Earl of Dartmouth, the Secretary of State for the Colonies, also named him to the council in South Carolina.[56] It was only then that Irving resigned

to have requested an exchange of posts with Charles Burdett, Collector of the Customs at St Augustine, East Florida, after 1767. Maxwell-Irving, "Irvings of Dumfries," p. 72. For Burdett, see Charles Loch Mowat, *East Florida as a British Province, 1763–1784*, University of California, Publications in History, vol. XXXII (Berkeley and Los Angeles, Calif., 1943), pp. 44, 163, 165. Burdett, at Gude Tulford, near York, recounted his experiences in the colonies in a memorial to Charles Watson-Wentworth, Marquis of Rockingham, the Prime Minister, 5 Apr. 1782, T 1/571, no. 268, PRO.

53 Irving's supplementary memorial, 9 Oct. 1787, AO 12/51, fols 158r–v PRO. Irving did not pay Saxby immediately but instead gave him an interest-bearing note; he attached to the memorial mentioned above an account of his payments against the note through Aug. 1787 (ibid., fol. 158v). As of 12 Sept. 1788 he was still paying the annuity to Mrs Saxby, whom he estimated then to be 58 or 60 years old. Irving's evidence of that date, AO 12/51, fols 164r–v, PRO. George Saxby was Receiver-General from 1742 to 1774; he had gone back home to London in 1772 because of ill health but he must have recovered somewhat for he was still alive in Jan. 1784. Ackerman, *South Carolina Land Policies*, pp. 112–113; Watson, "Quitrent System in Royal South Carolina," pp. 45–59 and passim; Irving's supplementary memorial, 9 Oct. 1787, AO 12/51, fol. 158v, PRO; Irving's evidence, 10 Oct. 1787, AO 12/51, fol. 163r, PRO.

54 Warrants, 1 Feb. and 2 Feb. 1774, T 28/1, pp. 235–236, 237, PRO; Irving's memorial, Mar. 1786, AO 12/51, fols 153r–v, PRO; Irving's evidence, 10 Oct. 1787, AO 12/51, fol. 162v, PRO. The warrant of 2 Feb. 1774 allowed him £70 for the hire of deputies, even though he later referred to it as salary.

55 In testimony on 10 Oct. 1787 Irving stated that "the office yielded to his predecessor [George Saxby] about £500 per annum." AO 12/51, fol. 163r, PRO. Compare the returns for the period 1735–1774 in Bond, *Quit-Rent System*, p. 346, n. 1. See also Saxby's account for the period 26 Mar. 1766–25 Mar. 1773, in T 1/504, fol. 36–37, PRO. "By a certif[icat]e from Mr Saxby the late Receiver General dated 23rd January 1784, whereby and by the rec[eip]t of the Dep[ut]y Auditor it appears that the p[er]centage from 26 March 1772, to 26 March 1783, amounted to £411 sterling which added to the salary w[oul]d make the emoluments to £480 per annum": so testified Irving, AO 12/51, fol. 163r, PRO. Compare Watson, "Quitrent System in Royal South Carolina," pp. 57–59.

Irving, at London, petitioned the Treasury, 22 Feb. 1774, to be allowed to make bond in Great Britain, as had been customary, rather than in the colony, as the Treasury was trying to institute. T 1/511, fol. 200, PRO. His petition was allowed. The bond of his predecessor, George Saxby, in 1742, had amounted to £2,000 sterling. Watson, "Quitrent System in Royal South Carolina," p. 70 and n. 6.

56 Commissioners for Trade and Plantations, meeting of 14 Feb. 1774, CO 391/81, fol. 10v, PRO; Commissioners for Trade and Plantations to Crown, Whitehall, 21 Feb. 1774, CO 5/381, fols 383–384v, PRO; Lt. Gov. William Bull to Sec. of State, 1 Aug. 1774, CO 5/396, fols 46–47v, PRO; Irving's memorial, Mar. 1786, AO 12/51, fols 153r–v, PRO. As a member of the Council, Irving was also a member of the Court of Chancery. *Records of the Court of Chancery of South Carolina, 1671–1779*, ed. Anne King Gregorie, American Legal Records, VI (Washington, DC, 1950), 624, 625, and elsewhere.

the office of Inspector-General.[57] It was also only then, in the early spring of that year, in his mid-thirties, secure in his new position, that he and Marion Corbet were married. The new Receiver-General of South Carolina and his wife quickly set out for Charleston, arriving there in mid-July. He was soon established in an office in Orange Street close to the center of town.[58]

Irving's year in South Carolina was not fruitful – or so he later claimed. He spent almost his entire tenure as Receiver-General trying to repair defects in the collection of the quit rents, and he struggled to prepare a new tax roll for that purpose. Before he had finished, the Revolution had taken hold and he could not profit from his labors. He made himself so unpopular among the patriot party, especially for his support of the Governor in the Drayton affair, that, for his health, "he was advized to try the sea air." Irving betook himself to the Bahama Islands and, as a consequence, began an odyssey unparalleled in the history of the American Revolution.[59]

Irving's luck had run out. In March 1776, in its first fleet engagement, the new navy of the newly United States attacked and captured the forts and town of Nassau, the capital of the Bahamas. The American forces stormed ashore on Sunday, 3 March; by early the next morning, after a bloodless battle, they were in complete control. Within two weeks they had ransacked the place of all military stores, but thanks to the ineptness of their commander, Esek Hopkins, they lost what they had come for – gunpowder

57 Irving's supplementary memorial, 9 Oct. 1787, AO 12/51, fol. 158v, PRO. James Murray replaced him. *Virginia Gazette* (Williamsburg), ed. Purdie and Dixon, 13 Oct. 1774, dateline Boston, 22 Sept.; *Georgia Gazette* (Savannah), 2 Nov. 1774, dateline Boston, 22 Sept. For Murray – whose papers are in the Massachusetts Historical Society – see *Letters of James Murray, Loyalist*, ed. Nina Moore Tiffany and Susan I. Lesley (Boston, 1901). Charles Steuart managed Murray's affairs for him in London during the war (ibid., p. 265, n. 1) just as he seems to have done Irving's.

58 *Georgia Gazette* (Savannah), 10 Aug. 1774, dateline Charleston, 22 July; *South Carolina Gazette* (Charleston), 17 Sept. 1774.

59 For his time in South Carolina prior to the Revolutionary War, see his memorial, Mar. 1786, AO 12/51, fols 153v–155r, PRO (quotation, fol. 155r); Watson, "Quitrent System in Royal South Carolina," pp. 60–61, 88–89, 205; Watson, "Placemen in South Carolina," pp. 27–30. For the Drayton affair and its aftermath, see the evidence of Thomas Knox Gordon, former Chief Justice of South Carolina, 10 Oct. 1787, AO 12/51, fols 163r–v, PRO. It was Gordon who described Irving as "a most active and zealous servant of the Crown." John Drayton, *Memoirs of the American Revolution, from Its Commencement to the Year 1776, Inclusive; as Relating to the State of South-Carolina* (Charleston, 1821), II, esp. 17; and William M. Dabney and Marion Dargan, *William Henry Drayton and American Revolution* (Albuquerque, NM, 1962), pp. 40–64. Earlier in the year Irving's acquaintance Charles Burdett had fled from St Augustine to New Providence. See Burdett to Rockingham, Apr. 5, 1782, T 1/571, no. 268. Daniel Chamier, Jr, another friend of Irving's who had fled from Charleston to Florida before Irving decamped, later wrote to his father in Boston to say that Irving had since gone to "Providence Island, for recovery from a bilious complaint, and he will remain there for some time if he is wise." Chamier to Chamier, St Augustine, 3–4 Oct. 1775, Intercepted Letters, 1775–1781, vol. I, p. 245, Records of the Continental and Confederation Congresses and the Constitutional Convention, 1765–1821, Record Group 360, National Archives, Washington, DC.

for George Washington's army. Governor Montfort Browne of the Bahamas had managed to send it all away to St Augustine, East Florida, because Hopkins had failed to press his advantage and to blockade the port. Hopkins, out of spite, carried away three important prisoners: Governor Browne; Browne's secretary; and, as luck would have it, Thomas Irving, Receiver-General and member of the Council of South Carolina. Someone among Hopkins' forces had recognized Irving or his name and reported him to Hopkins as "a dangerous person."[60]

Irving's trials did not end until two years later. Hopkins carried him to Connecticut on board the flagship *Alfred*. In Connecticut, Irving remained a prisoner until late 1776, despite his pleas to Governor Jonathan Trumbull, his letters to the Continental Congress, the intercession of both William Campbell, the former Governor of South Carolina, and of General William Howe, and even an arrangement for an exchange of prisoners that had General Washington's personal approval.[61] Finally granted a parole, Irving was freed by the Continental Congress in January 1777 and soon thereafter rejoined his family in South Carolina.[62] He had been home only a short

60 Irving's memorial, Mar. 1786, AO 12/51, fols 155r–v, PRO (quotation, fol. 155r). See also John J. McCusker, "The American Invasion of Nassau in the Bahamas," *American Neptune*, XXV (July 1965), 189–217 – revised as chapter twelve of the present book – and McCusker, *"Alfred": The First Continental Flagship, 1775–1778*, Smithsonian Studies in History and Technology, no. 20 (Washington, DC, 1973). It is within the realm of the possible that among those who recognized Irving, one was John Paul Jones, then serving as First Lieutenant on board *Alfred*. Whether he knew Thomas Irving or not, Jones must surely have known Thomas's younger brother, Joseph Irving of Borran.

61 Irving's memorial, Mar. 1786, AO 12/51, fols 155r–v, PRO; Washington, at "Head Quarters," to Col. Samuel John Atlee, at New York, 25 Nov. 1776, AO 13/130, fol. 42r, PRO, and as printed in *The Writings of George Washington*, ed. John C. Fitzpatrick (Washington, DC, 1931–1944), VI, 297n.; Campbell to Howe, 29 Nov. 1777, AO 12/51, fol. 161r–v, PRO. Irving and the two other prisoners were taken first to New London, Conn., where the fleet anchored on 8 Apr. 1776 They were paroled for twelve months on 12 Apr. with the provision that they agree "peaceably to abide within the limits" of the town of Windham, Conn., whence they were taken under escort on 18 Apr. *Connecticut Gazette* (New London), 12, 19 Apr. 1776; parole, dated 12 Apr. 1776, Revolutionary I Series, 1763–1789, V, fols 430, 432a, Connecticut Archives, 1636–1820, Connecticut State Library, Hartford; minutes of Connecticut Council of Safety, 15 Apr. 1776, [Connecticut (Colony)], *The Public Records of the Colony of Connecticut*, ed. James Hammond Trumbull and Charles Jeremy Hoadly, 15 vols (Hartford, Conn., 1850–1890), XV, 261–263. On 8 May 1776, the Continental Congress established a committee of seven members "to consider the situation" of the prisoners. [US, Continental Congress], *Journals of the Continental Congress, 1774–1789*, ed. Worthington Chauncey Ford *et al.*, 34 vols (Washington, DC, 1904–1937), IV, 334. Gov. Browne, with whom Irving was initially imprisoned, wrote later that, "I was sent to Norwich, Lebanon, Windham, and Hartford in Connecticut, and Lastly to Middletown where I did not experience the same hard usage I did at first, and at which place I remain'd till I was a few days ago exchanged." Browne, at New York, to George Germain, 5 Nov. 1776, CO 23/23, fols 107–109, PRO, and as printed in Malcolm Lloyd, Jr, "The Taking of the Bahamas by the Continental Navy in 1776," *Pennsylvania Magazine of History and Biography*, XLIX (Oct. 1925), 349–366.

62 *American Archives: ... a Documentary History of ... the North American Colonies; of ... the American Revolution; and of the Constitution of the Government of the United States*

while, however, when he was caught up by the "Test Act" there and made a refugee once again.[63] Forced to fly under pain of death, he and his family took the first available vessel from Charleston to Europe, a small sloop bound for Spain. But this sloop was captured by a ship of the Royal Navy, HMS *Brune*, and taken to St Augustine, from where Irving and his family had to make their way to New York, then in British hands. He became ill, again, at New York and he and his family did not get to London until June or early July 1778.[64]

Upon his return to England, the government came forward again to support him. A Treasury pension or allowance of £200 sterling per year was granted him, retroactive to 5 January 1778.[65] When the decision was made to reinstate the government in South Carolina after the capture of Charleston by Henry Clinton, Irving was ordered to return. From his arrival in mid-1781 until the time of the final evacuation in December 1782, he was active not only as Receiver-General but also as a member of the important Board of Police, Charleston's *de facto* civilian government during the British occupation.[66]

. . ., ed. Peter Force, 9 vols ([Washington, DC, 1837–1853]), 4th ser., V, 867, 5th ser., III, 619, 791–792, 838, 899; [US, Continental Congress], *Journals of the Continental Congress, 1774–1789*, ed. Worthington Chauncey Ford *et al.*, 34 vols (Washington, DC, 1904–1937), VII, 9; *Letters of Delegates to Congress, 1774–1789*, ed. Paul H. Smith, in progress (Washington, DC, 1976 to date), V, 687–690.

63 The 13 Feb. 1777 "Ordinance for establishing an Oath of Abjuration and Allegience" required that "all the late officers of the King" swear the oath or "within sixty days . . . be sent off from this state" to Europe or the West Indies. The state was to bear the cost. [South Carolina, Laws and Statutes], *The Statutes at Large of South Carolina*, ed. Thomas Cooper and David J. McCord, 10 vols (Columbia, 1836–1841), I, 135–136. In the late winter and early spring of 1777 committees visited suspected Loyalists to administer the oath; those who refused were banished. See *The Papers of Henry Laurens*, ed. Philip M. Hamer *et al.*, in progress (Columbia, SC, 1968 to date), XI, passim (e.g., p. 213 nn.). See also the similar stories of Thomas's brother Alexander and brother-in-law Archibald Baird (see nn. 8 and 10 of this chapter).

64 Irving's memorial, Mar. 1786, AO 12/51, fols 155r–v, PRO. For the log books of HMS *Brune*, 32 guns, Capt. James Ferguson, see Captains' Logs, Adm. 51/117, PRO, and Masters' Logs, Adm. 52/1619–1620, PRO.

65 Treasury Board, meeting of 5 Aug. 1778, T 29/47, fol. 150v, PRO; Irving to Germain, 12 Aug. 1779, CO 5/176, fols 46–47, PRO. See also Thomas Irving to Treasury, 24 Oct. 1780, Germain Papers, vol. 13, Clements Library; the copy in T 1/400, no. 180, PRO, is endorsed as having been read on 16 Nov. 1780. For the Treasury's reaction, see the minutes of the Board meeting, 16 Nov. 1780, T 29/49, fols 218v–219r, PRO. Irving estimated that between "the end of April 1775 when the collection of the Crown revenues ceased [in South Carolina] until his return to England in the year 1778," his expenses amounted to £1,500 sterling; his income was nil during the same period. Irving's memorial, Mar. 1786, AO 12/51, fol. 155v, PRO. Irving's old friend Charles Steuart drew on his personal account at Messrs Thomas Coutts and Co. for the sum of £75 on 12 Aug. 1778, in Irving's favor. Steuart Papers, MS 5037, fol. 39, National Library of Scotland. The allowance from the Treasury stopped in July 1780 upon his recall to South Carolina. Irving's case, May–June 1783, AO 12/99, fol. 282r, PRO. See also Sec. of State to Lt Gov. Bull, Whitehall, 6 July 1780, CO 5/408, p. 147, PRO.

66 For Irving's return to South Carolina, see George Germain, at Whitehall, to Irving, [17 July 1779], AO 12/51, fol. 161v, PRO, and as extracted in Irving, at Charleston, to Lt

THOMAS IRVING: LOYALIST AND CIVIL SERVANT

We know little of Irving's activities during the first three years after his return to London in 1783. Again he had not been well in South Carolina,[67] a complaint we hear more frequently as he grew older, and perhaps illness helps to explain this gap in our knowledge of his life. Later, in the 1790s, he mentioned that he had spent some time in the past traveling on the Continent, a trip that might have occurred in these years, perhaps in 1785. He petitioned the Loyalist Claims Commission in May and June 1783 and then again in March 1786 and October 1787; he could easily have devoted a considerable portion of his time over these months to preparing such petitions and gathering the necessary supporting materials.[68]

Gen. Alexander Leslie, 31 Jan. 1782, PRO 30/55/35, no. 4092, PRO. This and items cited subsequently from this collection are part of the Sir Guy Carleton: British Army Headquarters Papers, 1747–1783, PRO 30/55, PRO. There are photostats of these papers in the Colonial Williamsburg Foundation Library, Williamsburg, Va., and the Manuscript and Archives Division, New York Public Library, New York City; transcripts in the Public Archives of Canada, Ottawa; and microfilms in the Manuscript Division, LC. See also Thomas De Grey, at London, to Irving, 30 July 1779, AO 12/51, fol. 162r, PRO; Grey Cooper to Irving, [1779?], AO 12/51, fol. 162r, PRO; and Treasury Board, meeting of 4 Aug. 1779, T 29/48, fol. 209v, PRO. Irving, and, apparently, most of the rest of the civil officers took two years to get to South Carolina; they came out together in a fleet that first stopped at Virginia. *Royal Georgia Gazette* (Savannah), 14 June 1781, dateline Charleston, 6 June. Once in South Carolina, Irving spent a good bit of his time trying to secure from the military authorities the right to some of the revenues that they had begun to collect for their own purposes in lieu of any civil government. See the series of letters in the Carleton/Headquarters Papers, PRO 30/55/34, nos 3928, 3929, PRO; PRO 30/55/35, nos 4091, 4092, 4098, 4101, PRO; PRO 30/55/37, nos 4248, 4249, 4250, PRO. Copies of some of these appear in T 1/571, nos 316–327, PRO, and in CO 5/105, fols 13–40, PRO. The records of the Board of Police are in CO 5/513–526, PRO. See George Smith McCowen, Jr, *The British Occupation of Charleston, 1780–82* (Columbia, SC, 1972), pp. 13–42. Irving's own summation of the events of the period can be found in his case, May–June 1783, AO 12/99, fol. 282r, PRO; and in his memorial, Mar. 1786, AO 12/51, fols 155v–156r, PRO. See also Mary Beth Norton, *The British-Americans: The Loyalist Exiles in England, 1774–1789* (Boston, 1972), pp. 109–111; Watson, "Quitrent System in Royal South Carolina," pp. 62–64.

67 Irving, at Charleston, to Steuart, at London, 20 Dec. 1781, Steuart Papers, MS 5040, fols 223–224, National Library of Scotland. He had been sick in bed on and off from 22 June until 2 Oct.

68 For the European trip, see the discussion later in this chapter. The first claim to the Loyalist Claims Commission resulted in the award of an allowance of £100 per year. AO 12/99, fols 282r–283v, PRO.

Burke, *Landed Gentry*, ed. Townend, 18th edn, II, 338, reports that Irving was "King's Agent for W. Florida, 1772 . . . King's Agent for Florida 1774, Gov. of Leeward (or Windward) Islands ca. 1780 . . ." See also Irving, *The Irvings*, p. 86; and Maxwell-Irving, "Irvings of Dumfries," p. 72. My own researches confirm none of this. The standard authorities not only fail to indicate that Irving held any of these offices but also show other people in the offices at the stated times. See Cecil Johnson, *British West Florida, 1763–1783* (New Haven, Conn., 1943), p. 98n; Mowat, *East Florida*, p. 34; David P. Henige, *Colonial Governors from the Fifteenth Century to the Present: A Comprehensive List* (Madison, Wis., 1970). Most importantly, Irving himself made no mention of ever having held any of those positions in his presentations to the Loyalist Claims Commission; he was under an obligation to do so because he was supposed to show all of the sources of his income during the times for which he was making a claim for compensation. The Commission checked on such matters and the claimants knew it.

THOMAS IRVING: LOYALIST AND CIVIL SERVANT

In the same period we can identify Irving's endeavors in the successful campaign to keep the commerce of the British Empire closed to the United States. After the ending of the Revolutionary War, many on both sides hoped that the Americans could continue to trade in the same old ways with Great Britain and its colonies, especially with the West Indies. Yet strong arguments against such a breach in the principles of mercantilism prevailed and a series of Orders in Council promulgated in July 1783 and afterwards forbade American merchants a role in the British West Indian trade. Discussions continued, however, and arguments were heard on both sides. The most effective public tract in defense of the Orders in Council was Lord Sheffield's *On the Commerce of the American States* which went through several editions in the mid-1780s. Irving supplied material for the book but, in my estimation, his contribution went well beyond the few tables identified with his name. Sheffield, who had no first-hand acquaintance with the workings of the American economy, obviously relied heavily on people who had, one of whom was Irving.[69]

Irving performed a parallel service for government and we are able to document that more satisfactorily. The debate over the Orders in Council continued in Parliament as well as in the popular press. Through the spring of 1784 the Commissioners for Trade and Plantations held hearings to gather information on the West Indian–North American trade. Irving appeared before the committee repeatedly in the role of expert witness, presented with detailed questions one week and asked to return the next with all the answers. His data and commentary appear regularly in the surviving records of the committee.[70] Moreover, much of his data and the points he made about

69 The first edition of Sheffield's book was entitled *Observations on the Commerce of the American States with Europe and the West Indies* (London, 1783); the 6th, enlarged edition (London, 1784) is the fullest version. See Herbert C. Bell "British Commercial Policy in the West Indies, 1783–93," *English Historical Review*, XXXI (July, 1916), 429–441; Ritcheson, *Aftermath of Revolution*, passim. The nature and the extent of the relationship between Sheffield and Irving are not clear, largely because neither man has left behind a collection of his papers. There is the suggestion that the two families were on quite friendly terms in the 1790s but how old that friendship was, again, we can really only guess. See *The Girlhood of Maria Josepha Holroyd (Lady Stanley of Aderley). Recorded in Letters of a Hundred Years Ago: From 1776 to 1796*, ed. J[ane] H. Adeane (London, 1896), p. 367. Nevertheless it does seem reasonable to suppose, given the range and depth of their shared interests, that they would have sought each other out early and often. For Sheffield, see Namier and Brooke, *House of Commons*, II, 43.

70 Irving testified several times between Mar. and May 1784 before the Lords of the Committee of the Privy Council Appointed for the Consideration of all Matters Relating to Trade and Foreign Plantations. (This body was, in everything but name, the old "Commissioners for Trade and Plantations"; and it is sometimes, but inaccurately, called the "Board of Trade," a name that only applies later in Britain's history. For an impassioned plea that we all use the more accurate name – a call with which I am in sympathy – see K. G. Davies in his "Introduction" to the most recent volume of [GB, PRO], *Calendar of State Papers, Colonial Series, America and West Indies [1574–1739]*, by W[illiam] Noel Sainsbury *et al.*, 45 vols in 46 pts [London, 1860–1994], XLV, xiv.) The record of their proceedings is in BT 5/1, PRO. (There is a copy of this volume in the Liverpool

them turn up again in the expanded sixth edition of Sheffield's extremely influential book. Clearly, Irving's was an important voice in the drive to maintain the integrity of the British imperial system. What else he did between 1783 and 1786 we have yet to discover, but his activities – perhaps in this one sphere alone – were enough to catch the attention of government and again to earn for him an appropriate reward.

Thomas Irving began the last and longest phase of his public career when on 5 January 1786, he was appointed Deputy Inspector-General of Imports and Exports of Great Britain. Three months later, on April 7, he was promoted to Inspector-General, and began, in the words of George Clark, "a new era" in that office.[71] Clark's assessment is justified not only by the reforms that Irving instituted in the work of his own agency but also by the more active role that he as Inspector-General undertook in government as a whole.

The traditional task of the Inspector-General and his staff was to collect and compile trade statistics. From the middle of the 1690s onward, the end product of those labors had been an annual summary ledger of England's imports and exports, the comparative values of which were used to strike the nation's balance of trade. One problem with the import–export ledgers as Irving found them was that they were organized basically by countries traded with; to extract information about specific commodities required considerable retabulation. Beginning with 1792, imports, exports, and re-exports were

Papers, Add. MS 38388, BL.) Additionally, Irving's own testimony has been copied into Liverpool Papers, Add. MS 38345, fols 136–152, BL. Compare ibid., fols 153–155. For the papers he presented to support his testimony, see BT 6/83, pts i and ii, PRO. See also Irving's "Observations on the Trade carried on between the W[est] Indies and America," [21 Feb. 1788], Add. MS 59238, fols 122–123, BL. Compare Ritcheson, *Aftermath of Revolution*, pp. 12–13, 21, 213, 221, 224, 345.

71 Clark, *Guide to English Commercial Statistics*, p. 32, and his citations to T 11/34, pp. 261, 389, PRO. Irving once testified that "the Title of the Office is, Inspector General of the Imports and Exports of Great Britain and the British Colonies" (28 Mar. 1797). See [GB, Parl., Commons, Committee of Secrecy], *Third Report from the Committee of Secrecy [on the Outstanding Demands on the Bank of England]*, [Lambert 4717] ([London], 1797), p. 105. On another occasion, speaking more freely, he called himself the "Inspector General of the Commerce of the Empire." [GB, Parl., Commons, Select Committee on Finance], *Fourth Report from the Select Committee on Finance. Collection of the Public Revenue. Customs* [Lambert 4759] ([London],1797), p. 140. The previous Deputy Inspector-General, John Tomkyns, retired with a pension of £100 paid out of Irving's salary. Irving later complained not only about that £100 deduction, but also about several others that reduced his new annual income from the office from a salary of £780 to £272 10s. (£272.50). Irving's evidence, 10 Oct. 1787, 18 Sept. 1788, AO 12/51, fols 162v, 164v, PRO. See also the statement by John Tomkyns, 26 May 1785, in [GB, Commissioners for Taking, Examining and Stating the Public Accounts], *The Reports of the Commissioners Appointed to Examine, Take, and State the Public Accounts of the Kingdom*, ed. William Molleson and John Lane, 3 vols (London, 1783–1787), III, 432–433. The suppression of the sinecure and, by implication, the appointment of an active Inspector-General, had been one of the recommendations of the fourteenth report, 30 Dec. 1785, of the commission appointed under the Act of 20 George III, c. 54 (1780). See *Reports of the Commissioners*, ed. Molleson and Lane, III, 99, 105. For the broader context of these reforms, see Ehrman, *Younger Pitt*, passim.

compiled both by commodity and by country in a new series of six annual volumes. This reform was certainly Irving's.[72]

A second major problem with the import–export ledgers involved the valuations assigned to commodities. The Customs officials in the various ports sent to London the quantities of each commodity imported and exported. Clerks in the office of the Inspector-General multiplied quantity by unit value and entered both the total quantity and the total value of each commodity. The grand totals of these values of exports and imports added up by country gave, supposedly, the balance of trade between England and the places with which it did business. The difficulty was that the unit values used by the clerks had not been changed since the early eighteenth century and no longer reflected current market prices. Consequently the annual ledgers were useless for striking an accurate balance of trade.[73]

Knowledgeable contemporaries recognized and criticized this deficiency in the government's figures. In *The Wealth of Nations*, Adam Smith stated that "the custom-house books, I think, it is now generally acknowledged, are a very uncertain criterion [of the value of trade], on account of the inaccuracy of the valuation at which the greater part of goods are rated in them."[74] Irving noted the same defect: "the arguments held both in and out of Parliament, and the voluminous writing of various authors upon the subject

72 For a discussion of the early ledgers and the data in them, see John J. McCusker, "The Current Value of English Exports, 1697 to 1800," *W&MQ*, 3rd ser., XXVIII (Oct. 1971), 607–628 – revised as chapter ten of the present book. At least one copy of each of the ledgers still survives for the years down through 1780 (with the exceptions of the years 1705 and 1712); the most complete set is designated Customs 3, PRO. We can only theorize about the changes in 1792 because the 1814 fire in the London Custom House apparently destroyed the last eleven years of the older one-volume series and as much as the first twenty years of some of the new, post-1792 six-volume series. Clark, *Guide to English Commercial Statistics*, p. 31, speculated on the loss of the last eleven vols of the Customs 3 series. See also [GB, Royal Commission on Public Records], *Report of the Royal Commission on Public Records Appointed to Enquire into and Report on the State of the Public Records and Local Records of a Public Nature of England and Wales*, [HC Sessional Papers, Cmd. 6361, 6395–6396, 7544–7546, 367–369] (London, 1912–1919), I, pt ii, p. 47n. The guess about the post-1792, six-volume arrangement is my own based on the existing volumes in the several series Customs 4, 5, 8, 9, 10, and 11, PRO. From 1772 on, as a supplement to the Customs 3 ledgers, the Inspector-General's office also prepared an annual volume of tables summarizing the year's shipping, commercial, and revenue statistics. This is the series Customs 17, PRO. Irving's intentions in his reforms of 1792 were summed up in his annual report dated 12 Dec. 1791, Customs 17/12, pp. 1–5, PRO. There is a copy of this volume, identified as the "State of the Navigation, Revenues and Commerce of Great Britain in the Year 1790," MS 140, Palaeography Room, Senate House, Library, University of London.

73 McCusker, "Current Value of English Exports," passim. See also Irving's "A few general Observations on the Trade between Great Britain and Portugal and Spain," Dec. 1789, Add. MS 34429, fols 196–199, BL; and his testimony, in Mar., 1797, included in the *Third Report from the Committee of Secrecy [on the Outstanding Demands on the Bank of England]*, pp. 153–154.

74 Adam Smith, *An Inquiry into the Nature and Causes of the Wealth of Nations* (1776), ed. R[oy] H. Campbell, A[ndrew] S. Skinner, and W[illiam] B. Todd, 2 vols (Oxford, 1976), I, 475–476.

of commercial balances, chiefly founded upon the accounts of the inspector-general's office, are made upon false data."[75] His efforts to deal with this problem were less successful than in other areas because there seems to have been considerable difficulty in collecting the required prices. Only in the late 1790s did the office begin to use current market prices, and not until many years later, during his son William's time as Inspector-General, were Irving's ideas about how to strike the balance of trade fully implemented.[76]

Thomas Irving's services went far beyond collecting better data. His experience and his command of information equipped him to express knowledgeable opinions on many policy matters. Accordingly, his views came to be solicited on nearly every branch of the trade and shipping of the empire. His responses to inquiries are to be found throughout the papers of the Commissioners for Trade and Plantations and other governmental agencies.[77] John Ehrman, who has studied this period closely, found that Irving expressed influential opinions on everything from imported Portuguese wine and the boom in trade with Russia to the dangers of overexpansion in the early

75 Customs 17/12, p. 4, PRO. Irving had to have been aware of Smith's opinions.

76 "Commercial Accounts of Great Britain," pp. 3–40, in [GB, Parl., Commons], *Accounts and Papers Relative to the Commerce, Revenue, and Expenditure of the Kingdoms of Great Britain and Ireland*, HC Sessional Papers to 1801, Accounts and Papers, vol. XLIX, no. 981 [Lambert 5010] ([London], 1800). Thomas Irving supervised the preparation of these accounts and sent them to William Pitt over his signature; they are dated 31 Mar. 1800. Pitt presented them to the House of Commons on 2 Apr. 1800. Phyllis Deane and W[illiam] A. Cole, *British Economic Growth*, 1688–1959: *Trends and Structure*, 2nd edn (Cambridge, Eng., 1962), pp. 43, 315, checked some of Irving's work and concluded that he was both "careful" and "remarkably accurate." See also Albert H. Imlah, *Economic Elements in the Pax Britannica: Studies in British Foreign Trade in the Nineteenth Century* (Cambridge, Mass., 1958), pp. 24–25. For William Irving, see n. 83 of this chapter.

77 See nn. 70, 79, and 80 of this chapter. As an example of an important report, presented by Irving (in 1791) but later published only anonymously, see the unsigned answers to three questions about the ownership of colonial shipping in BT 6/20, fols 269r–273v, PRO. The author did identify himself (ibid., fols 270v–271r) as a pre-war Inspector-General of Imports and Exports and Register of Shipping in America but, more to the point, we know for certain that he was Irving because it was to him that the Commissioners for Trade and Plantations submitted the questions on 10 Dec. 1790, BT 5/6, fol. 195, PRO. There is a copy of this volume in the Liverpool Papers, Add. MS 38393, BL.

The data that Irving presented, which were considered significant enough by contemporaries to have been printed several times, become much more compelling because Irving compiled them. The committee to which Irving presented the material incorporated it into its published report (but, again, with no indication of its author). [GB, Commissioners for Trade and Plantations], A *Report of the Lords of the Committee of Privy Council, Appointed for All Matters Relating to Trade and Foreign Plantations, on the Commerce and Navigation between His Majesty's Dominions and the Territories belonging to the United States of America* ([London], 1791), pp. 31–33. The British government thought it important enough information to have suppressed the report, but not before Andrew Burnaby had a chance to extract some material from it, including the data referred to specifically here. Andrew Burnaby, *Travels through the Middle Settlements in North-America, In the Years 1759–1760 with Observations upon the State of the Colonies*, 3rd edn (London, 1790), p. 134. Thomas Jefferson also seems to have obtained a copy of the report; there is a précis of it in the Thomas Jefferson Papers, 1651–1856, LC, which was also edited and published. See [GB, Commissioners for Trade and Plantations], *Report of a Committee of the Lords*

1790s and the impact on the Customs reforms of William Pitt's attempts to make smuggling less attractive.[78] He appeared before the committee investigating the slave trade, played a part in discussions of Canadian–West Indian trade, testified before the committee looking into the Bank of England, formulated a plan for an extended free port system in the Caribbean, and commented on similar plans for the home ports.[79] In short, Irving was at the center of British governmental discussions on trade and commerce during the last fifteen years of the eighteenth century. John Ehrman has speculated that Irving may even have had the ear of the Prime Minister himself.[80]

We gain still another measure of the man from the evidence that he gave before the committee that examined British government finances in 1797. They had asked him to compare conditions at home and abroad. Irving was impressive. He cited conversations with men of affairs during his visit to

of the Privy Council on the Trade of Great Britain with the United States, January 1791, [ed. Worthington C. Ford] (Washington, DC, 1888), p. 16. "The Society of Ship-Owners of Great Britain" reprinted the original report several years later in their *Collection of Interesting and Important Reports and Papers on the Navigation and Trade of Great Britain, Ireland, and the British Colonies in the West Indies,* [comp. Nathaniel Atcheson] ([London], 1807), pp. 74–75. This, in turn, was the source of the still anonymous data reprinted in two contemporary American works: Adam Seybert, *Statistical Annals . . . of the United States of America* (Philadelphia, 1818), p. 290; and Timothy Pitkin, *A Statistical View of the Commerce of the United States of America,* 2nd edn (New Haven, Conn., 1835), p. 345.

78 Ehrman, *British Government and Commercial Negotiations with Europe,* pp. 11n., 12n., 94n., 191, 206n., 207n.; Ehrman, *Younger Pitt,* pp. 163, 247, 326n., 382, 503.

79 For the slave trade, see his testimony, 5 Apr. 1791, *Minutes of the Evidence . . . Respecting the African Slave Trade,* pp. 264–275. Compare *Remarks upon the Evidence given by Thomas Irving, Esq., Inspector General of the Exports and Imports to Great Britain before the Select Committee appointed to Take the Examination of Witnesses on the Slave Trade* (London, 1791). Many of the accounts relating to the slave trade prepared for Parliament in the 1780s and 1790s bore the signature of Thomas Irving. See, for example, "An Account of the Ships that have arrived from the Coast of Africa . . . ," 10 June 1799, Main Papers, 10 June 1799, Sessional Papers, House of Lords, HLRO. Compare *Documents Illustrative of the History of the Slave Trade to America,* ed. Elizabeth Donnan, Carnegie Institution of Washington, Publication no. 409, 4 vols ([Washington, DC], 1930–1935), II, li. For the other topics, see CO 42/12, esp. fols 111r, 113r, 133r, 135–137, PRO, and Gerald S. Graham, *British Policy and Canada, 1774–1791: A Study in 18th Century Trade Policy* (London, 1930), pp. 92, 94; *Third Report from the Committee of Secrecy [on the Outstanding Demands on the Bank of England],* pp. 153–156, 164–165; Frances Armytage, *The Free Port System in the British West Indies: A Study in Commercial Policy, 1766–1792* (New York and London, 1953); and *Fourth Report from the Select Committee on Finance. Collection of the Public Revenue. Customs,* pp. 139–140. For Irving's comments on a variety of other subjects between 1784 and 1799, see: Add. MS 34427, fols 346–365, BL; Add. MS 34429, fols 190–199, BL; Add. MS 38218, fol. 271, BL; Add. MS 38225, fol. 346, BL; Add. MS 38345, fols 208–213, BL; Add. MS 38348, fols 75–76, BL; Add. MS 38354, fol. 114, BL; Add. MS 59238, fols 62–76, 91–123, BL; MS. 57, Beinecke Collection of Manuscripts, Hamilton College Library, Clinton, NY. See also George Chalmers, *Considerations on Commerce, Bullion and Coin, Circulation and Exchanges; with a View to Our Present Circumstances* (London, 1811), p. 168.

80 Ehrman, *British Government and Commercial Negotiations with Europe,* p. 191; Ehrman, *Younger Pitt,* pp. 326n., 503, 510. There are numerous letters and accounts from Irving in Pitt's papers. See, e.g., PRO 30/8/147, fols 237–254, PRO, and PRO 30/8/286, passim, PRO. Compare Morris, *Diary and Letters,* I, 315.

France and the Low Countries a few years earlier and called upon his extensive reading in the published materials about the finances of those nations. The Dutch "Government [has] never possessed any collective View of the Revenues," and there was also much reason for concern about the completeness and accuracy of the French government's figures. In Irving's eyes, these were shocking deficiencies in statecraft. One infers that he held both governments to have deserved the chaos that such sloppy bookkeeping had brought upon them. In contrast, the British system merited respect and trust from every citizen because income and expenses were accounted for down to the last farthing, "with a mathematical Accuracy."[81]

This is the theme that seems to have run through Irving's entire career – in North America on the eve of the Revolution and thereafter. Great Britain, in his view, offered to its subjects the best of all possible worlds. As he said with specific reference to the Acts of Trade:

> I feel it perfectly within the Province of my official Situation . . . to remark, that under the Operation of these great fundamental Laws (commonly called Navigation Acts) our Trade, our Navigation, our Revenues, and our Manufactures, have flourished beyond the example of all other Nations.[82]

He devoted his mature life to preserving the integrity of an imperial system founded upon the Navigation Acts. His personal contribution consisted in turning to the defense of the empire the records of imperial trade, records the integrity and trustworthiness of which he strove to maintain down to the last barrel of flour, "with proper precision," "with a mathematical accuracy."

♦ ♦ ♦ ♦ ♦

Though not a man of first rank among the public figures of his time, Irving was no mere functionary. He was an innovative and effective administrator within his sphere – and more. At Boston, risking limb and life, he stepped

81 *Fourth Report from the Select Committee on Finance. Collection of the Public Revenue. Customs*, pp. 36–37 (quotation, p. 37). Compare, ibid., pp. 139–140. See also J[ohn] E. D. Binney, *British Public Finance and Administration, 1774–92* (Oxford, 1962), p. 255. This was, of course, a favorite subject of Irving's friend John Sinclair, who wrote the standard contemporary work on it, *The History of the Public Revenue of the British Empire*, [1st edn], 3 vols (London, 1785–1790).

82 *Fourth Report from the Select Committee on Finance. Collection of the Public Revenue. Customs*, p. 140. Compare his celebration of "the great System of our Commercial Regulations" in the "Report by Mr. Irving, Inspector General of Imports & Exports, to the Commissioners of the Customs upon a Correspondence refer'd to him between the Officers of the Navy and the Civil Officers in the West Indies," in Add. MS 59238, fols 91–123, BL, and as quoted by Michael John Craton, "The Caribbean Vice Admiralty Courts, 1763–1815: Indispensable Agents of an Imperial System" (Ph.D. diss., McMaster University, 1968), p. 125, n. 24; and the tenor of his testimony in Apr. 1791 to the "Select Committee appointed to take Examination of Witnesses on the Slave Trade," as recorded in the *Minutes of the Evidence . . . Respecting the African Slave Trade*, pp. 264–275.

beyond his official duties to become a pamphleteer in defense of King and country. His tenure as Inspector-General of Imports and Exports in London marked the end of that position as a sinecure and the beginning of reforms that were to outlive Irving by several decades. One hopes that he would have been pleased by his obituary notice in *The Times*:

> Died . . . At his house, in Middle Scotland-yard, on Sunday last, after a long and severe illness, Thomas Irving, Esq., Inspector General of the Imports and Exports of Great Britain. To Mr. Irving's able and indefatigable exertions the Public have been much indebted for the excellent and correct system which now prevails in the arrangement of the National Accounts. His loss, therefore, cannot be more deeply regretted by His numerous Friends, who knew his worth and could appreciate his virtues, than it must be felt by the Government and the Country, in being deprived of the useful services of this intelligent and valuable Man.[83]

83 *The Times* (London), 15 July 1800, p. 3. Compare *The Gentleman's Magazine*: "In Scotland-yard, after a long and severe illness, Thomas Irving, esq., inspector-general of imports and exports of Great Britain; an office in which his talents were invaluable." ["Thomas Irving Obituary"], *Gentleman's Magazine*, LXX (Aug. 1800), 798. Thomas Irving's will is dated 3 June 1800. PROB 11/1345, fols 94v–96r, PRO. He died on 13 July.

Bouts of ill health had plagued Irving throughout his life, while he was resident in North America and after. See, e.g., nn. 48, 67, of this chapter. In Apr. 1791 the "Select Committee appointed to take Examination of Witnesses on the Slave Trade," came to him at his house – in Middle Scotland Yard, off Whitehall, one presumes – to take his testimony because, as they acknowledged, he was "only lately recovered from a dangerous illness." *Minutes of the Evidence . . . Respecting the African Slave Trade*, pp. 264, 266.

Irving and his wife had at least three children, only two of whom lived to adulthood. In 1781 Thomas wrote of "my little William and Libby," but the daughter whom he mentioned in his will was named Marion, after her mother, and was herself called a "little girl" in 1796. "Libby" – most likely a diminutive for Elizabeth – probably died in the 1780s, perhaps in London. Her younger sister, Marion, who was probably born near the end of the same decade, later married a London West Indian merchant named Furness whom I have been unable to trace. Maxwell-Irving, "Irvings of Dumfries," pp. 73–74; Irving, at Charleston, to Steuart, at London, 20 Dec. 1781, Steuart Papers, MS 5040, fols 223–224, National Library of Scotland; Irving's evidence ("His family . . . consists of a Wife and two Children"), 10 Oct. 1787, AO 12/51, fol. 162v, PRO; *Girlhood of Maria Josepha Holroyd*, ed. Adeane, p. 367; PROB 11/1345, fols 94v–96r, PRO.

Son William, who died on 27 Aug. 1855 at age 78, had to have been conceived before Irving left Charleston for the Bahamas in the summer of 1775 and must, therefore, have been born in South Carolina in 1776. Death Certificate, Register of Deaths, Office of Population Censuses and Surveys, London. William Irving's will is dated 1 Mar. 1856. PROB 11/2227, fol. 176v, PRO. He succeeded his father as Inspector-General, taking over immediately despite his relative youth. He started work before the end of Oct. 1800. See William Irving, at Custom House, to the Earl of Liverpool, 20 Oct. 1800, Add. MS 38234, fol. 179, BL. See also *The Royal Kalendar*; or, *Complete and Correct Annual Register for England, Scotland, Ireland, and America for the Year 1800* (London, [1800]), p. 210; *Royal Kalendar . . . 1801* (London, [1801]), p. 255. Compare The *Court and City Register* (London, 1799), 2nd pagination, p. 211; *The Court and City Register* (London, 1800), p. 255. For the latter source, see Alizon M. Mathews, "Editions of the Court and City

THOMAS IRVING: LOYALIST AND CIVIL SERVANT

Economic historians have particular cause to be indebted to Thomas Irving, because those talents bequeathed an invaluable corpus of statistical data with which to illumine a crucial half-century of Anglo-American economic history.

Register, 1742–1813," *Bulletin of the Institute of Historical Research*, XIX (1942–1943), 9–12. William Irving retained the position until his retirement, shortly before his death. Maxwell-Irving, "Irvings of Dumfries," p. 73. Together, father and son served as Inspectors-General for nearly seventy years.

15

Jonathan Duncan: A Lesson in Administrative Survival

Neil Rabitoy

Jonathan Duncan does not belong to that relatively small group of British administrators in South Asia who, by virtue of personality and accomplishment, take up such a large part of South Asian historiography. Instead, he was a survivor—most of his colleagues would label him a mediocrity—who managed, by careful calculation, to serve a longer (1796-1811) term in office than any other Governor of the Bombay Presidency. As such his career offers the opportunity to look at practical features of British administration not often encountered in studies of the "great" Governor-Generals or Viceroys but yet not unique to Duncan, Bombay, or the period.

The label "survivor" is not used here in a derogatory fashion. Duncan was governor at a critical time[1] in the history of the presidency and left at least one important legacy to his successors: he was ultimately responsible for the preservation of hundreds of princely states in Western India, a political problem until 1947. And despite the opinions of most of his contemporaries, he was, if not exceptional, certainly not incompetent. It is simply that his greatest concern as governor was maintaining his position against very real and almost constant threats. The following pages examine the forces which operated on Duncan and explain how a mediocre governor manged to survive for fifteen years in a basically hostile environment.

In an attempt to simplify a complex problem, i.e., human motivation and behavior in a bureaucratic structure, I have divided the essay into two sections entitled "cognitive" and "mechanical" patterns. The first examines Duncan's perceptions of his situation and the attitudes which he brought to it while the second deals with the structure within which he operated. I approach both sections in the belief that the traditional historiographic technique of placing administrators in schools (e.g., utilitarian, paternalist, etc.) or of judging their careers on the basis of their policies (e.g., "Curzon the imperialist") are helpful but insufficient. It would be easy to easy to brand Duncan a paternalist and thereby presume to understand him and his administration. Unfortunately, as in every case, the reality of the administrative situation was much more complex than convenient and superficial labels.

Abbreviations: I.O.L. – India Office Library and Records
J.D.D. – Judicial Department Diary, M.S.A.
M.S.A. – Maharashtra State Archives, Bombay
R.D.D. – Revenue Department Diary

1. See P. Nightingale, *Trade and Empire in Western India* (Cambridge: University Press, 1970), passim. See also N. Rabitoy, "Sovereignty, Profits, and Social Change" (Ph.D. diss., 1972), passim.

Cognitive Patterns

There is always a large number of subtle, and not so subtle, influences which combine to determine how any person behaves. No one, and Duncan was no exception, is aware of all of these and thus it is difficult to establish a complete causal relationship between the attitudes he brought to his job and his behavior in it. We can, however, identify several prominent elements in his disposition which go far to explain his administrative policies.

The most important of these was that he needed the job. On two occasions he lost his entire fortune to embezzlers.[2] The second time, which involved a loss of some 30,000 pounds, occured three years after his appointment as Governor. His greatest concern, then, was to recover financially as soon as possible. A lesser position would prolong this recovery; recall to England would be a disaster. This natural preoccupation with his financial condition–he informed Wellesley that his need to remain in India was "no longer a matter of any choice. . ."[3] –was a major factor behind all that he did as Governor.

It meant, primarily, that he could not afford to alienate the Court of Directors and had to rely on his patrons, Robert Dundas and David Scott, to plead his case in London. Thus Duncan was an extremely cautious Governor who never took action without carefully weighing the impact in England. The tone of his administration was cautious, expedient conservatism. He deliberately resisted any attempts at innovation which could even remotely affect the regular receipt of the revenue or threaten internal peace. These were the concerns of the Court, and he made them his.[4] When he died in 1811, administration in the Presidency was as he found it in 1796 or as it was when ceded to the British between 1802 and 1805. He collected information but he did not experiment. It was too risky.

Duncan's need to satisfy his superiors went beyond, then, that which exists for any bureaucrat. His desire to survive was more than a matter of convenience, it was a necessity. He was a conscious survivor who worked hard at it.[5]

He had little choice since he knew that there were many plotting his downfall. Rarely did a year go by without a serious threat of replacement and recall.[6] He had very few friends and even Dundas and Scott found his constant need for reassurance exasperating.[7] In addition, a few in the Bombay civil service objected to Duncan's conservatism. One of these, Robert Rickards, a member of the Bombay Council after 1807, went to the extent of pleading his case against Duncan to the Court of Directors.[8] If this were not enough to ensure his discomfiture, Bombay was basically a commerical presidency when Duncan arrived and his

2. Guildhall Muniment Room, Michie Papers, Mss. 5881, Duncan to Michie, 6 May 1799. V.A. Narain, *Jonathan Duncan and Varanasi* (Calcutta: Firma K.L. Mukhopadhyaya, 1959), p. 22.
3. B.M., Wellesley to Duncan Corres., 13696:248, Duncan to Wellesley, 27 April 1799. I.O.L., Home Misc. Series, 729:451, Scott to Duncan, 17 April 1800.
4. In fairness to Duncan, this must be viewed in the context of his sincere paternalism.
5. He wrote to Dundas and Scott often to plead for their help. See, for example, I.O.L., Home Misc. Series, 731a:182, Duncan to Scott, 7 Sept. 1803.
6. For example, see: I.O.L., Home Misc. Series, 438:17, Ewer to Dundas, 30 Nov. 1796. I.O.L., Minto Papers, M499, Nepean to Minto, 20 Aug. 1812. I.O.L., Home Misc. Series, 741:97, Duncan to Gen. Ross, 19 April 1810.
7. I.O.L., Home Misc. Series, 729:24 Scott to Duncan, 9 March 1797.
I.O.L., Home Misc. Series, 730:116, Scott to Duncan, 9 Aug. 1798.
8. This was a prolonged and extremely bitter confrontation which extended over three years.

inexperience (his expertise was land revenue policy in Bengal) in this field alienated many in the business community.[9]

Therefore, even if he had been economically independent and inclined towards administrative experimentation, Duncan lacked the support to do so. The absence of a local social base from which to operate severely restricted his functional administrative parameters. With few friends he could do little more than wage a holding action against those with selfish commercial ambitions or notions of administrative reform. He was, then, out of his element. He enjoyed neither his job nor the people around him. He loved India, was skilled in its languages and culture, and enjoyed close contact with its people but wound up appointed Governor of a commerical presidency and spent fifteen years clinging desperately to that job for purely monetary reasons. In 1803, in the middle of his governorship, he confessed to David Scott that

"I fear that when I leave India, my happiest days will have passed over. Where indeed, can I find a country, so congenial to my present feelings, and habits, or probably to my health, as that in which I have spent such a number of years—as from 16 to 47 years of life! If therefore I could indulge my own wishes,. . .they would be, to pass the rest of my life. . .in a small district,with as many natives under my charge, as I could, by attending to them, make happy—which my schooling at Benares, renders me fully competent to—and thus, gently to let myself down the stream of life, of which, tho' my health remains robust—I began to feel that I have turned the corner."[10]

Duncan would have surrendered his job readily; he had no ambitions, either in or beyond it. Unfortunately for him, he could not. This attitude, again, reinforced his administrative conservatism.

This also explains his subsequent treatment by historians. Those who have examined him solely in the context of his career in Bengal where he was a close advisor to Cornwallis have, without exception, been, if not ecstatic, at least laudatory.[11] Others who have viewed him in the context of Bombay have been persuaded by Duncan's contemporary detractors. Kaye refers to him as "simpleminded" and the term "Brahminized Englishman" is frequently employed by historians.[12] Certainly Duncan did not work in a congenial environment and could not, as a consequence, have invested a great deal of enthusiasm into his job.

His general unease was compounded by the technically fluid administrative situation which prevailed in the Presidency after 1803. I will emphasize this in the next section. For now it is sufficient to point out that the territories acquired after 1803 were unknown to Bombay administrators, including Duncan. This meant that he had to rely, to a greater degree than would otherwise have been the case, on subordinates on the scene for information and advice. He had no established structure within which to operate or policies upon which to base decisions. Already uncertain and anxious about his position, he had, for reasons beyond his control, to depend on men who, in the creation of policy, had little, if any, prior experience in land revenue administration. This must have weighed heavily on him, especially since he admitted to being a ppor judge of character,[13] and no doubt added to his conservatism.

9. I.O.L., Home Misc. Series 438:14, 16, Ewer to Dundas, 30 Nov. 1796.

10. I.O.L., Home Misc. Series, 731a:171, Duncan to Scott, 3 July 1803.

11. See H. Furber, *Henry Dundas* (London: Oxford University Press, 1931), p. 134. David Kopf, *British Orientalism and the Bengal Renaissance* (Berkeley: U. of California Press, 1969), p. 29. Narain, *Duncan*, passim.

12. J.W. Kaye, *The Administration of the East India Company* (London: Richard Bentley, 1953), p. 553, S.T. Sheppard, Bombay (Bombay: Times of India Press, 1932), p. 48. James Douglas, *Bombay and Western India*, 2 (London: Sampson Low, Marston & Co., 1893), pp. 32-33.

13. Guildhall Muniment Room, Michie Papers, Mss. 5881, Duncan to Michie, 6 May 1799.

All of these factors–his need for a governor's salary, the consequent requirement that he please his employers, the threats from ambitious colleagues, his personal alienation from the commerical and social life of Bombay, his paternalist/orientalist learnings born of a respect for Indian culture, and the technically uncertain administrative character of the Presidency–combined to shape Duncan's view of how he should and could behave as Governor. They made him a cautious and expedient administrator and, for example, explain, as mentioned above, why the British recognized the sovereignty of hundreds of petty chiefs in Gujarat. Rather than risk the costs and disruption of resistance, he legalized the status quo–a permanent legacy to the empire left by an insecure, anxious, weak, and dependent Governor who naively trusted others with his money.

Mechanical Patterns

Regardless of Duncan's attitudes and fiscal problems, he operated in an environment which he could only partially control. There were many aspects of being Governor of Bombay at that time which simply came with the job and to which any Governor would have had to adjust. Perhaps the most important of these was Bombay's economic condition. The presidency was poorer than its Governor. It had operated in the red for years and continued to do so long after Duncan's death. It functioned only with financial assistance from Madras and Calcutta.[14] The sole reason for its existence as a presidency (Wellesley seriously considered its demise) prior to the cessions of 1803-05 was the cotton trade to China which originated in Southern Gujarat and was channeled through Bombay.[15]

Duncan, then, inherited a debtor government whose continued existence was problematical. His own financial interests were dependent on those of Bombay; if Bombay went under so would he. He therefore did his best to strengthen Bombay's financial position and thus ensure his own future. For example, he was instrumental in Bombay's "push to the north" after 1802 whereby it deliberately obtained control over the major cotton districts and ports in Western India.[16] This meant, aside from the commerical advantages, that Bombay needed an administrator versed in land revenue systems, which happened to be Duncan's specialty.

Thus Duncan actively pursued a policy of expansion in selected districts which benefited not only the Company but himself. He also rigorously collected the maximum land revenue justified by local custom.[17] Again, given the financial condition of the presidency, nothing could have pleased his superiors more than his annual report on increased land revenues. He had no choice but to be very concerned with the balance sheet and to judge possible actions accordingly.

The cessions of 1803-05 provided Duncan with some relief from the overriding problem of Bombay's debtor status. But they also resulted in an unavoidable structural complication in his administration. No one in the Presidency was more than just superficially aware of the

14. See: Great Britain, *Parliamentary Papers*, "East India Revenues" (no. 54), 1807, 5:15. Great Britain, *Parliamentary Papers*, "East India Revenues" (No. 60), 1802-03, 9:15.

15. P. Nightingale, *Trade and Empire in Western India* (Cambridge: University Press, 1970), passim.

16. *Ibid.*

17. M.S.A., R.D.D., 38:849, Proc. of Walker, 9 April 1803. Bom. Sels., 39, pt. 1:22, Walker to Duncan, 18 June 1804. See also Rabitoy, "Sovereignty, Profits, and Social Change" (Ph.D. diss., 1972), passim for greater details.

character and customs of the ceded districts. The new Collectors and Magistrates appointed in 1805 had not much more than common sense and their Indian assistants to guide them. Because of this ignorance and the consequent uncertainty as to how to proceed, it was a highly fluid administrative situation. Local precedent was, for the most part, followed in each of the three districts and problems were handled individually as they were discovered. The lack of a uniform or regular administrative system in the districts was a problem Duncan, or any Governor, could not avoid and enhanced his anxiety and caution. His solution was to resist experimentation and avoid strong personal commitments to any policy prior to the Court's approval.[18] He had little choice but to reserve judgment pending word on the views ultimately endorsed by the Court of Directors. In the meantime, he administered with less than complete confidence.

Confidence was further reduced by another repercussion of having to function in a fluid administrative situation. In such a circumstance, those who opposed Duncan on any question were a problem to him not simply because they prolonged the decision-making process or even that they could be correct in their argument but because there was a chance, much stronger given the administrative uncertainty, that they could be believed by his superiors. Duncan's enemies, discussed in the first section, had the advantage of being able to present their case to an audience less likely to have made up its mind in advance. Without a prevailing administrative conventional wisdom regarding the newly acquired territories, the Court of Director's reaction to any controversy was far less predictable. And rather than risk being on the wrong side, Duncan avoided action whenever possible.

His reluctance to innovate and regularize was sound for other than selfish reasons. Despite the shortness of the Bombay administrative hierarchy, there was a great deal of distortion between each level. Distortion occurs when information is exchanged in any bureaucracy but in Bombay, in large part due to the technically fluid character of the administration, the distortion was acute. This was especially true at the district level where the inexperienced British Collectors and Magistrates had to rely on Indian assistants. Families in each district engaged in a power struggle to gain the confidence of the new British official. A major key to success was to tell him what he wanted to hear in a believable fashion. To the winner went virtual control of the district.[19] The same information was passed on to Bombay for the consideration of Governor Duncan and his Council. Distortion at this intermediate step was less serious but still important; it was crucial to newly appointed and inexperienced district servants that they impress their superiors in Bombay.[20]

The information Duncan received, then, did not reflect reality at the district level and he therefore had sound reason to avoid precipitate administrative experimentation. He could not change or control this; it was a fluid structural feature of administrative life and was common to British administration in South Asia in general.[21] Nor was there much he could do about the caliber of those who worked under him. For the most part they were at least competent and a few were exceptional. But he also had a Collector in Surat who was washed out of the college at Fort William and was never able to learn an Indian language. At best the man was a mediocrity, yet he continued as Collector for seventeen years. In another instance a Magistrate,

18. This was his common strategy. See Rabitoy, "Sovereignty," passim.

19. *Ibid.*, ch. 3.

20. *Ibid.*, chs. 2 & 3.

21. See R. Frykenberg, *Guntur District, 1788-1848* (Oxford: Clarendon Press, 1965), passim.

a few days after his arrival in Kaira, decided that defecation in the streets was unhealthy and issued an order forbidding such activity. He also ordered that all cattle in the town would have to be tethered. Only a general strike by the local merchants persuaded him to back down.[22] In this case, Duncan did replace the Magistrate but, with that exception, he had to function within the limits of those serving beneath him.

All of these functional or mechanical features of Bombay administrative life combined to increase Duncan's natural caution and anxiety and limited his ability to act had he so desired. If these are combined with the cognitive patterns discussed above, we can appreciate Duncan's cautious conservatism. In the immediate sense he was free to act–London was a year away. But he needed his job for longer than two or three years; in 1810 he still talked of serving until 1813.[23] Therefore, the distance to London, so often mentioned as an important factor in British administration in India, was of no consequence in this case. The only advantage that Duncan derived from it was the ability to delay decisions until the Court had an opportunity to express its views on a problem. With luck, a problem would disappear in the interim. In this sense the distance/time factor operated as a temporal shock absorber which increased Duncan's ability to survive.

Conclusion

Duncan had no choice but to survive, and he was successful at it. The question is how a man of limited ability in a hostile environment managed to serve the longest governorship in the history of the presidency. The answer, at root, lies in the way in which Duncan's view of his job–the cognitive patterns–blended with the technical or structural features of the Bombay administration at that time. What he had to do to satisfy his own needs was compatible with what made good sense given the fluid technical situation. A cautious, expedient policy was quite appropriate in light of British inexperience in the ceded districts and the inexperience of the Bombay Civil Service in general. It was Duncan's good fortune that such a policy also furthered his selfish interests.

Therefore, his caution actually saved Duncan. The Court did not want a bold, decisive, and innovative Governor in a situation where the administrative parameters were unclear. If not exciting, Duncan was steady and predictable. He was also honest–even his strongest detractors admitted this[24]–and he posed a threat to no one. If he could have afforded it, he would have willingly retreated to a lesser post. Given all of this, Duncan, his employers, and Western India were well served.

I am reluctant to generalize from this. Certainly the general picture described above was a feature of many administrative situations, though they each contained their unique elements and combined the various ingredients in differing amounts. No doubt many of the better

22. M.S.A., J.D.D., 31;1616-26, Walker to Corsellis, 29 Sept. 1805. M.S.A., J.D.D., 32: 1978, Warden to Corsellis, n.d. M.S.A.,

22. M.S.A., J.D.D., 31:1616-26, Walker to Corsellis, 29 Sept. 1805. M.S.A., J.D.D., 32: 1978, Warden to Corsellis, n.d. M.S.A., J.D.D., 33:2475, Govt. Resolution, 20 Dec. 1805.

23. I.O.L., Home Misc. Series, 741:116, Duncan to Dundas, 5 June 1810.

24. I.O.L., Home Misc. Series, 438:14, 16, Ewer to Dundas, 30 Nove. 1796. Susheela N. Pradhan, "Jonathan Duncan's Contribution to the Foundation of the British Empire in India, 1772-1811" (Ph.D. diss., 1955), p. 1.

known British administrators needed their jobs and compromised their views, to whatever degree, to keep them and their policies were, to some extent, subservient to given administrative and human limitations. It is true that patronage played a much larger role early in the nineteenth century than after ca. 1860 and that Duncan could not have survived without personal support in London. Also, as the British became more confident, their administration became more regular and lost much of its technical fluidity. These two factors were so important in Duncan's administration that I am inclined to believe that the combination of conditions described in this essay could only have occurred at the level of Governor early in the history of British India.

Beyond this, however, there is always room for a mediocrity in a large bureaucracy if the demands made of a person are not too severe. Put such a person, who is also intent on holding his job, in a fluid administrative structure (local administration remained so until 1947) and his chances of survival are excellent. He may, in fact, have a better chance of survival since it is in his interest to maintain a low profile and keep his superiors satisfied, i.e., waiting to act until he knows their views. Mediocrities have an additional advantage over more dynamic administrators: people, including administrators, enjoy hearing what they want to hear. The more impulsive and self-confident often fail to consider this.

These factors are worthy of greater consideration by administrative historians. As mentioned in the introduction, the conditions described in this paper explain, to a large extent, the vast number of princely states in Western India, an explanation not found in any other work of scholarship with which the author is familiar. A similar approach to the careers of other British administrators could, perhaps, be equally useful.

Bibliography

Douglas, J., *Bombay and Western India*, 2, Sampson Low, Marston & Co., 1893.

Frykenberg, R., *Guntur District, 1788-1848*, Clarendon Press, 1965.

Furber, H., *Henry Dundas*, Oxford University Press, 1931.

Kaye, J.W., *The Administration of the East India Company*, Richard Bentley, 1953.

Kopf, D., *British Orentalism and the Bengal Renaissance*, U. of California Press, 1969.

Narain, *Jonathan Duncan and Varanasi*, Fi rma K.L. Mukhopadhyaya, 1959.

Nightingale, P., *Trade and Empire in Western India*, Cambridge University Press, 1970.

Pradhan, S.N., "Jonathan Duncan's Contribution to the Foundationof the British Empire in India," Ph.D. Diss., 1955.

Rabitoy, N., "Sovereignty, Profits, and Social Change," Ph.D. Diss., 1972.

Sheppard, S.T., *Bombay*, Times of India Press, 1932.

16

Politics, Patronage, and the Imperial Interest: Charles de Beauharnais's Disputes with Gilles Hocquart

Dale S. Standen

'JE SUIS UN VIEUX MILITAIRE,' wrote Charles de Beauharnais, the sixty-nine-year-old governor general of New France, 'd'age à savoir ne pas donner prise sur moy.'[1] The words were writtein in 1740 to Jean-Frédéric Phélypeaux, comte de Maurepas, the minister of the marine, in response to anonymous accusations of favouritism made at court the previous year. Students of New France will recognize immediately in this glimpse the personal pattern of colonial politics. They will also anticipate as part of the pattern a series of quarrels with the intendant, Gilles Hocquart, over precedence, jurisdiction, the distribution of patronage, any number of 'abuses' of royal offices, and, buried somewhere, policies on important public issues.

If it is a truism that the politics of the governors general of New France were highly personal and were often displayed in rancorous disputes with the intendants, the extent to which these disputes were institutionalized, or rendered unavoidable by the structure of colonial government, is more controversial. A century ago Francis Parkman concluded that conflict was not only inevitable but intentional. 'In truth,' he wrote of the governors and intendants of New France, 'their relations to each other were so critical, and perfect harmony so rare, that they might almost be described as natural enemies. The court, it is certain, did not desire their perfect accord; nor, on the other hand, did it wish them to quarrel: it aimed to keep then on such terms that,

The paper was first presented to a session of the Canadian Historical Association in London in June 1978. Much research for this paper was done for a doctoral thesis for the University of Toronto with the support of a Canada Council Doctoral Fellowship.

1 Archives Nationales [AN], Archives des Colonies, C11A 74, Beauharnais à Maurepas, 28 oct. 1740, 110–11

without deranging the machinery of administration, each should be a check on the other.'[2] The eye of Parkman, the Liberal, was drawn to the extensive evidence within the voluminous official correspondence that bared the less edifying aspects of the French absolute monarchy, but other historians have since come to the same conclusion.[3]

Still others have been impressed more by contrary evidence, also extensive and also in the official correspondence. Co-operation and harmony between governors and intendants, whether in the French provinces or in the overseas colonies, have led them to reject the notion that the crown sought deliberately to establish opposing authorities. Thus, Roland Mousnier found in Languedoc in the seventeenth century 'Une collaboration constante d'hommes qui concourent à une même fin, dans un esprit de confiance et d'estime réciproques, sans ombre de rivalité.'[4] Professor William Eccles has argued that 'The concept of checks and balances was completely foreign to French political thought under the old regime, and the king made it very clear to all the colonial governors and intendants that they were to cooperate in all things, not to serve as a check on each other.'[5] Here the focus is upon what we could too easily forget if buried only amidst the evidence of quarrels: that royal officials were among other things professional men, getting done the jobs that they were sent to do.

Elsewhere, attention has turned to the play of private interests among the colonial élite to explain political conflicts.[6] Guy Frégault, in his authoritative work on the politics of New France in the early eighteenth century, ventured some structural and social explanations that went beyond the attributing of disputes to personality clashes, occasional greed, or superficial quarrels over public honours:

> Tout pousse donc les deux personnages à entrer en conflit: leur formation, leurs ambitions, leur mentalité et la division imprécise des fonctions qui leur

2 Francis Parkman, *The Old Regime in Canada* (Boston 1902 [1874]), vol. 2, 64–5

3 For example, see Guy Frégault, 'Politique et politiciens au début du XVIIIe siècle,' *Ecrits du Canada français*, XI, 1961, reprinted in *Le xviiie siècle canadien, études* (Montréal 1968), 177.

4 Roland Mousnier, 'Les Rapports entre les gouverneurs de province et les intendants dans la première moitié du XVIIe siècle,' *Revue Historique*, CCXXVIII, 1962, reprinted in *La Plume, la faucille et le marteau* (Paris 1970), 203

5 W.J. Eccles, *The Government of New France* (Ottawa 1965), 1

6 See the discussion of recent historiography in Yves Zoltvany, *The Government of New France: Royal, Clerical or Class Rule?* (Scarborough 1971), chaps. 4–5. For a superb analysis of interest groups in Louisbourg see Terence A. Crowley, 'Government and Interests: French Colonial Administration at Louisbourg, 1713–1758' (unpublished PHD thesis, Duke University, 1975), chap. VII, *passim*.

sont attribuées. La Cour tient apparemment à ce qu'ils se fasse contrepoids, mais ne cesse de leur recommander de vivre en bonne intelligence ...

Bien que les disputes des deux chefs de la colonie aient fort defrayé la chronique, il reste que leur action commune, malgré tous les tiraillements qui l'ont accompagnée, conserve, après 1700, une importance bien supérieure à celle de leurs dissensions ... A y regarder de près, ces luttes d'influence prennent parfois l'allure, assez confuse à la verité, de luttes de parties, c'est-à-dire de chocs d'intérêts et d'idées.[7]

Here is the stuff of colonial politics, brilliantly exposed in the contests of the era of the intendants Raudot and the governor Philippe de Rigaud de Vaudreuil. Yet Frégault fails to come to grips with the ambiguity between conflict and harmony in the relationship between governor and intendant whch he, Parkman, and others perceived, or with the glaring contradiction in ministerial policy which expected at once mutual surveillance and peaceful co-operation in all things.[8]

One way of resolving the problem is to accept ambiguity and contradiction as inherent in royal government in the Old Régime. This is what Professor John F. Bosher has argued in an examination of the royal financial administration and, by implication, of government in general.[9] No understanding of politics in the Old Régime is possible without first discarding twentieth-century preconceptions about sophisticated distinctions between 'public' and 'private' interests:[10] 'It was left for the French Revolution to draw distinctions between the state and the nation, the executive and the legislature, the administration and politics, and to endeavour to protect the administration from outside pressure and interference.'[11] In the meantime, 'the administration as a whole was contained within a social system that continually interfered with it. Patronage, clientage, the use of public power to advance relations and friends ... were not abuses at all.'[12] The royal

7 Frégault, 'Politique et politiciens,' 177–8

8 For a more recent appraisal of the issues from the perspective of Vaudreuil see Y. Zoltvany, *Philippe de Rigaud de Vaudreuil: Governor of New France 1703–1725* (Toronto 1974).

9 John F. Bosher, 'Government and Private Interests in New France,' *Canadian Public Administration*, x, 1967, reprinted in J.M. Bumsted, ed., *Canadian History before Confederation: Essays and Interpretations* (Georgetown 1972), 116

10 The terminology of many historians who employ 'government' and 'administration' interchangeably reflects the ambiguity surrounding the functions of institutions of the *ancien régime*. For example, see the works of Lanctôt, Eccles, Frégault, and Zoltvany cited throughout.

11 Bosher, 'Government and Private Interests,' 123

12 Ibid., 122

'bureaucracy' consisted of officials whose regard for their offices retained a personal and proprietary quality earlier associated with the feudal bond.[13] The vision of the higher authorities who longed for more effective government – the vision often adopted by historians who read their dispatches – was blinded by this incapacity to view royal administration in other than personal terms: terms of the honesty, wisdom, ability, or integrity of individual officials: 'The machine-like qualities of an organization were as yet hardly perceived, so that in practice the government does not seem to have arranged or rearranged duties and men in order to increase their collective power or efficiency. The Secretaries of State for the Marine Department .. apparently [were] unaware of the mechanical advantages of complex articulation ... .'[14]

Strive as it might, the crown only groped clumsily toward a more efficient administration, toward more effective supervision and accountability. The determined attempts by Jean-Baptiste Colbert, Louis XIV's great minister, to reform the personnel of the Marine Department by redefining the separate responsibilities of *officiers de plume* and *officiers d'épée*, had their parallel in Canada with the measures taken to restrain Frontenac's behaviour within defined limits.[15] Functions and responsibilities were being separated after a fashion but the constitutional theory adhered to by the crown clung to the facade of indivisible authority and social order. The legitimacy of political expression seems not to have been acknowledged: to have done so would have implied acceptance of opposition to the royal will. Thus, denied an institutional arena of its own, politics – the play of interests – permeated all levels of the royal, or 'public,' administration. When these interests clashed, opponents often explained disputes in terms of each other's personal frailties. For example, Claude-Thomas Dupuy accused Beauharnais of raw ambition, greed, and capriciousness, and the governor replied that Dupuy had been the dupe of a small group of flatterers.[16] Examples of similar refusals to admit the legitimacy of politics, among low as well as higher officials, abound in the official correspondence.[17]

13 R. Mousnier, *Les Hiérarchies sociales de 1450 à nos jours* (Paris 1969), 81–2

14 Bosher, 'Government and Private Interests,' 123–4

15 R. Mémain, *La Marine de guerre sous Louis XIV* (Paris 1937), 266–9, 367–71. J. Tramond, *Manuel d'histoire maritime de la France* (Paris 1916 [1947]), 194–5. W.J. Eccles, *Canada Under Louis XIV* (Toronto 1964), 78–9, *passim*.

16 AN, Col. F3 11, Procès verbal, Dupuy, 6 mars 1727, 21v-22. AN Col. C11A 49, Beauharnais à Maurepas, 6 mars 1727, 58v; ibid., Beauharnais à Maurepas, 17 avril 1727, 69–69v

17 Frégault noticed the tendency to dismiss political opposition as 'cabales' and 'mauvais esprits': 'Politique et politiciens,' 232.

BEAUHARNAIS'S DISPUTES WITH HOCQUART 23

The disputes that emerged after 1737 between Charles de Beauharnais and Gilles Hocquart illuminate the degree to which the structure of colonial government, and the spirit which animated the structure, imposed conflict upon the governor and the intendant. These conflicts are noteworthy because they erupted after almost a decade of harmonious relations.

Charles de Beauharnais was a scion of the *officiers d'épée* in the navy and was well connected in the Department of Marine and Colonies.[18] His older brother, François, was *intendant de la marine* at Rochefort. His brother-in-law, Michel Bégon, was intendant at Le Havre and formerly in Canada. More imporant, a cousin, Jean-Frédéric Phélypeaux, comte de Maurepas, was minister of the marine responsible for colonies: his family had consistently favoured the Beauharnais since Louis Phélypeaux de Pontchartrain had become secretary of state for the marine in 1690.[19] It was Maurepas's protection in 1726 that had secured the governorship of Canada for Beauharnais who was then desperately seeking reprieve from a legal suit brought against him by his wealthy wife for the separation of their *communauté de biens*.[20] Once in Canada Beauharnais proved himself to be an able and conscientious general and an astute politician. In the first two years of his government he successfully managed three frontier crises and won a bitter political duel with the intendant, Claude-Thomas Dupuy, who was recalled in disgrace in 1728.[21] Like many military officers, Beauharnais was vain and sensitive: when pressed he could be petty, even vindictive.[22] Even so, he demonstrated an understanding of the limits of his powers, a measure of self-control, and a generally conciliatory approach in local issues.

Circumstances augured well for a peaceful relationship between Beauharnais and Gilles Hocquart who arrived to succeed Dupuy in 1729. In order to impress upon Hocquart, and all Canadian officials, the gravity of Dupuy's insubordination, the minister appointed Hocquart probationally as 'Commissaire général de la marine pour faire les

18 For a summary sketch of Beauharnais's background see S.D. Standen, 'Charles de Beauharnois de La Boische,' *Dictionary of Canadian Biography* [DCB] (Toronto 1974) III, 41–2.

19 S.D. Standen, 'Charles, Marquis de Beauharnais de LaBoische, Governor-General of New France 1726–1747 (unpublished PHD thesis, University of Toronto, 1975), 13–14

20 AN, Marine C7 20 pièce 50, Demandes et décisions: Canada, 11 jan. 1726

21 Jean-Claude Dubé, *Claude-Thomas Dupuy, Intendant de la Nouvelle-France 1678–1738* (Montréal 1969), chaps. XI, XII

22 For example, see Standen, 'Charles, Marquis de Beauharnais,' 170–2, 214–16, 230.

fonctions de Commissaire Ordonnateur.'[23] Only in 1731 did he receive the title of intendant. Both officials were forewarned with greater care than was customary not to infringe upon each other's prerogatives or to tire the king with petty complaints. For several years both officials praised each other enthusiastically. 'L'Experience,' wrote Beauharnais with Dupuy in mind, 'm'en fais gouter la douceur.'[24]

The agreeable personality of Hocquart, who behaved sensibly and knew how to command respect for his ability, further contributed to peace. Equally significant was his corporate association with the Marine Department which he shared with Beauharnais. Son of a former *intendant de la marine* at Le Havre, Hocquart had been *contrôleur de la marine* at Rochefort under François de Beauharnais whom he had befriended and whose influence he knew.[25] He had the wisdom to pass over as his subdelegates the two judges who had compromised themselves by their close association with Dupuy's cause, and chose instead Nicolas-Gaspard Boucault, king's attorney in the provost and admiralty courts in Quebec, and Honoré Michel de la Rouvillière, the new *commissaire de la marine* in Montreal.[26] These men were always warm friends of Beauharnais, who also remained on good relations with Louis Guillaume Verrier, attorney-general of the Superior Council and perhaps the most valued friend of Hocquart in Canada.[27] By happy coincidence a remarkable group of able, wise, compatible French officials converged for a lengthy period in Canada. Bound by common experience and influence through the Marine Department, their mutual respect was fundamental. The later conflicts between Beauharnais and Hocquart will have to be explained in terms other than personal or social incompatibility.

Although many of their quarrels reflected competition between Beauharnais and Hocquart and between their respective clients over the distribution and enjoyment of patronage, the root problem was a

23 AN, Col. B 53, 'Commission,' 8 mars 1729, 560v–70v

24 AN, Col. C11A 52, Beauharnais à Maurepas, 10 oct. 1730, 200–200v

25 Archives National de Québec [ANQ], Collection des pièces judiciaires et notariales [CPJN] 4179, Mayaud à Verrier, 14 mai 1729. D.J. Horton, 'Gilles Hocquart, Intendant of New France, 1729–1748' (unpublished PHD thesis, McGill University, 1974), 20–9

26 André Morel, 'Nicolas-Gaspard Boucault,' DCB, III, 74. AN, Col. C11A 53, Hocquart à Maurepas, 14 oct. 1730, 15-15v. Dupuy's subdelegates had been Pierre Raimbault in Montreal and Pierre André de Leigne of the Provost court in Quebec.

27 In 1739 Michel became related to Beauharnais by marrying a Bégon: Donald Horton, 'Honoré Michel de Villebois de la Rouvillière,' DCB, III, 444–5. See also ANQ, CPJN 4179, Mayaud à Verrier, 15 avril 1729; ibid., 4194, Hocquart (brother of intendant) à Verrier, 30 avril 1738.

fundamental disagreement over the priority to be given a number of military expenditures. What led finally to discord was an incompatibility between their *professional* responsibilities – Beauharnais's to defend the colony in face of increasing military insecurity, and Hocquart's to balance the colony's budget. In theory the two senior officials were to co-operate 'en bonne intelligence' in all things; in practice their contradictory official objectives, dictated from Versailles, strained even their essentially amicable dispositions.

In the late 1730s Beauharnais saw the colony's security in peril.[28] Since his arrival in 1726 he had been expected to contain the English on the New York and Ohio frontiers and to extend the French trade empire to the far northwest. In 1730 he had cause for cautious optimism. Fort Niagara served as a counter-measure to the English foothold on Lake Ontario at Oswego, and the Six Nations Iroquois recaptured the balance of power which served as a check against further English westward expansion from New York. Seizing an opportunity of momentary weakness among New Yorkers, Beauharnais built a strategic fort at Pointe-à-la-chevelure on Lake Champlain. At the same time he took advantage of a temporary victory in the long wars against the Fox Indians, who had successfully obstructed French expansion west of the Great Lakes, to launch Pierre Gaultier de Varennes de La Vérendrye on his ventures among the Crees, Monsonis, and Assiniboines.

It was not long, however, before Beauharnais's plans went awry. The Fox continued to defy chastisement and to intrigue among the French Indian allies. While expanding westward among the Monsonis and Assiniboines, Beauharnais failed to maintain peace with their bitter foes, the Sioux of the woods on the upper Mississippi River, and in 1737 the Sioux post had to be abandoned. At the same time the Chickasaws, situated between the Tennessee and Mississippi rivers and long-time trading partners of the Carolinian English, intensified their war against the Louisianan French and, in collusion with the Cherokees, intrigued among the Canadian allies of the Great Lakes region. On the Ohio River where, beginning in the 1730s, English traders put in a regular appearance, a concerted diplomatic campaign by the English colonies from New York to Carolina began to have its effects in dividing the Canadian allies. One result was the rekindling of an old feud between the Ottawas and Hurons at Detroit in 1738, raising the dreaded spectre of a general Indian war. Closer to home Beauhar-

28 I have examined Beauharnais's policies on defence and Indian relations in 'Charles, Marquis de Beauharnais,' chaps. III, V, and VI.

nais became alarmed by what he saw to be the growing independence of policy of the mission Iroquois at the Sault Saint-Louis whose role in the burgeoning illegal trade with Albany was rendering them unreliable as allies. In the handling of this problem, and that of resettling the Hurons of Detroit, Beauharnais was further frustrated by what he thought to be a contrary policy of the Jesuit missionaries.

In face of the deteriorating situation in Indian relations and the growing expectation of another colonial war with Great Britain, Beauharnais inclined to spare no expense to secure peace in the west. Experience had shown a policy of force to be unreliable, so he turned to appeasement. He authorized hugh increases in Indian gifts, the ordinary budget for which was fixed at 22,000 *livres* a year. From an average of 19,000 *livres* from 1729 to 1735, expenditures jumped to an annual average of 25,400 *livres* from 1736 to 1739, and of 59,500 *livres* from 1741 to 1744.[29]

Understandably, Beauharnais was in no mood to submit to a reduction in military expenditures. Maurepas, who always placed Canadian defence low on a long list of Marine Department priorities, issued stern, annual reprimands to his general about the cost of maintaining the Canadian frontier and the apparently meagre results. He may have wondered whether the only beneficiaries of the king's expenditures were the fortune-hungry officers at the western posts. Furthermore, he saw no evidence of success in his plan of the 1720s to effect economies in ordinary military administration and to reform the discipline of officers and soldiers alike in the colonial regular troops.[30] On major aspects of defence policy Beauharnais had nothing to offer that was not expensive. Like all governors he wanted a comfortable margin of security. Among other things he urged the doubling of the number of colonial regulars and the construction of a citadel and wall to protect the landward side of Quebec.[31]

From the perspective of the Marine Department, Maurepas's policy

29 The ordinary budget did not include the large Indian campaigns against the Fox and Chickasaw tribes, ibid., 328–9, n117.

30 AN, Col. B 49, Mémoire à Beauharnais, 7 mai 1726, 625–6v; ibid., B 48, Mémoire à Chazel, 1725, 747–9; ibid., B 74, Maurepas à Beauharnais et Hocquart, 12 avril 1742, 445; ibid., B 68, Maurepas à Hocquart, 13 avril 1739, 277-77v. AN, Col. C11A 71, Beauharnais à Maurepas, 4 oct. 1739, 37–37v; ibid., Beauharnais à Maurepas, 5 oct. 1739, 45v–6

31 AN, Col. C11A 61, Beauharnais à Maurepas, 10 oct. 1734, 307v–11v; ibid., 63, Beauharnais à Maurepas, nd (1735), 257–57v; ibid., 67, Beauharnais à Maurepas, 14 oct. 1737, 168v. These were always rejected: AN, Col. B 53, Mémoire à Beauharnais et Hocquart, 19 avril 1729, 524v–25; ibid., 64, Mémoire à Beauharnais et Hocquart, 15 mai 1736, 441v

of spending little on Canadian defence was in large measure justified by experience. The militia, a small corps of regulars, and many Indian allies had preserved the colony in the past, and there was little merit in squandering scarce funds on the defence of a colony which, from the mercantilist point of view, had proved to be of marginal value.[32] The governor of New France, on whose shoulders rested responsibility for defence, may be forgiven for seeing things differently. In the late 1730s amidst rumours of war, with the pacification of the west as elusive as ever and the minister's temper shortening with each dispatch, Beauharnais could believe that his needs had been woefully neglected.

Young, able, and ambitious, Gilles Hocquart regarded his Canadian appointment as a step towards higher office within the Marine Department in France.[33] He was chosen, it appears, for his ample virtues in financial administration rather than for experience in the law, of which he had little.[34] A cursory look at his instructions leaves no doubt that the minister's primary objective was to bring order to the colony's accounts.[35] Behind the stern, retrenching hand of Maurepas lay that of Cardinal Fleury whose ministry, coinciding almost exactly with Beauharnais's peacetime government, achieved a ruthless standard of budgetary stringency, if not parsimony, that was unprecedented in French royal finances.[36] After sending lucid, perceptive, frank reports to Maurepas concluding that both the king and the *trésoriers de la marine* had failed to reimburse the colony for past expenditures, Hocquart received nothing but denials.[37] He was advised to eliminate 'abuses' in colonial expenditures, to curb his 'facilité pour la dépense,' and to make good past deficits by effecting economies in ordinary items of current budgets. Underpaid, overworked, without adequate staff, the intendant was perplexed by the minister's cold reception of his

32 AN, Col. B 64, Maurepas à Beauharnais, 10 avril 1736, 421v

33 He was a bachelor of 36 years when appointed; ANQ, CPJN 4179, Mayaud à Verrier, 28 avril 1729.

34 AN, Col. B 53, Mémoire à Hocquart, 22 mars 1729, 471. ANQ, CPJN 4179, Mayaud à Verrier, 14 mai 1729

35 AN, Col. B 53, Mémoire à Hocquart, 19 avril 1729, 498v–504v. Donald Horton, however, sees Hocquart's paramount responsibility to have been the development of the colony's resources and commerce: 'Gilles Hocquart,' 1974, 53–6.

36 Marcel Marion, *Histoire financière de la France depuis 1715* (New York nd [Paris 1927]), I, 151–69. Penfield Roberts, *The Quest for Security 1715–1740* (New York 1963), 216–20. A.M. Wilson, *French Foreign Policy during the Administration of Cardinal Fleury* (Cambridge, Mass. 1936), 63–72, 95

37 AN, Col. B 54, Maurepas à Hocquart, 25 avril 1730, 466v; ibid., 63, 5 mai 1735, 496v, 497v–8; ibid., 64, 10 avril 1736, 422

labours.[38] Thus, Hocquart's task was unenviable and the mood at Versailles more than usually unreceptive to unpleasant truths about the state of the colony's finances. The intendant's inability to win acceptance for his proposed reform in the system of colonial payments, which would have helped him meet current expenses,[39] drove him to expedients that were not palatable to the governor.

After the colony's finances, Hocquart was to attend to a number of projects that might make Canada more profitable to the kingdom. Principal among these were an ironworks at Saint Maurice near Three Rivers and the construction of naval vessels at Quebec.[40] Whereas Maurepas was cautious and deliberate, wishing to be certain that such large-scale undertakings were feasible before committing his carefully budgeted funds, Hocquart was impatient to begin immediately.[41] In 1730 he obtained for the entrepreneur, Poulin de Francheville, co-proprietor of the Saint-Maurice seigneury, permission to construct an iron smelter and a monopoly of marketing iron in the colony. In subsequent reorganizations of the partnership the colony's leading merchant-financier, François-Etienne Cugnet, councillor, director of the *Domaine*, and Hocquart's trusted confidant, emerged as a principal shareholder.[42] Unfortunately for Hocquart the company did not live up to his expectations: after a decade the smelter had barely started to produce, yet Maurepas had been persuaded, largely by Hocquart, to lend 200,000 *livres* to the venture.[43] The minister was still reluctant to

38 AN, Col. C11A 55, Hocquart à Forçade, oct. 1731, 370v–4

39 AN, Col. C11A 58, Hocquart à Maurepas, 30 oct. 1732, 121–7; ibid., 60, Hocquart à Maurepas, 24 oct. 1733, 158–69; ibid., 62, Hocquart à Maurepas, 1 nov. 1734, 219–24. Primarily, Hocquart wished to increase the amount of card money and to raise the limit of 250,000 *livres* worth of *lettres de change* that he could authorize annually.

40 Proposals to stimulate an integrated economy based upon resources other than furs were revived before Hocquart arrived in the colony. J.-N. Fauteux, *Essai sur l'industrie au Canada sous le régime française* (Québec 1927), I, 200–10, 240–6. AN, Col. C11A 48, Dupuy à Maurepas, 21 oct. 1726, 310–12; AN, Col. B 50, Maurepas à Dupuy, 8 mai 1727, 515–18v; ibid., 52, Maurepas à Dupuy, 11 mai 1728, 484–84v; ibid., 54 Maurepas à Hocquart, 25 avril 1730, 469–49v. Jacques Mathieu, *La Construction navale royale à Québec 1739–59* (Québec 1971), 6–11. M. Fillion, *La Pensée et l'action coloniale de Maurepas vis-à-vis du Canada 1723–1749* (Ottawa 1972), 252, 267, 275–6

41 AN, Col. C11A 55, Hocquart à Forçade, oct. 1731, 372v

42 Cameron Nish, *François-Etienne Cugnet 1719–1751: entrepreneur et entreprises en Nouvelle-France* (Montréal 1975), 63

43 AN, Col. B 63, Maurepas à Beauharnais et Hocquart, 19 avril 1735, 479v–80v; ibid., Maurepas à Beauharnais et Hocquart, 10 mai 1735, 505–5v; ibid., 68, Maurepas à Beauharnais et Hocquart, 21 avril 1739, 280–80v

undertake shipbuilding until the colony's large deficit had been reduced, and increasingly expressed his displeasure over the high cost of fortifications, notably those of the Montreal wall and a new fort at Pointe-à-la-chevelure, Fort St Fréderic.[44]

In 1736 Hocquart returned to France to explain personally what he had failed to convey in writing over the past several years. Moreover, it was widely rumoured that he was hoping to procure a promotion in France.[45] But Maurepas was completely unsympathetic. Far from accepting Hocquart's claim that the colony had a deficit of 150,000 *livres*, he calculated that the budgetary position should have been in surplus by 185,000 *livres*.[46] It is not known whether Hocquart, when in France, was told flatly that the *sine qua non* for a promotion was his success in economizing in Canada. Henceforth he behaved as though this were the understanding. At first with circumspection, then with grim determination, he began systematically to retrench across a broad range of ordinary expenditures in the military budget. After 1738, therefore, it must have seemed to Beauharnais particularly unjust and perverse that vast sums were now being committed to promote iron production and naval ship construction. It was downright galling that Hocquart, whose administrative empire was thereby expanded, should at the same time choose to slice deeply into the defence budget.

After simmering for a year or more, the differences between Beauharnais and Hocquart boiled over in 1739. 'Je ne sçais pas,' Beauharnais wrote revealing the crux of the problem, 'ou En Est M. Hocquart pour les fonds, ny l'usage qu'il en fait ...'[47] The intendant's cutbacks affected pensions for Indian interpreters, blacksmiths among the Iroquois, officers' uniforms, the supply of gunpowder, the expenses of western post commanders, among other items. Disputes soon transcended the question of budgetary priorities. Beauharnais challenged his colleague's cherished terrain – the monopoly of Cugnet and the Saint-Maurice Ironworks Company – by supporting the proposal of the abbé Louis Le Page de Sainte-Claire, a would-be competitor.[48] A bustling entrepreneur already overextended on several developmental

44 AN, Col. B 63, Maurepas à Hocquart, 5 mai 1735, 499–501v

45 ANQ, CPJN 4194, Hocquart (frère) à Verrier, 26 avril 1733; AN, Col. C11A 66, Michel à Maurepas, 18 oct. 1736, 90–2v

46 AN, Col. B 65, Maurepas à Hocquart, 16 avril 1737, 404–4v; ibid., 68, Maurepas à Hocquart, 7 avril 1739, 271–3v; ibid., Maurepas à Beauharnais et Hocquart, 1 mai 1739, 306–6v

47 AN, Col. C11A 71, Beauharnais à Maurepas, 5 nov. 1739, 84–84v

48 Ibid., 71, Beauharnais à Maurepas, 28 oct. 1739, 72–3v

projects, the abbé now faced bankruptcy before his creditors who, Beauharnais accused, were acting in conspiracy with Cugnet and the Saint-Maurice Company.[49]

Why Beauharnais chose this moment to take Le Page as his client may be explained by a dispatch written by Hocquart on the first of October revealing how far the intendant was now prepared to sacrifice his concord with the governor for his own professional amibition. The former agent of the *trésoriers de la marine*, Nicolas Lanoullier, was still reeling beneath debts incurred while in office and Maurepas, recognizing that Lanoullier had in some measure been the victim of the system of Marine Department finances, pleaded with Hocquart to find further means within the colony of assisting him.[50] With the support of both governor and intendant, Lanoullier had already acquired the comptrollership of the *Domaine* and the seals of the Superior Council – both salaried positions and, though commissioned by the king, virtually the patronage of the intendant.[51] Lanoullier had also pleaded very strongly in 1733, 1734, and 1736 to be accorded the lease of the Tadoussac trade in the event that the king, as accurately rumoured, should wish to discontinue the *régie*.[52] In 1733 Hocquart had reservations about leasing Tadoussac, though promised to give it to Lanoullier should it become desirable to do so.[53] Later he was conspicuously silent about Lanoullier's proposal; one suspects he then had in mind his partner and protégé, Cugnet, to whom the farm in fact was accorded in 1737.[54] Now, in 1739, Hocquart did not blush to recommend without consulting the governor that Lanoullier be accorded the free exploitation of the trade at one of the western posts, Temiscamingue.[55]

Nothing could have demonstrated more convincingly Hocquart's new departure. As in all the western posts the arrangement of trade at Temiscamingue was largely the patronage of the governor. The post was unique in that it was exploited not by several *congé* holders, or

49 Ibid.; Aimé Despatie, 'Louis Lepage de Sainte-Claire,' DCB, III, 390

50 AN, Col. B 68, Maurepas à Hocquart, 7 avril 1739, 273v

51 S.D. Standen, 'Nicolas Lanoullier de Boiscler,' DCB, III, 352–3

52 AN, Col. C11A 61, Placet de Lanoullier à Maurepas, 17 avril 1733, 265–70; ibid., 62, Lanoullier à Maurepas, 10 oct. 1734, 300–1v; ibid., 66, Lanoullier à Maurepas, 9 oct. 1736, 119

53 Ibid., 60, Hocquart à Maurepas, 8 oct. 1733, 64v–5. Maurepas had advised his officials that Lanoullier should be given the preference of the lease, if granted at all: AN, Col. B 59, Maurepas à Beauharnais et Hocquart, 24 avril 1733, 433–33v.

54 AN, Col. B 64, Maurepas à Beauharnais et Hocquart, 10 avril 1736, 420; ibid., 65, Mémoire à Beauharnais et Hocquart, 10 mai 1737, 428v

55 AN Col. C11A 71, Hocquart à Maurepas, 1 oct. 1739, 144–5

paying licencees, but by a monopolist, Paul Guillet,[56] whose annual payment of 3000 *livres* formed part of the *congé* receipts distributed by Beauharnais to the unfortunate widows and daughters of notable colonial families. The post's geographical isolation from the volatile Indian feuds of the upper Great Lakes, coupled with the homogeneity of the region's native population, made a commanding officer and garrison unnecessary. The chief competition came from the English on Hudson Bay, and Guillet had demonstrated since Philippe Rigaud de Vaudreuil's government his ability to conduct the trade satisfactorily and to maintain the French interest there. Hocquart, recognizing Guillet's importance, proposed replacing only his Montreal outfitter, Louis Charly Saint-Ange, with Lanoullier.[57] The proposal was not outrageous; it was in the spirit of royal beneficence intended by the *congé* system. But the intendant knew that he was infringing upon the sensitive area of Beauharnais's patronage – 'ce seroit gêner ses liberalités.' Such a calculated indiscretion suggests that Hocquart was henceforth determined to conserve his own patronage for his own ends and, if he could, to shift to Beauharnais's *congé* fund cases of public charity like Lanoullier's.

The minister treated Hocquart's proposal with unusual delicacy – 'ce ne soit pas un expedient tout a fait praticable' – and lied to Beauharnais that Hocquart could offer no remedy for Lanoullier's predicament.[58] 'Mais on m'en a indiqué un,' he continued vaguely in outlining the scheme. 'J'ay prevû sur la simple propo'on, les raisons que vous avés à opposer à cet expedient.' Yet in the past Maurepas had not hesitated to instruct the governor as to the distribution of the *congé* receipts. Why should he now? The explanation may lie in the uniqueness of Temiscamingue. Vaudreuil had reserved its trade for his own account, with Paul Guillet either as agent or partner.[59] If Beauharnais had assumed the practice of his predecessor, with the knowledge of the minister, this could explain the tenderness with which everyone handled the Temiscamingue proposal of 1739. It would also enhance the significance of what Hocquart had undertaken.

Beauharnais reacted with predictable sensitivity. Disdaining even to mention Temiscamingue while making clear he knew that Hocquart

56 Guillet had two partners, Godefroy and Cullerier. Ibid., 75, Beauharnais à Maurepas, 26 sept. 1741, 185

57 Ibid., 71, Hocquart à Maurepas, 1 oct. 1739, 144v

58 AN, Col. B 70, Maurepas à Hocquart, 2 mai 1740, 347. Ibid., 70, Maurepas à Beauharnais, nd [2 mai 1740], 347v

59 Zoltvany, *Vaudreuil*, 151, 178, 192–3. The Council of Marine granted him the post in 1716; Maurepas wished to end this arrangement in 1724.

was the author, he parried the intendant's thrust with a proposal of his own aimed at the intendant's patronage: 'quoyque M. Hocquart en dise il auroit bien pû trouver les moyens de la [Lanoullier] soulager et même de retablir ses affaires, le Poste de Tadoussac en Etoit la véritable source.'[60] But Beauharnais riposted more vigorously still. Noting that in 1737 Hocquart had leased Tadoussac to François-Etienne Cugnet for the surprisingly modest sum of 4500 *livres* annually, he implicitly accused them of conspiracy to defraud the king: 'je pense que si le S. Cugnet n'avoit pas sçû y faire son profit, luy qui en Etoit le Régisseur depuis l'année 1719, il ne l'auroit pas demandé avec tant d'instance, et offert de donner 4,500 livres d'une ferme qui suivant ... [son] Exposé, ne devoit rien raporter que de l'Embarras.'[61] Lanoullier had offered 6000 *livres* for the lease in 1736 and Beauharnais's secretary, Jacques de Lafontaine de Belcour, in partnership with Guillaume Estèbe in 1737, publicly proposed to Hocquart to pay Cugnet 9000 *livres* in addition to the 4500 *livres* lease. But Hocquart 'garde le silence.'[62] The clincher in Beauharnais's exposé was a new offer conveniently submitted by Lafontaine to pay 10,000 *livres* in anticipation of a profit of more than 20,000 *livres*.[63] 'Il est aîsé de connoître,' concluded the governor, 'que cette ferme a Eté donnée à la faveur, ou avec bien de la facilité ... sans avoir observé les formalités d'une adjudication publique.'[64] In the past he had done more than Hocquart to aid Lanoullier, or so he was convinced. He now proposed to cancel Cugnet's lease, in view of the deception on which it was based, and to reissue it on terms that would allow ample assistance to Lanoullier without encroaching upon the *congé* fund.

The entrance of Lafontaine signifies another dimension of Beauharnais's quarrels with the intendant. Since 1729 Hocquart had continually complained that his office was under-staffed, that salaries of civil personnel were insufficient to attract highly competent men, and that the insecurity of untenured employees – those without royal *brevets* – led them to devote their best attentions to private business.[65]

60 AN, Col. C11A 74, Beauharnais à Maurepas, 9 oct. 1740, 40v. See also ibid., 74, Beauharnais à Maurepas, 20 oct. 1740, 95.

61 Ibid., 74, Beauharnais à Maurepas, 9 oct. 1740, 40v

62 Ibid., 74, Beauharnais à Maurepas, 20 oct. 1740, 94v. Apparently the highest offer Maurepas had heard before 1735 was 3000 *livres*. AN, Col. B 63, Maurepas à Beauharnais et Hocquart, 5 mai 1735, 496–96v

63 AN, Col. C11A 74, Beauharnais à Maurepas, 20 oct. 1740, 92

64 Ibid., Beauharnais à Maurepas, 20 oct. 1740, 93v–4

65 For example, ibid., 51, Hocquart à Maurepas, 25 oct. 1729, 273v–4; ibid., 62, Hocquart à Maurepas, 10 oct. 1734, 36; ibid., 70, Hocquart à Maurepas, 8 oct. 1738, 9–9v; ibid., 76, Hocquart à Maurepas, 30 oct. 1741, 69; ibid., 77, Hocquart à Maurepas, 17 sept. 1742, 332v–6v

His requests, however, were firmly rejected as too costly and frivolous.[66] Thus, part of Hocquart's reforms involved cleaning out deadwood from his staff to make room for other, more productive servants. Among the deadwood, apparently, were Lafontaine and another of Beauharnais's secretaries, Charles-René Gaudron de Chevremont.

Intelligent, ambitious, an eager client of Beauharnais, Jacques de Lafontaine earned his reputation in the colony as a sharp schemer in all that he undertook.[67] The governor's protection had brought him not only a seigneurial concession on the Richelieu River and a commerical one in the Labrador seal fisheries but a seat on the Superior Council and an appointment as *commis* in the intendant's office as well. No doubt Hocquart acceded to these last to please Beauharnais; by 1735 Lafontaine's numerous, time-consuming official and private activities provided an excuse to dismiss him as *commis*, though the intendant probably distrusted him as well.[68]

Like Lafontaine, Charles-René Gaudron came to Canada as Beauharnais's secretary and through his protection procured appointments within Hocquart's jurisdiction: *écrivain*, commis of the comptroller and royal notary in Montreal.[69] He, too, supplemented his income with a number of other employments. Although Hocquart had joined the governor in praising the quality and diligence of Gaudron's work, he apparently had reservations which led him in 1740 to dismiss him as *écrivain* and *commis*, noting, that he 'remplit très superficiallement son employ de Commis au Controlle.'[70] Beauharnais was indignant over the intendant's summary action, 'sans me faire la politesse de m'en parler.' He suggested to Maurepas that Hocquart had responded out of vindictiveness to an unflattering report that Gaudron had submitted following his special investigation in 1738 into the falling revenues at the king's posts of Frontenac and Niagara.[71]

In the years that followed the two officials agreed much less on

66 AN, Col. B 64, Maurepas à Hocquart, 10 avril 1736, 422

67 S.D. Standen, 'Jacques de Lafontaine de Belcour,' DCB, III, 338–41

68 AN, Col. C11A 66, Lafontaine à Maurepas, 15 oct. 1736, 131–2v; ibid., 70, Hocquart à Maurepas, 8 oct. 1738, 9v; AN, Col. B 63, Maurepas à Beauharnais et Hocquart, 19 avril 1735, 473v. Hocquart wrote of Lafontaine in his report on judicial officials in 1736: 'agé de 30 à 35 ans, à de l'Esprit et de la facilité pour les affaires, a fait cy devant soupçonner quelque derangement dans sa conduitte ...' AN, Col. D2D, carton 1

69 *Rapport de l'archiviste de la Province de Québec*, 1921–2, 42–3; AN, Col. E, carton 81, 27 juil. 1732; S.D. Standen, 'Charles-René Gaudron de Chevremont,' DCB, III, 239

70 AN, Col. C11A 61, Beauharnais et Hocquart à Maurepas, 26 oct. 1734, 250–1; AN, Col. E, carton 81, Beauharnais et Hocquart à Maurepas, 27 oct. 1735; ibid., carton 81, Chevremont à Maurepas, nd [1736?]; AN, Col. C11A 73, Liste des écrivains 1740, 300

71 AN, Col. C11A 73, Hocquart à Maurepas, 26 oct. 1740, 306–9v; AN, Col. B 68, Mémoire à Beauharnais et Hocquart, 1 mai 1739, 300v

matters of personnel. Hocquart was determined no longer to defer to the governor in recommending candidates for vacancies within the civil jurisdiction, or for bonuses or pensions, and Beauharnais, though he had no legitimate cause to complain, displayed resentment that his supreme position as the colony's elder patron, held since Dupuy's departure, was now being successfully challenged.[72] The governor, whose sensitivity surfaced, saw encroachments upon his prerogatives where formerly he would have been unconcerned: 'cet article me regardoit seul Etant de mon district ... c'Etoit compromettre mon autorité ... mes Predécesseurs ont toujours joüis de cette prérogative.'[73]

It was, however, against supposedly needless military expenditures in the west that Hocquart directed his principal campaign: 'dans la façon de penser de ce pays cy on s'imagine que les retranchments que je fais sur certaines dépenses sont autant d'injustices; on ne paye jamais assez généreusement, l'oéconomie n'Est point la vertue dominante du Militaire, surtout en Canada, d'un autre Costé vous sçavez que La pays Est miserable et que chacun cherche a tirer du Roy tous ce qu'il peut pour s'en faire une ressource.'[74] He grimaced at the cost of Indian gifts, though admitted that much of this was indispensable when large contingents from the western tribes descended to confer with the governor each year.[75] Claims for reimbursement submitted by post commanders for expenses undertaken in the king's name were a different matter. 'Ce pays cy,' Hocquart once wrote, 'est un pays de facilitez sous pretexte de la pauvreté de ceux qui l'habitent.'[76] These claims, it was safe to assume, were amply padded, and whereas commanders and interpreters were supposed to credit the king with all presents received in diplomatic exchanges with Indians, few did so in more than a token manner.[77] Furthermore, he thought the officers' contingents and gar-

72 For example, AN, Col. C11A 74, Beauharnais à Maurepas, 2 nov. 1740, 121–2; ibid., 79, Beauharnais et Hocquart à Maurepas, 14 oct. 1743, 60v–1v; ibid., 79, Beauharnais à Maurepas, 28 oct. 1743, 209–9v; ibid., 79 Hocquart à Maurepas, 9 oct. 1743, 344–4v; ibid., 75, Beauharnais à Maurepas, 31 oct. 1741, 236–7

73 AN, Col. C11A 74, Beauharnais à Maurepas, 8 oct. 1740, 36–9; ibid., 78, Beauharnais à Maurepas, 29 oct. 1742, 139–40; ibid., 79, Beauharnais à Maurepas, 19 sept. 1743, 140–1

74 Later, when explaining the budgetary deficits from 1739 to 1741, Hocquart attributed virtually all of them, amounting to 173,568 *livres*, to the western military establishment and the servicing of the Indian alliances. AN, Col. C11A 78, Hocquart à Maurepas, 14 oct. 1742, 307–8; ibid., 80, Hocquart à Maurepas 30 oct. 1743, 241–1v

75 AN, Col. C11A 73, Hocquart à Maurepas, 31 oct. 1740, 335; see also ibid., 81, Hocquart à Maurepas, 28 oct. 1744, 451v–2; ibid., 76, Hocquart à Maurepas, 30 oct. 1741, 57–8v, 65v

76 AN, Col. C11A 81, Hocquart à Maurepas, 28 oct. 1744, 451

77 Ibid., 78, Projet de Règlement, 3 sept. 1742, 304; AN, Col. B53, Maurepas à Beauharnais et Hocquart, 2 mai 1729, 536–6v

risons at the posts needlessly large, even unnecessary in most cases. The large shipment of provisions to the upcountry annually disguised an extensive, unauthorized trade.[78] With a general war threatening in Europe Maurepas became more budget-conscious than ever, insisting unsympathetically that Hocquart keep western expenses, even those relating to the Chickasaw war, within the ordinary budget and even to come up with 'revenant bons.'[79]

Hocquart responded in 1740 by rejecting requests from Beauharnais to compensate some officers for exceptional service in the Chickasaw campaign and, in subsequent years, slashed drastically post commanders' claims for compensation.[80] He tried to crack down on the double issue of soldiers' uniforms and provisions when garrisoned at the posts.[81] Finally he endorsed in 1741 the general recommendations for retrenchment submitted by his *contrôleur*, Jean-Victor Varin de la Marre, including, among other things, withdrawing the garrison at Fort Chambly, the reduction of those at Frontenac and Niagara, and the leasing to the highest bidder the trade at these last two posts.[82]

The proposal was brilliantly timed to win approval at Versailles where the glitter of projected savings blinded the financially distressed minister to all the shortcomings such a scheme had presented in the past.[83] Hocquart was aware of these, but being short-staffed with ships to build and an ironworks on the verge of bankruptcy, he would gladly relinquish responsibility for an operation that had provided nothing but headaches.[84] In 1742 Maurepas informed his officials that Niagara

78 AN, Col. C11A 82, Varin à Maurepas, 1 nov. 1744, 284–92

79 Ibid., 78, Hocquart à Maurepas, 14 oct. 1742, 28v

80 Ibid., 80, Hocquart à Maurepas, 30 oct. 1743, 242–2v

81 Ibid., 74, Beauharnais à Maurepas, 27 oct. 1740, 106–6v

82 Ibid., 76, Mémoire sur quelques parties de dépenses de Canada (Varin), 16 fév. 1741, 272–7

83 Simultaneously Maurepas authorized 200,000 *livres* more card money, extended the Montreal wall tax indefinitely, raised duties on liquor, and revived the idea of levying a direct tax on all colonists. AN, Col. B 74, Mémoire à Beauharnais et Hocquart, 30 avril 1742, 503–11; ibid., 76, Mémoire à Beauharnais et Hocquart, 31 mai 1743, 442v–3v

84 Earlier Hocquart had always supported the exploitation of Tadoussac, Niagara, and Frontenac directly by *régie*, rather than by lease, because of political or diplomatic considerations. Thus, he had agreed with Beauharnais. After 1737, however, fiscal and administrative expediency led him to reverse his priorities – a rather significant decision. See AN, Col. C11A 50 Beauharnais à Maurepas, 1 oct. 1728, 88v–9; ibid., 51, Hocquart à Maurepas, 25 oct. 1729, 284–5; ibid., 55, Hocquart à Fermiers Généraux, 27 oct. 1731, 359–62v; ibid., 59, Beauharnais et Hocquart à Maurepas, 1 oct. 1731, 71–8v; ibid., 62, Hocquart à Maurepas, 10 oct. 1734, 39–9v; ibid., Hocquart à Maurepas, 26 oct. 1740, 309–9v.

and Frontenac had been farmed out, and instructed them to lease to the highest bidder the trade at most other western posts as well.[85]

The new policy reflected the commonly-held assumption at Versailles that the costly military establishment in the west was not altogether necessary, and that the participation of officers in the fur trade greatly reduced the revenue that the king could extract from it. Garrisons were to be slashed to skeletal proportions and the practice of commanding officers taking with them their entire families and households at prodigious expense to the king was to be ended.[86] The complement of officers was to be reduced in most cases to the commander and his second. Most important, under no circumstances whatever were officers to engage in trade, on penalty of dismissal from service: 'S[a]. M[ajeste]. veut que ces Exploitations Soient données à l'avenir aux négocians et aux voyageurs de la Colonie ...'[87]

The decision to lease all the posts was certainly unexpected, but the normal ten-month delay in communications between France and Canada afforded Beauharnais the means of softening the impact. He repeated the principal objections he had made when the policy had first been proposed to him in 1728. The dictates of Indian diplomacy required officers and garrisons at the western posts. Leaseholders would enjoy an effective monopoly at their respective posts: there would be nothing to restrain them from raising their prices and therby disgusting the Indians, especially at Frontenac and Niagara, and driving them to trade with the English.[88] The great merit of the *congé* system, or so it had always been held, was to ensure competitive, low prices in the upcountry. Maurepas anticipated this objection using Varin's argument that the English at Oswego were the effective competition in the west and that leaseholders, acting out of self-interest, would keep their prices down or face ruin.[89] But Beauharnais projected a different image of mercantile behaviour: merchants would pay what they must for a lease, then do what they must to recover their costs plus profit, regardless of the king's interest.[90]

85 The specific posts to be leased were Rivière St Joseph, La Baye du Lac Alepimigon, Kamanistigoya, Michipicoton, Temiscamingue, Miamis, and Ouyatanons. AN, Col. B 74, Mémoire à Beauharnais et Hocquart, 30 avril 1742, 509–10

86 Ibid., 74, Maurepas à Beauharnais, 17 avril 1742, 456v

87 Ibid., 74, Maurepas à Beauharnais et Hocquart, 27 avril 1742, 495–5v; ibid., 74, Maurepas à Hocquart, 20 avril 1742, 478–9v

88 AN Col. C11A 77, Beauharnais à Maurepas, 5 sept. 1742, 94–7

89 AN, Col. B 76; Mémoire à Beauharnais et Hocquart, 31 mai 1743, 442–2v; ibid., 76, Maurepas à Beauharnais, avril 1743, 403

90 AN, Col. C11A 78, Extrait, Beauharnais et Hocquart à Maurepas, 8 oct. 1742, 388v; ibid., 79, Beauharnais à Maurepas, 22 sept. 1743, 144–6v

Neither argument did justice to the complexities of the western trade. Beauharnais probably exaggerated the degree of competition fostered by the *congé* system except at the entrepots of Michilimackinac and Detroit, where *congés* were to be retained under the new system in any case.[91] At other posts a single *congé* holder seldom had the resources to finance his trade alone and often went into partnership with others, usually including the post commander. For posts other than Frontenac, Niagara, Michilimackinac, and Detroit, the significant effect of the new policy was to replace one group of monopolists, including the post commander, with another group of monopolists excluding him.

On the other hand, the benefits of the lease system predicted by Varin and Maurepas were not entirely borne out. True, the time, worry, and costs of outfitting and managing the king's posts on Lake Ontario were now the problem of the leaseholder, François Chalet.[92] But the outbreak of war in 1744 rendered futile any conclusive assessment of the leasing experiment. Even before the effects of war Chalet was confronted with all the difficulties that had plagued the *régie* of Niagara and Frontenac: the overhead of maintaining a large inventory of trade goods at the post; the maintenance costs of ships and *batteaux* on the lakes; and the relentless competition from Oswego.[93] The major achievement of Chalet's lease was to have produced accurate accounts, leaving no doubt that the trade at Niagara was unprofitable.[94]

The exclusion of officers from the western trade was an ambitious reform, the implementation of which would have made more sense at the beginning of the long peace in 1713. Undertaken on the eve of war it was virtually doomed to failure. Military expenditures could not safely be cut and wartime risks reduced bids for post leases. Politically, the reform was ill-timed. It would have taken years for leaseholders to establish their credit and effectiveness as diplomatic agents of the French among the Indian tribes; in the meantime it was the officers who performed this indispensable function. The minister's option for fiscal expediency at a time when war was imminent and strategic considerations were pressing placed Beauharnais in an awkward

91 Ibid., 79, Beauharnais à Maurepas, 22 sept. 1743, 144v–5v; ibid., 78, Extrait, Beauharnais et Hocquart à Maurepas, 8 oct. 1742, 378v–80

92 The basic terms of Chalet's lease had already been decided in France. AN, Col. B 74, Maurepas à Beauharnais et Hocquart, 27 avril 1742, 495–5v

93 AN, Col. C11A 81, Beauharnais à Maurepas, 9 oct. 1744, 162v–4; ibid., 81, Beauharnais et Hocquart à Maurepas, 25 oct. 1744, 72–4; ibid., 81, Hocquart à Maurepas, 23 oct. 1744, 406v–7

94 Ibid., 87, LaGalissonière et Hocquart à Maurepas, 26 sept. 1747, 110

predicament. More than ever dependent upon his officers in the west, he was at the same time bound to hold them to a trade policy that had deliberately attacked their interests.[95] Small wonder that he felt victimized.

Beauharnais learned to live with the new order inaugurated by Hocquart – he had little choice in face of support from Versailles. He lost his bid to have Cugnet's lease of Tadoussac rescinded. Although Maurepas was willing to believe that the king had been cheated by this lease, Hocquart skilfully managed to discredit Beauharnais's exposé by alluding to the untrustworthiness of Jacques de Lafontaine on whose bid the governor had hung his case.[96] Nicolas Lanoullier continued for several years to receive 3000 *livres* from the Temiscamingue receipts.[97] Until the outbreak of war in 1744, when Beauharnais could justify the exercise of superior authority, Hocquart maintained tight rein on the defence budget. The experiment in leasing all the western posts continued until after the peace in 1748.

If examined out of context, the disputes that Beauharnais had with Hocquart might be interpreted only as struggles over the distribution and enjoyment of patronage, as quarrels over prerogatives, as manifestations of the governor's pique in face of his colleague's increased responsibilities in iron production and shipbuilding,[98] or as contests between opposing colonial vested interests represented by the officer corps on the one hand and by the mercantile developers on the other. These personal and private interests were all real and are prominently displayed in the evidence. But to dwell at too great length upon them is to risk overlooking the profound professional concern of both the governor and the intendant to serve the public interest as each saw it. Beauharnais, who thought of himself as 'un vieux militaire,' a professional soldier, sought the most effective policies by which to defend the colony, secure the Indian alliances, and expand the fur trade. Likewise Hocquart, a career *officier de plume*, formulated his policies by the requirements of fiscal responsibility and colonial development. Their relationship is interesting as an illustration of how matters of imperial

95 For example, AN, Col. C11A 79, Règlement 16 juil. 1743, 22–7

96 AN, Col. B 72, Maurepas à Hocquart, 16 avril 1741, 348–9; ibid., 72, Maurepas à Beauharnais, 26 avril 1741, 365v; AN, Col. C11A 76, Hocquart à Maurepas, 12 oct. 1741, 8–13

97 AN, Col. B 74, Maurepas à Hocquart, 17 avril 1742, 457; ibid., 81, Maurepas à Lanoullier, 5 mai 1745, 302–2v; ibid., 85, Maurepas à LaJonquière, 3 avril 1747, 208–8v

98 Donald Horton has argued that Beauharnais's conflicts with Hocquart stemmed largely from the governor's jealousy of the intendant's increased patronage: 'Gilles Hocquart,' 1975, 223–7.

policy, even though other circumstances were propitious for harmony, turned them into opponents and precipitated secondary conflicts that might otherwise have been avoided.

An explanation of this process takes us to the structures of colonial government. As in all overseas colonies, distance required that the crown delegate considerable executive authority and all administrative responsibility to local officials. The minister of the marine expected, as Eccles has noted, that the governor and the intendant would act in unison in both executive and administrative capacities: they were to decide in the local context how best to execute policies determined by Versailles, and they were to administer them.[99] The governor, as personal representative of the king, symbolized, and in time of crisis could exercise, the ultimate authority of the king, even in matters of police, justice, and finance, normally the jurisdictions of the intendant. Since the excesses of Frontenac's government, however, when Louis XIV attempted to clarify the constitutional relationship between governor and intendant, the governor's supreme authority was normally supervisory and limited to reporting any improper conduct on the part of other officials to the minister of the marine.[100] It is clear that with the exception of the Indian wars in the west, and until war with Britain was declared in 1744, both Beauharnais and Hocquart assumed that the intendant possessed effective power of the purse.[101]

There was, therefore, considerable strain placed upon the governor and the intendant to achieve the mutually exclusive objectives of fiscal retrenchment *and* military security in the circumstances of the 1730s. No doubt Maurepas understood this, but with larger joys and sorrows of which Canada was only a part he probably hoped that something of both objectives might be attained. If not, then the charge of abuses at the local level provided an excuse for failure – a persuasive one for those familiar with royal administration. Given the divided nature of executive authority locally, however, the intendant and governor were bound to have conflicting professional interests. Conflict arose not, as Frégault suggested in part, from the overlapping or imprecision of jurisdictions but from the fact that the executive had been divided at

99 The determination of policy at Versailles, of course, relied in some measure upon the advice and experience of colonial officials in the first place. Frégault, 'Politique et politiciens,' 179

100 AN, Col. B 49, Mémoire du Roy à Beauharnais, 7 mai 1726, 620–7v. W.J. Eccles, *Frontenac: The Courtier Governor* (Toronto 1959), 127 passim. Frégault, 'Politique et politiciens,' 170–80

101 The intendant's supremacy in financial matters is widely recognized. Gustave Lanctôt, *L'Administration de la Nouvelle-France* (Montréal 1971), 79–83, 160; Crowley, 'Government and Interests,' 370

all.[102] The fiscal and military responsibilities were separated as clearly as any could be. This dualistic nature of colonial government, arising partly from the crown's groping toward a means of effecting accountability in royal administration, did in one sense make governor and intendant, in Parkman's words, 'natural enemies.'

The crown's predictably authoritarian approach to accountability, rejecting any formal, public scrutiny of its policies and administration, aggravated conflict between officials in other ways. Opposing vested interests did line up to some extent behind Beauharnais and Hocquart. Although John Bosher has argued that the failure to remove this and other 'rampant private enterprise' from government was a great impediment to the development of a clear sense of public interest, both Beauharnais and Hocquart displayed some such discernment.[103] The idea that there exists an unsullied public interest separable from or incompatable with private interests may have strengthened in the past two centuries, but it can be misleading. Who, after all, is to define the public interest? Who has ever failed to equate his particular interest with the common weal? Certainly Frontenac, Beauharnais, Hocquart, and probably even Bigot drew this equation. The issue is less one of private *versus* public than of which combination among all interests, individual and corporate, colonial and metropolitan, should define the public one. What Bosher underscores is that the process of definition – politics – was allowed no separate institutional outlet:[104] consequently, the battle between 'private' interests over public policy could take place only through the appointed royal officials.

The pretense that politics were mere personal vendettas or expressions of greed and ambition, the result only of cabals or scheming advisers, followed logically from the fundamental nature of the absolute monarchy and its refusal to admit of legitimate opposition. While the colony remained small, its interests simple, and its dependence upon imperial defence overwhelming, Canadians and royal officials alike could live with the built-in tensions of its governmental structures. Principal among these was the tension between the *château* and the *palais*, at once the seats of supposedly indivisible authority and the unofficial political axes of competing imperial and colonial interests.

102 Others also have attributed conflict to overlapping authorities: Lanctôt, *L'Administration*, 162–3; Eccles, *Government*, 9–10. Crowley cites an imbalance of responsibilities between governor and ordonnateur at Louisbourg as contributing to conflict: 'Government and Interests,' 370

103 Bosher, 'Government and Private Interests,' 123–4

104 Lanctôt expressed a similar observation in more traditional liberal terminology: 'Il n'existe, en dernière analyse, aucune institution qui le [le peuple] représente ou qui lui permette d'exprimer ses opinions.' *L'Administration*, 162

Index